Patricia Jobe Pierce

Elvis Presley Day by Day

The Ultimate

ELVIS
ELVIS
ELVIS
ELVIS
ELVIS

Simon & Schuster   New York London Toronto Sydney Tokyo Singapore

SIMON & SCHUSTER
Rockefeller Center
1230 Avenue of the Americas
New York, New York 10020

Designed by Hyun Joo Kim

Manufactured in the United States of America

10 9 8 7 6 5 4 3 2 1

Library of Congress Cataloging-in-Publication Data

Pierce, Patricia Jobe.
    The ultimate Elvis: Elvis Presley day by day/by Pa-
tricia Jobe Pierce.
        p.   cm.
    Includes discographies, videographies, filmogra-
phies, bibliographical references, and index.
    1. Presley, Elvis, 1935–1977—
Chronology.   2. Rock musicians—
United States—Biography.   I. Title.
ML420.P96P54   1994
782.42166′092—dc20
[B]   94–4612
                                                        CIP
                                                        MN

ISBN 0-671-87022-X

SPECIAL ACKNOWLEDGMENTS

I am especially grateful and indebted to **Thomas J. Francis** and **Peter Guralnick** for candidly sharing their astute knowledge and profound wisdom; **William J. Hlavin** and **Lori Broughton** for their affable intuition; **Zoe Hollywood** for her research fortitude; **Patricia Jarvist,** archivist, The Liberace Museum, Las Vegas, Nevada, for graciously donating photographs and historical data; **Leonard Carl Jobe** (posthumously) for being avant-garde when it was not fashionable; **Ruth Baten Jobe** for her care and generous support; **Kathleen Knight,** who is attentive when it counts the most; **Christine Ruth Pierce** for her scholarship and stamina; **Matthew Jobe Pierce** for his thoughtful insights into rock 'n' roll, musical know-how, and quick wit; **Ken Roberts,** a unique and insightful agent, and our mutual sidekicks **Kurt Lauer** and **Kaycee Benton** for their inspiration; to America's most profound and patient editor, Simon & Schuster's **Chuck Adams,** and to his esteemed colleague **Cheryl Weinstein;** and to the generous **John Reible** of the Las Vegas News Bureau, who is living proof not everyone holds authors in contempt. I sincerely thank you all.

Courtesy of AP/Wide World Photos.

ACKNOWLEDGMENTS

I earnestly credit all of those who have had the patience and discernment to see this long-term project through to the end. Without you, this book would have been arduous to complete: ABC News; Aerosmith; Steve Allen; Ann-Margret; John and Mary Helen Armstrong; Roger Bailey, "This Old House"; Milton Berle; Chuck Berry; Bettmann (Kate Schellenbach); James Blackwood, Sr.; Billy Blanks; John Bon Jovi; Pat Boone; David Bowie; the Bradford Exchange (Ginny Sexon), Niles, IL; Dennis Buda; Prescott S. Bush, Jr.; Tom Carey; Pres. Jimmy Carter; Johnny Cash; CBS News; Trina Cefali, Elvis Presley Museum, Pigeon Forge, TN; James Chappell; David H. Chumlea; Cathy Clark; disc jockey Dick Clark; William A. Clark, *Detroit News;* President and Mrs. Bill Clinton; Joyce Cobb, Memphis; Douglas Colclough; Tim Collins, Collins Management; Russell Coltharp; John W. Corbett; Larry Corthell, U.S. Postal Service; Marco Cotsonas, guitarist; Country Music Foundation, Nashville; Country Music Hall of Fame, Nashville, TN; Bennett W. Crocker, "The Ed Sullivan Show"; Chet Darmsteader; Andie and John DeCosta; Stuart and Beverly Denenberg; Bo Diddley; The Dixon Gallery and Garden (Lisa Incardona); Jim Duane, Keyboard Systems, Salt Lake City, UT; Dr. Roger Dunn; Joe Dupuis, Strawberries; Elvis Presley Enterprises, Memphis, TN; Joe Esposito; Olga and Vic Firth; Keith Garde; Arthur Garrity; Jean and Kahlil Gibran; Julie Stuempfig of Goldmine; disc jockey Jay Gordon of WODS-FM 103.3, Boston; The Grand Ole Opry, Nashville, TN; Normma Guistiani; William P. Heidrich; John Heller; Steven Herman; James Hill; John Douglas Ingraham; Jamie G. James, James Agency, Los Angeles; Roland James; Bertyl V. Johnson, Jr.; Jim and Judith Kelley; Russell E. Kemppel; B.B. King; Jay King; Dale Kirby; George Klein, disc jockey for WHBQ, Memphis, TN; Steven C. LaVere; Nira and Leonard Levine; Jerry Lee Lewis; The Liberace Museum, Las Vegas, NV; *Life* (Debra Cohen); Little Richard; David Loehr; Lo-el Fine Art, Newport Beach, CA; Louis Lombardi; Los Angeles Times Syndicate (Judy Colbert); Terlock MacDonagh; Greil Marcus; Daniel McGlinchey; Memphis Brooks Museum of Art; *Memphis Commer-*

ACKNOWLEDGMENTS

cial Appeal (Judy Cross, Larry Coyne); Memphis Housing Authority; *Memphis Press-Scimitar;* Memphis Symphony League (Mary Stagg); Metropolitan Museum of Art; Ken Miller; Mitzi, Lucy, and Max; James and Marge Mohn; Scotty Moore; Todd Morgan, Graceland; Elisha Morrison, Isolar; National Archives and Records Administration, Nixon Presidential Materials Staff, Washington, DC; *National Enquirer;* National Screen Service Corp.; NBC News; *New York Times;* Willie Jay Nichols; Pres. Richard Milhous Nixon; Sherylanne Nordella; Opryland, USA, Nashville, TN; Roy Orbison (posthumously); Paramount Pictures; Kenneth V. V. Parks; Glenn Peck; Carl Perkins; Dr. Norman B. Pierce; Portraits of the Past, NH; The Preservation Society of Newport County; Peter F. Miller; Dee Stanley Presley; R&R Enterprises; Ross Ramsay; Thomas K. Ranft, Jr., Braintree, MA; Dan Rather; Jimmy Raye; RCA Victor Records; Frank Richelman; Geraldo Rivera; *Rolling Stone;* Sam Phillips Recording Service, Memphis, TN; John Samaras; Shelby County Mayor's Office (Ruth Ann Hale); Susan R. Shellmer; Shent; Chris Skinker, Country Music Foundation, Inc.; Jerry Lee Smith; Jack Soden, director, Elvis Presley Enterprises, Memphis, TN; Sotheby's, New York City; Bruce Springsteen ("The Boss"); Beth Stallings; Robin Steiner; Sheila Sullivan; Fate Taylor; James Taylor; Jimmy Thayer; *Time* (Rhonda Sturtz); Blanchard E. Tual; *TV Guide;* Steven Tyler; Jill Urbanus; University of Mississippi, Center for the Study of Southern Culture; John Urbanus; U.S. Postal Service, Washington, DC, and Accord Park, Hingham, MA; Jimmy Velvet; Jeanne Axtell Walker; Bill "Sugarfoot" Wallace; Janet Warren; Charles A. Wathen; Roger H. Weisensteiner of Kimball Piano; Alfred Wertheimer, photographer; Pamela Wilkins; Windsor Associates, Akron, OH; Writers Guild of America; Cleveland Young (The Gospel Christian Singers); Kyle Young, Country Music Hall of Fame, Nashville, TN; Peter F. Young; Peter Wade Young and Edward Shein.

DEDICATION

This book is dedicated to those talented musicians, composers, and entertainers who aspire to keep music alive and on the cutting edge by exemplifying and defining with distinction and integrity the purpose and meaning of rock 'n' roll, and to the fans who support rock 'n' roll's ever-growing legacy of excellence.

CONTENTS

CONTENTS

INTRODUCTION

Rock 'n' roll is a blues euphemism for "sexual intercourse." In the truest sense, the original harsh, raw, and alarming messages of rock 'n' roll entered the wombs of innocence, ignorance, and bigotry during the fifties and poked social awareness, in order to give birth to a thoughtful era of social action and reform.

Rock abruptly challenged people to act on issues that had been ignored, excused as "indecent" or "evil," or brushed under the already too crowded religious and political carpets. It forced the startled masses to reanalyze or discard revered taboos and to examine new avenues of awareness. It promoted free love, a drugged altered state, freedom of speech, civil rights, and liberties for all.

Adversaries criticized rock 'n' roll as an outrageous crusade of "social defiance" that had the purposes of shocking the masses and destroying a civilized sense of balance within the community at large. Rock appealed to those of us who had not been given an avenue upon which we could autonomously express ourselves and rebel or give the finger to suppressing rules and regulations that we secretly loathed.

Rock opened doors that had been bolted or camouflaged. It exposed murky bias, inhumane oppression, and sadistic discrimination that had been veiled with denial or carried on the bandwagons of blind intolerance and "politically correct" oratory.

The right wing dubbed rock 'n' roll's themes and lascivious performances as offensive, irreverent, and dangerous. Such criticism only made rock 'n' roll more attractive and seductive, especially when a sneering, swivel-hipped rocker named Elvis Presley led the way to emancipation like a leather-clad pied piper.

Rock 'n' roll divided society into adults versus teens, who screamed for individual identity and liberation. Educators and religious leaders didn't know how to deal with this new desire for total independence. Few so-called "experts" knew how to control or comprehend rock enthusiasts' disapproval of the establishment. Educators worried students would drop out of school, while religious groups rallied to declare rock 'n' roll an "act of the devil."

When Elvis Presley gained national attention, his music was as foreign as his look. He represented something outside the sheltered mainstream's experience. *He* wasn't a "product of the devil," as so many antagonists wanted us to believe. *He* wasn't the problem. Uncompromising judgment was! Elvis made us all grow up and take a long, hard look at ourselves, individually and collectively as a society.

Rock 'n' roll became the most unpredictable, diversified, and creative aspect of pop culture. Its music is rebellious and subversive, dynamic and alluring, merciful and cathartic. It purifies and stimulates, or it corrupts and taints. As out-and-out pandemonium, it is structured noise. As a release of emotions, it can be an upheaval of chaos, an unveiling of tragedy, or a soothing, rejuvenating proclamation of altruism and love. It has no specific rules. *That's* rock 'n' roll.

Rock erupted on a public platform when Elvis first appeared in 1954. It was a gravely different world back then.

Nineteen fifty-four signifies a turning point in American history. Although a conservative, cold-war American mentality seemed set in its ways, a high-tech era had begun that required attitudes and traditions to be revised and modernized.

In 1954, Dwight D. Eisenhower was president of the United States. Sen. Joseph McCarthy launched a modern-day witch-hunt by falsely accusing servicemen and Hollywood writers of being Communist spies. In 1954, the first nuclear-powered submarine was launched; the first oral contraceptive pill was developed; the Supreme Court ruled segregation in schools unconstitutional; gasoline prices averaged twenty-nine cents a gallon; and hamburgers were eleven cents.

RCA introduced the first color television, and by 1954 Lucille Ball and Jackie Gleason were household names. In 1954, *Sports Illustrated* was created and Hugh Hefner's *Playboy* was published, featuring a nude calendar picture of Marilyn Monroe. Liberace was one of the highest-paid musicians, and music-chart hits included songs by Ray Charles, Fats Domino, Chuck Berry, Pat Boone, Frank Sinatra, Perry Como, Bing Crosby, the Chordelles, the McGuire Sisters, Dean Martin, and Bill Haley & the Comets.

Marilyn Monroe, James Dean, and Marlon Brando were idolized "silver-screen stars," and many now-classic films were produced including *On the Waterfront* and *The Wild One* starring Brando, and Alfred Hitchcock's *Rear Window*.

In 1954, "Three Coins in a Fountain," "Mister Sandman," "Cross Over the Bridge," "Sh-Boom," "Shake, Rattle and Roll" (by Charles Calhoun), and "Papa Loves Mambo" were among the most popular single records in America. The music industry promoted sweet "nothingness" and seemed to ignore what was happening in the world around it. Teenagers were bored, ignored, and eager to find something to glorify and revere.

In 1954, Elvis cracked open what is now labeled "the generation gap" with his sexual, macho image and his chaotic sound. Elvis created chasms that transformed the performing and visual arts by capturing the imagination of the masses and accomplished what few artists dared to express. Not only did he enliven the music scene, he gave direction, energy, and shape to what was to become the Age of Rock 'n' Roll.

Elvis was the antithesis of society's morals. His wild performances broke from the bland American mainstream of "Ozzie and Harriet" or "Father Knows Best," and the oppressed, youthful minority went wild over this raunchy, flagrantly sexual boy from the wrong side of the tracks. He had the perseverance to take a stand and the spirit to tackle and combat incredible obstacles in order to achieve what he wanted.

Ironically, Elvis represented not only everything teens were taught to repress by parents, churches, and schools, but a healthy respect for family and his elders. As he ingenuously defied the system, his actions and sound revolutionized television and radio. He became a forerunner whom the youth could follow because he and his attitude were at the right place at the right time.

Elvis was a symbol of hope that best resembled the American dream, but he did not know it. His magnetism and message demanded public attention, admiration, loyalty, criticism, scorn, and hate. He was James Dean and Marlon Brando with a guitar. He pinched America's restrained libido with his slight leer, vibrating, gyrating, seductive groin movements, outlandish outfits, and a slicked-down ducktail hairdo framed by long sideburns. To add to all of that, his scandalous entry was unexpected.

Using the only language he knew—laid-back, incorrect grammar spoken with a shy, lower-class, Southern drawl—Elvis confessed he loved his mother, God, and country, then performed provocative movements onstage that jolted a world audience. Because he represented what sociologists, educators, and religious leaders considered to be "evil" and "decadent" in a humble, virtuous manner, teenagers' adoration for Elvis overpowered any disapproval from authorities, and fans encouraged the singer to do whatever he wished—the more outlandish the better. He embodied their most secret desires, and soon they called him "the King of Rock 'n' Roll." On August 26, 1977, a reporter for *The Tampa Tribune* aptly noted, "For some he was the devil risen up to claim the nation's children, for others he was incomprehensible, but for most of a rising generation he was a relief from the stale, quiet fifties."

He was *more* than that: Elvis Presley uniquely interpreted and communicated the frustrations, passions, and needs of those who had been emotionally held down. His "hillbilly" behavior and background, "Negro" sound, Southern dialect, handsome appearance, and unusual performance ability were a unique package wrapped with the bows of decency and dissent. Because he was a white man who sang black rhythm and blues, he helped to merge and liberate black and white music communities. At the same time, his charismatic, unruly presence onstage best expressed an era that was going through its own dramatic transformations, and the people Elvis served to emancipate put him on a pedestal to glorify.

Entertainers are expected to enthrall and delight vast audiences. Seen as "bigger than life," many cannot withstand the pressures placed upon them by fans and the ever-present media, so to tolerate fame they often turn to drugs or alcohol or become reclusive. The responsibilities prominence brings, and the sacrifices any person in the spotlight is forced to make, are many. If that person is young and naive and peers are not mindful of his or her feelings and needs, it can lead to disaster. If it hadn't been for his unique upbringing, Elvis might have died even earlier than he did.

Music from Southern fundamentalist churches, black rhythm and blues, and aspects of country music are directly linked to the birth of "rockabilly" or rock 'n' roll.

Gospel music gave Elvis a true respect for music and life, and a certain degree of inner solace. From its earliest beginnings, gospel has given the persecuted a sense of self-worth and the suffering a hope for consolation. Gospel music appealed to all the "rockabilly" artists, and to combine gospel with the blues was a natural course of events.

Black rhythm and blues was ad-libbed and spontaneous. Its lyrics and melodies changed continuously because up until 1935, few people from lower socioeconomic groups knew how to read music. No teachers were available to them. Their music came from the soul or out of stories or harmonies "from God." Rhythm and blues is mournful, honest, and direct. Many songs deal with becoming emancipated from slavery of any kind. It's from the gut.

Elvis's early performances show Pentecostal influences. At Pentecostal church meetings, a trancelike, almost hypnotic state of mind occurred when members became "possessed by the Holy Spirit" and "spoke in tongues." These churches represented places where a person could let go of inhibitions and release the spirit and the body from daily trials and tribulation. It was clean, exhilarating music. Audiences could stomp, clap, wail, or sing without censorship because it was a part of the religious experience.

Rockabilly artists were also influenced by country-western music. Country-western included black blues, religious songs, vaudeville, ragtime, and soul. It has sustained aspects of western swing, honky-tonk, bluegrass, blues, Cajun, and mountain-style vocal duets. Country-western music gave expression and relief to hardworking rural folk.

The black blues, country-western, and church music inspired and ignited Elvis's potential. While his unique performance style was understood by black people, it seemed "strange" to most whites. Elvis wanted to be as fine a performer as the gospel, blues, and country singers he respected, and by the time he reached his twenty-second birthday, those he revered stood to watch and applaud him as the innovative "King of Rock 'n' Roll."

Elvis was the first rock/pop singer to have a single record sell a million copies, the first to go platinum with an album in less than two weeks, the first singer to presell a million records before a release, the first entertainer to earn a million dollars for one concert performance, and the first young, Caucasian, Southern male to bring to international attention the relevance of black rhythm and blues. Elvis was the first white performer to gyrate with explicit sexual moves onstage. He was the first singer to convert sedate, middle-class, conservative audiences into a screaming, cheering, swooning, fainting mass of adoring fans. He was the first singer to command a million-dollar screen contract. He was the first music personality to have a TV performance broadcast worldwide via satellite. In 1993, he became the first rock 'n' roll star whose picture appeared on a commemorative U.S. Postal Service stamp (the largest stamp printing in history).

Elvis became a sex symbol of legendary status. His music and actions set off a teen rebellion that spread into all aspects of society. Despite his many flaws, Elvis's energy, magnetism, and genuine appeal captivated and transformed the conscience of the masses. He did what he had to do, and we reacted, one way or the other.

Today, rock 'n' roll has become a valuable corporate commodity, a stepping-stone for the talented or freaky and a platform for social reform and political and environmental activism. Rock 'n' roll is freedom born from restraint. It zigzags across race, morals, religious boundaries, and codes of ethics. It extols raw originality and singularity of purpose. It has the ability to guard the conventional and spotlight the unorthodox.

Rock 'n' roll, once unique and "new," has become mainstream. Some of its artists are unimaginative and seek stardom and the riches that go along with fame despite the talent or aptitude to be innovative or distinguished. Some of its advocates allow themselves to become pawns of greedy, narrow-minded promoters or managers who seek fast bucks and don't care about the art or the integrity of music. Some rockers have irresponsibly incited violence to express frustration and anger at a system that they view as deaf, dumb, and blind. And some rock devotees are inventive, sincere contributors who stalk the edge and crave to inspire through candor a better, more profound way of life. Others rebel to be distinctive or shocking for the sake of being eccentric or bizarre, and a few rock artists—such as Elvis—are sensitive, daring individuals who have the confidence, desire, and ability to test the limits, regardless of reward or criticism. Their bravery is charitable. These are heroic artists of the first order. Because of them, rock is alive and still rollin'!

QUOTATIONS

Quotes about Elvis

Steve Allen:

—"The fact that someone with so little ability became the most popular singer in history says something significant about our cultural standards."

—(later) "I happen to think he is a very solid performer and will be around a lot longer than his detractors think."

Paul Anka:

—"To command such a large following, he must be a great performer."

Chet Atkins:

—"He was electrifying. I don't think anything like this will ever happen again, at least not in my lifetime. And I don't think there will ever be another man like him."

James Blackwood:

—"Gospel music was his first love."

—"If he had gone into gospel . . . he would still be alive today."

Gov. Raymond Blanton (Tennessee):

—"He had a significant impact on the culture and consciousness of America."

Pat Boone:

—"There's no way to measure his impact on society or the void that he leaves. He will always be the King of Rock 'n' Roll."

James Brown:

—"He taught white America to get down."

Pres. Jimmy Carter:

—"Elvis Presley's death deprives our country of a part of itself. He was unique and irreplaceable."

Ray Charles:

—". . . on Beale Street in Memphis. That's where he saw the *black* people doin' that [shaking hips]. Ain't no way they'd let anybody like us get on TV and do that, but *he* could 'cause he's white."

Pres. Bill Clinton:

—"Elvis was the first and the best

of the rock 'n' roll era. He's my favorite."

Joe Cocker:
—"Elvis is the greatest blues singer in the world today."

Louis Couttelene of RCA:
—"He was the greatest legend of the modern entertainment world."

Bing Crosby:
—"He never contributed a damn thing to music."

—(later) "The things that he did during his career, the things that he created, are really something important."

John Crosby, *New York Herald Tribune*:
—"Where do you go from Elvis Presley—short of obscenity, which is against the law?"

—"[Elvis is] unspeakably untalented and vulgar."

Bob Dylan:
—"Elvis recorded a song of mine; that's the recording I treasure most."

Rev. Carl E. Elgena, Des Moines:
—"Elvis Presley is morally insane."

D. J. Fontana:
—"If it hadn't been for his mother,

he probably wouldn't have made it."

Jackie Gleason:
—"He can't last. I tell you flatly, he can't last."

Rev. Charles Howard Graff of St. John's Episcopal Church, Greenwich Village, NY:
—"Elvis is a whirling dervish of sex."

Rev. Billy Graham:
—"I wouldn't let my daughter walk across the street to see Elvis Presley perform."

Jack Gould, *New York Times*:
—"Presley had no discernible singing ability."

Peter Guralnick:
—" 'What do you think of Elvis Presley?' was the first business of social exchange, and your answer defined you politically, socially, and morally."

James Hamill:
—"I told him he couldn't sing harmony—and he couldn't."

—"[Elvis] copied his early gospel style from Jack Hess of the Statesmen."

Patsy Guy Hammontree:
—"Many people never quite gave up the idea that Elvis was an evil force unleashed upon the land."

Delores Hart:

—"Elvis [has] . . . an enormous capacity to love. . . . I think he's terribly lonely."

Skitch Henderson:

—"[Elvis is] the Beethoven of his field. . . . You can't quarrel with longevity. The public is a severe critic. . . . He established the form, the tradition, and the flair."

Buddy Holly:

—"Without Elvis none of us could have made it."

Bob Hope:

—"Are you kiddin'? When he started, he couldn't spell *Tennessee.* Now, he owns it!"

Hedda Hopper:

—"He may be the kingpin, but in Hollywood he is a square in a peg."

—"I consider him a menace to young girls."

—"He is the most obscene, vulgar influence on America today."

Janis Joplin:

—"Elvis is my man!"

Hal Kantor, *Variety*:

—"In the eye of the hurricane the young man took it all with unnatural good grace and humility."

Marion Keisker, Sun Studios:

—"This is what I heard in Elvis . . . 'soul,' this Negro sound. So, I taped it. I wanted Sam to know."

—"This boy has something that seems to appeal to people."

Ku Klux Klan member:

—"We've set up a twenty-man committee to do away with this vulgar, animalistic, nigger rock 'n' roller bob."

John Landau, *New York Times*:

—"There is something magical about watching a man who has lost himself find his way home."

John Lennon:

—"Nothing really affected me until Elvis."

—"Before Elvis there was nothing."

—"If there hadn't been Elvis, there would not have been the Beatles."

—"We just idolized the guy so much. . . . He was a legend in his own lifetime. . . . Tanks for ze music, Elvis—and long live ze King!"

Liberace:

—"Don't allow any critic or audience to get to the soul of your art. . . . If you sing to the Lord, all of the heavens will hear you, and maybe—along the way—the mortals will, too."

—"Don't let the vultures chew you to the bone."

Little Richard:
—"He was a rocker. I was a rocker. I'm not rockin' anymore and he's not rockin' anymore."

Look:
—"His gyrations . . . nose wiping, his leers are vulgar."

Paul McCartney:
—"Every time I felt low, I just put on an Elvis record and I'd feel great, beautiful."

Jim Morrison:
—"Elvis was the best. The most unique. He started the ball rolling. He deserves the recognition."

Eddie Murphy:
—"Elvis was the greatest entertainer who ever lived!"

Newsweek:
—"Elvis was somewhat like a jug of corn liquor at a champagne party [in Vegas] . . . and his bodily motions were embarrassingly specific."

Peter Ochs:
—"The only possibility in the United States for a humane society would be a revolution with Elvis Presley as leader."

Colonel Tom Parker:
—"We do not socialize. Our great social interest is money."

—"When I first met Elvis, he had a million dollars worth of talent. Now, he has a million dollars."

Helen Parmeler, *Ottowa Journal:*
—"Last night's contortionist exhibition . . . was the closest to the jungle I'll ever get."

Dewey Phillips, Sun Studios:
—"He's a good boy. . . . He's always afraid he'll hurt somebody's feelings."

Sam Phillips:
—"Just don't make it too damned complicated!"

—"I knew Elvis was going to be big, but I never knew he'd be that big!"

Gladys Presley:
—"All I want is for ya to be a good boy."

—"It jus' ain't like Elvis, payin' attention t'trash like that. It's all Parker's doin'."

—"They won't let me see Elvis. . . . They're just tearing my boy's clothes off and we don't know if he's going to come back alive. . . . And now I can't even feed my chickens. It's supposed to be bad for his image."

Priscilla Presley:
—"He was the King of Rock 'n' Roll . . . a very special human being who touched our lives, our consciousness . . . as few men have ever done."

Steve Sholes to RCA executives:
—"I'm tellin' ya, this kid's got it!"

Paul Simon:
—"I thought his name was about the weirdest thing I'd ever heard. I thought he was a black guy."

—"I grew my hair like him and imitated his stage act."

Frank Sinatra:
—"His kind of music is deplorable, a rancid-smelling aphrodisiac. . . . It fosters almost totally negative and destructive reactions in young people."

—"He was a tremendous asset to the music business."

Cardinal Spellman, Buffalo, NY:
—"A new creed has been patterned by a segment of the young people . . . a creed of dishonesty, violence, lust, and degeneration."

Spokane Review:
—"Youngsters . . . were stealing

soil from the stadium infield [on August 31, 1956]. Presley's feet had touched it."

Bruce Springsteen:
—"There have been contenders, but there is only one King."

—"He's as big . . . as the whole dream. . . . Nothing will ever take the place of that guy."

Rolling Stone:
—"Elvis Presley remains the quintessential American pop star . . . an enormous talent and a charismatic appeal beyond mere nostalgia."

—"When he sings gospel, the audiences feel his loss and grief. . . . He's real. . . . It's as if these songs are his offering to the public. His confessional is in the songs."

Dee Stanley (Presley):
—"Everyone around him lived a lie."

Ringo Starr:
—"He was just like one of us, none of the old Hollywood show-off thing."

Gordon Stoker:
—"Elvis never realized just how great he was. . . . He'd look at us and ask, 'What is it I got?' We'd always tell him . . . , 'You got what it takes, that's what you got.' "

—"Vegas is what brought an end to the good years. . . . He felt like a piece of meat being carved up for everybody else's benefit. Eventually, it . . . took its toll."

Ed Sullivan:
 —"[Elvis is] a real decent, fine boy."

J. D. Sumner:
 —"He . . . kept his feet on the ground whenever people tried to make him into some kind of god."

Tampa Tribune:
 —"For some he was the devil risen up to claim the nation's children."

Rufus Thomas:
 —"In my lifetime, I know of only one other person who could have that kind of magnetism, and that was Dr. Martin Luther King."

TV Radio Mirror:
 —"Rock 'n' roll came from his heart and it ran over into his arms, legs, and hips. He was the real McCoy."

TV Scandals:
 —"What's most appalling is the fans' unbridled obscenity, their gleeful wallowing in smut."

Photographer Al Wertheimer:
 —"He made the girls *cry*. . . . He touched emotion. . . . He is nostalgia. . . . Elvis is their youth."

—"He had this intensity and it was the foremost aspect of his character. He had the ability to make you feel important at any moment. . . . He was intense."

Red West:
 —"He really developed that professional country-boy act with women . . . we were routing them through his bedrooms two and sometimes three a day."

Robert Wilson (*Memphis Press-Scimitar*):
 —"The King will live forever as the legend of rock 'n' roll. Men die, but the legends they create are immortal. . . . He will be remembered as nothing short of a modern god."

Wolfman Jack:
 —"Two thousand years from now they'll still be hearing about Elvis Presley!"

Youth World (**an East German Communist newspaper**):
 —"Elvis Presley was a weapon of the American psychological war aimed at inflicting a part of the population with a new philosophical outlook of inhumanity."

Quotes from Elvis

From the Fifties

"We were broke, man, broke . . . and we left for Memphis overnight."

"The gospel is really what we grew up with more than anything else. It's just a *part* of you, if you think about it."

(To his mother): "I have a reverence for God, Mama, but it's just music. It makes me feel this way."

(At the Eagle's Nest nightclub): "Man, if I could ever get people to talk about me the way they talk about Liberace, I would really have it made."

(To a Memphis audience): "Those people [Eastern critics] ain't gonna change me none."

(At Gladys Presley's coffin): "I lived my whole life just for you. . . . Oh, God! Everything I have is gone."

(To Marion Keisker, Sun Studios): "I don't sing like nobody. . . . I don't sound like nobody."

(Interview with Hy Gardner): "I'd like to have the ability of James Dean . . . but I'd never compare myself to James Dean."

—"I don't feel I'm doin' anything wrong."

—"Well, sir . . . you got to accept the bad along with the good. . . . I know that I'm doin' the best I can."

(To the Memphis press): "There should be no draft."

"I ain't no saint, but I've tried never to do anything that would hurt my family or offend God. . . . I figure all any kid needs is hope and the feeling he or she belongs. If I could do or say anything that would give some kid that feeling, I would believe I had contributed something to the world."

"I have not sold my soul to the devil. It's only music!"

(Regarding Jerry Lee Lewis): "That boy can go! I think he has a great future ahead of him . . . and the way he plays piano just gets inside me."

(To his manager): "Sure, Colonel, whatever you say's okay with me."

(To the press): "I thought it was s'posed to get easier but it's gettin' worse. I hate havin' to read what people write 'bout me. I jus' hate it."

(To reporters in Las Vegas): "The colored folks been singin' and playin' it just like I'm doing now, man, for more years than I know . . . nobody paid it no mind until I goosed it up. I got it from them. . . . I used to hear Arthur Crudup bang his box the way I do now, and I said if I ever got to the place where I could feel all old Arthur felt, I'd be a music man like nobody ever saw."

(To the press): "My first love is spiritual music—some of the old colored spirituals from way back. [I know] practically every religious song that's ever been written."

(To Army buddies): "After my first picture for Hal Wallis, it's the non-musical for me!"

(Regarding the Army): "All I want is to be treated as a regular GI. I want to do my duty and I'm mighty proud to be given the opportunity to serve my country."

From the Sixties

(To John Lennon): "We pay the price for fame with our nerves, don't we?"

(To a Vegas reporter): "The image is one thing and a human being is another. . . . It's very hard to live up to an image, put it that way." When asked why he dyed his hair: "I just done it for movies 'cause it's really gray."

(To the press): "I've always liked challenges. I like to prove I'm better than I was yesterday. . . . There's no fun in making a hit unless you deserve it. I believe in that, and I'm trying to live by it."

"The world seems more alive at night. . . . It's like God ain't watchin'."

(About ministers on TV): "They'll all get theirs!"

(To the press): "You can't fool yourself or the public for very long."

(To the press): "Ya gotta sell what ya feel. That's success, man!"

(After Sinatra verbally bashed Elvis and rock 'n' roll): I admire the man. He has the right to his own opinions. . . . You can't knock success."

(**Admitting he thought of being an electrician**): "I got wired the wrong way."

(**To his friends**): "I never met anyone who learned by talking."

(**Answering Billy Graham's criticism**): "I wouldn't do anything vulgar in front of anybody.... My folks didn't bring me up that way. I just move with the music. It's the way I feel."

(**Regarding Jim Denny**): "That sumbitch don't remember when he broke my heart."

(**To the press**): "The only thing that's worse than watchin' a bad movie is bein' in one!"

(**In an interview**): "I know what poverty is. I lived it for a long time.... I am not ashamed of my background."

"Somebody once called me a sissy 'cause I was polite.... There's a 'man' in *manners*."

"Gossip is little talk for little minds."

(**Regarding fame**): "When you're the top gunslinger in town, everyone takes you on."

(**To Colonel Parker**): "I want to be a good actor because you can't build a whole career on just singing."

(**To the press**): "Rock and roll music is basically gospel, rhythm and blues—or it sprang from that. And people have been adding things to it, experimenting with it."

From the Seventies

(**Talking about Marion Keisker**): "That woman was the one who had faith, she was the one who pushed me ... Marion did it for me."

(**To the press**): "I happened to come along at a time in the music business when there was no trend. I was lucky. The people were looking for something different.... I came along just in time."

"Everyone's nuts! Some of us just see it more clearly, that's all."

(**When asked about being lonesome**): "I am and I was."

"It's more important to believe in God than goin' to church."

"If your head gets too big, it'll break your neck."

"When I was a boy, I was the hero in comic books and movies. I grew up believing in a dream. Now, I've lived it out. That's all a man can ask for."

"People always look good in their coffins."

"I'd rather be angry than bored."

(**Regarding divorce**): "You can . . . love someone and be wrong for them."

"The only time I feel alive . . . is when I'm in front of my audience, my people. That's the only time I really feel like I'm human."

"Dreams . . . tell us truths that we've got to be smart enough to interpret."

(**Regarding the press**): "A lot of these guys ain't reporters, they're marksmen."

(**To the Jaycees**): "I learned very early in life . . . without a song, the day would never end; without a song, a man ain't got a friend; without a song, the road would never bend; without a song, so I'll keep singing the song."

(**Elvis wore a Christian cross, a Star of David, and a Hebrew chi**): "I don't want to miss out on heaven because of a technicality!"

"A man [is] . . . just a little boy wearin' a man's body."

(**About sleep**): "I'd rather be unconscious than miserable."

(**Regarding discrimination**): "If ya hate another human being, you're hatin' a part of yourself."

"I withdraw not from my fans, but from myself."

"Life is more than just drawin' breath."

"Love makes crowds disappear when you're with someone."

"Country music was always a part of the influence on my type of music. . . . It's a combination of country music, gospel, and rhythm and blues. As a child, I was influenced by all of that."

(**To a Vegas fan who handed him a crown**): "I'm not king. Christ is king. I'm just a singer."

(To a friend): "I'm tired of bein' me."

"Animals don't hate, and *we're* supposed to be better than them."

(On meat at dinner): "I like it well done. I ain't orderin' a pet."

"Long after I'm gone, what I did today will be heard by someone. I just want them to get the best of what I had."

Photograph by Ernest C. Withers. Copyright © 1994 Mimosa Productions, Inc.

PART I

Chronology of Elvis

and His Era,

1 9 3 3 – 7 7

Courtesy of the National
Archives and Records, and
President Richard M. Nixon.

CHRONOLOGY OF ELVIS AND HIS ERA, 1933-77

Following a decade of ostentatious facades, the Great Depression of the thirties crippled the world economy and placed America's populace in a state of mental dejection and in dire financial straits.

In 1933, Franklin D. Roosevelt replaced Herbert Hoover as the thirty-second president of the United States, and Joseph Stalin's ruthless totalitarian regime controlled the Soviet Union. By 1934, Adolph Hitler advocated the creation of a pure Aryan German nation, and Nazi storm troopers eliminated the party's radical wing. In America, those who could afford to pay ten cents for an admission ticket marveled at the movie debut of a six-year-old singing sensation named Shirley Temple, laughed at the risqué humor of W. C. Fields and Mae West, and appreciated such films as *Treasure Island*, *The Count of Monte Cristo*, and *Of Human Bondage*.

1933

APR.: Gladys Love Smith, twenty-one, and Vernon Elvis Presley, seventeen, met at the First Assembly of God Church in East Tupelo, Mississippi, and began a whirlwind courtship.

East Tupelo was dominated by low-paid, white factory workers and unemployed blacks from the Shakerag area. Town folk were plagued with hookworm, TB, and intestinal disorders. People felt, if one of those disasters didn't befall them, something else would.

Composed of five streets bordered with tiny, wood-frame houses, East Tupelo was a lengthy, morose mile from Tupelo, separated by a levee, cotton and corn fields, and a run-down ghetto. Plumbing was "out of order," baths and showers were infrequent, few people had electricity, and roaches and rats routinely infested boxes of food, beds, and corners of shacks.

MAY: Gladys Smith wanted to marry Vernon Presley partially to escape her family's sickly, depressing environment. Gladys was one of nine children of a moonshining, sharecropping father (Robert "Bob" Smith) and an invalid, bedridden mother who suffered from tuberculosis (Doll Mansell Smith). Living in poverty on Luther Lummus's farm, Gladys's favorite musician became Jimmie Rodgers for his "Mean Mama Blues." The headstrong, kind, uncomplaining Gladys was never a well woman, even from birth, but doctors were a luxury the Smiths and Presleys couldn't afford.

Before marrying Vernon, Gladys was known in the Tupelo area as a high-kicking "buck-dancer," who performed the Charleston or danced to Jimmie Rodgers's "Corinna, Corinna." People thought of her as a "joyous, pretty" young girl.

Buck dancing brought Gladys instant gratification and attention. Her friends called her "Clara Bow," and their enthusiasm for her vigorous, rhythmic dancing gave Gladys a vehicle to bring joy to their lives, and it instilled in Gladys a perception of how glorious a life of entertaining could be. Her buck dancing brought her instant gratification and attention. Joan Crawford's performance in the film *Our Dancing Daughters* ignited in Gladys a short-lived hope to become a movie star. When reality sank in, Gladys picked cotton and worked in factories.

During her teen years, Gladys dated Pid Harris, rejected Rex Stamford's proposal of marriage, and fell in love with a married farmer. When her father became blind and then died suddenly from pneumonia, he was buried without ceremony in an unmarked grave at Smith Hill Cemetery with a borrowed winding sheet from a friend, Lily Mae Irwin. The Smiths were left to fend for themselves without savings or security. Mother, brothers, and sisters lodged wherever they could. Gladys lived at Kelly Street in East Tupelo, in a part of town known as "the poor-white-trash area."

The downcast Gladys worked twelve-hour shifts at Tupelo's Garment Center for $2 a day (1932–33) while she supported her ailing mother. Her three brothers were of no use to the family. Tracy (born deaf and mute), Travis (an alcoholic who eventually died when he was thirty), and Johnny (who was somewhat violent and a drinker) did not care if the family starved to death.

JUNE 17: Two months after Gladys met the appealing, unemployed, seventeen-year-old Vernon Presley, they eloped and were married. After borrowing $3 from a friend, Marshall Brown, they secured a marriage license in Pontotoc County (where Gladys was born). Gladys lied and claimed she was nineteen, not twenty-one. No birth certificate existed to disprove her "white lie." As a minor, Vernon eluded the law by giving his age as twenty-two. The couple forgot they had no place to live. Impulsive, carefree Gladys later recognized she and Vernon had run off like a couple of kids. Getting married had not been a mature, adult decision.

As a product of neglect and child abuse, Vernon had little chance of becoming a responsible husband or father. He married Gladys without giving the results of his actions much thought. Vernon was a youth with no ambition, no goals. Living with him did not improve status or well-being. It made matters worse. The only benefit of tying the knot was being able to have sex without guilt, but in their social setting everyone fooled around anyway.

JULY 19: Living on Kelly Street and then in a run-down flat (soon condemned) on Berry Street, Gladys wanted Vernon to build a cabin on his father's lot so they could have privacy. Taking a $180 loan from a hog and cattle broker, Orville S. Bean, Vernon (with the aid of some relatives) built a house with two tiny rooms on Old Saltillo Road, which he and Gladys often shared with his ill-tempered, drunk, and boisterous father, Jessie D. Presley (J.D.), Vernon's mother, Minnie Mae, Vester (his older brother), and four younger sisters—Delta, Nashville, Lorene, and Little Gladys.

Vernon's wife was called "Big Gladys" to avoid confusion, a name that Gladys Presley hated. There was always mayhem with nine penniless people crowded in two rooms.

Elvis's grandfather, J.D. was an abrasive, exceptionally good-looking alcoholic and womanizer, who was thrown in a one-room jail on Lake Street several times a year after cavorting with prostitutes or creating havoc during drunken brawls at local beer joints. J.D. openly criticized Vernon and did nothing to encourage ambition, a sense of security, or a desire to help support his family.

JULY 30: The Old Saltillo house was near completion and would be one of the only things Vernon would ever do to please Gladys. Vernon came from the worst part of town "above the highway." He had no particular skills but was handsome and somewhat dynamic. Vernon rarely held a job. Prior to his marriage to Gladys, he had a milk route, picked cotton, drove a truck, was a carpenter, sorted lumber at Tupelo's Leake & Goodlett Lumber Yard, and later he did odd jobs for the Works Project Administration (WPA). He had no savings or assets and was always financially "in the hole." He often gambled or drank his earnings down the tubes.

Having the reputation of "a good for nothin'," Vernon was lazy, uninspired, and a sparse provider. As far as on-lookers were concerned, Vernon was a loser who could do no right. He was the spitting image of his delinquent father, J.D. Presley, who thought of Vernon as spineless, weak, and work-shy. Yet, Vernon appeared to be a happy-go-lucky, polite man who loved people. His compassionate, religious nature was what endeared him to Gladys.

AUG.: Gladys and Vernon frequented roller-skating rinks, took long walks, and sang at church functions for entertainment. A major pastime in the South was to sing gospel music and church hymns on porches with friends. Gladys often entertained her neighbors at home while the ever-roving Vernon played pool, bowled, or shot the breeze at Clyde Reese's cafe. After Gladys became pregnant, Vernon behaved like J.D. and stayed out all night.

1934

In 1934, G-men killed feared gangsters John Dillinger, "Baby Face" Nelson, and "Pretty Boy" Floyd, and Bonnie and Clyde's trail of terror ended in death. Less violent, but just as deadly, the Depression continued its stranglehold on all levels of society, forcing everyone from the upper-middle class to the impoverished to live hand to mouth.

APR.: Gladys Presley became pregnant when the term *rock and roll* was first heard by audiences. The Boswell Sis-ters used the term in 1934, in the title song (Brunswick 7302) for the movie *Transatlantic Merry-Go-Around,* which starred Jack Benny.

Gladys was unusually large early during her pregnancy, and she suspected she was carrying twins. During her pregnancy, Gladys worked in Tupelo's Garment Center in the stitching and the seam-ironing sections until her swollen legs prevented her from standing and she was laid off.

1935

Adolph Hitler enacted the Nuremberg Laws, which forbid Aryans to marry Jews.

Hitler sought to prevent "racial pollution" and promised Germans a new order of ethnic cleansing, based on "racial purity." In America, the United Automobile Workers (UAW) held its first meeting, the Social Security Act was enacted, the Works Project Administration (WPA) was created to get the nation working productively again, and the CIO was founded to organize labor.

In 1935, the first canned beer was produced, Alcoholics Anonymous was founded, a tape recorder using plastic tape was invented, New York's Rockefeller Center opened, and Kodachrome for 16-mm movie cameras was introduced. In sports, the first Heisman Trophy was awarded, the Orange Bowl and Sugar Bowl premiered, and the first major-league night baseball game was played in Cincinnati's Crosby Field.

In the arts, the NBC Blue Network radio show "Fibber McGee and Molly" and "Your Hit Parade" (sponsored by Lucky Strike) were popular, *Mutiny on the Bounty* with Clark Gable and *David Copperfield* with Freddie Bartholomew and W. C. Fields were movie favorites of the year, while *The Bride of Frankenstein* with Boris Karloff frightened audiences from coast to coast.

The year Elvis was born, Benny Goodman opened at the Palomar Ballroom in Los Angeles with his swing band, and hit songs included "The Music Goes 'Round and 'Round," "Stairway to the Stars," "A Little Bit Independent," "I'm Gonna Sit Right Down and Write Myself a Letter," and "Red Sails in the Sunset."

JAN. 8: It was a bitter-cold night when Gladys Presley went into labor and began contractions at intervals of every two or three minutes. Gladys was assisted by a neighbor during labor, who called the office of Dr. William R. Hunt, which was above Riley's Jewelry Store in downtown Tupelo, and urged Hunt to "hurry" to the Presleys' home. Gladys had never seen a doctor during her pregnancy. She didn't have that much money "to waste." Of course, the Presleys had no health insurance.

Elvis Aaron Presley was born at four thirty-five A.M., weighing five pounds and measuring twenty inches. His arrival followed the stillborn birth of an identical twin brother, Jesse Garon Presley. They were delivered for a $15 fee (which went unpaid) at 306 Old Saltillo Road, in the impoverished township of East Tupelo, Mississippi, across from a run-down Methodist church.

The birth certificates for both Jesse Garon (spelled "Garion" on his birth certificate) and Elvis Aaron (spelled "Evis Aron" on his birth certificate) are dated January 10, *1936*, the day the doctor finally signed and filed the certificates with the county.

Elvis's astrological sign was Capricorn.

"Elvis *Aaron* Presley" is the correct spelling of the singer's name. "Elvis" derives from the Old Norse word *alviss*, which means "all wise," "considered sagacious," or "intelligent." To honor Vernon's friend Aaron Kennedy, "Aaron" became Elvis's middle name. *Aaron* is a Hebrew word meaning "exalted, qualified, enlightened." (Note: RCA used the incorrect spelling "Aron" on its 1980 LP *Elvis Aron Presley*.)

Contrary to belief, "Elvis" is not unique to Elvis Aaron Presley. It was Vernon Presley's middle name, and many men were named Elvis in Southern record books prior to 1935: Elvis McCall; Elvis Heaperly; Elvis Gordon; Elvis Smith; Elvis McCoy; Elvis McCoy, Jr. "Elvis" was the middle name of Alonzo Elvis Tony Alderman, a member of the twenties string band named the Hill Billies. (The term *hillbilly* came from this group's title. Coincidentally, one early nickname for Elvis was "The Hillbilly Cat"). "Elvis" is a positive anagram for *lives* and a negative anagram for *evils*.

"Jesse" (not "Jessie," because Gladys wanted her son's name to differ from Vernon's father's name, "Jessie" D. McClowell Presley) is a Hebrew name meaning "God's gift for grace; symbolic of wealth." "Garon" was purposely given to rhyme with "Aaron," a typical habit of naming twins in the thirties and forties.

There were other sets of twins in the Presley/Smith families: Gordon and Sales Presley, cousins of Vernon's, were fraternal twins. Elzie and Ellis Mansell, cousins of Gladys Presley's, were twins.

There are conflicting stories about what happened the morning Elvis was born. Some accounts claim incorrectly Elvis was born first. The doctor wrote in his medical journal that Gladys had delivered a stillborn male child at four A.M. and that Elvis was born at four thirty-five A.M. One story asserts Gladys had to tell the doctor another baby was inside her, but that seems unlikely. It is inconclusive whether Elvis and Jesse were identical or fraternal twins, but most authorities believe they were "identical," and Gladys often spoke to Elvis of his "identical twin brother."

Elvis was troubled throughout his life by his twin brother's passing. Why did Jesse die? Was Elvis the fittest and thus the survivor, and was there a purpose for his being on earth? At times, Elvis consciously blamed himself for Jesse's being stillborn. For certain, it was a loss never forgotten. Gladys mourned Jesse's death for twenty-three years, and the guilt surrounding his brother's demise tormented Elvis. Elvis would always feel detached and lonely, as if "something was missing" from his life. In later life, he visited the area where Jesse's unmarked grave was supposed to be and often talked to his lost twin brother, as if in prayer.

The doctor put Jesse Garon's body in a cardboard box, which Gladys kept on the mantle overnight. She sobbed herself to sleep. Vernon was out cavorting with his friends and did not know he had become a father.

JAN. 9: Jesse Garon Presley was buried in a cardboard box in the Priceville Cemetery, northeast of Tupelo, near other Presley family members "so he wouldn't be lonely." The family kept a small, white, empty casket at their home as a token of their love for Jesse. (There is a plaque at Graceland's Meditation Garden for Jesse, upon which his name is incorrectly spelled "Jessie.")

JAN. 10: The beginning of Elvis's existence was shrouded with heartache and discomfort. After the birth, Gladys was in poor health and Elvis looked weak, gaunt, and pale. After the delivery, an unattended Gladys hemorrhaged profusely. On January 10, a concerned friend, Mertice Finley, thought Gladys would die if she went without medical care. She had lost too much blood. Mertice insisted Gladys and Elvis go to the Tupelo Hospital. They remained in the charity ward for over three weeks.

Gladys's ignorance, injurious eating habits, a lack of nutrition, and the slipshod medical practices in and around East Tupelo probably assisted in Jesse Garon's demise. Gladys accepted her minister's explanation of the death as "God's will."

After burying Jesse, Gladys became obsessed with the idea that something terrible might befall Elvis. Because he remained the Presleys' only child, Gladys became an essential, overprotective, supportive force in his life, as well as a burden.

Losing a twin brother at birth equally affected Elvis. Many identical twins believe they are "half" of the other twin, or half a person.

In *Twins on Twins*, studies of separated twins show twin bonding takes place at birth. If one twin dies at birth, the other often feels abandoned and alone or dependent upon having people around him or her until he or she dies. A twin often feels uneasy being isolated or alone, thus he or she can become a demanding, dominant, clinging personality who suffers from separation anxiety. In later life, Elvis kept an entourage of people with him at all times, agonized in the extreme over the death or loss of any friend or family member, insisted relatives live with him throughout his life, and did not trust that anyone would remain loyal to him. Because of a lack of confidence in others, he never totally trusted anyone other than his mother.

1936

In 1936, Franklin Delano Roosevelt won a landslide victory, Shirley Temple was a box-office smash, *Life* magazine began publication, and the "new machine age" created jobs.

JAN. 10:   Dr. Hunt signed and filed the birth certificates of Elvis Aaron and Jesse Garon Presley.

APR. 5:   Gladys clung to her baby and huddled in fear in their small house while a devastating tornado twisted through Tupelo, killing 235 and injuring 350 residents. Remarkably, the Presleys were untouched. The tornado leveled St. Mark's Methodist Church across from the Presleys' home and flattened other shacks along the street. The Presleys had miraculously persisted through another disaster, and years later Gladys convinced Elvis that God saved him that day (and the day he was born) because God had determined Elvis was "born to be a great man."

Elvis attended church every day from the age of one month. His mother had found comfort and salvation at the Parkertown Church of God and Prophecy after its members gave her food during a community welcoming practice called poundings. The purpose of this church was to keep the oppressed calm and orderly, and to teach them to thank God they were alive.

The Church of God was a fundamentalist sect that included the First Assembly of God and the Church of God and Prophecy. Church preachers instilled the belief that misfortune and hardship can be combated with faith and confidence in God. If good fortune did not befall one in this life, it would come in the afterlife. This was Gladys's hope and she instilled it in her son.

Worshiping and singing with all her strength, Gladys "made a joyful noise unto the Lord" with baby Elvis at her side. Ministers played guitars, gyrated, and danced wildly while parishioners rolled in aisles, feverishly jumped about, and spoke in tongues. The church was where everyone let it all hang out!

Church participation was the closest thing Gladys had that resembled her dream of becoming a dancer or entertainer. But she accepted the reality of being a common laborer who would probably struggle until death to make ends meet.

1937

In 1937, breadlines grew longer as people struggled to keep themselves alive. San Francisco's Golden Gate Bridge opened, Amelia Earhart disappeared over the South Pacific, and the *Hindenburg*, the German zeppelin thought to be that country's symbol of technology and progress, was destroyed in a spectacular explosion. Actress Jean Harlow, oil tycoon John D. Rockefeller, and composer George Gershwin all died that year.

CA. JUNE: After suffering from tuberculosis, Gladys's mother, Doll, was buried beside her husband in an unmarked grave in Springhill, Mississippi.

MAY–AUG.:   Gladys picked cotton on Capp Shirley's land at Reese farm. She told Elvis stories while he nestled on top of a large, long duck sack. Pulling the sack alongside her, Gladys picked over one hundred pounds of cotton a day for $1.50. In the humid, hot, bug-infested outdoors, the only nursery rhymes Elvis heard came from the black and white workers in those cotton fields who made up songs to help pass time or to take their minds off aching muscles and to help lift their spirits.

With this background and that of the church, it was no wonder that Elvis at age two left his mother's side one Sunday morning to scramble up his preacher-uncle Gains Mansell's aisle at the First Assembly of God Church to sing with a makeshift choir. It made no difference Elvis didn't know the words to the hymns being sung. The environment was friendly and half the congregation was kinfolk. There was no reason to be shy or frightened. This was where people were "saved," and it was fun to sing to God in unison.

Elvis learned how to jump and wiggle from preachers at religious sing-ins and ceremonies from 1937–44. It was good, healthy, spiritual behavior. This is why, when years later critics called his moves onstage "suggestive animation little short of an aborigine's mating dance," Elvis tried to shrug it off. He thought critics were joking. When they judged his behavior "unholy" and "lewd," they were condemning his church in the same breath.

NOV. 1:   Travis Smith (Gladys's derelict brother), Lether Gable (a friend of Vernon's), and Vernon Presley were accused by Orville Bean of forging a check. Vernon pleaded not guilty. He claimed the check Bean gave him was to cover the sale of a hog, which Vernon alleged he had sold to his boss and mortgage holder, Orville Bean. Vernon claimed Bean had mistakenly given him $4 for the hog, instead of the agreed upon $14 sale price. Some accounts assert the three men forged the check from $4 to $40, which is more likely. The men allegedly put a blank check over one with Bean's signature and forged his name and the amount on that check.

NOV. 10:   Noah Presley, Vernon's uncle, offered Orville Bean double the amount of the forged check, but Bean was determined to have the three men "really *pay*" for what they had done. These were hard times and no one would get away with stealing through forgery. Forty dollars was two weeks' pay for some folks.

NOV. 17:   A grand jury indicted Vernon, Travis Smith, and Lether Gable, and they were soon found guilty of forgery. The story appeared in the *Tupelo Journal*, November 17, 1937, much to Gladys's chagrin.

NOV. 18:   Vernon spent eight months in jail before he was formally sentenced because no one could afford the $500 to bail him out. During this period, Gladys campaigned vigorously and unsuccessfully for his release. She spent every night sobbing and wailing, which must have frightened Elvis.

To pay for food, Gladys took any job offered to her for meager wages. Elvis was always nearby watching his mother toil.

1938

With the Depression in its ninth year, the entertainment industry tried to help people forget their troubles for a few hours with such films as *Robin Hood* with Errol Flynn, and Cary Grant and Katharine Hepburn in *Holiday* and *Bringing Up Baby.* The "King of Swing," Benny Goodman, opened at Carnegie Hall, Walt Disney's *Snow White and the Seven Dwarfs* was the first feature-length cartoon film, Action Comics introduced Superman, Mae West (and even her name) were banned from public radio, and Thorton Wilder published *Our Town.*

JAN. 8:   Gladys dressed Elvis in his finest attire and baked him a birthday cake to celebrate his third birthday.

MAY 25:   Vernon went to Judge Thomas H. Johnston's courtroom to receive sentencing. His case was docket #9756, *The State vs. Travis Smith, Luhter [sic] Gable and Vernon Presley.* Vernon and his two pals were sentenced to serve three years at the Parchman penal plantation, a Mississippi state penitentiary known for being "tough." Elvis and Gladys were left to live on welfare, and their only salvation was attending daily services at the First Assembly of God Church.

MAY 26:   Orville Bean kicked Elvis and Gladys out of the Old Saltillo house after Vernon was found guilty of forging Bean's check. He claimed no one could give him back payments owed on the loan of $180, which he had made to Vernon to build the structure. Reluctantly, Gladys and Elvis moved in with relatives, Ben and Agnes Greenwood, on Maple Street. Gladys almost immediately started working part-time as a seamstress and laundress.

JUNE 1:   Vernon Presley and his two

pals were driven down Highway 61 to the Parchman penitentiary, while Gladys sobbed farewell from a dirt road outside the sheriff's office.

It was at this time that Gladys began a lifetime of secretive, heavy drinking, causing her to become dependent upon Elvis. Like most children of alcoholics, Elvis became co-dependent but could not stop his mother's drinking. Feeling he should be able "to help her get well," Elvis felt guilty that his attempts to please and cure Gladys were not successful. And like many children of alcoholics, he attempted to ignore Gladys's illness, hoping it would disappear.

At Parchman, Vernon experienced a more severe life where chain beatings, shootings, and crude disciplinary actions were conventional practice. Parchman's national reputation was that of being primitive, brutal, and degrading. The chain gang was hell, with inmates required to pick two hundred pounds of cotton a day in steaming weather.

After June 1938, Elvis and Gladys's relationship became uncommonly close. Vernon was absent and could not provide for his family's well-being or emotional needs. While Elvis watched his mother's loneliness and despair grow, his attachment to her and his craving to satisfy her became all encompassing, and vice versa. She was humiliated when Vernon was put in jail to await trial and even more discouraged when he was sentenced. Somehow, she handled her feelings with an outward display of self-respect and did not lose sight of the fact that she had a child to feed and clothe.

JULY: With Elvis on her lap, Gladys took a bus to Parchman prison to visit Vernon. She was pleased to know he was all right and that the blues singer

Bukka White (arrested in a recording studio in Chicago and incarcerated for murder) provided prison entertainment.

1939

In 1939, the World's Fair opened in New York City, while Adolph Hitler attacked Poland and war erupted in Europe. Meanwhile, Hollywood's "Golden Age" saw the premiere of such classic films as *Gone With the Wind* and *The Wizard of Oz.*

Elvis and Gladys were together every minute of each day and night, attending up to three church services a day, singing on the porches of neighbors at sundown, and sleeping together in the same bed. They made monthly vigils to see Vernon at the penitentiary, and Gladys reminded Elvis daily that *he* had to be a good boy and *not* turn out like his father.

1940

By the middle of 1940, World War II was in full swing in Europe. With close to 15 percent of America's workforce out of jobs, President Roosevelt nevertheless won a third term of office in 1940. Gladys Presley was frantic that the war would last decades and that Elvis would be forced to serve and die overseas. Bringing Elvis with her, Gladys forgot her worries by going to church and the local movie house. Listening to radio music for hours every night, Elvis and Gladys knew all the lyrics to the 1940 hits "Beat Me, Daddy, Eight to the Bar," "Blueberry Hill," and "Back in the Saddle Again" (by beloved cowboy singer Gene Autry).

JAN.: Elvis and Gladys slept together in the same bed until Elvis was a teenager. During the thirties and forties, especially in impoverished families where one or no beds were in homes, incest was common. With her husband in prison, the only person Gladys showed affection to was her son, Elvis. Whether or not they had an incestuous relationship is speculative, but Elvis's undying devotion to his mother and his psychological behavior point in that direction.

From the outside, Elvis appeared moody and restrained. He did not mingle with outsiders because he was ashamed of his father's incarceration. He also worried that someone might discover that his mother, father, and grandfather had drinking problems. Fits of rage for no noticeable reason showed Elvis was insecure and angry, although he often pretended to be polite, well adjusted, and confident. He was totally dependent on Gladys's affection, and his only fulfillment came through pleasing her. He did anything and everything she asked of him. One of his only school friends was a very poor boy named Leroy Green.

OCT.: Gladys and Elvis lived on Reese Street in Tupelo with Vester, Clettes, and Patsy Presley. Within weeks, Elvis broke an arm sliding on ice.

Elvis's upbringing differed from that of middle- and upper-class children. He easily identified with destitute black musicians blowing through horns or stroking a guitar in dark, smoky clubs. He grew up with blacks and admired their many talents. He had no way of knowing how to associate with white men in suits who could rarely hum a jive tune and who did not comprehend the anguish and pain experienced from daily poverty.

Elvis had no experience with wealthy, educated society. Throughout his life, Elvis naively thought everyone behaved and believed in spirit as he and his parents did, and that all white people enjoyed black music.

CA. OCT. 10: Vernon was released from Parchman penitentiary. He had been scheduled for release January 4, 1941, but because of his good behavior, he was let out early. He soon learned that Elvis had become (and would remain) the dominant male figure in Gladys's life. Mother and son had become accustomed to sleeping together and often walked and talked in their sleep. After his prison term, Vernon rarely made love with Gladys, and slept on the floor without much complaint. Some people felt Vernon's lack of protest was because he had been sexually assaulted in prison.

1941

In 1941, the National Gallery opened, the Mount Rushmore Memorial in South Dakota was completed, CBS and NBC began commercial television broadcasting in New York City, *Citizen Kane* premiered in Hollywood, and America declared war on Japan.

During Vernon's incarceration, Gladys placed all her affection, needs, and dreams on Elvis's shoulders. Neighbors recall Elvis being a temperamental, distraught child who would bawl until he lost his breath. Visits to the prison, made after five-hour bus rides, hardened Elvis into realizing crime does not pay, while at the same time those trips highlighted Gladys's undying devotion to Vernon. Her stability kept a semblance of order within the dysfunctional family. Soon, Elvis vowed he would take care of Gladys's needs because his father was incapable of it. Elvis promised himself he would someday make enough money so his mother would not have to work with calloused, bloody hands in cotton fields.

It disturbed friends whenever they heard Elvis purr to his mother, "There, there, my little baby," or baby-talk with her. It was even more upsetting to hear Gladys pout and act infantile. A role reversal was taking place—Elvis had become the parent and Gladys the child. In some ways, it must have gratified Elvis to receive so much attention and affection from his suffering mother—a woman to whom no other man was charming—but it must also have been a burden to play the role of the man of the house when he was still a boy.

MAR.: Gladys removed the doorknob on the inside of the Presleys' bedroom because she feared Elvis would hurt himself while sleepwalking.

JUNE: Gladys, Vernon, Elvis, cousin Sales Presley, his wife, Annie, and their children lived in Pascagoula, a port near Biloxi in southernmost Mississippi on the Gulf of Mexico. Sales and Vernon worked in the shipyards. Enduring a humid, miserably hot climate, and living together in a one-room shack with screen walls, the tight-knit group's stay in Pascagoula lasted until September, when they returned to Tupelo.

SEPT.: Gladys enrolled Elvis in the first grade at the Lawhon Grammar School on Lake Street, East Tupelo (then named the East Tupelo Consolidated School). He was an avid comic book fan but was not a good student.

Every morning when other children marched off by themselves to school, Gladys Presley held Elvis's hand and guided him to class on Lake Street. Here, disciplinarian superintendent Ross Lawhon tried to focus on every child's ability to learn, and principal J. D. Cole enforced strict rules. Young Elvis was in the company of men who took responsibility seriously. He thought they differed greatly from Vernon and he was correct.

In school, Elvis escaped the overwhelming, stifling presence of Gladys for a few hours each day. Grammar school became a place of solace, an escape from tragic realities produced by family members.

CA. OCT.: Gladys's sister Rhetha died in poverty when a kerosene can blew up and torched Rhetha and leveled her home. The atmosphere inside the Presley house became almost unbearable after Rhetha's accident. Gladys threw herself on the floor, spoke in tongues, and sobbed day and night. It seemed as if the Presleys were doomed to suffer continuous catastrophe.

The music of Roy Acuff, Ernest Tubb, Ted Daffan, Jimmie Davis, Jimmie Rodgers, B. B. King, and Bob Wills consoled Elvis during years of personal stress, conflict, and heartache. When his mother caught him listening to "the wrong songs" on the radio ("Take the A Train" by Duke Ellington and Billy Strayhorn; "Why Don't You Do Right"

by blues writer Joe McCoy), she quickly changed the station.

In 1941, when Elvis was six, local radio station WELO was housed on Spring Street in Tupelo. Its first announcer, Charlie Boren, was a jack-of-all-trades whose calling card boasted he could round up for paying customers "call girls, jury bribes, bed pans, trash haulers, artificial insemination, elections rigged," and "black market surplus," among other things. Boren's avocations brought in enough money to support his low-salaried broadcasting career.

For some reason, Gladys allowed Elvis to wait for a ride on Canal Street from either Mertice Finley or Reggie Bell, to travel to WELO's broadcast station where Reggie Bell performed with the Lee County Ramblers. Up until the age of ten, Elvis watched Charlie Boren's WELO broadcasts. Each was a free-for-all "Saturday Jamboree" (also called the "Black and White Jamboree") held weekly at the Tupelo courthouse, and everyone performed live.

Gladys taught Elvis social manners that implied he came from a proper background. He was not to swear, steal, show disrespect, mention his father's prison term or any family problem. He was instructed to stand when an older person entered a room, never argue with or interrupt an adult, respond with "Yes, sir" and "No, ma'am" when being addressed, come home on time, and never fight in public. Throughout his life, Elvis rarely said anything negative about anyone or anything. His role was to *please* people, not make them sadder than they might already be.

DEC. 7: Pearl Harbor, on the Hawaiian island of Oahu, came under attack on Sunday, December 7. A total of 2,344 American soldiers were killed, and the nation was stunned to tears and silence. The USS *Arizona* had been sunk and the USS *Oklahoma* had capsized.

1942

World War II continued, with naval battles in the Pacific, and Eisenhower was given command of the European theater. James Cagney starred in *Yankee Doodle Dandy*, and Frank Sinatra, Glenn Miller, and the Andrews Sisters were giants in the music world.

APR.:   Gladys became pregnant again, which caused her to be overly emotional. Not able to understand why his mother was acting strangely, Elvis got in the habit of waking her up at night to talk. Soon Gladys was the *only* person to whom he confided his innermost thoughts and feelings.

JUNE: A sobbing Elvis accompanied his mother to a local hospital as she hemorrhaged with a miscarriage. In this kind of circumstance, no child is able to handle himself dispassionately, nor could Elvis. Gladys was hysterical. She had lost another child in birth. Elvis comforted her, while Vernon worked on a WPA construction sight seventy-three miles away in Como, Mississippi.

During Vernon's absence, Elvis guided his mother through weeks of agonizing melancholy and despair. He couldn't help but notice the small replica of Jesse's casket kept in the house. It was a constant reminder his twin brother had been stillborn. As Gladys kept reinforcing, "God help us, if anything should happen to you!" Elvis felt obligated to be with Gladys morning, noon, and night. Soon, a restrictive, reclusive lifestyle developed.

Whenever anyone died in the family or disappeared even for a day, Gladys became distraught, fearful, and ridden with anxiety. She commonly clutched on to Elvis for a false sense of security.

While Vernon worked for the WPA in Como, Mississippi, Elvis vowed to protect Gladys and fulfill her every need as if he were the head of the family. In later life, he talked of having dreams of Vernon throwing him out windows when a house was on fire, or throwing him over the side of a boat when a small leak was found in the hull. In other words, for Elvis, being around Vernon was psychologically dangerous and uneasy.

Because of Gladys's constant adulation and praise of Elvis, he became a person who felt secure only around flattery and applause. By 1942, his shy, fearful, vulnerable side was balanced with a more confident I-can-do-anything-because-my-mother-says-so side. Elvis fits Sigmund Freud's analysis: "If a man has been his mother's undisputed darling, he retains throughout life the triumphant feeling, the confidence in success, which . . . [can bring] actual success along with it." For certain, Gladys's protectiveness and her ability to cherish Elvis molded the personality of a superstar.

Elvis had no strong male authority to emulate. Whatever his mother told him to do he did because it seemed to please her. Elvis obeyed Gladys because she continuously instilled the fear that something terrible might happen to him. If he did not listen to her, he might be hit by a car. If he walked down a street without her, lightning might strike him. If he swam alone, he could drown. If he played in areas where she could not see him, he could be kidnapped or beaten to death. She had lost Jesse Garon and she vowed she would not lose Elvis. Gladys made it clear, if *any*thing horrible happened to Elvis, she would collapse and die of a broken heart.

Gladys's behavior caused Elvis to

feel vulnerable and apprehensive. He had a huge responsibility: he had to stay alive and well to keep Gladys functioning. *That* was his reason for living. Her overprotective nature and her trepidation for Elvis's safety caused him to become secretive and somewhat hostile in his teens, but during his early years he submitted to most of Gladys's demands.

Gladys insisted Elvis not become like his father, a derelict criminal who was usually absent and could not hold a job. Gladys wanted Elvis to become *some*body important. He could be a movie star or an electrician. Although Gladys did not have the upbringing to instill in her son a longing for an advanced education, she did induce him to believe he was special and unique because *God* had wished him to be of that magnitude. He had to be "somebody someday" or "God would be disappointed in him!" What a heavy load that would be for any child to carry. Not only did Elvis have to gratify Gladys, he also had to satisfy God.

Relief came in the form of *Captain Marvel* and a comic book series called "The Sivana Family Strikes Again". Elvis quickly decided the best way to handle the mourning and misery in his family was to suppress it. He pretended it did not exist and did not admit to outsiders the gruesome facts. He preferred to think of life as a *Captain Marvel* comic or a movie in which everything comes out perfectly in the end.

As an avid reader of comic books, Elvis related to characters who had *no* parents. These were youths who had no adults telling them what to do. These children could solve their own problems because they were superhuman. Anything was possible! They went against the odds and won. They did not have to answer to anyone. They took control of their own existences.

One fictional character Elvis admired was the tin woodsman in *The Wizard of Oz*, who had no heart but yearned to feel. Day after day, Elvis told classmates how Dorothy was swept away by a tornado to enter the world of Oz. He memorized the Tin Man's heroic line to the Wizard: "I will bear all the unhappiness without a murmur, if you will give me a heart." That sentiment summarized how Elvis felt about himself. He had to let everyone else's mistakes and tragedies bounce off him as if he were made of tin.

Elvis's feelings were repressed most of the time. He found salvation whenever he had enough backbone to sing. By nature, he was timid, but something about singing caused him to stand up in grammar school and belt out songs. In song, he could identify himself as an individual. He was especially proficient at singing church hymns.

Every morning a chapel service was held at the East Tupelo Consolidated School, and Elvis was one of the few students who could recite prayer after prayer, or song after song.

He became a "chapel regular," which prompted Gladys to think he might become a preacher.

DEC.: Elvis had been inundated with the live, earthy sounds of black R&B, jazz, soul, and gospel music. He heard it on the radio, in the streets, outside clubs, and from churches. Men strumming guitars, banjos, or fiddles or banging on drums, sheets of tin, barrels, or other devices accompanied the black music that stemmed from gospel or jubilee hymns or Shakerag (Tupelo) black rhythm and blues. Later Elvis would applaud the bluegrass banjo licks and fast rhythms of men influenced by Bill Monroe ("The Father of Bluegrass"), Lester Flatt, and Earl Scruggs.

1943

As World War II continued, the U.S. defeated Japanese troops at Guadalcanal, wages and prices were frozen in the U.S., and *Oklahoma* opened to rave reviews in New York City.

JAN. 8: Elvis's eighth birthday. Gladys Presley had instilled in her son the notion that he could become somebody "famous." If he studied hard and got good grades (which he had not proven capable of doing yet), he could be a charitable man of celebrated status. God would make certain his path would be on an upswing. Yet, no one guided him directly to the avenue upon which he could escape his shoddy existence, nor did anyone tell him if he became a celebrity, his life would change drastically. These things were not discussed in his family, probably because no one really believed dreams came true nor did they have knowledge of what famous people did, or how "stars" survived. Elvis was naive and sheltered. To become someone of vast consequence seemed possible only in a dream world of fiction.

Elvis rode with Reggie Bell and Mertice Finley to hear the Lee County Ramblers at WELO's broadcast station in Tupelo. Elvis befriended Mississippi Slim (Carbel Lee Ausborn), the only real country singer in Tupelo. Elvis knew Slim's brother, James, who was in Elvis's school.

Elvis received "the baptism of the Spirit" at the Pentecostal church.

JAN.–DEC.: Elvis and Gladys took the bus to church daily. Elvis sang by memory *any* gospel song anyone requested to hear. He consciously aspired to become a local, professional gospel-quartet singer.

Up until the early 1980s, mainstream white America identified gospel music as "Negro spirituals" sung in "ring shouts," while black rural communities commonly perceived gospel hymns as "anthems" sung in "walk-arounds" after a hard day's labor. As a byproduct of the white community's mentality, less lively, often sedate, gospel music replaced the more invigorating Negro spiritual in many Southern communities.

Gospel music is more optimistic than spirituals are. Gospel songs state happiness can be achieved on earth, and joy is a preparation for an even grander pleasure in heaven.

DEC. 8: Jim Morrison of the Doors was born in Melbourne, Florida.

1944

In 1944, Roosevelt was reelected and approved the GI Bill of Rights, 16 million Americans joined the war effort, Betty Grable was the GI pinup queen, and Bob Hope entertained troops overseas.

JAN.: Because his mother continuously played country-western music on the radio, Elvis could sing almost every song known in country by the time he was nine.

In 1927, possibly in jest or as a rebuttal to those in Nashville who were offended by the class of country represented, George D. Hay called the radio station WSM (which showed a preference for country tunes) "The Grand Ole Opry," and soon the popularity of country music blossomed.

Elvis memorized country music lyrics and yearned to be like Hank Williams and Jimmie Rodgers by the age of nine. Entertaining Gladys, he sang songs by such country music stars as the Carter Family, Jimmie Rodgers (nicknamed "The Singing Brakeman" and "The Father of Country Music"), Hank Williams, and Roy Acuff, among others.

OCT. OR NOV.: Elvis sang on WELO's "Black and White Jamboree," Tupelo, at the Lee County Courthouse, with Mississippi Slim on guitar. On one occasion, Elvis shyly took the microphone and sang "Old Shep," a song that had been popularized by Red Foley. He also sang an occasional gospel tune or a selection from Gene Autry. Whenever his first musical hero, Mississippi Slim, sang a hillbilly version of country music on WELO, Elvis was all ears. He followed Slim all over town whenever he could.

Flattered by Elvis's admiration, Mississippi Slim allegedly taught Elvis to play a few chords on the guitar. When Elvis asked Slim to back his performance with guitar on WELO, Slim couldn't refuse. Afterward, Slim told Archie McKay that Elvis did a good job but couldn't keep time. After that day, Slim made certain that Elvis learned and practiced sharps, flats, and minor chords.

From WELO broadcasts, Elvis saw how performers acted on and off stage. He was impressed with their carefree, humorous, often risqué behavior. In the uninhibited studio environment, life seemed to revolve around music and entertaining, not tragedy and oppression. The exact opposite from home! At WELO, Elvis heard the music of Jimmie Rodgers (who came from Meridian, Mississippi), the Nicolas Brothers, John Lee Hooker, B. B. King, McKinley "Muddy Waters" Morganfield, Big Bill Broonzy, and Jimmy Reed. The success and optimistic attitude of Mississippi Slim had an everlasting impact on Elvis.

By 1943, Slim had his own radio show, "Singin' and Pickin' Hillbilly," which ran five days a week for an hour. Slim's hits "Honky Tonk Woman," "I'm Through Cryin' Over You," and "Tired of Your Eyes" ranked among Elvis's early favorites, along with Hank Snow's music and the boogie-woogie swings of Ernest Tubbs.

By 1944, Elvis clung to fantasies and comic-book personas that had dual identities: Batman, Superman, Danny Colt, The Spirit, Plastic Man, and his favorites, Captain Marvel and Captain Marvel, Jr. Captain Marvel is both all-powerful and vulnerable, just like Elvis felt when he wanted to be everything to Gladys but could not stop her from drinking or give her peace of mind.

Elvis quickly wanted to emulate Captain Marvel's goal to save the world and provide for his family. In later life, Elvis incorporated Captain Marvel's lightning-bolt emblem into his own Taking Care of Business (TCB) logo. The lighthearted (but serious) goals set by leading comic-book characters who projected a dual existence instilled in Elvis a sense of peacefulness, strength, hope, and purpose. These fictional characters allowed the child in Elvis to remain ever-wandering, but the characters also enforced in him an unrealistic attitude of superiority, and a sense of being indestructible. If Captain Marvel could do anything and get whatever he desired and live through it, no matter what the odds or obstacles, so could Elvis.

1945

The B-29 bomber *Enola Gay* dropped an atomic bomb on Hiroshima in Japan, signaling the end of World War II. When the war ended in Europe, Nazi atrocities were finally revealed at such concentration camps as Auschwitz and Dachau. President Roosevelt died and Harry S. Truman took over.

JAN. 8: The facts concerning Elvis's first guitar vary. One account claims Elvis bought a $12.95 guitar from F. L. Bobo's Tupelo Hardware Company because he wanted to accompany himself when he sang at WELO. Bobo publicly stated the guitar cost $7.75 and had a two-cent tax. He contended Elvis paid for part of his tenth birthday present from money he earned doing odd jobs around the neighborhood. Bobo also alleged Elvis was more interested in purchasing a rifle, but Gladys feared he would shoot a playmate. Another story tells of the boy's desire to get a $55 bicycle. The price was too high and Gladys feared he would get hurt, even though Elvis drove his parents to and from church revival meetings in a rusted-out truck by the time he was ten.

Elvis did obtain a "chewing-gum guitar" (so inexpensive it could have been purchased with gum wrappers through a mail order) for his tenth birthday. A local preacher, Uncle Vester Presley, and John Smith allegedly helped the boy learn to play the instrument.

Tupelo resident Ewel Dixon claims he allowed Elvis to come to his shop and play a guitar, which he says he gave to Elvis (value $12.95).

JAN–DEC.: Vernon lived in Memphis doing odd jobs. He sent meager wages to Gladys and Elvis, who lived in Tupelo on Berry Street (Aug. 8, 1945–July 18, 1946).

SUMMER: Elvis rode horses at a farm in East Tupelo owned by Patrick and Velma Dougherty. During the summer months, he enjoyed swapping comic books with playmate Wayne Earnest, listening to music outside black clubs, and singing at church revival meetings.

JUNE: Approximately five thousand people in America owned television sets with bulky receivers and tiny, blurry screens that picked up a few stations with programs. When Elvis heard about the "box which had people moving inside it," he was fascinated and ached to see one.

AUG. 14: President Harry S. Truman declared victory over Japan and World War II ended.

AUG. 18: Returning from a war plant, Vernon was conned into "buying" a house owned by Orville Bean for $2,000 with a deposit of $200. Gladys showed astute insight when she did not trust Bean and was skeptical of Vernon's purchase.

Elvis listened to hillbilly music, which was sung along the streets, in honky-tonk bars and alleys near his home. He liked the music's beat and loose lyrics.

Hillbilly music is often referred to as country and western music, with slang words and sloppy musical phrasing. Hillbilly is the music of Appalachia, but it has often been dubbed incorrectly as "race music." It became popular in the South because many hillbilly songs told stories with explicit narratives about people and their backgrounds.

SEPT.: Gladys, Vernon, and Elvis sang gospel music as a trio for no pay in East Tupelo.

CA. OCT.: Vernon became a deacon in the First Assembly of God Church and he bragged his family was no longer to be classified "undeserving poor" (on welfare or in public works employment). The Presleys were now "deserving poor" and out of debt. Vernon now earned $18 a week at a local lumberyard.

OCT. 3: WELO broadcast the live performances and competitions held at the annual Mississippi-Alabama Fair and Dairy Show, held in Tupelo, Mississippi.

Much has been said about Elvis's winning a second-place prize at the age of ten at this fair, when he sang "Old Shep." Some accounts claim he accompanied himself on the guitar, but that is unlikely. He probably stood on a wooden box, pulled the microphone toward his mouth, and sang unaccompanied.

Shirley Jones Gallentine (first-place winner of a $25 war bond) claimed she and Elvis went to the fair by bus. Other accounts of the day place Shirley and Elvis in a duet singing "My Blue Heaven" and "Deep in the Heart of Texas," but that is not probable. Elvis's second-place prize was $5 and free admission to all the fair's rides. From that day forward, Elvis had a lifelong love for the Fairgrounds Amusement Park, located on the East Parkway (which became Libertyland). Up until the day he won the fair's second prize, Elvis couldn't afford to buy an admission ticket to any fair. Many years later, he would become the park's biggest donor and patron.

His winning song, "Old Shep," perfectly exemplified Jesse's passing. Its words imply that not even love can save a life from going to heaven when God calls. "Old Shep" tells the story of a boy and his best friend, a dog named Old Shep. The dog saves the boy's life at a swimming hole, but when the dog is near death, the boy cannot rescue Old Shep. The boy does not have the guts to shoot the dying dog, so Old Shep puts his head on the boy's knee, dies, and goes to heaven—if dogs go to heaven. "Old Shep" touched the audience and was a natural vehicle from which Elvis could emote.

It is ironic that Mrs. J. C. Grimes was the woman who was so moved by Elvis's interpretation of "Old Shep" that she insisted he go to the fair to compete. Mrs. Grimes was the daughter of Orville Bean, the man who pressed charges against Vernon Presley, which eventually sent him to prison! October 3 changed Elvis's life. J. D. Cole, the grammar-school principal, was so impressed with Elvis's rendition of the tear-jerking song during school rehearsals, he drove Elvis to the competition. Gladys couldn't pay the fair's admission, so she stayed at home. Vernon knew nothing of the event.

DEC.: Elvis listened to commercialized sacred music by the Willing Four Soft Singers (a group of five black women), the Gospel Writers, the National Christian Singers, and the Four Stars of Harmony.

1946

With the war over, Americans began to put their lives back together. In Germany the Nuremberg trials found nine of Hitler's henchmen guilty of crimes against humanity.

JAN.: One of the only "entertainments" Gladys and Elvis attended together were church-oriented sings and "shouts." Elvis found jubilees to be hopeful songs, for the Presleys felt enslaved in what seemed to be an irreversible lifestyle. Elvis also loved spirituals, a form of American folk that promoted the idea that if life's afflictions are endured happily, a person's reward will be found after death.

JAN.: Taking the cue from Mississippi Slim's four marriages, Elvis liked to flirt with girls and then leave them. It seemed impossible to have a steady girlfriend because his mother would disapprove. Elvis didn't want Gladys to think another female was taking her place in his life. It was customary in poor Southern townships for young boys to "date" or flirt feverishly with young girls. By his eleventh birthday Elvis "dated" Eloise Bedford. Caroline Ballard and Magdalen Morgan followed.

When his hormones began to rage, Elvis asked Gladys to stay across the street whenever she insisted on following him to school.

Unemployed cousin Harold Lloyd (son of Rhetha) moved in with the Presley group on Berry Street. Vernon's salary was devoured by the extra mouth to feed, and he no longer could make the $30 payments on his second house.

JUNE: RCA Victor introduced the vinyl plastic phonograph record.

JULY 18: Vernon was forced to sell the Berry Street home to Aaron Kennedy (to whom Vernon had deeded the property) for $3,000 in lieu of foreclosure. Vernon did not know Orville Bean held a lien on the property from

the moment the Presleys moved into the house. Bean was Vernon's Achilles' heel, or at the very least, his albatross. No one knows why Bean hated Vernon so much. Aaron Kennedy gave Bean a deed of trust, or mortgage. The Presleys left the house, lost their initial investment, and made no profit. Vernon's plan to better the family's social standing failed, and Bean was forced by the town to destroy the demolished and condemned Berry Street house within months of the transaction. The Presleys moved into a small, impoverished room on Commerce Street for a few weeks.

Elvis's grandparents, J. D. Presley and his wife, Minnie Mae, divorced, and J.D. fled to Kentucky. Minnie Mae moved into the Presleys' living quarters. Within days they packed their belongings and moved into an apartment at 510½ Maple Street with cousin Frank Richards, his wife, Leona, and their children.

AUG.: Due to overcrowded living conditions, Gladys, Vernon, Elvis, and Minnie Mae moved again to a house on Mulberry Alley located near the railroad tracks, the city dump, and the fairground. Vernon escaped by driving a truck for $22 a week for wholesale grocer, L. P. McCarty.

SEPT.: The Presleys survived on handouts. Elvis entered Milam Junior High School at Gloser and Jefferson streets in Tupelo where he completed the sixth, seventh, and part of the eighth grade.

OCT.–DEC.: Elvis entered competitions on the Emma Edmonds Auditorium stage but won no awards. He often sang "Devotions" and strummed a guitar. Peer jealousy ended in a fight that left his guitar stolen and its strings broken. One of his only friends was Mississippi Slim's brother, James Ausborn, with whom he fished, watched movies at the Strand and Lyric theaters, and flirted with girls.

Gladys tried to instill in Elvis the ideal to be like Roy Acuff, Gene Austin, or Jimmie Rodgers. She felt Elvis was paying too much attention to black gospel singers and rhythm-and-blues men who drew attention to themselves by wearing "zoot suits," angels' robes, and flowing gowns. Gladys disapproved of "religious singers" who developed ornate dance routines and wore flashy attire. Elvis liked the glitz and pomp.

Elvis admired the movies of Rudolph Valentino, Dean Martin, Bing Crosby, and Fred Astaire. He disregarded the First Assembly of God's rule, "It's a sin to go to the movies," because for Elvis, movies were an escape into "the dream."

Elvis became a member of the library and was a Boy Scout. He didn't participate in any sports.

1947

A Streetcar Named Desire was Broadway's hottest hit, and the Yanks faced the Dodgers in the first televised World Series game.

Gladys worked at Mid-South Laundry, and the Presleys moved to 1010 N. Green Street at the edge of Shakerag, a black section of town dominated by black

◀ An undated, early photo of Elvis and his friend, Betty McMahon. *Courtesy of photo archives, Mimosa Records Productions, Inc.*

nurses, cleaning people, and cooks wealthier than the Presleys. Within days, Gladys's sister Lillian and her family moved in with the Presleys. To get away from the noise and depression within his household, Elvis often walked to the black Sanctified Church (located in a tent nearby). There, guitars, a piano, drums, harmonicas, and tambourines accompanied the frenzied, intense church music.

Elvis befriended and ran errands for black truck drivers, who gave the Pres-leys food and secondhand clothing for his labors.

JAN. 8: David Bowie (born David Robert Jones) was born on Elvis's birthday. Other music celebrities born on January 8 include singer Little Anthony Gourdine (1941), guitarist Jimmy Page (1944), Terry Sylvester of the Hollies (1947), and Robbie Krieger of the Doors (1946).

1948

In 1948, the Supreme Court forbid prayer in schools, the U.S. recognized the state of Israel, McDonald's fast-food restaurants opened, and television debuted "The Milton Berle Show."

JUNE: Elvis sang "Leaf on a Tree" to his Milam Junior High School class the last day he attended school.

AUG.: Gov. Jimmie "Pappy" Davis, governor of Louisiana, bestowed the honorary title of "colonel" upon his friend Tom Parker after being pressured to do so by a staff member named Bob Greer. Parker would one day become Elvis's lifelong manager/promoter. Governor Davis was also a singer and songwriter. His most famous song is "You Are My Sunshine."

SEPT. 12: When the Presleys moved "overnight" to Memphis, by packing every possession they had on top of their green 1939 Plymouth, Elvis again learned that security is illusive. Trucking for a bootlegger, Vernon broke the law and was caught for the second time. A further humiliation came when he was fired from L. P. McCarty. Without warning, he told Gladys and Elvis they were moving to Memphis, where he hoped his luck would change.

Elvis was uprooted and not allowed to say good-bye to anyone. Heartbroken and worried they would probably die from disease in a rat-infested welfare project without food, Elvis had no way of knowing this change was for the best. The family moved into a rat-infested one-bedroom apartment in a crowded boardinghouse at 572 Poplar Avenue. Since they shared a bathroom with fifteen other families, baths became unheard of luxuries, if and when water was available, and cooking was done from a small community hot plate in a dingy kitchen. Somehow they survived these unhealthy, congested, rancid conditions until September 20, 1949.

To pay their $35 monthly rent, Vernon drove a truck and loaded boxes of canned goods on United Paint Company vehicles. Gladys became a factory seamstress and later worked part-time as a cafeteria waitress and a nurse's aide. Their combined incomes averaged $35 a week.

During this period, Elvis developed a love for honky-tonk music, and he listened to such hits as Ernest Tubb's "Walking the Floor over You" and Hank Williams's "I'm So Lonesome I Could Cry," "Your Cheatin' Heart," and "Hey, Good-Looking."

SEPT. 13:   Elvis enrolled in the eighth grade at the Christine School on Third Street, Memphis. People made fun of his appearance and his shabby clothes. When his voice began to change, Elvis thought the devil possessed him. Whenever he sang, his voice cracked at the most awkward moments. Frightened and apprehensive, he talked only when necessary, which promoted the image of his being overly introverted. Sitting at the back of classrooms, with his head down and rarely looking up, Elvis was a C student at best. His favorite class was English, in which he frequently earned a B.

NOV.:   When Elvis complained to Gladys that no one liked him, Gladys was confirmed in her belief that Elvis was "a cut above" the rest, and that *her* son would become someone great someday. Besides, *she* loved him. That's all that mattered. He was not to listen to, or take seriously, any child's nasty remarks, nor was he to trust anyone but her. Taking this to heart, Elvis's behavior reflected this attitude in later life. He trusted no one but his mother.

DEC.:   Memphis felt large and austere to Elvis. No one seemed to take to this unassertive, mannerly boy who dressed in out-of-date gabardine and spoke low-class, gutter English. Because no one liked him, Elvis planned on making "a statement" with his looks. For

sure, he did not want to be like any of them! He was determined to be noticed, but he was not certain how he could accomplish that goal.

In 1948, the Memphis black-music station WDIA was founded, and Elvis listened to WDIA or KWEM to hear black R&B, country, and inspirational music by the Sunset Travelers, the Southern Wonders, and the Spirit of Memphis. Whenever one of Elvis's two favorite female singers, Kay Starr and Mahalia Jackson, were on any station, he insisted everyone be quiet.

Near bankruptcy, WDIA hired black professor Nat D. Williams (Nat Dee) for the late-night-early-morning show "Tan Town Jamboree," which featured black R&B and began to attract a large audience. That show was followed by Dee's "Tan Town Coffee Club" at eight in the morning. The "Tan Town Jubilee" featured the gospel songs of Five Blind Boys and Dixie Hummingbird and was hosted by "Hard Rod" Hulbert, Maurice Hulbert, Jr. Elvis listened to Hulbert whenever he could. When Bible readings and inspirational messages were included in his "Sweet Talkin' Time," Hard Rod became "Maurice the Mood Man," and listeners, including Elvis and Gladys, became hypnotized listening to Hulbert's deep, sensuous, personal Bible messages, which were combined with riveting gospel "jubilees" and "shout singing" songs. WDIA's music had a major influence on Elvis's singing and style.

1949

In 1949, a power struggle between the Soviet Union and the West continued, Peking fell to Mao Tse-tung's Communist forces, *Death of a Salesman* won the Pulitzer Prize, "The Lone Ranger" made its television debut, and Carol Channing

starred in the play *Gentlemen Prefer Blondes.*

Elvis aspired to be a gospel singer and befriended the Sunshine Boys Quartet at "shouts" at the Memphis Auditorium. He became a pal of their singer J. D. Sumner, who later joined the Blackwood Brothers. Sumner knew Elvis's first love was gospel music.

Sumner suggests that Elvis copied the early gospel style of Jack Hess of the Statesmen before Elvis developed his own style. James Blackwood, a gospel super-star who formed the group Master V, said Elvis loved gospel music more than any other style. However, Elvis did not *copy* or imitate any one singer. By the age of eight, he had a body language all his own that had developed through both black and white church meetings.

JUNE: Elvis was elated when he heard he could watch the annual Cotton Car-nival along Main and Front streets in Memphis. Standing with anxious crowds, he and tomboy Betty McMann watched young girls wave to them from flowered floats. After the parade, he and Betty rushed to the carnival rides, and Elvis tried to win his date a stuffed animal by knocking over bottom-heavy bottles with a lopsided baseball.

JUNE 17: The Presleys qualified for financial aid from the Memphis Hous-ing Authority.

JULY–AUG.: Elvis and Gladys attended church services at the First Assembly, South Memphis, located at 1084 E. McLemore Street.

AUG.: Elvis borrowed sheet music from friends, to look at or to memorize lyr-ics, but he practiced piano without it. Elvis was an "ear" musician, not a "sheet" musician. He expected people to hear a song once and be able to sing or jam it in three-part harmony—just like the black R&B singers or gospel quartets in Tupelo.

Being too poor to take lessons, but wanting to learn how to play the piano, Elvis was largely self-taught. He could "almost play" western swing. Western-swing stars he admired included Spade Colley (who billed himself as "The

King of Western Swing"), the Maddox Brothers and Rose, and Bob Wills and his Texas Playboys.

AUG.: RCA introduced the small 45-rpm LPs that required large spindles, and CBS improved the long-playing vinyl plastic phonograph records that RCA had introduced in 1946.

SEPT.: Elvis entered Humes High School at 659 Manassas Street, an all-white, understaffed, ill-equipped school with 1,700 students from grades seven through twelve, some of whom re-jected newcomers like Elvis (who wore shoes with cardboard patches covering holes and pants that were too short).

Miss Elsie Marmann turned down Elvis for the school glee club, stating he did not fit in with the music's style. Elvis was hurt by her refusal to let him sing and vowed he would "show her" she was wrong.

SEPT. 20: The Presleys moved to a $35-a-month, two-bedroom, ground-floor apartment at the federally funded Lauderdale Courts at 185 Winchester Street where they stayed until January 7, 1953. Across the street were run-down shacks filled with the poorest black citizens of Memphis. Gladys did not get along with neighbor Mary Guy, who complained to the landlord that Elvis's loud singing and guitar playing late at night was annoying.

A half mile away was legendary Beale Street, home of the black blues. Bill E. Burk, a friend of Elvis's during the Humes years, erroneously claims Elvis learned his crazy, wild moves in the Courts, not from Beale Street. In truth, Elvis incorporated his "wild moves" first from preachers in East Tupelo churches, and then from sing-ers at WELO and the blues boys on Beale Street.

Frequenting pawn shops, black clubs, and stores along Beale Street, Elvis soon bought pink and black clothing to replace baggy gabardine slacks from the Lanksy Brothers, who specialized in zoot suits, pegged trousers, flat hats, and bizarre, brightly colored outfits. Bright pink shirts accentuated Elvis's long hair, which was sometimes slicked back with pomade, a trick learned from black men on Beale. Bright pink also set off his smoldering gray-blue eyes.

Elvis did not care what anyone thought of his attire. Although he appeared crude and outlandish to other white people, he thought his look was stylish because it copied great black musicians *and* it drew attention. If his look triggered people's imagination and comment, it was powerful. Only the blacks wore pink-and-black combos, and only truck drivers had long, greasy hair with long sideburns. It was "cool."

Most Memphis teens had the clean, crew-cut look of Ivy Leaguers or prep-school students. Elvis's ducktail hair (or *DA* for "duck's ass") was pompadoured, swirled, and stacked to perfection with brilliantine, with a typical spit curl hanging over his forehead to hide acne. It was also Tony Curtis's "do" (complete with forelock) in the 1949 film *City Across the River*, a film Elvis saw at the Suzore Number Two theater many times. White suede shoes (instead of black leather loafers) furthered his eccentric image. His dress code was loud and drew instant dissention and shocking comments.

Elvis looked like a social outcast whom the middle and upper classes loved to hate because his image copied black men's dress codes, his language sounded like theirs, and his movements looked like theirs. Elvis did not identify himself as any one color,

therefore it never occurred to Elvis he was different. Thus, criticism leveled against his appearance or mannerisms came as a shock. His new clothing instilled confidence in him.

Because few people understood him, Elvis became a loner in search of a secure, positive identity while he remained radically unconventional. His clothing and hair did not conform to social standards set by whites. His "look" was black and his "sound" came from their musical heritage.

In 1949, Elvis entertained girls with his guitar, and two admired females were Betty McMann (who lived in Lauderdale Courts, with whom he went to the movies) and Billie Wardlow, who insisted he buy her chocolates.

OCT.: Elvis was prone to nightmares about his father harming him, or of being savagely beaten by groups of male strangers. He often cried out in the middle of the night, sleepwalked into other people's apartments half-naked, or was awakened as he pounded on walls or doors. Something was obviously wrong, but he refused to admit he had any problems.

NOV.: Gladys Presley had heard about Billy Graham's Christian tent crusades and wanted to hear him speak in person. She never did.

BY DEC.: Elvis saw the movie *She Wore a Yellow Ribbon* with John Wayne and *Twelve O'clock High* with Gregory Peck numerous times with various girls in the back row of the local movie house.

1950

Americans and Europeans recovering from the death and destruction of war, hoped the fifties would bring world peace,

prosperity, and a sense of order. Nevertheless, President Harry Truman advised the Atomic Energy Commission on January 31 to proceed with the development of the hydrogen bomb.

In 1950, the first Xerox machine was produced and the Japanese created a state-of-the-art tape recorder. Televisions were becoming the "in" thing to have for the upper and middle classes, and people talked of the "high-tech" future in which machines would soon replace humans in factories.

Elvis's experience in the church cannot be overemphasized. In Memphis, the Presleys rejoined a fervent Pentecostal church that practiced faith healing and speaking in tongues.

The Presleys' Tupelo and Memphis congregations were white and lower income. Daily meetings started with prayers followed by a lively sermon during which members moved about the sanctuary, sang to guitar and piano accompaniments, fell on the floor in trances, or shouted deliriously whenever the Holy Ghost "possessed them." Moments of incoherent rapture and frenzy provided mental release from daily tribulations.

Those who became seriously ill in Elvis's neighborhood usually could not afford visits to doctors. In the Presleys' church, it was believed God moved through a laying on of hands in which individuals often "recuperated" divinely from a sickness or convalescent period.

Uninhibited parishioners became possessed with emotion, and their bodies and voices did whatever came naturally. No one said, "You can't do that with your legs and hips," or hinted any movement was "too sexual, provocative, or harmful." Thus, from his earliest experiences, Elvis daily observed family members and friends in churches acting out wild, untamed, haphazard religious ceremonies in which unruly, almost sadistic movements were routinely performed whenever strong emotions and passions summoned the Holy Spirit to enter their beings.

The gestures Elvis eventually employed onstage were almost a toned-down version of the typical contortions of preachers and churchgoers. Perhaps that is one

reason Elvis was sincerely astonished when critics and the public made a fuss about his gyrating groin or hips. Elvis considered his motions to be tame when compared to the wild dancing and commotion in Southern fundamentalist churches!

It is crucial we understand the *importance* of Elvis Presley's acceptance of black people and their musical heritage. Because he had not been conditioned by anyone to act "white," and because he did not discriminate against blacks, he was able (without consciously being aware of what he was doing) to begin to bridge the gap between those two races through his actions and his music.

In the truest sense, rock 'n' roll was delivered from the heartland of slavery and black blues. Rock 'n' roll became a dissenting force that made the messages contained in the blues become obvious social and moral dilemmas with which society had to reckon.

The fifties was an era of unrest. The predominantly racist South was a breeding ground where violence, hatred, favoritism, and discrimination festered. Drinking fountains, restaurants, lavatories, churches, and most social functions were segregated. Blues and soul music became the vehicle upon which a few talented black men and women developed a sense of pride, while at the same time they expressed the anguish and heartache of their daily lives.

The twelve-bar song form, with bent notes and candid attitude, comprises the blues. It is quintessential emotion deeply felt. It is pessimistic and optimistic. The blues (like early rock) erupts out of pain, loneliness, torment, abuse, oppression, and affliction.

Elvis was inspired by early blues, which followed irregular speech rhythms and could be inspired by call-and-response get-togethers. Acoustic guitars, harmonicas, a fiddle, or a piano often accompanied the work of Charley Patton, Blind Lemon Jefferson, Robert Johnson, and Lightning Hopkins. By the forties, big-band jazz fused with the Delta blues and spread across the country when amplified guitars added dimension to sound and attracted large audiences. Muddy Waters, Howlin' Wolf, Elmore James, Johnny Lee Hooker, each had national hits, while B. B. King and T-Bone Walker incorporated smooth jazz-guitar proficiency into their club acts.

The only national dialogue people of color had was music, and in particular, the blues. The blues speak of despair, poverty, unfaithful lovers, gambling, crime, punishment, addiction to alcohol or drugs, prostitution, racism, hard labor, unemployment, the struggle to survive, and of love. Blues was the black community's rock in times of despair. It was a communication primarily understood by brothers and sisters of color. Elvis comprehended it, too.

After the Depression, the boogie-woogie era (popular in the teens and the twenties) began to slip into obscurity. Western-swing bands formed to combine country, cowboy, jazz, and blues into electrifying music. Bob Will's Texas Playboys and Milton Brown's Musical Brownies were popular western-swing bands. But blues bands outnumbered and outtoured the swing bands. Blues singers traveled and performed at roadhouses, bars, diners, barbershops, bus and train stations, honky-tonks, public shows, houses of ill repute, churches, and on street corners.

Prolific blues composers (who often diversified into country music) included Arthur "Big Boy" Crudup, Jimmie Rodgers (James A. Lane), Dave Bartholomew, Jimmy Reed, Willie Dixon (a competent bass player who wrote songs for Howlin' Wolf), Muddy Waters, Bo Diddley, and Chuck Berry. Robert Johnson, Elmore James, Robert Nighthawk, Johnny Shines, and Big Bill Broonzy were all early Delta bluesmen who influenced the forerunners of rock 'n' roll.

In the Memphis area, blues acts could be heard or seen on radio broadcasts and at black blues clubs. WDIA, known as "The Mother Station of the Negroes," had white executives and black announcers—two of whom were B. B. King and Rufus Thomas. Elvis knew both men by 1950.

NOV.: Elvis worked in the school library after coach Rube Boyce, Jr., kicked him off the football team because he refused to cut his hair. Elvis was not a rebellious punk with a narrow outlook on life, but rather a conscientious, courteous person who wanted to learn. He felt Mr. Boyce was wrong when Boyce judged him on his appearance and not on his performance. After this happened, Elvis became more aware of the prejudice blacks faced daily.

Many unexperienced critics point a derogatory finger at Elvis's grammar and call his language that of an ignorant, lower-class youth. His grammar was lacking because his schoolteachers and parents did not correct it. The use of *ain't*, double negatives, and laid-back colloquialisms were common to the areas in which he lived. Up until the day he died, he added *man* to his sentences, such as, "I don't understand it, man," a trait that came from the black community. Later in life, his manager insisted he emulate an uneducated, poor-boy image to foster sympathy from middle- and upper-class teenagers. A poor boy making it to the big time was more appealing and promotable than a rich boy getting richer.

NOV. 1: President Truman survived an assassination attempt at Blair House, where he was staying while the White House underwent renovations. Elvis realized the world had entered an era in which famous, important people could be killed by a stray bullet from a crazed person. Thinking he might be that significant a man someday, he told Gladys he would always have bodyguards around him.

1951

In 1951, Julius and Ethel Rosenberg were convicted of espionage and sentenced to death, Hollywood's *The African Queen* broke box-office records, and television's *I Love Lucy* was an instant success.

In 1951, Jimmy Denson lived near the Presleys in the Lauderdale Courts and claimed, "Elvis was the biggest sissy in Memphis. . . . He was so helpless. Infantile. All the old women called him Baby Elvis. The kids called him queer—Mama's Titty Baby. He never grew up from the cradle to the grave. He was always physically protected by other human beings. . . . We had wanted to take him to the YMCA but Gladys wouldn't let us; she'd say, 'My baby's too frail.' Elvis was mute. You had to look directly at him and pull words out of him. . . . We got him to sing onstage at school; it was the bravest thing I ever saw him do—stand up there in front of all the kids who had been bad-mouthing him. . . . Elvis was a wallflower. . . . [Gladys] was disgraced when he started wiggling his ass." ("Elvis in the Projects" by Colin Escott, in *Goldmine*, 8/10/90.)

JAN. 8:   Elvis's sixteenth birthday. Girls were frightened of him because his appearance was so unconventional. Some felt he acted as if he had a nervous disorder while most agreed he had the manners of a hog in heat when he was around the opposite sex.

APR.:   Bill Haley's group the Saddlemen (which became the Comets) exhilarated audiences with songs like "Rock the Joint," which had a faster beat than most country songs. Haley later fused rockabilly with R&B into rocking hits like "Shake, Rattle and Roll" and "Crazy Man, Crazy."

MAY: The Presleys went to Rev. James E. Hamill's First Assembly of God Church, at 255 North Highland Street,

Memphis, where Elvis became friends with the minister's son and listened to gospel sings at the reverend's home.

JUNE: Ignoring criticism regarding his love for black music, Sam Phillips of Memphis had become known for finding great, new, unknown talents in the Memphis area (such as the black artists B. B. King, Howlin' Wolf, Bobby "Blue" Bland, and electric-harmonica player Little Walter). Chess records in Chicago and Modern records in Los Angeles asked him to find singers for them. Sam Phillips cut "Rocket 88" (which symbolized the new Oldsmobile 88 with rocket tails), a song put together by then-unheard-of Ike Turner (who had been a DJ in Jackson, Mississippi) and written by Jackie Brenston. "Rocket 88" is considered the *first* rock 'n' roll music ever recorded. "Rocket 88" had "a driving train-rhythm beat, hooting sax, and a lyric extolling a car" (*Encyclopedia of Rock and Roll*, p. 429). Elvis heard "Rocket 88," thought it was avant-garde, and admired Phillips for having the guts to cut it. It was No. 1 on *Billboard*'s chart during a seventeen-week stay. Its flip side was "Booted," sung by Roscoe Gordon, which reached No. 2 in a thirteen-week stay on the charts.

JUNE 3:   Elvis started work at Precision Tools (a company that made ordnance shells for the Army) for $30 a week, from seven A.M. until two-thirty P.M., five days a week.

JUNE 25:   CBS broadcast a color television program on a commercial basis for the first time. No one had color sets and black-and-white televisions couldn't pick up the color signals.

JULY 1:   Elvis was fired from Precision Tools when it was learned he was underage. Cousins Travis and John Smith had secured Elvis and cousin Gene Smith jobs at the company.

Elvis was friendly with Red West, George Klein, Bill Burke, Billy Smith, and Gene Smith from high school.

AUG.: Elvis went to the Ellis Auditorium to hear the Blackwood Brothers and other gospel groups perform. Having no inhibitions even around more accomplished musicians, Elvis often sat at a piano in the auditorium and accompanied himself as he sang gospel songs. One of the first well-known gospel stars to talk to Elvis was J. D. Sumner. Elvis gushed about how much he admired his voice. When Sumner invited him to his shows, Elvis confessed he couldn't afford the price of tickets to concerts, so Sumner ushered his fan backstage and eventually got Elvis a job selling soda pops from an ice chest (which Elvis carried through the crowd). Soon Sumner would introduce Elvis to the famous bass singer Jimmy Jones of the Harmonizing Four and R. H. Harris of the Soul Stirrers.

SEPT.: Elvis listened for hours to the soul and R&B sounds of Louis Jordan, Dinah Washington, Lloyd Price, Fats Domino, Sonny Boy Williamson, and Howlin' Wolf that were being played by the black disc jockeys on WDIA and KWEM radio in Memphis. KWEM's "Heebee Jeebee Show" featured these artists because it was programmed by the savvy "Beale Street Blues Boy," better known as B. B. King (who had MCed "Pay Day" for KWEM at 2074 Union Avenue, Memphis). Only on occasion did KWEM play white singers' music. When B. B. King left KWEM, Elvis was relieved his replacement was Rufus Thomas of the Rabbit's Foot Minstrels fame. Thomas also hosted the midnight program, "Hoot and Holler," and was an MC for the amateur talent shows at the Palace Theater on Beale Street.

WINTER: By the end of 1951, Elvis's musical friends and influences included disc jockey and bluesman B. B. King, Rufus Thomas, a tap-dancing singer and disc jockey, blues singer Big Ma Rainey (the "Mother of Blues"), and the Blackwood Brothers, four white gospel singers who attended the Presleys' church.

B. B. King met Elvis while King carried his cherished Gibson guitar "Lucille" to a black club on Beale Street. King's hefty ten-pound Lucille was a heavyweight compared to the four-pound guitar Elvis played.

Born in Itta Bena, Mississippi, on September 16, 1925, B. B. King was influenced by the works of Robert Johnson, Leroy Carr, Elmore James, and T-Bone Walker. He became a leading exponent of modern blues and soul in Memphis after 1948. Dubbed "the Beale Street Blues Boy," "Blues Boy" was shortened to "B.B."

Singing lyrics that best exemplified the true black experience, B. B. King's distinguished guitar playing and music kept the blues alive in America. His musical message has added meaning and significance to blues worldwide, and it benefited the musical growth of Elvis.

Elvis listened for hours to the live music of B. B. King as well as the broadcast sounds of King's cousin, the famous Delta bluesman and soul singer, Bukka White (Booker T. Washington). Elvis joined friends at the Green Owl club to hear the blues vocalist and harmonica player Junior Parker (who wrote Presley's 1955 classic "Mystery Train"); Rufus Thomas, a dancing bluesman and Memphis disc jockey; Ukulele Ike, a blues musician at the Gray Mule (a black beer joint in Memphis), whom Elvis may have attempted to imitate early in his career; and Ike Turner, whose 1951 band the Kings of Rhythm recorded "Rocket 88," on the Sun label

DEC.: Jackie Wilson (1934–84) with Billy Ward and the Dominoes were the first group to chart on *Billboard*'s Top 100 list with a black rhythm and blues song, "Sixty Minute Man" (Federal 12022; which is heard in the 1979 movie *Elvis*).

1952

In 1952, Truman signed the Korea War GI Bill, *Mad* comics made its debut, and Gen. Dwight D. Eisenhower was elected President.

JAN.: Elvis practiced the piano a great deal and wanted to accompany himself at clubs. Feeling his oats, he often invited girls to clubs, but few accepted because they weren't allowed to go inside such "raunchy" dives.

During the fifties, years of social denial started to unravel. Although it appeared to be a calmer, more relaxed environment than today's fast-paced, faxified world, the image of life projected was partially a facade—deep in the bowels of society there ticked several time bombs.

People were emotionally frustrated. Women wanted to break loose from male bondage and domination and be treated as equals. People of color were tired of being held back. Society was aching for emancipation but not recognizing or admitting it. The time was ripe for rock 'n' roll!

FEB.: World-famous singer Eddy Arnold and his manager, the infamous "Colonel" Tom Parker, split up when Arnold accused Parker of cheating him. The music world was shocked when Arnold left Parker, but the clever manager quickly established a quasi-office with Tom Diskin and Jim O'Brien in the lobby of the Grand Ole Opry's WSM radio headquarters and rallied around Hank Snow. WSM's Artist Service Bureau was inefficiently run by Jim Denny in the same building. Parker paid no rent and allowed phone bills to be paid in full without detec-

tion for years by unaware executives of the Opry's Service Bureau. The indie promoters Parker, Charley Brown, and Oscar Davis conducted business without overhead. When their activities were discovered, Parker moved his and Hank Snow's newly formed Jamboree Attractions to a room in Parker's home in Madison, Tennessee.

MAR.: Disc jockey Sleepy-Eyed John Lepley booked Elvis into Memphis's Palm Club on Summer Avenue. His gig went virtually unnoticed. Keeping up with all the newest records and sounds, Elvis frequented Poplar Tunes Record Shop at 308 Poplar Avenue and listened to 45s for hours.

CA. MAR.: James R. Denny fired Elvis's idol, Hank Williams, from Nashville's Grand Ole Opry because Williams missed a performance. Denny would one day reject Elvis at the Opry.

APR. 17: Elvis took a part-time ushering job at Lowe's State Theater, where he became mesmerized by Tony Curtis in heroic, swashbuckling epic films. James Dean and Marlon Brando soon became Elvis's favorite actors as he watched movies for free.

MAY 28: Elvis accepted free candy from an usherette at Lowe's. A snitch reported it to the boss; Elvis knocked the tattletale to the ground and Elvis was fired. Gladys, who worried Elvis was becoming like Vernon, was dismayed. Sudden bursts of rage surfaced throughout Elvis's life and were usually expressed physically rather than verbally. Partly this was because schoolmates had called Elvis "a sissy" throughout his childhood. Elvis reasoned, no sissy puts his dukes up and fights.

Elvis's defiant-looking appearance and his respectable manners in front of adults confused onlookers, who did not know how to react to him. From teachers, he stimulated devotion, special favors, and appreciation because he "kissed up" to them. From girls, he aroused coyness, aggression, and fear. Male peers often hated him, especially when they thought he was wooing authority figures in order to get out of work or obtain a higher grade at school.

Red West, a fellow slum resident who attended Humes, claims he saved Elvis from being severely beaten in a lavatory by a group of enraged boys. Although West didn't really like Elvis, he recognized Elvis's fear and occasionally protected him because he couldn't adequately defend himself.

Elvis's closest high school buddies included Red West (who eventually entered Jones County Junior College on a football scholarship); George Klein (president of Elvis's class, editor of the yearbook, and Humes's "most likely to succeed," who became a disc jockey and lecturer at Memphis State University); Bill E. Burke (writer and avid fan); Billy and Gene Smith (cousins); and Bill "Blackie" Black (whom he met in 1951 at the Lauderdale Courts and who performed with the Doug Poindexter Starlite Wranglers).

Prior to Elvis's professional debut, he and singer Johnny Burnette hung out together, listening to honky-tonk music at the Disc Shop at the junction of Main and Beale streets. Together, they sang for the Memphis Firemen. On occasion someone would see Elvis and yell, "Let's hear ya sing, boy," and Elvis raised the roofs with an unconventional, raw, rocking sound.

From 1950–53, Elvis played minimal guitar licks while he sang at the Odd Fellows Club and for the First Assembly of God Church in Memphis.

SPRING OF 1952:   The Presleys received an eviction notice from Lauderdale Courts.

AUG. 6:   Elvis started work at Upholsteries Specialties Company on West Georgia Avenue. To get the job, he lied about his age.

SEPT.:   Elvis worked at Marl Metal Manufacturing Company at 208 Georgia Avenue in Memphis, for $1 an hour from three to seven-thirty P.M. He was hired by Robert Bozoff to work in the fabricating division where dinette sets were made.

OCT.:   Sony introduced the first pocket-size transistor radio.

NOV.:   Gladys forced Elvis to quit his job at Marl Metal because teachers complained he slept in class.

DEC. 24:   Elvis sang "Old Shep" and "Cold, Cold Icy Fingers" at Humes's Christmas concert and received rave reviews. He was inspired by the applause he received.

DEC. 25–31:   Elvis watched Gene Kelly, Debbie Reynolds, Donald O'Connor, and Cyd Charisse in *Singin' in the Rain*. He also liked Grace Kelly and Gary Cooper in the classic cowboy film *High Noon* with its song "Do Not Forsake Me." Other favorite song releases of 1952 were Hank Williams's "Your Cheatin' Heart," "Count Your Blessings (Instead of Sheep)" by Irving Berlin, and "I Saw Momma Kissing Santa Claus" by Tommie Connor (a song that Elvis sang to Gladys on Christmas morning).

By the end of 1952, *Mad* magazine and the *National Enquirer* were popular newsstand items.

1953

In 1953, the Korean War ended, Marilyn Monroe was the cover and nude centerfold for the debut of *Playboy*, and Sen. Joe McCarthy and the House Un-American Activities Committee falsely accused hundreds of American citizens of being Communists.

JAN. 1: Hank Williams's sudden death devastated Elvis. Williams was a star, and stars were not supposed to die. Elvis listened for hours in tears to Williams's music.

JAN. 7: The Presleys moved to a small, $52-a-month poverty apartment at 398 Cypress Street, in a seven-room house split into four apartments. Elvis worked for the M. B. Parker Machinist Shop until September. He was a member of the Independent Order of the Odd Fellows, Memphis, during three years of high school and was a member of ROTC.

JAN. 8: Vernon and Gladys paid $50 for a 1942 Lincoln Zephyr coupe, which they gave to Elvis on his eighteenth birthday. He had his own wheels and that gave him independence, which was something Gladys had not considered. She did not know how to drive, so she used Elvis's new present as an excuse to be with him and asked him to drive her everywhere (which he did).

FEB.: Elvis had his hair trimmed at Blake's Coiffure, Memphis, by Blake Johnson. Elvis often complained, "Jeez, you cut it too short!" Johnson felt it was "way too long for a white boy."

MAR.: *Captain Marvel* and *Captain Marvel, Jr.* comic books were taken off the market. This, coupled with Hank Williams's recent death, forced Elvis to face the reality that nothing lasts forever. His real-life and fictional heroes died in 1953. He decided it would be wonderful if, somehow, he could take their places in the world by becoming a singing folk hero who could achieve astronomical feats in movies. Of course, it was only a dream.

▶ Elvis outside the Eagle's Nest nightclub in Memphis, Tennessee, around 1953. *Courtesy of Drew Canale and photo archives, Mimosa Records Productions, Inc.*

APR. 1: The Presleys moved to a duplex at 462 Alabama Street, across from Lauderdale Courts, renting an apartment for $50 a month plus utilities. Grandma Minnie Mae slept on a cot outside a bedroom in which Elvis, Gladys, and Vernon slept. At times, Elvis slept on a sofa near Minnie Mae. Rabbi Alfred Fruchter and his wife, Jeannette, lived upstairs and quickly befriended the Presleys. Elvis was impressed the rabbi owned a phonograph (from which he would loudly play music by famous cantors) and a telephone (which Elvis was allowed to use in emergencies).

APR. 9: Elvis sang a blues rendition of "Keep Them Icy Fingers off of Me" in Mildred Scrivener's "Annual Minstrel." He was listed in the program as No. 16, "guitarist, Elvis Prestly [*sic*]," at Humes High School. Much to his surprise, he received an encore and shyly returned to the stage to sing " 'Til I Waltz Again With You" (some sources claim the encore was "Old Shep," which caused teachers to cry). Elvis was so astonished his peers liked his performance, he started to stutter backstage and Mildred Scrivener had to push him back onstage for his encore. From the enthusiastic reception he received, Elvis realized singers were appreciated at a special level. It made no real difference if his name was misspelled on the program. The audience would remember *him*. New school chums included Bill Leaptrot (who became a photographer for the *Press-Scimitar*) and Jack Seelig.

MAY 26: A penniless, long-haired, guitar-carrying Elvis hitchhiked to, and sang at, the First Jimmie Rodgers Memorial Talent Show, held at the Lamar Hotel in Meridian, Mississippi (sponsored by the *Meridian Star*). The audience reacted to Elvis with disbelief, and winning a second-place guitar did not sit well with Elvis. He sang a country version of "I'm Left, You're Right, She's Gone" and a rock variant of "Baby, Let's Play House." When hillbilly purists "booed and laughed him off the stage," Curtis Robinson, a reporter for the *Meridian Star*, remembered, "Elvis got so mad he swore he would never come back to Meridian." Elvis's funky sound was a mixture of Southern gospel, rhythm and blues, and Jimmie Rodgers's country tradition, and his stage presence resembled a young Howlin' Wolf's. Elvis was *no* mainstream American youth. The Meridian audience didn't know what hit them.

From the beginning, Elvis gave the public a rock 'n' roll sound that was both black *and* white in origin. He broke all rules of decorum. He was sexy. He was dangerous. His bump and grind, lascivious looks, and impish grin caused the status quo to recoil and teenagers to applaud and swoon.

While Elvis concentrated on gospel singing and rhythm and blues, Gladys was going through a major mental transition. She was forty-one and thought she looked older than Vernon, which was true, but she did not want her age known. Noticing every tiny wrinkle, Gladys began dyeing her hair black, and whenever she gained weight, she took diet pills to reduce. She was still obsessed about Jesse's dying at birth and was angry the family was still poor. Her drinking caused her to become too loud in bars, and her behavior repulsed Elvis, who vowed never to touch alcohol.

Frustrated his mother was not acting "normal," Elvis began to reinforce his intentions to become a success. At one point, he skipped classes and eventually dropped out of high school for a short period—a move that pleased Vernon. Elvis reasoned a truck driver or a singer did not need a degree. His high school years were ending, and the pressure was on him to perform successfully. Perhaps a part of him was resigned that the Presley men would always live in poverty. No matter what the reason, Elvis neglected his studies in his senior year. But because Gladys insisted he finish high school, he did graduate with his class.

During this period, Gladys began to feel preseparation anxiety regarding Elvis. Elvis was in his eighteenth year and he might leave the family after graduation. Gladys's fears surfaced in uneasiness, a gain of weight, excessive drinking, and continuous gloom. Taking on extra jobs, and arguing continually with Vernon about his future, Elvis earned extra money and got out of the house by working a night shift at Marl Metal Manufacturing Company.

Singing was the one thread that kept Elvis from falling apart at the seams. He became an "entertainer" at high school parties and local clubs. If people forgot what song he sang, they would remember him in the future. He would make certain of that! During the fifties, most teens' "American dream" meant prosperity. For Elvis and the men on Beale Street, it signified survival.

JUNE 3: Elvis graduated from Class 202 at Humes High School. Mrs. Weir Harris administered to Elvis his General Aptitude Test batteries and his scores were average. She liked Elvis, so she gave Gladys Tipler at Crown Electric Elvis's name as someone reliable enough to drive a truck. Elvis was grateful, but his earnings were spent on new clothing bought from the Lansky Brothers rather than on the family, and this upset the ever-complaining Gladys.

JUNE: Bill Haley and the Comets started some static with "Crazy Man, Crazy" and bebop music became old hat.

JUNE: Bill Morris and Elvis attended all night gospel sings at the Ellis Auditorium in Memphis, where Elvis accompanied himself on a Knabe piano while singing R&B and gospel music.

While playing the Ellis Auditorium's piano, Elvis told Bill Burke, "Man, if I could ever get people to talk about me the way they talk about Liberace, I

would really have it made!" (*Early Elvis* by Bill Burke.) Elvis listened to Liberace's music for hours. Elvis had no way of knowing in 1953 that his own charismatic magnetism would hit the world like a nuclear explosion.

CA. JULY: Elvis may have performed in Frayser, Tennessee, at Red's Place, a small club, and at the Silver Stallion nightclub, located at 1447 Union Street. Through J. D. Sumner he met the black quartet the Swan Silvertones and was impressed with their harmonies.

CA. JULY: Elvis may have worked as a busboy while he sang at the Eagle's Nest nightclub on Lamar Avenue where photographs of him were taken in a busboy's uniform.

Elvis attended gospel sings at the Ellis Auditorium, where he listened to—and often joined—the Blackwood Brothers and their young singing side-

kicks, the Songfellows. The Black-woods' singing was uplifting, inspiring, and hopeful in an otherwise miserable existence. Gospel music's credo became an integral part of Elvis. He craved its message because it soothed and calmed him. He fantasized about becoming a great tenor gospel soloist with some famous quartet, and this dream was praised by Gladys.

During the fifties, Elvis often soloed at church with a choir accompanying him. From the genuine acceptance he received from church congregations, Elvis cultivated a yearning to become a professional singer.

James Blackwood allowed Elvis to listen backstage to the Songfellows and the Blackwood Brothers Quartet. Elvis began to identify with the Songfellows Quartet, and he appreciated the musical talents of Cecil Blackwood, Jim Hamill, Bobby Baugh, Eddie Reece (pianist), and Kert Higginbotham.

Elvis auditioned for the Songfellows and was mortified by their rejection of him. Jim Hamill advised Elvis to keep driving a truck because Elvis, in his opinion, could not hear harmony. He was "flat."

When Hamill spurned Elvis, images of being a failure like Vernon and his derelict grandfather frightened Elvis, and he became determined to become a huge success. He had to show those who misjudged his ability that one day in the near future he could become an original master of song.

For a short time, Elvis aspired to become an electrician because truck driving only paid $1.25 an hour. That did not cover his clothing bills! Gladys said electricians were "respectable."

JULY: Elvis worked long hours at Crown Electric Company as a truck driver and was a part-time helper at M. B. Parker Machinist Shop in Memphis. He also worked part-time for Precision Tool.

JULY: Elvis and Johnny Black (brother of Bill) visited the black clubs in Mem-phis and appeared with Johnny and Dorsey Burnette on Saturday nights in clubs whenever they could. Eddie Bond and the Stompers alleged Elvis sang with them at the Hi Hat Club in Memphis.

JULY: Gov. Frank Goad Clement conferred the honorary title of "colonel" on Tom Parker. In 1961, he would receive the same honor from someone else.

CA. JULY: Robert Henry brought Elvis to the Gray Mule Club in Memphis because Elvis wanted to watch blues singer Charlie Burse (Ukulele Ike) wiggle wildly onstage. Some people believed Elvis was influenced by Ukulele Ike's moves on the Gray Mule's stage.

SUMMER: Elvis recorded "My Happiness" and "That's When Your Heartache Begins" on a ten-inch acetate at Sam Phillips's Memphis Recording Service. He took the acetate with him and no copies were kept by the studio.

It is uncertain exactly when Elvis walked into Sam Phillips's crowded recording studio. Everyone in Memphis knew the kind of music Phillips liked. Most of the men on his roster were black, and Phillips was proud of Joe Hill Louis's "We All Gotta Go Sometime" and Rufus Thomas's "Bear Cat." Although Elvis knew he didn't sound like them, he had confidence in his *own* unique way of singing.

Elvis went into the recording studio and sat by Marion Keisker, the office manager (previously known as "Miss Radio of Memphis"), who took an immediate interest in the polite, strange-looking, sideburned kid. According to *Elvis and Gladys* and *The Legend of Elvis Presley*, their conversation went something like this:

Marion: What can you sing?
Elvis: Anything.
M: Who do you sound like?
E: I don't sound like nobody.
M: Hillbilly?
E: Yeah. I sing hillbilly.

◄ The Blackwood Brothers. *Courtesy of the Country Music Foundation Library and Media Center, Nashville, Tennessee.*

M: Who do you sound like in hill-billy?

E: I don't sound like nobody.

The polite, shy, innocent, yet confident answers given by Elvis intrigued Marion Keisker. She wanted to know more. She was enthralled with Elvis's untamed yet natural appearance and mannerly demeanor. He stood out from the crowd, and Keisker knew that unique is the stuff from which stars are born.

Going into a sound booth to be recorded on a ten-inch acetate, Elvis anxiously cut a cover of the Inkspots' "My Happiness" and a country tear-jerker, "That's When Your Heartache Begins." Although people have rumored Elvis later made a tape of the acetate, none has surfaced. He walked out of the session with the acetate in hand. Out of the four songs Elvis committed to acetate, only "That's When Your Heartache Begins" was recorded at a real studio session at a later date.

Marion Keisker secretly taped Elvis's efforts for Sam Phillips to hear. Keisker thought Elvis had soul, that "Negro sound" Phillips had been seeking. After the recording session, Elvis was unhappy with his performance. Marion Keisker took his address and wrote his name as "Pressley," adding "good ballad singer—hold." The telephone number Elvis gave Keisker was that of a friend since the Presleys had no phone. Although Keisker tried to encourage Sam Phillips to call Elvis and hear him sing live, Phillips did not immediately respond.

Displeased with his acetate and discouraged Sam Phillips had not been at the recording studio, Elvis sang with the Blackwood Brothers after church and at revivals. Elvis told his father the Songfellows said he couldn't sing harmony. Nothing was going well for him.

SEPT.:   Elvis quit his job at M. B. Parker Machinist Shop.

OCT.:   Dewey Phillips introduced Elvis at the Eagle's Nest in Memphis as "the poor man's Liberace."

WINTER: Elvis met Dixie Locke each week at the Rainbow Rollerdome. Elvis enjoyed her company and told his friends he wanted to marry her. Elvis appreciated Dixie because she listened to him complain without making too many comments. Dixie's father worked for the Railway Express terminal and was not impressed with the "greasy-haired, strangely dressed" Elvis, but Elvis won Dixie's parents hearts with "Yes, ma'am" 's and "No, sir" 's. The Lockes lived in South Memphis, and Elvis saved money for gasoline every week so he could pick up Dixie and go to a movie, listen to R&B, roller-skate, or attend local musical festivities. Lonnie Johnson's "Tomorrow Night" became one of "their songs."

DEC.:   Sam Phillips opened Sun Records, stopped working for WREC, and started to record black artists such as Howlin' Wolf, Rufus Thomas, and B. B. King. Within nine months, he was leasing black artists' work to RPM, Chess, and Modern labels. Every musician in the Memphis area took notice, including Elvis.

DEC.:   When Elvis decided to become a singer, Hollywood's star system was in effect, and it took huge sums of money, time, and effort to boost anyone to national recognition. Any singer who became nationally famous had an aggressive manager who had unique promotional ideas, a network of connections, and money to spend. Elvis eagerly searched for such a person.

It is important to remember what the fifties were like in order to understand how unusual it was for a poor boy from Memphis to become a singing sensation. In the fifties, local movie theaters showed two feature films with live entertainment during intermissions for twenty-five to fifty cents. Television was still in black-and-white, and there

▶ A 1954 portrait of Elvis taken by James R. Reid. *Courtesy of the Memphis Brooks Museum of Art, Memphis, Tennessee.*

were no cable television stations, no MTV, no cassette tapes or CDs, and no videos. If a person wanted to become famous, he or she had to tour continuously and perform live.

DEC. 31: When Sam Phillips's Memphis Recording Service recorded Johnny Bragg and the Prisonaires from a Tennessee state penitentiary, Elvis figured if Phillips approved of men who were incarcerated, then maybe he wouldn't disapprove of Elvis's father's serving time. Gov. Frank Clement liked the Prisonaires' hit "Just Walkin' in the Rain" so much, he pardoned the men and they were released from prison.

BY THE END OF 1953: Elvis admired the singing of Clara Ward and Sister Rosetta Tharpe (who had a major impact on Little Richard and Dinah Washington). He fraternized with the Songfellows (who now liked "this rhythm boy" because he could imitate black singers, but who still rejected Elvis as a member of their quartet) and knew almost every gospel and rhythm-and-blues singer in the Tennessee circuit. Elvis was their fan and they appreciated his enthusiasm for their talents and musical interests.

1954

In 1954, the Army-McCarthy hearings captivated the American public, the Salk polio vaccine was given to children, the Supreme Court ruled segregated schools were unconstitutional, and Marlon Brando starred in *On The Waterfront*.

JAN.: Elvis was called the Hillbilly Cat by disc jockey Dewey Phillips and black musician-friends. The name stuck. His white friends thought of him as a hillbilly who had come from the backwoods, and black acquaintances called him Cat (meaning "cool" or "sharp"). Elvis was apparently called the Hillbilly Cat for the lack of a more appropriate term.

JAN.: Gladys (on harmonica), Vernon, and Elvis (on piano) sang inspirational songs at their home for hours.

JAN.: Agent Keith Lowery, Jr., offered Elvis's talents to Lois Brown for $150 a night, but the owner of the New Orleans Cadillac Club rejected Lowery's offer. *No* newcomer was worth $150 a night.

JAN.–MAR.: Elvis frequented Taylor's Cafe near Sun's office, where he heard the latest music news and met agents, managers, disc jockeys, singers, and musicians. After Eagle's Nest performances with Jack Clement's band and singer Johnny Burnette, Elvis had some positive exposure in Memphis, and Taylor's Cafe was a good place to increase that exposure. Sam Phillips's office manager, Marion Keisker, often saw Elvis at Taylor's Cafe, prior to Elvis's cutting an acetate. Taylor's Cafe was where the action was. Gigs and records were planned and contracted over coffee and doughnuts.

JAN.–MAY: Elvis mowed lawns and drove a Ford pickup truck for Crown Electric Company.

JAN. 4: "I'll Never Stand in Your Way" (written by Fred Rose and Walter "Hy" Heath) was recorded on acetate by Elvis at the Memphis Recording Service at 706 Union street with "Casual Love Affair" (for $4 on a ten-inch acetate). He allegedly met Sam Phillips on or around this afternoon, but he made no impact on Phillips.

JAN. 8: Gladys threw a birthday party to celebrate Elvis's nineteenth year. She splurged and bought Pepsi-Cola to serve to guests. Pepsi-Cola had been advertised by James Dean and Nick Adams in 1951, and soon after, it became Elvis's favorite beverage. It was also the soda pop that inspired Otis Blackwell to write "All Shook Up."

FEB.: Elvis listened to Bob Neal's Memphis radio show, "High Noon Roundup," which featured country artists and the Blackwood Brothers gospel quartet, but he preferred the programming on "race stations" WDIA and KWEM. He frequented Wink Martindale's or Slim and Mary Rhodes's TV shows, and Robert Henry ("Mr. Beale Street") often accompanied Elvis when he visited black clubs on Hernando Street.

By 1954, WDIA had expanded from a 250- to a 50,000-watt transmitter. Its disc jockeys bragged on the air that this "Negro station" reached "1,237,686 Negroes—nearly ten percent of America's total Negro population." How the station came up with such an exact number was questionable, but the fact was that WDIA's success enabled it to reach three states. Thus, its music had a broad exposure.

Elvis was a fan of the weirdest man in Memphis radio—the white, odd-talking, lunatic jokester Dewey Phillips, from WHBQ, who broadcast from the Old Chiska Hotel. Dewey preferred to play boogie-woogie, jazz, rocking gospel, and any music that got a rise out of listeners. Dewey knew Elvis through Sam Phillips and B. B. King.

FEB.: WHHM disc jockey "Sleepy-Eyed" John Lepley booked Elvis and Jack Clement (composer/band leader/vocalist who later produced records by Johnny Cash, Carl Perkins, Roy Orbison, Jerry Lee Lewis, and Charlie Rich) into the Eagle's Nest ballroom on Highway 78 at Lamar Avenue for $10 a night. Lepley often complimented Elvis on his sensual, robust piano playing.

FEB.: Elvis's girlfriend, Dixie Locke, met Gladys and Vernon Presley and saw the conditions in which Elvis lived. She was aghast that the son played the father's role; the father acted "like a female"; and the mother acted like "a child." Dixie immediately understood why Elvis thought of her parents as wealthy "uptown" people; compared to the Presleys, they lived like kings. Dixie Locke later admitted that the Presleys were not willing to make new friends and that she believed Gladys wanted Elvis to be attentive only to his mother.

CA. MAY: After Marion Keisker suggested it to Sam Phillips, Phillips asked

Elvis to sing "Without You" (written by a white inmate at a Nashville prison, from whom Sam Phillips acquired the song during a recording session with the Prisonaires). Although Elvis tried desperately to please Phillips, Phillips was not impressed. Elvis attempted to sing "Without You" many times and tried to awe him with other songs. Phillips sent Elvis home, but he called guitarist Scotty Moore and bass player Bill Black and asked them "to work with the kid." They did. Elvis never formally recorded "Without You."

MAY: Bill Black (a proficient bass player with Poindexter's Starlite Wranglers) and Winfield Scot Moore ("Scotty" Moore, a well-known, accomplished session guitarist) worked with Elvis on "Without You" outside Sam Phillips's studios, but again, Phillips did not like Elvis's rendition. Throughout his life, Elvis gave Marion Keisker credit for pushing him into Sam Phillips's life, and Elvis often said if Keisker had not had faith in him, he would probably have remained a truck driver.

At Elvis's first rehearsal outside Sun studios near Belz Street (where Black lived), he arrived in a pink outfit with white suede shoes. The two musicians were not impressed by his clothes or his hair, but they liked his jittery behavior and shaking voice. Phillips, who later denied he was intrigued with Elvis, nevertheless had enough faith in the kid to eventually let him rehearse at Sun for no fee. He knew Elvis was "different."

By this time, Phillips had produced seven records by white artists and many more by black performers. It is inconceivable that Scotty Moore and Bill Black, two of the most competent white musicians in the Memphis area, who both performed with the Starlight Wranglers and Doug Poindexter, and who both held separate outside jobs, would have wasted time rehearsing with a nobody who they thought had no potential—just to be nice guys! Not

only did they rehearse with Elvis without other band members' knowledge of it (which later infuriated the band and caused it to break up), they spent months doing it. Elvis was not discovered overnight. It took work. For weeks Elvis, Moore, and Black rehearsed songs by Hank Snow, Marty Robbins, and Roy Hamilton, along with rhythm and blues numbers.

For weeks the three men experimented with new sounds. No one was impressed with their efforts, but something forced Phillips to keep pushing the trio to keep trying.

Elvis studied the "gutter" recordings of Big Bill Broonzy, Otis Spann, B. B. King, John Lee Hooker, Jimmy Reed, Chester Burnett, and Ukka White.

CA. MAY: At the Cotton Carnival, Elvis met the famous country singer Eddy Arnold (who had been managed by Colonel Tom Parker) and the Jordanaires, a white gospel group that had organized in Springfield, Missouri, and moved to Memphis in the early fifties. Eventually based in Nashville, the Jordanaires' four singers were Gordon Stoker, Hoyt Hawkins, tenor Neal Matthews (who later said Elvis was the most dynamic artist ever to step on a stage), and Hugh Jarrett. The group specialized in blues, rock 'n' roll, gospel, and peppy barbershop tunes. They had a reputation for being able to competently back any lead singer. As a frustrated quartet singer, Elvis realized how talented the Jordanaires were and he told Gordon Stoker, if he ever "made it," he would like the quartet to sing with him.

MAY: Marion Keisker nicknamed Elvis "Timothy Sideburns" and conceded Elvis was a kind, decent boy. During his career, he would be called a lot of things, including "Doll Face" by Danny Thomas and "a no-good-for-nothing device of the devil" by ministers.

By May, Elvis had performed at the Bel Air Club (located at 1850 South

Bellevue Street in Memphis) with Doug Poindexter and the Starlight Wranglers and with Jack Clement's band. Jack Clement and Elvis sang on the same bill at the Eagle's Nest on Lamar Avenue in Memphis.

JUNE: Elvis and Dixie Locke attended Dixie's senior prom at Humes High School. Elvis told many people he wanted to marry Dixie.

JUNE 27: Elvis, Scotty Moore, and Bill Black met at Moore's home to rehearse before recording at Sun Records.

Friends often had suggested to Elvis that he go to Sam Phillips's studio to cut a two-sided acetate for $4, but it had taken time for Elvis to muster the courage. Elvis fretted about singing in a restrictive, studio setting. It was nothing like jovial church settings or gospel sing-ins. There was something austere and cold about singing behind a partition and having a stranger turn knobs and set the volume before recording. What if the acetate recording sounded awful? That intimidating thought had been unbearable.

Nevertheless, Elvis entered (with his guitar) the recording studio one hot, busy Saturday afternoon in the summer of 1953. Sam Phillips had recorded almost all the black singers with whom Elvis fraternized. Rumor had it, Sam said he was looking for a white man who had the Negro sound and the Negro feel. He thought that combo would make his recording company a million dollars. Elvis fit that bill, or at least he thought he did.

Elvis felt he had nothing to lose by cutting an acetate for Sam Phillips because he had already been rejected at other music events and knew how it felt to be booed offstage. If Sam Phillips spurned him, he would survive it.

Many sources wrongly claim Elvis recorded his first songs to surprise Gladys on her birthday, but Gladys was born on April 25, not in a summer month. After he became famous, Elvis said he knew Gladys would appreciate

him singing for her. It was probable Elvis's future manager, Colonel Tom Parker, made up the story to intrigue and touch the hearts of millions of fans.

JUNE: Although Sam Phillips at Sun Records asked Elvis to record Johnny Lee Wills's "Rag Mop," Elvis never completed the project to satisfaction. There may be an unreleased tape of "Rag Mop," but it has not surfaced.

JUNE 30: Elvis admired the Blackwood Brothers, who by June of 1954 had an RCA record contract, had produced a hit, "The Man Upstairs," and had won first place on the "Arthur Godfrey Talent Scout Show." Because their schedule could be more proficiently handled with the use of an airplane, baritone R. W. Blackwood earned a pilot's license. On June 30, R. W. Blackwood, bass singer Billy Lyles, and a teenage boy were killed when the group's two-engine Beechcraft crashed. These deaths devastated Elvis, who cried like a baby at the news and during the funeral.

JULY: Elvis gave his first interview, arranged by Sam Phillips, with a national magazine editor, Paul Ackerman of *Billboard.*

JULY: Locals became jealous of the attention Elvis received. Their bashing of his music and looks annoyed him. His destiny in music was not actively predetermined or inherited. Up until now, the idea he would miraculously become "somebody" had only been imagined by Gladys. The instant attention he received was difficult for Elvis to comprehend, and he did not know how to handle admiration.

Elvis did not have the business background or the awareness required to prepare himself for the publicity, obstacles, social constraints, erratic scheduling, fishbowllike lifestyle, and potent criticisms that accompany the daily lives of most rising stars. Elvis was launched into the spotlight too fast. Unprepared, Elvis had difficulty answering accusers. The incredible flux of contradictory reactions to his first record left Elvis confused and almost overwhelmed.

JULY: Elvis sang "That's All Right, Mama" and "Blue Moon of Kentucky" at the Bon Air Club on Summer Avenue at Mendenhall Road in Memphis, backed by Doug Poindexter and the Starlight Wranglers with Scotty Moore and Bill Black.

JULY 1: Elvis planned to sing in the Mississippi-Chicago electric blues style of Arthur "Big Boy" Crudup and prepared some of Crudup's songs to sing for Sun: "Cool Disposition," "Everything's All Right," "Hey, Mama," and "Rock Me, Mama." Phillips had *no* intention of recording covers, regardless of how jazzed up Elvis's country-rhythm-and-blues-rock was going to sound.

Elvis, distraught and anguished, attended with Dixie Locke the wake of R. W. Blackwood, Bill Lyles, and their young companion, who had died on June 30.

JULY 2: Gov. Frank Goad Clement eulogized Bill Lyles and R. W. Blackwood at their combined funerals at Ellis Auditorium. J. D. Sumner replaced Bill Lyles in the Blackwood Brothers. Cecil Blackwood eventually left the Songfellows to replace R. W. in the Blackwood Brothers Quartet. Cecil told Elvis this would be Elvis's chance to become a professional gospel singer. He could try out for the Songfellows. Elvis was torn by the news. He told Sam Phillips he wanted to leave him and join the Songfellows, but Phillips refused to let him go. Elvis sorrowfully told Cecil that he had "to sing the blues" and wouldn't be able to try out for the Songfellows.

JULY 5–6: The temperature hit 101 degrees the day Elvis first recorded in Sun's un-air-conditioned studio. Phillips taped "That's All Right, Mama," "I Love You Because" (four takes), and "Harbor Lights." Elvis sounded woefully country with his western-styled trembling voice. During the recording period, Phillips was dissatisfied and turned off his taping machine. The group started to fool around. During their spontaneous playing a new sound was heard. Picking up his guitar, Elvis started singing a mean, high, bouncing version of Arthur Crudup's "That's All Right, Mama." Phillips was stunned as he listened in the control room. His heart began to pound and he taped Elvis without telling the group. Elvis was producing the sound Phillips had wanted to find! Scotty Moore said Elvis was jumping all around the studio, acting the fool. Phillips asked what they were doing. They didn't know. Phillips told them not to lose that sound. For hours, Elvis sang blues, gospel, country, and Dean Martin covers.

The final recording of "That's All Right, Mama" reveals a voice that is earnestly compelling, high in pitch, and uninhibited. It was from the gutter. It reeked of black dives on Beale Street. It was from a restless street cowboy who grew up on frenzied Fundamentalist revivals. And throughout this foreign sounding, relaxed, unrehearsed vocal, Scotty Moore's guitar was country. "That's All Right, Mama" was rhythm and blues with a country tinge. Raw as it was, it was the direction in which Sam Phillips wanted to go. "Harbor Lights" by Jimmy Kennedy and Hugh Williams was the *first* song recorded by Elvis at the July 5 commercial taping session at Sun Records. Because Sam Phillips thought the takes were too awkward, none were released until 1976 (take No. 2) for RCA's LP *Elvis—A Legendary Performer*, Vol. 2. With Scotty Moore on guitar, Bill Black on bass, and Elvis on guitar, the trio next recorded "I Love You Because" by Leon Payne. Sam Phillips did not release any of the five takes of "I Love You Because," but RCA spliced takes three and five together for its single (RCA 20-6639, September 1956) with the flip side "Tryin' to Get to Know You." After five takes, rock 'n' roll history was made!

JULY 6: Elvis, Scotty Moore, and Bill Black cut two surviving versions of "Blue Moon of Kentucky," written by Bill Monroe. Elvis strongly interpreted the song to be a country rocker in medium tempo. When Scotty Moore ran his fingers down guitar frets, Elvis took a high-strung breath and broke loose. Phillips shouted, "Fine, man! Hell, that's *different!* That's a *pop* song!"

The next take was faster paced, and Elvis's vocals became unconventional, whimsical, and almost bizarre. In that carefree atmosphere, Phillips realized Elvis's magnetism could be generated in unrehearsed, unpredictable, almost unconscious vocal deliveries. If he was allowed to do whatever he wanted to do, he was dazzling.

Phillips realized that pure country was too stifling for Elvis. The last take of "Blue Moon of Kentucky" was more like the Negro sound Phillips had been looking for. It would become the flip side of "That's All Right, Mama" (released July 19, 1954).

Whether it was by pure luck, a mistake, or fate, black music and white music were united when Phillips allowed Elvis, Scotty Moore, and Bill Black to discover the sound that had the potential of writing a new page in the book of music history during that unprecedented month in 1954.

Because of his close association with two country musicians (Moore and Black), Elvis Presley—"The Hillbilly Cat," the next "King of Western Bop"—and his new, hybrid style and sound were soon labeled "rockabilly" (which eventually evolved into rock 'n' roll).

Leading rockabilly artists in the fifties included Elvis, Johnny Cash, Jerry Lee Lewis, Buddy Holly, Roy Orbison,

Homer & Jethro, Tommy Blake & the Rhythm Rebels, Gordon Terry, Carl Perkins, Jimmy Dell, Hoyt Johnson, and others. Today's rockabilly artists include Creedence Clearwater Revival, Stray Cats, and Elvis Costello.

JULY 7: Sam Phillips distributed DJ demos to WMPS (Uncle Richard), WHHM (Sleepy-Eyed John Lepley), and WHBQ (Dewey Phillips for "Red, Hot and Blue"), and convinced each disc jockey to play Elvis's record. No demos were given to black stations because Phillips thought they wouldn't play them. The single acetate recording of "That's All Right, Mama" with the flip side "Blue Moon of Kentucky" was officially released July 19 and became a local hit, but did not chart nationally (Sun 209).

Dewey Phillips played "That's All Right, Mama" after nine-thirty P.M. while a nervous Elvis hid at the Suzore No. 2 movie theater, not knowing that WHBQ played "That's All Right, Mama" *fourteen times* in a row! Later that night, a nervous Elvis gave his first on-air interview with Dewey Phillips.

Gladys Presley was stunned to hear her son's name on the radio. Her dreams for Elvis were coming to pass and she couldn't believe it. A part of her was thrilled. A part of her was fearful Elvis would leave to tour and never come home. Gladys became so insecure about what Sam Phillips "was doing to her son," she called Sun studios every day to give advice. Overprotective to the bitter end, Gladys's continuous meddling in Elvis's musical life hindered as well as pleased him. It is lonely at the top, and as long as he had his mother, he knew he was not alone. She sincerely cared about his well-being, but did not know how to handle the future.

When Elvis gave his first interview for WHBQ, Dewey Phillips told him not to say anything "dirty." A microphone was turned on and the jittery singer had no idea when the interview started or stopped. The purpose of the short talk was to make certain the listening audience knew Elvis had graduated from an all-*white* high school, thus establishing he was not "a colored boy."

Five thousand requests came to WHBQ to hear Elvis, which staggered the Memphis music world. Scotty Moore quickly became Elvis's manager, to handle local bookings.

WDIA disc jockey Rufus Thomas disregarded his program director's instructions *not* to play "That's All Right, Mama." WDIA's phones rang off the hook, and listeners begged for more. Sam Phillips was stunned that his young, unknown, white singer was appreciated by a huge black audience.

JULY 8–13: Phillips, in his caution, had no records of Elvis to sell. A master still had to be cut. While Sam scurried to fill orders, Elvis returned to drive a truck for Crown Electric. At night, he joined the Starlight Wranglers at the Bel Air Club. Members of the band were infuriated Scotty Moore and Bill Black "went behind their backs" and cut a hit without asking them to join the effort. For years, Scotty defended the action as innocent. No one thought Elvis or his songs would amount to anything.

JULY 10: John Lepley of WHHM played Elvis's songs over and over, and Sam Phillips urged Scotty Moore to sign Elvis to a more formal one-year contract as part of a trio, before someone stole him. Elvis would receive half the royalties earned; Moore and Black would earn 25 percent each.

JULY 11: Elvis recorded "Mystery Train" for Sun with Scotty Moore (guitar), Bill Black (bass), Johnny Bernero (drums), and Elvis on second guitar. Although Junior Parker's version of "Mystery Train" is more the blues, Elvis's version is faster and more spirited.

JULY 12: Elvis and his parents signed a one-year contract with Scotty Moore. Gladys Presley warned Elvis to retain his reverence for God when he performed. Elvis told his mother that he was only singing music.

Elvis's behavior showed signs of an insecure narcissist. He continually combed his hair, grew long sideburns, dressed loudly, flirted with women, and drove loud-mufflered cars.

JULY 17: Radio disc jockey Bob Neal told Scotty Moore he would like to manage Elvis because he was "hot." Up-and-coming white singers were baffled and agitated by the press attention and fan adulation Elvis started to generate. Some would copy Elvis's hair and movements in attempts to jump on the rapidly escalating money-earning bandwagon, including Ricky Nelson, Frank Avalon, Paul Anka, Jimmy Clanton, Pat Boone, Bobby Darin, Ed "Kookie" Byrnes, Fabian, Bobby Rydell, and Lloyd Price. The impact of rockabilly artists who followed him paled in comparison to Elvis, partially because they weren't the original. There's a lot to be said about being *first*.

JULY 18: Members of the Jordaniares were impressed with Elvis's rendition of "Mystery Train" (Sun 223).

JULY 19: Sun Records officially released "That's All Right, Mama" and "Blue Moon of Kentucky" (Sun 209). "That's All Right, Mama" conspicuously placed third on the Memphis country-and-western charts. It hit charts in Nashville and New Orleans. The record quickly sold twenty thousand copies, even though some radio stations thought Elvis's sound was too black to play, while others said it was too country to air after five o'clock.

JULY 19: The first person ever to buy an Elvis record was Eldene Beard, who

purchased "That's All Right, Mama"/
"Blue Moon of Kentucky" at nine A.M.,
at Charles Records on Main Street in
Memphis.

JULY 20:   People bought Elvis's first
single and chased after him for an autograph. At first, Elvis thought it was
funny that people wanted him to sign a
record.

JULY 27:   Marion Keisker convinced
Edwin Howard, a leading entertainment reporter from the *Memphis
Press-Scimitar*, to interview the young,
new rockabilly star Elvis Presley. Elvis
entered Howard's office, disheveled
after driving a truck all day. His hair
was a mess and he wore blue jeans,
yet his polite mannerisms and shyness
appealed to Edwin Howard. This was
Elvis's first printed interview.

JULY 28:   "The Front Row" in the
Press-Scimitar featured Edwin
Howard's interview with Elvis Presley.
It said Elvis's Sun release "promises to
be the biggest hit that Sun ever
pressed," which thrilled Sam Phillips.
Quoting an enthusiastic Marion
Keisker, the paper printed that "both
sides [of the single] seem to be equally
popular on pop, folk, and race-record
programs. This boy has something that
seems to appeal to everybody. . . . We
got big orders yesterday from Dallas
and Atlanta." Stating Sun had forty
coast-to-coast distributors, the reporter
predicted Elvis's first record had a
chance to become "a big national
sale." Howard made certain his readers
knew Elvis would appear live at disc
jockey Bob Neal's hillbilly show at
Overton Park Shell on "Friday night
along with veteran entertainers from
the Louisiana Hayride." The Cat's star
was rocketing fast.

JULY 30:   Elvis performed in Memphis
at the Bon Air Club. Audiences went
crazy, which puzzled Elvis and angered
other performers. With applause often

comes criticism, and Elvis got more
than his share. When people complained that Elvis had no personal
style, it was a fact. He had garish taste
in clothes, furnishings, and jewelry.

JULY 30:   Bob Neal put Elvis in his first
large concert appearance at the Overton Park Shell with headliners Slim
Whitman, Billy Walker, and Ira and
Charlie Louvin. His performances of
"That's All Right, Mama" and "Blue
Moon of Kentucky" baffled the audience. His Sun release had only been
out eleven days.

AUG: Elvis performed at the Kennedy
Veterans' Hospital at 1030 Jefferson
Avenue in Memphis and sang "That's
All Right, Mama" and "Blue Moon of
Kentucky."

AUG 7:   Elvis, Scotty Moore, and Bill
Black performed as the Blue Moon
Boys at the Eagle's Nest in Memphis
(nicknamed Clearpool because its restaurant, open twenty-four hours a day,
had a swimming pool). *Billboard* reviewed "That's All Right, Mama" the
same day, giving it decent acclaim.

AUG 8:   After negative criticism about
his being "unholy," Elvis asked Sam
Phillips to release him from his contract. He decided he wanted to sing
gospel music after all. Phillips said no
and told him not to "talk religious" at
Sun. That was a rule—no one talked
religion in the music world.

AUG 10:   Elvis, Moore, and Black performed again unbilled at a concert at
Overton Park Shell in Memphis. Elvis
sang "Old Shep" and "That's When
Your Heartaches Begin" at the afternoon performance, and "That's All
Right, Mama" and "Good Rockin' Tonight" during the evening performance.
Slim Whitman and Carl Smith headlined with Webb Pierce on the bill. After Elvis received a huge response,
Pierce refused to perform.

The derogatory nickname "Elvis the Pelvis" developed from Elvis's untamed, dangerous-looking hip and leg movements, which critics viewed as a wild, animalistic bump and grind. The name amused Elvis but greatly upset Gladys.

Elvis knew he would not be able to sustain the strain and confusion that would accompany his entrance into music history and unfathomable fame without the aggressive promotional tactics of someone like a Colonel Tom Parker. Sam Phillips, Bob Neal, and Scotty Moore were not assertive enough for the job, so he started to look for professional management.

AUG 21: The Blue Moon Boys performed in Gladewater, Texas, to an older audience, which was at first shocked at Elvis's wild stage movements, but soon many young women started to yell out to him and their ardor turned him on even more (on and off stage). In the truest sense of the word, Elvis originated and encouraged the rock world's groupie culture. It is commonly known he rarely turned away a woman from his bedroom.

He often modestly claimed in a soft-spoken voice that he had no control over what was happening to him. He embodied an angelic quality that critics hated and fans adored. Resembling a virtuous rebel, he left audience members spellbound or disgusted. Concentrating on his anatomical moves and not on his music or voice, audiences believed he wasn't *all* bad, and more notable, he didn't appear to be *all* good!

AUG. 22: Elvis was perplexed by the applause he received during his concert with the Blue Moon Boys in Houston, Texas, but he admitted he liked it. The only time Elvis felt comfortable with people was when he was performing live. When he was not singing, he often felt inadequate and insecure, especially when he was questioned or reprimanded by the hounding press.

Throughout his life, he had been scorned by his peers as a loser who was "common" and "weird." It seemed an inconceivable twist of fate when young fans responded differently and "liked him."

AUG. 24: Elvis and the Blue Moon Boys performed a benefit show at the Kennedy Veterans' Hospital in Memphis. Oftentimes people would ask Elvis why he didn't sing a certain song. He commonly answered, " 'Cause it ain't me. It just don't move me. It just don't."

AUG. 27: With his reputation beginning to follow him, Elvis performed before a larger crowd at the Eagle's Nest in Memphis. Scotty Moore and Bill Black couldn't believe how many young women pushed and shoved to get closer to the stage to see Elvis.

SEPT.: Elvis heard Carl Perkins perform at the El Rancho Club in Jackson, Mississippi. He was impressed with Perkins's lively performance and musical talent.

SEPT.–OCT.: Country singer Tiny Dixon and his band The Eagles occasionally backed Elvis at Memphis's Eagle's Nest.

SEPT.–NOV.: Elvis and the Blue Moon Boys performed whenever they could at the Eagle's Nest and their local fans grew in number. After performances, Elvis and the boys would rent rooms and party with local girls.

SEPT. 9: Johnny Cash and Becky Yancey were in the audience to watch Elvis, Scotty, and Bill perform at the grand opening of Katz Drug Store (now named Scagg's). The boys earned a remarkably high $65 that night. For $10, Peter Morton rented a flatbed truck from Leonard McTyier upon which Elvis belted out rockabilly tunes. To everyone's amazement, the parking lot was filled with adoring, screaming teenage girls.

SEPT. 9: Marion Keisker organized a Memphis fan club for the Blue Moon Boys and their lead singer, Elvis Presley.

SEPT. 10: Every recording session came hard for Elvis, who wanted to sing pieces that were currently on the radio or being sung on tour by others. Phillips said no to Elvis's singing any cover song. Elvis had to perform new, original tunes. It was unfortunate Elvis did not like to write lyrics or music as did Phillips's other rising stars. Elvis did not prerehearse songs he presented to Phillips, and he never knew in advance what he wanted to record next, which made every session nightmarish for the other band members. What might have taken a few hours to record dragged on for days or weeks.

"Just Because" by Bob Shelton, Joe Shelton, and Sid Robin was recorded at Sun studios (RCA 20–6640), a song Elvis would perform at the Louisiana Hayride. Its flip side was "Blue Moon." "Good Rockin' Tonight" (by Roy Brown) was completed with Scotty Moore and Bill Black (Sun 210), along with its flip side, "I Don't Care If the Sun Don't Shine" (by Mack David). Its popularity on the EP "Any Way You Want Me" brought the song to No. 74 on *Billboard*'s Top 100 chart for a seven-week run two years later, in October 1956. Elvis recorded Jimmy Wakely's "I'll Never Let You Go (Little Darlin')," which was not released until 1956 by RCA. Its flip side was by Joe Thomas, "I'm Gonna Sit Right Down and Cry (Over You)" (RCA 20–6638). Elvis recorded Martha Carson's "Satisfied" at Sun after he sang "I'll Never Let You Go (Little Darlin')," but the tape has not surfaced and the song was never released. With Scotty Moore on guitar, Elvis recorded "Tomorrow Night," a simple rendition written by Sam Coslow and Will Grosz in 1939. As

an overdubbed song, it was released in 1964 on the LP *Elvis for Everyone*. The original cut was released by RCA in 1985 on the LP *Reconsider Baby*.

SEPT. 14: Sam Phillips wanted Elvis to perform at Nashville's Grand Ole Opry—the mecca of country singing. Elvis was dumbfounded by the news. It was hard to image *he* would have a chance to sing in Nashville's finest arena. Marion Keisker said, "For all of us, the Grand Ole Opry was the summit, the peak, the show you hoped you'd get eventually—not when you had just one record out" (*Look*, 5/4/71). Stars were paid a union wage of $30 a performance, despite crowded auditoriums and turn-aways of thousands of fans. Singing in Ryman Auditorium at the Opry was the golden moment Elvis had been waiting for all his life.

SEPT. 24: Sam Phillips, Marion Keisker, Elvis, Scotty, and Bill drove to Nashville, where Elvis and the Blue Moon Boys would entertain at the Grand Ole Opry. The performance would be aired twice on WSM radio and on "Ernest Tubb's Midnight Jamboree" (October 2).

Upon his arrival in Nashville, Elvis was disappointed at the shabby, unkempt appearance of the Ryman Auditorium. Marion Keisker said that Elvis kept asking, "Ya mean this is what I been dreamin' 'bout all these years?" It was nowhere near as grand or glamorous as he had imagined it to be.

SEPT. 25: The main attraction at the Grand Ole Opry was country singer Slim Whitman, so Sam Phillips ran a huge ad in the local Nashville papers that gave the impression that Elvis—a singer who had not joined the Musician's Union and probably did not know what it was—was coming to outsing everyone in town. This hype generated resentment at the Grand Ole Opry as Phillips's ad seemed arrogant to the older "regulars."

Jim Denny, the Opry's talent-office manager, was enraged when he realized no large band appeared with Elvis. Almost everyone who heard Elvis's songs thought the band's sound was so big, there had to be five to eight players with the singer. Denny didn't think a singer with two players could please *any* audience.

After Elvis appeared onstage at the Grand Ole Opry, Jim Denny hurt Elvis deeply by suggesting he should go back to truck driving. The audience did not respond to the hillbilly-gone-rocker, and Elvis never forgot Denny's unkind comment and the negative audience reaction at the Opry. Singer Ernest Tubb (the "King of Country Music") eased the pain by telling Elvis he'd done a fine job and that the Nashville audience just wasn't used to his unusual talent and style.

After the concert, Sam Phillips and the boys went to a club to hear a pianist. Elvis went in, turned around, went outside, and sat on the sidewalk. Still upset by Denny's remark, he told Phillips and Keisker his mother would disapprove of his sitting and drinking in a rowdy nightclub.

The band was disappointed with Elvis's reception at the Grand Ole Opry. A suitcase full of Elvis's clothes was mistakenly left at a gas station, and Elvis cried all the way home. It took him weeks to get over Jim Denny's rude comment. Years later, Denny put his arm around Elvis and claimed he "always knew Elvis would make it," and Elvis politely and politically replied, "Yes, sir, thank you, sir," but he turned to a friend and spewed, "The sum-bitch don't remember when he broke my heart" (*Look*, 5/4/71).

Nashville was not ready for what they were witnessing. Many adults in the audience said Elvis's performance revolted them, and other entertainers thought Elvis was crazy. Elvis left Ryman Auditorium feeling he had failed and never performed at the Grand Ole Opry again.

SEPT. 25: "Good Rockin' Tonight" and "I Don't Care If the Sun Don't Shine" (Sun 210) were released.

SEPT. 27: A major clash between Bob Neal, who worked for WMPS radio, and Elvis occurred when Neal refused to go against a WMPS station manager's orders that forbid any disc jockey to play Elvis's records on the air. It infuriated Elvis that Neal and WMPS had censored his music. Neal argued, if he played any song Elvis sang, he might be fired. Elvis told him he could easily find a new job. Neal replied he was known for playing softer, gentler country music.

SEPT. 28: Promoter Oscar "The Baron" Davis heard that Neal thought Elvis's music was too raunchy to play on radio. That appealed to the Baron, who knew anyone who had the power to be censored might become a major financial commodity.

The Baron had seen Elvis, Scotty, and Black playing at the Memphis Airport Inn, but he did not tell Bob Neal. The crowded audience of women shrieked and swooned. The Baron wondered if that was just a fluke or if it was a common occurrence.

OCT.: Oscar the Baron Davis noticed Elvis at Memphis's Eagle's Nest and took note of his appeal to women. Davis understood the importance of a frenzied audience reaction and appreciated the free publicity that an angry press, delirious radio DJs, or oversexed female fans could generate. Davis was famous for organizing and promoting circuses, fiddle contests, jamborees, rodeos, and stage shows throughout the South. He was the man who had convinced Hank Williams to allow his second wedding to be a public, media event at the Municipal Auditorium in New Orleans during two lavish ceremonies. The event grossed over $30,000.

Davis was looking for new talent for

Red Foley's show when he appeared at WMPS in Memphis. Meeting with Bob Neal, the Baron listened to tapes of Elvis, then was driven by Neal to hear Elvis perform live at the Eagle's Nest. Davis reported the "Elvis phenomena" to his boss, Colonel Tom Parker. It was the first time Davis had ever seen a white singer cause audiences to stand, scream, faint, and cry in ecstasy and uncontrolled fervor (outside a Holy Roller Church). Even Sinatra hadn't done that. The Colonel immediately decided to go to see "Elvis the Pelvis."

A brief meeting was held at Taylor's restaurant between Elvis, Scotty, Bill Black, the Baron, Bob Neal, and Colonel Parker. Parker left knowing he wanted to hook the shark, Elvis.

OCT. 2: Elvis was on Ernest Tubb's "Midnight Jamboree" radio program. His "Louisiana Hayride" performances were played over KWKH radio that same night, and Elvis didn't care about his debut broadcast on WSM's "Grand Ole Opry" from Nashville. He didn't want to be reminded of the Opry. Elvis told Scotty Moore that the "Hayride" had a much better attitude toward newcomers. No wonder it was nicknamed "The Cradle to the Stars."

OCT. 5: Elvis's hillbilly renditions were played on KNUZ's "The Old Texas Corral" from Houston and from KSIG in Gladewater, Texas.

OCT. 16: "Louisiana Hayride" (known as "The Junior Grand Ole Opry") was broadcast to the southern U.S. from KWKH (a CBS affiliate, over 190 CBS stations) every Saturday from eight to eleven P.M. from Shreveport's Municipal Auditorium. Each packed performance featured up-and-coming talents as well as old-timers. Adult admission was sixty cents; children thirty cents.

Elvis would appear *fifty* times on the "Hayride," in Shreveport, Gladewater and Waco. This early exposure of "the Cat" gave him instant recognition among peers and local audiences. Elvis was also aired over KSIG and KNUZ radio in Texas.

After Elvis's first appearance on "Louisiana Hayride" he met D. J. Fontana (who became his drummer). On the show Elvis sang "That's All Right, Mama" and "Blue Moon of Kentucky," after being introduced by Frank Page for the "Lucky Strike Guest Time." Elvis was noticeably nervous. Page told avid listeners that Elvis was nineteen and that the songs he sang for their program "skyrocketed right up the charts." Taking note of the Cat's "new, distinctive style," Page asked Elvis how he was. He replied, "Just fine. How're you, sir?" He displayed that innocence and polite charm for

▶ Elvis performing in Shreveport, Louisiana, 1954. *Courtesy of AP/Wide World Photo.*

which he would become famous. Elvis told Page he and the group thought it was "a real honor" to appear. Then, with the candor that enchanted millions, he blurted out, "We're gonna do a song for ya—you got anything else to say?" The audience reaction was so positive, KWKH instantly wanted Elvis, Scotty Moore, and Bill Black to return. They were a smashing success!

Elvis, Scotty, and Bill usually stayed at the Al-Ida Motel, on the tough side of Shreveport known as Bossier City, which had a three-mile strip of booze, drugs, and women. Although Elvis often told associates he would "marry a virgin," it is well known the Cat cruised nightly for available young females. One Houston woman insisted her baby was Elvis's and it may have been, but most of these "chickadees" (as Elvis called them) slept with so many men, it would have been close to impossible to prove who the fathers were.

OCT. 22: Elvis and the Blue Moon Boys gave a concert in New Orleans, followed by a concert in Sweetwater, Texas.

OCT. 23: Elvis performed at the "Louisiana Hayride" and was told to bring "an adult guardian or parent" with him to the next performance so contracts could be signed with "Louisiana Hayride" executives for a one-year gig.

NOV.: *Billboard*'s disc jockeys placed Elvis as the eighth most promising new hillbilly or country-western singer of 1954.

NOV. 6: Elvis, Moore, and Black appeared on "Louisiana Hayride" and advertised the only product they'd ever endorse, a company called Southern Made Doughnuts.

Horace L. Logan, station manager for KWKH had Elvis, Moore, and Black sign a one-year contract to appear on the "Louisiana Hayride" every Saturday night. Their salary for each performance: $18 for Elvis and $12 each to Moore and Black. Gladys and Vernon Presley witnessed the signing of the contract.

NOV. 13, 20, 27: Elvis and the Blue Moon Boys performed at "Louisiana Hayride" concerts, and their audiences got bigger and wilder each time they appeared. Drummer D. J. Fontana joined Elvis, Scotty, and Black and the group toured Texas. Elvis, impatient to get to places the band was going, was always full of nervous energy. He was unable to sit, for instance, without tapping his feet, shaking his legs, or rapping a pencil on a table. The group stopped at almost every roadside stand so Elvis could stretch and see what was going on. For someone who had been sheltered throughout his life, every day and every thing was a new and exciting experience.

Fontana grew up with drumsticks in his hands, and by the time he met Elvis, he had played in combos and appeared on nationally broadcast radio shows. Fontana first heard Elvis's "That's All Right, Mama" on a record in the office of Horace Logan, the producer of the "Louisiana Hayride," where Fontana was a session drummer. Because Elvis "came cheap," Logan had decided to sign him. Once teens found out Elvis was performing live at the "Hayride," audiences changed drastically.

NOV.: Trying to build up a major following, Bob Neal organized a concert tour for Elvis and the band throughout Texas including Boston, Lufkin, Longview, Odessa, and at the Memphis Airport Inn in November. At each concert the applause was thunderous. Because of the onslaught of negative publicity that preceded the concerts, fans bought tickets and eagerly anticipated Elvis to be lewd and sexual onstage. Elvis and the band members realized few fans came to hear the music. They were there to see the rock hero whom Hugh Thomson called "a bulldozer in the mating season" and "Mr. Over-Statement."

NOV.: Elvis received adulation and condemnation from Texas critics and from "Louisiana Hayride" followers. Disc jockey John Lepley vied for Elvis's contract, but Scotty Moore sent him packing.

DEC. 4, 11, 18: Elvis and his band performed at "Louisiana Hayride" appearances, which were carried live over KWKH, the "sizzling" radio station of Louisiana.

Bob Neal watched Elvis make people swoon. Neal licked his chops, hoping to become Elvis's guiding light. Neal claimed Elvis knew exactly what he wanted to do in the entertainment world, and that Elvis was itchy to quickly attain a huge following. Neal alleges Elvis decided to test the limits, become a movie star, and have it all. If this is true, Elvis was a better actor than most people believe. His image was that of an overwhelmed, humble, oftentimes politely shy, impoverished youth who was bewildered by his rapid climb up fortune's ladder. Elvis coveted the kind of superstardom country singers Hank Williams and Hank Snow had.

Hank Snow had been promoted through bookings obtained by Jamboree Attractions through the efforts of the flamboyant ex–circus barker Colonel Tom Parker. Neal knew Elvis might have kept Parker in the back of his mind as his next manager, but Neal wouldn't admit it now.

DEC. 10: "Milkcow Blues Boogie" (by James "Kokomo" Arnold) was recorded by Elvis at Sun Records with Elvis and Scotty Moore on guitar and Bill Black on bass. The single did not chart (Sun 215, released on January 8, 1955, with the flip side "You're a Heartbreaker").

"You're a Heartbreaker" was the first song Elvis sang accompanied by sheet music. It was written by Charles "Jack" Alvin Salle. Elvis's rendition did not chart.

DEC. 18: Elvis recorded "I'm Left, You're Right, She's Gone," by Stanley Kesler and Bill Taylor at Sun Records with Scotty Moore and Elvis on guitar and Bill Black on bass. Its original title was "You're Right, I'm Left, She's Gone" (so printed on LP *The Sun Years* and on the Jimmie Rodgers Memorial Day Celebration ads, May 25, 1955). The song never charted (Sun 217). A version of "My Baby's Gone" was sung but not released to the public. A few DJs received copies of it. During his "Louisiana Hayride" performance on December 18, Elvis may have been recorded singing "Tweedlee Dee" by Winfield Scott. During his December 18 performance, Jimmy Day played steel guitar. Elvis often sang "Tweedlee Dee" and it is on the LP *Elvis: The First Live Recordings* ("*Louisiana Hayride," December 18, 1954*). During the LP recordings, Moore, Black, Fontana, Floyd Cramer (piano) and Jimmy Day (steel guitar) are backup musicians.

DEC.: The Presleys moved to 2414 Lamar Avenue from Alabama Street. Gladys became more depressed during this period because Elvis was never around to take care of her. Although Gladys had always told her son he would become "a somebody" someday, she had no idea how his schedule, ego, and workload would directly affect her life.

DEC. 28: Elvis and the band performed in Houston, Texas, to a large, enthusiastic crowd. Critics noted that when women screeched and shoved to touch Elvis onstage, he egged them on.

▶ Elvis in the fifties. *Courtesy of Blue Light Studio and photo archives, Mimosa Records Productions, Inc.*

1955

In 1955, the U.S. sent military advisers to Vietnam, Albert Einstein and James Dean died, the minimum wage was $1, "Alfred Hitchcock Presents" and "Captain Kangaroo" premiered on television, and Bill Haley's "Rock Around the Clock" topped the *Billboard* chart.

JAN. 1: Elvis and Tommy Sands performed together at Eagle's Hall in Houston, a gig arranged by the ever-scheming Colonel Parker and Bob Neal. Although Parker was not officially working for Elvis's interests, it is obvious he planned taking over the young singer's promotion and management. Bob Neal later complained that the Colonel submerged him with staff calls, messages, and other actions.

Elvis bought his parents a 1954 Ford to replace a clunker 1942 Lincoln Continental with over three hundred thousand miles on its meter. He painted the Ford pink and white and used it for touring. It "died on the road" (burning out near Texarkana, Arkansas) the night Gladys predicted her "baby would be in a fire." Elvis then purchased a 1954 Cadillac (which Bill Black ruined in a collision with a truck). The group then used a 1954 Chevy Bel Air, which Scotty Moore and his wife bought for the group to tour in, which also "died." The group went through cars like soda pops. Their traveling schedule had become intense.

JAN. 1: Julies T. Paglin of the OK Group of New Orleans, Louisiana, hired Elvis for one-night radio appearances for $300 a pop.

JAN. 1: A simple management-type contract was handed over to Bob Neal. "The Baron" Davis had shown a lot of interest in Elvis, which meant the infamous Colonel Parker might follow suit. That seemed to imply money in Neal's pocket. Neal took 15 percent off the top of everything Elvis earned and 10 percent for promotional expenses. Knowing how attached the underaged Elvis was to his parents, Neal had them sign a consent form/contract that allowed Neal to manage Elvis. Gladys liked Neal, who announced Elvis's songs on his own radio show. He painted a few window cards advertising Elvis's singing engagements in local schools or auditoriums, booking him three to five shows a week. Each show would net between $200 and $400. Money started pouring in (for Neal) when teenage crowds began to push and shove to see the sexy hillbilly with the romantic eyes and bouncing crotch.

When greed set in, Neal convinced Elvis to take a salary, rather than 50 percent of the take. Scotty Moore and Bill Black were asked to take minimum wages, which outraged both of them. They threatened to quit working with Elvis, but neither did at that time. Somehow, Elvis lost sight of the fact that Scotty Moore and Bill Black were the backbone of the band's beat and sound. Probably because they didn't cause screams and yells from the young female fans, Elvis felt they did not deserve high salaries. That was shortsighted and unfair of Elvis.

Things had changed since Elvis sang at the annual Memphis Jamboree. There was no musical category he fit. In a later LP recording, "Elvis Answers Back," Elvis said that when he was frightened, especially during an encore for the Jamboree, Bob Neal screamed for him to get out on the stage and to do what he was doing before. Elvis asked what he had done! The audience was going crazy over his trembling, gyrating hip and leg movements. Elvis acted as if he were overwhelmed by the audience's response. He claimed he did not understand it, but he enjoyed every minute of it.

Sam Phillips watched as Elvis's popularity grew. The more bookings Neal secured, the more records were sold. Phillips encouraged Neal to book the band for one-night stands in Arkansas, Texas, Georgia, Louisiana, Virginia, Florida, Tennessee, and in Carlsbad, New Mexico.

Pat Boone, the singer who headlined in Cleveland, Ohio, when Elvis sang there in 1955, recalls Elvis's dual personality on and off stage: "Elvis came in from the 'Louisiana Hayride.' . . . He was the bottom of the bill for the night's act. . . . Seeing him was quite a surprise. He was *very* shy, *very*. He had on pants that were too long—a coat with the collar turned up. He was nervous. He mumbled—kept his head down. . . . I actually felt sorry for him. I couldn't conceive of this shy person being commanding enough to be a big star. So—I was feeling sympathy—felt it until he walked out on that stage and began to sing. . . . He was great! He was a big hit that night. I knew then that this would be the last time he would ever follow me on a bill. And it was!" (From *Elvis Presley—A Bio-Bibliography*, pps. 13–14.)

Elvis started to wear more garish clothing on and off stage. These were the days when black teardrops were sewn on Elvis's pink jackets and female teenyboppers would faint or go into a frenzy when Elvis walked on a stage. Boys reacted in a jealous, oftentimes violent manner, which Elvis could not understand. He was a competitive showman, but he claimed to be just one of the guys.

JAN. 2: Cleveland disc jockey Bill Randle (WERE) played an Elvis record.

CA. JAN. 7: Benjamin F. "Whitey" Ford asked the Presleys to consider letting Elvis sign a major management contract with Colonel Tom Parker. Ford was a talent scout who claimed he appreciated Elvis's uniqueness. In actuality, he had been primed for the evening by Colonel Parker.

JAN. 8: "Milkcow Blues Boogie" and "You're a Heartbreaker" were released on the Sun label.

JAN. 8, 15, 22: Elvis performed at "Louisiana Hayride" concerts.

During this period, Colonel Parker asked Hank Williams's son, Jimmy Rodgers Snow, to go watch Elvis perform at the Cotton Club and "study the kid" to find out what kind of personality he had. Jimmy did as he was asked and reported back that Elvis was provocative, sexy, and appealed to *all women*. This was all Parker needed to hear. It was time to make Elvis his personal property.

JAN. 12: Elvis's concert in Clarksdale, Mississippi, was large and the audience was wilder than it had ever been.

JAN. 13: In Helena, Arkansas, women tried to grab Elvis and lined up to get his autograph after his concert.

JAN. 16: WBIP radio carried parts of Elvis's concert in Booneville, Mississippi.

JAN. 17: Elvis and other members of Bob Neal's performing groups gave a concert in Sheffield, Alabama.

JAN. 18: Elvis was tired after his performance in Leachville, Arkansas. Sleep was becoming a rare commodity, and eating anything but junk food was unheard of in his entourage (which included Moore, Black, Fontana, and his cousins, Gene and Junior Smith).

JAN. 19: Elvis and the Blue Moon Boys performed in Sikeston, Missouri.

JAN. 29: Justin Tubb and Elvis toured to jam and sing at Houston's Eagle's Nest. Some of their performance may have been carried over KNUZ radio, Houston.

FEB.: Country and western reviews in *Billboard* favorably discussed Elvis's "Milkcow Blues Boogie" and "You're a Heartbreaker."

FEB.: Bill Haley's "Rock-a-Beatin' Boogie" was one of the first true rock 'n' roll songs. Its lyrics, which encouraged everybody to rock, probably inspired disc jockey Alan Freed to call Haley's music "rock and roll." Haley had often used the term. Haley and Freed should be given credit for introducing the term into pop language.

FEB. 4: Elvis and his group traveled to perform at Lake Pontchartrain, New Orleans, Louisiana. Colonel Parker called Steve Sholes at Nashville's RCA branch about the continued ecstatic audience responses to Elvis. Sholes was convinced the Cat was special, but RCA still didn't budge.

FEB. 5: "Baby, Let's Play House," which hinted at premarital sex, caused a major stir because female fans thought Elvis was inviting them to have sex with him! It was written by Arthur Gunter and recorded at Sun studios with Scotty Moore (lead guitar), Bill Black (bass), and Elvis (rhythm guitar), and it became the first charted song for Elvis when it hit *Billboard*'s Top 100 in July at No. 10. Its flip side was Bill Taylor and Stanley Kesler's "I'm Left, You're Right, She's Gone," and the single was released April 1, 1955, on 78 and 45 rpm.

The Colonel immediately called Steve Sholes and told him of Elvis's charted "Baby, Let's Play House," which aroused RCA's interest in the Cat.

FEB. 5: Robert Johnson wrote a three-column article on Elvis for the *Memphis Press-Scimitar*, and Gladys Presley was both astonished and worried that her son was making headlines.

FEB. 5, 12, 19: Elvis completed "Louisiana Hayride" appearances.

FEB. 6: Elvis and the Blue Moon Boys gave two shows at the Memphis Auditorium, after which they jammed and partied. When Elvis came home after five A.M., Gladys warned him that his lifestyle was "going to hell" and that she did not want his managers and the music world to destroy Elvis.

FEB. 14: Colonel Tom Parker entered Elvis's life and assisted Bob Neal in booking Elvis (via Parker's Hank Snow tours) in Carlsbad, New Mexico, where he performed a Valentine's Day concert. The Colonel was attracted to Elvis's unpredictable personality, the reactions he pulled from audiences, his driving, wild style, and the future possible money-earning power of the Cat. Soon the Colonel would be at policy meetings with Elvis, his parents, Bob Neal, the Baron, and Tom Diskin (the Colonel's gofer and sidekick).

FEB. 15: While Elvis performed in Albuquerque, New Mexico, his manager's circus entourage of dancing dogs, yelping hogs, and an elephant that displayed an ad about Elvis on its satin blanket-coat caught the public's attention.

FEB. 16: Elvis's concert in Odessa, Texas, was greeted by huge crowds of teenage girls who screamed, yelled, pushed, and shoved to touch him after the concert. Being away from home, he claimed he was lonely. Thus, several young women slept with him that night "for security."

FEB. 18: Elvis sang all of his Sun songs in Monroe, Louisiana.

FEB. 22: The Cat's performance in Hope, Arkansas, was sold out.

FEB. 24: Colonel Parker was pleased with the reports he received from his staffers that Elvis's concert in Bastrop, Louisiana, was another sell-out.

FEB. 26: Elvis was in Cleveland with disc jockey Bill Randle and performed at Circle Theatre/WERE "Circle Theatre Jamboree."

CA. MAR.: Chuck Berry met Muddy Waters in a Chicago club. After Berry played a few hot guitar licks, Waters sent him to Chess records to get signed. His hit "Maybellene" created a new sound combo of blues-based, country-inspired rock. Songwriter/producer Willie Dixon (and others) called Berry "the first rock and roller." He *was* the first rock guitarist, but Elvis predated Chuck Berry's singing debut into rock 'n' roll. Elvis would one day record "Maybellene."

MAR.: Elvis took his first plane flight ever, to New York City with Neal, Moore, and Black to audition for (and be rejected by) "Arthur Godfrey's Talent Scouts." Being turned away by the famous Godfrey crushed Elvis, who never forgot the incident. He and the boys visited the Apollo Theater where they enjoyed the music of Bo Diddley, whom they later met.

When Arthur Godfrey spurned Elvis, Parker told him not to worry about it. Parker promised Elvis that New York City agents would beg to book him and that Elvis would be "bigger than that old fool before long." This kind of positive input impressed Elvis and solidified his relationship with the ingenious Colonel. He made things happen.

MAR. 5: Elvis made his TV debut on a regional telecast of the "Louisiana Hayride," during which he was introduced by Horace Logan to an overcurious audience. The show was broadcast from Shreveport, Louisiana, from station KWKH-TV, a local CBS affiliate.

Elvis allegedly sang Bill Monroe's "Uncle Pen." No tape has surfaced.

MAR. 6–10: Elvis performed in Tennessee, Arkansas, Mississippi, Louisiana, and Missouri almost nonstop, while the Colonel's staffers hyped his show. During weeks of travel, Elvis, Moore, and Black did not sleep well and they often fought the flu, stomachaches, headaches, and other illnesses. The ever-watchful Colonel Parker sent comic Whitey Ford to keep the boys in line.

MAR. 12, 26: Elvis's audience grew at "Louisiana Hayride" appearances, and many performers refused to perform the same night Elvis was onstage.

MAR. 14: Elvis and the boys stopped in Washington, DC, where Elvis was interviewed by country singing star Jimmy Dean for the WMAL radio show "Town and Country Jubilee." After the interview they partied until dawn.

MAR. 19: Elvis's live appearance on the "Grand Prize Saturday Night Jamboree," telecast from the Eagle's Hall in Houston, Texas, on KPRC-TV, was sponsored by Grand Prize Beer (a product Gladys Presley did not want Elvis to be associated with). Elvis appeared on the eight-to-seven P.M. show with the Brown Brothers, Sonny Burns, the Dixie Drifters, and Tommy Sands.

"I Got a Woman" was recorded at the Eagle's Hall in Houston. The song appears on the LP *Elvis, the Hillbilly Cat (Houston, at the Eagle's Hall, March 19, 1955).*

MAR. 24: Robert Carlton Brown interviewed Elvis at the Warwick Hotel in New York City. The interview is on the LP *Personally Elvis* (Silhouette Music).

MAR. 28: Elvis performed at the Circle Theatre in Cleveland, which was filmed by disc jockey Bill Randle. He appeared on "Circle Theatre Jamboree," some of which was aired on WERE Radio, Cleveland. Randle and Alan Freed were the most popular DJs in America, and although Randle was the first disc jockey outside the South to play one of Elvis's records, he refused to play Elvis's music over any New York City station. After extraordinarily positive audience response to Elvis (from WERE Radio, Cleveland), Randle finally played Elvis in the Big Apple.

APRIL: "The Tennessee Rock and Roll" was recorded by Sons of the Pioneers (a western harmony group) in an attempt to cash in on Elvis's trend-setting performance style. Soon, Eddy Arnold cranked out "The Rockin' Mockin' Bird." Homer and Jethro spoofed "Blue Suede Shoes" with RCA's "Two-Tone Shoes." Steve Sholes discovered Janis Martin (nicknamed "the female Elvis"). She imitated Elvis's rockabilly techniques, while the black music community claimed Elvis stole their style and would have been overlooked had he been black. The entire music industry talked about the sensational "Elvis the Pelvis."

APR. 1: Sun released "Baby, Let's Play House" and "I'm Left, You're Right, She's Gone," and Elvis performed in Odessa, Texas. In July, "Baby, Let's Play House" emerged on a national best-seller chart, and Colonel Parker met with Elvis to convince him to leave Sun Records. Tom Diskin, the Baron, and probably Hank Snow told Elvis to leave Sam Phillips and sign with RCA. Somehow, in the interim, Parker managed to change Elvis's restrictive "Louisiana Hayride" contract. He wanted Elvis available for Saturday-night television spots or major shows outside Southern states.

APR. 2, 9, 23, 30: Elvis completed "Louisiana Hayride" appearances, while the scheming Colonel made certain his performances with them were

going to come to an end and that Parker would get a piece of the gross receipts of each show.

APR. 15: Steel guitarist/composer Stanley A. Kesler toured with Elvis from 1954 to 1955. Country singer Hank Locklin was on the same "Big D Jamboree" bill with Elvis in Dallas.

APR. 16: Elvis performed at the Sportatorium in Dallas, then he gave concerts in El Dorado, Texarkana, and Helena, Arkansas.

Colonel Parker kept telling Elvis to leave Sam Phillips and Sun because Phillips needed money to invest in other artists at Sun Records. Roy Orbison, Johnny Cash, Jerry Lee Lewis, and others needed attention. Phillips had offered Elvis's contract for $7,500 to Randy Wood, head of Los Angeles–based Dot Records, and Wood turned it down because he thought Elvis "was a flash in the pan." Wood put his efforts into the safer Pat Boone instead. After Wood's rejection of Elvis's contract, Sam Phillips was ready for *any* buyout, if it seemed "reasonable." The stage was set for Colonel Parker to make a swift and powerful business move.

APR. 16: Elvis gave his first performance for KRLD radio in Dallas, Texas.

CA. APR. 18: After Elvis's performance at the Arkansas Municipal Auditorium in Texarkana, Arkansas, Elvis was interviewed by Bob Neal for a local radio station. Neal worked for his own company, the Memphis Promotion Agency, and he often booked acts in the Texarkana area. Listeners heard Neal call Elvis "the King of Western Bop" and speak of Johnny Cash and Charlene Arthur costarring onstage with Elvis, Scotty Moore, and Bill Black. Mention was made of D. J. Fontana as the group's new drummer, Floyd Cramer (piano), and Jimmy Day (steel guitarist). Scotty Moore mentioned the group's new songs "I'm Left, You're Right, She's Gone," "Baby, Let's Play House," and "Maybellene" written by Chuck Berry. (*Note:* on the LP *Elvis Confidentially* [Arena Records ARAD 1008] the date for this interview is incorrectly given as May 6, 1955. Elvis was in Birmingham, Alabama, on May 6, 1955.)

MAY 1: Elvis performed in New Orleans and toured with Hank Snow's All-Star Jamboree for three weeks through Chattanooga. The Jamboree was run by Colonel Parker and his staffers, who controlled Elvis's actions. Elvis was not going to be allowed to "fall out of the net."

MAY 4–5: Elvis, Scotty Moore, and Bill Black's performance in Mobile, Alabama, was greeted with hostility and glee. Old-timers thought Elvis was "crude," but their teenage sons and daughters were enthralled.

MAY 6: Elvis's show in Birmingham, Alabama, went smoothly. Elvis's delivery was powerful—his performances either mesmerized audiences or caused mass delirium. After a few weeks on tour, no one wanted to close a show after Elvis.

MAY 7: After his concert in Daytona Beach, Florida, Elvis was physically and mentally exhausted.

MAY 8: Scotty Moore and Bill Black had become pros at following Elvis's erratic hip signals. The audiences in Tampa, Florida, went wild every time Elvis jerked his left leg or put his right fist in the air, followed with two shakes of his hips.

MAY 9: Elvis's performance in Macon, Georgia, was sold out. As audience members collapsed in hysteria, police officers rushed them out of the audito-

rium. It was mayhem and Elvis adored every moment of it.

CA. MAY: Elvis and the boys traveled with Sun's packaged shows, which eventually included Johnny Cash, Carl Perkins, Roy Orbison, Jerry Lee Lewis, and others. Admission to see them was $1. Traveling together by car or bus, in hot, humid weather, Elvis, Black, Moore, and Fontana played small clubs and bars whenever anyone showed interest. Sometimes their pay was a tank of gasoline for the car (which they often slept in) or a hot meal. It was tough, grueling work with little financial reward, but it gave the group a chance to get to know one another. Each club date served as a rehearsal session.

MAY 10: Elvis and the band performed in Ocala, Florida.

MAY: The new release "Baby, Let's Play House"/"I'm Left, You're Right, She's Gone" was distributed by Bob Neal and each song became a hit.

MAY 13: In Jacksonville, Florida, Elvis's performance at the Gator Bowl caused a riot, the first of its kind in rock 'n' roll history. Johnny Tillotson was in the audience that night and claimed "the riot story" was created by Colonel Parker. Hank Snow, Slim Whitman, and others watched in amazement and fear when audience members jumped onto the stage and began tearing Elvis's clothes off him. Critics claimed watching Elvis perform was like watching a striptease while sipping milk. He looked to be decent and lewd, proper and sexual, and steamy but cool.

Performing that night as backup vocalists were the Jordanaires and the Blue Moon Boys. Also appearing before Elvis were Phil Maraquin and Frankie Connors.

By this time, Scotty, Bill, and Elvis had traveled over one hundred thousand miles, the Hillbilly Cat (also billed as the King of Western Bop) and the Blue Moon Boys were recognized in cities and small hamlets throughout the South as a troublesome trio. After his incorrigible performance in Jacksonville, Elvis naively teased, "Girls, I'll see you backstage." Taking his cue, fourteen thousand fans grappled to leap onstage and rip off Elvis's pink shirt, white jacket, and shoes. While he thought the potentially dangerous situation was humorous, his mother became distraught when girls shoved police guards to the ground and entered his dressing room. Elvis told Gladys, "If you're going to feel that way, you'd better not come along to my shows because that stuff is going to keep right on happening—I hope." (See p. 256, *Elvis and Gladys.*)

Scenes like the one in Florida prompted Tennessee Williams to write *Orpheus Descending* (1957), the story of a god (Orpheus) whose musical powers tame savage beasts who eventually tear Orpheus to shreds. Set in a Tennessee hamlet, the Elvis-based character, Val Xavier (played in the 1957 play by Cliff Robertson), is a naive guitarist who is destroyed in a world of idolatry and corruption. (In 1960, Brando played the role in a movie retitled *The Fugitive Kind*, directed by Sidney Lumet.) Placing Elvis in pop-culture literature, Williams's stage play eerily predicted the dilemmas that ended up molding the singer's future.

Elvis did not comprehend the level of public adoration he had generated. All of a sudden, audiences were making it clear: he had become a *part* of them. He was an aspect of their needs and secret desires. He was their answer to years of sexual repression. He no longer belonged to himself, or to his family. Everyone literally wanted a piece of him.

When millions of teens rushed to buy Elvis-type blue jeans (creating a new fad), Jacob Potofsky, president of the Amalgamated Clothing Workers of America, said, "It is sad, but Elvis Presley has more influence on our young people than our educators." The Colonel saw an opportunity to make even more money on Elvis-related merchandise. In personal royalties alone, Elvis earned more than $400,000 from RCA in 1956, an unprecedented amount. The Colonel wanted that amount to triple within twelve months.

News reporters told mainstream America the unmanageable Jacksonville audience of screaming devotees ran to strip pieces of clothing from Elvis's body because *he* encouraged it. Police rushed Elvis outside before he was manhandled to death, and the Colonel realized this image of an audacious boy who loved his mother and God was potent.

When Gladys Presley scurried to a waiting car to leave the incredible Jacksonville mob scene, lipsticked names of girls covered the vehicle. Those hot-pink names pointed to a not-too-private future. Elvis was no longer "her boy." He belonged to the masses. They would take pieces of him whenever they got the chance, until he disappeared.

Mae Boren Axton (composer with Tommy Durden of "Heartbreak Hotel") saw Elvis perform with the Hank Snow All-Star Jamboree in Jacksonville.

MAY 14, 21: At "Louisiana Hayride" appearances, teenagers ran amuck and were difficult to manage.

Elvis was in a category by himself. No other entertainer caused this kind of fervor. Parker purposely created various ingenious gimmicks to keep the fire ignited under fans and to develop an even larger mystique around Elvis. Incorrigible, oversexed, out-of-control teen audiences stimulated free publicity. Record sales skyrocketed and money poured in.

MAY 16: Elvis's performance at the Mosque Theater in Richmond, Virginia, caused another audience stir, despite a heavy security force and an ever-growing press corp.

MAY 17: Elvis gave two shows in Norfolk, Virginia.

MAY 18: Elvis's two shows at the American Legion Auditorium in Roanoke, Virginia, left him pumped up and ready for trouble. He joked around until he fell asleep in the car that carried the group to New Bern.

MAY 19: Elvis and the band performed in New Bern, North Carolina, to a capacity crowd.

MAY 22: Elvis performed in Houston's Magnolia Gardens.

MAY 25: Elvis sang at the Jimmie Rodgers Memorial Day Celebration and performed in honor of Rodgers in Meridian, Mississippi.

MAY 26: There was an innocence in Elvis that appealed to Parker. To the Cat, opulence was having a $20 bill in his pocket after he paid his parents' rent. Elvis and his black friends thought being rich meant owning fancy cars, while Elvis's Holy Roller acquaintances thought having a home with running, hot water would be luxury. That, too, appealed to the Cat, so he told the Colonel he wanted to buy a lot of Cadillacs and have hot, running water in a house somewhere. Parker told him he would have those things.

CA. MAY 27: Elvis's performance in Chattanooga, Tennessee, was followed by a set on KOCA, a Kilgore, Texas, radio station.

MAY 28: Elvis gave two evening shows at the Northside Coliseum in Forth Worth and performed on KRLD "Big D Jamboree" radio.

MAY 29: Elvis gave an afternoon and evening show at the Sportatorium in Dallas. He also performed that week in Kilgore, Gainesville, and Breckenridge, Texas.

MAY 30: Elvis performed at the Fair Park Auditorium in Abilene, Texas, to an adoring crowd.

MAY 31: Elvis performed an afternoon concert in Midland, Texas, and that evening he made a live radio appearance on "The Roy Orbison Show" in Odessa, Texas. It may have been that after hearing Orbison sing, Elvis suggested he come to the Sun Records' studio to try out for Sam Phillips, because in 1956, Orbison signed with Sun.

JUNE: *Cowboy Songs* printed a feature article on Elvis.

JUNE 1: Elvis's concert in Guymon, Oklahoma, once again drove the girls to a frenzy. Elvis was not "Mama's lit-

▲ Roy Orbison. *Courtesy of Roy Orbison.*

tle angel" when Gladys was absent. When a *Goldmine* interviewer asked Jimmy Denson, "What transformed the shrinking violet into the Hillbilly Cat?" Denson gave a disturbing reply: "Drugs. He needed 'em to come out of himself. Dewey Phillips [the first DJ to play an Elvis record] gave them to him. I knew Elvis for seven years. He was lethargic. He took amphetamines and Benzedrine to give him energy. Dewey would slip them to him in an alley bar near the Chisca Hotel. We warned Elvis because we'd seen our brother Delmer take every drug imaginable for years." Denson claimed Elvis's sexual behavior was not lily-white: "One time in the summer of 1955, I saw Elvis, Scotty, and Bill. They'd outfitted the back of the Cadillac with pillows from floor up to seat level. I saw Elvis knock off two pieces [girls] there after one show. . . . Elvis would pop a handful of Benzedrine and drive all night."

JUNE: Colonel Parker told the Presleys the Sun label could not promote Elvis to superstardom, but he could. He assured Elvis's parents Elvis had a million-dollar talent that deserved to *earn* that amount and more.

The cunning Colonel vied for complete control, which he had to have in order to skyrocket Elvis to the top.

The Colonel found out quickly what would please Elvis more than anything. He would make certain Elvis's wishes were granted. Elvis insisted Vernon leave his part-time job at the paint factory, so that Elvis became the man of the house. The Colonel created an environment in which the Presleys were dependent upon Elvis's ability to earn money, and they were forced to tolerate the constant presence of the abrasive, wily Parker.

Vernon almost bowed down to the Colonel whenever Parker gave advice or orders. Vernon watched from the sidelines as Parker consumed Elvis's life. Lavishing Gladys with almost anything he thought she wanted to have, Elvis enjoyed seeing his parents finally

relax and not have to worry about money. But Gladys was not content, a fact that grieved Elvis, but he had no time to deal with her anxieties. His career was rocketing and he put it before all else.

As Gladys watched pensively, the Colonel's ingenious marketing techniques created the Elvis mystique. Gladys believed the Colonel purposely tried to ruin Elvis's image by telling the press fictionalized stories. She feared Elvis was becoming a prisoner of fame. She abhorred his long absences from Memphis and was jealous of the attention Elvis gave to his exasperating manager—an outsider—who now masterminded her son's career.

No longer was Gladys the focus of Elvis's concern. She knew once Elvis signed a contract with RCA, the Colonel would take over. And he did. Gladys could no longer be with the son she adored. After meeting the Colonel, it seemed to Gladys all Elvis wanted was to have his name in lights and hear the roar of applause.

JUNE 2:   Elvis's performance at the City Auditorium in Amarillo, Texas, was greeted with dissent from an angry crowd of parents and educators.

JUNE 3:   Elvis gave a rocking concert in Lubbock, Texas, and met acquaintances of Buddy Holly's.

JUNE 4, 11, 25:   Elvis completed "Louisiana Hayride" appearances.

JUNE 9–10:   After their performance in Lawton, Oklahoma, Scotty Moore approached Elvis about the unfair pay he and Bill Black were receiving. Elvis brushed him off.

JUNE 13:   Elvis and the band performed in Bruce, Mississippi, on the "cherry soda circuit" (a name derived from audiences so poor and musicians so desperate, bottle caps were exchanged for admission tickets. In the late forties, the Colonel accepted bottle caps from audience members and quickly turned the caps in to bottling companies for a return of $2–4 a day).

JUNE 14: Elvis and the band performed in Tupelo, Mississippi, for a huge, shrieking crowd that chanted, "Elvis! Elvis!" The audience's adulation made Elvis feel wonderful. His hometown had finally accepted him.

JUNE 15: Although Gladys and Vernon wanted to travel with Elvis to his concert in Gobler, Missouri, they stayed home. The Colonel did not want Gladys (in particular) to see what was happening between Elvis and his female fans.

JUNE 16: Elvis performed in El Dorado, Arkansas.

JUNE 17: Valerie Harms alleges she started the first Elvis Presley Fan Club, but Marion Keisker at Sun had already opened an Elvis Presley Fan Club in Memphis.

JUNE 18: Bob Neal and Colonel Tom Parker met at "Big D Jamboree" (station KRLD, Dallas). Country singers Martha Carson, Anita Carter, and June Carter (whose manager was the Colonel) toured with Elvis. Red West and Elvis broke into June Carter's house to eat and sleep, but she didn't mind. Elvis performed at the Sportatorium in Dallas and appeared on KRLD's "Big D Jamboree" radio broadcast in Dallas.

JUNE 19: Elvis performed at the Magnolia Gardens in Houston, Texas.

JUNE 20: Elvis gave two long shows in Beaumont, Texas.

JUNE 21: Elvis and the band gave three packed shows in Beaumont. Their dressing rooms were crowded day and night with fans, eager young girls, and curious onlookers.

JUNE 22: The performance in Vernon, Texas, went smoothly, and Elvis called his mother to tell her everything was "fine."

JUNE 23: His heated performance in Lawton, Oklahoma, caused someone to ask Elvis *what* he was doing onstage. He replied, "It's rock and roll. You rock and roll with the music."

JUNE 24: Tickets for Elvis's performance in Altus, Oklahoma, sold rapidly and local musicians couldn't believe any young jive singer could cause such a commotion.

JUNE 26: Elvis again performed in Biloxi, Mississippi, where he met June Juanico (whom he dated on and off for a year). Marty Robbins still accompanied Elvis on this tour. During this concert, Elvis ignored friends' advice to beware of the Colonel's controlling behavior.

It was no accident the Colonel and Elvis found one another. Musicians talked about the promotional skills and money-making antics of Tom Parker. It made no difference to Elvis *how* Parker did it, nor did it occur to Elvis that it might have been done improperly or with a greedy, selfish intent. If Colonel Parker's promises of fame and fortune could come true, Elvis was willing to do anything the Colonel asked of him. *That* was Elvis's tragic flaw.

After Elvis began to hit it big on the music circuit, he made it clear he planned to become a movie star like Valentino, James Dean, or Dean Martin. If his popularity in music was a flash in the pan, a career in films would satisfy his hunger for applause and financial reward.

Many people believe Elvis had little to do with his rise to stardom, but he knew exactly what he was doing when he hooked the Colonel into his net. He simply didn't know the fisherman could become the bait the fish would devour! Elvis admitted later in his career, "When I was a boy, I was the hero in comic books and movies. I grew up believing in a dream. Now I've lived it out. That's all a man can ask for."

Elvis, seeking a promoter and manager who knew the ropes, was flattered when the well-known, scheming Colonel was interested in him. Knowing Elvis admired Hank Williams and Jimmie Rodgers, the Colonel told the starry-eyed youth, "I can make you bigger than all of them!" The Colonel's seductive approach was, "Stick with me, kid. Do as I say and you'll have the world at your feet." It was too bewitching a proposal to pass up. Then he would add, "I got powers people dream 'bout havin'. Trust me," and Elvis did.

JUNE 27–28: Elvis and the band performed at the NCO Club at Keesler Air Force Base in Biloxi, Mississippi. Marty Robbins accompanied them.

JUNE 29–30: Elvis performed at the Radio Ranch Club in Mobile, Alabama, and sang in Marianna, Arkansas.

JUNE 30: By this time, rock 'n' roll was branded as a champion of juvenile deliquency, partially because of the film *Blackboard Jungle*, which featured Bill Haley's "Rock Around the Clock" (which sold 25 million singles and hit *Billboard*'s Top 100 chart for eight weeks at No. 1). "Rock Around the Clock" motivated teenagers to keep time with the music by using their whole bodies. Its beat evolved into a lively jitterbug, which was a version of the lindy. Haley starred in a movie titled *Rock Around the Clock* with the Platters, Freddie Bell and His Bellboys, and deejay Alan Freed. *Blackboard Jungle* gave America its first glimpse of undisciplined teenage gangs taking to the streets. Elvis and Haley's rock music were blamed for this new social curiosity and "disorder."

JULY 1: After his performance in Baton Rouge, Louisiana, Elvis insisted the band members jam in a gospel session until dawn.

JULY 2: Their "Louisiana Hayride" appearance was larger and the audience was wilder than it usually was. Elvis waved provocatively to the crowd, and teenagers leaped to grab his feet at the stage's edge.

JULY 2: Elvis and the band appeared on KEYS radio in Corpus Christi, Texas.

JULY 3: Because of their radio exposure, Elvis's audience was huge during his concert in Corpus Christi, Texas.

JULY 4: During a festive Fourth of July celebration, Elvis let himself go during a performance at the City Recreational Building in Stephenville, Texas.

CA. JULY 10–12: "I Forgot to Remember to Forget" (by Stanley Kesler and Charlie Feathers) was recorded by Elvis for Sun Records with Elvis and Scotty Moore on guitars, Bill Black on bass, and Johnny Bernero on drums. Its success showed in its forty-week stay on *Billboard*'s country chart, peaking at No. 1 (Sun 223). (*Note:* As a Sun Records singer, the only sheet music which Hi-Lo printed with Elvis's name is for "I Forgot to Remember to Forget," which also featured Toni Arden.) Its flip side was "Mystery Train."

JULY 11: Elvis recorded at Sun "Tryin' to Get to You" (written by Rose Marie McCoy and Margie Singleton) after an unsuccessful first attempt on February 5, 1955 (which was released by RCA on the LP *Elvis Presley*). He accompanied himself on the piano during some of the takes, but Frank Tolley has also been given credit for the piano backing. Scotty Moore (guitar), Bill Black (bass), and Johnny Bernero (drums) accompanied. The uncharted single was released in September 1956 (RCA 20-6639 with the flip side "I Love You Because").

JULY 22: Elvis gave a wild performance in Odessa, Texas, where he had developed a rather large teenage following.

The Colonel was planning to get rid of Bob Neal. He needed to buy Neal out of Elvis's contract completely. Parker told Neal the kid's contract should be sold above $40,000. Neal laughed at him and reminded the Colonel that Owen Bradley of Decca wouldn't pay $5,000; Mitch Miller, an A&R man from Columbia, refused to pay over $4,000; and Dot Record's Randy Wood would not pay $7,500. The Colonel said these men had no insight or intelligence and that he would get what he wanted, and that Neal would get a buyout cut.

The Colonel soon talked to one of RCA's biggest recording talents (and one of his own partners), Hank Snow, about getting Elvis a contract with RCA through the record company's Nashville man, Steve Sholes. According to the Colonel's explicit instructions, Snow was to contact his music publishers, Hill and Range, to come in on an RCA bid for Elvis's contract. Snow did this for the Colonel, thinking he would make a long-term profit and eventually comanage Elvis with Parker. Snow and Parker had split income from their tour-packaging agency, Hank Snow Attractions, for a long time. Nothing would change, or so Snow thought.

JULY 23: Elvis's performance at the Dallas Sportatorium was followed by a few songs on the "Big D Jamboree" over KRLD Dallas radio.

JULY 23: Elvis, Scotty Moore, and Bill Black performed for radio station KRLD, "Big D Jamboree," Dallas and at KECK in Odessa, Texas, for "Pioneer Jamboree" with Lee Alexander.

JULY 25: At a concert held in the 116th Field Artillery Armory, in Tampa, Florida, the original photo of Elvis dressed in a gold-lamé tuxedo was taken by William S. "Popsie" Randolph. The photo has appeared in numerous articles, on albums, and in advertisements since 1955 (the latest being *Rolling Stone*'s Nov. 14, 1992 cover).

JULY 26–27: Elvis performed in Orlando, Florida, and partied all night with local musicians in his hotel room.

JULY 28–29: Elvis's return performance at the Gator Bowl, in Jacksonville, Florida, was secured by police and guards throughout the auditorium. Although the audience was loud and happy, its behavior did not end in a riot this time.

JULY 30: Elvis's performance in Daytona Beach, Florida, was a success, and the boys looked at race cars in their spare time in the afternoon.

JULY 31: Elvis performed at the Community Center, Sheffield, Alabama, and became sick after the show. Too much junk food!

AUG: Elvis recorded some songs that Sam Phillips did not release. Phillips was always looking for ways to cut corners financially, and some people suspect he reused the original Elvis tapes for other artists' work. The songs that had been recorded by this date included "Always Late With Your Kisses," "Gone," "Night Train to Memphis," "Blue Guitar," "Cryin' Heart Blues," "Tennessee Saturday Night," "I Got a Woman," Chuck Berry's "Maybellene," "Down the Line," "Satisfied," "Give Me More, More, More," "Uncle Pen," "That's the Stuff You Gotta Watch," and perhaps others.

AUG. 1–2: Gladys and Vernon were invited to Elvis's performance in Little Rock, Arkansas. The Colonel set up a "spontaneous meeting" between the Presleys and Whitey Ford (known as the Duke of Paducah), so that Ford could once again tell the Presleys how important and respected his boss, the Colonel, was in the music world. The Colonel planned the event, although Elvis was not aware to what extent Parker had gone to get Whitey Ford to praise his managerial skills. The Colonel vied to get Gladys to "trust and like" him. She never did.

At the awkward meeting, Gladys asked what church the Colonel attended and he skirted the question. He did not go to church unless there was some kind of carnival at which he could make a buck.

Gladys didn't like the trickster, but Elvis (who kept calling the Colonel the "Admiral") told her he "was gonna be jus' fine. Ya'll see."

AUG. 3: Elvis and the Blue Moon Boys were graciously received by throngs of fans for their concert in Tupelo, Mississippi. The Presleys also attended this concert.

AUG. 4: After his concert in Tupelo, Elvis and the band got in their cars and drove all night to reach Camden, Arkansas, where they gave two performances.

AUG. 5: Elvis performed at the Overton Park Shell in Memphis with Webb Pierce, Charles Feathers, Johnny Cash (his first appearance with the Tennessee Two), Scotty Moore, and Bill Black in a Bob Neal Anniversary Jamboree.

AUG. 6: Sun Records released Elvis's versions of "Mystery Train" and "I Forgot to Remember to Forget" (Sun 223).

Although his Sun sessions were somewhat relaxed, Elvis knew he had to perform well. Phillips often yelled, "Just don't make it too damned complicated!" He realized the public identified with simple songs, but Elvis was always looking for new ways to sing them.

CA. AUG. 6: At the "Louisiana Hayride" Elvis sang Chuck Berry's "Maybellene," which can be heard on the LP *Elvis: The First Live Recordings*.

Although Sam Phillips was instrumental in placing Elvis on the musical map, Elvis was not loyal to him. Sun's Marion Keisker, Gladys Presley, and Scotty Moore believed the Colonel began to spread the rumor that Elvis intended to leave Sun Records before Elvis had a national tour or a bigger record company's serious consideration. Others claim Sam showed equal interest in Jerry Lee Lewis, Carl Perkins, Johnny Cash, Buddy Holly, Roy Orbison, and Gene Vincent. Elvis had no intention of remaining a regional fad. Phillips and Bob Neal had not pushed him to the top fast enough. He had to move on.

When Bob Neal complained Elvis's music was too "colored," Elvis reminded Neal his music was not as radical as Jerry Lee Lewis's. Lewis was known to be a redneck type whose lewd comments and marriage to his underage cousin (1958) were beneath reproach. Lewis came from a Pentecostal boogie tradition and practically lived in the corners of black dives. He was more "colored" than all the rockabilly singers, or so Elvis thought. Lewis knew no limits. He was storming his

way through rock with a vengeance, and he banged on the piano like a musical demon. His inspiring, outrageous energy and erratic mood swings were things to watch. Elvis did not want Jerry Lee to preempt his splashy entrance into the spotlight. To stay with Sam Phillips and Sun Records might permit that to happen.

There was also Johnny Cash ("The Man in Black") to worry about. He was coming up strong with Phillips and could write his own kick-ass music. He was going to make it big, and Elvis did not plan to wait to see who could climb faster up the charts.

There were a lot of white race singers when hard-liners professed Elvis was the only one. Jimmie Rodgers absorbed and transformed black music into his own style of country-blues and got away with it. So did Gene Vincent, Buddy Holly, and Johnny Burnette. If it hadn't been for alcohol abuse, Carl Perkins's rockabilly vitality might have gotten him to the title he billed himself as, "The King of Rock 'n' Roll." He had the talent but not enough seductive charisma to carry it off. Hank Williams, whom Elvis had idolized, had been a poet of worry who pressed country music to the edge with dignity. Good thing he had been incapable of feeling the exquisite wrath and fury in rockabilly. His music missed that soul of hillbilly that Elvis caressed. With a little bit of luck, Williams could have become the mythical figure Elvis yearned to become. Roy Orbison's voice crossed into so many octaves. He captured with ease a pure, ravishing sound. What if he started to compete openly with Elvis? That possibility was not alluring.

Elvis felt an urge to advance in popularity faster than the many other talented men in Phillips's organization. Charlie Rich, Roy Orbison, Billy Lee Riley, Carl Perkins, Johnny Cash, and Jerry Lee Lewis were too gifted and too eager to produce songs that could hit the charts or impact on listeners. If Phillips decided to spend money and promote someone, one of them could

transcend Elvis's sudden spurt of public acclaim. Elvis knew he had to leave Phillips in order to attain legendary status. Elvis was smarter and more shrewd than many people believed.

AUG. 8: Elvis appeared on KSIG radio in Gladewater, Texas.

AUG. 8–10: Elvis and the band performed in and around Gladewater, giving two performances a night.

AUG. 11: Elvis's performance at the Texas State Fairgrounds in Dallas, Texas, was followed by autograph signing and all-night parties in his room.

AUG. 12: Elvis gave a concert in San Antonio, Texas.

AUG. 13: Elvis performed in Houston, Texas, and complained of having stomach cramps and a headache. Few men could have sustained his energy level onstage after having traveled so many miles in so few days.

AUG. 15: Elvis signed another contract, which gave Colonel Parker the right to manage his career, but Elvis was still legally bound to Bob Neal's management for one more year. Bob Neal and Parker would work together to promote Elvis.

AUG. 16: The Colonel contacted Arnold Shaw, a well-known New York publishing-house manager, and had Shaw give Elvis's tapes to weekend New York disc jockey Bill Randle (who succeeded disc jockey Alan Freed in Cleveland). Randle said the music was not appropriate to play over New York radio, but he had played Elvis's music in Cleveland and it had received an incredible response. Now, the Colonel could tell RCA executives "his boy" was "hot" above the Mason-Dixon Line.

◄ Elvis performing at the Louisiana Hayride, sometime between 1953–54. *Private collection.*

AUG. 20: Elvis performed two shows at the Circle Theater in Cleveland, Ohio. Bill Randle was in the audience and took note of the Hillbilly Cat's overall improvements in singing and guitar playing. Elvis had lost his initial stage fright and seemed calmer, more confident, and humorous.

CA. AUG. 26 OR 28: Elvis was interviewed for radio WMPS by his former manager, Bob Neal, in Memphis.

AUG. 27: Elvis appeared at the "Louisiana Hayride."

AUG. 31: Elvis sang for WMPS radio in Memphis.

SEPT: Marion Keisker quit working for Sam Phillips at Sun and joined the Air Force, where she would later be promoted to the rank of captain. Before she left the armed forces she would work for the Armed Forces' TV Network and meet Elvis in West Germany.

"Mystery Train" entered *Billboard*'s country chart and peaked at No. 1 in a thirty-one-week stay.

Country Song Roundup featured Elvis in an article titled "Folk Music Fireball."

Like thousands of others, singer/composer Paul Simon said, "I thought his name was about the weirdest thing I'd ever heard. I thought he was a black guy." (See *Rolling Stone*, Special Edition, 1977, p. 6.) It was not Elvis's name that caused Simon to think Elvis was black, but his sound and the tempo of his music.

SEPT. 1: The Colonel instructed Elvis on how to behave in public and made certain "his boy" (whom he often called "son" when Gladys was not present) knew *he* was in control. He resembled the kind of authoritative father figure that Elvis had craved when he was younger. When told his schedule was going to be exhausting, Elvis said he would tour wherever

Parker thought he should. "That's good," the Colonel muttered, "or else I'll put a hex on ya and you'll self-destruct."

Elvis was mesmerized and somewhat terrorized by this kind of talk. It may have been the Colonel's subliminal "powers" that eventually controlled Elvis's every career move, or perhaps it was trepidation about what the Colonel would do to him if he did not obey.

It was difficult to learn the truth about the Colonel because even his enemies would not talk about him. A rumor went through the music and film worlds that the cost was much higher to say something negative about him than to shut up and do what you were told. His good points were many. He did not drink or take drugs. He gave large amounts of money to the Catholic church (to please his family). He was a loyal husband to his wife, Marie Ross Mott, and he was an excellent father to his stepson, Bobby Ross. The Colonel's three downfalls were gambling, overeating, and placing money before the well-being of the people he represented. He once told Eddy Arnold, before Arnold dismissed him, "You're my hobby, boy. Jus' a hobby."

SEPT. 1: While Elvis performed in New Orleans, Louisiana, the audience was so loud no one could hear him sing.

SEPT. 2: Elvis's two concerts at the Arkansas Municipal Auditorium in Texarkana, Arkansas, sold out.

SEPT. 3: Elvis gave a concert at the Sportatorium in Dallas, Texas, with others who toured in Bob Neal's troupe, and Elvis sang for Dallas radio station KRLD's "Big D Jamboree."

SEPT. 5–9: Rockabilly singer Eddie Bond and the Stompers toured with Elvis (with whom the Stompers had previously played clubs in Memphis in 1953–54). They performed in Forrest City, Arkansas, to a full house.

SEPT. 6:   Eddy Bond and the Stompers traveled with Elvis to Bono, Arkansas, where they all performed.

SEPT. 7:   Elvis arrived in Sikeston, Missouri, to perform after Eddy Bond and the Stompers' act.

SEPT. 8:   Audiences went wild when Elvis sang in Clarksdale, Mississippi. Eddy Bond and the Stompers followed the act.

SEPT. 8:   Elvis signed a one-year contract with "Louisiana Hayride," which was to begin Nov. 8. His salary was to increase to $200 a night (up from $18). The Colonel did not know about the contract signing until it was a done deal. *That* would never happen again.

SEPT. 9:   Elvis gave a concert in McComb, Mississippi, and his family moved to a rented house on Getwell Street. Elvis was proud to tell everyone they had a telephone and that his phone number was 48–4921.

SEPT. 10, 24:   Elvis and the Blue Moon Boys gave two concerts at the "Louisiana Hayride."

SEPT. 11–12:   Elvis sang for WCMS radio and gave a concert at the City Auditorium in Norfolk, Virginia.

SEPT. 14:   Elvis toured with country singer Lloyd "Cowboy" Copas to Asheville, North Carolina.

SEPT. 15:   With Lloyd Cowboy Copas, Elvis performed at the American Legion Auditorium in Roanoke, Virginia. The two men jammed country music before getting in their cars and driving to New Bern, North Carolina.

SEPT. 16:   Copas and Elvis performed separately in New Bern.

SEPT. 17:   Elvis's performance in Wilson, North Carolina, was met with great enthusiasm.

SEPT. 18:   Elvis preformed in Raleigh, North Carolina.

SEPT. 19:   Elvis and his band's concert in Thomasville, North Carolina, was followed by a night of gospel jamming.

SEPT. 20:   Elvis and the boys gave two concerts in Richmond, Virginia, and performed live for a radio broadcast for WRVA.

SEPT. 21:   Elvis was ecstatic during his performance in Danville, Virginia, because his manager had told him his records were "breaking *all* records" in sales.

SEPT. 22:   Elvis and the boys performed in Kingsport, Tennessee. After the concert, they drove home, spent a day in Memphis, and left for their next concert. Gladys was beside herself with grief. She told Elvis he cared more about touring in a car with a bunch of musicians than he did about his family. He reassured her that his efforts were only to benefit her and Vernon.

SEPT. 26:   Elvis performed to huge crowds in Wichita, Kansas.

SEPT. 27:   Driving all night, the performance at the Saddle Club in Bryan, Texas, was invigorating.

SEPT. 28:   The Cat gave an outrageous show in Conroe, Texas.

SEPT. 29:   Elvis's performance at the Sports Arena in Austin, Texas, was closely watched by the police and the press. The audience remained somewhat peaceful.

SEPT. 30: Elvis performed at Gonzales, Texas, not knowing his idol, film star James Dean, had been killed in a freak auto accident. When he heard the news a few days later, Elvis was stunned. But his grief turned to hope—with Dead dead, maybe he could make a break for Hollywood. It now seemed a real possibility, not merely a boyhood fantasy. He again told Colonel Parker he wanted to be a Hollywood actor.

OCT.: Toni Arden did the first Elvis cover of "I Forgot to Remember to Forget" (RCA 6346), one month before Elvis's reissue of the tune. The 1955 Hi-Lo Music Company's sheet music featured Arden (RCA) & Elvis (Sun) on the cover.

Atlantic Records unsuccessfully bid $25,000 for Elvis to sign with them.

OCT.: Wanda Jackson appeared on the "Hank Snow Jamboree" bill with Elvis from Abilene, Texas, to St. Louis.

OCT. 1, 8, 29: Audiences were thrilled to watch the Hillbilly Cat's uncontrolled body language at these three "Louisiana Hayride" appearances.

OCT. 9: Elvis performed in Lufkin, Texas.

OCT. 10–14: Elvis performed in Brownwood, Abilene, Midland, Amarillo, and Odessa, Texas. Floyd Cramer toured with Elvis. Soon a Bill Haley and the Comets–Hank Snow tour developed. Wanda Jackson, Floyd Cramer, Johnny Cash, Carl Perkins, and Elvis were billed together on the Jamboree billings from Abilene, Texas, to St. Louis.

OCT. 14: Buddy Holly's big break came when he opened a show at Lubbock's Cotton Club for Bill Haley and the Comets.

OCT. 15: Buddy Holly opened the show at the Cotton Club in Lubbock, Texas, but the audience was not impressed. When Elvis appeared onstage, he caused a frenzy. Buddy Holly, Mac Davis, and Elvis talked until dawn. Elvis encouraged Buddy Holly to take music seriously after they jammed on the back of a pickup truck that night. Holly gave Elvis credit for having been his inspiration and guidance.

Holly signed a record contract with Decca Records after agent Eddie Crandell discovered him. Although Holly and his band, the Three Tunes, were country singers who had no idea how to produce a rock sound, they found out that Decca was looking for another Elvis. Holly's first attempts at singing rock 'n' roll were so disastrous, Decca did not release several records.

OCT. 16: Elvis, Carl Perkins, Johnny Cash, and Floyd Cramer were billed together as they performed at Hub Motors in Lubbock, Texas. Elvis liked Johnny Cash's blunt, raw style.

OCT. 16: Singer/composer Webb Pierce said Elvis "can put us all out of business."

OCT. 17: Elvis, Carl Perkins, and Johnny Cash jammed for hours before their performance in El Dorado, Arkansas.

OCT. 19: Elvis performed in Cleveland with Roy Acuff and Kitty Wells at the Circle Theater. He and Acuff did not get along well because Acuff scoffed at Elvis's first Grand Ole Opry appearance.

OCT. 20: Elvis, Pat Boone (whose "Ain't That a Shame" just hit the charts), Bill Haley (who had seven Top 20 hits), and the Four Lads (who had released "Moments to Remember") sang at the Brooklyn High School and St. Michael's Hall in Cleveland, Ohio.

Elvis performed by request in front of a camera for the well-known Cleveland disc jockey Bill Randle, who produced a forty-eight minute documentary with a $4,000 budget titled *The Pied Piper of Cleveland: A Day in the Life of a Famous Disc Jockey*. Tom Edwards photographed Elvis and Bill Haley shaking hands at Cleveland's Brooklyn High School Auditorium.

At the evening performance at St. Michael's Hall, Elvis sang "That's All Right, Mama," "Blue Moon of Kentucky," "Good Rockin' Tonight," "Mystery Train," and "I Forgot to Remember to Forget." Randle's documentary was shown at Euclid Shore Junior High School and on WEWS-TV, Channel 5, in Cleveland.

OCT. 21–22:   Elvis and the boys gave an exhausting concert in St. Louis, Missouri.

OCT. 26–28:   Elvis performed at the fairgrounds in Prichard, Alabama.

OCT. 29:   Rumors spread Elvis was to become the new James Dean.

People gravitate to and want to taste forbidden fruit. It's human nature. Teenyboppers flocked to Elvis, who symbolized James Dean's impact and charisma.

As we look at the sensational popularity Elvis suddenly obtained, we must not take lightly James Dean's passing and how the behavior of millions of fans proved they *needed* to have and keep a hero they could glorify. Elvis automatically became that man, whether he perceived that fact or not.

Both Dean and Elvis were renegades whom the haughty establishment loved to misunderstand; both personified men who "needed to be taken care of" by some "mothering, caring" female; both wore blue jeans, rode loud motorcycles, and cried in public (a trait that endeared them to females and caused men to scoff). Both men were called "unpleasing signs of the time" and were rejected as "unfit" by restrained moralists. Both "rebels" tapped respectfully an essential nerve in the repressed youth of America for which each man was rewarded with applause, riches, infatuation, and obsessive devotion.

OCT. 29:   The first British Elvis imitator, Terry Dene, was signed on Decca Records with the backup team Dene-Agers.

NOV. 5, 19, 26:   Elvis and the band appeared on "Louisiana Hayride."

NOV. 6:   Elvis performed to a large crowd in Biloxi, Mississippi.

NOV. 7:   After they performed at the NCO Club at Keesler Air Force Base in Biloxi, Elvis, Scotty, and Bill went to a local diner after their concert and "pigged out."

NOV. 8:   Elvis performed in Amory, Mississippi.

◀ Actor James Dean. *Courtesy of the James Dean Gallery, from the collection of David Loehr.*

NOV. 10: Elvis went to the annual disc-jockey convention at the Andrew Jackson Hotel in Nashville to hear new demo songs. He promised Mae Axton he would record her song "Heartbreak Hotel" and secured the rights to record it. The Colonel warned the Cat *not* to do that again. He would select all of Elvis's music in the future. He knew how to do it so royalties to writers would be cut out. Elvis naively agreed.

NOV. 10–13: The Country and Western Disc Jockey Association named Elvis the Most Promising Country Artist. Elvis now had to tolerate being flaunted by the Colonel with a sideshow promotion of roaming elephants, clucking chickens, and filthy hogs. Elvis and the Blue Moon Boys were to fit in, just like any other animals.

NOV. 12: Elvis gave an exhausting afternoon show in Carthage, Texas, and he told his band about a great song he had heard called "Heartbreak Hotel."

NOV. 13: After giving two shows at the Ellis Auditorium in Memphis, Elvis energetically played football and then sang until the early morning. He had not had eight hours sleep in a night for weeks. With Elvis surrounded by musicians and groupies at all hours, it was obvious to his family that he was no longer thoughtful of their needs.

Elvis was known to sleepwalk whenever he was anxious about being accepted or whenever a person close to him was near death or died.

His obsessions also led to overeating and an acute prescription-drug dependency. Gladys kept warning Elvis to get some rest before he collapsed, and she continuously worried about his sleepwalking.

NOV. 14: Elvis performed in Forrest City, Arkansas, where the "boys" picked up women and brought them to hotel rooms. In *Elvis: What Happened?* ex-colleague Red West explains how it

was in the heyday of rock 'n' roll: "He really developed that professional country-boy act with women. In the later years it was no longer natural, it became his line . . . toward the end of 1955. . . . Elvis suddenly found that he was one helluva an attractive guy offstage as well as on. And he started to realize that women liked going to bed just as much as men did. . . . We came across two gals . . . pickups . . . and Presley disappeared with his girl into the bedroom of Mrs. Lois West. . . . Elvis had been prosecuting the act of love with such inspired vigor that he had broken the slab of wood under the mattress. The beautiful moment of ecstasy had been punctured by the sound of cracking timber. [Elvis broke the old bed.] . . . Imagine the girl. There she is getting it on and suddenly the whole world collapses under her. I went into the room and there they are half-assed dressed and giggling like schoolkids. . . . Once he discovered how easy he could get girls, we were routing them through his bedrooms two and sometimes three a day."

NOV. 15: Elvis performed in Sheffield, Alabama.

NOV. 16: Elvis performed in Camden, Alabama.

NOV. 17: Elvis's concert in Texarkana, Arkansas, was filled to capacity, and women lined the streets to get a glimpse or a photograph of him.

NOV. 18: Elvis performed in Longview, Texas.

NOV. 19: Elvis and Red West flew to New York City to meet with Colonel Parker and Jean and Julian Aberbach of Hill and Range Music. They discussed the company's plans for Elvis's music. Elvis listened to what the Colonel told him would happen and agreed to all of it without having a lawyer present. He virtually signed his life away, little by little, under the Colonel's tutelage.

NOV. 20: Elvis's Sun Records contract was purchased by RCA Victor for $25,000 via Steve Sholes (head of the artist-and-repertoire department in Nashville) and RCA Victor's president Frank Folsom. The Aberbach brothers' company, Hill and Range Music, bought Phillips's Hi-Lo Music publishing company for $15,000, and Elvis earned $5,000 as a bonus from RCA against future royalties. The total amount for Elvis's contracts was an incredibly high $40,000, and Steve Sholes put his career on the line when he claimed Elvis would become the greatest single asset RCA ever contracted. Prior to the signing of the contracts, negotiations were conducted by Colonel Parker, Bob Neal (on his way out of Elvis's life, although he did not know it), and Coleman Tipley III, an RCA executive. The contract for RCA took Elvis from Sun and placed him at RCA Victor.

The Colonel worded the contract in such a clever manner that he became Elvis's employer and agent. The Colonel signed the contract on behalf of Hank Snow Attractions. It is not precisely known how the cagey Colonel got rid of Snow in the deal, but it ended in a heated argument, after which they never spoke to one another again.

Sam Phillips was to fill orders of records already recorded for a period of one year. Phillips now had the opportunity to launch more forcefully the careers of Johnny Cash, Carl Perkins, and Jerry Lee Lewis (who many people believe was the most talented of all the Sun group). With the rights they purchased, Hill and Range bought "Blue Suede Shoes," "Mystery Train," and other hits from which they planned to make a fortune.

Claiming he still has no regrets, Sam Phillips did what he felt was best at the time. He released the hottest pop singing sensation the world has ever known because he needed quick up-front money to make Sun Records financially secure and perhaps, knowing of Elvis's tremendous goals, disengaged him so the Cat could make a more hopeful break for superstardom. There was no going back.

Elvis went from poverty to affluence, from obscurity to blossoming fame shortly after he met the Colonel. Living on Getwell Street in Memphis, he lavished himself and his parents with gifts, including a pink Cadillac for Gladys (although she couldn't drive). One of his biggest pleasures was being able to buy as many cheeseburgers, sliced-banana and crisp-bacon and peanut-butter sandwiches, and milk shakes as he could stomach. To be able to buy expensive junk food, without having to count nickels and dimes, was a sure sign of wealth and success! It also was the start of the bad eating habits for which Elvis would pay dearly.

NOV. 21: Elvis took his last unaccompanied walk down a city street in New York City on November 21. Before he was discovered staying in the Warwick Hotel and was swamped by phone calls, eager girls, and bags of mail, he strolled down the Avenue of the Americas toward Times Square, and the cultural icon confessed he got lonesome sometimes in the crowd. In times like those, he turned to sacred music for comfort.

Elvis had become a conglomerate of opposites. If audience members or critics became uncomfortable with "All Shook Up" or "Whole Lotta Shakin' Goin' On," it was difficult for them to criticize his soulful delivery of "Take My Hand, Precious Lord." He appeared to be dangerous, but he could look and sound so innocent. Elvis's style and personality were as diverse as his songs, and it both pleased and puzzled his fans and detractors, who were not sure what to make of this slicked-back hoodlum who sang gospel.

NOV. 22: Although Gladys Presley didn't trust Parker and advised Elvis not to sign with him, Vernon was for the move, and on November 22, Parker held a signed document entitling him to represent Elvis exclusively. He would dominate Elvis, just as Gladys had predicted. In the heat of the moment, Elvis was overanxious to become famous. He blindly trusted Parker and would probably have signed any contract Parker presented to him.

There may have been a contract between the Presleys, Bob Neal, Parker, and/or Hank Snow Attractions of Madison, Tennessee (where Parker lived). The November contract stated Parker was to act as general adviser and manager with Bob Neal for one year. Parker was to be paid $2,500 for two years to build Elvis as an artist, and Elvis was to pay all Parker's expenses. It was agreed that Elvis and his musicians would be paid a meager $200 per appearance for one year. If Elvis had left his management during that period, Parker had clauses in the contract to reimburse management for expenses. Elvis never knew how much money the Colonel received for his many concert performances, and he never asked.

NOV. 25: Elvis performed at the Woodrow Wilson Junior High School in Port Arthur, Texas.

DEC.: James R. Denny, the man who told Elvis he should stick to driving trucks (at the Grand Ole Opry on September 25, 1954), was named *Billboard*'s Man of the Year.

DEC. 2: Elvis performed in the Sports Arena in Atlanta, Georgia, and sang live for a WBAM radio broadcast.

Elvis told fans he was not the originator of rockabilly music, and that he was merely the man who brought it to national attention. Kentucky singer Lattie Moore (b. 1924) was singing a rockabilly style before the Sun-label men. Hank Williams *lived* and died his country message. Jack Guthrie, Tennessee

Ernie Ford, Arthur Smith, Merrill Moore, the Delmore Brothers, and many other musicians and singers performed straight-out boogie-woogie licks prior to Elvis's renditions. But Elvis had an edge. Somehow his persona tapped the conscience of millions of fans as no one else had previously done. Sam Phillips and his independent Sun Records, pulled everything there was to obtain out of Elvis's talent. The Colonel would yank out more. The result was mass hysteria.

DEC. 3: Elvis performed at the State Coliseum in Montgomery, Alabama, before a huge, screaming crowd. Although reporters chastised him for having led a revolt against America's revered, puritanical beliefs and behaviors, Elvis claimed to have no insight into what critics were talking about. The media began to place him as a dangerous American hero, who was becoming a sexual myth, and that was close to impossible to live up to.

When critics claimed Elvis's purpose was to corrupt, he acted as if he were internally wounded. He did not want to be conceived of as a reckless pied piper who was leading youth down a path of destruction. He did not think of himself as a courageous anarchist or bold revolutionary and had never knowingly stood up for a social cause in his life. He was merely a hometown boy who accepted Sam Phillips's notion that Negro music (unlike white music) had "freshness" left in it. To many onlookers, Elvis's sound and look seemed to be a mixture of barnyard country and vaudeville.

In 1955, songs that were opposite from the rock 'n' roll sound went gold on the *Billboard* Top 100 chart: "Love Is a Many-Splendored Thing," "Cry Me a River," and "Love and Marriage."

Elvis no longer called Gladys "Mama" or the strange nickname "Sattnin." He took on the role of a soothing parent who told his "baby" he would be safe in the midst of any storm.

The Colonel did not want Elvis to

date Dixie Locke. He insisted Elvis's image be that of a single, available bachelor, so that fans could imagine and fantasize he might love each one of them. Elvis soon stopped seeing the one girl whom he claimed he loved because it was considered a "good career move."

Elvis performed at Humes High School in Memphis, where he had once been scorned as a "sissy" and taunted as "a weird freak." The audience's acceptance of him was overwhelming, and black disc jockeys realized he was a white bluesman with a black attitude.

Elvis was impressed when the Jordanaires won an Arthur Godfrey Manhattan Talent Show with "Dig a Little Deeper." He had previously heard the group's Grand Ole Opry broadcasts of "Peace in the Valley" with Red Foley and was convinced this group's presence and sound could help his popularity rise. He vowed he would seek the group out and ask them to join him.

After RCA signed Elvis, they reissued all five of his Sun singles. Elvis often sang "Rock Around the Clock" at local club performances and at "Louisiana Hayride" concerts from 1955–56. To date no tape of these performances has surfaced. He also sang "Tennessee Partner" during 1955 club gigs and "Tennessee Saturday Night" at "Louisiana Hayride" performances, but no known tapes exist of these concerts.

DEC. 6:   Elvis told the Colonel it was refreshing not to have to "be nice" to him all the time, as he had been with Sam Phillips. "Just make me money, son, and I'll keep smilin'," was the Colonel's reply.

Elvis had been careful not to upset Phillips. When Jerry Lee Lewis entered Memphis, his beliefs and behavior ruffled Phillips's feathers. During Jerry Lee Lewis's recording session for "Great Balls of Fire" (the song John Lennon dubbed the "greatest rock 'n' roll song ever written"), the strictly orthodox Pentecostal Lewis interpreted "balls of fire" to mean the oncoming Judgment Day. Sam Phillips wanted

the song finished and coaxed Lewis, "Now look, Jerry, religious conviction doesn't mean anything resembling extremism. You mean to tell me that you're gonna take the Bible, you're gonna take God's word, and you're gonna revolutionize the whole universe? Jerry, if you think that, you can't do good, if you're a rock 'n' roll exponent. . . . You can save souls! . . . The point I'm tryin' to make is—if you believe in what you're singin'—you got no alternative whatsoever. . . . How do you interpret the Bible if it's not what you believe?"

Phillips was used to arguing with rockabilly ravers raised on gospel. He prevailed and "Great Balls of Fire" became the hit he believed it would become, but the concerns of Fundamentalists regarding blasphemy were at the center of the rock 'n' roll storm. Was it, or wasn't it music of the devil? That was the primary question. It is fascinating to note that Phillips convinced all his singers with Holy Roller backgrounds (and there were many) to do music *his* way and let God be the judge after records were released.

DEC. 10, 17, 31:   Elvis performed at "Louisiana Hayride" appearances to enthusiastic crowds. Colonel Parker told Tom Diskin it would be "wise to make some little tokens the girls can buy and take home as souvenirs."

DEC. 12:   Elvis told the Colonel he would be a good actor, if he was given the chance. Parker knew teens would flock to see him. Teen adoration kindled record sales, and those acetates would be played over and over again, reinforcing the bag of contradictions that the idol represented: a shy, polite hoodlum who assaulted the music world while praising God. The Colonel would make certain his presence would become legend. The Colonel's balance-sheet mind knew Elvis's photogenic face could earn more money. He was sexy. Illusive. Captivating. Outrageous. He was perfect.

DEC. 16: Elvis gave a concert at the "Louisiana Hayride" to benefit the Shreveport YMCA.

Although people said it was the Colonel who set the rule that Gladys Presley would not be allowed to attend Elvis's concerts, Elvis encouraged the Colonel to enforce it so that Elvis could be free of her overprotective supervision. The Colonel convinced Vernon that Gladys was too emotional. Her demands were too much for Elvis to handle. It ruined Elvis's performance. Gladys rarely saw her son perform outside of Memphis after that.

CA. DEC. 20: Colonel Parker insisted Elvis *never* meet any songwriters, thus Elvis never did (unless by accident). Parker did not want Elvis to agree he would sing a song *before* his manager had taken away a writer's royalty rights. This was extremely detrimental to Elvis's career because it limited the songs he would be offered.

Buddy Holly regrouped and formed the Crickets, and "That'll Be the Day" was recorded for Brunswick. When promoters thought the group was black, Buddy and the Crickets became the first white band to play (by mistake) at Harlem's Apollo Theater.

1956

In 1956, the cold war festered and Nikita Khrushchev's chilling threat, "We will bury you," put the U.S. on guard. Grace Kelly married Monaco's Prince Rainier, Eisenhower was reelected president, *My Fair Lady* opened on Broadway, the steamy novel *Peyton Place* was a bestseller, and Elvis Presley sold 7 million records.

JAN.: Elvis's American Guild of Variety Artists number was 165890.

JAN.: Carl Perkins's "Blue Suede Shoes" (which was inspired by Johnny Cash, its lyrics scribbled on a potato bag) was released through Sun. *Billboard* stated, "Perkins contributes a lively reading on a gay rhythm ditty with a strong R&B-styled backing. Fine for the jukes." The song stayed at the top of the charts for three months, and in March, Elvis's "Heartbreak Hotel" was No. 1 and Perkins's "Blue Suede Shoes" ranked No. 2 (selling twenty thousand copies a day). *Billboard* told readers Perkins was on seven charts and that Elvis and Perkins produced "mongrel music." Carl Perkins's ver-

sion of "Blue Suede Shoes" was the first record that combined blues, pop, and country to hit all three music charts.

JAN.: Eisenhower became president, but Elvis had supported Adlai Stevenson (although he never registered to vote in his life). The Academy Awards chose *Around the World in 80 Days* as Best Picture, and "Playhouse 90" competed with "I Love Lucy" for top TV awards. "American Bandstand" (owned by *The Philadelphia Inquirer* and seen on WFIL-TV) hired disc jockey Dick Clark (who had previously run the radio version of the show). A forty-six-date rock extravaganza billed as the "biggest rock tour of its kind" packaged only one white group, Bill Haley and the Comets, with black artists Clyde McPhatter, Bo Diddley, the Teenagers, Red Prysock's Orchestra, LaVern Baker, Big Joe Turner, Gene Vincent (with "Be Bop-a-Lula"), the Teen Queens, and the Drifters. Rock 'n' roll gathered steam.

JAN. 5: RCA recorded Elvis in its Nashville studios, after Steve Sholes put his career on the line and guaranteed RCA executives they would not lose money. As director of RCA's country-music division, Sholes met the Colonel when he managed Eddy Arnold's career. Sholes was instrumental in convincing RCA to purchase Elvis's contract from Sam Phillips. Knowing it would either catapult RCA sales into the history books or destroy his reputation in the music business and put RCA near bankruptcy, Sholes had faith in Elvis and changed the course of music history.

In the Nashville studio Elvis, Scotty Moore, Bill Black, D. J. Fontana, Chet Atkins, and the Jordanaires (with Gordon Stoker, Hoyt Hawkins, Neal Matthews, and Hugh Jarrett) assembled to record. The Jordanaires were known for writing backup arrangements on the spot during sessions. Abandoning the heavy emphasis on rockabilly for a more rocking pop sound, Elvis recorded the phenomenal hit "Heartbreak Hotel" as well as "I Want You, I Need You, I Love You," and "I Was the One." He strummed a guitar so hard, he broke its strings and his fingers bled, yet Elvis refused to stop the session. Elvis was a forerunner to almost everything that is common to modern record production. He was one of the first artists to work spontaneously in the studio and reworked songs up to thirty-five times.

JAN. 5: The Colonel made another swift and profitable move. He contacted Jean and Julian Aberbach of Hill and Range Music, and a five-year fifty-fifty partnership was established with the newly created Presley Music Inc. to publish songs Elvis recorded. It was good timing for Parker. By the previous September, three songs had hit national country-music charts, and by October Elvis had toured with his own jamboree, headlining over Johnny Cash, Floyd Cramer (who played the piano for Elvis), Wanda Jackson, Bobby Lord, and others. In mid-November, he had been "on display"

with Parker's animal act at Nashville's country-and-western disc jockey's convention. Elvis was sixteenth on the disc jockeys' most favorite artists list; thirteenth most played artist on radio; and number one on the most promising country-artist list.

JAN. 7: Elvis performed on "Louisiana Hayride" in Shreveport, Louisiana, to a standing-room-only crowd.

JAN. 8: Elvis's twenty-first birthday was spent on the road going to and from "Louisiana Hayride" appearances. The Colonel had told Elvis and the band something important was "in the wind" and to "prepare for it." They never knew what the devilish manager had up his sleeves, but they did as they were told.

JAN. 9: A tour was planned for Elvis, Scotty, D. J. Fontana, and Bill Black, with bodyguards Red West and Bitsy Mott. The Colonel announced that Jackie Gleason wanted Elvis to appear on "Stage Show," a New York CBS/TV weekly variety review. The Colonel knew that accepting Gleason's offer to appear would cause a tsunami in the building waves of Elvis mania.

JAN. 9: Elvis rehearsed "Heartbreak Hotel" prior to recording it. Elvis's sneer, his droopy smile, and smoldering eyes oozed with sex appeal, and young girls all over America wanted to take him away from Lonely Street and Heartbreak Hotel. They had no idea how forlorn Elvis really was.

"Heartbreak Hotel" was written after songwriter Tommy Durden read a *Miami Herald* article about a suicide victim who left a note that stated, "I walk a lonely street." The unidentified dead man inspired Durden to cowrite with Mae Axton the blues hit in the fall of 1955. On November 10 of that year, Axton took a demo tape of the tune (sung by Glen Reeves) to Nashville's DJ convention at the Andrew Jackson

Hotel, where Elvis heard it and promised to record it.

JAN. 10: At the Methodist TV, Radio and Film Commission at 1525 McGavock Street in Nashville, Elvis recorded for RCA "I Got a Woman" and "Heartbreak Hotel" with Scotty Moore (guitar), Chet Atkins (guitar), Bill Black (bass), Floyd Cramer (piano), D. J. Fontana (drums), and backup singers Gordon Stoker, Ben Speer, and Brock Speer. Although many writers claim the Jordanaires recorded these two songs with Elvis in Nashville, they did not. Even Elvis mistakenly gave them credit for the session at the Mississippi-Alabama Fair in 1956 (Gordon Stoker was a member of the Jordanaires, thus the confusion).

In the meantime, record executives (and Sun's Sam Phillips) thought Elvis was a quick fad. RCA viewed him as a poor-boy flash in the pan. Therefore, only cheap black and white promo shots were taken of Elvis, rather than the more expensive color photographs.

A headline in a 1956 issue of *Billboard*, "Sholes Has Last Laugh As Presley Rings Up Sales," made all Steve Sholes's and Elvis's detractors look foolish. Elvis's records were selling to the tune of $75,000 a day; releases of singles, fifty thousand a day; EPs and LPs sold up to eight thousand a day. Elvis Presley records soon accounted for 50 percent of RCA's business, and producers with Decca, Capitol, Columbia, and Sun Records scrambled to find their own teen idols. Singers all over the world would soon begin to imitate Elvis, but no one topped Elvis in popularity or charismatic charm.

Elvis's first RCA recording was Ray Charles's "I Got a Woman" at RCA's Nashville studios (which the Cat had performed during "Louisiana Hayride" shows in 1955 and on the Dorseys' "Stage Show," January 28, 1956). The song was released on the first LP, *Elvis Presley*, and later as an uncharted single in September 1956 (RCA 20-6637). The song was erroneously titled "I Got a Sweetie" in Great Britain.

JAN. 11: At RCA's Nashville studios, Elvis recorded the million-selling record "I Was the One" (by Aaron Schroeder, Hal Blair, Bill Pepper, and Claude DeMetrius) with backup vocals by Gordon Stoker, Ben and Brock Speer. The song hit No. 23 during a sixteen-week run on *Billboard*'s Top 100 chart (RCA 20-6420). Elvis sang the song on February 18, 1956, on TV's "Stage Show"; on December 16, 1956, at the "Louisiana Hayride"; and on September 1 in Vancouver. During the January 11 session, Elvis and the group recorded "I'm Counting on You" by Don Robertson (RCA 20-6637). It's flip side was "I Got a Woman."

JAN. 14: The boys completed "Louisiana Hayride" appearances to record-breaking crowds.

JAN. 15: RCA gave Elvis a new convertible.

JAN. 17: RCA released "Heartbreak Hotel" and "I Was the One" (RCA 20/47-6420). Sales were phenomenal.

When the Colonel heard Elvis record "Heartbreak Hotel," he devoted himself to the promotion (and guarding) of Elvis's career. Although no one knows for certain what the exact terms and financial arrangements were between Elvis and Parker, they were binding. Parker was a fast-buck master packager and peddler who saw Elvis as a potential gold mine. He told a trusting Elvis, "We do not socialize. Our great social interest is money." (*Chicago Daily News*, June 8, 1972.)

Parker made certain Elvis, the media, and the public thought he discovered and eventually "owned" Elvis. To the Colonel, Elvis was merchandise to be wrapped and sold. Parker knew the public adores what it cannot have, thus he turned Elvis into a sought-after singer no one could contact. Parker had every intention of putting Elvis in a caged environment like a circus act, and he did just that.

JAN. 21: Elvis's appearance at "Louisiana Hayride" nearly started a riot, and he was rushed from the premises.

JAN. 25: *Downbeat* described Elvis as a mix between Frankie Laine, Billy Daniels, and Johnnie Ray (one of the only white men whom black radio stations would play), which enthused lukewarm RCA Victor bigwigs.

JAN. 26: Elvis and his crew prepared for their appearance on "Stage Show." Elvis was visibly nervous when he met Milton Berle (who was disgusted Elvis was earning $1,250 for the appearance).

JAN. 28: On "Stage Show," Elvis sang "Flip, Flop and Fly" (by Charles Calhoun/Lou Willie Turner) as the ending of "Shake, Rattle and Roll" (by Jesse Stone or "Charles E. Calhoun"). A film clip of his performance (with drums overdubbed) is on the documentary *This Is Elvis*. He sang the same version of the song on April 3 on "The

Milton Berle Show" (RCA 20-6642, released Sept. 1956). Shocked viewers across America couldn't believe what they were seeing.

JAN. 29: Elvis performed at the Mosque Theater in Richmond, Virginia. Around this time, the now-famous line "Elvis has left the building" came into use. Elvis learned quickly to dash to a waiting car or limo outside concert halls, so that he would not be torn to pieces by adoring fans. The "Elvis has left the building" announcement was meant to calm overanxious audience members from trampling one another in attempts to dash after him.

JAN. 30: Sam Phillips admitted Elvis could wail the hell out of a guitar.

JAN. 30–31: At an RCA studio session in New York City, Elvis sang with backup players Scotty Moore (guitar), Bill Black (bass), Shorty Long (piano), and D. J. Fontana (drums). During this session "Blue Suede Shoes" was recorded. The group stayed and caused havoc at the Warwick Hotel for several weeks.

Criticized by New Yorkers for his speech and clothing, Elvis felt insecure.

Elvis's version of "Blue Suede Shoes" was released in September 1956, with the flip side "Tutti Frutti" (RCA 20-6636). The single did not chart, but it reached the No. 24 position during a twelve-week stay on *Billboard*'s Top 100 from the EP *Elvis Presley* (RCA EPA-747). Eight singles, five EPs, ten LPs, and twelve bootleg LPs carry "Blue Suede Shoes."

"One-Sided Love Affair" by Bill Campbell was Elvis's most admired country song on his first LP, *Elvis Presley*. Recorded on January 30, it was released as a single in September (RCA 20-6641) with the flip side "Money Honey" (by Jesse Stone). It was rumored that Elvis learned the song from Buddy Holly in Texas, dur-

◀ A collector's plate from the Bradford Exchange series: "Elvis Presley Hit Parade," featuring "Heartbreak Hotel." *Courtesy of the Bradford Exchange.*

ing a 1955 jam. Because of the song's popularity on the EP *Heartbreak Hotel*, it peaked at No. 76 on *Billboard*'s Top 100 chart during a five-week stay. The single of "Money Honey" did not chart after its September 1956 release.

Elvis finished Arthur Crudup's "My Baby Left Me" on January 30, and it enjoyed a fourteen-week stay on *Billboard*'s Top 100 chart, peaking at No. 31 (RCA 20-1974). Its flip side was "I Want You, I Need You, I Love You."

Elvis recorded Arthur Crudup's "So Glad You're Mine," which appears on the EP *Elvis*, Vol. 2 and LPs *Elvis* (RCA LPM-1382) and *Reconsider Baby*.

Arthur Crudup had a major influence on Elvis's overall singing style. Elvis sounded like the "Big Boy" when he sang "That's All Right, Mama." In 1945–46, Crudup had six songs on *Billboard*'s rhythm and blues charts on the Bluebird, RCA, and Victor labels. Elvis listened to Crudup daily. Compare Crudup's 1947 version of "That's All Right (Mama)" (RCA Victor 20-2205) or the LP/CD "Arthur Crudup: That's All Right (Mama)" (Relic 7036) with Elvis's version of the song and you will hear a remarkable similarity in style.

JAN. 31: "Tutti Frutti" (written by Dorothy LaBostrie after the flavor of an ice cream) was recorded by Elvis at RCA's New York City studio (RCA 20-6636), but many critics preferred Little Richard's earlier 1955 wilder version (Specialty 561). Joe Thomas's "I'm Gonna Sit Right Down and Cry (Over You)" was recorded by Elvis and did not chart (RCA 20-6638). Its flip side was "I'll Never Let You Go (Little Darlin')."

JAN. 31: Fred Danzig interviewed Elvis at RCA's New York studio during a recording session.

FEB.: Because of increased popularity and demand for his time, Elvis signed a contract that stipulated he pay $400 to the "Louisiana Hayride" for every missed performance.

FEB.: The Colonel tried to talk Jackie Gleason into putting his boy on major TV shows and specials. Jackie Gleason said about Elvis, "He's a Marlon Brando who can sing," and, "He can't last. I tell you flatly, he can't last." Elvis's six "Stage Show" appearances (which Gleason produced) would introduce "Heartbreak Hotel," "Shake, Rattle, and Roll," and Carl Perkins's "Blue Suede Shoes" to a growing, national audience.

FEB. 3: Elvis recorded "Lawdy Miss Clawdy" at RCA's New York City studio, but the single did not chart (RCA 20-6640. Its flip side was "Shake, Rattle, and Roll").

The *Charlotte News* hyped interest in Elvis's upcoming performance by running an article about him. Tickets sold out.

FEB. 4: Elvis appeared on the Dorsey Brothers' "Stage Show" on CBS-TV singing "Baby, Let's Play House" and "Tutti Frutti." Outraged conservatives were aghast at the lyrics in "Baby, Let's Play House," which seemed to urge girls across America to come and live with him. The program also featured comedian Joe E. Brown and a chimpanzee act. After watching the chimps perform, Elvis was determined to own one someday. He thought they were "cute" and "smart."

FEB. 5: Elvis performed at the Monticello Auditorium in Norfolk, Virginia, where people went wild listening to his country-oriented boogie music.

The Colonel used Chicago booker Al Dvorin (who commonly gathered midgets and freaks whenever Parker wanted to put on a side show) to find Elvis lucrative engagements. Often traveling with "The Elvis Presley Show" of 1956 were acrobats, jugglers, xylophone players, tap dancers, disc jockeys, full orchestras, and anyone else who would tag along for minimum wage. Most of the crew attached themselves to Elvis for no fee, and they acted as bodyguards, but the lack of appreciation and financial reward annoyed many of Elvis's entourage.

Red West's feelings about how Elvis treated him are typical of many people's reactions: "The work I did, there should have been some kind of payment because, man, I worked like a dog. All the odd jobs, all that damn driving, anything that nobody else wanted to do, I did. . . . I have seen [Elvis] give away some of the most incredible gifts imaginable. . . . Gifts are one thing. Money is something else. The point is that I believe somehow he believes money gives a person independence. He doesn't want people to have independence from him. He likes to be a father figure, or a God figure . . . above all, he needs to be needed. . . . It was almost as if it was a requirement to work for him you had to be broke. You had to need him more than he needed you. . . . There was no union for being a professional companion, and I could see myself being that for the rest of my life without getting paid. . . . Sometimes the hours on the road were really tough . . . man, how long could I go busting my chops like this and getting abused into the bargain? . . . I was too embarrassed to ask [Elvis] for anything." (See *Elvis: What Happened?*)

Why did the locals stay on Elvis's crew? Prestige. Women. To hope, somehow, Elvis would one day recognize their value and pay them what they deserved. It never happened.

FEB. 6: Elvis performed at the National Theater in Greensboro, North Carolina, giving shows at 2:30, 4:15, 7:20, and 9:30 P.M. He opened the concerts with Roy Brown's words, "Have you heard the news? There's good rockin' tonight." The teenage audiences went berserk while parents were horrified. The Colonel couldn't have been happier and told Elvis, "Keep makin' 'em squeal." As negative press grew, it only fueled the fans' fire and sent record

sales skyrocketing. The Colonel assessed accurately the value of protest. Marketed correctly, the reaction Elvis kindled was a superior promotional tool.

Disapproving authority figures and opposing press releases enabled Elvis to almost single-handedly transform the nation's clean-cut, monied teen society into a pack of howling, swooning, record-buying, concert-going maniacs!

FEB. 11: Ella Fitzgerald was the emcee when Elvis appeared on "Stage Show." *The Charlotte News* reported over six thousand teenage girls went "ga-ga" over the "hillbilly," who sang "Blue Suede Shoes" and "Heartbreak Hotel." Elvis said, "No, don't call me that. . . . I don't know what style I have. I never could answer that."

FEB. 15: "Mystery Train" and "I Forgot to Remember to Forget" both hit No. 1 on *Billboard*'s country chart (Sun 223). *The Tupelo Daily Journal* told Elvis fans that mobs were tearing Elvis's pink shirts and white jackets to shreds for souvenirs. The journalist placed the Cat in Sinatra and Johnny Ray's leagues and quoted Elvis as saying his rise to fame "just scares me."

FEB. 18: Elvis appeared on "Stage Show" to belt out "Tutti Frutti" and "I Was the One." The time changed from eight P.M. to eight-thirty P.M. for this show.

FEB. 21: Elvis performed at the Florida Theater in Sarasota, Florida, to a huge stomping, yelling crowd.

FEB. 22: "Heartbreak Hotel" entered *Billboard*'s Top 100 chart at No. 68. It also entered the Country's Best Sellers in Stores chart at No. 9.

FEB. 25: Crowds lined up outside the "Louisiana Hayride" to buy tickets for Elvis's performance. Elvis soon mastered how best to promote himself on radio.

FEB. 29: "I Was the One" hit *Billboard*'s Top 100 chart at No. 84.

MAR.: RCA Victor promoted a state-of-the-art, four-speed Victrola with Elvis's name stamped in gold. It was the Colonel's marketing idea, which was another first of its kind in the music world. It was packaged with *8 Hits by Elvis Presley* (a double EP, RCA SPD-22) for $32.95. A second gold-signature edition soon entered the market at $44.95 with an EP triple-pack (RCA-SPD-23). RCA raced to supply the demand. Elvis mania was a lucrative, hot commodity. RCA came out with a third machine, the Elvis Presley autographed, automatic, 45-rpm portable Victrola, boxed with a twelve-song album titled *Elvis Presley "Perfect for Parties" Highlight Album*, Vol. 1 (RCA SPA-7-37). The gold-autographed "specials" sold out at $47.95. That was a lot of money when hamburgers were nineteen cents and coffee was a nickel!

While RCA's main motivation was to pull in revenue by selling records and Victrolas to teenagers, Parker's brilliant maneuvers catapulted Elvis's image from that of a mere curiosity to the most influential media star of the era. "No publicity is bad publicity" was the Colonel's motto.

MAR.: Elvis bought a red and black German Messerschmitt automobile (ID# 56007), which he traded to Bernard Lansky for clothes in June.

MAR. 1: Elvis told Colonel Parker he would rather be a movie star than a rock star. He admitted he had taken his belligerent stance from Marlon Brando in *The Wild One*, and his pout from James Dean's sulk in the 1955 movie *East of Eden*.

Al Wertheimer became Elvis's photographer-companion until the King left for Germany. Wertheimer told the author on October 31, 1991, "The only book I saw in his house was a paperback about the loves of Liberace. Elvis knew everything about Liberace." In 1954, "Lee" became the first TV matinee idol, had his own Emmy-winning show, and toured the world packing concert halls and playing before royalty. His trademarks were a candelabra, a vivacious smile, a quick, clean wit, flamboyant keyboard tricks, diamonds and dazzle, and a tremendous humanity. It wouldn't be long before the two superstars would meet.

Colonel Parker spread the news "his boy" was to be called "the atomic-powered singer."

MAR. 1: RCA offices were overwhelmed with 362,000 advance orders for Elvis's first LP, *Elvis Presley*. The album consisted of five tracks recorded at Sun and seven from New York and Nashville RCA sessions from January 1956. Five EPs came from this album. First listed as No. 11 in *Billboard*'s Best-Selling Pop Albums, within six weeks it was No. 1. It remained on that chart for forty-nine weeks.

MAR. 3: Elvis completed a "Louisiana Hayride" appearance.

The critics, unaccustomed to seeing entertainers perform in what they considered to be an "indecent" or "immoral" fashion, tried to halt Elvis's exposure. The Colonel had created a national crisis with his boy at its nucleus. Elvis was becoming a hazardous commodity that some aspects of society would not tolerate. A Ku Klux Klan member said on a national news broadcast, "We've set up a twenty-man committee to do away with this vulgar, animalistic, nigger rock 'n' roller bob. Our committee will check with restaurant owners . . . to see what Presley records is on their machines and then ask them to do away with them."

Billboard named Elvis RCA's "hottest artist" for the week, and six of Elvis's records were on RCA's "Top 25 Best Sellers."

▶ Elvis on stage in 1956, as drawn by artist XNO. *Courtesy of Chet Darmsteader.*

MAR. 7: "Heartbreak Hotel" was No. 1 on *Billboard*'s Country Best Sellers in Stores chart.

MAR. 10: Elvis performed at the "Louisiana Hayride."

MAR. 13: *Elvis Presley*, Elvis's first album, was released (RCA LPM 4671) with the famous photo of young Elvis singing and strumming his guitar. This album was the first in history to sell a million copies. On the cover was a photograph taken at a Tampa, Florida, concert by William S. "Popsie" Randolph in July 1955. It was given to RCA by the Colonel (who was billed on the LP as "Art Director").

MAR. 14–15: Elvis gave six shows at the Fox theater in Atlanta, Georgia. Police lined the outside of the building and the aisles to keep order.

MAR. 15: Colonel Tom Parker became Elvis's official manager, taking the position from Bob Neal. Up until this date, Neal and Parker acted as comanagers of Elvis, with Neal earning 15 percent and Parker 25 percent of everything Elvis earned, plus expenses.

MAR. 17: On CBS-TV's "Stage Show," Elvis sang "Blue Suede Shoes" and "Heartbreak Hotel" (a repeat of his February 11 performance). On this St. Patrick's Day some older viewers had wished for something a little more "homespun" and complained to CBS about their "poor" programming. Elvis earned another $1,250.

MAR. 22: Elvis gave two shows at the Mosque Theater, Richmond, Virginia.

MAR. 23: Colonel Parker convinced movie producer Hal B. Wallis to give Elvis a screen test.
Elvis and the band went to New York City and stayed at the Warwick Hotel.

MAR. 24: On Elvis's final appearance on "Stage Show," he sang "Money Honey" and "Heartbreak Hotel." At the Warwick Hotel, Elvis was interviewed by reporters. The Cat talked of recording "My Happiness" for his mother, and said his favorite artists were Frank Sinatra, Roy Acuff, Mario Lanza, Pat Boone, and Sonny James (who toured with Elvis in 1955 and hit the charts in March 1956). He also said his favorite song was "I Was the One" (recorded in January 1956 with the flip side "Heartbreak Hotel") and spoke of the Colonel's help in his career. Elvis admitted he had a weight problem caused by bad eating habits and he mentioned his mother's failing health and the home he had recently bought his parents on Audubon Drive in Memphis.

MAR. 28: "Blue Suede Shoes" entered *Billboard*'s Top 100 chart at No. 88.

MAR. 30: Elvis, Carl Perkins, Little Richard, Jerry Lee Lewis, Chuck Berry, and Bill Haley generated a new sound in music that dominated record sales. Because of their success, everyone with a voice wanted to jump on the rock 'n' roll bandwagon, including

Bobby Vee, Fabian, Danny & the Juniors, Ricky Nelson, and Frankie Avalon. Even "old-timers" such as Perry Como, Dean Martin, Frank Sinatra, and Pat Boone attempted to "shake, rattle, and roll."

MAR. 31:   Elvis flew to Los Angeles, where he would make a television appearance and film a screen test for Hal Wallis for Paramount Pictures. He became ill on the flight.

Elvis's LP *Elvis Presley* was No. 11 on *Billboard*'s "Best Selling Packaged Records."

APR.:   "Heartbreak Hotel" topped the pop charts at No. 1 and stayed there for seven weeks. It was the second song to hit all three *Billboard* charts, remaining for twenty-seven weeks (No. 1 pop; No. 1 country; No. 5 R&B, the first Presley song on this chart), and the first Presley record to sell 1 million copies. Carl Perkins's "Blue Suede Shoes" was the first single to make three *Billboard* charts. It was *Billboard*'s No. 1 Single of 1956. It became the first cover of an Elvis tune sung by black artists (the hot rhythm and blues group from L.A., the Cadets), which they recorded with a flip side of "Church Bells May Ring" for Modern Records (Modern 985, 1956). Elvis's "Heartbreak Hotel" was on five singles, two EPs, eleven LPs, and over eighteen bootleg LPs. The album *Elvis Presley* was released by RCA as an extended play, double-extended play, and LP.

Nat "King" Cole was attacked by six men during an Alabama concert in front of an audience of three thousand white people. The assailants jumped on the stage and dragged Cole into the audience, claiming they hated "bop and Negro music." In protest, Bill Haley publicly announced he would not give concerts to segregated audiences, while Elvis told his fans many black musicians had inspired and influenced him.

Bill Haley closely associated with the black community and held no prejudices against anyone. He often toured with black entertainers and took a stand against segregation whenever he could. In this respect, Haley was more an activist than Elvis.

Little Richard was also making an impact on the music scene with his silver hair and bizarre singing style. "The Killer," Jerry Lee Lewis, copied many piano gimmicks from Little Richard's early moves.

While Little Richard was way out in left field, music fans made hits of Robert Guidry's "See You Later, Alligator" and Elvis's "Hound Dog," "Love Me Tender," and "Heartbreak Hotel" (which would soon break sales records).

Alfred Wertheimer photographed Elvis almost full-time.

APR. 1:   Elvis's first screen test for Hal Wallis included Elvis singing "Blue Suede Shoes" and acting in a scene from *The Rainmaker* with actor Frank Faylen. Not pleased with his screen test, Elvis requested to do a second test (probably shot on April 2 with Cynthia Baxter) on the Paramount lot.

Many people believe Elvis's thirty-three movies earned him over $200 million. He eventually made movies for Paramount, Twentieth-Century Fox, MGM, United Artists, Allied Artists, National General Pictures, and Universal. His first film's budget was $1 million.

Art Murphy of *Variety* wrote, "Colonel Parker made some smart deals. Elvis eventually got $1 million per picture and Parker made it so that Elvis co-owned the music-publishing rights—not the studios." Film writer Gerald Drayson Adams stated, "There were never any story conferences. They consisted of money—the first act, second act, and third act, money. They were all conducted by Colonel Parker." (*Look*, 1971.)

APR. 3:   Earning $5,000 to appear on the deck of the USS *Hancock* in San Diego, California, for "The Milton Berle

Show," Elvis sang "Shake, Rattle and Roll," "Blue Suede Shoes," and "Heartbreak Hotel" to servicemen and women, who adored every minute of it. In a comedy sketch designed by Berle, the old veteran called Elvis "Elvin" while Berle played his twin brother, "Melvin Presley." This show pinpoints the Colonel's willingness to place Elvis in *any* quandary without concern for the man's dignity.

APR. 4: Hal B. Wallis and the Colonel discussed Elvis's taking the role of Jimmy Curry in *The Rainmaker*, but Parker refused to allow Elvis to take the part. (Eventually, Earl Holliman played opposite Yvonne Lime in the film starring Burt Lancaster and Katharine Hepburn.)

The Colonel's automatic rejection suggests that Parker had *no* intention of ever allowing Elvis to become a fine actor. He wanted Elvis to remain a merchandising tool, not a credible acting talent, but Elvis did not figure that out until it was too late.

APR. 4–5: Elvis performed at the San Diego Sports Arena in San Diego, California, and signed photographs in a local record store. Audiences went berserk over this wild Cat from the South. Few people had seen anything like Elvis.

APR. 6: Elvis signed a seven-year, three-movie contract with Paramount Pictures. His salary was to escalate from $100,000 to $150,000 for his second movie, and to $200,000 for the third film. The Colonel renegotiated the contract for more money shortly thereafter.

Elvis's first movie was produced the year James Dean died. Hal Wallis discovered and signed both Dean and Elvis. Although Dean had major roles in only three films, he had reached colossal stardom, and his reputation grew after death. When movie magazines asked, "Is Elvis a new James Dean?"

or "Can Elvis fill James Dean's shoes?" the hick from the sticks was put in the uncomfortable spot of having to outdo a legend.

Because he was equated with Dean, Elvis fretted that his own fate might be a premature death. He knew it would be futile to try to be a better film actor than James Dean. He glorified Dean in the same way his fans idolized him: on an unrealistic pedestal. Dean represented the lonely, youthful, distraught rebel. He was a taunting, suffering martyr—an effigy with which Elvis easily identified.

APR. 7: Elvis performed at the "Louisiana Hayride" in Shreveport and prepared to travel to Vegas to entertain in the neon city he had heard so much about.

APR. 8: Colonel Parker negotiated Elvis's salary at $7,500–12,500 per week at The New Frontier Hotel in Las Vegas, where Elvis was touted as the "Atomic Powered Singer" (a name the Colonel invented). A fifty-foot cardboard replica of him was to be placed outside the hotel. Elvis was to perform in the Venus room with comedian Shecky Greene, Freddy Martin's band, and the Venus Starlet dancers. Elvis was enthusiastic about performing on The Strip. He believed he would be accepted in grand style. He was wrong.

APR. 10: Disc jockey Jay Thompson of KSTB radio's "The Hillbilly Hit Parade" taped an interview with Elvis in Wichita, Kansas. The interview can be heard on the LPs *The Sun Years* and *Elvis— A Legendary Performer*, Vol. 2. Justin Tubb was on tour with Elvis and complained Elvis was getting too much attention.

APR. 10: Riding in a plane that almost crashed, Elvis became exceedingly distraught. Unnerved, he was only able to record "I Want You, I Need You, I Love You" at RCA's Nashville studios before he returned at noon to Memphis. Splicing takes No. 14 and No. 17 together, the RCA single release peaked at No. 3 on *Billboard*'s Top 100 chart during a twenty-four-week run. The million seller hit No. 10 on the R&B chart and No. 1 for one week on the Country chart (RCA 20-6540, released in May 1956). Its flip side was "My Baby Left Me" by Arthur Crudup.

APR. 11: *Variety* claimed "Heartbreak Hotel" sold over 1 million copies.

APR. 13: After Elvis's performance at the Municipal Auditorium, San Antonio, Texas, Charlie Walker, disc jockey for WMAC radio in San Antonio, interviewed Elvis and called him "Elvis 'the Cat' Presley." Their talk is on the LP *The Sun Years*. Radio KSTB aired a taped April 10 interview of Jay Thompson and Elvis for "The Hillbilly Hit Parade" from Breckenridge, Texas.

APR. 15–16: Elvis performed at the Municipal Auditorium in San Antonio and in Corpus Christi. Audiences were uncontrollable at each performance, and cities complained about the extra cost of hiring security guards, while at the same time they loved this phenomenal new "tourist" attraction, Elvis the Pelvis.

APR. 17: Elvis performed in Waco, Texas, and visited Eddie Fadal, a deejay for KRLD in Dallas.

APR. 18: Elvis performed in Tulsa, Oklahoma, to a wild crowd of eight thousand people.

APR. 19: Elvis tried to sing above the audience's screaming while he performed in Amarillo, Texas.

APR. 20: Elvis gave a fine performance at the Northside Convention Center in Forth Worth, Texas, while Liberace got ready for Elvis's entrance into Vegas.

Not to be outdone by any young upstart, Liberace and his brother played boogie-woogie, classics, and hillbilly tunes, first at a gold piano and then at a black model with a $1,500 transparent-plastic top. The day before Elvis was to entertain in Vegas, Elvis watched Liberace, who was dressed in white lamé and seated at a gold-leafed piano, at the Riviera. He ended that show wearing a black jacket embroidered with 1,000,363 shining bugle beads. When Elvis first saw Liberace's act, he was left speechless! He was also quite obviously influenced by Liberace's flamboyant style, as Elvis's own gaudy costumes in his later career would show.

APR. 21: Elvis's performance in Dallas, Texas, was greeted with enthusiasm, but Elvis was exhausted from too much traveling and was nervous about his upcoming Vegas gig.

APR. 22: Elvis gave two shows before thousands of cheering fans at the Municipal Auditorium in San Antonio, Texas, and he appeared on WMAC radio to be interviewed by Charlie Walker, after which he and his entourage traveled to Las Vegas.

Elvis's exhausting schedule was taking its effects. In *Elvis: What Happened?* Red West speaks of Elvis's restless nights. Sleepwalking became a major problem: "In Las Vegas, there were nights when I sat up awake all night, just sitting by the window, while Elvis was asleep. I . . . stayed there because I was scared to hell he would walk in his sleep and jump out the window. It was a genuine fear."

APR. 23: *The Houston Press* said, "Squads of police kept the singer's blue suede shoes from being trampled" at the Texas concerts. Elvis told a reporter the screaming fans made him "work harder—I know they like me."

APR. 23–MAY 6: Elvis's Las Vegas debut at the New Frontier Hotel was not

▶ Colonel Tom Parker and Elvis at the New Frontier Hotel in Las Vegas, Nevada, April 30, 1956. *Courtesy of John Reible, Las Vegas News Bureau.*

well received. A four-week gig ended in two. Vegas represented the big time, and most of the singers or comedians who were lucky enough to be booked at prominent Vegas hotels felt they had finally made it to the top. Yet Elvis was apprehensive. Memories of Arthur Godfrey's rejection in New York haunted him. So did the rude audiences he remembered at Nashville's Grand Ole Opry. John Crosby of the *New York Herald Tribune* said typically, "Where do you go from Elvis Presley—short of obscenity, which is against the law?" Elvis's self-doubt and instability surfaced when he admitted, "If I screwed up b'fore, I only had to worry 'bout the audience throwin' things at me. Now I gotta worry 'bout what the papers will say and whether I'll ever get to go on TV again. I thought it was s'posed to get easier, but it's gettin' worse. I hate havin' to read what people write 'bout me. I jus' *hate* it." (See *A Boy Who Would Be King*).

The Colonel hoped Elvis would shake up the middle-class Vegas crowds who had come to gawk at this new pop phenomenon, but their response was practically nonexistent.

Elvis was so flabbergasted by one audience's cold shoulder he desperately cried out, "Thank you very much, ladies and gentlemen, we'd like to say it's been a sorta pleasure being in Las Vegas. . . . We've had a pretty hard time . . . ah—had a pretty good time while we were here! Now we've got a few little songs for ya, we have on record, in our style of singin' . . . . This song really tells a story, friends, it's not only sad, it's plumb pitiful!—plumb pitiful! . . . It's called 'Long Tall Sally' and I want ya to listen to this song, it really tells a story." (See *King! When Elvis Rocked the World.*) Elvis told the audience *its* lack of emotion was "pitiful."

Accompanied by a fast, country-rock beat, Elvis let go of an explosive, almost frantic version of "Long Tall Sally." This was pure social defiance. A dirty boogie of the first order. Everywhere he had sung it, people were unable to contain themselves. But if anyone in Vegas felt the music's pulsating emotion, they did not indicate it. The audience was a sea of stone-faced zombies!

Elvis announced that RCA had awarded him a gold record for the millionth sale of "Heartbreak Hotel," then jeered humorously, "And we're real proud of it because it made so much mon . . . ah—it's done so well for itself, and here's another one . . . called 'Get Outta the Stables, Grandmaw, You're Too Old to Be Horsin' around'!"

Turning to Freddy Martin's orchestra, Elvis wisecracked, "Do you know that song, Mr. Martin, 'Get Outta the Stables'? Ya do? Well, do you know that one about 'Take Back Your Golden Garter, My Leg Is Turnin' Green'? D'ya ever hear that one? Well, let's do Blue Suede—ah, sumpin'."

Seeing actor Ray Bolger and comic Phil Silvers in the audience, Elvis dedicated "Blue Suede Shoes" to them, but he was really hoping to get some response from the audience. It must have worked, because what was to be his last song was followed by "Money Honey" in his first and only Vegas encore. Although Elvis poured emotion into every performance, he completed two weeks under duress and embarrassment. By the end he was embittered.

In order to take his mind off his troubles, Elvis, Scotty, Bill, D.J., Red West, and a few others went to the movies, seduced all the women they could, rode motorbikes, and stuffed themselves with junk food. Elvis's crew (first called "El's Angels" and "Presley's Boys") became widely known as the "Memphis Mafia." Elvis's gang was the Cat's response to Sinatra's "Rat Pack."

APR. 23: *Variety* reported Elvis's "failure" in Vegas but took note of Liberace's influence on the Cat. Mr. Showman told the singing Southerner to "dress to please an audience," implying Elvis's appearance offended onlookers. Elvis's teeth had not yet been capped; he wore baggy jackets; and he had the skin problems of most teens. But most of that would change after his talks with Liberace. Soon, he would walk into a room and his attire would astound onlookers.

Movie Teen noted, "Every fan is interested in what he wears.... You could wrap him in a sheet like Gandhi" and fans would still go crazy over him.

MAY 13: Elvis performed two shows in St. Paul, Minnesota.

MAY 14: Elvis gave two shows at the Mary E. E. Sawyer Auditorium in La Crosse, Wisconsin.

MAY 15: Rows of police officers held back thousands of fans during Elvis's concert at the Ellis Auditorium in Memphis.

MAY 16: Elvis gave a concert at the Little Rock Auditorium, Little Rock, Arkansas.

MAY 17: Elvis sang at the Shrine Mosque in Springfield, Missouri.

MAY 18: Elvis gave two concerts in Des Moines, Iowa.

MAY 19: Elvis performed at the University of Nebraska's Coliseum in Lincoln, Nebraska.

MAY 20: Elvis gave two shows in Omaha, Nebraska.

MAY 24: Elvis performed in Kansas City, Missouri.

MAY 25: At Detroit's Fox Theater, Elvis performed three two-hour concerts.

MAY 26: Elvis gave two shows at the Veterans Memorial Auditorium in Columbus, Ohio.

MAY 27: Elvis performed two shows at the Fieldhouse, University of Dayton, Dayton, Ohio.

JUNE: RCA released an extended-play LP "Elvis Presley."

JUNE 3: Elvis gave two shows at the Oakland Auditorium, Oakland, California.

JUNE 5: Elvis's second appearance on the "Milton Berle Show," before which he posed with Irish starlet "Sheena" McCalla.

JUNE 6: Elvis played to standing room only at the San Diego Arena, San Diego, California.

JUNE 7: Elvis performed at the Long Beach Municipal Auditorium, Long Beach, California.

JUNE 8: Elvis's performance at the Los Angeles Shrine Auditorium caused a near riot.

JUNE 16–18: *Time* nicknamed Elvis "the Pelvis," the Boston Roman Catholic Church declared an Elvis boycott, *Newsweek* proclaimed teens "worshipped" Elvis as a "hero," *Variety* and *Billboard* discussed the controversy circling around the Cat's sex appeal.

JUNE 20: Wink Martindale of Memphis's KLAC-TV interviewed Elvis.

JUNE 22–24: Elvis performed ten shows at the Paramount Theater in Atlanta, Georgia. *America* and the *National Catholic Review* condemned Elvis as immoral, risque, and vulgar.

JUNE 25: Elvis gave two shows at the Savannah Auditorium in Savannah, Georgia.

JUNE 26: Elvis performed at the Charlotte Coliseum, Charlotte, North Carolina. In *Look*'s "The Great Rock 'n' Roll Controversy" the national reaction to Elvis's groin gyrations was discussed with chagrin. Rock 'n' roll was in its glory.

JUNE 27: At the Bell Auditorium in Augusta, Georgia, Elvis performed one concert.

JUNE 28: Elvis went back to Charlotte, North Carolina, to perform one more sold-out concert.

JUNE 30: Elvis gave a concert at the Mosque Theater in Richmond, Virginia.

JULY: Elvis performed on WNOE radio, New Orleans, LA, and *TV Scandals* reviewed Elvis's "unbridled obscenity."

JULY 1: Elvis appeared on TV's "The Steve Allen Show" wearing a tuxedo and singing "Hound Dog" to a basset hound! Rock purists were aghast and riveted when Elvis (playing the part of Tumbleweed), Andy Griffith, Imogene Coca and Allen performed a mundane skit to promote Tonto candy bars (see page 118). Elvis confessed it was *the* most humiliating moment of his career.

Channel 4's WRCA interviewed Elvis from his hotel room for "Hy Gardner Calling." The program was aired live on a split-TV screen. Elvis shyly confessed the media's bashing of him was confusing and that his mother approved of the way he moved and sang on stage.

JULY 2: Elvis and the Jordanaires recorded for RCA in New York City the smash hits "Hound Dog," "Don't Be Cruel," and "Anyway You Want Me (That's How I Will Be)." They all hit *Billboard*'s Top 100 chart, and Elvis became the second white singer to enter the R&B chart (Johnny Ray was the first) with "Hound Dog" and "Don't Be Cruel." Scotty Moore, Bill Black, and Shorty Long accompanied. Over six million copies of "Don't Be Cruel"/ "Hound Dog" were sold (RCA 20-6604 standard 78 rpm and RCA 47-6604 standard 45 rpm).

While teens picketed Steve Allen's offices for harming Elvis's reputation, Washington's WPGC formed "The Society for the Prevention to Cruelty to Elvis."

JULY 4: Elvis performed a benefit concert at the Russwood Park in Memphis before 14,000 fans.

JULY 16: *Newsweek* said Steve Allen dressed Elvis "like a corpse."

JULY 21: *Melody Maker* told readers *not* to buy Elvis records.

AUG.: While *Look* dubbed Elvis "Vulgar," *TV Guide* reviewed "Pelvic Appeal," *The New York Times* (Jack Gould) reported "Presley is . . . downright revolting," Carl Perkins and Elvis were on the cover of *Country Roundup*, and rock 'n' roll gained momentum.

AUG. 2: "Love Me Tender" and "Let Me" were recorded at Radio Recorders in Hollywood with Chuck Prescott, Red Robinson, and John Dodson as backup vocalists.

AUG. 3–4: Elvis gave six shows at the Olympic Theater in Miami and "Hound Dog" received three gold records.

AUG. 5: Elvis gave two shows at the Fort Homer Hesterly Armory in Tampa, Florida.

AUG. 6: Elvis gave three shows at the Polk Theater in Lakeland, Florida.

AUG. 7: Elvis gave three shows at the Florida Theater in St. Petersburg, Florida.

AUG. 8: Elvis gave two shows in Orlando, Florida.

AUG. 9: Elvis gave two day shows at the Peabody Auditorium in Daytona Beach, and he performed an evening concert in Pontchartrain Beach, New Orleans.

AUG. 10–11: Elvis gave five shows at the Florida Theater in Jacksonville, Florida. Jacksonville's Judge Marion W. Gooding ordered a perplexed Elvis to keep his act "clean," not "obscene." On August 11, Elvis was interviewed by Johnny Tillotson for WWPF radio.

AUG. 12: Elvis performed at the Municipal Auditorium in New Orleans.

AUG. 20: Elvis began filming Twentieth Century–Fox's *Love Me Tender* in Hollywood. Elvis portrayed Clint Reno. The film costarred Debra Paget, Richard Egan, and Mildred Dunnock, and was directed by Robert D. Webb. Elvis resided at the Knickerbocker Hotel on Ivar Avenue. *Downbeat* quoted an Elvis fan, "He's just ghastly . . . the doll!" and *that* sentiment showed the world why over 2,000 ardent devotees wrote daily or called Elvis at the film studios. Guards soon protected actors and film crews from mobs of Elvis fans.

AUG. 27: *Newsweek* talked of Elvis's "sex-hot flame," *Life* confessed Elvis's charisma caused fans to cry, and the Cat won the Apollo Award from the disc jockey and news reporters' association.

SEPT.: The LP *Elvis* was produced at Radio Recorders in Hollywood, and songs included "Love Me," "Playing for Keeps," "How Do You Think I Feel?" and "How's the World Treating You?"

▲ Imogene Coca, Steve Allen, and Elvis at the Hudson Theatre in New York City, performing on "The Steve Allen Show," July 1, 1956. *Courtesy of AP/Wide World Photos.*

SEPT. 1: Stanley A. Kesler's "Playing for Keeps" was recorded at Radio Recorders and take No. 7 was released by RCA. In the single's nine-week stay on *Billboard*'s Top 100 chart, it reached No. 34 (RCA 20-6800, released in January 1957 with the flip side "Too Much").

SEPT. 2: Little Richard wrote "Long Tall Sally," which hit the pop charts at No. 6 in 1956. Pat Boone's 1958 cover of it reached No. 8. Elvis recorded the song at Radio Recorders, and take No. 4 was released in LP form only, and curiously it did *not* list Little Richard as the songwriter, but Enotris Johnson. (Little Richard has often alluded to Elvis's "stealing" his songs.) Nevertheless, Elvis sang the song for the 1973 TV special "Elvis: Aloha From Hawaii," and it appears on the EP *Strictly Elvis* and five other LPs and two bootleg LPs.

"Old Shep"—the song that started his career at the age of ten—was first recorded on September 2, 1956, at Radio Recorders, and all takes featured Elvis on piano. A one-sided single of "Old Shep" was given to disc jockeys (RCA CR-15, released December 1956). The song's fifth take was released on the EPs *Elvis*, Vol. 2, and *Promotion Disc RCA PRO-12*, and on LPs *Double Dynamite, Elvis, Elvis Sings for Children and Grownups Too!* and *Separate Ways*.

Elvis sang "Paralyzed," which Otis Blackwell wrote for him, at Radio Recorders. Take No. 12 was released by RCA on an EP, and the song had a seven-week run on *Billboard*'s Top 100 chart reaching No. 59, but it was No. 8 on England's chart. In 1983, a single was released with the flip side "Little Sister" (RCA PB-13547, released June 1983).

RCA released take No. 12 of "Too Much," recorded on September 2, written by Lee Rosenberg and Bernard Weisman. The single peaked at No. 2 for four out of seventeen weeks on *Billboard*'s Top 100 chart (RCA 20-6800, released in January 1957 with the flip side "Playing for Keeps").

"When My Blue Moon Turns to Gold Again" (written by Wiley Walker and Gene Sullivan) was recorded and released on the EP *Elvis*, Vol. 1. It charted at No. 27 on *Billboard*'s Top 100 list during a fifteen-week stay. Elvis sang the song as a duet with Charlie Hodge during the dress rehearsal for his 1968 TV special and on the "Ed Sullivan Show," January 6, 1957.

SEPT. 3: Elvis recorded Joe Thomas's "Any Place Is Paradise" at Radio Recorders for the LP *Elvis*. Take No. 27 of "First in Line" by Ben Weisman–Aaron Schroeder and take No. 27 of "Reddy Teddy" (by John Marascalco and Robert "Bumps" Blackwell) were released on the EP *Elvis*, Vol. 2. Take No. 19 was released of "Rip It Up" (written by John Marascalco) as a single with the flip side "Little Sister" (RCA EP-0517, a twelve-inch promo disk). It did not chart. It is heard on the EP *Elvis*, Vol. 1 and LP *Elvis* (RCA LPM 1382).

SEPT. 3: Although his mother didn't drive, Elvis bought Gladys the now-famous 1957 pink Cadillac (originally blue, he had it painted pink). It remained at Graceland until Elvis died. Elvis changed the line "You may get religion" to "You may get a pink Cadillac" in the song "Baby, Let's Play House." Although he did not live long enough to make his promise come true, the King promised his daughter, Lisa Marie, the pink Caddy would be hers on her eighteenth birthday.

The Real Elvis extended-play album is released by RCA.

SEPT. 4: Actor Nick Adams and Elvis rode Harley-Davidson motorcycles through L.A. wearing black leather jackets, boots, and caps. It was no wonder rumors spread Elvis wanted to outact and outshine Brando—or at least imitate him.

In 1950, Brando made his screen debut playing a paraplegic in Stanley Kramer's *The Men*. From 1950 to 1954, Brando's roles in *A Streetcar Named Desire*, *Viva Zapata!* and *Julius Caesar* drew wide critical acclaim and Academy Award nominations. He won the New York Critics Award, the Cannes Film Festival prize, and the coveted Oscar for his 1954 performance in Kazan's *On The Waterfront*. *The Film Encyclopedia* states: "Young audiences acclaimed him as the rebellious, nonconforming prototype of the beat generation; older audiences often saw him as an antisocial menace, unkempt and unrestrained—but audiences and critics agreed he was one of the most original and compelling personalities to appear on the screen in a long time."

Elvis was most impressed with Brando's 1953 cult classic, *The Wild One*, in which Brando played a rough, leather-clad biker and gang leader who storms in to assault a middle-class California town. His character faces hostility and prejudice from irate citizens—thus Brando (like Dean and Elvis) becomes a martyr in the eyes of many fans. Elvis yearned to play these kinds of parts, but Parker demanded he perform singing roles.

SEPT. 5:   Elvis was nicknamed Teen Angel by fans. He admitted he liked Teddy Bears and paying taxes (a comment that aroused the interest of the IRS, which started a probe of Elvis's income). He also told fans his favorite animals were tigers, horses, and dogs.

According to an article in *Coronet* titled "A Craze Called Elvis," Elvis brought in over 50 percent of RCA's income, while he himself earned $25,000 a week. He weighed 185 pounds, traveled by limousine and planes, slept no more than four hours a night, and did not like snobby girls. *Modern Screen*'s Louella Parsons asked Elvis why he didn't drop acting "now." She warned him not to star in anything

in bad taste and saluted his work for charities.

"Don't Be Cruel" reached No. 1 on *Billboard*'s Top 100 chart.

SEPT. 7:   Ed Sullivan worried about what the public would think of his allowing Elvis to appear on his TV show. Sullivan feared Elvis would destroy ratings because his image was not that of a clean-cut teen. Sullivan was also appalled by the Colonel's unprecedented $50,000 fee. No one in show business history had been paid that much!

Ed Sullivan knew Elvis's music differed drastically from the more "acceptable" middle-of-the-road tunes of Perry Como, Pat Boone, or Frank Sinatra. Elvis's suggestive lyrics and hoedown rock sound was torrid, somewhat violent, and sexually outrageous. In "Baby, Let's Play House," the lyrics tell the female listener the singer would rather she were dead than with another man. One writer happily gloated that Elvis and his lyrics sucked the blood from audiences like "a vampire—pure evil, a rare treat." Yet when "That's All Right, Mama" was first aired, Dewey Phillips said, "He's a good boy. . . . He's always afraid he'll hurt somebody's feelings." (*TV Guide*, Sept. 22–28, 1956.)

SEPT. 8:   Elvis was featured on the cover of *TV Guide*. Inside, he was photographed with actress Cynthia Baxter. (Two more segments appeared on Sept. 22–28 and Sept. 29–Oct. 4.) *TV Guide* admitted Elvis's hips drove teenagers crazy and that "at the moment, Presley is perhaps the hottest name in show business. Wherever he goes he is mobbed. The sales of his records alone are making him a millionaire." Due to his exposure on the "Ed Sullivan Show," 2 million advance orders for "Love Me Tender" were received. Some people became angry to learn a poorly educated "hillbilly" was earning eight times what the president of the

United States made a year. By 1957, the Colonel demanded stations pay Elvis a cool $10,000 for a short radio appearance.

SEPT. 9: Thanks to publicity generated by the Colonel and thousands of over-sexed fans, Elvis's appearance on the "Ed Sullivan Show" stimulated the highest ratings in television history, which shocked the staid Sullivan, who had attempted to censor Elvis. Gladys, Vernon, and Elvis wonder why Elvis was the one being so persecuted. Elvis defended his image by telling Ed Sullivan and the press that he was "just singing."

Because Sullivan had publicly declared he would never have Presley on his show, he had to eat those words. Perhaps it was lucky for Elvis (and unlucky for Sullivan) that "Great Stone Face" was involved in an auto accident outside Seymour, Connecticut. Veteran actor Charles Laughton substituted for Sullivan in New York and introduced Elvis by saying, "Music hath charms to soothe the savage beast." Elvis sang "Don't Be Cruel," "Love Me Tender," "Ready Teddy," and "Hound Dog."

The Dallas Times Herald asked, "What Makes Him Tick? . . . One minute he is frantically singing and leaping about. The following moment he may slip into a mood of deep despondency. . . . He's unruly and wild and is a constant source of trouble for those booking his act. He is the physical epitome of a trouble-making teenager. . . . He is elected ruler of a cult of defiant fans, not king by talent or choice, but simply because he was born at the right moment. . . . Perhaps our civilization needs a Presley to hold up, inspect and study. It makes our advances more than satisfying."

SEPT. 10: According to the *New York Times*, Steve Allen did not try to compete with Sullivan for ratings when Elvis was on Ed's show. NBC gave Allen the night off and instead aired an English film. Noting that TV cameras concentrated on the singer's upper body and tried to avoid the rest, the *Philadelphia Inquirer* joked that Sullivan only got half of what he paid for.

SEPT. 11–20: Rumors spread that Natalie Wood and Elvis were dating. On September 13, the *Tupelo Daily Journal* announced: "Elvis, Actress Natalie Wood Are Twosome." Wood was quoted: "He's really great and the most totally real boy I've ever met. He's a real pixie and has a wonderful little-boy quality. . . . A wonderful dancer—and he sings all the time to me."

SEPT. 16: Elvis became upset when he heard the *New York Times* said he and the "lack of responsibility" of television had exploited teenagers. Stating Elvis played a "martyr" with a "strip-tease behavior," the writer alleged that Elvis "injected movements of the tongue and indulged in wordless singing that were singularly distasteful . . . almost hypnotic power." He then pointed a finger at those who promoted and sold Elvis to the public as "culprits" guilty of "selfish exploitation," which was "a gross national disservice."

SEPT. 19: *Downbeat* claimed that in Elvis's moves "the sexual suggestiveness comes across" to audiences, and his "antiformalism" appealed to teenagers, who sought releases from the staid patterns in life.

"Blue Moon" entered *Billboard*'s Top 100 chart at No. 87. At No. 1 in its Best Sellers Chart were "Hound Dog"/ "Don't Be Cruel."

SEPT. 20–21: Tupelo prepared for Elvis's return. Merchants put banners and signs in windows, and a key to the city was to be presented to the Cat. The *Tupelo Daily Journal* hyped the events on September 21. Although citizens begged Elvis to be in the town's parade, local police and Colonel Parker said it would be too dangerous. Elvis would be hidden until he walked onto a stage, otherwise he would be torn to shreds.

SEPT. 22: *TV Guide* (Sept. 22–28) discussed Elvis's family and friends and quoted people saying Elvis worked too hard.

SEPT. 24: Prior to Elvis's recording "Love Me Tender" at Radio Recorders, Hollywood, it had presold 856,327 copies. The prepublication plug on the "Ed Sullivan Show" goosed sales. The song replaced "Hound Dog" and "Don't Be Cruel" as No. 1 on the pop charts. With Chuck Prescott, Red Robinson, and John Dodson on backup vocals, Elvis sang "We're Gonna Move" and "Poor Boy" (both written by Ken Darby, *not* Elvis and Darby's wife, Vera Matson) for *Love Me Tender* at Radio Recorders. The EP of that title reached No. 35 on *Billboard*'s Top 100 chart in an eleven-week run.

Newsweek reported that Elvis's appearance on Ed Sullivan's variety show boosted ratings to an unprecedented 82.6 percent of the American viewing public.

SEPT. 25: Rumors of a romance between Debra Paget and Elvis ran rampant, and it was reported they would marry. Elvis also dated Yvonne Lime, Dolores Hart, Natalie Wood, Ann-Margret, and other actresses. Actor Richard Egan recognized Elvis was "an American heartthrob" and observed, "He is the male Monroe." (See *Elvis Album.*) *Movieland* gushed he was "the next great lover."

The people of Tupelo ruled that cars could not park downtown or on Main Street when Elvis performed. Town officials warned of "massive" crowds and told merchants to "get ready." The *Tupelo Daily Journal* ran a front-page headline: "The Welcome Mat Is Out for Presley Homecoming" and announced that newspeople, TV reporters, and representatives from Fox Movietone (who were there to record his performance) would have a special section at the Mississippi-Alabama Fair. Excitement filled every corner of Tupelo.

SEPT. 26: This was declared Elvis Presley Day in Tupelo. Elvis performed two shows at Tupelo's Mississippi-Alabama Fair and Dairy Show in a hand-sewn (by Gladys) velvet shirt. Nick Adams was with Gladys at the performance before twenty-two thou-

◀Hometown Tupelo fans cheer Elvis's performance at the Mississippi-Alabama State Fair, September 26, 1956. *Courtesy of AP/Wide World Photos.*

sand fans. Elvis was presented with a guitar-shaped key to the city by Gov. J. P. Coleman, and papers raved, "Hometown Folks Hail Elvis Presley With Rock 'n' Roll."

His triumphant homecoming resulted in pandemonium. Fans screamed, fainted, and were carried out on stretchers. The once-unpopular hometown boy, who came from poverty and despair, was now able to donate $10,000 to charity. In 1955, he left the Tupelo and Memphis areas wearing torn and tattered clothing, and by 1957 he would return in gold lamé.

Prior to Elvis, American audiences sat quietly to watch entertainers perform. But Elvis set them free! The *Detroit Free Press* noted: "The trouble with going to see Elvis Presley is that you are likely to get killed. The experience is the closest thing to getting bashed in the head with an atomic bomb." Through all the criticism and bad press, Elvis retained a sense of humor, which endeared him to fans across the world.

SEPT. 26: At the Alabama-Mississippi Fair and Dairy Show, Elvis was recorded singing "I Got a Woman," which is on the LP *A Golden Celebration.* For twenty years, this Ray Charles song was a Presley favorite.

The National Guard was called to control the mobs of hysterical, screaming fans in Tupelo. Elvis was swarmed by girls at his two-thirty and seven-thirty P.M. performances. On September 27, the *Tupelo Daily Journal* reported that fans tore silver buttons from Elvis's hand-sewn blue velvet shirt. The story also noted that reporters rushed to the stage for protection from the wild mob, and that some fans were nearly trampled. In the end, Elvis earned $5,000 plus 60 percent of the gate.

Gladys and Vernon Presley were in the audience and could not believe what was happening to their son. Gladys was appalled at the way audiences were clutching and screeching at

her baby boy. And why did Elvis seem to enjoy and encourage it? She had not raised him to be like this. Something terrible and dangerous was happening to her son.

SEPT. 29: *Billboard* spoke of the merchandising genius behind Elvis's rise to stardom and predicted he would sell $20 million worth of Elvis souvenirs before December 1956. "This will overcome Mickey Mouse, Hopalong Cassidy, and Davy Crockett. . . . There are approximately 200,000 fan club members. A magazine titled 'Elvis Presley Answers Back' will be sold for 50 cents."

Variety enlightened readers about Elvis's wiggle. Colonel Parker told anyone who would listen that a group of sailors attempted to beat Elvis to a pulp, thus he now had to have bodyguards at his side day and night.

SEPT. 30: Hoping to prevent Catholics from supporting Elvis, Cardinal Spellman said in Buffalo, New York, "A new creed has been patterned by a segment of the young people in America—a creed of dishonesty, violence, lust, and degeneration." Gladys Presley was distraught to learn a cardinal condemned her son, and she went into a deep state of depression.

Elvis Presley Enterprises was formed in conjunction with Special Projects, Inc. to market 185 Elvis-related promo products. Its offices were set up by Elvis and Bob Neal at 160 Union Street, Memphis. Tom Parker dissolved the company in 1957 and started his own merchandising empire.

Running his office from Madison, Tennessee, the Colonel hired Howard Bell and Hank Saperstein of Special Projects, Inc. to coordinate Elvis products and merchandising. Saperstein administered the Elvis Presley National Fan Club for the primary purpose of promoting and selling Elvis commodities.

The Colonel raised Elvis's TV appearance fee to $300,000 per show. There were no takers.

OCT.: *Variety* named Elvis the "King of Rock 'n' Roll." Meanwhile, Cardinal Spellman's public condemnation of Elvis reverberated around the country. A typical reaction to Elvis occurred at a Catholic high school in Chicago where students were "ordered by a Catholic action group to stay away lest their morals be corrupted." Presley was spreading a national juvenile mania called rock 'n' roll. Elvis's reaction: "I am not doing anything wrong!"

OCT.: After *Variety* named Elvis "the King" it established him as *the* king of rock 'n' roll in the minds of millions. However, not everyone would agree.

Little Richard said in *Life* (Dec. 1, 1992), "How can a white boy be King of Rock and Roll? . . . I, too, have been called King of Rock and Roll. I been called the Queen. I earned the throne 'cause I am the Originator, the Architect, the Emancipator—*The* Founding Father of Rock and Roll." It was unfortunate that Little Richard left the music world in 1957 to become a minister. His previous recordings set the pace and standard that others had to reach. Elvis eventually recorded many of Little Richard's songs including "Tutti Frutti" (Specialty 561, 1955), "Long Tall Sally" (Specialty 571, 1956), "Ready Teddy"/"Rip It Up" (Specialty 579, 1956), "Shake a Hand" (Specialty 670, 1957), and "Crying in the Chapel" (Atlantic 2181).

Elvis was on the October cover of *Rock and Roll* magazine. His newly acquired affluence prompted thousands of charitable institutions and greedy individuals to bombard Elvis with requests for money and gifts.

OCT. 1: Natalie Wood dated Elvis, but neither was ready to make a major commitment. Their careers came first.

House and Gardens ran an article titled "The War of the Generations," which stated television should not cen-

sor singers. It was *not* the music that upset adults, but the fact that teenagers represented a new, large body to be reckoned with. The writer states clearly that although parents wanted their children to identify with them, they "failed to inspire in them a respect for our own standards." Teens will always have idols separate from their elders'.

Modern Screen quoted a fan who compared Elvis to Apollo, the symbol of beauty and youth.

OCT. 3: "I Don't Care If the Sun Don't Shine" entered *Billboard*'s Top 100 chart at No. 77.

OCT. 8: Elvis turned down NBC-TV's suggestion he sing in a forthcoming special for the "Kraft Television Theatre" about a singing idol. *Newsweek* said NBC and CBS rejected Elvis's appearances because the new asking fee was too steep at $300,000.

Time magazine announced that RCA had an all-time-high advance sale of 1 million "Love Me Tender" records.

OCT. 9: The *San Francisco Chronicle* announced that Elvis and Jayne Mansfield were scheduled to star in a Twentieth Century-Fox movie titled *The Love Maniac*. The Colonel's reply: "Hogwash!"

OCT. 10: "Love Me Tender"/"Any Way You Want Me" entered *Billboard*'s Top 100 chart at No. 9.

OCT. 11: Elvis performed at the 71st State Fair at the Cotton Bowl Stadium in Dallas, Texas, before more than twenty-six thousand people. Police were everywhere and Elvis feared for his life when he started to exit the stage. The *Dallas Times Herald* reported that Elvis's secretive plans prior to his appearance infuriated overeager fans, who wanted to get to him. A plan to put a wire fence around the stadium got this reaction from fans: "We'll get wire clippers."

OCT. 12: Elvis performed at the Heart o' Texas Coliseum in Waco and saw Eddie Fadal of KRLD radio (Dallas). Surrounded by an eight-foot fence and accompanied by ninety-five police officers, Elvis was driven onto the Coliseum floor to the fifty-yard line. His entire performance was drowned out by yelling and screaming.

The *Dallas Morning News* headlined, "Elvis Presley Disturbance Surely Hit Seismic Scale," and told of a Dallas County deputy sheriff who served Elvis and his management with a $38,000 lawsuit that alleged Elvis's management broke a contract. A reporter asked Elvis why he was humble. "I know that the Lord can give and that the Lord can take away," he replied. "I might be herding sheep next year."

OCT. 13: Al Hickock of radio station KEYS in Corpus Christi, Texas, interviewed Elvis (offered on a 78-rpm KEYS record, 1956; also on the LP *Elvis Confidentially*, ARAD 108, Arena Records, which gives the incorrect date of November 2, 1956. Elvis was not in Texas on that date). During the interview, Elvis said his rock 'n' roll was revolutionizing the pop music world.

The Cat complimented Debra Paget's and Richard Egan's work in the film *Love Me Tender* and bragged about his ten-movie contract.

Elvis performed in San Antonio before five thousand screaming, hysterical fans. San Antonio critics complained the Cat attracted too many "undesirable elements."

Disc jockey Charlie Walker interviewed Elvis after his two concert performances and stated he was "the hottest show business personality in the whole world in the last twenty years" while in the background five thousand fans chanted, "We want Elvis." Walker discussed the necessity for police during Elvis's concerts and the possible danger of the fans' delirium. He also spoke of Elvis's recent movie contract, studio sessions, and

his upcoming concert in Corpus Christi, Texas.

OCT. 14: Elvis's concert in Houston was so loud and unruly, authorities feared people would be crushed to death and that Elvis, too, might be killed in the madness.

OCT. 15: Elvis was exhausted, but his concert at Corpus Christi was as energetic and animated as the rest of his tour. He left the audience of frenzied youth wanting more.

The *San Francisco News* ran a front-page story titled, "What Makes Elvis Roll On? Story of a Jelly-Kneed Kid." RCA was so busy filling Elvis record orders, it hired Decca and MGM to press records for them. The director of *Love Me Tender* said Elvis "was very cooperative . . . flexible, took directions like a trouper. . . . Once in a while someone comes along—an Edison or Bach, who's been tapped on the shoulder, who's got a great gift. This boy's got it. . . . We loved him." Twentieth Century-Fox made 575 prints of *Love Me Tender*, the most it had ever released for any film.

OCT. 16: Part II of the *San Francisco News*' series on Elvis talked of his fans' adoration. They loved him so much they would have torn him to shreds, if they could have.

OCT. 17: *Variety* headlined, "Baptist Minister vs. Elvis: He'll Hit the Skids." The minister said Elvis represented the turmoil and confusion in teenagers.

Part III of the *San Francisco News*' series talked of the humble, God-fearing Elvis and quoted his dismay over a minister in *Life* magazine who denounced him: "That hurt me bitter-. . . . God gave me my voice. I never danced vulgar in my life. I've just been jigglin'." Nick Adams said, "He's the greatest guy I've ever met."

OCT. 18: Critics eagerly pointed out that Elvis was not perfect when, on

October 19, the *San Francisco Chronicle*, the *Tupelo Daily Journal*, and the *New York Times* reported that Elvis had hit the owner of a gas station. On October 18, Elvis pulled into a Memphis gas station, and naturally his presence caused a near riot. Who else drove a $10,000 Cadillac in that part of town? Ed Hopper, the owner of the gas station, didn't want any trouble and hit Elvis in the head and told him to leave the station. Fans crushed Hopper against the pumps. Elvis retaliated and defended himself, and when Hopper's assistant came to Hopper's aid, Elvis belted him, too. A Memphis judge found Elvis an innocent victim of an assault and battery.

OCT. 19: The LP *Elvis* (RCA LPM-1382) was released.

OCT. 20: "Love Me Tender" entered *Billboard*'s Top 100 chart at No. 12.
The *New York Times* announced Elvis's innocence in the gas station fight of October 18.

OCT. 22: Elvis watched television while fans tore the upholstery of his white Cadillac and wrote lipsticked love messages all over the car. The story was covered by the *San Francisco Chronicle*.

OCT. 24: Elvis earned his fifth gold record in one year, and *Variety* announced Ed Sullivan would present it to him (for "Love Me Tender"). The front page of *Variety* announced, "Elvis a Millionaire in One Year," and said merchandisers expected $40 million in domestic sales of fifty-one Elvis-related items within fifteen months. *Variety* projected Elvis's income for 1956–57 at $2.5 million. *Variety* reprinted an RCA trailer that said Elvis "walks like Marilyn Monroe but at home he is a model son!"
Elvis told United Press that he received his draft questionnaire at the beginning of October. The story was covered by the *Tupelo Daily Journal*, which quoted Elvis as saying, "I'm no different from anyone else. . . . When they want me [the Army], I'm ready. I'll have a ball until they call me and after they call me."

OCT. 26: *Collier's* ran an article titled "Rock 'n' Roll Battle: Boone vs. Presley" and claimed erroneously that Pat Boone was gaining in popularity on Elvis.
Elvis tried to save the job of the forty-two-year-old gas station attendant who had fought Elvis on October 18, but the man was fired. The story was covered in the *Tupelo Daily Journal*.

OCT. 27: "Army to Give Elvis Presley a G.I. Haircut" was run on the front page of *Billboard* and caused fans to panic from coast to coast. It reported incorrectly that Elvis would join the Special Forces "under as much secrecy as possible."
Someone unofficially leaked a story from the Fort Dix, New Jersey, Army base to *Billboard* that Elvis would soon join the Special Services and entertain troops. Elvis had no idea where that notion originated. The Army and the Colonel denied they had anything to do with the publicity stunt. Elvis said earlier he supported Adlai Stevenson for president and made it clear "there should be *no* draft." (See *New York Daily News*, September 1956.) This bold statement encouraged young men across America to burn draft cards.

OCT. 28: Elvis's second appearance on the "Ed Sullivan Show" confused the host, who couldn't comprehend why teenagers in his otherwise sedate audience were screaming. Sullivan went so far as to accuse Elvis of attaching and wiggling a cardboard tube from his crotch to make the girls go crazy.
As Elvis sang "Don't Be Cruel," "Love Me Tender," "Love Me," and "Hound Dog," fans screamed, parents

shook their heads, and ratings rose. Elvis was presented with a gold record for "Love Me Tender," which conveniently plugged the movie of the same name. Because TV cameras did not show enough of Elvis's pelvis, hundreds of thousands of letters were sent to the TV station scolding the camera crew and Sullivan for having tried to censor Elvis's performance. Yet when the camera did occasionally show him full-length, viewers also complained. It seemed Elvis caused a controversy no matter what he did or didn't do.

Pop artist Andy Warhol first painted Elvis.

Elvis settled out of court with Robbie Moore, who objected to having her photograph taken with Elvis.

OCT. 28/29: The *Tupelo Daily Journal* announced Elvis wanted to buy Vernon Presley a farm because "Daddy was raised in a cotton patch."

OCT. 29: The *New York Times* reported, "Presley Receives a City Polio Shot," and that he was "personable, quick-witted, charming and polite" to surprised reporters. "He is setting a fine example for the youth of the country," gushed the writer.

OCT. 30: The *Tupelo Daily Journal* reported that "evangelist Billy Graham said today singer Elvis Presley would make a great evangelist."

OCT. 31: Elvis appeared on WMPS radio.

Elvis started to date Barbara Hearn.

Elvis became a marketing phenomenon. Elvis photo buttons, bubble-gum cards, scarves, pins, stick-on sideburns, posters, records, hats, dolls, and other items were sold; as well as Chu-Bops, Elvis rings, perfume, charm bracelets, and guitars. Elvis earned $25,000 an appearance (and more), which topped Dean Martin and Jerry Lewis's zenith price of $10,000.

Priscilla Beaulieu bought her first Elvis album, *Elvis Presley*, at a PX in Austin, Texas.

An honorary "Captain of the Louisiana State Highway Patrol" badge was bestowed on Elvis.

NOV.: Rainbo Records of Lawndale, California, cut a single 78 rpm released as "Elvis Presley Speaks—In Person" (Rainbo Records), which included an undated interview with Elvis. Rainbo Records also produced in November 1956 "Elvis Presley: "The Truth About Me,'" which was the same as their first issue of November. Both records were attached to the magazine cover "Elvis Answers Back."

Elvis was all over the newsstands: *Dig* magazine ran four pages and a cover on Elvis; *Hollywood Rebels* featured Natalie Wood and Elvis on its cover; *Motion Pictures* ran gossip columnist Hedda Hopper's revulsion over Elvis's gyrations; while *The New Yorker* in "The Current Cinema" negatively reviewed *Love Me Tender*.

Elvis, Vol. 1, and *Elvis*, Vol. 2, (EPs) and *Elvis* were released by RCA Victor.

NOV. 1: Natalie Wood flew to Memphis to visit Elvis, and wedding rumors were reported in the *San Francisco News*.

NOV. 5: *Newsweek* reported Elvis would be a GI at Fort Dix, New Jersey, by December; his hair and sideburns would be cut; and he was to have extensive dental work done.

NOV. 7: "Love Me" (from the LP *Elvis*, Vol. 1) entered *Billboard*'s Top 100 chart at No. 84. The LP *Elvis* entered *Billboard*'s Best Selling Packaged Records–Popular Albums chart at No. 7. "Love Me Tender" peaked at No. 1 on *Billboard*'s Top 100 chart. It was a *good* day for Elvis!

Variety reported that RCA was spreading Elvis's earnings over a ten-year period to save him from paying too much in taxes. RCA guaranteed him $1 million each year for ten years.

The *Tupelo Daily Journal* took note of the *New York Times*' favorable review of Elvis and quoted him saying, "You know, there's a verse in the Bible that says you will reap what you sow. I believe it, and I try to be careful about what I sow."

NOV. 8: The *Tupelo Daily Journal* stated that Elvis tore up the original RCA contract regarding his earning $1 million a year for ten years and rewrote it to read $1,000 a week for 20 years.

NOV. 13: *Look* ran the article "The Great Elvis Presley Industry," highlighting Colonel Tom Parker's and Hank Saperstein's involvement.

NOV. 14: Elvis was in the audience at Liberace's Riviera concert. When Liberace spotted Elvis, he paid a piano rock 'n' roll tribute to the Cat. After the show, Elvis and Liberace exchanged jackets and instruments and the press had a heyday.

Variety talked of teenagers crowding the lobbies of the Heritage and Andrew Jackson hotels in Nashville because of a rumor Elvis was coming to town.

Colonel Parker threw a tantrum and wanted to know who told the *Tupelo Daily Journal* Elvis was considering a two-to-four week tour at Empress Hall in London, England, for $11,200.

NOV. 15: *Love Me Tender* opened in five hundred theaters and became a smash hit, despite weak reviews. The *Harvard Lampoon* conferred on Elvis an undeserved Worst Supporting Actor Award, while one *New York Times* critic described Elvis as "turgid" in a "horse opera" film. A fifty-foot-tall cardboard picture of Elvis stood outside the Paramount Theater.

The *Los Angeles Times* reported that Liberace and Elvis were fond of each other and that the pianist jovially remarked, "Elvis and I may be characters—he with his sideburns and me with my gold jackets—but we can afford to be!" Because Liberace was respectful and courteous toward the rock 'n' roller, Elvis instantly considered Liberace a confidant because he was not threatened by Elvis's rising star. Liberace told Elvis to make certain he kept his "head above water."

Liberace and Elvis both came from poverty and both adored gold, cars, mansions, and money as these implied security to them. By the end of 1956, both men were millionaires. Liberace convinced Elvis to change his image from that of a country hick to that of an alluring star who sparkled in the spotlight. Elvis would soon be featured on record covers wearing a gold-lamé suit with shiny gold shoes.

"When My Blue Moon Turns to Gold Again" (on the LP *Elvis*, Vol. 1) entered *Billboard*'s Top 100 chart at No. 94.

NOV. 16: Elvis and the Liberace brothers appeared before the press at the Hotel Riviera, Las Vegas. Elvis sent Liberace a guitar made of flowers for every opening Liberace had until Elvis died. Liberace said Elvis told him, "I only send them to people I love, you know." Reflecting on being an entertainer, Liberace said, "You have to work at it, be surprising, find new things to make that audience sit up and take notice. . . . You're only as good as your last show or the one you're doing now. . . . An audience wants only one thing. To be entertained." (See *San Antonio Light*, Feb. 8, 1987.)

A critic for the *New York Times* criticized other actors in *Love Me Tender* and said Elvis did a better job than all of them. The Colonel, Hal B. Wallis, and Elvis were elated.

NOV. 17: The *Tupelo Daily Journal* headlined, "Judge Upholds School's Right to Expel Boy for Wearing Elvis

Presley Haircut; Mother May Appeal."
On page 7, it quoted a doctor who
claimed Elvis's music soothed Iowa
Mental Health Institute patients.

NOV. 19: Presley Pressed Down (a pomade for unruly hair) and Hound Dog
lipsticks (and others) are discussed in
the *Toledo Ledger-Enquirer*. The article also reported the riot outside of
Paramount's theater in New York City,
when fans became wild buying *Love
Me Tender* tickets.

NOV. 20: A local paper dispelled the
rumor Elvis was buying a farm for Vernon in Hickory Flat, Mississippi.

NOV. 21: Colonel Parker removed Bob
Neal from Elvis completely and made
Neal sign yet another contract to that
effect. Hank Snow was paid an unknown sum to agree not to feel he was
owed a finder's fee for Elvis. The Colonel owned "his boy," lock, stock, and
barrel.

NOV. 23: Unemployed steelworker
Louis John Balint was fined $19.60 for
attacking Elvis at the Commodore
Perry Hotel in Toledo, Ohio, asserting
his wife loved the singer and because
of her passion for him broke up their
marriage. The story was reported in
the *San Francisco Chronicle*, the *New
York Times*, and the *Ledger-Enquirer*
(which claimed the Elvis "rage" was
"spreading to lipsticks").

The Cat gave two performances at
Toledo's Sports Arena before wild
crowds. Elvis decided to carry a gun to
protect himself from jealous husbands
and boyfriends of fans who had fallen
in love with him.

Shelby (Tenn.) County sheriff Roy
Nixon swore Elvis in as a special deputy so he could carry a firearm. As his
world became more confining, Elvis
turned to gospel music as a release
and started to read Kahlil Gibran's *The
Prophet*, the Bible, *Siddhartha* by Herman Hesse, *Autobiography of a Yogi*
by Paramahansa Yogananda, *The Mystical Christ* by Manly Palmer Hall, and
*The Life and Teaching of the Masters
of the Far East* by Baird Spalding.

NOV. 24: Elvis flew to Cleveland, Ohio,
and performed before a packed house.

◄ Liberace and Elvis at the
Riviera Hotel in Las Vegas on
November 14, 1956. *Courtesy
of the James Agency and the
Liberace Foundation.*

NOV. 25: Elvis performed at the Armory in Louisville, Kentucky.

CA. NOV. 25: Twentieth Century- Fox offered Elvis the starring role in *The Way to the Gold*, with a salary of $150,000 and 50 percent of the profits. The Colonel insisted upon $250,000 and 50 percent of the gross profits. Fox turned him down.

NOV. 28: *Love Me Tender* entered *Variety*'s National Box Office Survey chart at No. 2.

DEC.: Elvis and Ed Sullivan appeared on the cover of *TV and Radio Mirror*. RCA Victor released the extended-play album *Love Me Tender*.

Cosmopolitan ran the article "What Is an Elvis Presley?" Eddie Condon wrote: "It isn't enough to say that Elvis is kind to his parents, sends money home, and is the same unspoiled kid he was before all the commotion began. That still isn't a free ticket to behave like a sex maniac in public."

TV World asked, "Singer or Sexpot?" and *Photoplay* ran a multiple cutout, pinup of Elvis's pictures and announced "Presley Takes Hollywood," while *Motion Picture* called him "the Big Noise from Tupelo" and spoke of fans lining the film lots, writing and calling Elvis on film sets, and acting like mad lunatics in his presence. He is noted as an "explosion" onstage and "a shy, uncertain country boy" offstage. At the Knickerbocker Hotel in Hollywood, he received up to 237 calls a day.

The ever-scheming Colonel promoted Elvis bubble-gum cards featuring questions about Elvis on one side and photos of him on the flip side. Of the sixty-six cards in the collection, twenty had scenes from *Love Me Tender*. (Sixty-six cards in all were distributed.)

DEC. 1: *Melody Maker* ran an article titled "Let's Be Fair to Mr. Presley"

and gave Elvis a good review for his debut performance in *Love Me Tender*.

DEC. 3: The words of Rev. Carl E. Elgena of Des Moines, Iowa, unnerved Elvis: "Elvis Presley is morally insane. The spirit of Presleyism has taken down all the bars and standards. We're living in a day of jellyfish morality."

It is important to note that Elvis was the first entertainer to openly admit teenagers could be the center of a rock star's life. He gave them a powerful salute of recognition by stating publicly teenagers were the reason for his triumphant success. When Elvis hailed them as special and thanked them for helping him "make it," teens across the world worshiped him. Their continuous adulation, and the adult world's negative response to it, created a superstar.

Colonel Parker asked Ed Sullivan for $250,000 for any program upon which Elvis would appear. (See *Tupelo Daily Journal*.)

DEC. 4: The Million Dollar Quartet sessions were recorded at Sun Records, Memphis, with Elvis, Jerry Lee Lewis, Carl Perkins, and Johnny Cash, who came together to belt out white country spirituals. On the original recording Johnny Cash is not heard, but a photograph of the session suggests he participated in the jam session. The photograph probably was a publicity shot, and although Elvis is seated at Sun's piano in the photograph, he and Lewis played the piano during the session.

It is the only time the four stars sang together, and they performed fifteen gospel tunes or parts of tunes, and a few country and pop songs.

For the Million Dollar Quartet session, Elvis walked into Sun studios with nineteen-year-old Vegas dancer Marilyn Evans. Elvis sat at the piano and began playing "Blueberry Hill." Carl Perkins, Jerry Lee Lewis, and perhaps Johnny Cash joined him. Jack Clement, realizing the importance of the session, began to tape it. *Press-*

Scimitar reporter Robert Johnson wrote the next day: "The joint was relly [*sic*] rocking before they all got thru. Elvis is high on Jerry Lee Lewis. 'That boy can go,' he said. 'I think he has a great future ahead of him . . . and the way he plays piano just gets inside me.' " Without the Colonel's supervision, Elvis's candor came out during this session when he proudly spoke of a performer named Jackie Wilson who imitated Elvis in Vegas: "There's a guy out there who's doin' a takeoff on me—'Don't Be Cruel.' He tried so hard, 'til he got much better, boy—much better than that record of mine. . . . He was a colored guy. . . . [He] grabbed that microphone, went down to the last note, went all the way down to the floor, man, lookin' straight up at the ceiling. Man, he cut me—I was under the table when he got through singin'. . . . Wooh! Man, he sang that song. . . . I went back four nights straight and heard that guy do that. Man, he sung the hell outta that song." The Colonel told Elvis to watch his mouth and not advertise his love for "race music" or "niggers." Elvis had been called "the white nigger" and that was bad enough.

Sam Phillips sent a press release to disc jockeys with a photograph taken by George Pierce stating "our little shindig—it was a dilly." It has never been told how many songs were sung spontaneously in that December 4 session. The album was released November 1980. The songs included "Brown-Eyed Handsome Man" (by Chuck Berry) sung by Elvis; a few lines of "Crazy Arms" by Elvis and Jerry Lee Lewis; "Down by the Riverside/When the Saints Go Marching In" sung by Elvis, Lewis, and Carl Perkins; Lewis on piano and vocals for "End of the Road"; "Farther Along" sung by Elvis, Carl Perkins, and Jerry Lee Lewis; "Home, Sweet Home" by American John Howard Payne (during which Elvis spontaneously sang, "You know what it takes, you've got it, baby," from "When It Rains It Really Pours"); "I Hear a Sweet Voice Calling" with Elvis, Jerry Lee Lewis, and Carl Perkins; "I Just Can't Make It by Myself," a gospel in harmony with Elvis and Jerry Lee Lewis; "I Shall Not Be Moved" sung by Elvis, Jerry Lee Lewis, and Carl Perkins; Elvis doing a few lines of Hank Snow's "I'm Gonna Bid My Blues Goodbye"; Elvis imitating Ernest Tubb in the Tubb song "I'm With a Crowd (But Oh So Lonesome)"; Elvis singing "Is It So Strange" to Lewis and Perkins; a piano solo by Jerry Lee Lewis of "Jerry's Boogie"; Elvis and Lewis singing harmony on "Jesus Hold My Hand"; "Just a Little Talk With Jesus" with Elvis and Lewis singing in harmony; "Keeper of the Key" sung by Carl Perkins, with Elvis and Lewis in harmony; Elvis imitating Bill Monroe as he sang "Little Cabin on the Hill"; Elvis, Perkins, and Lewis doing "On the Jericho Road"; Elvis singing a few lines of "Out of Sight Out of Mind"; Elvis, Perkins, and Lewis singing "Paralyzed"; "Rip It Up" sung by all; the gospel song "Softly and Tenderly" with Elvis on lead and Jerry Lee Lewis on harmony; Perkins and Elvis singing a line from "Summertime Has Passed and Gone"; Perkins singing harmony during "Sweetheart You Done Me Wrong" with Elvis on lead; Elvis and Lewis doing "That Lonesome Valley"; Elvis singing "That's My Desire"; "When God Dips His Love in My Heart" by Elvis with Perkins on harmony; "When the Saints Go Marching In" with everyone there singing; Elvis accompanying himself on guitar for "You Belong to My Heart"; and Jerry Lee Lewis accompanying himself while singing "You're the Only Star in My Blue Heaven."

DEC. 11: *Look* compared Elvis's features with those of the discus thrower Discobolus and Michelangelo's David.

DEC. 15: Elvis gave his last show for the "Louisiana Hayride" to nine thousand fans, which the *Shreveport Times* called "an unforgettable performance." A press conference followed his show.

One fan club member was quoted: "Elvis is the living denial of the notion teenagers should be seen and not heard." *That* was the big secret behind his appeal and his success.

The *Shreveport Times* reported the next day: "The gyrating rotary troubadour was seldom if ever heard by an audience screaming like Zulus every time he moved a muscle. The Pelvis applies more 'Body English.' . . . No entertainer in history has worked under greater audience handicaps, not even Sinatra at the Palace. Elvis's mere appearance on the 'Hayride' stage last night set off a veritable atomic explosion of photographic flashbulbs and squeals from teenagers which crescendoed into pandemonium."

By 1957, because the crowds became too desperate to see Elvis, touch him, and take a part of him home with them, he would stop touring and his world would flip upside down. He felt threatened by his enemies while fans almost adored him to death. He needed space; a place to hide and reflect.

Although he had become the highest-paid superstar in America, Elvis felt critics' remarks toward him were cruel and unfounded. Bigotry and censorship hindered him from performing freely when the urge struck him. There were no concert halls large enough to satisfy the ever-growing crowds, and no income was too big for the Colonel to bank. Fans and cameras followed him everywhere. Millions of his records sold and RCA had a hard time keeping up with demand.

DEC. 17: The *New York Times* quoted a Greenwich Village minister who called Elvis "a passing fancy" and rebuked him as "a whirling dervish of sex" who earned more money than the president of the United States.

DEC. 19: From the LP *Elvis*, Vol. 1, the singles "Old Shep," "Poor Boy," and "Paralyzed" entered *Billboard*'s Top 100 at Nos. 47, 54, and 78.

CA. DEC. 20: After reviewing Elvis's sudden rise to fame, musician Spike Jones wondered if Elvis had the ability to stay fresh. Jones speculated Elvis would probably not be creating "Hound Dog" 's twenty years from this day—he would most likely be counting Cadillacs. Unfortunately, Jones's prediction would come to pass.

DEC. 22: Elvis and B. B. King were on radio's WDIA "Goodwill Review."

Elvis appeared onstage at the Ellis Auditorium in Memphis at an all-black function. WDIA disc jockey Rufus Thomas noted the audience went crazy over Elvis. At the "Goodwill Review" the night belonged to B. B. King, Bobby "Blue" Bland, Little Junior Parker, and Earl Malone. Elvis was photographed on Beale Street with Little Junior Parker (1927–71), Bobby "Blue" Bland (1930–?), and other black singers and musicians.

DEC. 24: *The New Republic* stated "A Star Is Born" in *Love Me Tender* and recognized Elvis's talent.

DEC. 25: Elvis adored Christmas. He liked to give and he liked to receive. His homes always resounded with Christmas music and were overdecorated in typical, ostentatious Presley fashion with trees, ornaments, rows of lights, wreaths, holly, and Santa Claus figures. Drinking nonalcoholic beverages and eating peanut-butter and banana snacks, employees were given presents and Christmas bonuses. Elvis received thousands of gifts from fans, and each Christmas ended with hours of hymns sung around a piano.

DEC. 31: Elvis made a nonsinging TV appearance for "Holiday Hop" on KLAC-TV in Memphis, for a special presentation. Host Wink Martindale briefly interviewed Elvis.

The *Wall Street Journal* took notice of the money being made in the merchandising of Elvis Presley: 12,000 pair of Elvis jeans were sold from one outlet in New York and 350,000 charm bracelets were scooped up by fans in three months.

By the end of the year, the images of Mickey Mouse, Jesus, and Elvis had been reproduced more than any others. Confused by the $22 million earned by Elvis Presley Enterprises and the Colonel's souvenir line, the December 1956 issue of *Cosmopolitan* asked, "What is an Elvis Presley?"

The Colonel watched from the sidelines as Elvis handled ever-growing, hysterical crowds with the panache of an eager, evangelist minister at a fundamentalist convention, who purposely touched and singled out members of each audience to caress with a look or a gesture. When Elvis sang lyrics that asked listeners to never say good-bye and promised he would never leave them, fans felt he was directing sentiments to each of them. It was personal. Intimate. Salable.

By the end of 1956, a tightly knit entourage of security guards, hardnosed businessmen, and flashy, guncarrying PR men surrounded Elvis. They followed him wherever he went, and few outsiders were allowed in. Ironically, while Elvis was becoming the public's symbol for independence and freedom of expression, he was

carefully being isolated and kept under strict guard. The intimidating Colonel's domination was all-encompassing. "Do as I say and your dreams will come true," was one of his magical lines to Elvis, and Elvis swallowed it, hook, line, and sinker.

Elvis's ability to create the convincing illusion of being a happy, carefree person who was in command of his destiny was, in fact, his highest acting achievement. He never felt a sense of deliverance from repression, nor had he ever been given a chance to let go completely. He was simply taken from one repressive life circumstance into another.

DEC. 31:   Elvis called Liberace to discuss a mutual interest in Cadillac Eldorados and pianos. Liberace connected Elvis with George Barris of Kustom City automobiles, located at 10811 Riverside Drive, in North Hollywood.

Elvis gave sixty-one concerts in 1956.

Fourteen-year-old Martin Ritchie died of electrocution while he hung an effigy of Elvis in Chicago to protest censorship. Elvis wept when he heard the news. He told friends that no entertainer's actions or songs were worth anyone's life.

1957

In 1957, the Teamsters union was headed by Jimmy Hoffa, Rev. Martin Luther King, Jr., headed the Southern Christian Leadership Conference, Russia sent *Sputnik* into space with the first living creature (a dog), and Barbie was introduced by Mattel toys.

In 1957, Chuck Berry released "School Days," which told of students rejecting books for the wild sides of street life. The play *West Side Story* and Elvis's film *Jailhouse Rock* gave middle America its first

glimpses of street-gang activity. Balancing the scene, "sweet" songs like "April Love," "Young Love," "Bye, Bye Love," "Tammy," and "Old Cape Cod" became hits.

JAN.:   Elvis was amused when he watched the last film Jerry Lewis and Dean Martin made, *Hollywood or Bust*, because a huge billboard in the film advertised Elvis in Vegas. After the bad reviews he had received there, Elvis

► Gladys, Elvis, and Vernon
Presley in 1957. *Courtesy
of private collector.*

thought the free plug was hysterically
funny.

Jerry Lee Lewis contended he was
the *only* pianist in the rockabilly Memphis crowd, but Elvis had performed
without criticism at the National Guard
Armory in Florida in front of thousands and was considered "a decent
piano player." Elvis played piano for
enjoyment, and if he tickled the ivories
in front of an audience, it was when he
was feeling confident and relaxed.

Many movie magazines labeled Elvis
"the world's most eligible bachelor."
Elvis was on the cover of *Dig* magazine.

By this time, bans against Elvis and
his music had been posted across
America. San Antonio critics said he
"attracted undesirable elements." Asbury Park's (NJ) Mayor Roland Hines
prohibited rock concerts in city halls,
and Santa Cruz, California, officials
followed New Jersey's rulings. The
New York Daily News suggested no
teenager should be allowed to dance in
public without parental consent and
advised the city enforce a midnight
curfew. Elvis's antagonists had become
radical!

Somewhat threatened by Elvis's
popularity, Frank Sinatra denounced
him and rock 'n' roll: "His kind of music is deplorable, a rancid-smelling aph-

rodisiac. . . . [Rock 'n' roll is] the most
brutal, ugly, degenerate, vicious form
of expression it has been my displeasure to hear. . . . It fosters almost totally negative and destructive reactions
in young people. It smells phony and
false. It is sung, played, and written for
the most part by cretinous goons, and
by means of its almost imbecilic reiter-
ations and sly, lewd—in plain fact—
dirty lyrics, it manages to be the
martial music of every sideburned delinquent on the face of the earth."

JAN. 1:   The rumor spread that Elvis
was going to be drafted into the United
States Army. Fans flocked in protest to
his home. Because of the commotion,
neighbors near the Audubon Drive
house loathed the Presleys' presence.
In a frantic effort to oust them from
the neighborhood, a public nuisance
suit was filed against them, but a court
ruled Elvis was not liable for the noise
or actions of spirited fans. Not wanting
to move, Elvis tried to buy all the
homes on the street, but neighbors refused to sell. It humiliated him when
neighbors called his family "poor white
trash." Elvis said, "Our house is the
only one paid in full around here!"

JAN. 2:   Despite Elvis's newly acquired
fame, Audubon neighbors asked the

Presleys to move. Elvis was furious. Gladys felt the Colonel had caused her son to become bitter and egotistical. But Elvis told Gladys she was the one who had changed for the worse. Her incredible mood swings, bloated legs and feet, and her difficulty walking indicated to Elvis she was drinking heavily, but he chose to ignore it.

JAN. 3: The neighborhood's hostility depressed Elvis. After spending most of his money on too many cars, trinkets, and appliances, the thrill of purchases faded, and it was perplexing what to *do* with his vast wealth. Bored with his neighbors complaints, Elvis told the Colonel he was going to buy a mansion.

JAN. 4: Elvis reluctantly went to the Memphis draft board to clarify his status. His preinduction Army physical was at Kennedy Veterans Hospital, Memphis, where he was accompanied by Vegas dancer Dorothy Harmony and Cliff Gleaves. Capt. Leonard Click conducted the physical.

At the time the Army rumor hit the news, Fred Sparks of the *New York World Herald* said of Elvis, "He is the soil himself, like Will Rogers or Carl Sandburg," and John C. Wilson of the *New York Times* applauded Elvis's "distinct talent." The kid from nowhere had gone somewhere, and the press was beginning to take him seriously. He was no longer called a joke, a freak, or a sideshow in the Colonel's circus.

Many people question how the Colonel came into the Elvis picture. Although at first the Colonel seemed out of his league in the presence of Hollywood magnates, his ability to make incredible, precedent-setting record deals and keep a tight grip on the rights to use Elvis's name and image were underestimated by his critics.

JAN. 5: Las Vegas dancer Dorothy Harmony said good-bye to Elvis and left Memphis.

JAN. 6: Elvis's last TV appearance on the "Ed Sullivan Show" was watched by millions. Elvis sang "Hound Dog," "Love Me Tender," "Heartbreak Hotel," "Don't Be Cruel," "Too Much" (after which Elvis told the audience he had received 282 teddy bears from fans for Christmas), "When My Blue Moon Turns to Gold Again," and Thomas A. Dorsey's "Peace in the Valley." Sullivan told listeners of Elvis's concern for the Hungarian relief efforts and that Elvis was planning a benefit concert to support that cause, which he never did. He admitted Elvis was "a real decent, fine boy" and that he had "never had a pleasanter experience . . . with a big name. . . . You're thoroughly all right," Sullivan said, beaming at Elvis, who nodded.

JAN. 8: Vernon, Gladys, the Jordanaires, Scotty Moore, Bill Black, D. J. Fontana (all of whom debuted in *Loving You* with small scenes), and Elvis traveled by train to Hollywood on Elvis's twenty-second birthday. They ate a birthday cake on the train.

Elvis's role in *Loving You* is of a young pop star in quest of stardom in the Southwest. The Colonel insisted Elvis be given top billing. During the film, his character's fame outshone band members, so he dumped his loyal musicians. Elvis, in real life, followed suit after the movie.

JAN. 9: "Inside Paradise" by Hal Kanter of *Variety* stated the Colonel had confined Elvis, who entertained and then disappeared from view. The Colonel, said Kanter, told the singer/ actor it was not safe for him to be in public. Kanter felt sorry for Elvis being controlled by such a tyrannical manager and wrote of the life Elvis seemed to lead: "In the eye of the hurricane the young man took it all with unnatural good grace and humility. . . . He was enjoying himself . . . that evoked a strange magic on audiences, whipping them into a frenzy of appreciation no entertainer in his time had been able to match. But after a year . . . Mom and Dad had nothing left to desire, for they had all they could use. . . . [After a concert he is] dripping wet, dives headlong into the backseat of a patrol car. The door slams . . . other police join the entourage to form a bodyguard. . . . Inside the room [he] falls exhausted on his bed. . . . He stares at the ceiling in silence."

CA. JAN. 11: Army captain Elwyn P. Rowan held a press conference and announced to disappointed fans that Elvis was "an A profile, and that's as high as you can go." Elvis's new occupation: GI. His status: private with ROTC training.

JAN. 12–14: Elvis performed at recording sessions at Radio Recorders in Hollywood. On January 13, he recorded "Peace in the Valley," written by Chicago-based gospel master Rev. Thomas A. Dorsey (who died in January 1993). Take No. 9 is the RCA master. Gordon Stoker played backup organ. The EP hit No. 39 on *Billboard*'s Top 100 chart (ten weeks). The four-song EP *Peace in the Valley* was released in March 1957. It consisted of the title song, "Take My Hand, Precious Lord," and two sacred compositions written by Rev. Thomas A. Dorsey. "I Believe" and "It Is No Secret" completed the LP, which became the top-selling gospel record of all time. Some fans wanted to start the Elvis Presley Church.

JAN. 12–13: Otis Blackwell wrote "All Shook Up" in the office of Shalimar Music. David Hill and Vicki Young recorded it prior to Elvis's singing it at Hollywood's Radio Recorders with Dudley Brooks on piano (RCA 20-6870) with the flip side "That's When Your Heartache Begins" (recorded January 13 and written by William J. Raskin, Billy Hill, and Fred Fisher in 1940). Elvis stated during the Million Dollar Quartet session that he had recorded the song earlier on acetate in 1953, and that he sang it during the Sun session

on January 4, 1954. "All Shook Up" became No. 1 for eight weeks on *Billboard*'s Top 100 chart after charting for three weeks. It entered the chart at No. 25 and stayed on the Top 100 chart for thirty weeks. Hitting the R&B and country charts, "All Shook Up" was the first single by Elvis to hit the British charts. There were five singles, two EPs, eleven LPs, and nine bootleg albums with these two songs.

Take No. 9 on January 12 of "Got a Lot o' Livin' to Do" (by Aaron Schroeder and Ben Weisman) was used in *Loving You*. Take No. 5 of "Tell Me Why" (by Titus Turner) was selected for release by RCA, but it wasn't until December 1965 that it came out as a single.

On January 13, Elvis recorded "I Beg of You," written by Rosemarie McCoy and Kelly Owens, using take No. 34 (not the master take No. 12). It peaked at No. 12 on *Billboard*'s Top 100 chart during a twelve-week stay. It was No. 2 on the country chart and No. 4 on the R&B chart (RCA 20-7150). Its flip side was "Don't."

"Mean Woman Blues" by Claude DeMetrius was completed on January 13. Take No. 14 was released in October 1957 (RCA 47-7066) and it did not chart. However, Roy Orbison's 1963 version hit No. 5 on the Top 100 chart and No. 8 on the R&B chart (Monument 824). "Mean Woman Blues" can be heard on the LP *Elvis Aron Presley—Forever* and on the documentary *This Is Elvis*.

JAN. 13: Rumors ran rampant about whether or not the Army would make Elvis cut his famous hair, which had been insured for $1 million. The Army reassured all those concerned, it would all come off! Even worse, his dark hair could not be dyed in the Army.

The Elvis Midget Fan Club, organized by the Colonel, distributed Elvis ads and pamphlets.

JAN. 14: Elvis was on the cover of *Mirabelle*. The inside article proclaimed he was the epitome of an "Adonis with a heart of gold and a darker purpose." He dressed and spoke poorly, but his polite, soft-spoken manners made girls swoon. No one could figure him out. That was his appeal and ultimately caused his loneliness.

JAN. 19: Elvis recorded the sensational "Blueberry Hill" (written by Al Lewis, Larry Stock, and Vincent Rose) at Radio Recorders and take No. 9 was released by RCA only in album form. Recordings by Glenn Miller, Gene Autry, Louis Armstrong, and Fats Domino made the song popular by 1956. On January 19, take No. 15 was the best of "Have I Told You Lately That I Love You" (by Scott Wiseman). With its flip side "Mean Woman Blues" it was released in October 1957 (RCA 47-7066). Elvis also finished Faron Young's "Is It So Strange," with take No. 12 released by RCA in LP and EP formats. "It Is No Secret (What God Can Do)" by Stuart Hamblen, included on the EP *Peace in the Valley* (take No. 13), was also recorded.

JAN. 20: Hal B. Wallis observed Gladys Presley's possessive and jealous nature. Whether it was on purpose or by mistake, he decided to allow Gladys and Vernon to appear in an audience scene during the shooting of *Loving You* in which Elvis bumped and grinded out "Got a Lot o' Livin' to Do" to a predominantly female crowd of worshiping fans. This was Gladys's only screen appearance.

JAN. 21: Elvis began Paramount's *Loving You*, directed and written by Hal Kanter and produced by Hal B. Wallis. It costarred Lizabeth Scott, Wendell Corey, and Delores Hart. The Jordanaires and the Blue Moon Boys provided vocal and musical backups.

During the filming Elvis dated Rita Moreno, and Sal Mineo visited Elvis on the set. Debra Paget supposedly "resisted his [Elvis's] charm despite a proposal of marriage." (See *The Elvis Album.*) The film was hyped as "Mr. Rock 'n' Roll in the story he was born to play." During the filming, Wallis decided the Ken Darby Trio should replace Scotty Moore and Bill Black as Elvis's band. Wallis did not want "Southern hillbillies" to ruin the film's image. Typically, Elvis did not defend those who had helped him make it to the top and allowed Darby's trio to replace the two men who had been with him from the beginning. The Colonel went along with Wallis's decision because he felt Scotty and Bill were getting too close to Elvis.

Love Me Tender and James Dean's *Giant* (with Elizabeth Taylor and Rock Hudson) were the top-grossing films of 1956. Gladys would not watch *Love Me Tender* because Elvis's character died in the movie and Gladys could not stomach that possibility even in fiction.

JAN. 24: Knowing Elvis was to cut "Teddy Bear," the Colonel lied and told reporters Elvis collected teddy bears which prompted fans to send thousands to add to his nonexistent collection. Elvis donated truckloads of teddy bears to the National Foundation for Infantile Paralysis, and during the rest of his career he tossed stuffed teddies to audience members. "Loving You" and "Mean Woman Blues" were also popular numbers from *Love Me Tender*.

At Hollywood's Radio Recorders, Elvis recorded Dave Bartholomew and Pearl King's "One Night of Sin" (not released until 1983 on the LP *Elvis—A Legendary Performer*, Vol. 4). He may have played the piano for this version. On the 1983 LP, the lyrics speak about paying for one night of sin (recorded for LPs on Feb. 23, 1957). A "clean" version was recorded January 24, and during its seventeen weeks on *Billboard*'s Hot 100 chart, it reached No. 4, also No. 10 on R&B and No. 24 on the Country charts (RCA 20-7410, released in October 1957).

Elvis also recorded "Teddy Bear" (by Kal Mann and Bernie Lowe) for *Loving You*, which he would also sing for the CBS-TV 1977 special "Elvis in Concert." The million-seller "Teddy Bear" was No. 1 for seven out of twenty-four weeks on *Billboard*'s Top 100 chart, and No. 1 on the R&B and Country charts for one week. With "Don't Be Cruel" and "Jailhouse Rock," "Teddy Bear" was the only other single to hit No. 1 on all three charts (RCA 20-7000, released in June 1957, with the flip side "Loving You").

JAN. 30:   Executives for NBC-TV's "Kraft Television Theatre" asked Elvis to star in *The Singing Idol*, but the Colonel refused to let Elvis play the part, which obviously hit too close to home for the Colonel. In the film, Tommy Sands portrayed a singer named Ewell Walker (an Elvis clone), who is controlled by his evil manager and is kept far away from his roots. Sands sang "Teen-Age Crush" (which sold over 1 million records) and "Hep Dee Hootie."

JAN.–APR.:   Yvonne Lime was one of Elvis's steady dates, but he also spent time with the sweet and charming Dolores Hart. Hart retired from films in 1963 after making ten movies and became a nun. She is Mother Dolores at the Regina Laudis in Bethlehem, Connecticut. In 1959, *Photoplay* published Hart's article, "What It's Like to Kiss Elvis." Despite rumors to the contrary, Hart and Elvis were not a serious item. During *Loving You* he also dated starlet Lizabeth Scott. Many movie insiders thought Scott was "a threat" to the single Elvis.

FEB.:   An Elvis Presley board game was created by the Colonel.

FEB. 23:   "Don't Leave Me Now" written by Aaron Schroeder and Ben Weisman was recorded twice by Elvis, on February 23 and on April 30, 1957. The February take No. 29 is on the *Loving You* LP, recorded at Radio Recorders. Elvis recorded "Hot Dog" by Leiber-Stoller and sang it three times in *Loving You*. "I Beg of You" by Rose Marie McCoy and Kelly Owens was also recorded on Feb. 23. Released in January 1958, it was on *Billboard*'s Top 100 list for twelve weeks and reached No. 12, while reaching No. 4 on R&B and No. 2 on the Country charts (RCA 20-7150). "I Need You So" by Ivory Joe Hunter, take No. 8, was recorded and released on the EP *Just for You* and the LP *Loving You*. Elvis also recorded "True Love" and take No. 20 was released on RCA's *Loving You* LP and the EP *Loving You*, Vol. 1.

FEB. 24:   Principal O. T. Freeman warned the all-female student body at the Wichita Falls Senior High School in Kansas that the school would not "tolerate Elvis Presley records . . . blue jeans, or ducktail hairdos." In defiance, many of the students rushed to buy every possible Elvis record and product available.

FEB. 24–25:   Elvis recorded "Lonesome Cowboy" by Sid Tepper and Roy C. Bennett, and two versions of Mae Robinson's "Party," for *Loving You* at Radio Recorders. No single was released. The Leiber-Stoller title song for *Loving You* was completed on February 24 by Elvis and take No. 21 was released. "Loving You" peaked at No. 24 on *Billboard*'s Top 100 chart during a twenty-two-week run. With its flip side, "Teddy Bear," "Loving You" was No. 1 for one of eight weeks on the Country chart and No. 1 on the R&B chart for one week before Jerry Lee Lewis's "Whole Lotta Shakin' Goin' On" replaced it. The "Teddy Bear"/"Loving You" single was the first to be distributed and sold in Great Britain, selling over 1 million copies (RCA 20-7000, released in June 1957).

Elvis recorded "When It Rains, It Really Pours" (written by William Robert Emerson) at Radio Recorders. He had attempted to record the song in July 1955, but wasn't pleased with the takes. Take No. 8 from the February 24 session was released on the LPs *Elvis for Everyone* and *Reconsider Baby*.

MAR. 2: Gladys and Vernon Presley took the train from Hollywood to Memphis. On March 5, while driving through the southern part of Memphis called Whitehaven with real estate broker Virginia Grant, they spotted the house of their dreams. Graceland was a twenty-three-room limestone and brick mansion badly in need of repair, secluded and set back from the street on 13.8 acres.

Graceland was named in the late 1930s after Grace Toof, the aunt of its builder, Dr. Thomas Moore. The land upon which Graceland is built had been a farm during the Civil War. The mansion is located at 3764 Elvis Presley Boulevard (previously Highway 51 South), Memphis, Tennessee 38116. It had previously been operated as the Graceland Christian Church.

MAR. 3: Elvis discussed playing the part of James Dean in a movie called *The James Dean Story*. The Colonel turned down the project as an Elvis vehicle because Warner Brothers was planning to film it as a documentary.

MAR. 5–6: Gladys and Vernon showed Elvis Graceland and told him to buy it. At first, Elvis was uncertain he could maintain the mansion. He talked with Liberace, who applauded the purchase. Elvis thought the property could provide seclusion and privacy. Gladys, in particular, could no longer tolerate being called "poor white trash" by Audubon neighbors. Elvis felt a change—far from the maddening crowd—would be healthy for all of them. The move was, in fact, a hindrance of sorts, but Elvis viewed it as a chance to show the world he had finally attained class.

Within the confines of Graceland, life became illusory, even more isolated, and Gladys was even lonelier.

MAR. 7: Elvis outbid the YMCA with its $35,000 offer to buy Graceland by tell-

ing the owner, musician Ruth Moore, he would pay $102,500. His real estate broker, Virginia Grant, was shocked that he paid that price, but happy to make the commission. It would become his rock 'n' roll palace.

MAR. 8: To buy a refuge from the outside world, Elvis paid $40,000 in cash; another $25,500 came from the $55,000 sale of the Audubon house; and Elvis secured a $37,000 note with Equitable Life at 4 percent. Promising Gladys that he would convert Graceland into a huge farm where she could raise chickens (she wanted to collect eggs without paying for them!) and where all their relatives could find sanctuary, Elvis's pledge rekindled a short-lived happiness in Gladys.

Immediately redesigning aspects of the two-story structure to suit his tastes, Elvis added pillars to the front of Graceland, and a tall, ornate, double iron Music Gate at the driveway's entrance decorated with musical notes and guitars (which Hank Williams had done at one of his properties years before). Over the years, Elvis added a thick wall of Alabama fieldstone, a private recording studio, several recre-

▲ Graceland. *Courtesy of the author's collection.*

ation rooms, a barn, garages, racquet ball courts, horse stables with fenced-in fields, chicken coops, vegetable gardens, and a forty-foot-long trophy room.

Elvis garishly decorated his new home with lavish velvets, gold trims, mirrors, shag carpets, and ostentatious, cheap furniture. He originally painted parts of the mansion glow-in-the-dark gold and blue, and he flooded the edifice with pale blue lights at night. He planned to make his bedroom a dark blue with one mirrored wall. He wanted to decorate the entrance hall with a facsimile sky—clouds painted on the ceiling for daytime, little lights that blinked for stars at night (an idea from Liberace). As his whims (or women) changed, so did the decor and Graceland's huge staff.

Only four entertainers are reported to have seen Elvis's upstairs bedroom: Brian Wilson of the Beach Boys, Bill Medley of the Righteous Brothers, singer Roy Hamilton, and actor Nick Adams. Hundreds of young women were sighted going in and out at all hours of the night, even when Priscilla lived in the mansion, and all the members of Elvis's entourage came and went as they pleased.

MAR. 12:　The Colonel proved he was in control of Elvis, despite Elvis's purchase of Graceland without his permission. Parker filled Elvis's schedule with out-of-town engagements and negotiated new high-salaried film deals for the Cat.

MAR. 18:　The atmosphere at Graceland soon resembled a human zoo. Elvis said any member of the Memphis Mafia, reliving the youth they never had, could live at Graceland (in tents, trailers, mobile homes, in the basement), where they would play football, ride motorcycles, wrestle, swim, sing gospels in the music room, eat junk food to their heart's desire, bed as many women as possible (after Gladys was sound asleep), watch television and

movies, play pool and racquet ball, barbecue, and capture the innocent hearts of girls during Elvis's Bible readings in the parlor!

Charlie Hodge moved to Graceland and stayed seventeen years. Along with Hodge, Alan Fortas, Lamar Fike, Red and Sonny West, band members, backup singers, and a variety of musicians, bodyguards, and starlets lived at Graceland (on and off, or in back of the main house) and continuously surrounded Elvis (day and night), which upset Gladys. She was no longer the center of Elvis's world.

Uncles Travis Smith and Vester Presley became gatekeepers with the primary responsibility of keeping hundreds of fans from crawling over the walls to invade the Presleys' "privacy."

CA. MAR. 21:　RCA presented Elvis with a gold-lamé suit.

MAR. 25:　Marine Hershel Nixon claimed Elvis pulled a toy pistol on him at the Salvation Army's USO at 174 North Third, Memphis.

MAR. 27:　Elvis and his band flew to Chicago.

MAR. 28:　After Elvis's concert at the International Amphitheater in Chicago, the audience went out of control. Chicago's Catholic archbishop, Samuel Cardinal Stritch, sent a letter to the huge Catholic constituency in Chicago that denounced rock 'n' roll as "tribal rhythms."

MAR. 29:　Elvis performed at the Kiel Auditorium in St. Louis in the gold-lamé suit recently presented to him by RCA (designed by Nudie Cohen of Nudie's Rodeo Tailors, Hollywood). The outlandish outfit started a trend-setting uproar. A fan was so taken with his new look she stole the golden shoelaces out of the King's $1,000 gold shoes.

As his tour progressed, rumors regarding the price of his gold tuxedo grew. The *Fort Wayne News Sentinel* reported the jacket cost $2,000. In Canada, the suit's value climbed to $4,000. By 1960, the suit was said to have cost $10,000. A person could have purchased six new cars for that amount in 1957. Calling his costuming a gimmick that reinforced his notorious nature, critics had a heyday with Elvis's lamé look, and some reporters seemed to resent the young singer's confidence and bold dress code, while others thought he looked and acted "too black."

MAR. 30: The *St. Louis Post-Dispatch* reviewed Elvis's ostentatious golden look: "Elvis Presley, shimmering in sequins and metallic gold cloth, writhed and sang last night in Kiel Auditorium convention hall before a capacity crowd of about 11,000 spectators. . . . Rhinestones embedded even in the laces of his gold-colored, raised-heel shoes added to the dazzling sight. Girls screamed and hundreds of flashbulbs were discharged, making the hall look as if it were under an artillery barrage. . . . His contortions were ecstatically received."

Australian promoter Lee Gordon said the gold suit had cost $2,500. "It's real gold, with impregnated unborn-calf skin, or something of the sort," he jeered. "He looked like a young man being dutifully attentive to his fans, who have provided him with a life as golden as his suit."

MAR. 30: Wearing gold lamé, Elvis nearly caused a riot with his performance in Fort Wayne, Indiana.

MAR. 31: Elvis wore gold lamé during his two concerts at Detroit's Olympia Stadium.

MAR. 31: Terri Taylor claimed that on this date she conceived Elvis's child, which was born December 22, 1957. Elvis sent her flowers when the child was born.

APRIL: *Harper's* correctly observed, "From a strictly Marxist-Leninist viewpoint, he [Elvis] is a typical example of capitalist exploitation." From Colonel Parker's point of view, that was the beauty of it all.

APR. 1: Performing in his gold-lamé jacket, Elvis wowed a huge audience in Buffalo, New York.

APR. 2: Elvis gave two shows at the Maple Leaf Garden in Toronto, Canada, where he sang "Butterfly" by Bernie Low and Kal Mann. Wearing lamé jackets and touring with his matching gold Cadillac, Elvis's minitour caused thunderous, often dangerously wild responses. His popularity had grown too rapidly, and security guards could not hold back zealous fans from mobbing the superstar. In Buffalo, New York, Ottawa and Toronto, Canada, and Philadelphia, teenagers destroyed auditoriums, tore off each other's clothing, or pushed and shoved to stand close to Elvis. One reviewer shuddered: "The trouble with going to see Elvis Presley is that you're liable to get killed. . . . When he made his grand entrance, pandemonium broke loose and carnage waited in the wings. . . . He was asked whether he worried about his popularity waning. 'If they forget me, I'll just have to do something worth remembering,' he said. . . . [He wore] a gold jacket, gold shoes, and a gold string tie, [and] dashed onstage to the hysterical shrieks of unleashed bedlam." (See *Elvis Album*.)

APR. 3: Elvis gave two shows in Ottawa, under heavy police guard. Ottawa's Notre Dame Convent for Girls forced its students to boycott Elvis's Canadian show. Thousands of young women responded in anger, which resulted in the *Hit Parader*'s contest for some "lucky" girl to win a date with Elvis. They received thousands of replies.

APR. 5–6: Elvis performed two shows nightly at the Sports Arena in Philadelphia to wild, chanting crowds.

APR. 9: Elvis's wardrobe was becoming as wild and lavish as his performance. At the Municipal Auditorium, in Wichita Falls, Texas, the guards wondered if the lamé suit was really solid gold. It was difficult keeping thieves from Elvis's dressing room.

APR. 10: "All Shook Up" was No. 1 on *Billboard*'s Top 100 chart for eight weeks (the longest-running Elvis record at No. 1).

CA. APR. 13: Elvis and his entourage arrived by train in California and prepared to shoot *Jailhouse Rock* in Culver City. Elvis played the part of Vince Everett, a two-bit punk with a bad attitude who reformed in prison and became a singing sensation. Elvis's part was advertised as "his first big dramatic singing role. Elvis Presley at his greatest."

As a decent punk who rocked "lean and mean," Elvis choreographed the wild dance number seen during his rendition of the title song. It was his first and last attempt at choreography.

APR. 14: Elvis met with *Jailhouse Rock* composers Jerry Leiber and Mike Stoller. They were impressed with Elvis's craftsmanship and knowledge about black music. Stoller remembered: "Between takes, Elvis would go to the piano and play a few simple chords and sing hymns. Or he'd rap his guitar." (See *Life*, Dec. 1, 1992.)

APR. 19: Actress Yvonne Lime visited Elvis during Easter week and they posed together for the press outside Graceland.

APR. 28: Elvis had become rich beyond his wildest dreams and a god to some of his more obsessive fans. His life was not his own anymore. To protect himself and feel comfortable, he formed his own "country club" (the Memphis Mafia) a circle of salaried bodyguards and companions to watch over, comfort, and basically agree with him. The main entourage included Red and Sonny West, Lamar Fike, George Klein, Army buddies Joe Esposito and Charlie Hodge, Dave Hebler, his cousin Gee Gee Gambill, and others. Watching over *them* like hawks were the Colonel and Vernon Presley.

Producers, actors, and the press were disturbed by the "low-class" behavior of Elvis's entourage. In a moment of disgust, film director Philip Dunne labeled them Elvis's "fart catchers." Not only did the boys step in when anyone had anything negative to say to Elvis on a set, they jumped to fill his every demand and in doing so disrupted film shoots.

APR. 30: The instrumentals for Leiber and Stoller's "(You're So Square) Baby, I Don't Care" for *Jailhouse Rock* were laid down at Radio Recorders, and Elvis recorded the vocals a few days later. Dudley Brooks played the piano for rehearsals, and Stoller played for the take used on the record. The second recording of "Don't Leave Me Now" (see February 23) was for *Jailhouse Rock*, in which Elvis sang the song three times, and take No. 11 of Leiber-Stoller's "I Want to Be Free" was released. "Jailhouse Rock" was recorded by Elvis, but no one knows for certain who played the piano on the released take No. 6. It was either Mike Stoller (who had a bit part in the film as a pianist) or Dudley Brooks.

On the chart twenty-seven weeks, "Jailhouse Rock" entered *Billboard*'s Top 100 chart at No. 15 and leaped to No. 1 in three weeks (where it stayed for seven weeks). It sold over 3 million records within twelve months and entered as No. 1 (a first!) on England's charts (RCA 20-7035, released in September 1957). Its flip side was "Treat Me Nice" by Leiber-Stoller (the movie's version was recorded on April 30 and the single's version on September 5). Elvis recorded twenty-three takes of "Young and Beautiful" (written by Abner Silver and Aaron Schroeder) for *Jailhouse Rock.*

MAY 13: Elvis began filming MGM's *Jailhouse Rock* earning 50 percent of its gross profits plus a $250,000 salary. It was directed by Richard Thorpe, produced by Pandro S. Berman, and costarred Judy Tyler, Mickey Shaughnessy, Vaughn Taylor, Jennifer Holden, and Dean Jones. Scotty Moore, Bill Black, D. J. Fontana, and Mike Stoller (piano) formed the band.

MAY 14: Hollywood was not prepared for the odd eating, sleeping, and late-night habits of Elvis and his Memphis boys. Staffers for the kitchen during *Jailhouse Rock* had to restock the refrigerators with mashed potatoes, dark brown gravy, crisp bacon, peanut butter, and apple pies. Elvis was a junk-food addict.

Elvis was rushed to Cedars of Lebanon Hospital, California, with chest pains after inhaling a porcelain cap from one of his teeth during a dance number in *Jailhouse Rock.* (Elvis had a habit of sucking on the caps.)

MAY 15: Gladys had Graceland completely renovated to surprise Elvis upon his return from Hollywood. Her changes included a white shag carpet, pure white walls, strange-looking fabrics, and long drapes at every window. Gladys had also added a chicken coop and hog pen behind Graceland. Vernon had taken up gardening and learning to cook vegetables and fruits.

MAY 20: Gladys was discontented in the huge mansion. Its rooms were too empty. Elvis was always gone. She missed the porch parties in East Tupelo. At Graceland, she was stranded with her chickens and she hated living in isolation.

By March, Gladys developed a severe liver ailment associated with cirrhosis. She had gallstones, suffered from nausea and deep despair, and became dependent on vodka and diet pills in efforts to drown her sorrows and lose weight. Poor health, emotional distress, and worrying about Elvis's safety cheated her of enjoying her son's celebrity. She coveted what he could no longer give her: time. Whenever she saw Elvis, he was dashing from place to place, followed by the Memphis Mafia. She warned if Elvis didn't slow down, he would die before he was thirty.

MAY 29: Debuting in *Jailhouse Rock* was the voluptuous Jennifer Holden, who had a three-minute love scene with Elvis, which took four hours to shoot. Elvis and Holden became close friends, and when a small heater ignited a fire in her dressing room, the valiant Elvis carried his leading lady to safety.

JUNE: A manufacturer of shortwave radios, Hallicrafters, distributed a promo sampler of shortwave radio broadcasts that included "Loving You" by Elvis ("The Amazing World of Shortwave Radio," Hallicrafters N2MW-4434).

▲ A Delphi collector's plate from the "Elvis Presley: Looking at a Legend" series featuring "Jailhouse Rock." *Courtesy of the Bradford Exchange.*

JUNE 2: Elvis dated starlets, including Ann Neyland. The crew of *Jailhouse Rock* spread rumors that Elvis was in love with Jennifer Holden.

JUNE 10: A rumor spread in Hollywood that Elvis was planning to get rid of the Colonel. Parker quickly made certain everyone knew that could *never* happen and took even tighter control over Elvis's life. The Colonel was not liked in Hollywood, but he did not care if he was appreciated or hated by outsiders.

JUNE 14: *Jailhouse Rock* was completed but Elvis was not comfortable with the result. The movie's plot focused on the one issue that had been kept undisclosed in the Presley mystique: a young rebel is imprisoned at the same age Vernon was sent to prison. This hit a little too close to home for Elvis, and during some scenes, his behavior was unbearable. In *Elvis, What Happened?* Red West stated firmly Elvis's ego and temper went out of control (which no one had seen before). West alleged they shared everything up until *Jailhouse Rock*, even women, but after the film Elvis expected to be treated as "special." It annoyed everyone around him and caused friction.

JUNE 15: Gladys turned Graceland into a tomb when she heard Elvis was taking a twelve-day vacation in Biloxi and would stay at the Sea and Sand Hotel with the Memphis Mafia. She was not invited. She drank herself into oblivion and did not take the medications prescribed for her by Dr. Evans. Alcohol made an already acute liver disorder worse. The Presleys did not tell Dr. Evans of Gladys's drinking problem because the doctor might have spoken to the press. Sadly, Elvis's career was put before all else.

JUNE 28: "All Shook Up" was recorded at Radio Recorders in Hollywood, with Scotty Moore, D. J. Fontana, Bill Black, Dudley Brooks (piano), and backup vocals by the Jordanaires. Words and music were credited to Otis Blackwell and Elvis with a copyright of 1957, Unart Music Corporation (but Elvis did not write the song).

JULY: Elvis purchased the white Knabe piano (white with gold-leaf trim, not to be confused with the gold-leaf 1928 Kimball grand piano) he liked so much from the Ellis Auditorium and bought them a new grand piano.

JULY 3: During the shooting of *Jailhouse Rock*, Elvis became friends with starlet Judy Tyler, who played the part of Peggy Van Alden. When Tyler (age twenty-four) and her husband (Gregory Lafayette) were killed in a Wyoming automobile accident on July 3, 1957, Elvis went into a state of shock. Kenny Baker recorded "Good-bye Little Star" as a tribute to Tyler's tragic death. Elvis did nothing but grieve. He told his father, "Nothing has hurt me as bad in my life. . . . All of us boys really loved that girl. . . . She meant a lot to all of us. I don't believe I can stand to see the movie we made together now, just don't believe I can." (*Memphis Commercial Appeal*.)

JULY 5: Helen Parmeler of the *Ottawa Journal* wrote: "[Elvis's] contortionist exhibition at the Auditorium was the closest to the jungle I'll ever get."

JULY 9: The Presleys, Elvis, and Anita Wood attended the midnight showing of the premiere of *Loving You* at the Strand Theater in Memphis.

CA. JULY 10: Vernon was rarely at Graceland during the summer. He may have been having an affair. Elvis's career was so demanding, he, too, had become a stranger at Graceland.

JULY 24: Elvis attended a Blackwood Brothers concert.

In *Lost on Tour* Elvis spoke fondly of the Blackwood Brothers, who were all members of his Memphis church. Elvis habitually visited the Brothers backstage at Memphis's Ellis Auditorium, where the Blackwoods hosted all-night gospel sings. Elvis told how gospel music calmed his nerves and relaxed him enough to go to sleep after a concert: "After we've done two shows . . . we'll go upstairs . . . and just sing 'til daylight . . . gospel music. . . . [It] puts your mind at ease. . . . Otherwise you couldn't sleep. . . . It takes at least four or five hours just to unwind. . . . Back when I was fifteen . . . I was a big gospel music fan, we'd listen all night. . . . One of the secrets [is] not to let 'um get old."

JULY 27: Charles O'Curran worked with Elvis for Paramount and claimed Elvis chose "Teddy Bear" and the rest of the songs in *Loving You*. O'Curran appreciated the fact Elvis was still "unspoiled and unaffected." (*Melody Maker*, July 27, 1957.) That would soon change.

During this period, Elvis felt like "a visitor" in Hollywood. Actors were polite to him, but they refused to accept him as an equal. Although publicist Stan Brossette was under pressure to force Elvis to attend Hollywood functions, he rarely went. He brought his own continuous party with him from Memphis.

"Teddy Bear" hit No. 1 on *Billboard*'s Top 100 chart for seventeen weeks. It remained on the chart for a total of twenty-four weeks. It was No. 1 for one week on both the R&B and Country charts. With "Jailhouse Rock" and "Don't Be Cruel" it was one of three songs of Elvis's to hit all three charts. It sold well over a million records.

JULY: Elvis was on the covers of *Photoplay*, *TV Life*, and *Star Parade*.

JULY–AUG.: Elvis and Dewey Phillips of WHBQ had a falling out. Elvis could no longer tolerate Dewey's "low-class" behavior, and Dewey felt Elvis had become a Hollywood snob. There was some truth in both men's opinions.

AUG.: Tennessee governor Buford Ellington conferred the honorary title of "colonel" on Elvis. "Colonel" Parker was *not* amused. Elvis thought it was hilarious.

To refute rock 'n' roll's surge forward, the middle class ran to record stores to make hits of Paul Anka's "Put Your Head on My Shoulder" and "High Hopes."

AUG. 27: Elvis prepared to travel to Spokane, Washington's Memorial Stadium to begin a tour through the Pacific Northwest and Canada from which he would earn $147,000 per performance. The Colonel told Elvis not to take so many "aides" on the tour because it cost too much. Elvis promised he would try to cut down on expenses. His dedication and allegiance to the cutthroat, often abusive, and certainly restrictive Colonel was puzzling to outsiders. But his manager had kept from the public the deep, dark secret of Vernon's prison stint and Gladys's addictions to drugs and alcohol. If the press knew the truth, the Colonel kept reminding Elvis, it could devastate and possibly end Elvis's career. If used as a blackmail tactic, perhaps this was the clandestine detail that kept Elvis loyal to his Svengali-like manager.

AUG. 30: The stadium literally shook when twelve thousand fans went wild during Elvis's concert at the Memorial Stadium in Spokane, Washington. Elvis, dressed in a gold jacket, collapsed to his knees, playing to pink footlights that illuminated his pouting sneer. As the audience became wild, police and reporters became hostile, and stadium officials tried to stop obsessed teenagers from stealing clumps of soil from the infield.

AUG. 31: Elvis sang over screams in the Empire Stadium in Vancouver, British Columbia. Police and air cadets could not control the audience, and by the end of the evening, girls were carried out unconscious, fistfights erupted, and teens battled police officers for a chance to touch Elvis. The *Spokane Review* wrote: "Presley Whips 12,000 into Near Hysteria . . . youngsters . . . were stealing soil from the stadium infield. Presley's feet had touched it."

AUG. 31: In an interview with Red Robinson at the Empire Stadium in Vancouver, Elvis talked of his love for football and especially the Cleveland Browns (his favorite team). In this same interview, Elvis said Pat Boone was "the finest voice out now, especially on slow songs."

Unfair criticism and unkind remarks from other top entertainers seemed to upset Elvis almost more than all else. Once Bob Hope joked about Elvis's fortune with an audience member who yelled, "How much does Elvis Presley make?" Hope replied, "Are you kiddin'? When he started, he couldn't spell *Tennessee.* Now, he owns it!" Hedda Hopper defended Elvis by stating, "He owns twenty-six gold records! It's an all-time record!" Elvis tried to take it all in stride, but it did bother him.

Mobs poured onto the stage after Elvis's concert at the Empire Stadium where critics accused Elvis of purposely whipping the audience into a frenzy. Teenagers battled police, and many were charged with disorderly conduct.

SEPT. 1: Elvis's concert at the Tacoma Stadium in Tacoma, Washington, was packed with hysterical women and their impatient boyfriends. Parents complained Elvis's behavior had a negative, violent impact on their children. As stage lights flashed on and off, many teenagers passed out and were

carried backstage. Rock 'n' roll was here to stay.

SEPT. 2: Elvis played to unruly crowds in Seattle's Rainier Ballpark.

SEPT. 3: Elvis's two explosive shows at the Multomah Stadium in Portland, Oregon, ended in chaos. His presence in a gold-lamé, sequined suit before fourteen thousand people caused bedlam and such a loud roar, few could hear him sing.

SEPT. 4: Twentieth Century-Fox talked again to Elvis and the Colonel about the possibility of Elvis's playing a lead comedy role opposite sex kitten Jayne Mansfield in *The Love Maniac.* Elvis liked the idea, but the film was never made.

SEPT. 5–7: Elvis recorded songs for the LP *Elvis' Christmas Album* with backup singer Mildred Kirkham of the Jordanaires. This album was inspired by the Colonel's belief that his boy needed to show the public he was a loving, devout, conscientious Christian. The album's songs included "Santa Claus Is Back in Town," "White Christmas," "Here Comes Santa Claus," "I'll Be Home for Christmas," "Blue Christmas," "Santa Bring My Baby Back," "O Little Town of Bethlehem," "Silent Night," "Peace in the Valley," "I Believe," "Take My Hand, Precious Lord," and "It Is No Secret." The LP was so popular it was reissued in 1958 and again in November 1970.

SEPT. 5: The No. 3 take of Elvis's version of "Blue Christmas" was sung at Radio Recorders. The single was released years later in November of 1964 (RCA 447-0720) with the flip side "Wooden Heart." The single's version of "Treat Me Nice" was No. 15, recorded on September 5. The million seller reached No. 27 on *Billboard*'s Top 100 chart during a ten-week run; was No. 1 on the R&B chart for five weeks; it reached No. 1 on the Country chart during a nine-week stay (RCA 20-7035, released in September 1957). Its flip side was "Jailhouse Rock."

SEPT. 6: Although many takes were done of "My Wish Came True" (Jan. 23, 1958, Feb. 1, 1958), take No. 28 from September 6 was released by RCA. Elvis's version reached No. 12 during an eleven-week stay on *Billboard*'s Top 100 chart. Its flip side was "Big Hunk o' Love" (RCA 47-7600).

Elvis asked Leiber-Stoller to write "Don't." Elvis wanted it flawless. Advance orders climbed over 1 million for the song (RCA 20-7150). Take No. 7 out of twenty-six was used. "Silent Night" was also recorded that night and was backed by Dudley Brooks on piano and "Millie" Kirkham on vocals. It was the first time Elvis used a woman as a major voice in recording sessions. Take No. 9 of "Silent Night" was released. After this session, Elvis was exhausted. "Don't" was No. 1 on the Top 100 chart and remained on the chart for twenty weeks. It was No. 4 on R&B and No. 2 on the Country charts. The flip side of "Don't" was "I Beg of You."

RCA selected take No. 2 of "Here Comes Santa Claus (Right Down Santa Claus Lane)" for release after Elvis recorded it on September 6. No single was made of Elvis's version.

"White Christmas" (written in 1942 by Irving Berlin for the film *Holiday Inn*) was recorded by Elvis based on the Drifters' 1954 record (Atlantic 1048). Bing Crosby was furious that Elvis sang "his" song. Take No. 9 was released on the LP *Elvis' Christmas Album* and was criticized as too raunchy to play on the radio! It also appears on the EP *Christmas With Elvis*.

SEPT. 7: "I'll Be Home for Christmas" was recorded by Elvis at Radio Recorders. Take No. 15 was released by RCA. He also completed "O Little Town of Bethlehem." Take No. 4 was used on the EP *Christmas with Elvis*

and the LP *Elvis' Christmas Album*. Take No. 9 of "Santa, Bring My Baby Back" was included on the EP *Elvis Sings Christmas Songs* and the LP *Elvis' Christmas Album*. Take No. 7 of "Santa Claus Is Back in Town" (a Leiber-Stoller song written for Elvis) was released on an uncharted single with the flip side "Blue Christmas" (RCA 447-0647, released in November 1965). It was reissued with "Merry Christmas Baby" as its flip side (RCA PB-14327, released in November 1985).

SEPT. 17: Vancouver music critic Dr. Ida Halpern reviewed the Cat's concert there: "The performance had not even the quality of true obscenity, merely an artificial and unhealthy exploitation of the enthusiasm of youth's body and mind."

SEPT. 22–27: Scotty Moore and Bill Black left Elvis's tour (coming back 1960–68) because of low salaries and no credit. They played for three more recording sessions.

SEPT. 27: Elvis gave one smashing concert at Tupelo's Mississippi-Alabama Fair and Dairy Show, to benefit the Elvis Presley Youth Recreation Center. He wore a gold-lamé jacket with tiny beads at the cuffs and lapels, but preferred regular black pants to the more cumbersome lamé slacks, which stuck to his skin whenever he perspired.

SEPT. 28: Elvis's first LP was No. 1 on *Billboard*'s extended-play-album chart six weeks out of its sixty-eight weeks on the chart, from September 28, 1957 to January 10, 1959.

OCT. 17: The Presleys attended the Memphis premiere of *Jailhouse Rock* in Memphis. Elvis played a convict, yet the jacket of the album stated Elvis's "style shows more than a little gospel influence." The film grossed $4 million in twelve months.

OCT. 23: Elvis was interviewed by George Klein on WHBQ, Memphis.

OCT. 26: Thousands of young people bought tickets to see one of two Presley shows at the Civic Auditorium in Oakland, California. Outside the concert, teens held signs that told adults to stop attacking "the King."

One important key to Elvis's popularity was that his teenage fans believed the adult world was purposely trying to destroy anything *they* liked independently. Elvis allowed them to be themselves. Teens felt the adult world and its staunch critics did not accept or care about their wants, desires, or beliefs, *but* Elvis *did* and that endeared him to millions of frustrated teenagers. One sympathetic reviewer later remembered Elvis's performances in *Movie Teen Illustrated* (1962): "You can't win every last person in an audience unless you have warmth. To a natural warmth, Elvis adds genuineness. He makes you believe him. . . . The sexy, passionate voice that makes a song an individual allurement to every girl listener gets across the same feeling when delivering dialogue in the movies. Elvis comes right out of the screen for every girl in the audience. When he holds a girl in a romantic scene and when he kisses her, he's holding and kissing every girl in the theater. . . . Top director Don Siegel . . . calls Elvis electric with no reference to the wire on his guitar. . . . Siegel says Elvis has the same magnetism that still draws people to the grave of Rudolph Valentino."

OCT. 28: At his Pan-Pacific Auditorium concert in Los Angeles, Elvis let loose, as if he were liberating himself from his more insipid film roles. As the rebel surfaced one more time, Elvis was blasted for acting out obscene gestures onstage, such as rolling around on the floor with "Nipper," a statue of the NBC dog. No one had ever seen a white performer move like Elvis. It was outrageous. He opened jaded, star-studded eyes in Los Angeles, even though he knew it would cost him respect at home. After the concert ended, he innocently told the press he was "in a trance" and couldn't account for his actions during a performance. He gave his soul to rock 'n' roll! No Elvis disciple could ask for more.

Elvis was cocky and sure of himself, and his lamé outfit caused audiences to screech out of control. One fan was mesmerized for years by his glamour and wrote in *Movie Teen Illustrated* (April 1962): "Just his name fires up a party. [He wore] a sparkling golden suit . . . the center of the universe. . . . His performance that night was one of his greatest."

The timid boy who once bought secondhand clothes on Beale Street was now starting fashion trends. First, he caused a national fervor for blue jeans. Later in his career he introduced and made popular bell-bottom pants and jumpsuits and open-throat shirts studded with jewels and lined with gold. Teenage boys across the world started to grow their hair long and—if they couldn't grow sideburns—glued on Colonel Parker's paste-ons. However, RCA's exorbitant gold-lamé tuxedo caused the largest sensation until Elvis's later Las Vegas extravaganzas. In the fifties, the gold-lamé tux was the most costly outfit in rock 'n' roll.

OCT. 29: For his second night at the Pan-Pacific Auditorium in Los Angeles, Elvis *did* give his fans more to cheer, including Cher, who was in the audience.

Police and cameramen lined the Pan-Pacific stage anticipating chaos if Elvis disobeyed the authorities, who warned him not to provoke the audience with any sexy moves. Elvis diminished his movements to a twitch of a finger, and the audience still went berserk.

A Los Angeles reporter wrote an article, "Elvis Wiggles, Fans Scream at Pan-Pacific," and quoted Elvis saying he "yells" (not sings) at concerts. Even though Elvis was put on the defensive, when given the chance, he did *not* bash the popular, well-liked Sinatra, even though Old Blue Eyes had publicly knocked rock 'n' roll. Elvis's incorruptible essence of innocence emerged, and he conquered another reviewer when he purred, "I admire the man. He has the right to his own opinions. . . . You can't knock success."

OCT. 30: The Colonel was promoting Elvis's next stint, which would take place in Honolulu. Promotional items were circulated outside Elvis's hotel, and by the time the concert opened the Colonel had sold thousands of Elvis-related items. No bookkeeping for these merchandised items was shown to Elvis, and it is suspected by many that Parker pocketed millions of dollars without giving Elvis his fair share. The statement "It was brown-bagged" came from the Parker era, when money was stuffed into brown bags and carried off without declaring a dime to the IRS (or to Elvis).

NOV. 1: English singer Tommy Steele was nicknamed by the press "The English Elvis Presley."

Buddy Holly's "Peggy Sue" hit the *Billboard* Top 100 chart for nine weeks.

NOV. 1: Elvis and his entourage flew to Hawaii to rehearse for their extravagant show, complete with orchestra.

NOV. 8: *Jailhouse Rock* opened nationally.

NOV. 10: Elvis gave two shows at the Honolulu Stadium to sold-out, standing-room-only crowds.

NOV. 11: Elvis pleased crowds during his concert at the Schofield Barracks, Pearl Harbor, Hawaii. He and the boys partied until dawn with as many female fans as they could fit in their hotel rooms.

NOV. 21: In New York City, *Jailhouse Rock* caused riots in the streets. It grossed a profit within three weeks. That was another all-time first, unprecedented by any other actor or performer in the film world.

DEC.: Elvis was on the cover of *Hep Cats*.

Elvis, Sonny and Red West, a girl named Linda Mulinex, and several cousins played cards at the Rainbow Rollerdome in Memphis.

The releases of the LPs *Elvis Sings Christmas Songs* and *Elvis' Christmas Album* puzzled critics. Many disc jockeys refused to air his rendition of "White Christmas" (take No. 9, which was recorded in September 1957) because it sounded "too colored." Disc jockey Al Priddy was fired from Portland, Oregon's, KEX radio station after he dared to air the song. Disc jockey Dick Whittinghill of Los Angeles' KMPC radio told people that to play *any* Christmas song by Elvis would be as ludicrous as stripper Tempest Storm's giving presents to children. Fans across America banned together and bought every Christmas album they could find. Teenagers were proving they could censor the censors by doing exactly the opposite of what they were told.

DEC. 14: Elvis established the Elvis Presley Youth Recreation Center at the site of his birthplace, East Tupelo. Officials of the town forced Orville Bean to sell several plots of land to Elvis for $500, including the lot that Bean had forced Vernon to sell for a financial loss years before. What goes around comes around!

DEC. 17: Army and Navy recruiters met with Elvis at Graceland, offering him special status. Chief Petty Officer D. U. Stanley promised to shape the "Elvis Presley Company" with Memphis soldiers, the purpose of which would be to entertain the troops. Elvis passed, saying he would take his chances. The Colonel told Elvis there was *no* way he was going to sing "for nothing for the Army." Although it may have been a ploy of the Colonel's, Elvis's attitude affirms he probably welcomed being treated like any other soldier. He did not invite or accept exceptional privileges. He told the press he would miss his parents but that he was "kinda proud of it. It's a duty I've got to fill and I'm gonna do it." That strong and patriotic attitude endeared him to fans.

DEC. 18: Elvis told his parents he was going to put his singing and acting on hold to serve in the Army. The news ruined Christmas and Gladys sobbed for days. She feared Elvis would be killed, despite his reminders that there was *no* war.

DEC. 19: Elvis received his draft notice at Graceland from Memphis Draft Board #86 chairman Milton Bowers. That Christmas was spent setting off $1,800 worth of firecrackers. Elvis gave thousands of dollars to his aides and staff and spent as much time as possible surrounded by his entourage. In the background, his mother was fading. Elvis gave Gladys a pink lounging gown, but no gift could alleviate the pain she felt.

DEC. 20: When the reality of Elvis's going into the Army sank in, Gladys clutched her little Boston bulldog and told a friend she was "the most miserable woman in the world. . . . They won't let me see Elvis. They're always keeping him working somewhere or other. They're just tearing my boy's clothes off and we don't know if he's going to come back alive. . . . And now I can't even feed my chickens. It's supposed to be bad for his image." (See *Elvis and Gladys*).

DEC. 21: Fans sent letters by the basketful, begging Elvis to join the USO and entertain troops. The Army also requested Elvis join the Special Ser-

vices to perform in front of troops, free of charge for two years, but the Colonel refused to let that happen. No one hired Elvis for nothing, not even the government!

Parker flew to Washington, DC, to explain in detail to the commander of the Fifth Army (Lt. Gen. William H. Arnold) why Elvis should be "just one of the regular boys" and that "Elvis did not want to be treated in any special way." Although Elvis went along with whatever the Colonel said, the real reason his manager did not want him to become a performing soldier was because it would not pay.

The Colonel planned to release records during Elvis's tour of duty, to keep the home fires burning. Making $1 replicas of Elvis's Army dog tags, the Colonel showed everyone how to turn the Army into a lucrative business venture.

DEC. 21: While Elvis filmed *King Creole* for Paramount, its production chief (Frank Freeman) got a sixty-day Army deferment for Elvis, so he could finish the film. It was one of Elvis's best performances.

At a *King Creole* session, Elvis and his entourage sang spirituals until the noon break. Gordon Stoker said, "All these officials and technicians were standing around, just dying. . . . They came over to us and told us they were terribly upset, that the session was costing them a fortune, and for us not to sing spirituals with Elvis when he came back [from lunch] and sat down at the piano. . . . Well, he really got mad at that. He said, 'Look, if I want to bring you guys to Hollywood to sing spirituals all day long, *that's* what we'll do.' And with that, he turned and walked out of the studio!"

Drummer D. J. Fontana admits Hollywood executives were afraid to ask Elvis to stop singing gospels: "I told one of these people, 'He's the guy who pays me. And if he wants to sing gospel all day long, I'll play it.'" (See *Elvis in Private*).

DEC. 25: Elvis gave Anita Wood a French poodle for Christmas.

DEC. 26: Elvis gave another truckload of teddy bears to the National Foundation for Infantile Paralysis.

DEC. 27: All of Paramount was excited about Elvis's being able to finish filming *King Creole*. Elvis's role in *King Creole* paralleled his life, and it became his favorite movie. During the final days of filming, Elvis diehards sobbed from coast to coast, fearing something would happen to their favorite singer if he entered the Army. To keep the public calm, Elvis announced, "All I want is to be treated as a regular GI. I want to do my duty and I'm mighty proud to be given the opportunity to serve my country." (See *Elvis, Image of a Legend*). All of a sudden, Elvis's image changed. Critics and conservatives suddenly didn't know what to make of this rock 'n' roll crazy "cat" turned red-blooded American patriot.

DEC. 28: Elvis's movies had captured a more mature following than his music. If his popularity held out, Elvis would have to gravitate to the older audiences when he returned. Elvis joined the Army willingly, though his enemies thought he would "never make it through." Critics felt he didn't have the discipline. What they didn't know was, Elvis respected authority figures and relished being around large groups of friends. He felt safe in a group atmosphere. The Army was the perfect place for him.

Elvis feared only one thing: losing his popularity back home during a two-year absence. The Colonel reassured Elvis that he would have a viable career after he served in the Army. But Parker did not like the idea of losing control over Elvis, and Elvis was unnerved to have to leave the well-structured, supervised environment that the Colonel had built around him. Yet, the strict military dominion appealed to him, and Elvis truly enjoyed his tour of duty.

DEC. 31: His concert in St. Louis, Missouri, left Elvis exhausted and fans aching to see more of him.

By 1957, Elvis wore gold-lamé suits with $1,000 gold shoes, had a fleet of cars, a "zoo of animals," a mansion named Graceland, and could buy anything he desired. He had been criticized and adored by almost every viable voice in America, was nearly burnt out by the age of twenty-one, and the Colonel still wanted his last drop of blood.

In his desire to keep audiences who had paid to see Elvis happy, the Colonel paraded Elvis around with satin-draped elephants and bands of midgets. Art imitated life in the words of Deke Rivers (the character Elvis played in the movie *Loving You*): "That's how you're selling me, isn't it? A monkey in a zoo. Isn't that what you want?" Nothing was too humiliating or absurd if the Colonel thought it could turn a buck. By the end of 1957, the Colonel managed to export Elvis T-shirts to Japan, New Guinea, and Tibet. The world was his for the taking.

Elvis was dubbed "The King" of rock, a name that May Mann alleged she gave to Elvis in *Fabulous Las Ve-*

▲ Drummer D. J. Fontana and Elvis. *Courtesy of the Country Music Foundation Library and Media Center, Nashville, Tennessee.*

gas magazine, but a title *Variety* probably first coined for the Cat in 1956. Mann, a former Miss Utah, wrote the syndicated column "Going Hollywood with May Mann." She also wrote an article titled "I Want to Get Married to Elvis Presley, As Told to May Mann" for *Movieland*. May Mann was one of the only reporters/writers authorized by the Colonel to interview or even talk to Elvis.

J. D. Sumner of the Stamps Quartet remembers fondly one night Elvis was called "King": "One night in Las Vegas something happened. . . . I'll never forget it. A woman ran down to the front of the stage, and Elvis leaned forward like he usually did to kiss her. As he did so, he noticed that she was carrying a crown on a small pillow. 'What's that?' he asked her. 'It's for you,' she said breathlessly. 'You're the King.' Elvis smiled and took her hand. 'No, honey,' he said. 'I'm not King. Christ is the King. I'm just a singer.' For me, Elvis was not just a singer. He was *the* singer of our times. We shall not see his like again." (See *Elvis in Private*).

Elvis was chosen one of "The Stars of 1957" along with Kim Novak, Rock Hudson, and George Stevens. He was named as the fourth top box-office draw for 1957 by theater owners. A Gold Medal Award was given to him by *Photoplay* magazine.

Elvis won the Pops-Rite Popstar award for being the star who stimulated the sale of more popcorn than anyone else during the 1956–57 season. He received the award from the Mayor of Popcorn Village, Tennessee, Jim Blevins.

1958

By 1958, few men in entertainment had so affected the world through music in such a short time. Elvis belonged to the public. He was their liberator. They were his salvation.

Teenagers continued to rebel against the mainstream as slacks and tight-fitting clothes were banned on girls in school while boys tried desperately to emulate their hero in blue jeans and sideburns.

Rock 'n' roll declared loudly and clearly to the world that it was here to stay, but the middle class made certain *their* music hit the charts, too: "Volare," "Sugartime," "Twilight Time," "Catch a Falling Star," and "The Chipmunk Song" were all hits of 1958, and the Kingston Trio and the Everly Brothers were popular "easy-listening" music groups.

JAN.: Fans knew almost all there was to know about Elvis by his twenty-third birthday. His favorite foods were apple pie, fried potatoes, banana and peanut-butter sandwiches, milk (which he called "butch"), doughnuts (the greasier the better), burnt bacon, lemon meringue pie, corn bread in buttermilk, corn pone, pork chops, cheeseburgers, brown gravy, beans, and Whammy ice creams. He hated runny eggs and detested the smell of fish. His favorite colors were blue, pink, white, black, and gold. Joe Turner's "Flip, Flop and Fly" was one of his favorite songs. His toothpaste was Colgate. His favorite cologne was Brut by Fabergé. He washed his face (but did not like showers or baths, unless necessary) with Neutrogena. He had a pet turkey named Bow Tie. His maternal great-great-great-grandmother was Morning White Dove, a Cherokee Indian. His voice was classified as a tenor with baritone touches.

JAN. 1: Elvis celebrated the New Year with his Memphis buddies at Graceland.

JAN. 3: Elvis flew to California for recording sessions.

JAN. 12: Elvis's ninth take of "I Believe" (by Ervin Drake, Jimmy Shirl, Irvin Graham, and Al Stillman) was released by RCA on the LPs *Elvis' Christmas Album* and *You'll Never Walk Alone* and on the EP *Peace in the Valley*. The song was recorded at Radio Recorders. It had previously been made famous by Frankie Laine in 1953 (Columbia 39938).

JAN. 15–18: The sound track for *King Creole* was taped at Radio Recorders in Hollywood.

"Crawfish" was sung by Elvis and Kitty White for *King Creole* at Radio Recorders on January 15. Take No. 7 is on the EP *King Creole*, Vol. 2. Elvis also recorded the first of his songs to be aired on BBC radio, "Hard Headed Woman," written by Claude DeMetrius, which became Elvis's first British gold record on August 11, 1958. It was No. 15 when it entered *Billboard*'s Top 100 list, and in seven days it was No. 3. It peaked at No. 2 during a thirteen-week stay, and it was No. 2 on the Country and R&B charts. Its flip side was "Don't Ask Me Why." Take No. 5 of the Sid Tepper–Roy C. Bennett song "New Orleans" was released in the film.

JAN. 16: "As Long As I Have You" by Fred Wise and Ben Weisman, "Lover Doll" (backed by the Jordanaires) by Sid Wayne and Abner Silver, and "Steadfast, Loyal and True" (written by Leiber-Stoller and later overdubbed with a Jordanaires' backup) were completed by Elvis at Radio Recorders for *King Creole*. On bootleg LPs *From the Beach to the Bayou* and *The Rockin' Rebel*, alternative takes No. 4 and No. 5 and one shorter take of "As Long As I Have You" include Elvis's piano as the sole accompaniment.

For the same sound track, "Dixieland Rock" (by Aaron Schroeder and R. Frank) was completed by Elvis. (*Note*: the EP *King Creole*, Vol. 2 incorrectly lists Claude DeMetrius and Fred Wise as the composers.)

Fred Wise and Ben Weisman wrote "Don't Ask Me Why," and Elvis's rendition hit *Billboard*'s Top 100 at No. 24 during a nine-week stay. It reached No. 2 on the R&B chart (RCA 20-7280). Its flip side was "Hard Headed Woman," recorded the day before.

JAN. 20: Paramount Picture's *King Creole* was produced by Hal B. Wallis and directed by Michael Curtiz. It costarred Elvis, Walter Matthau, Carolyn Jones, Dolores Hart, and Dean Jagger.

Elvis's sentimental, boy-with-a-grudge role in *King Creole* is that of a misfit, who becomes involved with gangsters in New Orleans and too many women. In the end, the character drags himself up by the boot straps and conquers incredible odds. In many ways, *King Creole* paralleled Elvis's own triumph over adversity and his rise from poverty to untold fame and fortune. Singing eleven songs in the film, Elvis was smooth, cool, and the ultimate rebel. But it's important to note that this film marked the *end* of his bad-boy image on-screen.

JAN. 23: At Radio Recorders, "Danny" (by Fred Wise and Ben Weisman) was finished by Elvis for *King Creole*, but the song was not used. It was first released on the 1978 LP *Elvis—A Legendary Performer*, Vol. 3.

"Doncha' Think It's Time" (by Clyde Otis and Willie Dixon) was not satisfactory. Redoing "King Creole," Elvis's take No. 13 was okayed for release for the movie. Take No. 15 from the January 15 session is on bootleg LPs. Elvis recorded "Young Dreams" for *King Creole* (written by Aaron Schroeder and Martin Kalmanoff) and take No. 8 was released for records.

JAN. 25: *Picturegoer* said Elvis's acting got better and better in *Jailhouse Rock*.

FEB. 1: Elvis resang "Doncha' Think It's Time" at Radio Recorders and it became No. 21 on *Billboard*'s Top 100 chart in a six-week stay (RCA 20-7240). Its flip side was finished that same day, "Wear My Ring Around Your Neck" (written by Bert Carroll and Russell Moody). By April, the song entered *Billboard*'s Top 100 list at No. 7 and peaked at No. 3. It stayed on the chart for fifteen weeks. Elvis recorded "Your Cheatin' Heart" (written by Hank Williams) with many alternative takes. The song is on the EP *The EP Collection*, Vol. 2, and the LPs *Elvis for Everyone* and *Welcome to My World*.

FEB. 3–24: Elvis rehearsed scenes, grew a beard, and studied the script for *King Creole*.

MAR.: Elvis did not like social functions. At a Paramount Pictures party he hid in a corner to play a piano and then guitar. He enjoyed accompanying himself on "Lawdy Miss Clawdy," "One-Sided Love Affair," and "I'll Hold You in My Heart" when he was not jamming with gospel.

MAR. 5: During the filming of *King Creole*, director Michael Curtiz (who allegedly did not get along with Elvis) told the actor he was too fat. Elvis dieted for fourteen days and lost ten pounds. Seeing himself on film after Curtiz's comment made him uncomfortable. Even when he was slender, he thought he looked fat.

CA. MAR. 7: During the filming of *King Creole*, Elvis and his friends were told to leave the Beverly Hills Hotel because of their loud and unruly behavior. He then rented a house at 565 Perugia Way in Bel Air (where Elvis held Bible readings).

MAR. 9: Elvis and the *King Creole* crew flew to New Orleans. Elvis became a friend of costars Carolyn Jones, Walter Matthau, Dolores Hart, Vic Morrow, and Dean Jagger, whom he introduced to Southern hospitality in clubs, restaurants, dives, and strip joints whenever he could. The Hollywood group was shocked at the way people behaved in New Orleans, but Elvis and his Memphis gang fit right in.

MAR. 10: *King Creole* ended shooting in New Orleans, where Elvis and his friends enjoyed the wilder nightspots.

MAR. 11: The cast and crew of *King Creole* flew back to Los Angeles.

MAR. 13: Elvis and his entourage caused havoc on a train from Los Angeles to Memphis, much to the delight of all the girls on board.

MAR. 14: Elvis arrived at Union Station, Memphis, greeted by girlfriend, Anita Wood. All of the Memphis-Tupelo area had prepared for his "comeback" to Tennessee. Banners, placards, and cheering crowds lined the streets.

MAR. 15: Elvis was accompanied by Anita Wood to the Mississippi-Alabama Fair and Dairy Show in Tupelo. When Anita Wood kissed Elvis in front of thousands of fans, the Colonel saw the negative reaction Wood's moment of passion caused, and Parker ended the relationship (although it was rumored they would marry). Once again, Elvis would say good-bye to a person he professed to love because the Colonel demanded it.

Elvis gave two performances (with Hank "Sugarfoot" Garland on guitar) at Russwood Park in Memphis. These would be his last live performances in America until 1961. Security was placed every twenty feet, and Gladys Presley could not bear to see her son "torn to shreds" by oversexed women.

After the crowds dispersed, the Memphis Mafia set up lights in a field and played football with the King. Elvis egged on cheering fans who jumped up and down at the sidelines, watching every move the Cat made. If Elvis liked what he saw, he sent Red West into the mob to ask young girls to visit Graceland. Time had no value. Nor did most people. Elvis sent his bodyguards for hamburgers, malts, and women. Rarely, if ever, did he stop to fulfill a simple need of someone else in his entourage. He was the center of his universe.

MAR. 16: Elvis donated $25,000 of the proceeds from the Memphis concerts to the Elvis Presley Youth Recreation Center in Tupelo.

MAR. 17–22: Elvis tried to calm Gladys, who fretted over his impending absence in the Army. Though he lavished his mother with gifts, nothing seemed to please her. Every night he went off and did not return until Gladys was sound asleep. Vernon disappeared frequently after Elvis became famous.

MAR. 23: Elvis rented the Rainbow Rollerdrome in Memphis for $70, so his family and friends could skate.

A fan named Judy Powell Spreckles presented Elvis with the Pops-Rite Popstar Award.

MAR. 24: Elvis was inducted into the United States Army, accompanied by Judy Powell Spreckles. Leaving an income of hundreds of thousands of dollars a month to earn $78 a month, a smiling, 185-pound Elvis entered A Company, Second Medium Tank Battalion, Second Armored Division, U.S. Army. Elvis posed for the press holding Gladys. She had become so ill with hepatitis, her skin had turned yellow and dark, sunken circles framed her eyes. Elvis kissed his grieving, sickly mother good-bye in front of a huge crowd while twelve recruits stood by.

Elvis reported for duty March 24, 1958, as a private E-1 and traveled by Greyhound bus to Fort Chaffee, Arkansas, U.S. soldier number 53310761. It was the first time he had lived without his parents—but the Colonel was there to handle publicity shots.

The press named March 24 "Black Monday," the day Elvis was inducted into the Army. Fans wept from coast to coast.

MAR. 25: Elvis was given an Army haircut at Fort Chaffee, Arkansas, from James Peterson, while a myriad of press took photographs of "the historic moment." When his famous pompadour hair was "scalped," Elvis joked, "Hair today, gone tomorrow!"

MAR. 26: Sgt. Calvin Rhoades gave Elvis an Asian flu shot.

MAR. 27: At Fort Chaffee, Elvis was inoculated for typhoid and tetanus.

Ex-lover Kitty Dolan wrote "How Elvis Made Love to Me" for *Movie Mirror*, which infuriated Elvis. The Colonel warned the Vegas entertainer to never make a public statement about "his boy" again. She never did.

▶ Elvis in an army chow line, March 29, 1958. *Courtesy of AP/Wide World Photos.*

MAR. 28: Elvis traveled with his battalion to Ford Hood for basic training under Sgt. William Fraley. Lt. Col. Marjorie Schultern sent Parker packing. Although he did not openly gripe, the Colonel knew it was potentially dangerous for the singer to live in barracks with the troops. Inside strict Army confines, the Colonel could not supervise Elvis's life. Elvis *was* different, despite his aspiration to be just one of the men. He was a legendary celebrity, and the Colonel did not want to chance Elvis's safety.

Elvis and other Army recruits stopped at the Coffee Cup restaurant in West Memphis, Arkansas, to eat. Elvis ordered spaghetti but fans interrupted the meal.

During basic training to become a tanker, Elvis called Gladys every night, and reports claimed he longed to have family and friends around him. He was not embarrassed to cry in front of Master Sergeant Bill Nowood when he was homesick, but when he broke his finger playing football with Army buddies, he assured physicians it "didn't hurt bad."

MAR. 30: "Hy Gardner Calling" (a repeat of the July 1, 1956, show) was telecast from New York on station WABD, Channel 5, because so many fans cried out to "save Elvis" before the Army took him from them.

APR.: Promoting the "golden" image, *Elvis' Golden Records*, Vol. 1 (RCA PM-1707), was released (14 million distributed). The gold-lamé tux appeared on the LP jacket of *A Touch of Gold*, Vol. 1 (released April 1959); *50,000,000 Elvis Fans Can't Be Wrong—Elvis' Gold Records*, Vol. 2 (released September 1959), featured sixteen views of Elvis in the gold-lamé suit; *A Touch of Gold*, Vol. 2 (released October 1959), displayed two figures of Elvis in the gold-lamé tuxedo; and volume 3 (released February 1960) had three views of Elvis in the gold suit. *Elvis' Golden Records*, Vol. 3 (released

in September 1963), showed Elvis smiling through the middle of a golden disk. Many more "gold" promotions developed.

APR. 26: Elvis was dubbed The King of Hearts with an award from the National March of Dimes, for which he introduced a "Teens vs. Polio" campaign.

MAY 1: The Colonel discovered a soldier could live off the post if he had dependents living in the area. Elvis was the sole supporter of his parents, thus they qualified as "dependents." Delighted to find this out, Elvis moved Gladys and Vernon and five friends into a rented house in Killeen, Texas, for three months. He drove to and from duty in a sports car, while his parents cooked, kept house, and watched over a menagerie of houseguests. The drive from Memphis to Killeen nearly killed the weakened Gladys. Elvis hadn't considered how the humid, steamy heat might affect his mother. He thought being near him would cure her ailments.

SUMMER: Janis Darlene Martin came out with the LP *Janis and Elvis* in 1958 (Teal Record label, South Africa). RCA approved the release, which featured six of Elvis's songs, but Parker demanded the LP be withdrawn from the market and it was. (In 1985, the album was released legally.)

JUNE: In the summer of 1958, Elvis stayed with Anita Wood at the Waco, Texas, home of his friends Eddie and LaNelle Fadal while stationed at Fort Hood. The Fadals knew of Elvis's love for the piano, so they built an extra room and put a piano in it for their weekend guest. Eddie Fadal recorded Elvis while he sang along with records and accompanied himself on piano, including "Happy, Happy Birthday, Baby," which he sang seven times over the Tune Weavers' 1956 recording of the song (Checker 872), "I Can't Help It," and "Just a Closer Walk With Thee." Elvis was also recorded singing "Don't You Know" (written by Fats Domino and Dave Bartholomew) over Fats Domino's Imperial recording (Imperial 5340). Elvis accompanied himself on piano and sang Pat Best's "I Understand (Just How You Feel)" and sang a line from "Tumbling Tumbleweeds" by Bob Nolan. With Anita Wood, Elvis sang "Who's Sorry Now?" twice as he played the piano. These are all on the LP *Forever Young: Forever Beautiful* (Waco, TX, 1958), a Paul Lichter bootleg.

Elvis was on the cover of *Teen* magazine.

Jerry Lee Lewis ruined his career when critics rebuffed the former ministry student for conducting himself in an "immoral and incestuous" manner when he married his thirteen-year-old cousin, Myra Gale. To make matters worse, Lewis was two weeks short of a final divorce from his second wife, Jane.

JUNE 1: Gladys felt cramped and uncomfortable in the Killeen house (which had no air-conditioning), but she did not complain about her failing health. Her looks faded and she gained weight and drank too much liquor. She was playing the role of a domestic to Vernon, Elvis, and his buddies. No one seemed to care about her at all.

JUNE 10: On leave from the Army, Elvis and the Jordanaires (with Murray Buddy Harmon on bongos and Ray Walker, who replaced Hugh Jarrett) rushed to Nashville to record at RCA's studios, where Elvis sang Clyde Otis and Ivory Joe Hunter's "Ain't That Loving You Baby," which was not released until 1964. In its ten-week stay on *Billboard*'s Top 100 chart it peaked at No. 16, but RCA claimed it sold 1 million records (RCA 47-8440). The song eventually became a hit from the movie *Roustabout*. While on leave, Elvis wanted to record as many songs as

possible. Take No. 3 of "A Big Hunk o' Love" (written by Aaron Schroeder and Sid Wyche) was recorded June 10 and was released in July 1959, with the flip side "My Wish Came True" (RCA 47-7600). "A Fool Such As I" by Bill Trader was recorded with bass singer Ray Walker of the Jordanaires. The song hit *Billboard*'s Top 100 list for fifteen weeks where it peaked at No. 2, made it to No. 16 on the R&B chart, and stayed in the No. 1 spot for five weeks in England. It almost instantaneously sold a million copies (RCA 47-7506, released March 1959). Its flip side, "I Need Your Love Tonight" (by Sid Wayne and Bix Reichner) was recorded that day. Take No. 14 was released on RCA 47-7506, which peaked at No. 18 on *Billboard*'s Top 100 chart during a thirteen-week run. Another million records were sold.

JUNE 11: "I Got Stung" (by Aaron Schroeder and David Hill) was recorded by Elvis at RCA's Nashville studios. Take No. 24 was released (RCA 20-7410, October 1958), and during its sixteen-week stay on *Billboard*'s Top 100 it hit No. 8. The million seller peaked at No. 1 for three weeks in Great Britain. Its flip side was "One Night."

CA. JUNE 20: A very ill Gladys Presley was returned to Memphis for treatment—an action that stunned Elvis. It became obvious to him that in the midst of serving his country and partying with his entourage, his mother had been neglected. He had not noticed she was failing mentally and physically. Trying to put up with her son's career and the antics that went along with it, she had been forgotten by him.

Gladys longed for the days when she and Elvis used affectionate language when addressing one another. "Put your yittle duckling in da sooties" meant "Put your little feet in the water" in Presley terminology. The French word *beaucoup* became "boocups"; *toophies*, "teeth"; *butch*, "milk";

toasties, "warm"; *sugar puss*, "sweet person"; *yuv*, "love"; *nungen*, "young one"; and *Sattnin*, the intimate name Elvis and his mother called each other, later used for Elvis's wife, were words used daily.

JULY 1: Upon *King Creole*'s release, Elvis was elated by a *New York Times* review that called him a decent actor. After this review, he had dreams of becoming as good an actor as Dean or Brando and told the Colonel he didn't want to do concert tours again.

JULY 2–AUG. 4: Elvis trained to become a soldier. Although fans sent thousands of letters to every base at which he was stationed, and members of the press tried to interview him through fences and by telephone, Elvis attempted to be "one of the guys" within his Army unit.

AUG. 5: Elvis was told his mother had been taken to the hospital. Elvis threatened to go AWOL if the Army did not grant him a leave of absence to be at his mother's side. Elvis obtained his leave and flew from Texas to be at Gladys's bedside, despite her pleas for him not to come.

AUG. 7: Elvis went to Memphis's City Methodist Hospital to be with Gladys. Elvis and Vernon kept a vigilant watch over her.

AUG. 11: "Hard Headed Woman" sold a million copies and Elvis received his first RIAA Gold Disc Award from the Recording Industry Association of America (RCA 20-7280).

AUG. 12: Elvis exhausted himself grieving as he watched his mother slip further away. The end was near and the doctors and the family could do nothing. Her misuse of alcohol and barbiturates contributed to her early death—a fact the Colonel made certain was kept

secret for years. He had built an image of the loving son with a perfect mother, and nothing was going to change that if the Colonel could help it. But the fact was, Gladys took diet pills so Elvis would not be embarrassed to introduce her to his Hollywood friends, and she abused alcohol when she was left alone.

Because Elvis had not had any rest in days, he returned to Graceland where he slept for over twenty-four hours.

AUG. 14: Gladys Presley died of a heart attack in Room 688 at Memphis's Methodist Hospital. Cousin Billy Smith informed Elvis of his mother's death after Vernon called Graceland with the sad news. After arriving at the hospital, Elvis rushed to Gladys's room. He refused to leave his mother alone and claimed he had nothing more to live for.

Gladys's death was brought on by acute hepatitis, at three A.M., August 14, 1958. It was the most catastrophic event in Elvis's life, partially because he felt so guilty about having left her stranded at the end of her life, and partially because she was the *only* person to whom he had confided his real feelings. Claiming his mother was "his

baby" and that his purpose and goals had been "for her," Elvis went into a state of shock when she died. Vernon organized the lavish, $20,000 funeral, pastored by the Reverend James E. Hammill of the First Assembly of God Church.

According to the authors of *Elvis World*, "He grieved like he sang, racked with emotion, oblivious to the judgments of others." Gladys's absence created a lonely void that would forever go unfilled.

AUG. 15: Elvis became distraught. Funeral directors had a difficult time tearing the singer away from his dead mother. Vernon, Billy Smith, and members of the Memphis Mafia did all they could to ease his pain, but nothing helped. Elvis sobbed until he had no breath. The *Press-Scimitar* ran Clark Porteous's story about Gladys Presley's death in the article "A Lonely Life Ends on Elvis Presley Boulevard."

AUG. 16: Elvis became overwrought at his mother's funeral at Forest Hill Cemetery, three miles south of Memphis. The *Tupelo Daily Journal* revealed, "Elvis cried without shame." He wailed for hours at Gladys's coffin. He began to sleepwalk nightly and had horrifying nightmares. He lost his will to live and "they couldn't get him to stop touching her . . . they were afraid for him, you know," sighed a family friend. Elvis believed the dead could *see* what the living were doing, and that was even more upsetting to him. Now, he could have no secrets from his dead mother's spirit. She would know *every*thing he did.

While combing his mother's hair over and over again, he insisted she be placed in a glass-topped casket so that he could see her and continue to mutter baby talk to her, and he caressed the lifeless body inside the coffin and told his mother who was coming to the funeral parlor to pay respect. Wanting to leave everything as Gladys had left

it, Elvis ordered all her belongings to remain as they were and directed a window she had broken when she had fallen be left untouched.

Four hundred guests attended Gladys's funeral while 3,300 fans mourned outside the Graceland gates. The Blackwood Brothers (Gladys's favorite gospel quartet) flew to Memphis from North Carolina to sing "Rock of Ages," "In the Garden," "I Am Redeemed," and "Precious Memories."

As sixty-five policemen held back crowds, Gladys was laid to rest beneath a ten-foot marble monument with two kneeling angels and a life-size statue of Jesus on the cross with arms outstretched. The original grave markers read "Presley" and "Not mine but thy will be done." Weeks later a larger marker was placed at the grave site that read:

Gladys Smith Presley
April 25 1912–August 14 1958
Beloved Wife of Vernon Presley
and Mother of Elvis Presley
'She was the sunshine of our home.'

Unable to leave the grave site, Elvis was overheard moaning, "Oh, God! Everything I have is gone." His main supporter, the woman who loved him enough to protect and nurture him, was no longer available to watch over him or guide and applaud his actions. There was no one else he wanted to impress with his accomplishments. No one else to bestow riches upon. No one else to do everything for. She died at the wrong time—during a period when she had felt neglected and unloved. He wanted to make it up to her, but it was too late.

AUG. 16: Elvis locked himself in a room at Graceland for eight days, barely eating and refusing to talk to anyone. This was the most unbearable, lonely period of his life.

AUG. 18: Elvis forbid everyone in his entourage to watch *Loving You* or mention the movie in his presence because Gladys appeared in one scene.

◀ A devastated Elvis and his father, Vernon, mourn the death of Gladys Presley, August 14, 1958. *Courtesy of AP/Wide World Photos.*

AUG. 20: Elvis came out of his room to sing gospel hymns at a piano with Charlie Hodge. His eyes were swollen from crying. Elvis admitted he held himself responsible for Gladys's death. During his climb to fame and fortune he had neglected the only person he loved, his mother.

AUG. 22: Elvis learned his Army battalion was being sent to Germany and that he must return to basic training.

CA. AUG. 23: Elvis piloted a helicopter from Graceland, according to Eddie Fadal. Elvis had been given a few lessons.

AUG. 24: Elvis returned to basic training and told reporters at Dallas's Love Field his father would accompany him to Germany because his mother's last wish was for them to stay together.

AUG. 25: Despite the tragedy of his mother's death, Elvis was an exceptional recruit. He worked diligently to complete work efficiently and well, and he was generally liked by his peers, but as a celebrity he could not behave as others did. The Colonel had warned him to watch his language and actions.

SEPT.: Elvis's cousin Carrol "Junior" Smith died. Smith had toured with Elvis for months. Elvis was again numb with grief. Smith died three weeks after Gladys.

SEPT. 19: Elvis traveled from Fort Hood to Brooklyn, New York, with his Army unit and was greeted by a huge crowd and hundreds of reporters.

SEPT. 20: Elvis had an impact on daring youths in Chemnitz, East Germany. When police would not allow Elvis's records to be played, fans rioted and seventeen teenagers were arrested in Scholssteich Square.

SEPT. 22: Elvis and his Army unit boarded the USS *General Randall* from the Military Ocean Terminal in Brooklyn to head for the open seas. Saluting their most famous soldier, an Army band played "All Shook Up" at dockside while fans sobbed.

The ship was to carry the unit to their combat-ready Second Armored Division "Mailed Fist" of NATO, stationed at Bremerhaven, West Germany. As Elvis boarded, thousands of fans screamed, fainted, and pushed to touch their hero. Elvis smiled and waved and told the press the scene was as wild as anything back home. He could not believe so many people had come to Brooklyn to bid him farewell. After his departure, thousands of young recruits wanted to join the Army. Elvis had once denounced the draft; now, he made it popular to become a soldier.

At the dock, a reporter wondered if Elvis had difficulties with other recruits. He responded, "No, I expected it because in civilian life I sorta get harassed, but when they saw me pull KP and everything else, they treated me fine."

Elvis was interviewed by Pat Hernon in the library of the USS *General Randall* (which is included on the EP *Elvis Sails*, released in December 1958). Elvis's voyage to Bremerhaven was a good time for the young star. He read the book *Poems That Touch the Heart* while he nibbled on a cheesecake that model Lillian Portnoy had given him as he boarded the ship.

SEPT. 22–23: Photographer Al Wertheimer watched Elvis leave the docks in New York. In the aftermath of his departure, fans were numb. Wertheimer told the author, "Flocks of fans gravitated to Elvis. He made the girls *cry*. They were unashamed *en masse*. He touched emotion, triggered and released crying mechanisms. He's still popular because all those girls remember how he touched their inside feelings. He is nostalgia. All the Elvis memorabilia brings back the memories of the times fans released their emotions in the past. Elvis is their youth. . . . He was a real natural, and that ability was brought to the broad audience via TV and then the silver screen. After '56, the Colonel pulled down the curtain around Elvis. My photographs are some of the only natural candids of the singer because of that fact. Everything was posed with a purpose after Elvis entered the Army. The last time I was with him was in Brooklyn, the day he left for Germany. Before the Colonel controlled every move he made, Elvis was oblivious to the camera. He needed action around him at all times. He couldn't sit still. His activities were more important to him than any camera ever was. He had this *intensity* and it was the foremost aspect of his character. He had the ability to make you feel important at any moment. . . . He was intense."

SEPT. 30: By this date, the Colonel had turned down offers for Elvis to sing at Carnegie Hall, the Boston Pops, and in Europe because he couldn't negotiate record-setting fees for Elvis. Or did the Colonel reject eminent career opportunities on Elvis's behalf so his boy would not become *too* powerful? The Colonel had said yes to almost every other plausible promotional gimmick, regardless of how absurd or degrading. Perhaps Parker feared the classier the venue the more sophisticated Elvis's tastes might become, and in the circus-like atmosphere that Parker had created for his star attraction, that might have been a disaster.

OCT.: *Photoplay* told Elvis's grieving fans, "Elvis' last words to you before going overseas, 'Please don't forget me when I'm gone.' " The Colonel frequently sent out press releases at random without Elvis's knowledge or consent.

OCT. 1: Elvis's ship arrived in Bremerhaven where hundreds of curious rock 'n' roll fanatics lined the docks to glimpse their idol. Elvis donated blood along with 180 other GIs of the Second Armored Division. German Red Cross nurse Marie Everle did the honors.

Vernon and Minnie Mae Presley first stayed at Ritter's Park Hotel in Bad Homberg, West Germany, before they moved in with Red West and Lamar Fike at the Gruenwald Hotel in Bad Nauheim. Soon afterward they moved to a rented house at 14 Goethestrasse. The Presley group had a bad local reputation for starting fights and getting into trouble (the group was asked to leave the Gruenwald Hotel by hotel manager Herr Schmidt when West and Elvis started a fire and had shaving cream and water-gun fights). Before they left, Vernon met Dee Stanley (who would become his future wife).

Elvis was on the cover of *TV Movie* in his Army uniform.

OCT. 2: Elvis was interviewed at a large press conference in the men's canteen at the Thirty-second Armored Battalion in Friedberg, Germany.

Richard Atcheson served in the Seventh Army in Bad Nauheim when Elvis was there. In *Lear's* (May 1991) he revealed how screened and isolated Elvis may have been in Germany: "They kept Elvis in a house in town and wouldn't let him go out except under armed guard. I know—there were newsreels of it at the time, but more to the point, my cousin Sylvester was a master sergeant in what they called the Elvis unit, which existed to guard and wait on him. 'They kept the poor son of a bitch like a prisoner,' Sylvester told me. . . . Colonel Parker [kept] breathing over his shoulder all the time." However, Parker never left America.

OCT. 5: Because of the crush of fans and the media, all fans and reporters were banned from the Army base.

OCT. 6: Elvis obtained an Army pass and moved members of his family and the Memphis Mafia to Ritter's Park Hotel located outside Bad Homburg, Germany.

OCT. 7–8: Elvis and his entourage moved to Hilberts Park Hotel in Bad Nauheim, but because oil sheik Ibn Saud, who was also staying at the hotel, received as much attention as Elvis, the Cat soon moved to the elegant and lavishly decorated Gruenwald Hotel at 10 Terrassenstrasse, Bad Nauheim.

OCT. 7: Elvis briefly dated a sixteen-year-old German girl, and a German actress named Vera Tschechowa. He also dined with a Berlin starlet. Elvis's unsatiable appetite for the opposite sex grew even stronger after Gladys's death, as if he were trying to fill the gap she'd left. Like many of the rockabilly singers from Tennessee, he gravitated toward young girls rather than mature women. Elvis may have felt uncomfortable with older women or those his own age. His lack of confidence and his often juvenile antics insulted more seasoned women. He had to be the domineering person in any relationship.

OCT. 10: Elvis moved off the base into a three-bedroom house at 14 Goethestrasse, in Bad Nauheim until March 1960, with his father, Minnie Mae Presley (whom he nicknamed The Dodger), Red West, and Lamar Fike. Many people "visited" for weeks on end. Elvis moved a piano, television sets, and a refrigerator filled with pounds of hamburger, bacon, and rolls into the house. "No soldier was ever more obedient to his country or his kin." (See *Elvis World.*)

OCT. 23: Elvis attended Bill Haley and the Comets' concert at a cinema house in Frankfurt. The two rock stars posed for the press in Haley's dressing room.

OCT. 29: Elvis attended Bill Haley and the Comets' concert in Mannheim.

NOV.: During Army leaves, Elvis, Lamar Fike, Rex Mansfield, Joe Esposito, Red West, and Charlie Hodge partied at after-hours clubs in France. Elvis's entourage tolerated his every whim because Elvis bought them anything they desired, from girls and cars to booze and pills. The group became his extended family, while at the same time the men shielded his more risqué actions from public view. A plethora of young, pretty, oversexed women were ever-present in West Germany and in the United States. Elvis automatically gravitated to burlesque dancers, with whom he spent many nights. Recent photographs have been discovered of Elvis cavorting with strippers in Paris and other forms of "night life."

NOV. 1: Russian leaders called Elvis "public enemy number one" and accused the U.S. of using Elvis as a psychological-warfare "weapon."

▲ Elvis being kissed by Margit Burgin in Frankfurt, Germany. *Courtesy of AP/Wide World Photos.*

NOV. 1: Elvis wrote only three letters while he served in the Army: to George Klein (now lost); to ex-girlfriend Anita Wood; and to longtime pal "Hog Ears" Alan Fortas, in which he said he was lonely, the training area was miserable, he was dating a German "chickaloid" named Margrit Buergin (a German typist), and that he missed Memphis.

Actress Venetia Stevenson flew to West Germany to see Elvis.

NOV. 20: Because Elvis's publicists (via the Colonel's tight control) handled his Army duties with dignity, fans stayed loyal and supportive. No less than five hundred to a thousand letters a day poured in for him at the Ray Barracks, Friedberg, Germany, post office. Some were addressed to "General Presley." This avalanche was seen as a blessing by Colonel Parker.

NOV. 22: In snowy, cold, blustery November, the thirty-second Battalion actively maneuvered by the Czechoslovakian border. Unaccustomed to the long waking hours soldiers keep, Elvis was first exposed to drugs (Dexedrine pills to stay awake), allegedly given to him by an Army sergeant.

NOV. 27: Elvis was promoted to private first class in Germany.

NOV. 28: Elvis bought a small dog named Cherry. He insisted that the hotel management at the Hotel Gruenwald care for the dog when he was at the Army base.

DEC.: The *Guinness Book of World Records* listed Elvis for having the most gold disc awards. *Guinness* stated Elvis surpassed Bing Crosby as the most successful recorded singer of all time.

The EP *Elvis Sails* was released and sold out.

Elvis bought a great deal of gold jewelry for himself, girlfriends, and for friends. Eventually, he gave members of his entourage gold chains with a gold thunderbolt inscribed with the letters *TCB*. Red West explained to newcomers it meant "taking care of business" and "everyone who wears it knows that it means just that. . . . When [Elvis] nodded, they jumped to see what he needed." (See *Elvis the King.*) Although his golden crown was invisible, the King ruled his court.

For 1958, Elvis was awarded the World's Outstanding Popular Singer, the World's Outstanding Musical Personality, and Favorite U.S. Male Singer.

DEC. 20: Elvis bought a used BMW 507 sports car for $3,750 from Bavarian Motor Works of Munich. In exchange for the low price, he agreed to pose for promotional photos.

DEC. 25: Elvis did not like spending Christmas in Germany, and he complained continuously that he missed his mother.

DEC. 26: Elvis attended a Holiday on Ice performance in Frankfurt, autographed fans' programs after the show, and posed with female skaters for promotional photographs.

1959

In 1959, a huge payola scandal placed suspicion on the radio industry and disc jockey Alan Freed, *Ben-Hur* was voted Best Picture, and TV's *The Untouchables*, *Dobie Gillis*, and *Bonanza* became popular. Dick Clark started his now-famous "Dick Clark's World of Talent" tour, and Top 10 singers included newcomers

Frankie Avalon, Johnny Horton, Paul Anka, Dodie Stevens, Paul Evans & the Curls, Lloyd Price, and others.

By 1959, Elvis and Cliff Richard ("Traveling Light") had become American and British "rock icons." British producer Jack Good said, "I don't think Cliff Richards would have existed at all as a singer without Elvis," but most critics realized both men had rejected rock 'n' roll for more sedate music by the end of 1959.

JAN.: Donald Rex Mansfield dated Elisabeth Stefaniak, a young secretary who lived in Elvis's German house. Mansfield alleged that Elvis bought (or was given) amphetamines from soldiers in Bad Nauheim, January 1959. (See *Elvis the Soldier.*)

Elvis posed with Robert Stephen Marquett (son of an Army master sergeant), who had polio. The photo became a 1959 March of Dimes poster.

JAN. 1: German newspapers reported Elvis had died in a car accident after Vernon Presley crashed Elvis's black Mercedes into a tree. Vernon, who was on the way back from the Army PX in Frankfurt with Elvis's secretary Elisabeth Stefaniak, walked away from the wreck, but Stefaniak was temporarily paralyzed.

JAN. 4: Elvis rented a piano for $40 a month from the Kuehlwetter Music Shop and moved it to his house at 14 Goethestrasse.

JAN. 8: Dick Clark's "American Bandstand" dedicated its program to Elvis on Elvis's twenty-fourth birthday. Ricky Nelson and Elvis were two of the only rock stars who never appeared on "American Bandstand." On January 8, Clark talked by phone to Elvis and told the soldier he had been voted Best Singer of the Year and that "King Creole" had won Best Song of the Year. Elvis was pleased he had not been forgotten.

JAN. 16: Elvis donated blood at the Red Cross in the presence of German nurse Marie Everly. *Bravo* and newspapers across Europe carried the story.

FEB. 3: Buddy Holly, Ritchie Valens (often billed as "the next Elvis," with hits like "Donna" and "Let's Go"), Jiles Perry Richardson ("The Big Bopper"), and pilot Roger Peterson were killed in a plane crash outside Mason City, Iowa, on their way to the Winter Dance Party in Moorhead, Minnesota.

Elvis sent Holly's family in Lubbock, Texas, a telegram. He was extremely upset by the deaths of these friends and fellow rock 'n' roll artists.

APR.: Elvis and his Army unit erected a war memorial in Steinfurth. During a press conference at the Ray Barracks in Friedberg, Elvis reported how well he and the other soldiers worked.

MAY: Elvis briefly dated a young girl named Janie Wilbanks in Friedberg.

JUNE 1: Elvis was promoted to specialist fourth class.

JUNE 3–9: Elvis was hospitalized at the Frankfurt Military Hospital, Frankfurt, Germany, with tonsillitis.

CA. JUNE 10: After winning an Elvis Presley contest, Pim Maas (an aspiring fourteen-year-old actress from Holland) visited a cordial Elvis at his home in Bad Nauheim. German newspapers carried the story.

JUNE 12: Elvis was recorded playing the piano and singing "He's Only a Prayer Away" (which was released in 1984's *A Golden Anniversary, West Germany 1958–60*) as he entertained guests and members of his entourage in his rented house. Other known recordings of Elvis playing the piano while he sang are limited.

JUNE 17–26: Elvis enjoyed a ten-day furlough with members of the Memphis Mafia. They stayed three days in Munich with eighteen-year-old actress Vera Tschechowa and her parents. Tschechowa told reporters she was disenchanted with Elvis after meeting the loud and unruly members of his ever-present entourage.

JUNE 21: Elvis, Charlie Hodge, Lamar Fike, and Rex Mansfield flew a chartered plane to Paris. The Colonel, not wanting Elvis to have too much fun or get in too much trouble, sent attorney Ben Starr and music publisher Jean Aberbach to chaperon the four men. The group went to the Lido nightclub to hear George and Bert Bernard sing. Seeing Elvis, they called him to the stage, and he played an impromptu piano version of "Willow Weep for Me." The boys visited the Louvre, the Eiffel Tower, and a Grand Prix race in Reims. At the Folies-Bergère, Elvis socialized with the black singers in the Golden Gate Quartet, headed by Bill Johnson (the Jordanaires and Elvis had been influenced by this group's music.) Elvis later cut his own versions of the group's 1953 Columbia songs "His Hand in Mine," "White Christmas," and "Silent Night."

Using the hotel de Galles on Avenue George V as a base, the group soon included Joe Esposito. Together they frequented the Folies-Bergère, the Carousel, the Moulin Rouge, the 4 O'Clock Club (where they conned the entire Blue Bell chorus line into going back to their hotel to party), and the Café de Paris. Singing along the Champs-Élysées one night, Elvis and company were told by police to go back to their hotel. Elvis hired an $800 limousine to drive them back to the Army base. Afterward, the men laughed about the $10,000 cost of their ten-day vacation, all of which Elvis paid in full.

JUNE 23: Singer George Bernard remembered Elvis's talent and charisma during a casual moment at the Lido club in Paris: "I heard a piano being played—softly and very skillfully. . . . Then a voice started to sing—so quietly . . . a soft blues number called 'Willow Weep for Me.' . . . There he was— and surrounding him were a whole group of people, absolutely mesmerized. . . . They were getting—for nothing—what no one else in Europe could get for a fortune: a show from Elvis Presley. . . . But it wasn't the Elvis we then knew on records. This was a suave, sophisticated songster at the piano, making magic at the keyboard and singing in a soft, well-modulated, superbly controlled voice. . . . A dreamy, contented expression was on his face. He was really enjoying himself. . . . He was a very fine pianist indeed." (See "Making Magic at the Lido" in *Elvis in Private.*)

JULY: Elvis in Army fatigues was the cover of *TV Star Parade* and many other international magazines.

JULY 7: Elvis drove his BMW to Friedberg to purchase a lawn mower from a man named Samen Herman. He gave the lawn mower as a gift to his landlord, Frau Pieper, and insisted she mow the lawn of his rented house. When she refused, Elvis told Rex Mansfield and Charlie Hodge to keep the lawn mowed.

AUG.: Elvis visited an English-speaking German from Mainz named Siegrid Schutz, and together they saw movies and went to clubs in and around Bad Nauheim. They did not have a romantic relationship.

AUG. 20: Lee Gordon (an Australian promoter) told the press that Elvis and Colonel Parker had accepted a large fee for Elvis to sing live in Australia for five or six days. Elvis denied it and the concert never took place.

OCT. 24–29:   Elvis was again hospitalized with tonsillitis, at the General Hospital in Frankfurt.

NOV.:   U.S. Air Force airman Currie Grant introduced fourteen-year-old Priscilla Beaulieu to twenty-four-year-old Elvis in West Germany at an Army party. Grant, who worked for Air Force intelligence at the 497th Reconnaissance Technical Squadron at Schierstein near Wiesbaden, and his wife, Carole, escorted Priscilla to the party. Grant was influential at the Eagle's Club, a military dive in Wiesbaden. Contrary to more romantic versions of their meeting, Grant claims Priscilla asked him at the Eagle's Club if he knew Elvis and asked to meet him. Priscilla wore a blue-and-white sailor outfit with white socks. Calling her "Cilla," Elvis took her to a local theater, accompanied by Vernon and his girlfriend Dee Stanley (a Tennessean who was in Germany with her husband and family, and in the process of getting a divorce). Dee became Vernon's steady date, which annoyed and frustrated Elvis, who thought Vernon should have grieved the loss of Gladys longer.

NOV.:   Elvis took karate lessons from German instructor Jurgen Seydel. He had his photograph taken in a karate *gi*, with a white belt. Years later the Cat asked for, and allegedly received

permission from Seydel, to paint the white belt in the photo black!

NOV. 2:   Elvis hired Monsieur Laurenz of the De Fleur Clinic of Johannesburg, South Africa, as an exercise and fitness instructor. Elvis paid Laurenz $15,000, as well as for his stay at the Rex Hotel. But when Elvis became uncomfortable with some of Laurenz's massages, he accused Laurenz of being gay. He then fired him and ordered Lamar Fike and Red West to throw him out of town. Laurenz threatened to sue but never did.

NOV. 3–20:   Elvis visited the Friedberg home of twenty-three-year-old Ingrid Sauer, and together they attended Frankfurt's Casino de Paris and other clubs. During this period, Elvis invited fifteen-year-old Siegrid Schutz and her friends to his rented house to listen to music and to party.

DEC: Albert Hand published *Elvis Monthly* in Great Britain. Peter deVecchi wrote the first book about Elvis's stay in Germany.

DEC. 25:   Elvis donated $1,500 to the Landesjugendenheim Steinmuehle orphanage near Friedberg.
 Elvis met Priscilla Beaulieu's parents and often took the young girl to local festivities.

1960

The sixties applauded the genius rhythm and blues of pianist/singer Ray Charles; Roy Orbison finally hit the UK charts with "Only the Lonely," "Blue Angel," and "Today's Teardrops"; while the cha-cha was the new dance craze and the twist phenomena was boosted by Chubby Checker. The Beatles made their debut on the BBC; Bob Dylan premiered with thir-

teen songs on the CBS label in March 1961; the Rolling Stones first appeared at London's Marquee Club in July 1962; the Doors hit the charts and Motown's Supremes delighted audiences.
 The sixties ushered in an onslaught of British blues and rock bands including the Beatles, the Who, and the Rolling Stones, while Motown and Atlantic Records intro-

duced soul music to both sides of the Atlantic. Ike and Tina Turner and the Righteous Brothers brought refreshing, new music to the foreground, while the Beach Boys and Pat Boone pushed to keep a clean-cut commercial sound on the charts.

The sixties' hippie generation urged its followers to "turn on, tune in, and drop out." Drugs were the newest, fastest, and easiest way to appreciate the psychedelic sounds produced by the Doors, the Grateful Dead, David Bowie, Frank Zappa and the Mothers of Invention, and the Jefferson Airplane. The *Rock 'n' Roll Years* claimed: "Soon the drugs led to deaths, and a decade which produced more innovation than any other seemed to be slipping into a self-induced oblivion."

JAN.:   Rumors in Hollywood reported that United Artists wanted Elvis to play the lead role in *West Side Story* and that Colonel Parker turned it down because the character dies a brutal death. It was also reported that Elvis, Paul Anka, Fabian, Bobby Darin, and Frankie Avalon would play members of opposing street gangs, the Sharks and the Jets, in the same film.

Elvis posed with March of Dimes poster girl Mary Kosloski.

Before he returned to Elvis's group, Scotty Moore produced and played guitar for Jerry Lee Lewis's "Sweet Little Sixteen," "Hello, Josephine," "Good Rockin' Tonight," and "Be-Bop-a-Lula."

JAN. 2:   Elvis visited fifteen-year-old Siegrid Schutz in Bad Nauheim.

JAN. 20:   By orders of Army lieutenant Thomas S. Jones, Elvis was promoted to sergeant. He received a $22.94-a-month raise.

FEB.:   Elvis was on the cover of *Popular TV Movie & Record Stars*. The fan magazine *Elvis Monthly* was released in America.

Wall Beene of *Stars and Stripes* was the only reporter who interviewed Elvis while he was in the Army.

FEB. 17:   Although the LP *Elvis* (RCA LPM-1382) had sold over 3 million copies by this time, the RIAA only gave it a gold-record certification on this date.

FEB. 28:   Anita Wood stayed with Elvis at his rented home but was quickly spirited away when Elvis learned Priscilla was coming to say good-bye.

MAR.:   *Photoplay* ran a cover shot of Elvis in his Army fatigues and printed a "letter from Elvis" (allegedly written February 1, 1960, but probably from the Colonel's hand): "It won't be long now, before I'm home again. . . . Some people say the Army's tough—but it's a lot tougher if you try to fight it instead of making the most of your two years. I've tried to make the most of mine, and I think I've benefited by it. Sure, I had my share of troubles, like the time I put a tank in reverse gear by mistake . . . and crashed it. . . . I want a quiet homecoming, like any other soldier . . . just a small get-together with my friends and family in Memphis, I don't want any fuss or a brass band waiting for me. Other soldiers don't get one, so why should I?"

MAR.:   After playing straight roles in Army post shows, Elvis told Army buddies, "The kind of acting I expect to do in Hollywood . . . after my first picture for Hal Wallis [will be a] nonmusical for me." (*Photoplay*.)

Men watched their girlfriends and wives swoon at the mere mention of Elvis, and they wondered, "What's he got that I don't have?" There are not enough pages in any one book to answer that completely, but *TV Radio Mirror* reported how Frank Sinatra felt about Elvis in March 1960: "Say 'Elvis' and the sparks fly. Rumor had it Elvis's career would be damaged and over by his two-years stint in the Army. It didn't bother him."

Frank Sinatra booked Elvis for an appearance on an ABC-TV special in 1960 and continuously boosted Elvis's image. He said, "This boy believes, he believes right down to his bones. . . . Most of the others who came up after him copied a little of his style. . . . They're riding the gravy train of a new fad, rock 'n' roll. But Elvis has been singing all his life . . . church music, western music, folk music. Singing means everything to him. . . . Rock 'n' roll came from his heart and it ran over into his arms, legs, and hips. He was the real McCoy. . . . How can you sell him short?"

Movie columnist Eunice Field quoted a more mature Elvis, who felt the doubting, cynical press thought he was complacent: "I've always liked challenges. I like to prove I'm better than I was yesterday. When I made it as a rock 'n' roller, folks said I couldn't do ballads. Well, I did, and they liked it. Same with songs like 'Peace in the Valley.' . . . If I come out on top, fine. I'll be happy. If I lose out, nobody will hear me complain. There's no fun in making a hit unless you deserve it. I believe in that, and I'm trying to live by it." (*TV Radio Mirror.*)

While Elvis served in Germany, Paul Anka, Frankie Avalon, Edd Byrnes, Jimmy Clanton, Bobby Darin, Fabian, Ricky Nelson, Lloyd Price, and Bobby Rydell were trying to take his glory and remove him from the pop charts. The March 1960 *TV Radio Mirror* held a contest asking who would reign as King of rock 'n' roll. Elvis won, hands down.

Life magazine wanted to run Elvis on its cover with a feature story, but rejected the idea when Colonel Parker demanded $25,000. *Life* ran a story about the making of *G.I. Blues* in a later issue.

MAR. 1:   At nine A.M. at the Services Club of the Third U.S. Armored Division at Friedberg, Elvis held a press conference. Marion Kiesker, formerly of Sun Records, attended.

MAR. 2:   Elvis left Germany from Wiesbaden Airport, leaving behind a tearful Priscilla, who did not expect to see him again. After a brief stop at Prestwick Airport, Scotland, the DC-7 carrying him landed on March 3 at McGuire Air Force Base at Fort Dix, New Jersey, in a blizzard. Nancy Sinatra greeted him.

MAR. 3:   Elvis received $147 in out pay at the McGuire Air Force Base in Fort Dix, New Jersey. Elvis left the Air Force base, traveled to Fort Dix, and was discharged. Nancy Sinatra was by his side. Tina Louise covered the homecoming on the Mutual Broadcast Network.

MAR. 3:   A photo of Elvis in uniform, waving to the crowds, plastered the front page of papers across America and Europe. Telling the press there was "no one special" in his love life, Priscilla assumed there was nothing between them.

MAR. 5:   Elvis was discharged from the U.S. Army as a 170-pound buck sergeant. He had lost weight in the service. Photographs of Elvis's return show him in a uniform with the extra stripe of staff sergeant, but he did not

earn that rank. After his time in the Army, he rarely wore blue jeans and seemed more reserved and conservative.

Sen. Estes Kefauver (Democrat, Tennessee) paid tribute to Elvis in the *Congressional Record*.

MAR. 14: *Life* printed an article about the girls Elvis left behind and gave this gloomy report: "He is now a decent, God-fearing, country-loving all-American. He tells news reporters he will sing rock songs only if fans want to hear it and confesses: 'I want to become a good actor, because you can't build a whole career on just singing. Look at Frank Sinatra. Until he added acting to singing he found himself slipping downhill.' "

MAR. 15–18: Colonel Parker instructed Elvis about what was going to take place in his career over the next year, from how to dress to what to say. Parker was a controlling force in Elvis's life to be reckoned with.

MAR. 20: Elvis completed "Soldier Boy" (written by David Jones and Larry Banks) and Otis Blackwell's "Make Me Know It" (the first song he sang after he returned from the Army) on the LP *Elvis Is Back* at RCA's Nashville Studios.

MAR. 21: With 1,275,077 advance orders of *any* record he would produce, Elvis went into RCA's Nashville studios and recorded his first pure stereo release, "Fame and Fortune" by Fred Wise and Ben Weisman. Staying on the Top 100 chart ten weeks, it peaked at No. 17 (RCA 47-7740). Completed that day was the single's flip side, "Stuck on You" by Aaron Schroeder and Leslie McFarland. It peaked at No. 1 on *Billboard*'s Top 100 chart with a sixteen-week stay. It was No. 6 on R&B charts and No. 27 on the Country chart. He also recorded "It Feels So Right" by Fred Wise and Ben Weisman, which

peaked at No. 55 on *Billboard*'s Hot 100 chart (RCA 47-8585). Its flip side was "(Such an) Easy Question." Elvis completed the Doc Pomus–Mort Shuman song "A Mess of Blues." The million seller peaked at No. 32 on *Billboard*'s Hot 100 chart (RCA 47-7777, released in July 1960). Its flip side was "It's Now or Never." Elvis also recorded "Slicin' Sand" by Sid Tepper and Roy C. Bennett, for *Blue Hawaii*. Take No. 19 was released for the LP of that title.

At the Nashville recording sessions, advance PR men used the name "Sivle Yelserp" for "Elvis Presley" to make hotel and plane-flight reservations (*Sivle Yelserp* is "Elvis Presley" spelled backward.) He also traveled under the name Dr. John Carpenter.

A 1960 *Life* reporter noted: "The Elvis Presley everyone thinks he is—isn't. . . . He is no longer the sneering, hip-swinging symbol of the untamed beast that resides in 17-year-old breasts." Elvis seemed to have lost his enthusiasm for life. Something inside of him had died, and it was obvious to everyone around him. He refused to tour in concert. He wanted to prove he could act, but the gusto was gone. Hollywood's glamour bored him. He preferred going for hamburgers and malteds rather than to flashy Hollywood dinner parties. The rebel rocker with an attitude was gone. Fans wondered where their bad boy of rock 'n' roll had disappeared to and waited for him to return. Instead, he recorded "Are You Lonesome Tonight?" and "It's Now or Never," two songs that stated how he felt about a life going off course.

MAR. 23: To capitalize on Elvis's return, the Colonel planned a trip for Elvis that would resemble the campaign train rides of presidents. The press followed Elvis as he boarded a train to Miami Beach to videotape a show for Frank Sinatra. Every few hours, the Colonel had Elvis stand and wave to anxious fans along the route. Scotty Moore recalls, "In every little

◀ A young Priscilla Beaulieau holding Elvis's photo in Frankfurt, Germany, March 1960. *Courtesy of AP/Wide World Photos.*

town along the way, the tracks were lined. Twenty-four hours a day. The whole trip. Photographers. Cameramen. Kids. I don't know where they came from." (See *Look*, 1971.)

MAR. 26: "The Frank Sinatra–Timex Special" (the final Sinatra special of the 1959–60 season) was taped with Sinatra and Elvis for ABC-TV in the Grand Ballroom of Miami Beach's Fontainebleau Hotel. Elvis's salary for a six-minute appearance was $125,000. Four hundred fans showed up at the Fontainebleau and were in the audience of seven hundred when the King sang "Fame and Fortune" and "Stuck on You."

The show opened with Elvis and the cast singing "It's Nice to Go Traveling." In a rare duet with Nancy Sinatra, Elvis sang her hit "Witchcraft." Sinatra tried his rendition of "Love Me Tender." Other guests were Sinatra Rat Pack members Sammy Davis, Jr., Peter Lawford, and Joey Bishop, as well as the Tom Hansen Dancers and the Nelson Riddle Orchestra. Despite this collection of stars, the Nielsen rating was 41.5, not as high as Elvis's performances for the "Ed Sullivan Show."

MAR. 27: An article in *Bild am Sonntag* exposed the conflict between Monsieur Laurenz of the De Fleur Clinic and Elvis. Laurenz alleged that Elvis attacked him with a knife and claimed Lamar Fike and Red West beat him.

APR.: Elvis said he had not changed his style after he retained the title of Most Popular Singer Worldwide. Although Bobby Darin had naively said (when Elvis left for Germany) it was close to impossible for fans to be loyal to any one singer for more than a few months, Ricky Nelson admitted publicly, "When Elvis returned from Germany, the competition was rather tough for all young male singers." (See *The Rock 'n' Roll Years*.)

Elvis was on the cover of *Movieland*

and TV Time. He also appeared on the cover of *Movie Stars*.

The Easter release "Crying in the Chapel" earned a gold-record disc in Britain.

APR. 3: The release of the LP *Elvis Is Back* (RCA LPM-2231, with songs recorded in March and April 1960 at RCA Studios in Nashville) included a few demo recordings produced by Phil Spector. The album opened like a book, with song titles on the jacket and bonus photos of Elvis inside. Sales climbed to over $1 million within two months. For three weeks the album was No. 2 on *Billboard*'s Best-Selling chart (where it stayed fifty-six weeks). The album was Elvis's first stereo album. It stayed on *Billboard*'s Best-Selling stereophonic LP chart for fourteen weeks, reaching No. 9.

Elvis had asked Freddie Bienstock of Hill and Range to rearrange Tony Martin's "There's No Tomorrow" while Elvis was in West Germany. Bienstock contacted Aaron Schroeder and Wally Gold, who did the rewrite via a demo tape with vocals by David Hill. Newly named "It's Now or Never," the original song was based on the Italian song "O Sole Mio." Elvis recorded "It's Now or Never" at RCA's Nashville studios. It sold 2 million copies and hit *Billboard*'s Hot 100 chart at No. 44 and within five weeks was No. 1. It remained on that chart for twenty weeks, was No. 7 on the R&B chart, and was No. 1 for eight weeks in England. It was *Billboard*'s Vocal Single of 1960 and has sold over 23 million copies to date (RCA 47-7777). Its flip side was "A Mess of Blues." Elvis also recorded Jesse Stone's "Like a Baby," which is heard only on the LP *Elvis Is Back*.

APR. 4: "Dirty, Dirty Feeling" by Leiber-Stoller was in the *Tickle Me* sound track of 1965, but it was recorded at RCA's Nashville studios on April 4, 1960, with "Fever" by John Davenport (Otis Blackwell's pseudonym). First titled "The Girl Next Door" and later "The Girl Next Door

Went-a-Walking" (written by Bill Rice and Thomas Wayne), "Dirty, Dirty Feeling" was completed on April 4, and it is on the LP *Elvis Is Back*. Elvis also sang "The Girl of My Best Friend" (by Beverly Ross and Sam Bobrick) and "Thrill of Your Love" (by Stan Kesler) which are on the LP *Elvis Is Back*. "I Gotta Know" by Paul Evans and Matt Williams was recorded. The single (RCA 47-7810) peaked at No. 20 during an eleven-week run on *Billboard*'s Hot 100 chart. Its flip side was "Are You Lonesome Tonight?" "Are You Lonesome Tonight?" was sung because the Colonel wanted Elvis to record it. The song hit *Billboard*'s Hot 100 chart at No. 35 and within seven days took the largest leap upward in history, to No. 2. It stayed on that chart for sixteen weeks. It was No. 22 on the Country chart and No. 3 on the R&B chart. It was No. 1 in Britain for four weeks. "Are You Lonesome Tonight?" received three Grammy nominations but won none. Elvis also sang a duet with Charlie Hodge during " I Will Be Home Again" by Bennie Benjamin, Raymond Leveen, and Lou Singer. It appears on the LP *Elvis Is Back*.

"Such a Night," written by Lincoln Chase, was finished by Elvis, and take No. 4 was selected for its single release. It peaked at No. 16 during an eight-week stay on *Billboard*'s Hot 100 chart (RCA 47-8400, released in July 1964, with the flip side "Never Ending").

"Reconsider Baby" (by Lowell Fulson) was recorded (but many bootleg LPs have the version that was recorded on March 25, 1961, from the Bloch Arena in Honolulu).

APR. 27–28: At RCA studios in Nashville, Elvis recorded the sound track for *G.I. Blues*. The purpose of the film was to promote the idea that soldiering is "fun." Advertisements for the movie promoted Elvis as the perfect all-American boy: "The idol of the teenagers is the idol of the family." Elvis was now the young man parents wanted their daughters to bring home!

APR. 27: "Didja Ever" (by Sid Wayne and Sherman Edwards for *G.I. Blues*) was recorded by Elvis at RCA's Hollywood studio with the Jordanaires as backup vocalists. Doc Pomus and Mort Shuman's "Doin' the Best I Can," "G.I. Blues" by Sid Tepper and Roy C. Bennett, "Frankfort Special" (not released until 1978) by Sid Wayne and Sherman Edwards, and "Whistling Blues" instrumental (but no vocal by Elvis) were completed. The *G.I. Blues* film version of "Frankfort Special" had horns and extra voices added.

APR. 28: A slow version of "Big Boots" by Sid Wayne and Sherman Edwards was recorded at RCA's Hollywood studio for *G.I. Blues*. A faster take was made on May 6. Aspects of both versions were used in the film's sound track. During this session, "Wooden Heart" was recorded for *G.I. Blues* with Jimmie Haskell on accordion (RCA 1226), and it was released in the United Kingdom, where it remained on the pop charts twenty-seven weeks. It was released in the U.S. in 1964, but it never charted, despite sales of over 1 million records. Elvis recorded "Pocketful of Rainbows" (written by Fred Wise and Ben Weisman for *G.I. Blues*), but this version (with a few lines sung by Juliet Prowse) was not used in the movie. It does appear on a British boxed EP, *The EP Collection*, Vol. 2. Elvis also completed "Tonight Is So Right for Love" and the eighteen-second "What's She Really Like" (both by Sid Wayne and Abner Silver) for the film.

MAY: Elvis appeared on the cover of *TV Movie Screen*.

MAY 1: Paramount Pictures canceled a hundred-city tour with Elvis because the crowd control was impossible to arrange.

Elvis and his bodyguards arrived at the Beverly Wilshire Hotel and prepared to shoot *G.I. Blues*. D. J. Fontana and Scotty Moore appeared in the film's rathskeller scene.

MAY 2:   Elvis began filming *G.I. Blues*, in which he played a GI named Tulsa McLean.

The film has become one of the five top video rentals of Elvis's films. All of Elvis's scenes were shot on a Paramount lot. A camera crew went to West Germany for location shooting.

Elvis played host on the Paramount lot to the king and queen of Thailand, the king and queen of Nepal, and several royal princesses from Norway, Denmark, and Sweden. He called Liberace to brag, knowing "Lee" often entertained royalty. Elvis felt as if he had really shown the world he had class.

MAY 6:   At the Radio Recorders recording session for *G.I. Blues*, Elvis was unhappy with the music he was being forced to sing. He wanted to be an *actor*, not a Pat Boone clone. This sound track became RCA's first video disc. The record for the film stayed on the charts 111 weeks, despite the fact it is inferior. Rock fans were disappointed with the rather bland and conservative music in the film.

After failing to record correctly the song "Shoppin' Around" (by Sid Tepper, Roy C. Bennett, and Aaron Schroeder) for *G.I. Blues* on April 27,

Elvis's seventh take on May 6 was deemed okay for release. Horns were later added to the movie version. "Tonight's All Right for Love" (by Sid Wayne, Abner Silver, and Joe Lilley) was recorded, but it was released later on the 1974 LP *Elvis—A Legendary Performer*, Vol. 1.

MAY 7–13:   An issue of *TV Guide* featured Elvis and Sinatra on the cover. By this time, the two men were having a "cold war" because Elvis briefly dated Juliet Prowse, who was the fiancée of Frank Sinatra. Insiders believed Sinatra was jealous of Elvis's return to being "the King" of the music world. For certain, Elvis gave Old Blue Eyes a run for his money.

MAY 12:   The entire nation watched ABC-TV's showing of "Welcome Home, Elvis," the final Frank Sinatra–Timex TV special. Fans cringed when they saw Elvis blending too comfortably with Sinatra's laid-back style. Elvis no longer seemed dissenting or dangerous. He wore first an Army uniform and then a tuxedo.

MAY 13:   Critics claimed Elvis had deserted rock 'n' roll. Others said he had gotten lazy and did not care about mu-

▶ Elvis in *G.I. Blues*, July 4, 1960. *Courtesy of AP/Wide World Photos.*

sic. Some said he had matured, after having faced grief and losses. Life no longer was a bright-eyed adventure for Elvis. He had seen too much and had been hounded to death by the press and the public. Nothing was sacred anymore. His actions seemed mechanical and he knew it.

MAY 15:   RCA had an unprecedented 1,430,000 presold records of whatever Elvis decided to record after his Army return.

MAY 20–30:   Elvis rehearsed and filmed *G.I. Blues*. When scenes ended, his bodyguards formed a phalanx around him and escorted him to a waiting car. Next stop, the hotel, where the Memphis men would eat until they couldn't move.

JUNE: The June cover of *Movie Mirror* stated, "The King of Rock 'n' Roll Is Dead!" One reporter said, "Rocker Doffs the Cool Duds—A Conservative Elvis!" His fans were horrified that their hero, the man who showed the world how to rock 'n' roll, was now being looked at as nothing more than a wealthy, commercialized, conventional entertainer accepted by the same critics who had once defiled him. This turn of events did not sit well with die-hard rock enthusiasts.

Elvis allegedly "earned" a first-degree black belt in karate, but no one was teaching him at that time!

JULY 3:   Elvis refused to attend his father and Dee Stanley's wedding. Dee had three sons (Billy, David, and Rick Stanley) and was Vernon's junior by ten years. Vernon and Dee were married at Richard Neely's Huntsville, Alabama, home (Neely was best man and the brother of Dee). Elvis still mourned the death of his mother and felt Vernon's marriage was inappropriate. He vowed never to accept Dee or treat her with any respect.

JULY 17:   Elvis and James Brown met at the Continental Hotel in Hollywood and became lifelong friends. They sang all night at a piano together. Although Elvis wanted to record with James Brown's band, the Famous Flames, Colonel Parker said, "No!" Thus, they never recorded together.

CA. JULY 19:   Elvis finished filming Paramount's *G.I. Blues.*

JULY 20:   Vernon brought his bride back to Graceland. Dee told this author in June 1991: "It was a nightmare of all nightmares, with Elvis parading all his women, people with drugs by the bagfuls, and odd friends in and out of the house every night. We soon moved out of Graceland to Dolan Avenue, thank goodness. Elvis's home was *no* place to raise young boys! It was dreadful." Living in Graceland were Vernon, Dee and her sons, Elvis's grandmother and aunt, a cook, seven members of the Memphis Mafia, and a few other relatives.

JULY 24–AUG.:   Elvis received the script *Flaming Star* and memorized everyone's lines. He never carried a script on the set.

AUGUST (EARLY):   Elvis completed songs for *Flaming Star*'s sound track at Radio Recorders in Hollywood. "Flaming star" alludes to a vision some Indians declare they see as a sign of approaching death.

AUG. 8:   "Britches" by Sid Wayne and Sherman Edwards was recorded by Elvis at Radio Recorders in Hollywood. It only appears on the LP *Elvis—A Legendary Performer*, Vol. 3, (released in 1978). It may have been during this session he recorded "Cane and a High Starched Collar" by Sid Tepper and Roy C. Bennett. It was released years later in 1976 and is heard on *Elvis—A Legendary Performer*, Vol. 2. Take No.

2 was a false start; take No. 3 was used in the movie *Flaming Star*. The film's title song by Sid Wayne and Sherman Edwards peaked at No. 14 during a seven-week stay on *Billboard*'s Hot 100 chart.

AUG. 9: "Summer Kisses, Winter Tears" by Fred Wise, Ben Weisman, and Jack Lloyd was cut from the movie *Flaming Star*, but it was recorded on August 9 and appears on the EP *Elvis By Request* and the LP *Elvis for Everyone*.

AUG. 16: Elvis began filming *Flaming Star*, starring as "Pacer Burton." Film locations included San Fernando Valley ranches, the Conejo Movie Ranch outside Thousand Oaks, California, and Twentieth Century-Fox's Stage 14 (interiors).

Marlon Brando and Frank Sinatra were originally asked to play the two Burton brothers (instead of Elvis and Steve Forrest), but they declined.

Because Elvis's character was the son of a white father and an Indian mother, the film was banned in South Africa. During a fight scene with Elvis, Red West (portraying an Indian) broke an arm.

AUG. 17: Tests were made with Elvis wearing brown-tinted contact lenses, but he discarded them because they were distracting. This was the first time Elvis became aware that he might be slightly nearsighted.

AUG. 18: Going against the Colonel's wishes, Elvis refused to sing on horseback in the film, yet he crooned during a party scene and sang over the titles. Though his acting was somewhat proficient in *Flaming Star*, Elvis began to look like anyone in a crowd. His roles were predictable. He was *not* Brando.

He had lost a relevant, unique dynamic when he allowed the Colonel to run his life for him.

AUG. 18: A sneak preview of *G.I. Blues* was well received at the Majestic Theater in Dallas, Texas, but critics panned it as an insipid effort to show an old-fashioned and charming GI surrounded by lovesick young women. Even the film's rendition of "Blue Suede Shoes" was lifeless and dull. Hoping for the best, audiences poured into movie theaters. Remarkably, the movie was the biggest box-office draw in a decade. *Billboard* voted "It's Now or Never" the hit of the year, which pleased die-hard Elvis devotees.

CA. AUG. 20: While shooting a scene for *Flaming Star*, Elvis fell off a horse but was not seriously hurt.

AUG. 30: Elvis did not please the crew or the director of *Flaming Star*. Director Don Siegel called Elvis "insecure" and "unsure of himself" and remembered after shooting *Flaming Star*, "I was never interested in Elvis after the picture because . . . he was so removed! To try and submit another property for him in a dramatic vein . . . I mean, he did his usual shtick, which was to sing twelve songs in a terrible film." (*Florence* (Calif.) *Morning News*, Oct. 5, 1977.)

SEPT.: The Mexican government banned all future Elvis films because a showing of *G.I. Blues* in Mexico City caused a riot that left the theater in shambles.

SEPT. 15: A Hollywood AP reporter wrote: "Elvis Presley, who once wore long sideburns and gold-lamé jackets that even Liberace wouldn't be caught dead in, has become a fashion plate. Movie stylist Sy DeVore disclosed yesterday that he has fashioned a new wardrobe for the onetime Beau Brummell of the black leather jacket and motorcycle boots set. DeVore said the new Elvis took his place alongside such conservative and stylish men as

Frank Sinatra, William Holden, Peter Lawford, and even JFK himself. The stylist announced, 'He could pass as a Wall Street Banker. . . . he flipped when he saw the clothes. He loved them. . . . Elvis, I discovered, doesn't wear underwear.' "

Colonel Parker set the stage for *any* reaction to Elvis. During Elvis's Army tour of duty, Parker sold millions of dollars' worth of Elvis dog tags, photographs, and other gimmicks to sorrowful supporters who missed him. Parker didn't saturate the market because he believed you can't give a starving horse a bale of hay. You have to keep it hungry, wanting more. The Colonel's photographs of the brave Elvis on duty by a tank, of the courageous Elvis with rifle and ready to fire, and of the uniformed Elvis, ready to fight for his country, kept millions of fans yearning to buy new records and tickets to his films.

OCT. 4: The filming of *Flaming Star* ended. Elvis spent several nights with wardrobe assistant Nancy Sharp.

OCT. 30–31: The *His Hand in Mine* LP was recorded in RCA's studio B in Nashville.

An all-night session with the Jordanaires resulted in thirteen gospel songs recorded plus the secular tune "Surrender." The LP *His Hand in Mine* was released in December. It combined the blues with a rocking country ensemble of religious songs: "His Hand in Mine," "I'm Gonna Walk Dem Golden Stairs," "In My Father's House," "Milky White Way," "Known Only to Him," "I Believe in the Man in the Sky," and on side two, "Joshua Fit the Battle," "Jesus Knows What I Need," "Swing Down, Sweet Chariot," "Mansion Over the Hilltop," "If We Never Meet Again," and "Working on the Building." The album was reissued in January 1976.

OCT. 30: "It's Now or Never'" hit the U.K. charts at No. 1 and remained

there for eight weeks. "I Believe in the Man in the Sky" by Richard Howard was completed by Elvis in RCA's Nashville studios (RCA 447-0643). It never charted. Mosie Lister's "His Hand in Mine" (RCA 74-0130, which did not chart) and take No. 10 of Lister's "He Knows What I Need" (on the LP *How Great Thou Art*) were released, and "How Great Thou Art" is also on the LP reissue *His Hand in Mine* and mistitled "Jesus Knows What I Need" (RCA 447-0670). Ira Stanphill's gospel song "Mansion on the Hilltop" was recorded, and take No. 3 is heard on the LP *His Hand in Mine*.

Elvis recorded Doc Pomus and Mort Shuman's English adaptation of Dean Martin's Italian hit "Torna a Sorrento," retitled "Surrender." Take No. 4 was released and reached No. 1 on *Billboard*'s Hot 100 chart during a twelve-week run, and No. 1 for four weeks in England. Over 5 million copies of the record were sold, despite the fact it was the shortest No. 1 hit in the history of pop music (one minute, fifty-one seconds). Its flip side was "Lonely Man" (RCA 47-7850, released in February 1961). Elvis recorded the standard gospel tune "Milky White Way," but its single did not chart (RCA 447-0652, released in March 1966, with the flip side "Swing Down, Sweet Chariot").

OCT. 31: With the Jordanaires as backup vocalists, Elvis recorded "Working on the Building" at RCA's Nashville studio. The Jordanaires had previously recorded the song in 1950 (Capitol 1254). Elvis's version is heard on the LP *His Hand in Mine*. "Crying in the Chapel" was also completed that day. In 1965, RCA released the single with its flip side "I Believe in the Man in the Sky" (RCA 447-0643). "Crying in the Chapel" hit No. 3 during a fourteen-week stay on *Billboard*'s Top 100 chart. In May, it became No. 1 on the Easy-Listening charts and lasted seven weeks in that position. In England, it was No. 1 for two weeks.

Needless to say, it sold over 1 million copies.

"If We Never Meet Again," a gospel written by A. E. Brumley, the spiritual "I'm Gonna Walk Dem Golden Stairs," "In My Father's House" by Aileene Hanks, and "Joshua Fit the Battle" by Marshall Bartholomew with its single flip side Stuart Hamblen's "Known Only to Him"(RCA 447-0651) were completed for the LP *His Hand in Mine*.

The old, standard black gospel song "Swing Down, Sweet Chariot" was recorded by Elvis with the Jordanaires as an uncharted single (RCA 447-0652, released in March 1966, with its uncharted flip side "Milky White Way").

NOV.: Despite phenomenal success and international fame, Elvis had become an exceedingly lonely, moody man who had developed extremely odd eating, sleeping, and personal habits. He detested seeing himself in movies because he thought of himself as "too fat," but he would gorge himself on junk food and he often went for weeks without taking baths. Elvis's sleepwalking habits endangered him. One night he was found in a parking lot. On another occasion, he walked down a hotel corridor until he slammed into a wall. The Colonel gave an ultimatum to members of the Memphis Mafia: guard and protect him or you'll be out. Elvis was watched twenty-four hours a day. If he started to sleepwalk, the guard would awaken him, soothe him, read to him, and put him back to bed.

NOV. 1–6: Elvis memorized the script *Wild in the Country*.

NOV. 7: At Radio Recorders, Elvis cut "Forget Me Never" and "In My Way," both written by Fred Wise and Ben Weisman, and two versions of "Lonely Man" by Bennie Benjamin and Sol Marcus for *Wild in the Country*. "Lonely Man" and "Forget Me Never" were not used in the movie. "Forget Me Never" and "In My Way" are on the LPs *Elvis*

for Everyone and *Separate Ways*. The single "Lonely Man" climbed to No. 32 on *Billboard*'s Top 100 chart during a five-week run (RCA 47-7850, released in February 1961, with the flip side "Surrender").

Elvis's take No. 19 was released in May 1961 and peaked at No. 26 on *Billboard*'s Top 100 (RCA 47-7880). Its flip side was "I Feel So Bad," which also charted.

NOV. 8: For *Wild in the Country*, Elvis recorded "I Slipped, I Stumbled, I Fell" by Fred Wise and Ben Weisman at Radio Recorders. Take No. 13 was released.

NOV. 11: Fabian was rejected and Elvis was cast as Glenn Tyler in Twentieth Century-Fox's *Wild in the Country*, which began filming November 11. It costarred Hope Lange, Tuesday Weld (whose singing voice was dubbed by Connie Francis), Millie Perkins, Rafer Johnson, John Ireland, and Gary Lockwood. Red West played Hank Tyler, his first, small speaking role.

In Hollywood, Elvis's and his entourage's reputation as womanizers preceded them. Many Memphis Mafia members used Elvis's fame to lure women into their own rooms. One starlet said, "Nobody'd talk. All these guys . . . there was a pecking order . . . [guys would go from one woman to another and finally] girls were supposed to get to Elvis, although it never worked out that way." (See *Look*, May 18, 1971).

When Elvis threw a tantrum to get his way, an aide would handle the situation. Elvis's moods did not sit well with anyone, and he was becoming more like Gladys in her final days, dyeing his hair with L'Oréal Excellence blue-black, popping diet pills, and being up one minute and down the next. One of the Memphis Mafia confirmed, "One day he'd be the sweetest person in the world, the next day he'd burn holes in you with his eyes. It was hard on the guys. One time he fired every one of them, told them to get their asses back to Memphis, and they packed and left. By the time they'd got to the airport, Elvis changed his mind. . . . Elvis told them to get their asses back, they were on the payroll again." (See *Look*, May 18, 1971.)

People around Elvis responded as he did. If he frowned, they frowned. If he laughed, they did. If he wanted to watch television all night, they did. When he wanted a girl, Joe Esposito or Red West found one (or more). Elvis rarely ventured outside his Hollywood residences. In the privacy of his rented homes, he could do whatever he wanted to do, to whoever allowed it. And everyone seemed to allow it, if they dared to enter.

NOV. 23: *G.I. Blues* was released nationally to sell-out crowds.

NOV. 23: Twentieth Century-Fox's *Flaming Star* was sneak-previewed in the Loyola Theater in Westchester, California, featuring two songs. On November 25, a version of the film with four songs was shown. The two-song version was released to the general public, who appreciated the performances of Elvis, Barbara Eden (who played Roslyn Pierce), and Steve Forrest (playing Clint Burton). The picture hit *Variety*'s list of top-grossing films at No. 12.

DEC.: Elvis watched the movie *Let's Make Love* (1960) and was delighted to hear Marilyn Monroe, Yves Montand, and Frankie Vaughan sing about him and the Colonel in a song titled "Specialization." Monroe knew who he was, and this pleased Elvis. Although he wanted to meet the sex goddess, he never did.

DEC. 3: Elvis was treated for boils on his rump. He went home to Memphis to recuperate, leaving the set for *Wild in the Country*.

DEC. 8: Fabian visited Graceland and

Elvis drove him through town in his Cadillac with gold-plated interior. Its license number was 2X 139. The Cadillac 75 limousine was painted with diamond dust and gold flakes, had gold-plated bumpers and hubcaps, interior record players, a TV set, shoe buffer, telephones, and a "gold" electric razor. Oriental fish scales and crushed diamonds reportedly composed the forty coats of exterior paint on the Cadillac. Gold-lamé interior curtains hid backseat passengers from the view of any driver.

CA. DEC. 9: Elvis convinced Priscilla Beaulieu's parents in West Germany to allow their daughter to spend Christmas with him in Graceland.

DEC. 20: The premiere of Twentieth Century-Fox's film *Flaming Star* was held in Los Angeles, and it was well received.

DEC. 21: Elvis posed in front of Graceland for a photo shoot. Alongside him was a new Rolls-Royce (license number ULL 501).

DEC. 25: Priscilla Ann Beaulieu stayed in the east wing of Graceland, and also with Dee and Vernon Presley in a house behind the mansion, while she shared Christmas with Elvis. In the east wing, she was separated from Elvis, who often saw other young girls and women after Priscilla went to bed.

Priscilla (born May 25, 1945) is a gray-eyed beauty of five feet three inches, the daughter of Ann Beaulieu and Navy lieutenant James Wagner. Her biological father died in a plane crash when Priscilla was six months old. When her mother remarried Air Force captain Joseph Beaulieu, he adopted Priscilla. In 1960, the family lived in Germany.

Elvis convinced "Cilla" 's parents to allow her to visit him in Los Angeles while he filmed a new movie, and they reluctantly agreed. Because his mother and one of his "old loves" (Debra Paget) had black hair, Elvis persuaded Cilla to dye her hair the same color.

Prior to Elvis, Priscilla had known no other lovers. At fifteen, she was young and naive and had no idea whether or not Elvis's lifestyle was "normal," but she felt it was not.

CA. DEC. 27: Elvis was inducted into the Los Angeles Indian Tribal Council by Chief Wah-Nee-Ota for his portrayal of a man with Indian blood in *Flaming Star*.

DEC. 28: Although he did not drink alcohol, take hard drugs, or smoke cigarettes (although there are photographs of Elvis smoking), Elvis was still considered by authorities to be "a corrupt, bad influence" on society. In reprisal, Elvis recorded the album *Fifty Million Fans Can't Be Wrong*, but the disparaging critics did not stop and antagonists continued to torment him.

DEC. 31: As the fourteenth top-grossing film, *G.I. Blues* earned Para-

mount Pictures $4.3 million in 1960, and it reached No. 2 in *Variety*'s weekly list of top-grossing pictures.

The LP *A Golden Celebration* (*West Germany, 1958–1960*) revealed songs Elvis had sung privately in West Germany: "Earth Angel" by Jesse Belvin, "Danny Boy," "The Fool," "Soldier Boy," and "He's Only a Prayer Away."

1961

Bob Dylan was discovered in the folk clubs of Greenwich Village and his haunting and thoughtful lyrics reflected the changing times and shifting moods of his generation and the nation, while "We Shall Overcome" became the marching hymn for civil rights groups and social activists worldwide. Thousands peacefully protested racial discrimination at the side of civil rights leader Dr. Martin Luther King, Jr.

Citizens across America watched in horror as Southern police armed with weapons and vicious dogs fought peaceful black and white demonstrators who marched with King.

In the eye of the storm was deep-seated racial hatred on both sides of the issue, and although King's noble goals and contributions resulted in major benefits to the black and white communities, racial unrest, bigotry, hypocrisy, poverty, and segregation were not eliminated.

The government and the mainstream did not take seriously what was happening within the inner cities or within the liberal youth cultures of America and Europe. Simple solutions could no longer

▲ Elvis celebrates Christmas at Graceland, 1960.
Courtesy of Wide World Photos.

solve imposing, mammoth social dilemmas.

JAN.: Elvis tried to take courses at UCLA, but college officials refused to let him into classes for fear that the students (and his fans) would get out of control.

Elvis was asked to sing for the 1961 annual presentation for British royalty, but Colonel Parker turned down the invitation because Parker could not attend. Once again, the Colonel put himself before Elvis, and the Cat was gravely disappointed.

JAN. 2: Priscilla Beaulieu returned to Germany after staying up all night to celebrate the New Year with Elvis.

JAN. 3: Elvis returned to Los Angeles to finish *Wild in the Country*. Dating a costume assistant and actress Hope Lange, he seemed to have quickly forgotten Priscilla Beaulieu. Ads for his next movie stating he "Sings of Love to Three Women!" were close to the truth, and rumors spread he was dating Nancy Sinatra, too.

JAN. 8: Elvis celebrated his birthday with Hope Lange on a Twentieth Century-Fox set, but he was in a bad mood because the Colonel forced him to sing in *Wild in the Country* and he had been told it was a nonsinging role. When Colonel Parker changed his mind and said, "You'll sing. There's more money if you sing," Elvis complied.

JAN. 10: While in Los Angeles, Elvis called Germany to speak to Captain Joseph Beaulieu, Priscilla's stepfather. Elvis asked that the captain allow Priscilla to move to Tennessee and finish her education in a private school in Memphis. The captain was not agreeable at this time.

JAN. 18: Elvis finished filming *Wild in the Country* and spent a few days with a current girlfriend, wardrobe assistant Nancy Sharp.

FEB.: Elvis spent a few weeks resting at Graceland. On February 1, he told the Colonel he wanted to sing live again. Parker arranged two performances at Memphis's Ellis Auditorium, but told Elvis he was to concentrate on acting.

FEB. 25: Tennessee governor Buford Ellington proclaimed the day Elvis Presley Day.

Elvis performed two shows at the Ellis Auditorium and gave $51,612 to charities. He was interviewed by the press in the Empire Room at the Claridge Hotel in Memphis.

MAR. 8: Gov. Buford Ellington bestowed the title of "honorary colonel" to Elvis before the General Assembly, the state's legislature. Elvis was delighted.

MAR. 12: Woody Harris's "I Want You With Me" and "Gently" by Murray Wizell and Edward Lisbona were recorded by Elvis at RCA's Nashville studios. Both are heard on the LP *Something for Everybody*. "Give Me the Right," by Fred Wise and Norman Blagman, and Chuck Willis's "I Feel So Bad" were completed. Floyd Cramer backed Elvis on piano and Boots Randolph played sax. "I Feel So Bad" had a nine-week run on *Billboard*'s Top 100 chart and reached No. 5, while it peaked at No. 15 on the R&B chart (RCA 47-7880). Its flip side was "Wild in the Country." "I'm Comin' Home" by Charlie Rich (with Floyd Cramer on piano), "In Your Arms" by Aaron Schroeder and Wally Gold, and "It's a Sin" by Zeb Turner and Fred Rose were completed. They are on the LP *Something For Everybody*.

MAR. 13:   Teddy Redell's "Judy" was recorded by Elvis at RCA's Nashville studios, and its five-week stay on *Billboard*'s Hot 100 chart peaked at No. 78 (RCA 47-9287, released in August 1967). Its flip side was "There's Always Me," recorded the same day, written by Don Robertson. RCA didn't release the song until August 1967. It had a six-week run on *Billboard*'s Hot 100 chart and climbed to No. 56 (RCA 47-9287). Elvis also recorded "Put the Blame on Me" (written by Fred Wise, Kay Twomey, and Norman Blagman for *Tickle Me*). "Sentimental Me" (written by Jimmy Cassin and Jim Morehead) was recorded and appeared on the LPs *Double Dynamite*, *Separate Ways*, and *Something for Everybody*. Elvis recorded "Starting Today" by Don Robertson, which appears on the LP *Something for Everybody*.

MAR. 14:   Elvis and his entourage flew to California.

MAR. 15:   Angela Lansbury left Broadway's "Taste of Honey" to play Elvis's mother in *Blue Hawaii*.

MAR. 17:   Elvis began filming Paramount's *Blue Hawaii* which costarred Joan Blackman, Angela Lansbury, Nancy Walters, Roland Winters, and John Archer. Red West played a party guest. Vocal accompaniment was provided by the Jordanaires. The film was shot on Oahu, with scenes at Waikiki Beach, the Honolulu International Airport, the Ala Moana Park, Hanauma Bay, the Ala Wai Yacht Club, the jail at Honolulu's Police Department, the Tantalus area, the Waiola Tea Room, and at Paramount's California studio lots.

MAR. 17–20:   Elvis entertained Juliet Prowse, Pat Fackenthal (whom he kissed in the movie), and Joan Blackman during the filming of *Blue Hawaii*. Although Juliet Prowse was supposed to play the part of Maile Duval, she made too many demands and on March 13 was replaced by Joan

Blackman. This not only infuriated Elvis and Prowse, it angered Prowse's fiancé, Frank Sinatra.

MAR. 21:   "Hawaiian Sunset" by Sid Tepper and Roy C. Bennett; "K-u-u-i-p-o" by George Weiss, Hugo Peretti, and Luigi Creatore; "No More" by Don Robertson and Hal Blair; and "Playing With Fire" by Fred Wise and Ben Weisman (cut from the film) were completed by Elvis for *Blue Hawaii* at Radio Recorders in Hollywood, with backup vocalists the Surfers. In the movie's version of "K-u-u-i-p-o" a group of women back Elvis. He sang the song without an audience for the broadcast of "Elvis: Aloha From Hawaii," which was aired April 4, 1973, but the song was not included on that LP. It was later put on the LP *Mahalo From Elvis* (Honolulu, Jan. 14, 1973).

MAR. 22:   At the Hollywood Radio Recorders studio, Fred Wise and Ben Weisman's "Almost Always True" was recorded by Elvis for *Blue Hawaii*. It appears on the album of that title and on four bootleg LPs. "Aloha Oe" was split in two takes for commercial use. The seventh take of "Blue Hawaii" (written by Leo Robin and Ralph Rainger) was used for the film and record. No singles were made. "Hawaiian Wedding Song" by Charles E. King (English lyrics by Al Hoffman and Dick Manning); "Ito Eats" and "Island of Love (Kauai)," both written by Sid Tepper and Roy C. Bennett; "Moonlight Swim," composed by Sylvia Dee and Ben Weisman; and "Steppin' out of Line," written by Fred Wise, Ben Weisman, and Dolores Fuller, were finished on March 22 for *Blue Hawaii*. The film's version of "Steppin' out of Line" used take Nos. 8 and 19; take No. 17 was on the *Pot Luck* LP; but the piece in full was cut from the main body of the movie and added to the end.

MAR. 23:   For *Blue Hawaii*, Elvis sang "Beach Boy Blues," written by Sid Tepper and Roy C. Bennett. Take No. 3

was used for a release. "Can't Help Falling in Love" by George Weiss, Hugo Peretti, and Luigi Creatore was also recorded. It took many takes to sing it correctly, and take No. 29 (RCA 47-7968) was finally used for the single (which peaked at No. 2 during a fourteen-week run on *Billboard*'s Top 100 chart). Also recorded was its flip side, "Rock-a-Hula-Baby," written by Fred Wise, Ben Weisman, and Florence Kay. Take No. 5 was used for the single, which hit the Top 100 chart at No. 23 for a nine-week stay (RCA 47-7968). *Note:* A rare compact 33-single release played 33⅓ rpm (RCA 447-7968).

MAR. 24:   Elvis became self-conscious about his looks on film. In *Blue Hawaii* scantily clad starlets pranced around a disenchanted, overweight Elvis who wore tight-fitting swim trunks. Director Norman Taurog often compared Elvis with Clark Gable, but he regretted Elvis had not stretched to reach his potential in acting. Elvis was still controlled by the Colonel, and Parker didn't care if his protégé was a poor, mediocre, or excellent actor unless his performances lowered his films' grosses.

Elvis and his group flew to Hawaii.

MAR. 25:   Elvis gave a benefit concert for the USS *Arizona* Memorial Fund at Bloch Arena at Pearl Harbor, Hawaii, and donated $5,000 of $62,000 to the Memorial. Elvis was accompanied from the airport to the hotel and the arena by country entertainer Minnie Pearl, who told reporters later that Elvis's success was so huge that it endangered his safety in public. She felt sorry for Elvis.

Over two thousand fans greeted Elvis at the airport. Minnie Pearl felt they would be killed by overanxious women who chased Elvis, but Elvis loved every minute of it. Going into his hotel, the Colonel and members of the Memphis Mafia had covered the windows to his room with aluminum foil (to shield him from light, so he could sleep in the daytime) and had food

waiting by the side of a king-size bed.

Elvis sang nineteen songs before four thousand wild fans at Bloch Arena. The concert was the longest of Elvis's career—and it would be his last concert in front of a live audience until July 31, 1969.

From the Honolulu concert "Reconsider Baby" by Lowell Fulson was recorded and included on the LP *Elvis Aron Presley* (USS *Arizona Memorial, March 25, 1961*).

APR.:   *TV Star Parade* and *TV Movie Screen* featured Pat Boone and Elvis on their covers and asked if they were feuding or if they were friends. They were friends. Elvis believed that Pat Boone had the better voice.

APRIL 18:   An exhausted Elvis and his entourage flew from Hawaii to Los Angeles.

MAY: Following Elvis's lead, Pat Boone wore a gold-lamé suit for his LP *Pat Boone Sings Guess Who?* (Dot DLP 3501).

Movie TV Secrets showed Elvis on the cover with the lead article, "Don't Make Me Marry Tuesday Weld."

MAY 26:   Bill Fury of *Melody Maker* interviewed and wrote about Elvis.

JUNE 15:   *Wild in the Country* premiered in Memphis. Two endings were filmed—one in which Hope Lange's character dies, the other in which she lives. At the sneak preview, the audience voted to keep Hope Lange alive in the film.

JUNE 22:   *Wild in the Country* opened nationally and rumors spread Elvis was going to marry Tuesday Weld.

JUNE 25:   Elvis's first Gold Standard Series original was "Kiss Me Quick" by Doc Pomus and Mort Shuman, which Elvis recorded at RCA's Nashville studios. The single reached No. 34 on *Billboard*'s Hot 100 chart in 1964. The Jordanaires provided backup vocals (RCA 447-0639). Its flip side was "Suspicion."

JUNE 26:   The million seller "(Marie's the Name) His Latest Flame" was recorded by Elvis at RCA's Nashville studios. Its eleven-week stay on *Billboard*'s Top 100 chart peaked at No. 4, but in England it was No. 1 for four weeks. It is the opening song on the 1981 documentary *This Is Elvis*. The single's flip side was the million seller by Doc Pomus–Mort Shuman "Little Sister," recorded by Elvis the same day (RCA 47-7908). It peaked at No. 5 on the Top 100 chart but hit No. 1 in England. Elvis recorded "I'm Yours" by Hal Blair and Don Robertson; it was released four years later in the movie *Tickle Me*, 1965. In August 1965, the million-selling single was on *Billboard*'s Hot 100 chart and peaked at No. 11 during its eleven-week run and was No. 1 on the October Easy-Listening chart for three weeks. Its uncharted flip side was "(It's a) Long Lonely Highway" by Doc Pomus and Mort Shuman, recorded in June (RCA 47-8657).

JULY 1:   Elvis and Anita Wood attended Red West and Patricia Boyd's wedding. Boyd was Elvis's secretary.

JULY 5:   "Angel" by Sid Tepper and Roy C. Bennett; "I'm Not the Marrying Kind" by Mack David and Sherman Edwards; "Sound Advice" by Bill Giant, Bernie Baum, and Florence Kaye (the credits incorrectly say Giant and Anna Shaw are composers); "What a Wonderful Life" by Sid Wayne and Jay Livingston; and "A Whistling Tune" by Sherman Edwards and Hal David (not used in the movie) were completed by Elvis at RCA's Nashville studios for *Follow That Dream*, along with the title song by Fred Wise and Ben Weisman. "On Top of Old Smoky" was re-

corded on the movie set. "A Whistling Tune" was eventually used in the film *Kid Galahad*.

JULY 6–7:   Elvis and his Memphis group took a bus from Nashville to Florida, where they bought two cars and a large speedboat.

JULY 9:   While in Crystal River, Florida, Elvis memorized the script for *Follow That Dream* in a matter of hours. Elvis memorized entire scripts very rapidly— every part. If any actor missed a line or cue, he would tell him or her the forgotten line.

JULY 11:   Elvis began filming *Follow That Dream* (United Artists) in Crystal River, Florida. Other scenes were shot in Tampa, Ocala, Yankeetown, Inverness, Bird Creek, Florida, and in Culver City, California. It was directed by Gordon Douglas (the only director to have worked with both Elvis and Frank Sinatra) and produced by David Weisbart. The film costarred Arthur O'Connell, Anne Helm, Joanna Moore, and Alan Hewitt. Red West played a bank guard.

JULY 15:   The gambling scenes in *Follow That Dream* were some of the Colonel's favorites. He loved to gamble. But in 1961, gambling was illegal in Florida, so the props were allegedly smuggled onto sets by mobsters.

AUG.:   Hank Snow sued Colonel Parker for a piece of Elvis's contract and lost the suit. (See *Journal American*, 9/26/61.) Parker and Snow had created the Hank Snow Jamboree Attractions, which toured such country staples as Minnie Pearl, Webb Pierce, Jimmie Rodgers, the Carter Family, and others. Because Bob Neal and Oscar Davis insisted, the Colonel had booked Elvis through Snow's promo business, Jamboree Attractions, but the Colonel shrewdly eliminated Snow from earning a dime of Elvis's take. No one knows for certain what role, if any, Hank Snow had in discovering and promoting Elvis early on, but he did talk to RCA's Steve Sholes about Elvis. Whatever Hank Snow did was veiled by the aggressive Colonel Parker, who usually took credit for what everyone around him had achieved.

SEPT.: Elvis was in Hollywood.

OCT. 12: Elvis flew to Nashville to record.

OCT. 15: Elvis recorded "Anything That's Part of You" by Don Robertson, which was eventually released in March 1962 and reached No. 31 during eight weeks on *Billboard*'s Top 100 chart and No. 6 on the Easy-Listening chart. It was recorded at RCA's Nashville studio with the single's flip side "Good Luck Charm" (which was Elvis's last No. 1 single until 1969) by Alan Schroeder and Wally Gold (RCA 47-7992). The single "For the Millionth and Last Time" (by Sid Tepper–Roy C. Bennett) was completed by Elvis with Gordon Stoker on accordion.

OCT. 16: Elvis recorded "I Met Her Today" by Don Robertson and Hal Blair at RCA's Nashville studio. No single was released. It appears on the LPs *Elvis for Everyone* and *Separate Ways*.

OCT. 18: Elvis flew back to Los Angeles.

OCT. 26–27: Elvis recorded "Home Is Where the Heart Is" by Sherman Edwards and Hal Davis for *Kid Galahad* at Radio Recorders in Hollywood. Take No. 21 is a more robust version, heard on the uncharted disc-jockey promo demo (RCA SP-45-118, released May 1962). Its flip side is "King of the Whole Wide World" by Ruth Batchelor and Bob Roberts. Elvis couldn't sing the original arrangement, so it was re-

arranged and resung on October 27, with a sax solo by Boots Randolph (which was later removed). Master take No. 31 is only heard on bootleg LPs. In *Kid Galahad*, the song was placed over the credits. Even though RCA never released a single of "King of the Whole Wide World," it reached No. 30 on *Billboard*'s Top 100 list and enjoyed a seven-week stay because of the popularity of the EP *Kid Galahad*.

On October 27, Elvis recorded "I Got Lucky" by Dolores Fuller, Fred Wise, and Ben Weisman. Although the master take was No. 6, take No. 2 was released for *Kid Galahad* because it was thirty-eight seconds longer. "Love Is For Lovers" by Ruth Batchelor and Sharon Silbert was completed for the same film as a duet with the Jordanaires. It is not available on any record to date. Different takes of "Riding the Rainbow" were combined for the movie, and take No. 10 of "This Is Living" (both songs by Fred Wise and Ben Weisman) was for release.

NOV.: Elvis began filming *Kid Galahad*. The film costarred Gig Young, Lola Albright, Joan Blackman, Charles Bronson, and Ned Glass. Elvis's Memphis buddy Sonny West played a bit part. Other than for some scenes shot in an Idylwild, California, resort area, most of the interior shots were filmed on MGM/UA's Culver City studio lots.

Elvis and Tuesday Weld were on the cover of *Datebook*.

NOV. 5–14: Elvis was coached for *Kid Galahad* boxing scenes by Mush Callahan (a former world junior-welterweight boxing champion) and assisted by the rugged Al Silvani (cornerman/trainer for Floyd Patterson, Rocky Graciano, and Jake LaMotta). Ed Asner (with a full head of hair) made his film debut in *Kid Galahad*, playing the bit part of Frank Gerson.

MID-NOV.: Elvis sang "Husky Dusky Day" with Hope Lange, and it was recorded during their scene on the film set for *Wild in the Country* as they drove in a car. The song was not released by RCA, but it is heard on two bootleg LPs, *Eternal Elvis* and *From Hollywood to Vegas.*

NOV. 21: Paramount's film *Blue Hawaii* opened nationally. By the end of the year it had grossed $4.7 million and was a huge hit throughout the U.S. for over a year. But it upset Elvis when *West Side Story* was named Best Picture of 1961 because the Colonel made him turn down its leading role. Elvis admitted it was better than any film he had ever done.

NOV. 30: Colonel Parker refused to allow Elvis to play the lead of John Wakefield in *Too Late Blues*, directed by John Cassavetes. Bobby Darin was given the role and costarred with Stella Stevens.

DEC.: *Teen* magazine readers voted Elvis and Tuesday Weld "The Damp Raincoat Award" for Most Disappointing Performers of 1961, while the theater owners voted Elvis the *tenth* top box-office draw for 1961.

1962

In 1962, the Cuban missile crisis almost resulted in war, while television news brought Vietnam into living rooms across the country. Rev. Martin Luther King crusaded for civil rights, John Glenn became the first American to orbit the earth, and Marilyn Monroe died on August 5.

JAN.: "Write to Me From Naples" by Alex Alstone and Jimmy Kennedy was recorded by Elvis at Graceland. It appears on the LP *A Golden Celebration* (*Graceland 1960s*).

JAN. 8: On his broadcast of "American Bandstand," Dick Clark dedicated the program to Elvis's birthday.

FEB.: Colonel Parker persuaded Elvis to turn down the part of Chance Wayne in the film *Sweet Bird of Youth*, which had been based on Tennessee Williams's play of the same title (Paul Newman played the role). Parker did

not like Tennessee Williams's obsession with Elvis's real-life persona. Once again, the Colonel made the wrong decision for Elvis, and the Cat accepted it without argument.

MAR.: For *Girls! Girls! Girls!* Ruth Batchelor and Bob Roberts wrote "Because of Love," finished by Elvis at Radio Recorders in Hollywood. It never became a hit or a single. "Bourbon Street," "Just for Old Times' Sake," and "The Walls Have Ears" (all by Sid Tepper and Roy C. Bennett) were recorded for the film. The Leiber-Stoller song "Dainty Little Moonbeams" was recorded but was not released. Less than a minute of Elvis singing the song is in *Girls! Girls! Girls!* The Tepper-Bennett song "Earth Boy" reveals Elvis and the Tiu sisters switching from Chinese to English lyrics. Take No. 3 of the title song by Leiber-Stoller and the splice of three tapes is the recorded version heard in *Girls! Girls! Girls!* "I

Don't Wanna Be Tied" by Bill Giant, Bernie Baum, and Florence Kaye; Janice Torre and Fred Spielman's "I Don't Want To"; Doc Pomus and Alan Jeffries's "I Feel That I've Known You Forever"; "Return to Sender," written by Otis Blackwell and Winfield Scott; "Song of the Shrimp," written by Sid Tepper and Roy C. Bennett; and "Thanks to the Rolling Sea" by Ruth Batchelor and Bob Roberts were completed for *Girls! Girls! Girls!*

"Return to Sender" sold over 1 million copies and the single reached No. 2 for five weeks on *Billboard*'s Hot 100 chart during a sixteen-week run; No. 5 on the R&B chart during a twelve-week stay; and was No. 1 for three weeks in Great Britain (RCA 47-8100, released in October 1962, with the flip side "Where Do You Come From"). "Where Do You Come From" by Bob Roberts and Ruth Batchelor peaked miserably at No. 99 on *Billboard*'s Hot 100 chart.

CA. MAR. 2:　Elvis sang "Mama" by Charles O'Curran and Dudley Brooks for *Girls! Girls! Girls!* at Radio Recorders, but Elvis's version was cut from the movie. It is heard on the LPs *Double Dynamite* and *Let's Be Friends*.

MAR. 18:　Elvis, Red West, and Charlie Hodge wrote "You'll Be Gone," which Elvis recorded at RCA's Nashville studio. Produced as a single with the flip side "Do the Clam," it never charted (RCA 47-8500). It was released in February 1965.

During that session, Otis Blackwell and Winfield Scott's "(Such an) Easy Question" was recorded and was included in the movie *Tickle Me*. The song was released in May 1965 as a single and peaked at No. 11 on *Billboard*'s Top 100 chart during an eight-week run. In July, it was No. 1 on the Easy-Listening chart for two weeks (RCA 47-8585). "Fountain of Love" by Bill Grant and Jeff Lewis; "Gonna Get Back Home Somehow" by Doc Pomus and Mort Shuman; and "Something

Blue" by Paul Evans and Al Byron were finished, but no singles were made. They can be heard on the LP *Pot Luck*. The Doc Pomus–Mort Shuman song "Night Rider" was recorded on March 18, but was released in the 1965 film *Tickle Me* (heard on the EP *Tickle Me* and LP *Pot Luck*).

MAR. 19:　The Leiber-Stoller song "Just Tell Her Jim Said Hello" was recorded by Elvis at RCA's Nashville studios. The single was released in July 1962 and peaked at No. 14 on the Easy-Listening chart and No. 55 on *Billboard*'s Top 100 chart (RCA 47-8041). Its flip side, "She's Not You," was written by Leiber–Stoller–Doc Pomus and was recorded the same day. Its single reached No. 5 on *Billboard*'s Top 100 chart during a ten-week run; No. 2 on the Easy-Listening chart; No. 13 on the R&B chart; and No. 1 during three weeks on the English chart. The Doc Pomus–Mort Shuman song "Suspicion" was completed by Elvis and the Jordanaires on March 19. It was first released on the LP *Pot Luck*, and in 1964 did not chart as a single (RCA 447-0639).

MAR. 27:　Elvis recorded "We'll Be Together," written by Charles O'Curran and Dudley Brooks; "We're Coming In Loaded," written by Otis Blackwell and Winfield Scott; and "Plantation Rock" by Bill Giant, Bernie Baum, and Florence Kaye at Radio Recorders. "Plantation Rock" was first released in a spliced-tape version on the bootleg LP *Plantation Rock*. In 1983, RCA released it on the LP *Elvis—A Legendary Performer*, Vol. 4. "Potpourri" by Sid Tepper and Roy C. Bennett and "Twist Me Loose" were recorded and cut from *Girls! Girls! Girls!*

MAR. 30:　Having listened to records by Elvis and bluesmen Blind Lemon Jefferson and Son House, Eric Clapton made his first public appearance as a guitarist in a small club in southern England.

APR.: *Movie Teen Magazine* told readers: "No matter how big Elvis gets as an actor, there's still too wide a following for his singing for him ever to drop the lucrative record part of his career. It's a kind of two-way parlay. . . . The bigger he gets as an actor, the more popularity there will be for his records—the more records sold, the more demand to see him, too, in movies. With Elvis as singer and actor, it's a case where us fans, for once, can have our cake and eat it, too."

APR. 7: Elvis flew into Hawaii and was mobbed at the airport by several thousand fans, who took a diamond ring, a tie clip, and a watch from him. He and members of the Memphis Mafia lived in the Kona Coast village of Milolii, Hawaii, and at the Hawaiian Village Hotel on Oahu. He dated briefly Laurel Goodwin and socialized with many local beauties.

APR. 8: Elvis met with film crews and went over the script for *Girls! Girls! Girls!* on location. After rehearsing a few scenes, he demanded a piano be delivered, so he and his friends could sing gospel music "to relax" between scenes.

APR. 9: Elvis began filming Paramount's *Girls! Girls! Girls!* in Hawaii,

which was directed by Norman Taurog and produced by Hal B. Wallis. It co-starred Stella Stevens, Jeremy Slate, and Laurel Goodwin. Memphis Mafia member Red West played a bongo player–crewman in a tuna boat. Vocal accompaniment was by the Jordanaires.

APR. 11: *Follow That Dream* premiered in Ocala, Florida.

APR. 12–30: In between shoots for *Girls! Girls! Girls!* Elvis and various starlets rode around the island and kept late hours together. Many of the young women liked being with Elvis but resented the constant presence of Red West, Charlie Hodge, and other members of the Memphis gang.

MAY 15: Elvis and his crew returned to Culver City, California, to finish *Girls! Girls! Girls!*

MAY 23: Elvis's film *Follow That Dream* opened nationally. It did not do well at the box office. Elvis hated the movie because he thought he looked "fat." He had gained a jelly roll around his waist and it showed.

JUNE: Priscilla Beaulieu stayed with auto dealer George Barris and his wife in Beverly Hills while Elvis secretly dated starlets. Elvis later became angry with Barris when Barris did not give him a "Celebrity Series" Cadillac as he did to Liberace.

JUNE–JULY: Elvis filmed with the Paramount Pictures crew.

AUG. 1: Elvis started to read a new script, *It Happened at the World's Fair.* Priscilla was forbidden to visit Elvis on the set. The press would have had a heyday if they had known Elvis was dating such a young girl. The Colonel worried about Elvis being compared to Jerry Lee Lewis, whose

▲ Elvis backstage with a fan at Johnny Ray's opening at the Dunes Hotel in Las Vegas, January 26, 1961. *Courtesy of John Reible, Las Vegas News Bureau, Las Vegas, Nevada.*

marriage to his thirteen-year-old cousin destroyed his career.

AUG. 25: During a wardrobe fitting (which he detested) Elvis learned his clothing for *It Happened at the World's Fair* cost $9,300 and included thirty shirts, ten suits, fifty-five ties, two cashmere coats, ten pairs of shoes, fifteen pairs of slacks, and "other essentials." After the movie was completed, he gave members of the Memphis Mafia the wardrobe, which annoyed studio executives.

AUG. 27: Elvis began filming MGM's *It Happened at the World's Fair*, which costarred Joan O'Brien, Gary Lockwood, Vicky Tiu, and H. M. Wynant. Though it was filmed primarily in Culver City, the monorail scenes were shot in Seattle, Washington.

AUG. 29: United Artist's *Kid Galahad* opened nationally. By the end of 1962, it had grossed $1.75 million.

SEPT.: For *It Happened at the World's Fair*, Elvis sang "Beyond the Bend" by Fred Wise, Ben Weisman, and Dolores Fuller at Hollywood's Radio Recorders with the Mello Men as backup vocalists; "A World of Our Own" by Bill Giant, Bernard Baur, and Florence Kaye, with Don Robertson on piano; and "One Broken Heart for Sale" (by Otis Blackwell and Winfield Scott) with the Mello Men. "Cotton Candy Band" by Ruth Batchelor and Bob Roberts was finished. A string accompaniment and a shorter ending for "Cotton Candy Band" was recorded for the film. "Happy Ending" by Ben Weisman and Sid Wayne had vocal backups by the Jordanaires. "One Broken Heart for Sale" hit *Billboard*'s Hot 100 chart, reaching No. 11 during a nine-week run, and it was No. 21 on the R&B chart (RCA 47-8134, released in February 1963, with the flip side "They Remind Me Too Much of You").

SEPT. 8: Elvis traveled to Seattle to film scenes for *It Happened at the World's Fair*. He roomed on the eleventh floor of the New Washington Hotel where nightly parties disturbed other visitors. Members of the hotel's cooking staff couldn't believe the amount of junk food Elvis ordered and devoured.

SEPT. 8–13: People lined the streets hours early to catch a glimpse of their hero prior to his appearance on the film sets in and around the Seattle World's Fair. Over one hundred police and six special Pinkerton plainclothes bodyguards were hired to protect Elvis during every minute of his filming. Colonel Parker regretted that he had not set up a huge Seattle concert to coincide with the Fair. Instead, he sold hundreds of photographs of Elvis at premium prices outside the fairgrounds.

SEPT. 15–18: Elvis was physically burning out. Because he was fatigued, his temper was short and erratic, and fellow actors wondered if he was going to become violent or if he was on some kind of medication. The Colonel told him to behave himself or take a long vacation.

SEPT. 20: Elvis flew back to Hollywood.

SEPT. 22: Elvis sang "I'm Falling in Love Tonight," composed by Don Robertson, with the vocal backup of the Mello Men at Radio Recorders in Hollywood. "They Remind Me Too Much of You" by Don Robertson and "Relax" by Sid Tepper and Roy C. Bennett were recorded for *It Happened at the World's Fair*. "They Remind Me Too Much of You" had a four-week run on *Billboard*'s Hot 100 chart and peaked at No. 53 (RCA 47-0134, released in February 1963, with the flip side "One Broken Heart for Sale").

OCT.: Elvis dated Yvonne Craig, whom he met during film shoots for *It Happened at the World's Fair*. In this movie, a young Kurt Russell kicked Elvis in the shin. (Russell would one day play Elvis in a movie.) Red West played Charlie (while acting as Elvis's real-life bodyguard while on the set in *It Happened at the World's Fair*.) Joe Esposito, another Memphis friend, portrayed a carnival man.

With her parents' permission, Priscilla Beaulieu moved from Germany to Graceland. Elvis's stepmother, Dee, and his grandmother assured Captain and Mrs. Beaulieu she would be safe, happy, and strictly supervised. Upon her arrival, she enrolled at Immaculate Conception High School, and her presence at Graceland was kept somewhat quiet.

OCT. 31: *Girls! Girls! Girls!* premiered to a full house in Honolulu.

NOV. 1–20: Elvis spent an unusual three weeks at Graceland, getting accustomed to Priscilla's presence, trying to cope with Vernon's new family on the property, and trying to find music to record. He had become overweight, and dieting was making him cranky.

NOV. 21: The film *Girls! Girls! Girls!* opened nationally and grossed $2.6 million by the end of the year.

DEC. 25: Elvis gave Priscilla a musical "Love Me Tender" cigarette case. "Love Me Tender" was the first song she had heard Elvis sing.

DEC. 31: Elvis rented the Manhattan Club in Memphis for a party.

Elvis was voted the fifth top box-office draw for 1962 by theater owners.

Elvis received three Norwegian silver records for "Good Luck Charm" from the Norwegian consulate in Los Angeles.

Sometime in the sixties, Elvis accompanied himself on the guitar and recorded at Graceland "Tears on My Pillow" (never released) and "Mona Lisa" by Jay Livingston and Ray Evans (heard on the LP *Elvis—A Legendary Performer*, Vol. 4). During a home recording in the sixties, Elvis also sang "My Heart Cries for You" by Carl Sigman and Percy Faith (released only on the LP *A Golden Celebration*). He also recorded "Primrose Lane," written by George Callender and Wayne Shanklin. There was no release of the song. He also is known to have recorded at Graceland "Sixteen Tons" (accompanying himself on the guitar), a Merle Travis original made famous by Tennessee Ernie Ford in 1955. Elvis's rendition of "Sixteen Tons" has never been released and may be lost.

1963

1963 saw both triumph and tragedy. Rev. Martin Luther King's "I Have a Dream" speech was heard by over two hundred thousand people of all-colors at the foot of the Lincoln Memorial in Washington, DC, and in November Pres. John F. Kennedy was assassinated and a stunned nation mourned.

Although Elvis's acting took precedence over his music in 1963, he was not in the most memorable films of the year (*The Birds, Lilies of the Field, The Great Escape*, and *Tom Jones*) nor was he aware of the popularity and impact British bands had upon American musicians and their fans.

Jerry Lee Lewis's rendition of Little Richard's "Good Golly Miss Molly" and Ricky Nelson's "Poor Little Fool" ranked high on U.K. charts. Chuck Berry, Bo Did-

dley, the Everly Brothers, and the Rolling Stones first toured the U.K. The Beatles (who traveled with Roy Orbison and Little Richard) produced the first U.K. million-selling album, *With the Beatles*, and Cliff Richard's title song from *Summer Holiday* topped the charts to replace the Beatles' single "Please, Please Me."

Closer to home, in California, Janis Joplin sang in North Beach clubs, Frank Zappa opened Studio Z in Cucamonga, California, and the Turtles organized in Redondo Beach. Social activists such as Joan Baez and Bob Dylan appeared at the Monterey, California, and Newport, Rhode Island, folk festivals.

JAN.: Elvis's favorite sports were touch football and karate. Although Elvis claimed he was "a black belt" in tae kwon do, he was *not* a legitimate black belt.

George Barris was commissioned by Elvis to customize a forty-foot-long Greyhound touring bus, which took four months to complete. Elvis eventually gave the bus to country singer T. G. Sheppard.

JAN. 22: Elvis began recording the sound track for the film *Fun in Acapulco* at Radio Recorders in Hollywood with backup vocalists the Amigos. On January 22, Elvis sang Leiber and Stoller's "Bossa Nova Baby," the single of which reached No. 8 on *Billboard*'s Top 100 chart during a ten-week stay. It was the last Elvis single to hit the

R&B chart, No. 20 (RCA 47-8243). The only other bossa nova song to hit the charts was Eydie Gorme's "Blame It on the Bossa Nova" (Columbia 42661) in 1963. The flip side of Elvis's recording was "Witchcraft." Elvis finished a duet with Larry Domasin during the song "Mexico" by Sid Tepper and Roy C. Bennett; sang "Marguerita" by Don Robertson; and did "Vino, Dinero y Amor" (by Sid Tepper and Roy C. Bennett) for the film.

"The Bullfighter Was a Lady" by Roy C. Bennett and Sid Tepper and "I Think I'm Gonna Like It Here" by Don Robertson and Hal Blair were also recorded for *Fun in Acapulco*.

JAN. 23: The Giant-Baum-Kaye song "El Toro" for *Fun in Acapulco* was finished at Radio Recorders, along with the film's title song, written by Wayne-Weisman; "(There's) No Room to Rhumba in a Sports Car" by Fred Wise and Dick Manning; and "You Can't Say No to Acapulco" by Sid Feller, Dorothy Fuller, and Lee Morris. Strings were added for the film version of the title song.

JAN. 28: Filming began for Paramount's *Fun in Acapulco*. It costarred Ursula Andress (with whom Elvis allegedly had an affair). Some shots were filmed in Acapulco, but Elvis's scenes were filmed only on Paramount's Hollywood lots. Red West played a poolside extra.

FEB.: Elvis filmed *Fun in Acapulco* and partied in Hollywood at various locations.

FEB. 27: At Radio Recorders, Elvis, the Jordanaires, and the Mello Men completed "Guadalajara" for *Fun in Acapulco*.

MAR. 5: Lloyd "Cowboy" Copas, Patsy Cline, and Harold "Hawkshaw" Hawkins were killed in a plane crash and

▲ Elvis and Willa Monroe at WDIA radio. *Photograph by Ernest C. Withers. Copyright © 1994 Mimosa Records Productions, Inc.*

Elvis was grief stricken. He and Copas had toured together in 1955, and Patsy Cline was a good friend.

MAR. 15: *Fun in Acapulco* was completed. As a promotional stratagem, Paramount distributed promo passports. The poster for the movie included passport number 483473.

APR.: Folk singer and social activist Bob Dylan gave his first one-man concert at New York's Town Hall.

APR. 3: MGM's film *It Happened at the World's Fair* opened in Los Angeles.

APR. 10: *It Happened at the World's Fair* opened nationally and grossed $2.25 million by the end of 1963.

MAY 26: Elvis recorded "Witchcraft" at RCA's Nashville studios, and the single peaked at No. 32 on *Billboard*'s Top 100 chart and enjoyed a seven-week stay (RCA 47-8243). Over a million records were sold. This song is not to be confused with the "Witchcraft" that Frank Sinatra cut in 1958 (Capitol 3859), which Sinatra and Elvis sang in the Timex special on May 12, 1960, for ABC-TV.

Elvis also recorded Bill Grant, Bernie Baum, and Florence Kaye's "(You're the) Devil in Disguise," which reached No. 3 on *Billboard*'s Top 100 chart during an eleven-week stay, No. 9 on R&B, and No. 1 on Britain's pop chart. It sold over 1 million copies in a year (RCA 47-8188). Its flip side, "Please Don't Drag That String Around" by Otis Blackwell and Winfield Scott was recorded the same day and did not chart. It was released June 1963.

"Echoes of Love" by Bob Roberts and Paddy McMains; "Once Is Enough" by Tepper-Bennett; and "One Boy, Two Little Girls" by Giant-Baum-Kaye for *Kissin' Cousins*; "Finders Keepers, Losers Weepers" by Dory and Ollie Jones; and "Love Me Tonight" by Don Robertson (heard on the LP *Fun in Acapulco*) were recorded. He also recorded "Never Ending," written by Buddy Kaye and Phil Springer (RCA 47-8400, released in July 1964 with the flip side "Such a Night"). "What Now, What Next, Where To" (written by Don Robertson and Hal Blair) appears only on the LPs *Double Trouble* and *Separate Ways*.

MAY 27: At RCA's Nashville studios, Elvis recorded "Ask Me" written by Domenico Modugno. This recording has not been released. He completed "Blue River" by Paul Evans and Fred Tobias (which hit No. 95 during a one-week stay on *Billboard*'s Top 100 chart). The flip side of "Blue River" is "Tell Me Why" (RCA 47-8740), released in December 1965. Elvis recorded "Memphis, Tennessee" written by Chuck Berry (this version has not been released). For the movie *Tickle Me* (released two years later) Elvis recorded "Slowly but Surely" (written by Sid Wayne and Ben Weisman). As a "bonus song" for the film *Speedway*, Elvis sang the Sid Tepper–Roy C. Bennett song "Western Union."

MID-JUNE: Elvis visited the Colonel's home for the first time in Bel Air, California. *Pix* ran an article, "Elvis, the Colonel . . . ," June 29, 1963.

The Rolling Stones released their first single, a Chuck Berry song, "Come On."

Ann and Bernie Granadier built the Meditation Gardens at Graceland.

JUNE 14: Priscilla graduated from the Catholic all-girls high school Immaculate Conception (1725 Central Avenue, Memphis), while Elvis waited outside. Elvis gave her a Corvair for graduation. Priscilla took ballet lessons at the Jo Haynes School of Dancing at 4679 Highway 51 South.

JULY: At Radio Recorders, take No. 14 of Elvis's recording of "Night Life," written by Bill Giant, Bernie Baum, and Florence Kaye; "Santa Lucia," written by Teodoro Cottrau; and "Viva Las Vegas" by Doc Pomus and Mort Shuman were recorded for the film *Viva Las Vegas*. Overdubbing of Ann-Margret humming during "Santa Lucia" was added from the movie set. The million-selling title song spent seven weeks on *Billboard*'s Hot 100 chart, reaching No. 29 (RCA 48-8360, released in April 1964 with the flip side "What'd I Say"). Ray Charles wrote "What'd I Say" and the single had a six-week stay on *Billboard*'s Hot 100 chart, topping at No. 21.

JULY 9: For *Viva Las Vegas*, at Radio Recorders Elvis completed "If You Think I Don't Need You" by Red West and Joe Cooper.

JULY 10: At Radio Recorders, Elvis sang "Do the Vega" for the film *Viva Las Vegas*. The song was written by Bill Giant, Bernie Baum, and Florence Kaye. It was eventually cut from the film. "I Need Somebody to Lean On" by Doc Pomus and Mort Shuman and "Yeah, Yeah, Yeah" by Jerry Leiber and Mike Stoller (which disappeared and still has not surfaced) were recorded for the film.

JULY 11: RCA okayed take No. 10 of Elvis and Ann-Margret's duet "The Lady Loves Me" (by Sid Tepper and Roy C. Bennett), which was completed at Radio Recorders for *Viva Las Vegas*. Its first release was on the 1983 LP *Elvis—A Legendary Performer*, Vol. 4. He also finished many takes of "Today, Tomorrow and Forever" by Giant-Baum-Kaye. Master take No. 4 was used in the movie *Viva Las Vegas* and is heard on the EP by that title. Elvis also recorded for the movie "The Yellow Rose of Texas/The Eyes of Texas." "The Eyes of Texas" was included in the 1969 film *The Trouble With Girls*.

JULY 15: Elvis began shooting MGM's

Viva Las Vegas, directed by George Sidney, who produced the film with Jack Cummings. During this film, Elvis and Ann-Margret had an affair in the Sahara Hotel's Presidential Suite.

Scenes for *Viva Las Vegas* were shot in the University of Nevada–Las Vegas gym, McCarran Airport, Henderson, Nevada, the skeet-shooting range at the Tropicana Hotel, Las Vegas, and the swimming pool at the Flamingo Hotel, Las Vegas.

JULY: Elvis and Joan O'Brien were on the cover of *Film Review*.

AUG.: Elvis allegedly "earned" a second-degree black belt in karate, via some "unknown" instructor.

Elvis and Ann-Margret appeared to be dating. It was rumored that Ann-Margret entered Elvis's suite at the Sahara Hotel in the evening and often exited in the late morning or early afternoon. For certain, Ann-Margret was falling in love with Elvis, which Priscilla Beaulieu had a hard time accepting.

AUG. 8: "It Looks Like Romance for Presley & Ann-Margret" by Bob Thomas appeared in the *Memphis Press-Scimitar*. The article hurt and infuriated Priscilla, who waited patiently at Graceland for Elvis to pay attention to her.

Ann-Margret and Elvis were on the cover of *Movieland*.

Riding the wave of rock enthusiasm in America, many British bands later toured the U.S., including the Searchers, Gerry and the Pacemakers, the Who, The Yardbirds, the Moody Blues, Cream, Pink Floyd, Traffic, the Beatles, and the Rolling Stones. The U.S.A. was where the action (and the money) was.

Priscilla enrolled in Patricia Stevens Finishing School, but did not apply to college.

AUG. 28: Elvis watched the televised coverage of Dr. Martin Luther King,

Jr.'s stirring delivery of the "I Have a Dream" speech at the Lincoln Memorial in Washington, DC. He was especially touched by Mahalia Jackson's singing prior to the speech.

SEPT. 16: With a banjo player and the Mello Men on backup vocals, Elvis sang "Take Me to the Fair" by Sid Tepper and Roy C. Bennett at Hollywood's Radio Recorders for the film *It Happened at the World's Fair*.

OCT. (EARLY): Elvis began recording at RCA's Nashville studios the sound track for *Kissin' Cousins*. Elvis filmed the movie during sixteen days in October. Director Gene Nelson suggested to the Colonel the script was terrible and needed to be changed. Parker proposed adding a talking camel! He had just the camel the film company could use . . . for a fee. If it would make a few extra bucks, he was all for it. Thankfully, no camel was added.

OCT. 3: "Anyone (Could Fall in Love With You)," written by Bennie Benjamin, Sol Marcus, and Louis A. DeJesus; "Barefoot Ballad" by Dolores Fuller and Lee Morris; "Smokey Mountain Boy" by Leonore Rosenblatt and Victor Millrose; "There's Gold in the Mountains" by Giant-Baum-Kaye; and "Tender Feelings" by Giant-Baum-Kaye were recorded by Elvis at Radio Recorders for *Kissin' Cousins*. "Catchin' on Fast" by Giant-Baum-Kaye was also cut for the same film.

OCT. 5: MGM's *Kissin' Cousins* began production, directed by Gene Nelson and produced by Sam Katzman. Elvis portrayed both Josh Morgan and Jodie Tatum. The film, budgeted at $800,000 was shot on MGM lots in Culver City and at Big Bear Lake, California. Joe Esposito played Mike (a bit part).

CA. OCT. 7: Fred Wise and Randy Starr wrote the song "Kissin' Cousins"

for Elvis, but it is not in the movie. Elvis recorded the song in RCA's Nashville studios, and the single reached No. 12 on *Billboard*'s Hot 100 chart during a nine-week run (RCA 47-8309, released January 1964). Its flip side was "It Hurts Me." Elvis cut a completely different "Kissin' Cousins" for the movie (which appears only on the LP by that title) written by Bill Giant, Bernie Baum, and Florence Kaye. No single was released of that version.

OCT. 21: *Kissin' Cousins* was completed in Culver City.

NOV. 22: President John F. Kennedy was assassinated in Dallas, Texas, leaving the world horrified. John Lennon and Paul McCartney's "I Want to Hold Your Hand" (the Beatles' first U.S. hit) took the country by storm.

NOV. 27: Paramount's *Fun in Acapulco* premiered nationally. In six weeks it had grossed over $1.5 million. In twelve weeks receipts doubled.
　　Ann-Margret and Elvis were on the cover of *Movie Life*.
　　Elvis stopped dating Ann-Margret when she announced to the press they were planning to get married.

DEC.: Colonel Parker refused to allow Elvis to sing in the film *Bye Bye Birdie*, which was about an Elvis-like rock 'n' roll idol.

DEC. 11: *Love Me Tender* was first shown on television.

DEC. 13: Elvis bought fifty tickets at $12.50 each for Priscilla, himself, and friends to attend the premiere of *Cleopatra* in Memphis.

DEC. 31: Elvis rented the Manhattan Club in Memphis to party.

Those around Elvis (such as Sonny West) felt the Colonel used mind control to orchestrate Elvis's every move and to control certain members of the Memphis Mafia. West said, "He would make us all get down on all fours and tell us that we were dogs . . . snapping at each other." (See *Elvis: What Happened?*) Steve Binder confirmed in an interview with Albert Goldman: "The Colonel used to sit at a meeting with those cold steel-blue eyes . . . trying to get a subliminal message into my brain. . . . He did convince me that there is such a thing as *mind control*. That strange hypnotic way he had of exercising total control and power over Elvis. That kind of hold is totally unexplained in terms either of deals or loyalties between people."

Parker did not want Elvis to be interviewed or to mingle with outsiders. "You don't have to be nice to people on the way up, if you're not coming down," was one of the Colonel's more revealing statements. By controlling Elvis's every move, Parker turned an unknown commodity into an international legendary entertainer. One *Time* reviewer savagely remarked, "Barker, merry-go-round operator, candied-apple dipper, ice-shaver for snow cones, and general man-about-the-midway . . . profitably managed Gene Autry, Hank Snow, and Eddy Arnold before he found the boy with the coin in the groin." Regardless of how disparaging the views of the Colonel are, he must be given credit for placing Elvis in a major spotlight and never allowing his presence on the national scene to fade. Even after Elvis left rock 'n' roll to act, the Colonel promoted Elvis, his films, and his music to unprecedented profitability.

Pop artist Andy Warhol painted Elvis for the second time (the first being of his shoe in 1956). According to *Art News* (March 1992), the appraised value of Warhol's *Elvis* (*eleven times*) is currently a cool $5 million. It hangs in the Andy Warhol Museum in Pittsburgh, Pennsylvania.

Theater owners named Elvis the seventh top box-office draw for the 1963 movie season.

1964

In 1964, President Lyndon Baines Johnson signed a landmark civil-rights act while race riots broke out in New York City; the Surgeon General declared cigarette smoking a health hazard; Teamsters union chief Jimmy Hoffa was found guilty of fraud; and the Warren report claimed Lee Harvey Oswald acted alone in the assassination of President Kennedy. Popular movies included *Dr. Strangelove* and *Mary Poppins*. "The British invasion" began with the arrival of the Beatles in February and has never stopped.

In the sixties, rock stars' (as well as their fans') primary concerns were sex, drugs, and rock 'n' roll. But it was also a decade of phenomenal change and upheaval, from political and moral issues to

◄ Ann-Margret. *Courtesy of the author's collection.*

fashion and style, and of course, music. British bands brought with them a flood of new sights and sounds from across the sea, even though most of the bands had been indirectly influenced by Elvis as well as black rhythm and blues. Teens were ready for change, and their music and looks were a force to be reckoned with. Bands like the Beatles and the Rolling Stones were a real threat to groups and performers with a fifties sound which seemed stale and outdated. In the sixties, rock 'n' roll became a matter of the survival of the fittest.

JAN. 1: George Hamilton was chosen over Elvis to play the role of Hank Williams in the film *Your Cheatin' Heart* because Williams's widow, Audrey, felt her husband's life would be overshadowed by Elvis's presence.

JAN. 8: Elvis did not want to celebrate his birthday. He was extremely upset about the way his career was going. With celebrity came vast disappointment and loneliness. He became almost violent when too many papers ran stories about his professional or personal life.

JAN. 12: Recordings for MGM's *Kissin' Cousins* were held at the RCA studios in Nashville, with the purpose of acquiring a real Southern country-western sound. Elvis again recorded "Ask Me" (RCA 47-8440), which hit No. 12 during a twelve-week stay on *Billboard*'s Top 100 chart. One version is with the Jordanaires and Floyd Cramer on organ. "It Hurts Me" by Joy Byers and Charlie Daniels was also recorded, and it peaked at No. 29 on *Billboard*'s Top 100 chart during a seven-week run. For the second time, Elvis recorded Chuck Berry's "Memphis, Tennessee," and it is heard on the EP *See the USA, the Elvis Way* and the LP *Elvis for Everyone*.

JAN. 14: Fans were upset when the *Memphis Press-Scimitar* ran the story

"Elvis Rocks to a $20-Million Roll." He was not "rock 'n' rolling," he was "rolling" poorly in predictable, senseless flicks. The article claimed Elvis had earned $75 million in eight years.

JAN. 30: Elvis bought the yacht *Potomac*, once owned by Pres. Franklin D. Roosevelt, and donated it to Danny Thomas's St. Jude's Children's Hospital on February 15.

FEB.: February's issue of *Movie Life* confused fans with the article "Elvis and Ann-Margret Wed!" which was about their wedding in the movie *Viva Las Vegas*.

FEB. 7: The Beatles arrived at New York's Kennedy Airport from Liverpool, England, where they were greeted by mobs of screaming teenagers. They stayed at New York's Warwick Hotel, and Elvis sent them a congratulatory telegram.
  The ever-watchful Colonel told Elvis he had better cut some first-class records or else the Beatles would take money out of his pocket.

FEB. 18: The Beatles went to see *Fun in Acapulco* at a Miami drive-in theater.

FEB. 21: A sneak preview of MGM's *Kissin' Cousins* was seen in North Long Beach, California.

FEB. 24–28: Elvis started to record songs for the sound track of *Roustabout* at Radio Recorders in Hollywood. Mae West was originally asked to play Maggie Morgan in the film, but she turned down the role, which Barbara Stanwyck took. During the shooting, stuntman Glen Wilder mistakenly hit Elvis, who went to a local hospital and received nine stitches in his head.

CA. FEB. 28: "Hard Knocks" by Joy Byers, Jerry Leiber–Mike Stoller's "Little Egypt," "One-Track Heart" by Giant-Baum-Kaye, and "Wheels on My Heels" by Sid Tepper and Roy C. Bennett were completed by Elvis for *Roustabout* at Radio Recorders.

MAR.: Lee Morris, Dolores Fuller, and Sonny Hendrix wrote "Big Love, Big Heartache," which Elvis recorded at Radio Recorders for *Roustabout*. No single was released. "Carny Town" by Fred Wise and Randy Starr; "It's Carnival Time" by Ben Weisman and Sid Wayne; "It's a Wonderful World" (the only song by Elvis to be considered for an Academy Award nomination) by Sid Tepper and Roy C. Bennett; "Poison Ivy League" and "Roustabout," both by Giant-Baum-Kaye; and "There's a Brand New Day on the Horizon" by Joy Byers were recorded for *Roustabout*. *Note:* Although the Mello Men sang backup vocals for "Roustabout," the Jordanaires were credited. The uncharted single "Roustabout" was released with "One-Track Heart" in November 1964 as a promo disc (RCA SP-45-139).

MAR. 6: A sneak preview of MGM's *Kissin' Cousins* was seen in Phoenix, Arizona.

MAR. 9: Elvis began filming Paramount's *Roustabout*, directed by John Rich and produced by Hal B. Wallis (who had been nominated 121 times for Oscars and had won 32 Academy Awards). The film costarred Barbara Stanwyck, Joan Freeman, Leif Erickson, and Sue Ann Langdon. Red West played a carnival worker. Vocal accompaniment was by the Jordanaires. *Roustabout* was filmed on various Paramount lots and in Thousand Oaks, California.

MAR. 11: Elvis was given an Americanism award from Shelby County and Memphis business leaders.

MAR. 18: Elvis purchased a Rolls-

Royce Phantom V from Coventry Motors in Beverly Hills (license number ULL501). Sonny West was his chauffeur.

APR.: MGM's *Kissin' Cousins* opened nationally. During 1964, the film grossed $2.8 million.

APR.: Volume 1, #1, of *The Elvis Echo* (newspaper) was released. It was edited by Paulette Sansone.

APR. 20: Elvis finished filming *Roustabout* for Paramount. *Viva Las Vegas* premiered in New York City to capacity crowds.

APR. 30: Larry Geller was working on Johnny River's hair at Jay Sebring's Beverly Hills, California, salon when the phone rang with a message: go to Elvis's Bel Air home and cut his hair. He did, and a close, but strange relationship began that concerned Parker.

At times, Elvis was ambivalent about religion, and people often took advantage of that fact. Larry Geller, his hairstylist turned spiritual guru, allegedly witnessed Elvis surrounded by awards and gold records, in tears because he wasn't "one of the chosen ones." At one time, Elvis considered changing his religion to Judaism. Another time, he pondered becoming a monk. In a moment of gloom, he talked of his desire to be a Buddhist. Geller convinced Elvis he should be a student of the occult and the mystical world. Geller quickly replaced Sal Orfice as Elvis's personal hairstylist.

By the time Elvis was best man at high school chum George Klein's Jewish wedding ceremony, he knew a lot about Judaism. As the rabbi officiated, Elvis repeated in Hebrew every word the rabbi said. People were flabbergasted to hear the Cat from Tupelo recite whole verses in ancient Hebrew!

Larry Geller, the self-proclaimed "healing" influence in Elvis's life, introduced the singer to the Self-Realization

Fellowship Center on Mount Washington in the Hollywood Hills and inspired Elvis to read all he could on metaphysics. Parker, paranoid when Geller's influence on Elvis seemed to be getting out of hand, made certain someone was present whenever Geller was with Elvis. By 1966, Vernon Presley and the Colonel ended the relationship and discarded any book that related to the occult in the library.

MAY: An issue of *Movielife* featured Elvis and Ann-Margret.

For *Frankie and Johnny*, Elvis sang Sid Tepper and Roy C. Bennett's "Beginner's Luck" and "Petunia, the Gardener's Daughter" in a duet with Donna Douglas at RCA's Nashville studios. No single was released. "Harum Holiday" by Peter Andreoli and Vince Poncia, Jr., and "Chesay" by Fred Karger, Sid Wayne, and Ben Weisman were completed for the same film at Radio Recorders. David Hess's "Come Along" was completed by Elvis, but it was never released.

At Radio Recorders, the adaption of "Down by the Riverside/When the Saints Go Marching In" by Giant-Baum-Kaye for the film *Frankie and Johnny* was sung as a medley. "Everybody Come Aboard" by the same composers and the title song were completed. Sue Ann Langdon, Harry Morgan, and Donna Douglas were a backup chorus for "Everybody Comes Aboard." The title song, "Frankie and Johnny," peaked at No. 25 on *Billboard*'s Top 100 chart during an eight-week run.

JUNE: Colonel Parker announced on the set of *Girl Happy* he was conferring the title "honorary Colonel" on singer Sergio Franchi, which annoyed Elvis.

JUNE–JULY: Elvis sang at *Girl Happy* recording sessions, in Hollywood's Radio Recorders. For *Girl Happy*, take No. 13 of the title song was finally released. "Cross My Heart and Hope to Die" and "The Meanest Girl in Town" by Joy Byers were finished. Take No. 36 of "Do Not Disturb" by Giant-Baum-Kaye was used in the film. "Do the Clam," written by Sid Wayne, Ben Weisman, and Dolores Fuller was completed that day. The single sold well in Japan (RCA 47-8500) and hit No. 21 of *Billboard*'s Top 100 chart in an eight-week stay. Its flip side was "You'll Be Gone." "Fort Lauderdale Chamber of Commerce" by Tepper-Bennett and "I've Got to Find My Baby" by Joy Byers were completed for *Girl Happy*. Elvis also recorded "Puppet on a String," written by Sid Tepper and Roy C. Bennett, for *Girl Happy*. The single release reached No. 14 on *Billboard*'s Hot 100 chart during a ten-week stay and was No. 3 on the Easy-Listening chart (RCA 447-0650, released in October 1965 with the flip side "Wooden Heart").

JUNE 17: *Viva Las Vegas* opened nationally, after having premiered in New York City and overseas. It set box-office records in Tokyo, Manila, and many Far East cities, but it was banned in Gozo (sister island of Malta) because the Gozo College of Parish Priests censored the film as "indecent." Malta, however, showed the film and it sold out every night. The film grossed $4,675,000 in 1964.

JUNE 22: Elvis began filming MGM's *Girl Happy*. The Clam, choreographed by David Winters, was introduced as a new dance in the movie but did not become a fad. Vocal accompaniment was by the Jordanaires. Filming took place on MGM Culver City studio lots and in Fort Lauderdale, Florida. Miss America of 1959, Mary Ann Mobley and Shelley Fabares costarred with Elvis. Red West played an extra in the Kit Kat Club.

JULY: A gold record for "Kiss Me Quick" was awarded to Elvis from South Africa on the MGM lot of *Girl*

Happy. At Radio Recorders, "Spring Fever," written by Giant-Baum-Kaye, was recorded by Elvis for *Girl Happy* as a duet with Shelley Fabares. Elvis also recorded "Startin' Tonight" by Lenore Rosenblatt and Victor Millrose and "Wolf Call" by Giant-Baum-Kaye for the same movie.

JULY: Ann-Margret and Elvis were on the cover of *Movie World.* The press did not want to let go of a possible romance between Ann-Margret and Elvis, but Ann-Margret's personality was too strong for Elvis to handle. She was not the submissive, quiet type who would do anything and everything he told her to do. Thus, their romance was doomed from the start—Elvis wanted complete control.

JULY 7: Take No. 5 of Joy Byer's song "C'mon Everybody" was finished by Elvis at Hollywood's Radio Recorders for *Viva Las Vegas.*

JULY 30: The Beatles were the most popular rock band in America.

AUG.: Elvis appeared with two bathing beauties on the cover of *Film Review.*

AUG. 1: Elvis's close friend, singer Johnny Burnette, drowned in California. When Elvis heard the news, he sobbed.

AUG. 2: Elvis added vocals to "Drums of the Island" by Sid Tepper and Roy C. Bennett and completed "Sand Castles" by Herb Goldberg and David Hess for the film *Paradise, Hawaiian Style* at Radio Recorders.

AUG. 4: The duet with Elvis and Donna Butterworth of "Datin' " by Fred Wise and Randy Starr for *Paradise, Hawaiian Style* was completed at Radio Recorders after July 26 instrumentals were finished. Take No. 14 was used in the film. That same day "A Dog's Life"

by Sid Wayne–Ben Weisman was finished for the movie.

AUG. 6: AP reporter Bob Thomas wrote an article that stated, "It Looks Like Romance for Presley and Ann-Margret." Thomas and almost every tabloid in America had a field day when Ann-Margret confessed their serious love relationship would culminate in marriage. Elvis declared to the press and to Ann-Margret that no one would announce he was going to marry anyone.

AUG. 28: The Beatles appeared on the cover of *Life.*

CA. SEPT: Jim Morrison, who would establish the band the Doors, moved to California to become a film student at UCLA. Morrison was a sexy, brooding, mysterious poet with a dark side. His music reflected his genius and his pain. Like Elvis, whom he idolized, Morrison would often allow the negative to overtake the positive.

OCT.: Elvis began filming *Tickle Me* for Allied Artists, which was directed by Norman Taurog and produced by Ben Schwalb. For this rather dull role, Elvis earned $750,000 plus 50 percent of the gross profits. Saving Allied Artist's from financial doom, the reel sale for the film was the largest in the film company's history. The budget for the movie was $1,480,000. Although twelve songs were scheduled for the movie, only nine were used.

Larry Geller introduced Elvis to Sri Daya Mata, head of the Self-Realization Fellowship Center on Mount Washington in the Hollywood Hills. Elvis kept her book *Only Love* in his religious library.

OCT. 10: Raquel Welch debuted in *Roustabout.* She appeared in the last five minutes of the film as a college girl. Elvis barely noticed her.

NOV. 11: Paramount's *Roustabout* opened nationally. By the end of 1964, it grossed $3 million.

NOV.: This issue of *Movie Teen Illustrated* featured Elvis and the Beatles on the cover and ran a story about the popular singers.

DEC.: Elvis gave $68,000 to Memphis charities for Christmas.

Elvis (with "Kissin' Cousins") and the Beatles (with "I Want to Hold Your Hand") appeared on the U.S. Marines' LP titled *Sounds of Solid Gold*.

DEC. 31: Theater owners named Elvis the sixth top box-office draw of the 1964 movie season.

Elvis's favorite movie was *Dr. Strangelove*, which starred Peter Sellers. Elvis saw the movie many times.

Tennessee state senator LeRoy Johnson named Elvis the state's Entertainer of the Year and presented him with an award.

1965

1965 was a turbulent year. The riots in the predominantly black Los Angeles community of Watts shocked the world. The Vietnam War began to polarize the nation, and on February 21, black leader Malcolm X was silenced by an assassin's bullet in New York City. Mainstream America was horrified and wondered what was next.

CA. JAN: Priscilla modeled at the Piccadilly Cafeteria at 123 Madison Avenue in Memphis.

JAN. 8: Elvis signed a three-picture contract with MGM. There was some talk of him doing a film titled *Baby, the Rain Must Fall* but Steve McQueen ended up playing Henry Thomas, an ex-con who had a band called the Rockabillies. In the movie, one of McQueen's lines was, "Maybe I'll be a big movie star like Elvis Presley."

JAN. 24: Colonel Parker received $1,300,000 for two of Elvis's movies in a contract with United Artists.

FEB.: Bob Dylan's "Like a Rolling Stone" became his first major hit.

Elvis started recording the sound track for the movie *Harum Scarum* at RCA studios in Nashville. "Go East, Young Man" and "Shake That Tambourine," both by Bill Giant, Bernie Baum, Florence Kaye; "Golden Coins" by Bill Giant, Bernie Baum, and Florence Kaye; "Hey, Little Girl" by Joy Byers; "Kismet" (not the same as the theme song from the 1955 movie *Kismet*) by Sid Tepper and Roy C. Bennett; "Mirage" by Bill Giant, Bernie Baum, and Florence Kaye; "My Desert Serenade" by Stan Geller; Joy Byer's "So Close, Yet So Far (From Paradise)"; and "Wisdom of the Ages" by Giant-Baum-Kaye, which was not used in the film but appears on the LP *Harum Scarum*, were recorded by Elvis for *Harum Scarum*.

FEB. 5: Claiming she had rights to the song "Roustabout," exotic dancer Little Egypt sued Paramount Pictures and Elvis Presley Music in the New York Supreme Court for damages (seeking

an injunction to stop the distribution of the film *Roustabout* and its LP). She lost the case.

MAR.:   Bob Dylan had a sell-out U.K. tour.

MAR. 7:   To refute those who blamed Elvis for having perverted society with rock 'n' roll, the *Commercial Appeal* of Memphis raved about Elvis: "Unlike some other superstars, Elvis is a genuine nice guy. He never makes news by insulting people, by brawling, nightclubbing or running with the Hollywood status packs. . . . His manners are a source of amazement to those meeting him for the first time. He is . . . universally described . . . as 'polite,' 'nice,' 'humble,' 'sincere,' and 'thoughtful'."

It is an unfortunate twist of fate that those whom society idolizes often become isolated and reclusive. (A case in point is Michael Jackson, who has been portrayed by the press as an eccentric recluse.)

In a 1965 interview, Elvis denied he sequestered himself: "It's not true. . . . Of course, I don't get out like I used to . . . because I'm so busy. . . . I withdraw not from my fans, but from myself. After work, I just give out. I like to come back here [to Graceland] to think and relax. I guess in that respect I have

withdrawn, but here it's quiet and I can reevaluate myself and see where I am going."

The truth was obvious. Elvis did not socialize or attend public functions. His celebrity was too immense. By the end of his life he hid within the walls of Graceland.

MAR. 7:   The press continued to attack Elvis for every conceivable reason. He answered back, attempting to set the record straight in an unpretentious, almost noble manner: "My team has been my millions of fans. There have been thousands of stories about me that were not true. I don't really object because I know what it is to scratch and fight for what you want. . . . I can never forget the longing to be someone. I guess if you are poor, you always think bigger and want more than those who have everything when they are born. We didn't. So our dreams and ambitions could be much greater because we had so much farther to go than anyone else. . . . I know what poverty is. I lived it for a long time. But my mama and daddy kept struggling. They did everything possible for me. . . . I am not ashamed of my background, or the fact I drove a truck. In fact, I am proud that in America we have the opportunity to fight for a way of life. . . . I don't regard money or position as important. It is what a man does that is important." (See the *Commercial Appeal*, 3/7/65.)

MAR.:   "Scatter," a forty-pound chimpanzee, was Elvis's most troublesome pet. Members of the Memphis Mafia enjoyed dressing Scatter like a human. The chimpanzee often traveled with Elvis.

MAR. 15:   Elvis filmed *Harum Scarum* for MGM. The movie was directed by Gene Nelson and produced by Sam Katzman. Mary Ann Mobley, in her second film with Elvis, costarred.

▲ Elvis holding a young Carla Thomas on stage at Ellis Auditorium, Memphis, Tennessee. *Photograph by Ernest C. Withers. Copyright © 1994 Mimosa Records Productions, Inc.*

APR. 14: MGM's *Girl Happy* was released. It grossed MGM $3.1 million in 1965. Critics thought Elvis was horrible.

With the William Morris Agency and the Colonel supervising his every move, Elvis made too many dull, predictable films, and he became tired, complacent, and angry because he was getting terrible reviews and he deserved most of them. He also abhorred the music. His management had become antiquated and self-serving. The Colonel's tactics were starting to break down. Even dyed-in-the-wool fans disliked some of Elvis's films. There was nothing noble, outstanding, or innovative about any role he took.

MAY: An AP article in the *Memphis Press-Scimitar* titled "Elvis' Popularity Puzzling to Hollywood 'Insiders'" said Elvis lived a "Garbo-like" existence because he purposely hid himself from the public. However, the truth was he could not tolerate or combat criticism, and because his natural response was to fight back verbally, the Colonel isolated him. *Movie News* insisted, "Elvis beefed about the circus that always surrounds him . . . and . . . caused friction in the company [at MGM]."

Gossip columnists continuously mentioned a "mystery woman" who kept most of the West Coast guessing, and they wondered if she was Nancy Sinatra, Barbara Eden, or Laurel Goodwin. It may have been Priscilla Beaulieu or Cybill Shepherd.

The sound track for *Frankie and Johnny* was started at Radio Recorders in Hollywood. Because talk of riots in the Los Angeles area ran rampant, the Colonel instructed every person around Elvis to carry a firearm.

Elvis recorded Fred Wise and Randy Starr's "Look Out, Broadway"; "Shout It Out" by Bill Giant, Bernie Baum, and Florence Kaye; and "What Every Woman Lives For" by Doc Pomus and Mort Shuman. No singles were made.

Elvis was on the cover of *Film Stars* and *Movie News*. While gossip ran rampant about Elvis and his many "affairs of the heart," the U.S. was in a state of confusion and hostility. Protests against the Vietnam War became violent, but Elvis kept his feelings about the war private.

A reporter asked Elvis for an opinion about protest songs. He said he didn't think every song had to have a message. He was not a student of current affairs, nor did he keep up with national or international issues, wars, or politics. He felt uncomfortable answering questions that might make him look foolish or ignorant, therefore he purposely would not remark on another person's stand. Nor did he make statements for or against anything. For the most part, he kept his beliefs and comments to himself.

MAY 25: Elvis began filming *Frankie and Johnny* for United Artists, but it was shot at MGM. The film was directed by Frederick de Cordova and produced by Edward Small with a budget of $4.5 million. Thomas Hart Benton's original murals of the legendary Frankie and Johnny hang in the Missouri State Capitol Building. Reproductions were hung in the MGM lot.

MAY 28: Elvis's film *Tickle Me* premiered in Atlanta, Georgia.

MAY 30: Hairstylist Larry Geller claimed Elvis was so despondent he wanted to join a monastery and flee publicity of any kind. Geller alleged that he talked Elvis out of it.

CA. JUNE: To be near the home of Colonel Parker, Elvis built an $85,000, Spanish-style, white stucco home on Chino Canyon Road in Palm Springs, California, which also had a small recording studio. Elvis would eventually will the home to his daughter, Lisa Marie, who would sell the home in 1979 to singer Frankie Valli for $385,000.

AUG.: Elvis was on the cover of *Screen Stars.*

The Elvis Presley Appreciation Society was founded in Luxembourg and held its first "annual awards" meeting.

AUG. 2–3: For *Paradise, Hawaiian Style*, Elvis recorded "House of Sand" and "Stop Where You Are," both by Bill Giant, Bernie Baum, and Florence Kaye; and "Paradise, Hawaiian Style" (same composers) at Radio Recorders (RCA used splices of take Nos. 3 and 4 for release). Instrumentals for the songs had been finished on July 27, 1965. For the movie, take No. 2 was released of "Scratch My Back (Then I'll Scratch Yours)" by Giant-Baum-Kaye.

AUG. 4: Elvis and Donna Butterworth sang a duet for the film *Paradise, Hawaiian Style* during "Queenie Wahine's Papaya" (written by Bernie Baum, Bill Giant, and Florence Kaye), which they recorded at Radio Recorders in Hollywood. Splices from take Nos. 2 and 6 were used in the film.

AUG. 7: Elvis began filming *Paradise, Hawaiian Style* in Hanauma Bay, for Paramount, which was directed by D. Michael Moore and produced by Hal B. Wallis. During the filming, Elvis and his group from Memphis stayed in Suite 2225 at the Ilikai Hotel in Hawaii. The film was shot in Honolulu, Kauai (at the Hanalei Plantation Resort), Maui (Maui Sheraton Hotel), on the Kona Coast, Paramount Studios in Hollywood, and at the airport in Torrance, California.

CA. AUG. 8: "Please Don't Stop Loving Me" was recorded for the film *Frankie and Johnny* at Radio Recorders. It was written by Joy Byers and it charted at No. 45 during an eight-week stay on *Billboard*'s Hot 100 chart (RCA 47-8780, released in March 1966 with the flip side "Frankie and Johnny").

AUG. 9–10: Elvis disappeared from the *Paradise, Hawaiian Style* set. His Memphis cronies claimed he had stomach cramps, while others spread the rumor he was "vacationing" with an eager starlet who wanted to know him better.

AUG. 11: Elvis's mood swings and sudden outbursts of temper shocked associates on the set of *Paradise, Hawaiian Style* and provoked criticism from columnist Hedda Hopper. Prior to this day's shooting, the so-called "stomach cramps" from August 9–10 had kept Elvis from the set. Some people thought he was popping pills. Others blamed his discomfort on junk food. Elvis was becoming exceedingly reclusive, and *Movie News* reported: "The only person he would see was a 'mystery' visitor from Hollywood—a nineteen-year-old blonde, whom he did not introduce . . . During his self-imposed isolation [he] grumbled about the way his privacy was always being disturbed."

AUG. 15: The Beatles performed before 55,000 fans at Shea Stadium in New York, the largest rock-concert crowd in history. Those closest to Elvis tried to shield him from knowing how big the Beatles were becoming, but he knew. The "Ed Sullivan Show" filmed the Beatles at Shea Stadium, and TV offers came pouring in. The British-beat invasion dominated the charts in America.

Colonel Parker and Elvis placed two wreaths (with 1,177 carnations—one carnation for each man who died there on December 7, 1941) at the USS *Arizona* memorial.

AUG. 19: Peter Noone, the lead singer of Herman's Hermits, interviewed Elvis. From October 1964 to August 1965, Herman's Hermits had eight *Billboard* Top 100 hits that charted at No. 10 and above. Elvis did not chart during that period. Although Noone had the chance of a lifetime to ask Elvis relevant questions about why he allowed himself to slip out of the vanguard of rock, he did not ask one pertinent question. When Elvis became bored with Peter Noone, he wished him luck and exited.

AUG. 27: The Beatles and their manager, Brian Epstein, went to Elvis's Bel Air home on Friday, August 27. Elvis and the Beatles fooled around with various songs, including Cilla Black's smash hit, "You're My World." Jokingly, the Beatles asked Elvis to become the fifth member of their group, as the Colonel and Brian Epstein played roulette in an adjoining room.

Elvis was not bashful about his musical ability. He played piano in front of such famous personalities as Tom Jones, Nancy Sinatra, Redd Foxx, Sammy Davis, Jr., and many others. After meeting Elvis, John Lennon of the Beatles declared, "We spent about four hours talking, listening to records, and jamming. During the jam session Elvis played piano and drums. We ate a lot, shot some pool, and had a ball. The whole time we were jamming he had the tape machine running." (See *Elvis, the Illustrated Record.*) To date, no tape of this meeting has surfaced.

When the Beatles came to America, they idolized Elvis. Although the Beatles and Elvis tried to respect one another (and at first they did), Elvis regrettably condemned them as a "subversive group." Elvis's stint in the Army and his years in Tinsel Town rubbed a conservative tinge into the cocky, lovable wonder boy of rock. By calling the Beatles "subversive," it was obvious Elvis had lost his edge. On the British TV show "Juke Box Jury," the Beatles ruled, "Elvis has gone down the nicks [tubes]."

The Beatles became the most popular group of the sixties. The Beatles asked the Colonel to be their manager after Brian Epstein died. When Parker told the Beatles Elvis would always be number one in his book, the Beatles decided not to join Parker's promo-tions, which was probably a good decision.

SEPT.: *Teen Scrapbook* asked, "Is Elvis Presley Really Worth a Million Dollars [per movie]?" The answer: "Yes," as far as movie producers were concerned. Elvis never lost anyone a dime, and that is what counted in Hollywood.

OCT. 21: After being hospitalized three times, Bill Black, one of the Blue Moon Boys, died of a brain tumor during surgery at the Baptist Memorial Hospital, at the age of thirty-nine. The news of Black's passing devastated the Memphis rockabilly artists, but Elvis seemed to ignore Black's death. It hit too close to home. Vernon Presley went to the funeral and gave Elvis's saddest condolences to Black's wife, Evelyn, and his three daughters.

After Bill Black left Elvis in 1958, he bought a recording company across the street from the American Sound Studios in Memphis, appeared in the movie *Teen-age Millionaire* (a 1961 film that included Chubby Checker and Jackie Wilson), and organized the Bill Black Combo, which recorded for Memphis Hi-Records a version of "Don't Be Cruel" (Hi 2026).

NOV.: Jim Morrison and the Doors performed at Odine's, a stylish New York club on Fifty-ninth Street. Morrison was brooding, elusive, and charismatic. He patterned himself after the man he admired the most: Elvis Presley. Both men had sexual charisma, that special star quality that cannot be learned. Both men had voracious sexual appetites, and both men eventually allowed drugs to destroy them.

NOV. 24: *Harum Scarum* premiered in Los Angeles.

DEC.: Elvis moved from Perugia Way in Bel Air to a mansion at 10550 Rocca Place in Stone Canyon.

DEC. 31: Theater owners voted Elvis the sixth top box-office draw of the 1965 movie season. Remarkably, pop polls named Elvis the number one singer and number one musical personality over the Beatles and the Rolling Stones (who dominated the charts).

1966

As antiwar protesters marched on Washington, DC, B-52 bombers hammered Hanoi hoping to defeat North Vietnam, "black power" split civil rights groups, race riots inflamed Chicago and Atlanta, and Truman Capote's *In Cold Blood* probed the minds of cold-blooded killers.

In 1966, Jimi Hendrix introduced the electric guitar in Europe, while the Beatles' album *Revolver*, Bob Dylan's *Blonde on Blonde*, the Beach Boys' *Pet Sounds*, and the Byrds' "Eight Miles High" hit the charts, and the made-for-TV Monkees entertained a new generation of music fans.

FEB.: The Fred Wise–Randy Starr song "Adam and Evil" was recorded at Hollywood's Radio Recorders by Elvis for the movie *Spinout*, with "All That I Am," written by Sid Tepper and Roy C. Bennett. "All That I Am" (RCA 47-8941) hit *Billboard*'s Top 100 chart at No. 47 and was No. 9 on the Easy-Listening chart. Its flip side was the film's title song, "Spinout," written by Sid Wayne, Ben Weisman, and Dolores Fuller. "Spinout" hit No. 40 on the Top 100 chart. Reportedly, each song sold over 1 million copies by 1968.

It took seven takes for Elvis to perfect "Am I Ready," written by Sid Tepper and Roy C. Bennett.

FEB. 15–17: "Stop, Look and Listen" by Joy Byers and "Beach Shack" by Bill Giant, Bernie Baum, and Florence Kaye were finished at Radio Recorders for *Spinout*. No single was released. On February 16, Elvis recorded "Never Say Yes" by Doc Pomus and Mort Shuman at Radio Recorders for *Spinout*.

On February 17, Elvis sang Sid Wayne and Ben Weisman's "I'll Be Back" for *Spinout*.

CA. FEB. 18: Elvis recorded for *Spinout* "Smorgasbord" (written by Sid Tepper and Roy C. Bennett) at Radio Recorders.

FEB. 20: Elvis began filming MGM's *Spinout*, set in Santa Barbara, California. It was directed by Norman Taurog and produced by Joe Pasternak. To commemorate Elvis's ten years in film, MGM distributed Elvis photographs, posters, and booklets about his gold Cadillac with a twenty-one-page anniversary story about their top-grossing star. Five thousand radio stations received promo copies of the single "Spinout."

CA. FEB. 26: Pres. Lyndon Baines Johnson visited Elvis on the set of *Spinout*, and Elvis made certain everyone took notice of how important he had become. Some people on the set thought Elvis was obnoxious during this episode, although he was exceedingly gracious to the president.

FEB. 28: Elvis dated actress Deborah Walley.

CA. MAR.: Elvis, Sonny West, and Jerry Schilling filed a UFO sighting, which they claim they had seen in December from Elvis's home on Perugia Way in Bel Air, California.

MAR.:   MGM sponsored an essay contest on "The Perfect American Male." Prize winners received Elvis records.

Elvis was bored filming *Spinout* because he did not like the music and felt he was too fat.

MAR. 31:   In Baton Rouge, Louisiana, *Frankie and Johnny* was released. To promote the movie, Elvis's 1960 Cadillac (advertised as "solid gold") toured the U.S.

CA. APR.:   Elvis, Priscilla, and the gang went to John Huston's premiere of the film *The Bible*, which Elvis hated. He walked out during intermission leaving Priscilla behind.

APR. 6:   MGM's *Spinout* was completed.

MAY: A 16–mm short was released as a promotional tool for *Paradise, Hawaiian Style*, showing how the movie was made. It was distributed to churches, schools, travel agencies, and other groups.

Felton Jarvis negotiated with the Colonel to produce Elvis's next album, a religious LP. Jarvis was concerned that Elvis's music had slipped to an all-time low, and he wanted to rectify the situation.

While at a nightclub on Sunset Strip in Los Angeles, the Doors lead singer Jim Morrison noticed a man named Gerard Malanga wearing tight, black leather pants. Morrison wanted to make an impression on the West Coast as Elvis had done in 1954–55, and soon black leather became Morrison's trademark. Because of Morrison's successful, sexual image in black leather, designer Bill Belew designed an almost identical leather jacket and slacks for Elvis to wear during his TV comeback in 1968.

MAY 25:   *How Great Thou Art* began production with Henry Slaughter on piano and organ. Felton Jarvis produced the LP. Jake Hess and the Imperials (with Hess, Jim Murray, Gary McSpadden, Armand Morales) were backup singers. Recordings were made in Nashville's RCA Studio B and the LP was released in March 1967. Side one includes "How Great Thou Art" (one of Elvis's favorite songs), "In the Garden," "Somebody Bigger Than You and I," "Stand By Me" (which Elvis sang when he was depressed); side two contains "So High," "Where Could I Go but to the Lord," "By and By," "If the Lord Wasn't Walking by My Side," "Run On," "Where No One Stands Alone," "Crying in the Chapel." Much to the Colonel's delight, Elvis's decision to sing gospel music pleased fans, and the record put him back on the top of pop charts.

Elvis recorded "How Great Thou Art" at RCA's Nashville Studio B (released in April 1967, RCA 74-0130, which did not chart). Its flip side was "So High." He also recorded "Run On" (an old gospel classic arranged by Elvis), which appears on the LP *How Great Thou Art*.

MAY 26: "Down in the Alley" by Jesse Stone was recorded by Elvis for *Spinout* at RCA's Nashville studio. He also completed Edward Heyman and Victor Young's "Love Letters," with Floyd Cramer on piano. It peaked at No. 19 on *Billboard*'s Hot 100 chart and No. 38 on Easy-Listening (RCA 47-8870, released in June 1966, with the flip side "Come What May"). Elvis also completed the gospel song "Where No One Stands Alone" by Mosier Lister, recorded for the LP *How Great Thou Art*. Elvis recorded Bob Dylan's "Tomorrow Is a Long Time." Elvis's version is heard on the *Spinout* LP and the LP *A Valentine Gift for You*.

"Stand by Me" was recorded by Elvis at RCA studios in Nashville on May 26, and its lyrics best expressed how Elvis felt about God's protection and the trials of life.

MAY 27: Elvis sang "Beyond the Reef," which was written by Red West and Charlie Hodge and recorded at RCA's Nashville studios with West as lead singer, Elvis as second tenor and at the piano, and Charlie Hodge as first tenor. A bad recording, it was never used. Elvis also recorded "By and By," a gospel tune that is on the LP *How Great Thou Art*. "Somebody Bigger Than You and I," written by Johnny Lange, Walter "Hy" Heath, and Joseph Burke; "Farther Along"; "So High" and "In the Garden" by C. Austin Miles; and "Without Him" by Myron Lefevre were recorded for the LP *How Great Thou Art*.

MAY 28: "Come What May" by Franklin Tableporter was recorded by Elvis

at RCA's Nashville studio (RCA 47-8870) and was released June 1966. Also recorded was "Fools Fall in Love" (RCA 47-9056) by Leiber and Stoller; neither song charted. Elvis also completed "If the Lord Wasn't Walking by My Side" by Henry Slaughter (who played organ) and "Where Could I Go but to the Lord" by James B. Coats.

JUNE: *Seventeen Magazine* selected *Paradise, Hawaiian Style* Picture of the Month.

For the film *Double Trouble*, Elvis recorded Joy Byers's "Baby, If You'll Give Me All of Your Love" at Radio Recorders, and take No. 3 of "City by Night," written by Bill Giant, Florence Kaye, and Bernie Baum, was used in the sound track. Randy Starr's "Could I Fall in Love" was completed at this session. The Doc Pomus–Mort Shuman song "Double Trouble"; "I Love Only One Girl" by Sid Tepper and Roy C. Bennett; "It Won't Be Long" by Sid Wayne and Ben Weisman; "Long Legged Girl (With the Short Dress On)," written by J. Leslie McFarland and Winfield Scott; "Old MacDonald," arranged by Randy Starr; and "There Is So Much World to See," written by Tepper and Weisman, were completed for *Double Trouble*. Take No. 5 of "Long Legged Girl" was released and reached No. 63 during five weeks on *Billboard*'s Hot 100 chart. It was the shortest song Elvis ever recorded for a single—one minute twenty-six seconds (RCA 47-9115, released in May of 1967, with its flip side "That's Someone You Never Forget").

JUNE 9: *Paradise, Hawaiian Style* sneak-previewed in Memphis to sell-out crowds.

JUNE 10: RCA studios in Nashville started recording sessions with Elvis backed by Henry Slaughter on organ/ piano. "Indescribably Blue," written by Darrell Glenns, was completed, and it peaked at No. 33 on *Billboard*'s Top

100 chart during an eight-week run (RCA 47-9056, released Jan. 6, 1967). Its flip side was "Fools Fall in Love." Elvis also recorded Red West and Glen Spreen's uncharted song "If Every Day Was Like Christmas" with the flip side "How Would You Like to Be" (RCA 47-8950).

CA. JUNE 10: Elvis completed sound tracks for the film *Double Trouble* at Radio Recorders in Hollywood. Although ads for the movie claimed Elvis sang nine songs, one was cut, "It Won't Be Long."

JUNE 11: Elvis began filming *Double Trouble* for MGM, directed by Norman Taurog and produced by Judd Bernard and Irwin Winkler. George Klein, a member of the Memphis Mafia, had a bit part. All scenes took place on MGM's studio lots in Culver City, California. Elvis's male cousin Billy Smith doubled for Elvis's costar, actress Annette Day, in a scene! Billy was kidded about that for months.

JUNE 15: A sneak preview of *Paradise, Hawaiian Style* opened in New York City to enthusiastic crowds.

JUNE 25: Red West wrote "That's Someone You Never Forget" for Elvis, which he recorded at RCA's Nashville studios on June 25, 1961. It took six years for RCA to release it as a single (RCA 47-9115), in May 1967 with the flip side "Long Legged Girl (With the Short Dress On)." Elvis's rendition of West's song climbed to a low No. 92 on *Billboard*'s Hot 100 chart with less than one week on the list. It can be heard on the LP *Pot Luck*.

JUNE 29: Elvis's relative Travis Smith, who had been a gatekeeper at Graceland, died after a long hospitalization. Elvis did not attend the funeral.

JULY 6: *Paradise, Hawaiian Style* opened nationally. It grossed over $2.5 million in 1966.

JULY 8–26: Elvis filmed various scenes for *Double Trouble*.

JULY 29: When Bob Dylan broke his neck vertebrae and landed in the hospital with a concussion after a motorcycle accident, Elvis decided motorcycles were too dangerous to ride outside Graceland.

AUG.: Elvis filmed *Double Trouble* and caused havoc at his Bel Air home with members of the Memphis Mafia.

AUG. 29: The Beatles gave up touring in concert after their gig at San Francisco's Candlestick Park. Together with the Rolling Stones and Bob Dylan, they dominated the U.S. and U.K. pop charts.

SEPT. 1: Elvis started memorizing the script *Easy Come, Easy Go*.

SEPT. 5: *Double Trouble* was finished.

SEPT. 7–13: *Weekend* speculated Priscilla and Elvis had secretly been married, which caused some of Elvis's fans to cringe and others to applaud.

SEPT. 10: "Big Boss Man," written by Al Smith and Luther Dixon, was recorded at RCA's Nashville studio by Elvis, after the backups and instrumentals had been recorded at Western Recorders during the third week of June. It was for the sound track for *Spinout*, and the strings were added February 22, 1967. On September 11, the record version was sung by Elvis. "Big Boss Man" hit No. 44 of the Top 100 chart and had a six-week stay, while it reached No. 34 on the Easy-Listening chart. Its single flip side was "You

Don't Know Me" (RCA 47-9341), released September 1967, which was written by Eddy Arnold and Cindy Walker in 1955. Jerry Vale hit the Top 100 chart at No. 14 with his version of the song in 1956.

SEPT. 12: Elvis began filming Paramount's *Easy Come, Easy Go*, directed by John Rich and produced by Hal B. Wallis. It costarred Dodie Marshall and Pat Priest, among others. Vocal accompaniments were by the Jordanaires.

SEPT. 13: Presley family members went to the sneak preview of *Spinout*. The King was in Los Angeles, acting in yet another predictable movie.

SEPT. 16: NBC's "Tuesday Night at the Movies" had a disagreement with Paramount Pictures and had to pull *Blue Hawaii* from airing on television. It was replaced by Dean Martin's movie *Living It Up*.

SEPT. 26–29: Elvis began taping *Easy Come, Easy Go* sound tracks, at Radio Recorders in Hollywood. Jerry Scheff played bass. On September 28, Elvis recorded "The Love Machine" for *Easy Come, Easy Go* at Radio Recorders. Written by Gerald Nelson, Fred Burch, and Chuck Taylor, it is heard on the EP *Easy Come, Easy Go* and the LP *I Got Lucky*. On September 29, at Radio Recorders, Elvis sang "I'll Take Love" by Dolores Fuller and Mark Barkan; "She's a Machine" by Joy Byers; and "Leave My Woman Alone" by Ray Charles, for *Easy Come, Easy Go*. "Leave My Woman Alone" was not put in the film nor was it released on any record.

SEPT. 30: Elvis recorded at Radio Recorders for *Easy Come, Easy Go* the song "Yoga Is As Yoga Does" as a duet with Elsa Lanchester. It was written by Gerald Nelson and Fred Burch and is

on the EP by that title and the LP *I Got Lucky*. For the movie *Easy Come, Easy Go*, Elvis sang the title song, written by Sid Wayne and Ben Weisman, at Radio Recorders.

CA. OCT. 1: "You Gotta Stop," written by Bill Giant, Bernie Baum, and Florence Kaye (the instrumental for which was recorded September 28–29), and "Sing, You Children" by Gerald Nelson and Fred Burch were recorded by Elvis for *Easy Come, Easy Go*.

OCT. 28: Shooting ended for *Easy Come, Easy Go*.

NOV. 1: The LP *Elvis Presley* received a platinum certificate from the RIAA for having sold 1 million copies.

NOV. 23: *Spinout* was released nationally.

DEC.: Colonel Parker told producers Elvis would not take the lead in *The Fastest Guitar Alive*, which eventually starred Michael Moore, Roy Orbison, and Sammy Jackson. Elvis was disappointed the Colonel said no, despite the fact he was not the "fastest" or the best player around.

CA. DEC. 8: Colonel Parker had a heart-to-heart talk with Elvis, and then Vernon Presley. There were too many rumors in Hollywood that Elvis led a life of "sin" and some people suspected he was gay because he never went anywhere without his Memphis men around him. The Colonel told Elvis it was time he got married. The Colonel had decided Priscilla Ann Beaulieu would be his bride. Elvis did not want to marry anyone at this time, but Parker insisted that Elvis either ask Priscilla to marry him or get rid of her. The public did not approve of Elvis living with her unmarried. The

Colonel promised to take care of everything—the couple would not have to lift a finger. It was settled.

DEC. 24: Elvis's proposal of marriage to Priscilla Ann Beaulieu came at the insistence of his manager. It is hard to know if Elvis was capable of feeling deeply for anyone but his mother. His behavior with Priscilla was not that of a man committed to keeping marriage vows or treating any wife with respect. In fact, had she not insisted that he give her *some* attention, she may not have received any at all.

Priscilla had dreamed of being Elvis's wife without knowing exactly what that would entail. Like so many young women, she thought marriage would change him. She had rarely traveled with him and had never seen him perform live, thus she had not seen Elvis in his greatest moment—on stage—which was the only place he ever felt totally at ease. He was America's most sought after male—a handsome, sensuous, talented, controversial, wealthy superstar. Priscilla had been sheltered for most of her life and

was ten years Elvis's junior. She had lived in Graceland since October 1962, sequestered far from Elvis's room. Even in the Bel Air house she was secluded from the action and Elvis.

During her life at Graceland, Elvis bedded many women, while members of the Memphis Mafia shielded Priscilla from the facts. Members of the Memphis Mafia were vehemently against the marriage because they knew Elvis did not want to marry anyone. And if Priscilla insisted on going on the road with them, Elvis would become impossible to live with. Elvis needed freedom. He was accustomed to having as many women as he wanted when he wanted them. Because the Memphis Mafia members were so opposed to the marriage, the Colonel told Elvis they would not be invited to the wedding.

DEC. 31: Theater owners named Elvis the tenth top box-office draw of the 1966 movie season. He never again made the list. For the years 1957–65, John Wayne beat Elvis in the polls and Rock Hudson beat him all but two years (1965 and 1966).

1967

In 1967, Albert DeSalvo, the "Boston Strangler," was sentenced to life in prison, three astronauts burned to death in the Apollo tragedy, Muhammad Ali was stripped of his world heavyweight championship for resisting the military draft, Detroit race riots were the worst in U.S. history, and thousands of antiwar protesters marched to the Pentagon.

Meanwhile, flower children flocked to San Francisco for a summer of love, which started at the Monterey Pop Festival, while rock fans gravitated to the raucous music of Janis Joplin, the Grateful

Dead, the Mamas and the Papas, Jimi Hendrix, the Doors, and the Animals.

JAN.: Elvis's personality began to change when he felt his popularity was in decline. He was uncomfortable playing to cameras instead of live audiences. Insisting he needed medication to help ease his depression and physical pain, he was introduced by Red West to Dr. George Nichopoulos, of Tennessee. Most critics claimed Dr. Nichopoulos prescribed too many amphetamines and barbiturates without diagnosing or curing real, physical ailments. Perhaps the thought of his impending marriage turned Elvis to drugs. Perhaps it was the guilt he was feeling because another woman was replacing Gladys. Perhaps he was beginning to feel owned, which was a reality whether he wanted to believe it or not. Whatever the reasons, his intake of medications and drugs increased right before he was to be married.

JAN. 2: Eroding his image as Mr. Nice Guy, Elvis's temper tantrums caused some colleagues in the film industry to think he was psychotic. Elvis hated the movie roles he was given and said he was going to quit show business. Alarmed by this attitude, Parker decided to renegotiate their original contract. Having insisted Elvis marry Priscilla, Parker knew a wife might try to manipulate, spend, or control assets. In the new contract, Parker's managerial fee was set at 50 percent of every dollar Elvis earned and was to run through January 22, 1976. The William Morris Agency of California received 10 percent over and beyond Parker's commission, and many perks were added to Parker's 50 percent. The agency handled the details of Elvis's contracts and collected fees and royalties due him. The Colonel also received royalties from Hill and Range, Boxcar, and other enterprises connected to Elvis.

JAN. 8: Marty Lacker, Charlie Hodge, and other members of the Memphis Mafia gave Elvis a tree-of-life medallion for a birthday present, which Elvis often wore.

FEB.: Keith Richards and Mick Jagger of the Rolling Stones were arrested on drug possession charges in Britain. The heavy jail sentences they received were suspended on appeal, and rock 'n' rollers rallied to support that decision. As "bad boys" the Stones' behavior would soon pale in the face of the more outrageous rockers of the seventies.

FEB. 3: Band leader Skitch Henderson said Elvis was "the Beethoven of contemporary music" and that no one should quarrel with the importance of longevity, but Elvis never wrote music. Henderson asserted, "The public is a severe critic.... He established the form, the tradition, and the flair" for rock 'n' roll and contemporary music. (See *Memphis Press-Scimitar*, 2/3/67.)

FEB. 9: Elvis bought the Circle G Ranch in Walls, Mississippi. Nash Prichett (sister of Vernon Presley) first lived with her husband at Elvis's Circle G Ranch in Walls and then moved into a trailer on the northeast side of the Graceland estate, where her husband, Earl, was a maintenance man.

Nash Prichett eventually became a minister for the Assembly of God Church, and Elvis was exceedingly generous to her. In the video *Elvis Presley's Graceland*, she claimed, "Elvis ... told me [in 1969] he knew I needed a piano for the church ... and he said he'd like for me to have the gold one [the 1928 Kimball grand] because he no longer needed it.... The piano was really too large for the church and I asked him if I could trade it for a smaller one. He said whatever suited our needs was fine with him because he gave it to me. My husband pulled the tractor up in front of the house and moved the piano out on the dip of the tractor."

FEB. 21: Elvis started recording the sound tracks for the movie *Clambake* at RCA studios in Nashville. The title song for *Clambake* (written by Sid Wayne–Ben Weisman); "The Girl I Never Loved," written by Randy Starr, with strings added for the film; and "Who Needs Money," written by Randy Starr and sung as a duet with Ray Walker of the Jordanaires, who sang for the lip-synched Will Hutchins, were recorded.

FEB. 22: The Sid Tepper–Roy C. Bennett songs "A House That Has Everything" and "Confidence" were recorded by Elvis at RCA's Nashville studios for *Clambake*. A children's chorus accompanied Elvis in the film version of "Confidence." Cut from the film was Elvis's recording of the Sid Wayne–Ben Weisman song "How Can You Lose What You Never Had."

MAR.: Elvis gave Annette Day (his co-star in *Double Trouble*) a blue-and-white Mustang.

Colonel Parker busily planned Elvis and Priscilla's wedding.

MAR. 10: Filming for *Clambake* in Los Angeles was delayed when Elvis fell in a bathroom and suffered a minor concussion. A stand-in for Elvis was used for scenes shot in Miami. After Elvis returned to finish the film, the $10,000 white suit he wore in it was cut into pieces and sold with the four-record boxed set *Elvis: The Other Sides—Worldwide Gold Award Hits*, Vol. 2.

MAR. 11: Elvis stayed in the Los Angeles County Hospital suffering from a minor concussion while the Memphis Mafia guarded his room. Doctors, nurses, and the hospital staff became angered with the bodyguard tactics of Elvis's entourage, and some complained to United Artists.

MAR. 15: During an argument with actors on the set of *Clambake*, Elvis became moody. If anyone dared to differ with him, or challenge him, he became morose and discouraged, and he was often accused of acting like a child. His friends and family felt defenseless in Elvis's presence because he had become increasingly nervous, distraught, and unhappy. The lines he would later sing about being caught in a trap would, tragically, best define the predicament Elvis felt he was in.

MAR. 22: Paramount's film *Easy Come, Easy Go* opened nationally. By the end of the year, the film had grossed over $1.95 million.

MAR. 26: *Clambake* was directed by Arthur H. Nadel and produced by Arnold Lavin, Arthur Gardner, and Jules Levy. It costarred Shelley Fabares and Bill Bixby. Charlie Hodge, Red West, and Joe Esposito had small parts.

Memphis Mafia members were given bit parts because Elvis refused to act without members of his entourage on the set. Without them he would feel alone and vulnerable. Wherever Elvis went, the Memphis Mafia was close behind.

RCA released a "Special Palm Sunday Programming," which was a reissue of many previously released religious tunes.

APR. 5: The film *Double Trouble* was released and grossed $1.6 million within a few months.

APR. 27: After production on *Clambake* was finished, Elvis was greatly relieved, although he joked he would miss his friend Flipper the dolphin more than anyone in the cast. Perhaps all those beach scenes with Shelley Fabares were not as enjoyable as they appeared. Fabares and Elvis did not kiss until the last scene of *Clambake*, and rumors had it neither of them was impressed with the other. Another rumor spread that the Colonel told Elvis *not* to look as if he enjoyed it, on or off the screen—he was about to be married.

APR. 28: Elvis invited Redd Foxx to attend his May 1 wedding breakfast in Las Vegas.

MAY 1: Elvis wed Priscilla Beaulieu at the Aladdin Hotel in Las Vegas, Nevada, at 9:41 A.M., in a private ceremony in Milton Prell's suite (Prell owned the

▶ Elvis and Priscilla cut their wedding cake at the Aladdin Hotel in Las Vegas, May 1, 1967. *Courtesy of John Reible, Las Vegas News Bureau, Las Vegas, Nevada.*

Aladdin). They obtained a marriage license from Justice of the Peace David Zenoff. The Colonel forbid the Memphis Mafia from attending and had convinced Elvis there was no room for all of them. Of course, there was too much room and the place looked barren, which greatly disturbed Elvis. The Presleys' marriage license, number A 175632, appeared in the county clerk's book 248/405256. The word *obey* was purposely removed from their wedding vows, per Elvis's request. Priscilla's sister, Michelle Beaulieu, was maid of honor. The bride wore a long white gown with a veil mounted on her dyed-black beehive hair, which Elvis demanded she have in order to resemble Debra Paget (the woman who had rejected his advances for those of an even richer man, Howard Hughes). The couple cut into a five-foot-high, six-tiered wedding cake as photographers snapped photos.

As people vied to see the three-carat diamond ring on Priscilla's finger, Elvis was looking at young women in the hallways of the Aladdin.

MAY 2–6: Elvis and Priscilla flew in Frank Sinatra's jet to honeymoon in Palm Springs, California. Along for the ride were the ever-present Memphis Mafia. It was there Priscilla was told Elvis wanted to live in California to make more movies. To his new bride, that only meant one thing: Elvis would be surrounded by beautiful starlets, while she waited impatiently at home for his return.

Priscilla became pregnant on their wedding night. She later revealed that their sex life, at the very best, was not a good one, and that after she became pregnant, Elvis's entire personality changed drastically. He no longer wanted to make love with her.

MAY 7: Elvis, Priscilla, Joe Esposito, and Richard Davis moved from the newlyweds' rented honeymoon suite at 10550 Rocca Place to a huge multilevel home with three bedrooms at 1174 Hillcrest Road in Beverly Hills, California, in order to accommodate all of Elvis's male friends. The $400,000 mansion had an Olympic-sized swimming pool. In the guesthouse, various Memphis Mafia members and relatives would come and go as they pleased. They included Red and Sonny West, Gee Gee Gambill, Jerry Schilling, George Klein, Lamar Fike, and Charlie Hodge.

If and when Priscilla asked Elvis to be alone with her for an extended period of time, Elvis went into a tirade, comparing Priscilla to his mother, the only woman he ever really loved. Priscilla had *no* way of measuring up to Gladys's image. Despite Gladys's alcoholism, constant complaining, and overpossessiveness toward Elvis, he described her as the closest thing to perfection he had ever known. Gladys had sacrificed for him but she died unfulfilled, and Elvis would live the rest of his life atoning for that shortcoming.

Priscilla had heard many stories about the day Elvis threw himself on top of Gladys's casket and sobbed he had lived his life for her and her alone. Dee Presley and others had hinted to Priscilla, before her marriage to Elvis, that Elvis and his mother once had an incestuous relationship, but Priscilla never believed them. Not knowing if she could compete with Gladys's memory for the affections of Elvis, Priscilla was willing to give it a shot, even though it seemed an impossible feat.

MAY 12: Elvis and Priscilla traveled to their 163-acre Circle G Ranch. At that time, Vernon Smith (Elvis's uncle) was gatekeeper at the two-laked property. Located at the corner of State Highway 301 and Goodman Road, west of Walls, Mississippi, and Bull Frog Corners, it was located in De Soto county in Mississippi. The newlyweds enjoyed a few days of horseback riding. During one trip to the ranch, Priscilla lost her diamond engagement ring and it was never found.

MAY 29: Because many people complained to Elvis that he had purposely excluded them from the Las Vegas wedding, Elvis and Priscilla performed a second wedding ceremony at Graceland complete with wedding cake, bridal gown, tuxedo, and minister. The reception was catered in the blue room by Monte's Catering Service at 3788 Summer Avenue, Memphis.

CA. JUNE: One of Elvis's fifties guitars was exhibited at the 1967 World Fair in Montreal, Canada.

JUNE: Vernon's sister Delta Mae Presley moved to Graceland.

The Beatles' LP *Sgt. Pepper's Lonely Hearts Club Band* was released and became a worldwide No. 1 hit.

Priscilla contended with reporters from *TV and Movie Guide*, who asked, "Will Nancy Sinatra Steal Elvis From Priscilla?" Nancy Sinatra (and other females, who disguised their voices or used code names) often called the Bel Air home and Graceland, and Nancy

Sinatra seemed to "pop up" wherever Elvis was.

The issue of *Weekend* showed the newlyweds on the cover.

For *Speedway*, Sid Tepper and Roy C. Bennett wrote "Five Sleepy Heads," which Elvis recorded at the MGM studios in Culver City, California. It was cut from the film. The date for Elvis's recording of "He's Your Uncle, Not Your Dad" by Sid Wayne and Ben Weisman and his duet with Nancy Sinatra of "There Ain't Nothing Like a Song" by Joy Byers and William Johnston for *Speedway* occurred in June; the exact dates are uncertain.

JUNE 21: For *Speedway*, Elvis recorded "Suppose," written by Sylvia Dee and George Goehring at MGM's Culver City studios. It was cut from the film. Another version of the song appears on the boxed set *A Golden Celebration* (Graceland, 1960s).

JUNE 24: For *Speedway*, Elvis recorded the title song by Mel Glazer and Stephen Schlaks at MGM studios in Culver City. It appears on the LP *Speedway*.

JULY: Elvis was on the cover of *Movie News*.

Priscilla was pregnant and did not understand why Elvis suddenly did not want to sleep with her anymore. Elvis felt that Priscilla was no longer his girlfriend or even just his wife—she was now going to be a mother. And "a mother" meant something much different to Elvis. As he had put his own mother on a pedestal, so, too, would Priscilla now be viewed by him as untouchable and almost holy. He stopped making love to her as soon as she got pregnant.

This was disheartening for Priscilla, but she would have to deal with it for the rest of her marriage to Elvis. (See "How to Live With a Legend" in *Woman's Day*, an interview with Priscilla, Nov. 27, 1990.)

JULY 29: British TV's "Juke Box Jury" voted Elvis's "Long Legged Girl" a hit.

AUG.: Elvis and Priscilla were on the covers of *Movie Life, Cineavance,* and *Movieland.*

AUG. 27: Elvis sent the Beatles a telegram on the death of their manager, Brian Epstein.

SEPT.: Elvis and Priscilla were on the cover of *Silver Screen.*

SEPT. 8: Elvis finished shooting scenes for the movie *Clambake.* During the filming of this movie, the newlyweds had many conflicts. Elvis was not home enough and was becoming increasingly secretive. Gossip columnists savagely wrote rumor-filled stories about the young couple and speculated on the "other loves" of Elvis.

SEPT. 9: Joe Esposito and Elvis flew to Nashville, leaving Priscilla in Bel Air.

SEPT. 10–11: Elvis sang Jerry Reed's "Guitar Man" at RCA's Nashville studios, while Reed played lead guitar. The song placed No. 43 during a six-week stay on *Billboard*'s Top 100 chart (RCA 47-9425) with the single's flip side "High Heel Sneakers" by Robert Higginbotham, which Elvis recorded September 11 with Charlie McCoy on harmonica. It did not chart. The version of "Guitar Man" that is on the LP by that title was remixed by Felton Jarvis on October 6, 1980, at Young'Un Sound, Nashville. Elvis also recorded the song on June 29 and 30, 1968, for his TV special.

On September 11, Elvis recorded "Just Call Me Lonesome" by Rex Griffin, which is on the LPs *Clambake* and *Guitar Man* (with an overdubbed instrumental track), and the Sid Tepper–Roy C. Bennett song "Mine," which is heard only on the LP *Speedway.* The

stirring gospel song "We Call on Him" by Fred Karger, Sid Wayne, and Ben Weisman was recorded, but the single did not chart (RCA 47-9600, released in April 1968 with the flip side "You'll Never Walk Alone"). Some claim it sold over 1 million records.

On September 11, Elvis completed "You'll Never Walk Alone," written by Oscar Hammerstein and Richard Rodgers in 1945 for their play *Carousel.* Elvis's single topped at No. 90 on *Billboard*'s Hot 100 chart during a two-week run (RCA 47-9600, released in April 1968 with the flip side "We Call on Him"). It was reissued in 1982 and hit No. 73 during four weeks on the country chart (RCA PB-13058 with the flip side "There Goes My Everything").

SEPT. 19: Elvis fired his gardener, Troy Ivy.

Gov. Buford Ellington of Tennessee declared this date Elvis Presley Day.

SEPT. 21: Elvis recorded "Singing Tree" (written by A. Solberg and A. Owens) at RCA's Nashville studios. It appears on the LP *Clambake.*

OCT. 2: For *Stay Away, Joe,* Elvis recorded Joy Byers's song "Goin' Home" and the title song by Sid Wayne and Ben Weisman at RCA's Nashville studio. His few lines of the song "Lovely Mamie," (which is heard on the bootleg LP *From Hollywood to Vegas*) were recorded on the film set. He also recorded for *Stay Away, Joe* and the Tepper–Bennett song "Stay Away." The single reached No. 67 during a five-week stay on *Billboard*'s Top 100 chart and sold over a million copies (RCA 47-9465, released in March 1968 with the flip side "U.S. Male"). "All I Needed Was the Rain," written by Sid Wayne and Ben Weisman, was completed. It first appeared on the LP *Elvis Sings Flaming Star.*

OCT. 18: Elvis began filming *Stay Away, Joe* near Sedona, Arizona. The film was directed by Peter Tewksbury and produced by Douglas Laurence. Joe Esposito and Sonny West had bit parts, and vocal accompaniments were provided by the Jordanaires.

OCT. 25: Rumors spread that actress Quentin Dean and Elvis were having a romantic fling. Quentin was a blond beauty who appeared in *Stay Away, Joe*. The ad for the movie, "Elvis goes West . . . and the West goes wild!" did not amuse Priscilla.

NOV.: *Screen Life*'s cover showed Elvis stating, "I'm Going to Be a Father."

NOV. 22: The film *Clambake* was released to poor reviews.

Elvis churned out three bad films a year for nine years and allowed his music to grow stale, while Bob Dylan, the Doors, Cream, the Beatles, Jimi Hendrix, Janis Joplin, and the Rolling Stones ruled the rock world. Somehow, it did not bother Colonel Parker that Elvis had had *no* No. 1 hits on the charts since 1962—Elvis was making too much money making inferior films.

DEC.: Priscilla and Elvis moved from Hillcrest to a two-story home at 144 Monovale St., Bel Air, in the Holmby Hills area of Los Angeles. The $400,000 house, surrounded by a rambling lawn and orange groves, was hidden behind a tall fence and had a pool table, soda fountain, and film projection room. Sonny West (with his wife, Judy, and their son) moved into the house with Priscilla and Elvis, which was comforting for the young bride, who was always left alone.

Homer Gilliland, Elvis's new hair-dresser, received the King's famous gold-lamé jacket as a gift (currently housed at the Country Music Hall of Fame, Nashville).

DEC. 3: "Seasons Greetings From Elvis" was aired as a special RCA show over national radio.

DEC. 8: CBS-TV premiered *Tickle Me* (Allied Artists, 1965) on "Friday Night at the Movies."

DEC. 10: A repeat of the LP "Seasons Greetings From Elvis" stimulated record sales.

DEC. 31: Elvis rented Memphis's Manhattan Club and invited five hundred guests to a New Year's Eve party, which he did not attend. He was despondent. He had not been at the top of the pop charts since 1962, and his movies had become flops.

Elvis received a Grammy for Best Sacred Performance for "How Great Thou Art" and was named by a pop poll the No. 1 Male Singer and the No. 1 Music Personality in America. But Elvis thought he was unloved and he knew his music was going nowhere.

Steve Sholes was elected into the Country Music Hall of Fame. It was Sholes who convinced RCA to sign Elvis in 1955. Because Sholes allowed Elvis to do his own thing in recording studios, he brought out Elvis's hidden talents and stimulated creativity.

Negative press came when the Hollywood's Women's Press Club conferred on Elvis the Sour Apple Award for Least Cooperative Actor of 1967. Natalie Wood took the dubious honor for Sour Apple Actress.

1968

It was a year filled with unrest and upheaval. While the Vietnam War raged, antiwar protest grew louder, stronger, and more violent—Chicago's Mayor Daley used sixteen thousand tear-gas carrying police officers to squelch 50,000 demonstrators; Jerry Rubin and Abbie Hoffman gave birth to the yippies, a more radical offshoot of the hippie movement; and the Black Panthers fought their own bloody battles for equality and justice. Dr. Martin Luther King, Jr. was assassinated; Robert Kennedy was murdered in California; and Richard Nixon was elected President. The most popular film was *2001: A Space Odyssey*.

The music, too, was getting more intense and experimental as fans experimented with mind-altering psychedelics such as LSD and with heroin. The most visible sign of the fervent times was seen in the rock musical *Hair*, about a hippie's rebellion against the establishment.

JAN.: Abe Lastvogel handled Elvis's bookings and contracts from the offices of the William Morris Agency, with Colonel Parker overseeing every move. The IRS searched through Elvis's finances, although he was well known for paying taxes in advance. His peak tax bracket was 91 percent.

JAN. 2: Elvis planned a singing tour through Europe. Priscilla was to give birth in February, so she would stay home. Not only was Priscilla upset by the idea of a European tour without her, it enraged Parker because he could not obtain a passport. Parker made certain Elvis's plans did not materialize.

JAN. 3–8: Elvis and Priscilla's marriage was already showing strain, and members of Elvis's entourage did not want Priscilla around them. Their job was to keep Elvis happy, and when he and

Priscilla fought, it made their job even harder. Elvis was a legend who belonged to everyone, and if he was unhappy, Elvis's fans blamed Priscilla. If she didn't like the way women swarmed over her husband, she had little to say about it. If she spoke her mind, she was perceived as a nagging wife—if she didn't speak out, she was considered callous and cold. It was a no-win situation.

Elvis's mediocre films and sound tracks had become tiresome. His career deteriorated while his earnings skyrocketed. The public wanted to see him perform live in concert—something he had not done since 1961. Could he compete with the provocative Jim Morrison of the Doors? Could he outdo the Beatles? Could he outsing Mick Jagger of the Rolling Stones—the hot band that mixed soul music with a black bluesy rockin' beat and made Elvis's once-outlandish lyrics and moves look like child's play? Elvis had a *lot* to worry about, but he knew one thing: *he* was not taking illegal drugs on or off stage like the rest of these rock 'n' roll stars. He believed audiences would respect him more than other groups, and millions of fans did.

Elvis films had grossed over $135 million, and RCA claimed it had sold more than 100 million of Elvis's records valued at over $150 million. *Look* quoted an MGM studio executive talking about Elvis's films: "They don't need titles. They could be numbered. They would still sell." (May 18, 1971.)

January's issue of *Disc* asked, "Elvis and the Oscar?" Although the question was flattering, Elvis knew he would not be nominated for any Oscar.

The Colonel signed Elvis for a 1968 special performance on NBC-TV and began to publicize that the King was coming back.

Elvis, not knowing if he would be able to recapture his old self or give fans what they wanted, began to diet for the NBC-TV special. He told those closest to him that he was terrified.

JAN. 15: Elvis recorded Chuck Berry's "Too Much Monkey Business" at RCA's Nashville studios with Jerry Reed on lead guitar. In 1980, Felton Jarvis over-dubbed the song at Young'Un Sound with Reed on guitar, which is on the documentary *This Is Elvis*.

JAN. 18: At RCA's Nashville studios, Elvis recorded "U.S. Male," written by Jerry Reed. The single peaked at No. 28 on *Billboard*'s Top 100 chart during a nine-week stay and was No. 55 on the Country chart (RCA 47-9465, released in March 1968 with the flip side "Stay Way").

FEB.: *Elvis' Gold Records*, Vol. 4, was released.

FEB. 1: People have claimed that the happiest day in Elvis's life came when his daughter, Lisa Marie, was born at 5:01 P.M., exactly six hours and nineteen minutes after Priscilla and Elvis entered the fifth floor of the east wing of Baptist Memorial Hospital. The baby weighed six pounds, fifteen ounces and was twenty inches long. Delivered by Dr. T. A. Turman, Lisa Marie was Elvis's only legitimate child.

After the birth, the superstar became even more distant from Priscilla. For the rest of their married life, Priscilla strove unsuccessfully to regain Elvis's affection, even though she felt unloved, unwanted, betrayed, and out of place living with him and his many male friends. Being a responsible mother, Priscilla soon realized that she did not want to be part of a continuing ad campaign for Elvis or the Colonel. It was not a good atmosphere in which to raise her child.

Lisa Marie was named after Colonel Parker's wife, Marie Mott Ross Parker (whom he called Miz Rie, after *misery*).

FEB. 7: Elvis's close Hollywood friend Nick Adams committed suicide with an overdose of pills, which threw Elvis into deep depression. Nick's wife, Carol Nugent, and their two children, Jeb and Allyson, were devastated. Although some of Elvis's bodyguards claimed Nick and Elvis had a homosexual relationship, there is no proof of it. Other Hollywood rumors claimed James Dean and Nick Adams were lovers.

FEB. 8: Elvis was honored in *Playboy* magazine's annual feature on the year's music scene.

EARLY FEB.: Nancy Sinatra gave a baby shower for Priscilla.

FEB. 28: After Lisa Marie's birth, Priscilla realized Elvis had mentally abandoned them. He became displaced and distracted by Nick Adams's death and began mourning the loss of his mother again. He talked of loneliness and desertion and claimed only to be happy when surrounded by his fans and staff members. A one-on-one rela-

tionship with Priscilla was not possible, probably because he was not able to be truly intimate and he did not want to deal with *real*, personal, vital issues that burdened her or him.

Elvis did not know how to deal with the inner struggles of others because he had no handle on how to deal with his own internal pain. There were many secrets in his life that no one was to unveil or scrutinize. The Colonel had buried most of them and that was the way it was going to remain. Elvis had to look and act like "the King" at any cost, despite the pain he and his loved ones might be feeling. His mother died under that credo. If she was indirectly sacrificed for his career, no one else would be able to destroy any aspect of it. If Priscilla wanted to complain, she had to keep it to herself. Confronting Elvis sent him packing, physically and emotionally.

MAR.: Felton Jarvis left RCA to dedicate his time and efforts to Elvis's career. In many respects, he took Chet Atkins's place in Elvis's recording life. In 1960, Atkins was A&R man for RCA, and in 1968 he became a vice president of RCA. Jarvis knew the quality of songs being offered to Elvis had deteriorated for a reason—he discovered the Colonel had established two publishing companies (Elvis Presley Music and Gladys Music) and had hired the Aberbach brothers of New York City to circulate music to those companies for the sole purpose of filtering percentages of song writers' royalties to Elvis and the Colonel. Elvis and the Colonel had also signed a contract with Hill and Range to buy complete song rights or to give them a cut of any writer's royalties. Many songwriters refused to make that sacrifice. Jarvis was instrumental in changing that and rescued Elvis's recording career from disaster. Although Jarvis selected some socially relevant songs for Elvis to sing and saw to it that songwriters were treated fairly, many fine writers still shied away from Colonel Parker, whose greedy management tactics corrupted Elvis's image in the trade.

MAR. 5: Elvis flew to California to record.

MAR. 7: The instrumentals for the film *Live a Little, Love a Little* began with Rick Bonfa and Randy Starr's "Almost in Love" (RCA 47-9610) at Western Recorders in Hollywood. Elvis added vocals at a later date. The song stayed on the Top 100 chart two weeks at a miserable No. 95. The flip side of the record was "A Little Less Conversation," which had a mediocre selling spree. "Edge of Reality" by Giant, Baum, and Kaye was completed, but it did not chart (RCA 47-9670). "Wonderful World" by Guy Fletcher and Doug Flett was finished and appears on the LPs *Elvis Sings Flaming Star* and *Singer Presents Elvis Singing Flaming Star and Others*. All in all, Elvis was not singing well enough because he was depressed.

MAR. 8: *Stay Away, Joe* was distributed nationally.

MAR. 9: For *Live a Little, Love a Little*, Elvis recorded "A Little Less Conversation" by Billy Strange and Mac Davis at Western Recorders. The song reached No. 69 on *Billboard*'s Top 100 chart during a four-week run (RCA 47-9610, released on September 15, 1968, with the flip side "Almost in Love").

MAR. 13–19: Elvis, Priscilla, and Lisa Marie were on the cover of *Weekend*.

The cover illustration of Elvis, Priscilla, and Lisa Marie on *Photoplay* was accompanied by the article "The Birth of Lisa Marie Presley." A similar cover appeared on March's *Movie Mirror*.

APR. 4: Civil rights leader Dr. Martin Luther King, Jr., was assassinated on the balcony of a Memphis motel room

◀ Elvis, Priscilla, and the newest Presley, Lisa Marie, at Graceland, February 1969. *Courtesy of AP/Wide World Photos.*

by James Earl Ray. Elvis was terribly disturbed that King was killed by a bullet in *his* city. It made his own life seem fragile, but the Colonel refused to allow Elvis to speak publicly about the loss of Dr. Martin Luther King, Jr.

MAY 20: Elvis flew to Hawaii with members of his entourage, where wild parties and late nights were frequent.

MAY 25: Elvis attended a karate tournament in Honolulu, where he met karate expert Mike Stone and suggested Stone teach Priscilla martial arts. Although most sources claim Priscilla met Stone in 1972, it is likely they met in 1968.

CA. MAY 26: While Elvis was in Hollywood, Priscilla purchased and had gold-leafed in twenty-four karat (inside and out) a 1928 Kimball grand piano (serial #377589, which weighed fifteen hundred pounds). She gave the Kimball to Elvis on their first wedding anniversary. Now housed at the Country Music Hall of Fame, from 1980 to 1981 it was displayed at Nashville's Opryland, and from 1982 to 1991 it was exhibited in the music room at Graceland. The Kimball was equipped with an unusual Lowrey Organo system with a gold-leaf amplifier and bench. The Organo system enhanced the piano's sound to resemble that of an organ or full orchestra. The gold-leaf Kimball is referred to and shown in many articles and books including the *Memphis Press-Scimitar* (January 9, 1968, which implies the piano was in Graceland prior to the couple's anniversary); in *Elvis, We Love You Dearly; Elvis, A Tribute to His Life; Elvis, My Dad*, which talks of Lisa Marie sneaking up to the gold piano while Elvis played it; and in the video *Elvis Presley's Graceland*, where Priscilla sits at the gold-leaf Kimball.

JUNE: *Screen Stories* linked Nancy Sinatra and Elvis romantically. Elvis was also on the cover of *TV Radio and Movie Guide.*

The bootleg LP *Elvis Rocks and the Girls Roll* from a dress rehearsal for the TV special "Elvis" in June 1968 features a recording of Elvis singing the Leiber-Stoller song "You're the Boss." Ann-Margret and Elvis had recorded the song in July of 1963, for *Viva Las Vegas*, but it was not used in the film because of the poor quality of the tape. RCA never released the song. Also on the bootleg is "Young Love," written by Carole Joyner and Rick Cartey, which was included in a medley with "Blue Moon" and "Oh, Happy Day."

JUNE 5: Following a victory celebration after scooping up 172 delegate votes for the Democratic nomination

▶ Elvis's 1928 gold-leafed Kimball grand piano, now on display at Nashville's Country Music Hall of Fame. *Courtesy of the Country Music Hall of Fame and Windsor Associates of Akron, Ohio.*

for president, Sen. Robert F. Kennedy was assassinated by Sirhan Bishara Sirhan in a Los Angeles hotel. Elvis was in Los Angeles when the catastrophe occurred.

JUNE 8:   Priscilla was angry that Elvis was going to star in the film *Speedway* with Nancy Sinatra because Priscilla believed the press would link them together romantically.

JUNE 12:   Elvis began filming *Speedway* for MGM and was given his own office on the MGM lot. The role of Susan Jacks, played by Nancy Sinatra, was first offered to and rejected by singer Petula Clark. Sonny and Cher also turned down roles in the film. *Speedway* was directed by Norman Taurog, produced by Douglas Laurence, and the Jordanaires sang backup vocals.

JUNE 15:   Without notifying officials they were coming, Elvis and Priscilla flew to Honolulu to see the *Arizona* Memorial at Pearl Harbor, which Elvis's 1961 benefit concert helped fund. Although Elvis was slender and handsome during this period, a June *TV Times* reporter said Elvis's fans did not scream with admiration as they used to. Once again, Elvis sank into despair, and he became anxious and paranoid about his future. Critics picked on his personal and professional life. Could he do no right? Vernon blamed the Elvis bashing on Parker's poor judgment.

JUNE 17–19, 21, 22:   Elvis rehearsed for the "pit" segment that would be in his forthcoming, highly publicized NBC-TV special, "Elvis" (June 17, 18, 19). He worked with prerecorded tapes at Western Recorders from June 17 to 19 and again on June 21 and 22. No formal vocals were laid down.

JUNE 20:   At NBC-TV studios Elvis taped "It Hurts Me" for the 1968 TV special, but it was not on the program. The song was used on bootleg LPs in various versions, one omitting the Jordanaires and leaving Floyd Cramer on piano with Elvis soloing. He also sang "Your Time Hasn't Come Yet, Baby" by Joel Hirschhorn and Al Kasha and "Who Are You (Who Am I)" by Sid Wayne and Ben Weisman for *Speedway*. The single charted for seven weeks and hit No. 72 on *Billboard*'s Top 100 chart. It hit No. 50 on the Country chart. Its flip side was "Let Yourself Go" (RCA 47-9547).

JUNE 20–21:   *Speedway* sound tracks were laid down with Elvis at MGM studios in Culver City, California, and again on June 26.

JUNE 20 OR 21:   "Nothingville," written by Mac Davis and Billy Strange, was recorded by Elvis for his 1968 TV special at Western Recorders. It was included in a medley of "Guitar Man," "Let Yourself Go," and "Big Boss Man" on the TV special. It is heard on the LP *Elvis—TV Special* and bootleg LP *The '68 Comeback*. Elvis completed "Where Could I Go but to the Lord" as a medley, which is heard on the bootleg LP *The '68 Comeback*.

JUNE 27:   Jimmy Reed's song "Baby, What Do You Want Me to Do?" was sung in concerts by Elvis in the sixties. The version heard on his 1968 TV special was taped on June 27, at six P.M., during a shoot of the TV show. No single has been made. "One Night" was recorded at six P.M. During his six and eight P.M. shows, Elvis sang "Lawdy Miss Clawdy," and the take from the eight P.M. performance was used on many LPs.

JUNE 27–30:   The NBC-TV "Elvis" special was taped in Studio 4, in Burbank, California (to be aired on December 3). Steve Binder was NBC's producer. Going against the Colonel's idea that Elvis sing fourteen Christmas tunes and then say goodnight, Binder convinced Elvis to go for broke and kick ass in black leather. Elvis was apprehensive. He felt his huge popularity would decline if he went out on an edge, and he did not want to chance failure. Binder proved to Elvis that he was not as "hot" as Elvis had been made to believe by convincing Elvis to sit in front of the Classic Cat (a topless bar) along the Sunset Strip, where Elvis went virtually unnoticed. His B movies had damaged his reputation, and it was time for a drastic change. Elvis was forced to admit he had a *lot* at stake when the program aired on December 3. He supported Binder's ideas for the special and wisely rejected the Colonel's Christmas notions.

The first show was taped at six P.M. on June 27. A second take was done at eight P.M. with a different audience. Elvis grabbed a microphone and within seconds unleashed a roaring personality as fresh and vital as it used to be.

JUNE 29: Two sessions for the '68 special were taped. The final production was completed on June 30. "Blue Suede Shoes," "Don't Be Cruel," and "It Hurts Me" were performed. Instead of singing a Christmas carol at the end of the show, per the Colonel's instructions, Elvis, in a tailored white suit, sang "If I Can Dream,"'a poignant tribute to the memories of Pres. John F. Kennedy, his brother Sen. Robert Kennedy, and Dr. Martin Luther King, Jr. During the special, the Claude Thompson Dancers and the Blossoms supported large production numbers, while Scotty Moore, Alan Fortas (tambourine), D. J. Fontana, and Charlie Hodge backed up Elvis in the pit segments.

"That's All Right, Mama," "When My Blue Moon Turns to Gold Again," "Love Me," "Tryin' to Get to You," and "Santa Claus Is Back in Town" were recorded but not included in the special. Because Elvis didn't do a vocal track for the prerecorded musical track for "A Little Less Conversation," it was excluded.

JUNE 29: Binder filmed Charlie Hodge, Scotty Moore, D. J. Fontana (who used the top of a guitar case to obtain a drum sound), and Alan Fortas (dressed in a red Nehru suit like Moore, Hodge, and Fontana) and a black-leather-clad Elvis Presley in front of a live rehearsal audience. The stage was tiny and intimate.

One of the finest bootleg LPs *Elvis Presley, the Complete Burbank Sessions*, Vol. 1, Audifon, was recorded in June at a warm-up performance for the NBC special. Elvis was carefree, fun-loving, and alive again! He and an excited band got into a stomping "Lawdy, Miss Clawdy." Elvis traded guitars with Moore to groove a lead and belt out "Baby, What Do You Want Me to Do?" When the tune went too high, Elvis stopped and confessed something was on his lip. It took a moment for the joke to sink in. Elvis responded, "I've got news for you, baby. I did twenty-nine pictures like that!" Elvis then ripped through "Trying to Get to You" and tore up "Baby, What Do You Want Me to Do?" a second time. He propped a leg on a chair, leaned into a guitar while standing, and told the audience he would sing one more song, "One Night With You." The audience moaned because the show was almost over. Elvis smiled and said, "Man, I just work here!" and then let loose. Elvis was again in charge. He gave this performance everything he had.

Although Elvis was insecure about the 1968 TV comeback performance, he nevertheless did the unconventional and combined rock 'n' roll with sacred music. He and Binder knew that would please everyone. In the middle set, Elvis inserted three gospel songs and told the audience gospel music was the root of rock 'n' roll. He sang "Saved," "Up Above My Head," and "Where Could I Go but to the Lord?" (These are found on *Elvis, NBC TV Special*, LPM 4088.) Aroused by the audience's positive response, he sang "Who Am I?" at his next session with American Sound Studios.

Elvis recorded a few lines from

Jimmy Webb's "MacArthur Park" and ended his 1968 TV-special taping with "If I Can Dream," which would be recorded on June 29 at Western Recorders in Hollywood. It hit No. 12 on *Billboard*'s Top 100 chart during a thirteen-week stay and became a million seller. The single's flip side was "Edge of Reality" (RCA 47-9670).

CA. JUNE 29: "Memories" by Mac Davis and Billy Strange was recorded by Elvis at Western Recorders for his 1968 TV special "Elvis." The single reached No. 35 on *Billboard*'s Top 100 chart during a seven-week stay, No. 7 on Easy-Listening, and No. 56 on the Country chart (RCA 47-9731, released in March 1969 with the flip side "Charro"). It was included during closing credits of *This Is Elvis* and *Elvis on Tour*. During the June 29 concert, Elvis kidded around and sang a line from "Tip-Toe Through the Tulips (With Me)" at his eight P.M. taping.

CA. JUNE 29 OR 30: Elvis recorded "Up Above My Head" at Western Recorders in Hollywood as part of a medley. It is heard on the LP *Elvis—TV Special* and the bootleg LP *The '68 Comeback* (*studio take*).

JUNE 30: Joy Byers's "Let Yourself Go" was completed by Elvis for *Speedway* at Western Recorders, Hollywood, after the instrumentals were finished June 21. The song was to be sung in a bordello scene for Elvis's 1968 TV special but was censored from the show. Its single peaked at No. 71 on *Billboard*'s Top 100 chart (RCA 47-9547). Its flip side was "Your Time Hasn't Come Yet, Baby." Elvis also recorded for the TV special "Little Egypt" and "Trouble," both of which had been written earlier by Leiber-Stoller for *King Creole*.

JULY: Columnist Dorothy Collins wrote about Elvis's live performances in NBC's Burbank studio for the TV special: "The incredible thing about Mr. Presley is not really that he is still popular fifteen years after he wriggled onto the pop record scene. What is most astounding is that the onetime Southern 'hood' youth who was denounced as a moral threat to the world's young people is now a respected sort of elder statesman." What Collins apparently overlooked was that the "young people" to whom she referred had gotten older along with Elvis and that he, almost single-handedly, had influenced an entire generation of performers such as Jim Morrison, Bob Dylan, Bruce Springsteen, the Beatles, Eric Clapton, and the Rolling Stones. Elvis was no longer just "a singer" or "an actor." He was an icon. A living myth. A legend.

JULY: Elvis began filming MGM's *Live a Little, Love a Little*, which was shot in Los Angeles. Vernon Presley was an extra in the film, which was directed by Norman Taurog (his last film) and produced by Douglas Laurence. It costarred Michele Carey, Don Porter, Rudy Vallee, and Dick Sargent. During the filming, Norman Taurog gave Elvis and Priscilla a yellow bassinet for Lisa Marie. Elvis's own Great Dane dog, named Brutus, was "Albert" in the movie, which pleased Elvis.

JULY: Priscilla was melancholy because she rarely saw Elvis. It seemed Elvis was paying too much attention to a former Miss USA, Susan Henning, who played a bit part in *Live a Little, Love a Little*. Priscilla often accused Elvis of living too much and loving too little!

Being Elvis's wife meant being trapped in a fishbowl existence, and Priscilla was expected to gleefully lose her individuality and identity. She had difficulty leaving their Bel Air home or Graceland because reporters turned simple shopping sprees into media events. Elvis never went outside without bodyguards, police protection, and secrecy. And always present was the

Memphis Mafia, who kept the facts of Elvis's life on the road far from Priscilla's ears. Each man's ego was strengthened, starved, or fed daily by Elvis, not Priscilla.

JULY 4: Elvis donated his 1964 Rolls-Royce to a charity auction, where it brought $35,000.

JULY 22: Elvis began growing a beard and rehearsing scenes for the film *Charro!* near Apache Junction, Arizona. Directed by Charles Marquis Warren with Harry Caplan as executive producer, it costarred Ina Balin, Victor French, Lynn Kellogg, and Barbara Werle. During the filming Elvis and his group stayed at Superstition Inn outside Phoenix. The states of Louisiana, Texas, and Oklahoma declared Charro Days when the movie came to local theaters, and in twenty-five states promoters ran Charro Girl contests. Winners of the Charro Girl contests appeared both in Dallas and Austin to be honored.

AUG.: The Democratic Convention in Chicago was marked with bloody police confrontations during which ten thousand demonstrators protested the rising death toll caused by the Vietnam War.

AUG. 9: New backing tracks for Red West and Charlie Hodge's song "Beyond the Reef" were done with Norbert Putnam (bass), Jerry Byrd (steel guitar), Buddy Harman (drums), and Ray Edenton (guitar). It was released in 1980 on the LP *Elvis Aron* [sic] *Presley.*

AUG. 23: At United Recorders in Los Angeles, Elvis sang "Clean Up Your Own Back Yard" by Bill Strange and Mac Davis, while "Sign of the Zodiac" (only on bootleg LPs) was sung as a duet with Marlyn Mason for the movie *The Trouble With Girls.* "Clean Up Your Own Back Yard" charted at No. 35 on the Top 100 list and hit No. 37 on Easy-Listening (RCA 47-9747). In 1980, Felton Jarvis redubbed the instrumentals for the *Guitar Man* LP. The original song's single flip side was "The Fair Is Moving On" by Doug Flett and Guy Fletcher. Elvis also recorded "The Whiffenpoof Song," which was in the movie *The Trouble With Girls* and is on the bootleg LP *Behind Closed Doors* (alternate take, in a medley with "Violet, Flower of NYU.")

SEPT. 30: Elvis attended Dewey Phillips's funeral in Memphis. For some unknown reason, Elvis started to giggle during the funeral and couldn't stop.

Meanwhile, Priscilla and Elvis's marriage was beginning to unravel. It was a reclusive, lonely existence for her, but Priscilla was expected to maintain a pleasant demeanor, a solid identity, and retain her sanity in order to bolster her husband's image.

Living in the unrealistic, savagely cruel world of the superstar, Priscilla watched her husband's ego grow as the public almost deified him. The press fought to interview Priscilla only to obtain knowledge of Elvis. If she said the wrong thing, she was considered an albatross around his royal neck. When Priscilla wanted to be alone with Elvis or get his undivided attention, her desires were rarely, if ever, satisfied. She began to feel guilty, as if she were too demanding or too unreasonable, but her needs were not being met. She often felt like a discarded object, not a vital aspect of her husband's life.

OCT.: The citizens of Bremerhaven, Germany, erected on a dock a life-size statue of Elvis, which was eventually moved to Bad Nauheim and is now somewhere in England.

Screen Life featured Priscilla and Elvis on the cover and ran a story titled, "Why Elvis and Priscilla Want Another Baby Now."

"Also Sprach Zarathustra," the theme song for Stanley Kubrick's 1968 film *2001: A Space Odyssey*, became one of Elvis's favorite songs. After Deodato's rock hit of the song (No. 2 on the charts), Elvis opened Vegas shows with it, accompanied by a full orchestra.

OCT. 2: Everyone thought Priscilla was a competent mother, but Priscilla knew any child needed the nurturing of two parents. She could not triumph as a mother or a wife, no matter how sincere, capable, or supporting she was, without Elvis's cooperation. Priscilla confronted Elvis about the matter, which only caused him to disappear more frequently.

OCT. 14: At United Recorders in Hollywood, Elvis recorded "Almost," written by Ben Weisman and Buddy Kaye, and "We Both Went Our Ways" for *The Trouble With Girls*. Two versions of each were recorded.

OCT. 14 OR 24: Elvis recorded "Violet, Flower of NYU" to the tune of "Aura Lee" (fifteen-second song) for the movie *The Trouble With Girls*. It is heard on the bootleg LP *Behind Closed Doors*. RCA did not release the song.

OCT. 23: The film *Live a Little, Love a Little* was released.

OCT. 24?: Elvis recorded the film version of the old standard Negro spiritual "Swing Down, Sweet Chariot" for the film *The Trouble With Girls* at United Recorders in Hollywood. Take No. 10 was used in the movie. He had previously recorded the song as a single in 1966, which did not chart.

CA. OCT. 26: With the Jordanaires, drummer Carl "Cubby" O'Brien, and Hugo Montenegro's Orchestra, Elvis sang the title song "Charro" by Mac

Davis and Billy Strange for the film *Charro!* probably at the Samuel Goldwyn Studios. The instrumental tracks were recorded on October 15. The flip side of the single was "Memories" (RCA 47-9731). "Charro" did not chart. Also recorded for *Charro!* was "Let's Forget About the Stars" by Al Owens, with Carl "Cubby" O'Brien on drums.

OCT. 28: Elvis began filming *The Trouble With Girls* for MGM. The film was directed by Peter Tewksbury, produced by Lester Welch, and costarred Marlyn Mason. In the film the Jordanaires provided backup vocals, Joe Esposito played a gambler, and Jerry Schilling played a deputy sheriff.

NOV.: The Colonel flatly turned down the role of Joe Buck for Elvis in *Midnight Cowboy*.

DEC.: Elvis was on the cover of *TV Times* dressed in black leather.

DEC. 3: The NBC-TV special "Elvis" aired at nine P.M. and was the highest-rated program of the week. The Singer Company paid $400,000 to sponsor the show and later shelled out an additional $275,000 for a rebroadcast. Executive producer Bob Finkel received the Peabody Award for the show.

The Colonel had hyped the special since January 1968, and it seemed as if everyone in the world wanted to watch "Elvis" on December 3. Elvis's wardrobe was designed by Bill Belew of Memphis for a multithousand-dollar price tag. Songs included "Trouble"/ "Guitar Man"; "Lawdy Miss Clawdy"; "Baby, What Do You Want Me to Do?"; "Heartbreak Hotel"/"Hound Dog"/"All Shook Up"; "Can't Help Fallin' in Love"; "Jailhouse Rock"; "Love Me Tender"; "Are You Lonesome Tonight?" (several lines only); "Where Could I Go but to the Lord?"; "Up Above My Head"; "Saved"; an encore of "Baby, What Do You Want Me to Do?"; "Blue

Christmas"; "One Night"; "Memories"; "Nothingville"; "Big Boss Man"; encores of "Guitar Man"; "Trouble" and "Little Egypt"; and the impassioned "If I Can Dream."

Darlene Love, Jean King, and Fanita James of the Blossoms (regulars on the ABC-TV series "Shindig") sang "Sometimes I Feel Like a Motherless Child," "I Found That Light," and "Yes, Yes, a Yes."

After the 1968 special, Elvis asked the Blossoms to tour with him, but they declined. The Sweet Inspirations later joined him.

During a special taping at his eight P.M. concert for the TV show, Elvis sang "Tiger Man," which appears on the LP *Elvis Sings Flaming Star.*

Elvis assessed his music and rock 'n' roll during the filming of "Elvis" and said, "Rock and roll music is basically gospel, rhythm and blues—or it sprang from that. And people have been adding things to it, experimenting with it."

DEC. 4: After seeing Elvis's TV special, John Landau of the *New York Times* marveled: "There is something magical about watching a man who has lost himself, find his way home. He sang with the kind of power people no longer expect from rock 'n' roll performers. And while most of the songs were ten or twelve years old, he performed them as freshly as though they were written yesterday."

DEC. 5: After seeing his TV special,

fans rushed to record stores and bought hundreds of thousands of Elvis's records.

DEC. 9: Elvis had first heard the term *taking care of business* on a NBC-TV special that bore that title. The show featured Diana Ross, the Supremes, and the Temptations.

Lee Ableseron designed fourteen-karat gold bracelets featuring the initials TCB and lightning-bolt insignia. Elvis gave each member of the Memphis Mafia one to wear, and each bracelet had the member's nickname engraved on its reverse side. The TCB emblem with the lightning bolt would eventually be placed in the Meditation Gardens at Graceland. Elvis claimed he witnessed lightning strike an object in the garden, and he thought God was sending him a message to take care of business.

DEC. 31: "Elvis," which aired in America on December 3, was shown without commercials on BBC-2 in Great Britain.

The Presley New Year's Eve party for two hundred was held at the Thunderbird Lounge in Memphis, with the band Flash, and the Board of Directors with B. J. Thomas (a singer whom Elvis admired), Ronnie Milsap, and Billy Lee Riley.

Elvis told Colonel Parker he wanted to sing live more often and that he was considering leaving Hollywood.

◄Elvis dressed in black leather during his NBC-TV comeback special, "Elvis," December 1968. *Courtesy of the Bettman Archives.*

1969

The war raged on while Nixon sent more troops to Vietnam, and a fanatical, violent cult led by Charles Manson made bloody, terrifying headlines.

It was a year of pride for America when Neil Armstrong landed on the moon, and one of scandal and tragedy for Sen. Edward Kennedy when Mary Jo Kopechne was found drowned at Chappaquiddick.

Public television premiered "Sesame Street" in November 1969. Major films included Paul Newman and Robert Redford in *Butch Cassidy and the Sundance Kid*, Dennis Hopper in *Easy Rider*, John Wayne and Glen Campbell in *True Grit*, and antiwar protester Jane Fonda in *They Shoot Horses, Don't They?*

Song hits included the Beatles "Get Back," the Rolling Stones' "Honky Tonk Women," Bob Dylan's "Lay Lady, Lay," and Burt Bacharach's "Raindrops Keep Fallin' on My Head" (for *Butch Cassidy and the Sundance Kid*). This, too, was the year almost three hundred thousand young people enjoyed three days of peace, drugs, and music at the Woodstock Festival, while murder and mayhem at Altamont signaled the beginning of the end of the "love" generation.

JAN.:   A black female group known for gospel-soul, the Sweet Inspirations, backed Elvis in his Las Vegas tour and warmed up audiences with spirituals. The women, called "the Sweets," included Estelle Brown, Sylvia Shenwell, Cissy Houston (mother of Whitney Houston), and Myrna Smith (wife of Jerry Schilling). In 1969, J. D. Sumner and the Stamps joined Elvis's shows. No matter where he traveled, Elvis made certain competent gospel singers were within hearing distance, and whenever he wanted a jubilant gospel singing session, everyone jumped to it.

JAN. 13–23:   Elvis booked the American Sound Studios in Memphis to

record thirty-six songs that would be included in the LP *From Memphis to Vegas/From Vegas to Memphis*, then had laryngitis four recording days out of ten.

Another Elvis take was his rendition of Chuck Berry's 1958 hit "Johnny B. Goode." After Elvis sang the song at the International Hotel in Vegas on August 22, 1969, it was included on the *From Memphis to Vegas/From Vegas to Memphis* LP. (It can also be heard on five other LPs and three bootleg LPs).

JAN. 13:   The first song Elvis recorded at American Sound Studios was Bobby George's "Long Black Limousine." No single was released. It is heard on the LPs *From Elvis in Memphis* and *The Memphis Record*. Elvis completed "This Is the Story," written by Chris Arnold, Geoffrey Morrow, and David Martin, which appears on the LPs *Back in Memphis* and *From Memphis to Vegas/From Vegas to Memphis*.

JAN. 14:   Elvis recorded "A Little Bit of Green" by Chris Arnold, Geoffrey Morrow, and David Martin at the American Sound Studios in Memphis. It is heard on the LPs *Back in Memphis* and *From Memphis to Vegas/From Vegas to Memphis* only. He also recorded "You'll Think of Me" by Mort Shuman, which did not chart (RCA 47-9764, released in September 1969, with the flip side "Suspicious Minds"). "Wearin' That Loved On Look," written by Dallas Frazier and Al Owens, appeared only on the LPs *From Elvis in Memphis* and *The Memphis Record*.

JAN. 15:   "Gentle on My Mind" was recorded by Elvis at the American Sound Studios in Memphis, with Ronnie Milsap on piano and Ed Kollis on harmonica. Elvis also sang "I'm Movin' On" by

Hank Snow (later retracked by Felton Jarvis at Young'Un Sound, Nashville, 1980).

JAN. 16: Eddie Rabbitt's "Inherit the Wind" (no single was made), Shirl Milete's uncharted "My Little Friend" (RCA 47-9791), and "Mama Liked the Roses" (with backup vocals by Sandy Posey and others) by Johnny Christopher were recorded by Elvis at the American Sound Studios. "Mama Liked the Roses" was on *Billboard*'s Top 100 chart for twelve weeks and hit No. 9 (RCA 47-9835, released in May 1970, with the flip side "The Wonder of You").

JAN. 20: "Rubberneckin'" by Dory Jones and Bunny Warren was finished by Elvis at Memphis's American Sound Studios. During a five-week stay on *Billboard*'s Top 100 chart, it reached No. 69 (RCA 47-9768). Its flip side was "Don't Cry, Daddy," which did better on the charts.

JAN. 21: Elvis sang Mac Davis's "In the Ghetto" at American Sound Studios. It peaked at No. 3 during a thirteen-week stay on *Billboard*'s Top 100 chart, reached No. 60 on the Country chart, and hit No. 2 in Great Britain. By June 25, it received its RIAA gold certificate. Its original flip side was "Any Day Now" (RCA 47-9741). Although many critics felt he had developed a crooner sound, "In the Ghetto" had a robust groove. The song chronicled life in the Chicago slums and was one of Elvis's rare social-commentary tunes. Sammy Davis, Jr., and the Righteous Brothers had rejected the piece prior to Elvis's being offered it.

On this same day, Elvis recorded "From a Jack to a King" by Ned Miller and Mac Davis's "Don't Cry, Daddy" (RCA 47-9768), which was released in November 1969. During a thirteen-week stay on *Billboard*'s Top 100, it peaked at No. 6 and was No. 13 on the Country chart. Its flip side was "Rubberneckin'."

JAN. 23: Elvis accompanied himself while recording "I'll Hold You in My Heart" at the American Sound Studios. Elvis also recorded a song that would become a standard for him, "Suspicious Minds," written by Mark James. Horns were later overdubbed on the spliced final release. In November 1969, it was Elvis's longest million-selling hit and was No. 1 for one out of fifteen weeks on *Billboard*'s Top 100. It would be Elvis's *last* No. 1 charted song (RCA 47-9764, released in September 1969, with the flip side "You'll Think of Me"). Elvis recorded "Without Love (There Is Nothing)," written by Danny Small, which appears on the LPs *Back in Memphis*, *From Memphis to Vegas/From Vegas to Memphis*, and *The Memphis Record*.

"I'll Be There (If Ever You Want Me)" by Bobby Darin was recorded by Elvis at the American Sound Studios (the studio incorrectly gives composing credit to Gabbard and Price). The song is heard on the LPs *Double Dynamite* and *Let's Be Friends*. "I'll Hold You in My Heart (Till I Can Hold You in My Arms)" was recorded with Elvis on piano.

CA. JAN. 28: The Beatles' hit "Hey Jude" was recorded by Elvis at American Sound Studios after the instrumentals were laid down on January 22. Elvis often sang "Hey Jude" in concert. There is no single of Elvis's version. It was first released on the LP *Elvis Aron Presley* (Las Vegas, August 1969, in a medley with "Yesterday"). The recorded version on the LP is from the January 1969 session.

FEB. 9: "Do You Know Who I Am," written by Bobby Russell, was recorded by Elvis at the American Sound Studios.

FEB. 17: Elvis recorded (with Reggie Young on electric sitar) Percy Mayfield's "Stranger in My Own Home Town" at American Sound Studios. It appears on the LPs *Back in Memphis*, *From Memphis to Vegas/From Vegas to Memphis*, *The Memphis Record* and an alternate mix is heard on *Reconsider Baby*. Elvis also completed "True Love Travels on a Gravel Road" by Dallas Frazier and Al Owens, which is heard on the LPs *From Elvis in Memphis* and *The Memphis Record*.

FEB. 18: Elvis recorded "After Loving You," written by Eddie Miller and Johnny Lantz, at American Sound Studios. In 1980, at Young'Un Sound in Nashville, Felton Jarvis laid a new instrumental background for the song. The original 1969 song is heard on the LPs *From Elvis in Memphis* and *The Memphis Record*. The new track is on the LP *Guitar Man*. Elvis also recorded "And the Grass Won't Pay No Mind" by Neil Diamond. "Power of Love" by Bill Giant, Bernie Baum, and Florence Kaye was completed and appeared on the LPs *From Elvis in Memphis* and *The Memphis Record*.

FEB. 19: Elvis recorded "Kentucky Rain" by Eddie Rabbitt and Dick Heard at American Sound Studios with Ronnie Milsap as backup harmony. In a nine-week stay on *Billboard*'s Top 100 chart, it peaked at No. 16. It also reached No. 31 on the Country chart (released in February 1971). Its flip side, "My Little Friend," did not chart.

FEB. 20: At the American Sound Studios, Elvis recorded Johnny Tillotson's "It Keeps Right On A-Hurtin'" and "Only the Strong Survive" by Jerry Butler, Kenny Gamble, and Leon Huff, both of which appear on the LPs *From Elvis in Memphis* and *The Memphis Record*.

FEB. 21: Elvis recorded "Any Day Now," written by Bob Hilliard and Burt Bacharach, at American Sound Studios, but it did not chart or sell well. Its flip side was Mac Davis's "In the Ghetto."

"The Fair Is Moving On" by Doug Flett and Guy Fletcher was finished that same day, along with "If I'm a Fool (for Loving You)" by Stan Kesler (on the LP *Let's Be Friends*).

FEB. 22: At American Sound Studios, Elvis recorded the gospel song "Who Am I" for the LP *He Walks Beside Me*.

MAR. 5–6: Elvis laid down sound tracks for the film *Change of Habit* at Decca Recording studios in Universal City, California. The film's title song was written by Ben Weisman and Buddy Kaye for Elvis. Instrumentals were cut on March 5 or 6. It is on the LP titled *Let's Be Friends*.

"Have a Happy" by Ben Weisman, Buddy Kaye, and Dolores Fuller; "Let Us Pray" by Weisman and Buddy Kaye; and "Let's Be Friends" by Chris Arnold, Geoffrey Morrow, and David Martin were recorded for *Change of Habit*.

MAR. 10: Elvis began filming *Change of Habit* for Universal and NBC in Los Angeles. It was directed by William Graham, produced by Joe Connelly, and costarred Mary Tyler Moore, Barbara McNair, Jane Elliot, Leora Dana, and Ed Asner.

In *Change of Habit*, Elvis played a young doctor working in a ghetto clinic where a nun (played by Mary Tyler Moore) falls in love with him. In a cleverly filmed segment, Elvis sang in front of an altar and the camera flipped back and forth from Elvis's face to that of Jesus on a cross.

MAR. 13: The movie *Charro!* was released and fans went nuts when they saw the bearded, rugged Elvis.

APR.: Gospel singer Clara Ward visited Elvis on the set of *Change of Habit*. The King was so excited to see Ward, he stopped production of a scene to sing gospel music with her at a piano.

▶ Elvis and the Jordanaires. *Courtesy of the Country Music Foundation Library and Media Center, Nashville, Tennessee.*

The camera crew became upset, but Elvis did not care.

CA. APR. 20: The blues singer whom Elvis admired most, Mahalia Jackson, visited Elvis on the set of *Change of Habit*, which thrilled him beyond words. Many papers said he was influenced by Jackson's voice and the sound of the Ward Gospel Singers, which was true.

MAY 2: *Change of Habit* was finished. Elvis, having played the part of Dr. John Carpenter, used the name when he traveled to avoid being mobbed.

MAY 8: Elvis told the Colonel that he would not act in another movie because the roles were too terrible and he no longer respected himself. The Colonel told Elvis he would set up a huge promotion for Elvis's reentry into Las Vegas.

MAY 21: Elvis sold the Circle G Ranch to Lou McClellan and moved its horses to Graceland. Elvis had allegedly paid Jack Adams $535,000 for the ranch and sold it for a loss at $410,000.

MAY 23–28: For a few pleasant days, Priscilla and Elvis rode horseback side by side around Graceland's fields. At night, Elvis rented theaters, invited up to fifty friends to watch movies with him until dawn, and played the role of a lazy, casual homeowner—an image that caused Colonel Parker to recoil. Elvis looked like a man who no longer seemed inspired or driven to *do* anything astonishing.

Photographer Al Wertheimer told the author in 1991 that Little Richard visited Graceland and remarked, "He got what he wanted and he lost what he had." Other onlookers claimed marriage ultimately destroyed Elvis's motivation and severed his bonds with members of the Memphis Mafia, most

of whom resented Priscilla as someone who stood between them and Elvis.

JUNE: The Jordanaires left Elvis stating that they did not want to perform in one of Colonel Parker's overdone Vegas shows. They had appeared in *Loving You, King Creole, G.I. Blues,* and *Blue Hawaii,* as well as on many "Louisiana Hayride" gigs with Elvis, and the Milton Berle and Ed Sullivan shows. They had recorded with Elvis "Crying in the Chapel," "All Shook Up," "That's All Right, Mama," "Suspicious Minds," "Blue Suede Shoes," "Return to Sender," "Mystery Train," "Love Me Tender," "An American Trilogy," "I Can't Help Falling in Love," and more. When the Jordanaires said they would no longer work with him, Elvis took it as one more betrayal from people whom he felt he had treated well.

JUNE 1: Elvis's behavior became somewhat nasty when he was forced to diet and get in shape for his Vegas concerts, scheduled for July 31 to August 28. The Colonel insisted he get rid of "his belly" and "flab." Thus, everyone at Graceland was told "to watch Elvis"

and to make certain he did not sneak junk food. Although he made miserable anyone who disciplined his eating, Elvis lost the weight.

JUNE 15: RIAA certified the single "In the Ghetto" gold.

JUNE 20: At Western Recorders, Elvis sang the Leiber-Stoller gospel song "Saved." He had previously performed the song in a medley for the 1968 TV special. The June 20 take is heard on the LP *Elvis—TV Special* and the bootleg LP *The '68 Comeback.*

JUNE 20–22: At Devonshire Downs, Northridge, Connecticut, the '69 Newport music festival drew over 150,000 fans to watch Jimi Hendrix, Creedance Clearwater, Jethro Tull, Spirit, Joe Cocker, Ike and Tina Turner, the Byrds, and others perform. Although a motorcycle gang was hired (the Street Racers) for security, gate-crashers became violent and locals vowed never again to run a festival.

JULY: An issue of *TV Times* featured Elvis on the cover and stated, "The fans don't scream like they used to." This did not set well with the dieting King of Rock.

JULY 1: Colonel Parker was in Vegas planning the triumphant return of "his boy" to the city of neon and glitz. Parker planted six thousand posters on everything from taxicabs to light poles and placed full-page ads in every newspaper. He talked about Elvis on every channel and inundated the airwaves with Elvis's "second coming." Once again, the Colonel made a deal that left heads and casino wheels spinning. The stakes he played were high—on and off the crap tables. When he rolled the dice, Elvis's life and career hung in the balance. It was rumored the more Parker lost gambling, the more Elvis was required to earn.

JULY 3: Elvis prepared to travel to Las Vegas and went on a crash water diet for two days, which resulted in a bad temper and dizziness.

JULY 3–6: Some members of the Memphis Mafia suggested to Elvis he appear at the Newport Jazz Festival in Rhode Island, but the idea was rejected. The festival drew 78,000 fans to hear rock, jazz, and blues by Jeff Beck, Ten Years After, Led Zeppelin, James Brown, Jethro Tull, and Blood, Sweat and Tears.

JULY 5: Brian Jones of the Rolling Stones overdosed and was found dead in a pool the day Elvis returned to Las Vegas to rehearse for his opening at the International Hotel. Elvis shed his black-leather image for a much more garish wardrobe, the likes of which no one had ever seen before. He was now the "rhinestone cowboy" who rocked.

JULY 20: Elvis wanted his Las Vegas performances to be the greatest shows on earth. Coming out of his musical dark age, and leaving his less than inspired world of film, Elvis's concerts were polished and professional. He had become an accomplished stylist who proved he could combine rock, country, rhythm and blues, and gospel music into a fine, balanced act. Myrna Smith of the Sweet Inspirations admitted, "He's gorgeous, really handsome, real trim, and a real doll to work with," while her counterpart Sylvia Shenwell said, "He's just like the boy next door. Still shy, polite, and an absolute knockout." Cissy Houston insisted Elvis "was still the greatest entertainer we had ever met. At the very first rehearsal you could see that . . . [it was] as if he had never been away." (See *Elvis '69—The Return.*)

Elvis's entourage arranged his costumes, which filled twenty-five trunks (along with makeup, pills, and junk food). The streets were buzzing with the news of Elvis's return to Vegas, which was the same day NASA landed a man on the moon. When Elvis stepped off the plane, hundreds of fans were there to greet him.

JULY 24: Giant marquees announced Elvis would begin to perform at the International on July 31, with Sammy Shore, the Imperials, the Sweet Inspirations, the Bobby Morse Orchestra, and a rock band consisting of James Burton (once Ricky Nelson's guitarist), drummer Ronnie Tutt, bassist Jerry Scheff, keyboard player Larry Muhoberack, and guitarists/vocalists John Wilkinson and Charlie Hodge (who also served as scarf protector and water boy).

JULY 25: A buzz spread across Vegas that Elvis would wear a new forty-pound, rhinestone-encrusted jumpsuit. Some people claim Priscilla suggested that Elvis wear the glittering jumpsuits, but Elvis told reporters he got the idea after taking karate lessons for years (although his jumpsuits are not similar to karate *gis*). The ostentatious jumpsuits became Elvis's performing trademark after 1969, and they were copied by a new generation of stars (such as Wayne Newton, Michael Jackson, and many others). Elvis humorously named his jumpsuits: Sundial, Burning Flame, Blue Aztec, Inca Gold, Mad Tiger, American Eagle, Red Lion, King of Spades, and Blue Rainbow.

JULY 27: Priscilla had *never* seen her husband perform live until his July 27 rehearsal. With perspiration streaming down him and rings glistening on his fingers, his shows were fresh, spirited, and provided a venue in which he could release bottled-up energy. This was a different sound from that of the rockabilly rock 'n' roller he once was.

During Vegas rehearsals, photographers hid from the Colonel and huddled in the balcony to sneak shots of the King. Having lost weight during a month's preparation for Vegas, Elvis looked the finest he had in years. Priscilla claimed this was Elvis at his best, but she had not seen his scandalous, brilliant beginning!

JULY 27–29: Over six thousand telegrams arrived in Vegas for Elvis from all over the world. He was an instantaneous phenomenon. Dionne Warwick, Dick Clark, Carol Channing, Ed Ames, Paul Anka, Angie Dickinson, Burt Bacharach, Pat Boone, Fats Domino, Ann-Margret, George Hamilton, Henry Mancini, Sam Phillips, Liberace, and Wayne Newton came to Elvis's dress rehearsals, and fans pushed and shoved to stand in line hours early for every performance. Conspicuously missing was Tom Jones, who had headlined in Vegas in 1968 and had become friendly with Elvis. Elvis's magnetism overshadowed Jones's act and Elvis commanded larger audiences so Jones stayed in his room, which was next to Elvis's, and rumors spread that Elvis paid Jones's hotel-room bills.

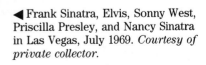

◀ Frank Sinatra, Elvis, Sonny West, Priscilla Presley, and Nancy Sinatra in Las Vegas, July 1969. *Courtesy of private collector.*

JULY 31: Elvis appeared in Vegas at the International Hotel (the opening of which was used in the 1979 TV movie *Elvis* produced by Dick Clark, who was in the audience). The moment Elvis entered the stage, the audience (which included Liberace and Herb Alpert) was *his*. This was the beginning of an eight-year span of 1,126 shows, and he never played to an empty seat! To salute man's first steps on the moon, the Sweet Inspirations opened Elvis's first Vegas show with "How High the Moon." The audience went berserk, just as in the fifties. Elvis was older, and he looked different, but he was back, and that's all that counted to fans.

While Elvis fanatics from all over the world flew to Las Vegas to see him perform on The Strip, Parker was busy selling T-shirts, stuffed animals, and other items in stores and on streets throughout the city. "Operation Elvis" was in full swing, with the Colonel in a white laboratory coat stamped forty times with "Elvis International in Person"!

Elvis performed to audiences of two thousand every night at eight P.M. and midnight for twenty-nine nights, amidst an array of psychedelic light effects.

The Colonel's promise to him, "You stay in shape and I'll make us rich as rajahs," became a reality. Cash receipts at the International for tickets alone were over $1.5 million. Parker told Elvis to "end the decade" with a successful reentrance into the music world, and that's exactly what he did. He felt at home in front of audiences. Out on a stage, he was bare to the world. It was *his* show and no one could ruin it for him. He had never felt secure in front of a camera, nor did he like directors telling him how to act or what to do.

JULY 31: Elvis was recorded singing the Bee Gees' song "Words." During his International Hotel performances Elvis forgot some of the lyrics to "Are You Lonesome Tonight?" and started to laugh. A take of this version can be heard on *Elvis—A Legendary Performer*. A few lines from "More" and all of "Sweet Inspiration" were recorded at this concert, which appear on the bootleg LPs *The Monologue L.P.* and *To Know Him Is to Love Him*. He also was recorded singing "Oh, Happy Day," which is heard on various bootleg LPs.

AUG.: Elvis often sang Johnny Cash's 1955 hit "Folsom Prison Blues" at his Vegas concerts. It appears only on four bootlegs.

AUG. 1: Elvis told Vegas reporters he was planning a world tour, which again infuriated the Colonel and Priscilla. When Priscilla was told she would have to stay home and take care of the baby, she quickly returned to Memphis.

Elvis introduced Johnny Cash to the audience in Vegas that night, and Cash received thunderous applause from enthusiastic fans.

The masses and the press realized Elvis saw other women, and they wondered if Priscilla purposely looked the other way or if she was just naive. Some fans believed she stayed with Elvis to spend his money and bask in the shadow of his glory; others thought she was just a symbol of marriage and that she had her own fleet of lovers.

After Nick Adams died, rumors spread Elvis was gay. He spent too much time with men and was known to have refused to make love with Priscilla. Some people wondered how *close* he *was* to members of the Memphis Mafia, and others pondered if Elvis was bisexual. Eyebrows lifted often because he was with his male friends more than he was with his wife. They even slept in his room when Priscilla was not present. Everyone knew Elvis never slept alone. If Priscilla became paranoid, she said nothing publicly. She was smart enough to understand fans would not have tolerated or listened to anything negative about Elvis. Priscilla had learned to keep opinions to herself. Elvis was "a rock god"; she was merely human.

AUG. 2: Elvis earned a "gold belt" at the Las Vegas International Hotel for holding "the world's championship attendance record." The belt with its huge, gaudy gold buckle, soon emphasized his expanding waistline. Elvis's capes and costumes, dripping with gold, silver, and jewels, were supposed to exemplify glory, wealth, and power.

In *Elvis World*, Samuel Roy's gushy observation from *Elvis, Prophet of Power* is quoted: "It was as if he were a momentary gift, too special to be real, too precious to be deserved, too illuminating to last."

AUG. 9–11: Critics had a heyday with Elvis's Vegas shows. One antagonist from the *Record Mirror* narrowly labeled him a "cabaret artiste," while *Newsweek* declared on August 11, "The pasty-faced enchanter quickly settled down to work his oleaginous charms, backed by a thirty-piece orchestra, a five-man combo, and a chorus of seven. . . . Oozing the sullen sexuality that threw America into a state of shock in the fifties, he groaned and swiveled . . . [and] it was hard to believe he was thirty-four and no longer nineteen years old."

AUG. 9: Elvis was in Las Vegas when Charles Manson and his followers brutally murdered actress Sharon Tate and four others. A leery, paranoid Elvis ordered tight security around his family and himself. He bought more guns and hired extra guards. After the Manson butchering spree, Elvis became so distrustful, he wore a bulletproof vest onstage in Las Vegas.

AUG. 10–11: A Las Vegas newspaper ran the story "Elvis: An Artistic Renaissance" in which Elvis told a reporter, "I was studying to be an electrician in the fifties . . . but I got wired the wrong way!"

In one August press conference in Vegas, someone asked Elvis about his reclusive nature. He smiled and said, "It's not secluded, honey. I'm just sneaky." (*Elvis '69—The Return.*) Whenever Elvis "opened up" to the press, he was scolded by Parker, who forbid him to make decisions pertaining to his career without Parker's permission.

During this same press conference, Elvis was cocky, friendly, and full of himself. Dressed in light blue, he flaunted a black cape and his incredibly conspicuous gold belt, yet his manner was sweet and sure. Alex Shoofey (manager of the International) offered Elvis a four-season contract for a reported $5 million which the Colonel turned down. Stars and showgirls flocked to hear Elvis sing or get his private attention after hours—regardless of Priscilla, who had left Vegas after a brief stay.

Many claimed Elvis became the essence of Las Vegas. *Rolling Stone* asserted he was supernatural. *Variety* renamed him "a superstar." *Newsweek* praised his staying power. The King of Rock had captured the hearts and minds of everyone who lived in or had visited the show biz city.

During one Vegas press conference a reporter asked Elvis, "Are you satisfied with the image you've established?"

"Well, the image is one thing and a human being is another."

"How close is the image to the man?"

"It's very hard to live up to an image, put it that way."

"What about your image as a shy, humble country boy?"

Elvis stood and exposed the silver-and-gold belt and said *it* was *not* humble and shy, which cued the Colonel to abruptly end the interview. Elvis became too candid and that was not allowed.

Elvis was also asked why he dyed

his hair black. He laughed and said, "I just done it for the movies . . . 'cause it's really gray." Comments like these did not endear Elvis to his manager, who knew the world expected Elvis to stay young forever. Fans could wither away and wrinkle, but their idols had to stay fresh.

AUG. 15–17: While Elvis was causing an uproar with his comeback in Las Vegas, some three hundred thousand "flower children" congregated at the Woodstock Music & Art Festival at Max Yasgur's farm to celebrate free love, rock 'n' roll, and drugs.

Woodstock was plagued with problems, from traffic jams to heavy rains and huge crowds that broke down all security barriers, but these were minor flaws in what was ultimately a remarkably peaceful gathering.

Woodstock featured a stellar group of performers including Jimi Hendrix, the Who, the Grateful Dead, the Butterfield Blues Band, Canned Heat, Sly and the Family Stone, Joe Cocker, Joan Baez, the Band, Santana, Ritchie Havens, the Jefferson Airplane, and others.

AUG. 17: In a rebroadcast of the "Elvis" TV special, the song "Blue Christmas" was replaced with "Tiger Man," which had been recorded live on December 3, 1968.

AUG. 22: Elvis introduced John Wayne's son, Patrick, onstage at the International Hotel in Las Vegas. The Bee Gees' "Words" and Chuck Berry's "Johnny B. Goode" were sung by Elvis and also recorded. Vocals for "Words" were placed over film footage from a July 1970 MGM rehearsal and included in *Elvis—That's the Way It Is*. "Johnny B. Goode" was for the LP *From Memphis to Vegas/From Vegas to Memphis*. Elvis sang the Berry song many times, and it appears on other LPs in a variety of renditions from live concerts (January 14, 1973; June 6, 1975; June 19 and 26, 1977; August 22, 1969).

"Runaway," written by Max T. Cook and Del Shannon, was recorded and is heard on the LP *On Stage—February, 1970*.

AUG. 22: NBC-TV's special "Elvis" was rerun and earned top ratings.

AUG. 24: Elvis was recorded live at the International Hotel singing "My Babe" by Willie Dixon and Charles Stone. This night's performance is on the LP *From Memphis to Vegas/From Vegas to Memphis*. Other performances can be found on *Elvis Aron Presley* (*Las Vegas, August, 1969*) and *Elvis in Person* (*Las Vegas, August 25, 1969*).

AUG. 25: The John Lennon–Paul McCartney masterpiece "Yesterday" was performed by Elvis in a medley with another Beatles' song, "Hey Jude," at the International Hotel, and they are heard on the LP *On Stage—February, 1970*. Vocal overdubs occurred on April 1, 1970. A different take of "Hey Jude" from another live concert is heard on the boxed set *Elvis Aron Presley*. No single was released.

AUG. 26: "Tiger Man" was recorded during Elvis's concert and is heard on the LP *Elvis in Person* in a medley with "Mystery Train."

AUG. 27: Elvis had a hard time sleeping in Vegas. Many young men and women entered and left his room after hours, and the International Hotel staff was discreet in keeping the activities on his floor as "private" as possible.

Elvis flirted with showgirls and overzealous fans whenever he was alone in Hollywood, Vegas, or on the road.

If Priscilla had rebelled against Elvis's lifestyle, he may have left her and she knew it. It did not occur to the King that men were admiring Priscilla, feeling sorry for her, and making advances. No men in his presence had ever "gotten the girl" if Elvis wanted or had her. No one would dare to touch his wife, or so he believed. Everyone had been told that Elvis would blow the head off of any man who even tried to flirt with Priscilla. It had nothing to do with *her*. He was protecting his image and his pride.

AUG. 28: Exhausted and despondent, Elvis finished the last of fifty-seven concerts at the International Hotel in Las Vegas, but Colonel Parker was not satisfied. He wanted more money to be earned, even though record releases were taking in huge sums: "How Great Thou Art" (April); "In the Ghetto" and "Any Day Now" (April); *Elvis Sings Flaming Star* (April); *From Elvis in Memphis* (May); "Clean Up Your Own Back Yard" and "The Fair Is Moving On" (June); "Suspicious Minds" (a huge million-seller hit, which exemplified Elvis's new singing style) and "You'll Think of Me" (September). Recordings were finished and ready to be released for "Don't Cry Daddy," and "Rubberneckin' " (November); *From Memphis to Vegas/From Vegas to Memphis* (November); and others.

AUG. 29: While some fans weren't pleased with Elvis's glitzy Las Vegas comeback, some acknowledged Elvis was setting yet another trend. The old Cat could do whatever he wanted—*he* was *the* originator. His earlier rock act had mellowed, but his voice was energetic, melodious, clear, and expressive. He was still the consummate showman. It was his *image*—a merchandised product that exemplified the ostentatiousness and the commercialism of Las Vegas and Hollywood—that disappointed true rock 'n' rollers. He was no longer nineteen nor was he innocent. He had become a product and he belonged to the public.

SEPT. 3: The film *The Trouble With Girls* was released, and many friends told Elvis he was having "girl trouble" at home, but he refused to believe it.

If Elvis did not want to be a true

husband to her and a loving father to Lisa Marie, Priscilla would find love and attention elsewhere. She wasn't sure where that would be, but she was determined to have a more fulfilling life.

NOV. 10: The film *Change of Habit* with Mary Tyler Moore was released.

NOV. 16: *From Memphis to Vegas/ From Vegas to Memphis* was released with sides one and two taken from recordings made during Elvis's International Hotel concerts in August 1969. The LP sold well and the King was on top again and he knew it. Mass hysteria followed him wherever he went. The public accepted Elvis back with open arms. He still represented the youthful dreams and secret aspirations of his audiences.

NOV.: "Suspicious Minds" hit No. 1 on *Billboard*'s Top 100 chart. After a seven-year absence from that position, Elvis was back.

DEC.: Elvis's temper tantrums put everyone on guard. Yet, he was as calm as a lamb when they all stood to join in gospel sings in Graceland's music room. *Elvis World* states, "Visitors to Graceland often spent their evenings listening to Elvis's extensive collection of religious records, or listened to Elvis himself praising God at the gold piano in his music room."

DEC. 6: The Rolling Stones gave a free concert at the Altamont Speedway before three hundred thousand fans. Also appearing with the Stones were Jefferson Airplane, Santana, the Flying Burrito Brothers, and Crosby, Stills, Nash and Young.

As the crowd became wilder, members of the Hell's Angels (hired to guard the Rolling Stones) beat several fans and stabbed eighteen-year-old Meredith Hunter to death in front of the stage. Three other deaths occurred.

DEC. 12: Elvis's LP *From Memphis to Vegas/From Vegas to Memphis* was awarded a gold record from the RIAA. It had sold $1 million worth of records and peaked at No. 12 on *Billboard*'s Top LP chart during a twenty-four-week stay and was on the Country chart peaking at No. 5.

DEC. 31: Elvis threw a party at Chenault's restaurant at 1402 Bellevue Boulevard South in Memphis. After dinner, the party traveled to T.J.'s Club in Memphis, where Billy Lee Riley, country singer Ronnie Milsap, and the Short Kids entertained.

DEC.: Ned Miller's "Dark Moon" was recorded by Elvis at Graceland with the Cat on guitar. It can be heard on the LP *A Golden Celebration (Graceland: 1960s)*.

Sometime in the sixties, Elvis made a home recording of "I'm Beginning to Forget You," which is heard on the LP *Elvis—A Legendary Performer*, Vol. 4.

1970

The seventies proved to be a turbulent period of change that saw contrasting types of music emerge. Heavy-metal bands such as AC/DC, Led Zeppelin, Judas Priest, and Black Sabbath were loud, raw, and raunchy. Less raucous but unique in their original styles were the new-wave rockers Talking Heads, the Pretenders, and Elvis Costello. Even more innovative, and certainly different, was the style of David Bowie, Queen, Kiss, T. Rex, Alice Cooper, and others. Among the most popular British rock groups and singers were Elton John, Pink Floyd, the Police, the Beatles, the Rolling Stones, Cream, and Fleetwood Mac.

While the Bee Gees and John Travolta ushered in the glitzy disco craze, the angrier and more passionate music of punk rock was being thrown into listeners' faces by such performers as Patti Smith, the New York Dolls, Blondie, Lou Reed, and the Ramones.

In 1970, dissent over the U.S. invasion of Cambodia ended with four dead at Kent State University and the first Earth Day made people more aware of the health of their environment, which resulted in the creation of the Environmental Protection Agency. By this time, the sexual revolution was in full swing, forc-ing people to question and reevaluate certain traditional values and morals that were slowly being replaced by divorce, communal living, feminism, and homosexuality. And rock 'n' roll was being blamed for most of it.

▲ Elvis in the 1960s. *Courtesy of the author's collection.*

JAN.: Elvis organized the TCB (Taking Care of Business) Band to entertain himself. Members included Pat Houson (trumpet), Glen D. Hardin (piano), Ronnie Tutt (drums), Hal Blaine (drums), Jerry Scheff (guitar), James Burton (lead guitar), John Wilkenson (rhythm guitar), Joe Osborne (bass), and Marty Harrell (trombone).

JAN. 10: Colonel Parker prepared for Elvis's next exhausting concert tour through the United States. One of Elvis's most successful concerts was at New York's Madison Square Garden. Elvis sold out every performance in advance. Screams and hysteria followed him wherever he went, but he hoped to be able to influence his fans in a more positive light—violence, drug and alcohol abuse, divorce, and promiscuity were not the answers. During this period, Elvis gave great sums of money to children's foundations and charities and preached to audiences about the values of Jesus' teachings.

JAN. 21: "Don't Cry Daddy" sold a million copies and received RIAA's Gold Record certification.

JAN. 22: Elvis feverishly rehearsed for the opening of fifty-seven shows, which were scheduled to run from January 26 to February 23 at the International Hotel in Las Vegas. Once again, the hype was high and tickets sold as rapidly as they were printed.

JAN. 26: Because Dean Martin was in the audience at Elvis's International Hotel opening, Elvis sang "Everybody Loves Somebody" (Martin's big hit) to honor him. A *Variety* review claimed Elvis's acts were "the essence of Kabuki drama." No move or action, no costume or prop, went unnoticed or without purpose, whether he threw karate punches while singing an old rock song, or closed his eyes, held his head high, and emotionally delivered a gospel song.

Elvis's emotional versions of "How Great Thou Art" and "Glory, Glory, Hallelujah" caused eyes to tear and hearts to pound. To devoted fans, Elvis was a superhero with sentiment. It made no difference if he was beginning to be encumbered by weighty layers of fat, cloth, sequins, jewels, and gold chains. Elvis was the consummate entertainer. He knew exactly when to manipulate with meticulous precision every member of the audience, and he left them wanting more. He was theirs, and more important, *they* were *his*.

FEB. 1: Dissatisfied with his physical appearance, with age creeping in, and being abandoned by friends and family members, Elvis became lazy, egotistical, and discontented. He complained life had not imitated the silver screen he first saw in Tupelo when he was a boy. Men did not become noble heroes, living the roles he revered back in 1950. Women had not turned out to be sweet, virginal, and tolerant. Life did not have a golden lining and there seemed to be no happy endings. Rock 'n' roll had not given Elvis the inner peace and personal satisfaction he had thought it would.

The tragic flaw that helped to destroy Elvis and others like him was that he did not understand or accept himself fully *before* he started his journey to the top. Thus, his career was spent searching for the man inside himself, and when that man was not found, or when aspects of him seemed unsuitable, Elvis began to self-destruct on drugs, while at the same time he induced audiences to worship him.

FEB. 1: Elvis talked to his audiences about how damaging the news media had become and informed fans he was becoming overweight and could barely fit into costumes. He started to deliver religious readings to fans, who only wanted to hear music, and put on karate demonstrations. He ended his two-hour concerts with riveting renditions of the "American Trilogy."

Elvis began to sing in cities throughout the United States once again. Drained, but motivated to perform to as many people as he could, Elvis's grueling schedule continued for years.

FEB. 17: Elvis often sang "Let It Be Me" in Las Vegas concerts. His February 17 performance at the International Hotel was recorded and can be heard on two LPs: *Elvis—A Legendary Performer*, Vol. 3 and *On Stage—February, 1970*. At this concert, he sang "The Wonder of You" by Baker Knight, and the single sold over 2 million copies and reached No. 9 during a twelve-week run on *Billboard*'s Top 100 chart, while it placed at No. 37 on the Country chart and was No. 1 for six weeks in Great Britain (RCA 47-9835, released in May 1970, with the flip side "Mama Liked the Roses"). "Proud Mary," written by John Fogerty, and "See See Rider," written by Big Bill Broonzy (some albums credited Elvis as arranger) were recorded and are heard on the LP *On Stage—February, 1970*.

FEB. 18: At the International Hotel in Las Vegas, Elvis was recorded live singing Tony Joe White's "Polk Salad Annie," which is on the LP *On Stage—February, 1970*. "Release Me" by Eddie Miller and W. S. Stevenson and Joe South's "Walk a Mile in My Shoes" were recorded and appear on the LP *On Stage—February, 1970*. "Release Me" is on the LP *Welcome to My World*. All but "Walk a Mile in My Shoes" are in the documentary *Elvis—That's the Way It Is*.

FEB. 23: This was to be Elvis's last performance at the International Hotel.

FEB. 25: Elvis and his crew flew to Houston, Texas.

FEB. 27–MAR. 1: Elvis gave two shows a night (six in all) at the Houston Astrodome during the Texas Livestock Show. He broke previous records by singing to 207,494 fans.

FEB. 28: Elvis told the press that the acceptance of country music was "fantastic" and added, "You see, country music was always a part of the influence on my type of music anyway. It's a combination of country music, gospel, and rhythm and blues. As a child, I was influenced by all of that."

MAR. 1: Elvis's last concert in Houston was wild and exuberant, but the King was too tired to notice. Complaining that his eyes bothered him, he decided to fly back to Memphis and rest.

MAR. 3–6: Elvis checked into the Baptist Memorial Hospital in Memphis for three days. It was discovered that he had glaucoma in his left eye (a disease that can cause sudden blindness). Elvis was so disturbed he cried for hours and could not sleep. He was afraid he would go blind.

A single issue of a magazine titled *Glen Campbell/Elvis Presley* was published and sold out almost immediately.

APR.–MAY: Elvis remained at Graceland in a deep depression. Terrified that he might go blind, he accused everyone around him of not realizing he was sick.

APR. 20–23: Elvis slept nearly twelve to fifteen hours a day and insisted he was going blind. He entertained himself playing the piano and singing gospel songs, or he played with Lisa Marie for short periods before telephoning Liberace, Nancy Sinatra, Redd Foxx, and other friends for consolation.

MAY: Elvis prepared to make a documentary titled *Elvis—That's the Way It Is* because he was promised he would have complete control over its content.

Some of the scenes had already been filmed at the International Hotel in Las Vegas in August with footage of Dale Robertson, Charo, Xavier Cugat, Juliet Prowse, Cary Grant, and others at the hotel to see Elvis perform.

JUNE 1: Members of the Memphis Mafia tried to cheer up Elvis, but little helped. Not only did Elvis think he would be blind by the end of the year, he couldn't seem to control his weight. After many hours of talk, the Colonel convinced Elvis to record some sessions in Nashville.

JUNE 2: Elvis and a few friends drove to Nashville from Memphis.

JUNE 4–8: At RCA's Nashville studios, Elvis accompanied himself on the piano during one take of "How the Web Was Woven," which was recorded for the sound track of *Elvis—That's the Way It Is* (1970). The song appears on the bootleg LPs *The King—From the Dark to the Light* and *That's the Way It Is.*

JUNE 4: "Cindy, Cindy" by Florence Kaye, Dolores Fuller, and Ben Weisman was recorded at RCA's Nashville studio. It can be heard on the LP *Love Letters From Elvis.* "The Fool" by Naomi Ford was also completed (it had previously been taped with Elvis on piano and a friend on bass in West Germany). He also recorded "I've Lost You" by Ken Howard and Alan Blaikley, which peaked at No. 32 during a nineteen-week stay on *Billboard*'s Top 100 chart; at No. 5 on the R&B chart; and at No. 57 on the Country chart (RCA 47-9873, released in July 1973). Its flip side was "The Next Step Is Love." Elvis completed Bill Monroe's "Little Cabin on the Hill," which is heard on the LP *Elvis Country.* "The Sound of Your Cry," written by Bill Giant, Bernie Baum, and Florence Kaye, was completed. The single, released in September 1971, with the flip side "It's Only Love," did not chart. Elvis recorded "Twenty Days and Twenty Nights," written by Ben Weisman and Clive Westlake, which appears on the LP *That's the Way It Is.*

JUNE 5: Elvis put his heart and soul into the recording of "Bridge Over Troubled Waters" at the RCA Nashville studios. He identified with the words. The June 5 version, with an applause overdub, is heard in the 1970 documentary *Elvis—That's the Way It Is.* In the 1972 documentary *Elvis on Tour,* a live performance from April 14, 1972, was used. During a studio jam, "Got My Mojo Working" by Muddy Waters was sung with "Keep Your Hands off Her" (but this was not meant to be recorded). RCA later overdubbed voices and instruments and released the two songs on the LP *Love Letters From Elvis.* "How the Web Was Woven" by Clive Westlake and David Most was recorded and used in *Elvis—That's the Way It Is,* but the visuals in the documentary were taped in July 1970. On June 5, Elvis also recorded "I'll Never Know" by Fred Karger, Ben Weisman, and Sid Wayne. Elvis also completed "It's Your Baby, You Rock It" by Shirl Milete and Nora Fowler, released by RCA on the LP *Elvis Country.* "Mary in the Morning" by Johnny Cymbal and Michael Rashkow was recorded and is heard on the LP *That's the Way It Is* as a studio recording and in the documentary *Elvis—That's the Way It Is.*

JUNE 6: "Heart of Rome" by Geoff Stephens, Alan Blaikley, and Ken Howard was recorded by Elvis at RCA's Nashville studios (RCA 47-9998). The single did not chart. Its flip side was "I'm Leavin'." He also finished "It Ain't No Big Thing (but It's Growing)," written by Merritt-Joy-Hall (on the LP *Love Letters From Elvis*); and "Life" by Shirl Milete, which had a seven-week stay on *Billboard*'s Top 100 chart and reached No. 53, but peaked at No. 8 on the Easy-Listening chart and No. 34 on the Country chart (RCA 47-9985). Its flip side was "Only Believe." Elvis also recorded "This Is Our Dance" by Les Reed and Geoff Stephens, which appears on the LP *Love Letters From Elvis*. He also sang "You Don't Have to Say You Love Me" by V. Pallavicini and P. Donaggio. The piano introduction was cut from the final release, and the song was filmed and recorded during an MGM rehearsal and is in *Elvis— That's the Way It Is*. Peaking at No. 11 during a ten-week stay on *Billboard*'s Top 100 chart, it was No. 1 on Easy-Listening during an eleven-week stay and it peaked at No. 56 on the Country chart (RCA 47-9916, released in October 1970 with the flip side "Patch It Up").

JUNE 7: "Faded Love" by Bob and John Wills was completed at RCA's Nashville studios by Elvis. It was edited for its album release. At Nashville's Young'Un Sound, Felton Jarvis laid a new instrumental background to the song (RCA PB 12158, released in January 1981). It did not chart. Elvis also recorded Willie Nelson's "Funny How Time Slips Away." "I Really Don't Want to Know" by Don Robertson and Howard Barnes, which was included in the 1977 TV special "Elvis in Concert," was recorded, and during its nine-week stay on *Billboard*'s Top 100 it peaked at No. 21. The million seller was No. 9 on the Country chart and was a hit with "There Goes My Everything," written by Dallas Frazier (RCA 47-9960). "There Goes My Everything" hit the Easy-Listening chart and peaked at No. 2. "I Washed My Hands in Muddy Water" by Joe Babcock was recorded, and an alternative mix is heard on the LP *Elvis Country*.

"The Next Step Is Love" by Paul Evans and Paul Parnes was recorded on June 7 and is included in the 1970 documentary *Elvis—That's the Way It Is*. The live footage and the recording are two separate entities. The single peaked at No. 32 on *Billboard*'s Top 100 chart during a nine-week run; No. 5 on Easy-Listening during a ten-week

stay; No. 57 on the Country chart during a six-week stay (RCA 47-9873, released July 1970). Its flip side was "I've Lost You."

Elvis recorded Han Cochran's "Make the World Go Away" with two mixes. The alternative mix was released on the LPs *Welcome to My World* and *Country Memories* with the master mix on *Elvis Country*.

Elvis recorded "Tomorrow Never Comes" by Ernest Tubb and Johnny Reed for the LP *Elvis Country*, and "When I'm Over You" by Shirl Milete for the LP *Love Letters From Elvis*.

JUNE 8: At RCA's Nashville studios Gerald Nelson's "If I Were You" was recorded, which is on the LP *Love Letters From Elvis*. Elvis also finished "Only Believe" by Paul Rader. Its single reached No. 95 during a two-week stay on *Billboard*'s Top 100 chart (RCA 47-9985, released May 1971 with the flip side "Life"). Elvis also sang "Patch It Up" by Eddie Rabbitt and Rory Bourke. The single had a three-week run, peaking at a miserable No. 90 on *Billboard*'s Hot 100 chart.

JULY: During a rehearsal at MGM Studios for *Elvis—That's the Way It Is*, Elvis sang Buck Owen's "Crying Time," but RCA has never released it. His rehearsal takes of "Little Sister" and "I Just Can't Help Believin' " by Barry Mann and Cynthia Weil were recorded and used in the documentary.

JULY (2ND WEEK): *Elvis—That's the Way It Is* went into MGM rehearsals. Previously filmed shows at the International Hotel were completed September 9 with concerts in Phoenix, Arizona, at the Veterans Memorial Coliseum. Bill Belew designed Elvis's wardrobe. Backup vocals were performed by the Imperials, the Sweet Inspirations, and Millie Kirkham. Musicians with Elvis included Charlie Hodge, Ronnie Tutt, John Wilkenson, Jerry Scheff, Glen Hardin, and James Burton.

During the filming, Elvis was introduced to a one-hundred-year-old female fan.

Sammy Davis, Jr., was in the audience while *Elvis—That's the Way It Is* was being taped during a rehearsal at the International Hotel. Elvis gave Davis a $30,000, 157-carat black sapphire ring from his own hand at that Vegas concert.

AUG.: The album *Worldwide 50 Gold Award Hits*, Vol. 1, was released. On the bootleg LP *The Hillbilly Cat "Live"* Elvis sings "Ava Maria" in a medley with "I Got a Woman" from the live concert at the Vegas International Hotel.

AUG. 10: Elvis began his fifty-eight-concert contract with the International Hotel in Las Vegas. By this time, members of his group had convinced him that he was not going blind, so he felt better about life and had regained enthusiasm.

AUG. 10: Elvis's performances of "Mystery Train," "Suspicious Minds," "Tiger Man," and "Sweet Caroline" at the International Hotel in Las Vegas were used in *Elvis—That's the Way It Is*. The 1955 Sun release of "Mystery Train" and an April 1972 performance of "Suspicious Minds" would be included in the documentary *Elvis on Tour*. "Suspicious Minds" from Elvis's 1973 TV special is on the 1981 documentary *This Is Elvis*. One of his backup groups, the Imperials, included Jake Hess, Jim Murray, Gary McSpadden, and Armand Morales.

AUG. 13: The live version of "Get Back" that is heard on the LP *Elvis Aron Presley* was recorded at the International Hotel, Las Vegas. Elvis often sang the song in Vegas concerts in a medley with "Little Sister." "Patch It Up" was also recorded at this concert for *Elvis—That's the Way It Is*.

AUG. 14: At his Las Vegas performance in the evening, Elvis was recorded singing "Oh Happy Day" for the second time. The song is on bootleg LPs *Command Performance* and *From Hollywood to Vegas*. He also sang "You've Lost That Lovin' Feelin'," written by Cynthia Weil and Barry Mann, which appears on the LP *That's the Way It Is*. A rehearsal performance in Vegas is shown in the documentary of that title.

In one of these Vegas concerts Elvis was recorded singing "The Twelfth of Never," written by Paul Francis Webster and Jerry Livingstone. His performance is on the bootleg LP *Elvis Special*, Vol. 2.

AUG. 19, 20, AND 24: Elvis sang in concert "When the Snow Is on the Roses," written by Bryan Fustukian, which appears on the bootleg LPs *Special Delivery From Elvis Presley* (August 19), *From Hollywood to Vegas* (August 20), *Sold Out* (August 24), and with Elvis's solo on piano for *The Hillbilly Cat "Live"* (August 1970).

AUG. 21: Elvis sang Jerry Leiber and Mike Stoller's 1959 hit "Along Came Jones" at the International Hotel.

AUG. 21: Hollywood waitress Patricia Parker filed a paternity suit against Elvis, claiming that her son, Jason, who was subsequently born on October 19, 1970, was his. Priscilla Presley was deeply disturbed by the allegations.

George Melly stated in *Revolt Into Style:* "He was the first white male singer to propose that fucking was a desirable activity in itself and that, given sufficient sex appeal, it was possible for a man to lay girls without any of the traditional gestures or promises. . . . He was the master of the sexual simile, treating his guitar as both phallus and girl, punctuating his lyrics with the animal grunts and groans of the male approaching an orgasm. He made it quite clear that he felt he was doing any woman he accepted a favor."

AUG. 26: To answer those who complained he had rejected rock 'n' roll for a more conservative singing style, Elvis said he chose more relevant songs to sing in Vegas, using as examples "In the Ghetto" and "Yesterday," and asked his accusers to compare the importance of those songs with the silly lyrics of "Hound Dog." Elvis felt he had grown as a man and a performer. Elvis's rendition of "Yesterday" is on the LP *On Stage—February, 1970,* which was recorded at the International Hotel August 25. The box set *Elvis Aron Presley* (middle name misspelled by RCA) has a different version of "Yesterday." It can also be heard on two bootleg LPs.

SEPT. 1: Elvis became a special deputy in Tennessee in order to carry guns legally.

SEPT. 1: The bootleg LP *Long Lost Songs (Las Vegas, September 1, 1970)* has Elvis's live performance of "San Antonio Rose," written by Bob Wills, at the International Hotel.

SEPT. 7: Elvis finished his fifty-eight concerts at the International Hotel, knowing his marriage was on the rocks and critics were beating him up.
　　Although the Elvis of 1970 differed greatly from the Cat of 1956, he nevertheless personified for fans the essence of the rebel, the liberator, and the musical wonder-man. Psychic George Dareos prophesied in *The Private Elvis* that Elvis was "becoming a holy man, a religious leader. It will come about through his gospel singing. Elvis can become governor of Tennessee and bring order and brotherly love to the whites and blacks. One day the South will nominate Elvis Presley to become President of the United States."
　　Regardless of accolades or disapproval, Elvis was the symbol of the true American dream, and he played the role well in public. A reporter once asked him in Vegas if he would rather be anyone else. Elvis placed his hands (which glittered with diamond rings) to his mouth and replied, "Are you kidding?"

SEPT. 8: Elvis, Priscilla, Vernon, and Dee Presley were in Las Vegas to see Nancy Sinatra open at the International. Directly after the performance Elvis flew to Arizona and Priscilla returned home.

SEPT. 9: With his performance at the Veterans Memorial Coliseum, in Phoenix, Arizona, the filming for *Elvis—That's the Way It Is* was complete.

SEPT. 10: Elvis performed at the Kiel Auditorium in St. Louis.

SEPT. 11: Capacity crowds filled the Olympia Stadium in Detroit, Michigan, to hear Elvis.

SEPT. 12: Flying to Miami Beach, Elvis gave two energetic performances at the Miami Beach Convention Center.

SEPT. 13: Elvis gave two shows at the Curtis Hixon Hall in Tampa, Florida.

SEPT. 14: During his Mobile, Alabama, concert at the Municipal Auditorium, Elvis sang a moving rendition of Hal David and Burt Bacharach's "Close to You."

SEPT. 18: Jimi Hendrix died and Elvis told friends how much he had admired Hendrix's diversified talent. Hendrix, one of the music world's most significant and innovative rock guitarists, died in London on September 18 at age twenty-eight from a drug overdose.

SEPT. 20: Elvis and his entourage flew to Hollywood.

SEPT. 22: Elvis recorded "Rags to Riches" at RCA's Hollywood studios. The single reached No. 45 on *Billboard*'s Top 100 chart during a five-week stay (RCA 47-9980, released in February 1971 with the flip side "Where Did They Go," recorded that day). During this million seller's seven-week stay on the Top 100 chart, it hit No. 33, reaching No. 18 on Easy-Listening, and No. 55 on the Country chart. The EP *Elvis Country* included Elvis's recording (with Harold Bradley on guitar) from September 22 of "Snowbird."

The first time Elvis was recorded singing "Whole Lotta Shakin' Goin' On" was on September 22. He sang it later for his 1973 TV special "Elvis: Aloha From Hawaii," and an alternative mix appears on the RCA Record Club *Country Memories*. It was never released as a single.

OCT.: Elvis was on the cover of Australia's *Women's Weekly*.

OCT. 4: Rock singer Janis Joplin was found dead in a room at the Landmark Hotel in Hollywood from "an accidental heroin overdose."

OCT. 13: UPI reported Elvis carried a pistol, and fans worried that someone was trying to kill him.

NOV.: RCA released two separate LPs from the four-sided LP release of November 16, 1969, *From Memphis to Vegas/From Vegas to Memphis*. The original sides one and two were retitled *Elvis in Person at the International Hotel, Las Vegas, Nevada*, and sides three and four were retitled *Back to Memphis*.

Elvis told reporters his marriage had "difficulties."

NOV. 4: While performing at the Forum in Englewood, New Jersey, Patricia Parker handed Elvis court documents that proved she was suing him. She still alleged her child was his, and she wanted Elvis's financial support. The suit was dropped when Elvis passed a lie detector test and blood test on January 6, 1971.

NOV. 10: Elvis gave a gutsy performance at the Oakland Coliseum in Oakland, California.

NOV. 11: Elvis Presley Day in Portland, Oregon, where Elvis performed at the Memorial Coliseum.

NOV. 11: The premiere of *Elvis—That's the Way It Is* was seen by capacity crowds in Phoenix, Arizona, and was well received.

NOV. 12: Elvis performed at the Coliseum in Seattle, Washington.

NOV. 13: Elvis performed at the Cow Palace in San Francisco.

NOV. 14: After two shows at the Los Angeles Forum, in which the crowds seemed overly anxious to get to their idol, Elvis became so paranoid he bought $38,000 worth of guns from Kerr's Sporting Goods in Beverly Hills.

NOV. 15: Elvis performed at the Sports Arena in San Diego.

NOV. 16: During his performance at the State Fairgrounds Arena in Oklahoma City, Oklahoma, rumors spread that Elvis carried a gun onstage. Not only did he carry weapons, he bought arsenals of guns and was planning a visit to the FBI headquarters in Washington, DC.

NOV. 17: Elvis performed at the Denver Coliseum in Denver, Colorado.

DEC.: Elvis toured with a portable library of over 150 spiritual books.

By this date, Elvis had spent over $200,000 on his recording studio at Graceland.

In appreciation of what Felton Jarvis had done for him and his music, Elvis gave Jarvis the money for a kidney transplant operation.

DEC. 1: Vice President Agnew and Elvis met to talk about the rock 'n' roll world and how it (or Elvis) may have indirectly influenced drug problems in America.

DEC. 3: Elvis donated $7,000 to the Los Angeles Police Department so it could purchase toys for poor children for Christmas and uniforms for L.A. police officers.

DEC. 20–21: Flying on American Airlines (after he decided his own plane would cause too much commotion) and using the name Jon Burrows, Elvis flew to Washington, DC, with Jerry Schilling and Sonny West. They stayed at the Washington Hotel (Elvis was in Room 506). Elvis was determined to see President Nixon, but did not think it was necessary to get an appointment. He handwrote a letter to Nixon, which was delivered by Sen. George Murphy. The letter read:

Dear Mr. President.

First I would like to introduce myself. I am Elvis Presley and admire you and have Great Respect for your office. I talked to Vice President Agnew in Palm Springs three weeks ago and expressed my concern for our country. The Drug Culture, The Hippie Demonstrations, the SDS, Black Panthers, etc. do *not* consider me as their enemy or as they call it the Establishment. *I call it America* and I love it. Sir, I can and will be of any service that I can to help the country out. I have no concern or motives other than helping the country out. So I wish not to be given a title or an appointed position. I can and will do more good if I were made a Federal Agent at Large, and I will help out by doing it my way through my connections with people of all ages. First and Foremost I am an entertainer, but all I need is the Federal credentials. I am on the plane with Senator George Murphy and we have been discussing the problems that our country is faced with. So I am Staying at the Washington Hotel Room 505-506-507. I have two men who work with me by the name of Jerry Schilling and Sonny West. I am registered under the name of Jon Burrows. I will be here for as long as it takes to get the credentials of a Federal Agent. I have done an in-depth study of drug abuse and Communist brainwashing techniques and I am right in the middle of the whole thing where I can and will do the most good. I am Glad to help just so long as it is kept very private. You can have your staff or whomever call on me anytime today, tonight or tomorrow. I

was nominated this coming year one of America's Ten Most Outstanding Young Men. That will be in January 18 in my home town of Memphis, Tenn. I am sending you the short autobiography about myself so you can better understand their approval. I would love to meet you just to say hello if you're not to [*sic*] busy.

Respectfully,
Elvis Presley

P.S. I believe that you Sir were one of the Top Ten Outstanding Men of America also.

I have a personal gift for you also which I would like to present to you and you can accept it or I will keep it for you until you can take it.

Mr. President
These are all my PVT [private] numbers.

Beverly Hills	278-3496
	278-5935
Palm Springs	325-3241 PVT
Memphis	397-4427
	398-4882
	398-9722
Col. P.S.	325-4781
	[Colonel in Palm Springs]
Col. B.H.	274-8498
	[Colonel in Beverly Hills]
Col. OFF. Mgm	870-0370
Washington Hotel/Phone me	85900
PRIVATE	Rm. 505-506

AND CONFIDENTIAL
UNDER THE NAME OF
JON BURROWS
Attn. President Nixon
via Sen. George Murphy
from
Elvis Presley

If the rock 'n' roll world had known of this letter's contents, it would have felt deeply betrayed. Elvis visited the deputy director of the Narcotics Bureau in Washington DC, before going to the White House. Nixon met Elvis at twelve-thirty P.M., December 21, after Elvis arrived unannounced at the White House gates. With H. R. Haldeman's permission Elvis entered the White House carrying a gun. Additionally, he gave Nixon a commemorative World War II Colt .45 pistol in a wooden box. Nixon conferred a Narcotics Bureau badge on Elvis (for which the president was criticized). It is unclear if Elvis ever used it in any undercover investigations. Elvis introduced Jerry Schilling and Sonny West to Nixon.

Colonel Parker refused to allow Elvis to perform at the White House upon Nixon's request in 1974 because Nixon refused to pay Elvis a $25,000 performance fee. The White House pays no one to perform. Even at this level, the Colonel had convincing clout with the singer.

Many people have speculated since Elvis's death in 1977, that he actually went underground as a federal agent and faked his own death.

DEC.: Elvis purchased more guns from Kerr's Sporting Goods in Beverly Hills, California.

DEC. 25: Elvis gave a stranger named Mrs. Mennie L. Person an $11,500 gold-and-white Cadillac Eldorado and a check to purchase a new wardrobe to match its interior.

DEC. 30: Elvis toured FBI headquarters with William L. Morris in Washington DC, and got permits to carry firearms in every state.

◄President Richard Nixon and Elvis at the White House on December 21, 1970. *Courtesy of the National Archives and Records, and President Richard M. Nixon.*

1971

President Nixon called for a "new revolution" in which "power is turned back to the people," while war protesters marched on Washington. The subversive antiwar group the Weathermen took responsibility for bombing the Capitol, and the *New York Times* printed the Pentagon Papers, winning the battle between Nixon and the news media over the government's right to secrecy and the public's right to know.

In 1971, Elvis gave 168 performances in fifteen cities, received the Jaycees' Award and the Bing Crosby Award, made the cover of *Look*, and watched his marriage fall apart. *A Clockwork Orange, The Last Picture Show, Klute, Carnal Knowledge, Bananas,* and *Fiddler on the Roof* were popular films. John Denver, Olivia Newton-John, Carole King, and Joni Mitchell competed with the Bee Gees' "Lonely Days," the Rolling Stone's album *Sticky Fingers*, the Who's LP *Who's Next?* and John Lennon's album *Imagine*.

JAN.: Elvis's mild glaucoma caused him dire anguish. When he learned glaucoma was the eye disease that blinded Ray Charles at the age of seven, Elvis wept like a baby.

With his marriage on the rocks, Elvis became dependent on uppers and downers to remain calm. The only people he was loyal to were his fans, but even they began to see a deterioration in Elvis.

As early as 1971, those close to Elvis were forced to admit his drug problem. Those around him revealed he had to get high to enhance lovemak-

ing or even play sports. Using massive amounts of Hycodan (a cough medicine), Elvis and an unidentified female companion (named Jane Robertson at the hospital) almost overdosed after making love at Graceland in 1971. Not only did the incident nearly kill them, Priscilla and everyone around Elvis were disgusted and dismayed by the event.

JAN. 9: The Jaycees voted Elvis one of the Ten Outstanding Young Men of America in Memphis. This tribute brought tears of joy to his eyes and it was the *only* award Elvis had ever accepted in person. He said he was "humbled" to receive it with the other nine men honored. As Priscilla watched, Elvis told an attentive audience at the Jaycees' prayer breakfast: "I learned early in life that, without a song, the day would never end; without a song, a man ain't got a friend; without a song, the road would never bend; without a song, so I'll keep singing the song. Good night." (Yes, he said "good night" at the breakfast.)

JAN. 15: Elvis was gravely despondent. He told his friends he wanted to do something to stop drugs from infiltrating into the youth culture. He called Washington, but government officials refused to use him as an undercover agent.

▶ Elvis at the Jaycee's award ceremony for "Ten Outstanding Young Men of America," January 9, 1971. *Courtesy of AP/Wide World Photos.*

JAN. 26–FEB. 23: Elvis gave fifty-seven shows at Las Vegas's International Hotel. With members of the Memphis Mafia, Elvis held nightly vigils in his International Hotel suite with as many young dancers, singers, and starlets as he could. Whenever possible, he visited Liberace, Tom Jones, and other headliners. Almost every week he gave away thousands of dollars' worth of rings and bracelets, as well as money to charities, and cars and other items to fans, strangers, friends, fellow performers, and staffers at the International. Because he was known for being a generous man, people took advantage of him.

Elvis played to standing-room-only crowds and gave two shows each night throughout this Las Vegas stay, missing Lisa Marie's birthday. Priscilla was home during this period.

FEB. 27: Elvis stayed in Vegas a few extra days and flew back to Memphis, where he remained approximately seven days. Then, he drove with his pals to Nashville.

MAR. 15: Elvis cherished the gospel song "Amazing Grace," which he recorded at RCA's Nashville studios. The song was released on the LP *He Touched Me.* That same day Elvis finished his first recording of "Early Morning Rain" (which he would record on other occasions) and "For Lovin' Me," both by Gordon Lightfoot.

"The First Time Ever I Saw Your Face" by Ewan McColl was recorded in a duet with Temple Riser, but it did not chart (RCA 74-0672, released in April 1972).

MAY 4: Elvis appeared on the cover of *Look* magazine. *Look*'s May 4 and 11 issues ran Jerry Hopkins's accounts of Elvis from a book dedicated to Jim Morrison and written by Hopkins in 1971, titled *Elvis: A Biography.*

MAY 6: Members of Elvis's entourage complained they were underpaid. This was a grievance Elvis heard throughout his life because he underpaid everyone. He preferred controlling staff members by giving them gifts. Paying them minimum salaries kept them in need of his help.

MAY 15: Red West and Glen Spreen wrote "Holly Leaves and Christmas Trees," which Elvis recorded at RCA's Nashville studio with "If I Get Home on Christmas Day," written by Tony Macaulay and John MacLeod; "It Won't Seem Like Christmas (Without You)" by J. A. Balthrop; "Merry Christmas, Baby" by Lou Baxter and Johnny Moore; and "Silver Bells" by Jay Livingston and Ray Evans. They all are on the LP *Elvis Sings the Wonderful World of Christmas* (RCA LSP-4579). "Merry Christmas, Baby" was an uncharted single release (RCA 74-0572, released in December 1971, with the flip side "O Come, All Ye Faithful"). "Padre" by Paul Francis Webster was completed and is heard on the LPs *Elvis* (RCA APL 1-0283) and *He Walks Beside Me* (RCA AFL1-2772).

MAY 15–21: Elvis completed recording sessions at RCA studios in Nashville of thirty-one sacred and secular songs, which appear on *Elvis Sings the Wonderful World of Christmas.* A five-by-seven color postcard was included inside the album jacket. Elvis played the piano during the rehearsals for some takes of "It's Still Here," "I'll Take You Home Again, Kathleen," and "I Will Be True," all released on *Elvis* (RCA APL 1-0283).

MAY 16: *Look* ran an article on Graceland.

Elvis recorded Bob Dylan's 1963 song "Don't Think Twice, It's All Right" during a fifteen-minute jam session at the RCA Nashville studios (not yet released in its entirety). A shorter version (two minutes and forty-five seconds) is on the LP *Elvis*; an eight-and-a-half minute version is on *Our Memories of Elvis*, Vol. 2.

Elvis sang the following Dylan songs, which were not released: "Blowin' in the Wind," "She Belongs to Me" (a 1970 Ricky Nelson hit), "Mr. Tambourine Man," and "It Ain't Me Babe." Dylan and Elvis recorded "Blue Moon," "I Can't Stop Loving You," "A Fool Such as I," "Can't Help Falling in Love," "Early Morning Rain," and "Let it Be."

MAY 16: "The First Noel," "I'll Be Home Christmas Day," and "O Come, All Ye Faithful" were completed at RCA's Nashville studios. Elvis also recorded for the LP *Elvis Sings the Wonderful World of Christmas* "Winter Wonderland" and "The Wonderful World of Christmas."

MAY 17: Elvis could identify with the lyrics in the Kris Kristofferson–Fred Foster song "Help Me Make It Through the Night," which he recorded at RCA's Nashville studios after the instrumentals were completed on May 16. No single was released of Elvis's version. Elvis also recorded "Lead Me, Guide Me" by Doris Akers. In April 1972, Elvis sang the song backstage with the Stamps. The moment is recorded in the documentary *Elvis on Tour*.

MAY 18: For the LP *He Touched Me*, Elvis recorded C. M. Battersby and Charles H. Gabriel's "An Evening Prayer" at RCA's Nashville studios. Johnny Mercer and Rube Bloom's "Fools Rush In" (based on Ricky Nelson's arrangement) and "He Touched Me" (a gospel number by William J. Gaither) were completed. When it was first released in March 1972 (RCA 74-0651), the single of "He Touched Me" played at 33⅓ rpm on a larger 45-rpm record. RCA quickly replaced the records, but it did not chart. Its flip side was "Bosom of Abraham."

MAY 19: Elvis accompanied himself on the piano when he sang Ivory Joe Hunter's "I Will Be True" at RCA's Nashville studios. That same day he recorded "I'll Take You Home Again, Kathleen" by Thomas Westendorf and Ivory Joe Hunter's "It's Still There," which are on the LP *Elvis*; and Lee Denson's "Miracle of the Rosary," heard on the LPs *Elvis Now* and *He Walks Beside Me*. "Seeing Is Believing," written by Red West and Glen Spreen, and "A Thing Called Love," written by Jerry Reed, were released on the LP *He Touched Me* (RCA LSP-4690).

MAY 20: "I'm Leavin' " (by Michael Jarrett and Sonny Charles) was recorded at RCA's Nashville studios. Selling over a million copies, the single peaked at No. 36 on *Billboard*'s Top 100 chart during a nine-week stay, and it was No. 2 on the Easy-Listening chart (RCA 47-9998). Its flip side was "Heart of Rome," which didn't chart. "It's Only Love" by B. J. Thomas was recorded that day, and it had a six-week run on *Billboard*'s Top 100 chart, reaching No. 51, but on the Easy-Listening chart it peaked at No. 19 (RCA 48-1017, released in September 1971). "We Can Make the Morning," written by Jay Ramsey, was released as a single with the flip side "Until It's Time to Go," and the pair had a seven-week run on *Billboard*'s Easy-Listening chart, peaking at No. 9 (RCA 74-0619, released in January 1972).

MAY 21: At RCA's Nashville studios, Elvis recorded for the LP *Elvis* "Love Me, Love the Life I Lead" by Roger Greenaway and Tony Macaulay.

MAY 21: "Suspicious Minds," recorded by Elvis in 1959, was named the most Outstanding Single to be recorded in Memphis.

JUNE 1: Elvis's birthplace in Tupelo was opened to the public.

A stretch of Highway 51 South in

Memphis, which passes in front of the Graceland mansion, was officially renamed Elvis Presley Boulevard.

Graceland became a shrine to which people swarmed to glorify Elvis. He was the "King," but no one seriously thought of Priscilla as "the Queen." Love letters and gifts arrived every day from women all over the world, and everyone wondered how long the Presleys' marriage would survive.

Threats upon Priscilla's and Lisa Marie's lives were common from fans' jealous boyfriends and husbands, and Elvis became paranoid. He bought an arsenal of guns and hired armed guards to watch over his family.

JUNE 8: Elvis recorded at RCA's Nashville studios Gene MacLellan's "Put Your Hand in the Hand" and "Reach Out to Jesus" by Ralph Carmichael. The first is on the LPs *Elvis—A Canadian Tribute* (RCA KKL1-7065) and *Elvis—Now* (RCA LSP-4671). The latter is heard on the LP *He Touched Me*. Elvis also recorded "Until It's Time for You to Go" by Buffy Sainte-Marie. The single peaked at No. 40 during a nineweek stay on *Billboard*'s Hot 100 chart, was No. 68 on the Country chart during a two-week stay, and was No. 9 during seven weeks on the Easy-Listening chart (RCA 74-0619, released in January 1972, with the flip side "We Can Make the Morning").

JUNE 9–10: "Bosom of Abraham" was recorded by Elvis at RCA's Nashville studios (RCA 74-9651). Its first release in March 1972, played at 33⅓ rpm on a larger 45 rpm record. RCA recalled the records and reissued it. It didn't chart.

On June 9, Elvis recorded "He Is My Everything," a gospel song by Dallas Frazier and "There Is No God but God," which are heard on the LP *He Touched Me*. "I John" by William Johnson, George McFadden, and Ted Brooks was completed on June 10. On June 9, Geraldo Rivera emceed Elvis's press conference at the Las Vegas Hilton Hotel.

CA. JUNE 11: At RCA's Nashville studios, Elvis recorded "I've Got Confidence," a gospel song by Andrae Crouch, which appeared on the LP *He Touched Me*.

JULY 3: Jim Morrison was found dead in a Paris bathroom at the age of twenty-seven from a drug overdose.

JULY 10: Priscilla and Elvis fought continuously. Every aspect of their lives was made public, whether they liked it or not. When Elvis gained weight, it was her fault for not feeding him properly. Any eating disorder was blamed on everyone else's inability to satisfy him. When it was rumored Elvis was dependent on drugs, fans asked why Priscilla allowed it to happen. Every mishap in Elvis's life was *her* fault because the superstar was seen by fans as a victim of the circumstances around him. All his frailties were excused as the fault of someone else's shortcomings.

CA. SUMMER: Elvis paid $55,000 for a stretch limo after he saw the one in the movie *Shaft*.

JULY 20–AUG. 2: Elvis gave twenty-eight shows at the Sahara Tahoe Hotel, Stateline, Nevada.

Whenever an audience member handed him a Bible, Elvis stopped the show to read the Holy Scriptures. As a student of many religions, Elvis searched for inner solace, meaning, and answers for existence. Compelled to read about all religions, he found consolation and significance in the beliefs of Judaism, Buddhism, yoga, Hinduism, pyramid power, Taoism, and spiritualism. For years he wore a gold *chai* (a Hebrew letter and word meaning "life") on a chain around his neck.

JULY 27: Rock journalist Mike Farren saw Elvis at the Sahara and said, "He seemed to start seeing himself as some sort of messiah, believing that his shows were not so much entertainment as holy events, during which he could commune with his disciples and they, in turn, could worship him. Religion apparently took hold of him, and he had bouts of reading the Bible to his hangers-on. At extreme moments, he even suffered from delusions that he could heal the sick, and control the weather, by an effort of will." (See *Elvis, the Illustrated Record* by Carr and Farren.)

JULY 29:   Elvis became openly dependent on pills to cure everything from insomnia to stomach problems and depression. He became so medicated he did not remember promises made, nor did he care about family responsibilities.

While throngs of people assisted Elvis with his every whim or fancy, no one fulfilled Priscilla's needs. She had become an afterthought. If Priscilla was discontent, Elvis felt guilty and often thought his wife was ungrateful. He believed he had given her every possession she had asked for, and he felt she should have been thrilled to be living with him. He complained that Priscilla was the only female who didn't think of him as a lovable sex god.

Like many who acquire wealth too soon, Elvis felt that buying objects for people was a way to show love for them. He bought lavish gifts for those he did not know. His mother and Priscilla, however, had wanted time. with the man they loved, not gifts. Unfortunately, Elvis was unable to give them what they needed from him the most.

AUG.:   *Elvis: The Other Sides—Worldwide Gold Award Hits*, Vol. 2 was released (RCA LPM-6402).

AUG. 1:   Paul Anka and Elvis exchanged pleasantries at Elvis's Sahara concert. Elvis eventually sang Paul Anka's hit "My Way" in 1973, and "Until It's Time to Go."

AUG. 3:   As Elvis prepared for and survived another Vegas extravaganza, Priscilla asked him to take some responsibility for Lisa Marie. Elvis fled his home continuously, and Priscilla was not expected or required to be with him. She had become a hindrance because he could not act freely when she was around. Instead of sharing life (and love) with her, he found one-night partners with whom to sleep. Strangers professed love and were easy to get rid of in his world. They served as diversions or recreation and nothing else.

After a few years of leading the life of Elvis Presley's wife, the ideals Priscilla had about a loving partnership were not realized, and her dream of a gratifying marriage became a nightmare. She no longer knew Elvis. He had become a stranger, while she represented dull normalcy to him.

AUG. 9–SEPT. 6:   Elvis performed fifty-seven shows at the Hilton Hotel in Las Vegas, Nevada.

Priscilla may have taken karate lessons from Mike Stone while Elvis was in Vegas. It should not have surprised anyone when she fell in love with the handsome karate instructor. Stone treated her with gentle respect. He claimed to admire her courage and strength of character. For the first time in her life, a man was paying attention to Priscilla.

AUG. 14:   "I Need Your Loving (Every Day)" by Don Gardner and Bobby Robinson was recorded during Elvis's performance in Las Vegas and is heard on the bootleg LPs *From Hollywood to Vegas* and *Sold Out.*

During many of Elvis's Las Vegas performances, tapes were made of songs, some of which appear on the bootleg LP *Susie Q.* "You Can Have Her (I Don't Want Her)" by Roy Hamilton is one of these songs.

AUG.:   The Imperials left Elvis to perform with singer Jimmy Dean.

J. D. Sumner & the Stamps joined Elvis's touring group. With the addition of a flashy light show, Elvis's movements became more animated. In his glittering costumes, every inch of the man sparkled and shook.

SEPT. 1: Elvis bought his first Stutz Blackhawk coupe for $38,500 from Jules Meyers. Frank Sinatra bought the second one issued. Elvis eventually owned three Stutz Bearcats. He gave one to Dr. Elias Ghanem in Las Vegas.

SEPT. 8: The National Academy of Recording Arts and Sciences presented the Bing Crosby Award to Elvis (later to be named the Life Achievement Award). Previous winners had been Irving Berlin, Frank Sinatra, and Duke Ellington.

SEPT. 20: Those around Elvis began to paint a grotesque picture of his deteriorating lifestyle and daily temperament. His marriage was crumbling. Priscilla seemed distant. Elvis told his father no one cared about him. All anyone wanted was what Elvis could not give them. Colonel Parker was continuously badgering him to make more money and to do more concert tours. Band members and backup vocalists wanted more promotional coverage, more prominent billings, and increases in salary. Members of the Memphis Mafia complained about not being treated fairly. Vernon Presley was no longer happy with his second wife, and Elvis told Vernon he didn't approve of Vernon's actions.

OCT.: The LP *Elvis Sings the Wonderful World of Christmas* was released.

OCT. 24: Jerry Hopkins wrote and Ron Jacobs produced a twelve-hour radio show titled *The Elvis Presley Story,* which was narrated by Wink Martindale.

Elvis was furious when the *National Insider* stated he had a drug problem.

NOV. 5: Elvis performed at the Metropolitan Sports Center in Minneapolis, Minnesota, to a capacity crowd.

NOV. 6: Elvis gave two sellout shows at the Public Hall Auditorium in Cleveland, Ohio.

NOV. 7: Elvis performed at Freedom Hall in Louisville, Kentucky.

NOV. 8: Elvis performed at the Spectrum in Philadelphia, where he stayed in the Bellevue-Stratford Hotel.

NOV. 9: Elvis gave a sellout concert at the Baltimore Civic Center in Baltimore, Maryland.

NOV. 10: Elvis's performance at the Boston Garden was sold out. Wearing simpler costumes than those he wore in Las Vegas, he was stunning in an all-black outfit garnished with touches of red.

NOV. 11: Elvis performed at the Cincinnati Gardens in Cincinnati, Ohio. Prior to his arrival, ticket scalpers were having a heyday outside the Gardens, and Colonel Parker made a fortune selling photographs and T-shirts.

NOV. 12: Although he was becoming physically fatigued, Elvis performed a flawless concert at the Hofheinz Pavilion in Houston, Texas.

NOV. 13: Elvis's concert at the Dallas Memorial Auditorium in Dallas, Texas, was sold out weeks in advance, and crowds lined up outside the Auditorium to catch a glimpse of the King as he walked from his limo to a backstage area.

NOV. 14: Elvis gave a superior performance at the University of Alabama Field House, in Tuscaloosa, Alabama.

NOV. 15: Elvis's concert at the Municipal Auditorium in Kansas City, Missouri, was sold out.

NOV. 16: The flight to Salt Lake City frightened Elvis, but his concert at the Salt Palace was energetic and well received.

NOV. 20: Elvis flew to Palm Springs for a rest with the Colonel and various members of the Memphis Mafia, then flew to Beverly Hills, where Lisa Marie and Priscilla were staying. Visiting his family for a few hours, he then left and partied with friends.

DEC. 23: *Rolling Stone* paid tribute to the King: "The magnificence of Presley's performance lies in its presentation of him as royalty. He is the one entertainer in the world who doesn't have to take out any insurance on his fame, success, grandeur, or greatness. He is the one and only performer who can simply revel in it and us with him."

DEC. 28: Priscilla Presley was maid of honor and Elvis served as best man at Sonny West and Judy Morgan's wedding at Trinity Baptist Church in Memphis.

DEC. 31: Elvis handed envelopes of money to his staff and family for Christmas.
   Screen Star issued the "Elvis, 1971 Presley Album" with every page devoted to Elvis. It sold for fifty cents a copy.

1972

This was a tempestuous year for Elvis. The strain of his marriage finally took its toll, and divorce proceedings began. Meanwhile, Elvis toured twenty-five cities (hitting some of them three times) to complete 156 shows.

It was the beginning of the end for President Nixon when the Watergate scandal rocked the capital and the nation.

Look and *Life* magazines stopped publishing by 1972 and *Ms.* began. Times were changing. Elvis's favorite movies of the year were *Deliverance*, *The Godfather*, and *Cabaret*. Stars to watch in the music world were Don McLean, Elton John, and Jim Croce, and the Colonel complained too many teenagers were buying disco music instead of Elvis's latest records.

JAN: By 1972, Elvis had acquired a large law-enforcement badge and gun collection. Priscilla became frustrated with the convoy of males who protected, provided for, and kept the secrets of her husband. Elvis had known his bodyguards and attendants before he met Priscilla, and they knew how to please him, and unlike Priscilla, they rarely complained in front of him. Any wish Elvis had was their command to fill. They were with him twenty-four hours a day. Priscilla's role in his life was significantly reduced.

JAN.: Rock star David Bowie stunned fans when *Melody Maker* announced he was gay. Wearing futuristic clothing, bizarre makeup, and spiking his orange-colored hair, Bowie dazzled the rock world with outrageous theatrics and brilliant music. *The Rise and Fall of Ziggy Stardust and the Spiders from Mars* sold over 1 million copies. Elvis was amused by Bowie's taste in clothes, lyrics, and names because they reminded him of comic-book characters.

CA. JAN. 2: Elvis gave Muhammad Ali a $10,000 robe inscribed "The People's Champion." Ali wore it on March 31, 1973, when Ali lost to Ken Norton.

JAN. 26–FEB. 23: Elvis gave fifty-seven stunning, energetic, sold-out shows at the Las Vegas Hilton Hotel. During this period, Elvis met with Mike Stone in Las Vegas. Stone was a temporary bodyguard for producer Phil Spector. Elvis had no idea Stone was having an affair with his wife.

JAN. 30: Elvis felt he could teach audiences the virtues of clean living, but his sermons disturbed them when his preaching became insufferable. *The Rock 'n' Roll Years* stated: "Elvis Presley is the subject of rumors . . . he is either sick, messed up on drugs, dying, or gay. He is currently the undisputed hot number as far as the U.S. show biz scandal sheets are concerned, and each week at least two dozen of them are offering hot poop on Elvis' alleged illegitimate kids or terminal cancer.

"Not that he's been taking this lying down—during his last season at the Las Vegas Hilton, Presley's act became a marathon of denials and denunciations with songs fitted in between. He launched into long diatribes . . . and showed the audience the badge and certificate the Federal Bureau of Narcotics gave him when they made Elvis an honorary narc in an attempt to prove that he'd never used drugs."

FEB.: Mike Stone's wife of six years, Fran Stone, sued him for divorce. The couple had two children. At the time of their separation, Stone made approximately $22,000 a year. Fran Stone won custody of the couple's children (Lorie and Shelley) and ownership of their home.

It was Red West who told Elvis that Stone and Priscilla were having an affair. Elvis became violent and vowed he would kill Stone. It took many members of the Memphis Mafia to calm the enraged singer and to convince him not to murder Mike Stone.

FEB. 16: Elvis's rendition at this evening's Las Vegas concert of "The Impossible Dream" was used on the LP *He Walks Beside Me*. The night's performance of "It's Impossible" appears on the bootleg LP *The Legend Lives On*.

FEB. 17: The single release of "An American Trilogy" was taken from a live concert at the Las Vegas Hilton. Although "An American Trilogy" stayed on *Billboard*'s Top 100 chart for six weeks, it did not go higher than No. 66, or No. 31 on Easy-Listening (RCA 74-0672). Three singles, five LPs, and six bootlegs carry the trilogy.

FEB. 22: Elvis sang one line of "Carry Me Back to Old Virginny" before singing "Never Been to Spain" at his Vegas concert. He was in a terrible mood during this concert. He thought Mike Stone was going to send someone to kill him, so Elvis wore a gun underneath his costume.

FEB. 23: A mentally distraught Elvis and a somewhat calm Priscilla legally separated after he discovered her affection for Mike Stone.

MAR.: Priscilla left Graceland with Lisa Marie and moved into the Presleys' 144 Monovale St. home in Holmby Hills, Los Angeles, for a few weeks before they moved into a two-bedroom apartment at Huntington Beach, California. Later, Mike Stone moved in with them, and when Elvis learned of his wife's actions, he told the Colonel to prepare the papers for a divorce. He told everyone it was "immoral" for Priscilla to be living with Stone in the presence of Lisa Marie, but he never reprimanded himself for the lifestyle he fashioned around his daughter. Elvis went into mourning and refused to eat for days.

MAR. 27–29: At studios in Hollywood, Elvis completed sessions for *Elvis on Tour*, which was first titled *Standing Room Only*. The opening monologue is by comedian Jackie Kahane. Disc jockey George Klein introduced "Suspicious Minds" during scenes of Graceland. In its first week the film grossed $494,270 in 187 theaters.

An unknown voice on *Elvis on Tour* says, "We have to figure out how to get a piano in each room . . . for these guys to sing after the show." Elvis demanded a piano be present wherever he toured. Everyone knew the rules. Before and after every concert or recording session the group sang sacred music for hours.

During a take of "For the Good Times" on March 27, Elvis, a film director, and a member of the Stamps discussed gospel music and Elvis's personal roots. Charlie Hodge sang harmony during one take and a smooth rendition of "Lead Me, Guide Me." The Stamps joined Elvis in "Sweet, Sweet Spirit" and "Nearer My God to Thee." After the gospel jam, Elvis and the session men sang "Burning Love."

Elvis confided to codirector Pierre Adidge during *Elvis on Tour* that acting in low-rated films had made him physically ill. Elvis felt Hollywood producers had cultivated the wrong image of him, and he claimed he could not do a thing about it.

Why was he so powerless? He was a superstar. A rock legend and a very rich man. Why did he allow himself to star in a series of predictable, sugary love stories? Most of the blame has to go to Elvis and his inability to stand up to Parker. W. A. Harbinson observes in *The Legend of Elvis Presley:* "And the star himself . . . will grow fat and lazy . . . and as the films pile up like more stones on his grave, he'll recede farther back into the shelter of Graceland, back into his mysterious and shadowed thoughts, back to his memories."

MAR. 27–29: "Always on My Mind" (RCA 74-0815, with the flip side "Separate Ways") was written for Elvis by Mark James, Wayne Carson, and Johnny Christopher. He first recorded the song on March 27, at RCA's Hollywood studios. It hit No. 16 on the Country charts during a thirteen-week stay. RCA released four LPs with the song and five singles of it with various flip sides. The original flip, "Separate Ways," was written by Red West and Richard Mainegra when Elvis and Priscilla broke up in 1972. Elvis recorded two takes of the song on March 29. "Separate Ways" hit the Top 100 Chart at No. 20 with a twelve-week stay, reached No. 3 on Easy-Listening, and No. 16 on the country chart.

"For the Good Times," written by Kris Kristofferson, is yet to be released. Elvis's June 10, 1972, Madison Square concert version of the song can be heard on the LPs *Elvis as Recorded at Madison Square Garden* and *Welcome to My World*. He also recorded "Where Do I Go From Here," written by Paul Williams, released on RCA's LP *Elvis* (RCA APL 1-0283).

On March 28, "Burning Love" by Dennis Linde was finished with Linde on guitar. The song reached No. 2 during a fifteen-week stay on *Billboard*'s Top 100 chart (RCA 74-0769). The RIAA certified "Burning Love" as a million seller. Its flip side was "It's a Matter of Time." The version of the song that is heard on *Elvis on Tour* was re-

▲ Elvis and George Klein of 56/WHBQ radio, Memphis, Tennessee. *Courtesy of George Klein, Memphis, Tennessee.*

corded live from a concert in April 1972. He also recorded "Fool" by Carl Sigman and James Last, which had a twelve-week run on *Billboard*'s Top 100 chart, peaking at No. 17, reaching No. 12 on Easy-Listening and No. 31 on the Country chart. The flip side of "Fool" was "Steamroller Blues" (RCA 74-0910).

"Steamroller Blues" was written by folksinger James Taylor for his LP *Sweet Baby James* in 1970. It was recorded during one of Elvis's 1971 or 1972 concerts and released as a single in April 1973, peaking on the Top 100 chart at No. 17 during a twelve-week stay, and No. 31 on the Country chart (RCA 74-0910).

MAR. 29: Elvis recorded Clive Westlake's "It's a Matter of Time." The song hit No. 9 on the Easy-Listening chart and was No. 36 during a thirteen-week stay on the Country chart (RCA 74-0769).

APR.: "An American Trilogy," recorded at Elvis's performance on February 17 at the Las Vegas Hilton, was released. "Trilogy" is a medley of three songs: "Dixie," "The Battle Hymn of the Republic," and "All My Trials." It made *Billboard*'s Top 100 chart for six weeks, peaking at No. 66, and it reached No. 31 on the Easy-Listening chart (RCA 74-0672).

APR.: Twelve gospel songs for the LP *He Touched Me* were recorded. The title song reached No. 79 on *Billboard*'s Top LPs chart during its ten-week stay.

APR. 5: Elvis performed in Buffalo, New York, at Memorial Auditorium. The beginning of this live concert was filmed for *Elvis on Tour*. Aspects of every performance through April 19 were filmed. The final *Elvis on Tour* was seen at 187 theaters in 105 cities. In one week it grossed $494,270.

APR. 6: Elvis gave an excellent performance to a capacity crowd at the Olympia Stadium in Detroit, Michigan.

APR. 7: Elvis performed at the University of Dayton Arena, in Dayton, Ohio.

APRIL 7 OR 8: Elvis gave two shows at the Stokely Athletic Center in Knoxville, Tennessee. A backstage rehearsal performance of "I John" was taped with the Stamps for *Elvis on Tour*. It may have been during this period that rehearsals for "Portrait of Love," written by Cyril Ornadel and David West, were recorded for the bootleg LPs *Special Delivery From Elvis Presley* (*Las Vegas rehearsal?*) and *Susie Q* (*Las Vegas rehearsal?*). This may also have been when "Proud Mary" was recorded for *Elvis on Tour*.

APR. 9: After singing "I Got a Woman," Elvis customarily sang "Amen." He performed the songs at the Coliseum in Hampton Roads, Virginia. They were recorded in Dallas on June 6, 1975, and first included on the LP *Elvis Aron Presley*. "You Gave Me a Mountain" was recorded this night at the Coliseum and is heard in *Elvis on Tour*. Elvis performed the song at his 1973 Aloha concert and elsewhere. This night's performance of "Lawdy Miss Clawdy" (recorded several other times) and "Polka Salad Annie" were also used in *Elvis on Tour*.

APR. 9: "An American Trilogy" is heard on *Elvis on Tour*, from a live performance given on April 9 at Hampton Roads, Virginia.

Elvis on Tour features a more defiant rocker who belts out twenty-nine selections with the Imperials as backup. Producers Bob Abel and Pierre Adidge wanted to veil the Vegas image as an aging pop star gone sour and instead showcase the vigorous rebel, the man who had caused riots during the genesis of rock 'n' roll.

APR. 10: Elvis performed at the Coliseum to sell-out crowds in Richmond, Virginia. "Never Been to Spain" was recorded for *Elvis on Tour*.

APR. 11: Elvis was presented the key to the city by Mayor Roy Webber prior to his performance at the Civic Center Coliseum in Roanoke, Virginia.

APR. 12: Elvis performed at the Fairgrounds Coliseum to a capacity crowd in Indianapolis, Indiana.

APR. 13: Elvis performed at the Coliseum in Charlotte, North Carolina. Although he was beginning to feel the stress from his concert tour, he did not disappoint fans.

APR. 14: Elvis sang "Bridge Over Troubled Water" and "Funny How Time Slips Away" at the Coliseum concert in Greensboro, North Carolina. These songs are heard on the documentary *Elvis on Tour*.

During a limo ride, Elvis was recorded singing "Rainy Night in Georgia," which was included in *Elvis on Tour*.

APR. 15: Elvis gave two enthusiastic shows at the Coliseum in Macon, Georgia.

APR. 16: Elvis gave two shows at the Veterans Memorial Coliseum in Jacksonville, Florida.

APR. 17: Elvis performed in the Little Rock Convention Center in Little Rock, Arkansas.

APR. 18: Elvis performed at the T. H. Barton Coliseum in San Antonio, Texas.

APR. 19: With his performance at Tingley Coliseum, Albuquerque, New Mex-

ico, the filming of *Elvis on Tour* ended.

MAY: Mike Stone told Elvis when he could and could not see Lisa Marie, which incensed the superstar.

JUNE 1–5: Elvis rehearsed for his opening at Madison Square Garden on June 6, and attempted to diet.

JUNE 9–11: During a major press conference Elvis dressed in a tux before he performed to four sold-out performances at Madison Square Garden in New York City.

JUNE 10: During the afternoon show at Madison Square Garden, Elvis was recorded singing "I'll Remember You" and "Reconsider Baby," which are on the LP *Elvis—A Legendary Performer*, Vol. 4. "The Impossible Dream," "Never Been to Spain," and "You've Lost That Lovin' Feelin'" were recorded for the LP *Elvis as Recorded at Madison Square Garden* (RCA SPS-33-571).

JUNE 12: Elvis performed at the Memorial Coliseum in Fort Wayne, Indiana, to standing room only.

JUNE 13: Elvis performed at the Roberts Memorial Stadium in Evansville, Indiana, and was mobbed by fans as he tried to enter his limo to drive to the airport.

JUNE 14–15: Elvis gave several performances at the Milwaukee Arena in Milwaukee, Wisconsin. All were sold out.

JUNE 16–17: Elvis gave one performance on the sixteenth and two sell-out concerts on the seventeenth at Chicago Stadium.

JUNE 18: Elvis performed at the Tarrant County Convention Center in Fort Worth, Texas.

JUNE 19: Elvis performed at the Henry Levitt Arena, Wichita, Kansas.

JUNE 20: Elvis performed at the Civic Assembly Center in Tulsa, Oklahoma. Distressed over his weight and for having lost Priscilla to a karate instructor, he was in a bad mood throughout the evening.

AUG. 4–SEPT. 4: Elvis gave sixty-three shows at the Hilton Hotel in Las Vegas. Sammy Davis, Jr., visited him backstage many times.

AUG. 4: A medley of "Little Sister"/ "Get Back" and "My Babe" appear on the bootleg LP *Command Performances* (*Las Vegas: August 4, 1972*).

AUG. 7–14: Elvis saw many young starlets after his performances each night. He was, in the truest sense, a man on the rebound.

AUG. 18: Elvis filed for divorce from Priscilla in Santa Monica, California. Elvis's attorney was E. Gregory Hookstraten and Priscilla's was Robert Brock.

Elvis's life was in turmoil. He began taking too many diet pills, kept late-night hours, suffered from a chronic sleeping disorder, and obsessed about the loss of his twin brother, his mother's untimely death, and now the loss of Priscilla. The Cat had become surrounded by dominating, selfish people who wanted him for themselves, without much care for the man himself. He had watched the music world be taken over by a new generation of flamboyant artists, and his associates confirmed the only salvation Elvis found was singing gospel songs at a piano.

Elvis communicated through gospel his losses and his personal grief. Elvis

felt he could count on God and that was a comfort to him.

AUG. 30: John Lennon yelled out at a Madison Square Garden benefit concert, "I love you, Elvis!" The audience went crazy.

SEPT. 4: Elvis finished an exhausting performance schedule in Las Vegas. He began to eat too much and gained a lot of weight within a few months. Food had become one of the only pleasurable aspects of his life.

OCT. 20: The network TV premiere of *Change of Habit* was seen on NBC's "Friday Night at the Movies."

CA. NOV.: Prior to his divorce becoming final, Elvis allowed Linda Diane Thompson (voted Best Dressed Coed at Memphis State University, Miss Liberty Bowl, Miss Memphis State, and third runner-up as Miss Tennessee in the Miss USA Pageant) to move into Graceland. Almost immediately, Thompson began to redecorate. Elvis lavished jewelry and cars on Linda Thompson. No longer could he tell Priscilla she was living in sin with Mike Stone; he had followed Priscilla's lead.

NOV. 1: *Elvis on Tour* was released. It focused on Elvis's tour of fifteen cities from April 5 to April 19, 1972. Production costs for the documentary totaled $1.6 million. Elvis's salary was a sweet $1 million. The montage supervisor was none other than Martin Scorsese!

Gordon Stoker of the Jordanaires claimed Elvis only lost his temper once during the documentary's filming. Many times Elvis and his entourage went to a recording studio and sat with Elvis at the piano to sing spirituals all night. Sometimes, they never recorded anything. If anyone complained that he was wasting time, Elvis threw a tantrum.

NOV. 8: Elvis performed at the Municipal Coliseum in Lubbock, Texas, and more young woman than usual were at the concert. Each vied for the King's attention. Everyone knew he was going through a divorce. Many fans sent him teddy bears, love letters with photographs of themselves, and other objects of love. Again, he was considered "the most eligible man in the world." Little did they know. . . .

NOV. 9: Traveling all night, Elvis performed at the Community Center Arena in Tucson, Arizona. After relaxing for a few minutes, it was back to Texas for the next night's performance.

NOV. 10: Elvis performed another sold-out concert at the Coliseum in El Paso, Texas. Elvis had wanted to stop and see some horses in El Paso, but the Colonel had already booked him in California for the next day.

NOV. 11: Elvis performed at the Coliseum in Oakland, California.

NOV. 12–13: Elvis gave three concerts at the Swing Auditorium in San Bernardino, California, to capacity crowds. Members of the Memphis Mafia lined up females for themselves, but Elvis was stuck with Linda Thompson. Although Thompson was beautiful, patient, and kind, Elvis was still bitter that Priscilla "dumped him for a nobody." No matter how many gorgeous beauty queens or starlets were around him, he had been rejected by his wife.

NOV. 14–15: Elvis performed at the Long Beach Arena in Long Beach, California.

NOV. 16: Elvis and his entourage flew to Hawaii and Elvis complained of headaches. His schedule was taking its toll.

NOV. 17: Elvis performed at the Honolulu International Center in Honolulu, Hawaii, before a mob scene.

NOV. 18: Elvis gave two shows at the Honolulu International Center, and hundreds of women lined the streets, hotel lobbies, and concert parking lots trying to get to the King.

NOV. 26: Elvis flew back to Los Angeles, California.

NOV. 28: Elvis purchased a Colt Detective Special revolver and other guns from Kerr's Sporting Goods store in Beverly Hills. He also bought guns from Charles Church in Memphis.

DEC.: Elvis affixed the "International Kempo Karate Association—IKKA" emblem to his guitar, which he used in the TV Special "Elvis: Aloha From Hawaii" in 1973. Elvis's karate belts had been given to him purely for show. He paid sizable sums to any karate instructor who would give him an advanced karate degree.

Linda Thompson and Elvis had become an unpopular item in the tabloids. Thompson clung to his side, and many fans believed she was just another gold digger.

Elvis won a Grammy for Best Inspirational Performance for the album *He Touched Me*, 1972. He was extremely pleased with the honor, although he was not at the Grammy ceremonies to receive it.

Elvis on Tour was voted Best Documentary of 1972 by the Hollywood Foreign Press Association. It was the highest award any Presley film received, and Elvis felt vindicated. His *singing*, not acting, received praise. His decision to leave dull scripts was the right one.

DEC. 25: Elvis lavishly decorated each of his homes for Christmas, sent various people out to buy Lisa Marie too many toys, and presented Linda Thompson with hundreds of thousands of dollars' worth of opulent gifts. He sent Liberace, Sammy Davis, Jr., and others huge bouquets of flowers and gave over $100,000 to children's charities.

DEC. 31: Elvis threw a huge party at Graceland to celebrate the New Year. He was in a good mood because his work had been applauded by peers in the music world.

1973

In 1973, Elvis gave 169 performances in twenty cities. Due to illness (in February and May) he missed several scheduled events. After *Elvis on Tour* won the Golden Globe Award, Elvis felt his future was looking up. In some respects, he felt it was *he*—not the production staff—who had caused the film to win the Golden Globe.

Americans celebrated the cease-fire in Vietnam on January 28, and the last U.S. troops left Southeast Asia on March 29. With the Watergate break-in exposing Nixon and his staff to possible criminal indictment, Vice President Agnew resigned on October 10, and on December 6, House Republican leader Gerald R. Ford took Agnew's place.

Popular films included *Paper Moon, Last Tango in Paris, American Graffiti, The Paper Chase,* and *The Way We Were.* Stevie Wonder's "Superstition" and "You Are the Sunshine of My Life" were single pop hits; Jim Croce's "Bad Bad Leroy Brown" was a smash; Elton John had two hit LPs—*Goodbye Yellow Brick Road* and *Don't Shoot Me, I'm Only the Piano Player;* the Rolling Stones came out with *Goat's Head Soup;* and former Beatle George Harrison hit the charts with the LP *Living in the Material World.*

JAN. 9: Elvis arrived by helicopter at the Hawaiian Village Hotel in Honolulu. Swamped by eager fans, he barely made it into the hotel clothed.

▶ Elvis performing in Hawaii.
Courtesy of a New York collector.

JAN. 10–11: Rehearsals for the TV show "Elvis: Aloha From Hawaii" were long and tiresome. Elvis demanded perfection from everyone. He was in control.

JAN. 12: Dress rehearsals for the TV special were performed in front of six thousand fans at the Honolulu International Center Arena. Elvis debuted his version of Hank Williams's "I'm So Lonesome I Could Cry" during the TV special and told the audience it was the saddest song he had ever heard. During this performance, Elvis also sang "Something," written by George Harrison for the Beatles in 1969, and "What Now, My Love," both included in the TV special and the EP/LP *Aloha From Hawaii via Satellite* (RCA DTFO-2006). "Something" was included on the LP *The Alternate Aloha* (RCA 695B-1-R).

JAN. 13: Elvis Presley Day in Honolulu, Hawaii. Elvis was the best promotion for tourism Hawaii had ever seen.

Elvis anxiously awaited his January 14 telecast, which was to be shown worldwide. Members of his entourage had a difficult time guarding Elvis from hundreds of eager fans attempting to climb into his room (or pants).

JAN. 14: "Elvis: Aloha From Hawaii" was beamed worldwide by a Intelsat IV communications satellite to approximately one *billion* people in forty countries at twelve-thirty A.M. (Honolulu time). Remarkably, people in Communist China were able to see Elvis in action! Although the production cost $2.5 million, it was well worth the expense. Special performers with Elvis included J. D. Sumner & the Stamps, Kathy Westmoreland, the Sweet Inspirations, and the Joe Guercio Orchestra.

Ninety-two percent of the TV audience in the Philippines watched the show, and it was the first time music enthusiasts in Japan, South Korea, New Zealand, South Vietnam, Thailand, the Far East, and Australia could see the legendary Elvis. It was a true triumph for everyone involved.

Elvis recorded five songs for the U.S. edition of the concert after the Hawaiian audience left the building: "Blue Hawaii," "Ku-u-i-po," "Hawaiian Wedding Song," "Early Morning Rain," and "No More" (which was not used on the LP). His most popular costume to date was a white, gem-studded, tight-fitting two-piece jumpsuit, adorned with stars and the American eagle. Its cape was thrown into the audience, which caused near hysteria. Bruce Spinks, sportswriter for the *Honolulu Advisor*, caught it. Throughout the concert, Elvis tossed sweat-soaked scarves to eagerly awaiting fans.

Songs in the worldwide telecast were "Paradise, Hawaiian Style" (with opening credits); "Also Sprach Zarathustra," accompanied by the Joe Guercio Orchestra; "See See Rider"; "Burning Love"; "Something"; "You Gave Me a Mountain"; "Steamroller Blues"; "Early Morning Rain" (only on U.S. telecast); "My Way"; "Love Me"; "Johnny B. Goode"; "It's Over"; "Blue Suede Shoes"; "I'm So Lonesome I Could Cry"; "I Can't Stop Loving You"; "Hound Dog"; "Blue Hawaii" (in U.S. only); "What Now My Love"; "Fever"; "Welcome to My World"; "Suspicious Minds"; "I'll Remember You"; "Hawaiian Wedding Song" (in U.S. only); "Long Tail Sally"/"Whole Lotta Shakin' Goin' On"; "Ku-u-i-po" (in U.S. only); "An American Trilogy"; "A Big Hunk o' Love"; and "Can't Help Falling in Love". "Elvis: Aloha From Hawaii" was a benefit concert for the Kuio-kalani Lee Cancer Fund.

Elvis's live version of Don Gibson's "I Can't Stop Lovin' You"; Kuiokalani Lee's "I'll Remember You"; "It's Over" by Jimmie Rodgers; "No More" by Don Robertson and Hal Blair; "See See Rider" by Big Bill Broonzy; and "Welcome to My World" by Ray Winkler and John Hathcock were recorded and released on LPs, which included *Aloha From Hawaii via Satellite* and Pickwick's *Mahalo From Elvis.*

JAN. 15: A rebroadcast of "Elvis: Aloha From Hawaii" was shown in twenty-eight European countries.

JAN. 18: Elvis and his crew, band, and backup vocalists flew to Las Vegas.

JAN. 20: Elvis started rehearsals for his opening in Las Vegas's Hilton Hotel, January 26.

JAN. 26: Elvis began fifty-four performances at the Las Vegas Hilton. He missed three concerts due to extreme fatigue. Linda Thompson nursed him back to health, along with a team of doctors.

FEB. 13: Dr. Sidney Boyers treated Elvis during his concert engagement in Las Vegas. In appreciation, Elvis bought Boyers a Lincoln Continental.

FEB. 14: For his Valentine's Day concert in Las Vegas, many fans gave the King paper and chocolate hearts. It was a romantic, frantic night.

FEB. 20: At the Las Vegas Hilton, Elvis sang one line of "Alfie," which had been written by Hal David and Burt Bacharach in 1966, for the film of the same name. Elvis never officially recorded the song.

FEB. 23: Elvis, physically and emotionally drained, finished fifty-four concerts in Las Vegas. He told the Colonel he needed to go back to Memphis or Palm Springs to relax, and that he would not be seen in public for at least four weeks. His stomach, eyes, and head were bothering him.

FEB. 25–?: Elvis recuperated in Memphis at Graceland with Linda Thompson and members of the Memphis Mafia.

APR. 4: "Elvis: Aloha From Hawaii"

was expanded to ninety minutes and aired as a TV special (with four songs not aired on January 14) by NBC-TV to the United States.

APR. 20: Elvis and his large staff and crew flew to Phoenix, Arizona, to rehearse for their upcoming concert. Elvis was feeling better and was in good spirits. Linda Thompson accompanied him.

APR. 22: Elvis's performance at the Veterans Memorial Coliseum in Phoenix, Arizona, was inspired, and the sell-out audience was thrilled to see Elvis well again.

APR. 23–24: Elvis gave three concerts at the Anaheim Convention Center in Anaheim, California.

APR. 25: Elvis gave two shows at the Selland Arena in Fresno, California.

APR. 26: Elvis performed at the Sports Arena in San Diego, California, to a wild, sold-out crowd.

APR. 27: Elvis performed at the Memorial Coliseum in Portland, Oregon, to a sell-out crowd.

APR. 28: Elvis's two shows at the Coliseum in Spokane, Washington, were greeted enthusiastically, and the King was in a good mood during the break between the shows.

APR. 29: Elvis gave two shows at the Seattle Civic Center in Seattle, Washington.

APR. 30: Elvis performed at the Denver Coliseum, Denver, Colorado, before a huge, young crowd.

MAY 4–16: Elvis was scheduled to play twenty-five shows in Stateline, Nevada, at the Sahara Tahoe Hotel. Before his contract with the hotel was complete, he had to cancel concerts due to exhaustion, stomach cramps, and severe headaches. Popping pills and ignoring advice from Linda Thompson, members of his staff, or doctors, Elvis went into deep depression.

MAY 7: Former Beatle George Harrison visited Elvis in Las Vegas (and many times thereafter).

MAY 13: In memory of his mother (at a special Mother's Day concert) Elvis donated money from his Lake Tahoe performance to the Barton Memorial Hospital.

MAY 18: A physically ill Elvis traveled back to Memphis.

MAY 29: Priscilla refused the original divorce proposal, which stipulated she would receive $1,000 a month, plus $5,000 in child support yearly, with a lump sum of $100,000. Priscilla filed a suit of extrinsic fraud via attorney Arthur Toll demanding $11,800 monthly. She finally received $2 million, plus $6,000 a month for ten years, $4,200 a month alimony for one year, $4,000 a month in child support, $250,000 from the sale of their Bel Air home, and 5 percent of two of Elvis's publishing companies. Priscilla took her favorite horse, Domino, from Graceland to southern California along with many other possessions.

SUMMER: When Bill "Sugarfoot" Wallace, world middleweight karate champion, injured his left leg in a karate competition, Elvis invited him to Graceland, where Wallace was treated by an acupuncturist. He eventually became a bodyguard for Elvis for a short period.

JUNE 18: The Colonel had convinced Elvis to reenter an arduous concert schedule. The Colonel wasn't con-

cerned if the schedule was too much for the singer and his crew, and Elvis, ever the obedient boy, left for Mobile, Alabama, to rehearse.

JUNE 20: Elvis performed at the Mobile, Alabama, Municipal Auditorium.

JUNE 21: Elvis performed at the Omni in Atlanta, Georgia.

JUNE 22: Elvis performed at the Nassau Coliseum in Uniondale, New York.

JUNE 23–24 Elvis gave three shows at the Nassau Coliseum to sell-out crowds. While singing "Heartbreak Hotel," he substituted "Holiday Inn." He never lost his sense of humor. This version does not appear on any record to date.

JUNE 25–26: Elvis performed at the Civic Center Arena in Pittsburgh, Pennsylvania.

JUNE 27: Elvis performed at the Cincinnati Gardens to sell-out crowds in Cincinnati, Ohio.

JUNE 28: Elvis performed at the Kiel Auditorium, St. Louis, Missouri.

JUNE 29–30: Elvis gave three shows at the Omni in Atlanta, Georgia.

JULY 1: Elvis gave two shows at the Municipal Auditorium in Nashville, Tennessee, and partied all night after the concerts, jamming with local musicians in his hotel.

JULY 2: Elvis performed at the Myriad Convention Center in Oklahoma City, Oklahoma.

JULY 3: Elvis performed at the Omni in Atlanta, Georgia, and directly after the concert he flew to Memphis.

JULY 4: Elvis allegedly gave a ninety-minute karate demonstration at Red West and Bobby Mann's martial-arts studio at 1372 Overton Street, Memphis.

CA. JULY 5: Elvis gave his friend Jimmy Velvet his 1969 Mercedes 600 limo.

JULY 21: At Memphis's Stax Studios, Elvis recorded Jerry Leiber and Mike Stoller's "If You Don't Come Back," "Three Corn Patches" by Leiber-Stoller, and Arthur Kent's "Take Good Care of Her," which had a seven-week run on *Billboard*'s Hot 100 chart, topping at No. 39, but it was No. 4 on the Country chart and No. 27 on the Easy-Listening chart (RCA APBO-0196). Its flip side was "I've Got a Thing About You, Baby."

JULY 22: In Memphis at Stax Studios, Elvis recorded "Find Out What's Happening," written by Jerry Crutchfield. No single was made of the song. He also completed Tony Joe White's "I've Got a Thing About You, Baby," which peaked at No. 39 during a twelve-week stay on *Billboard*'s Hot 100 chart; reaching No. 4 on the Country and No. 27 on the Easy-Listening charts (RCA APBO-0196). Its flip side was "Take Good Care of Her." "Just a Little Bit," composed by John Thornton, Ralph Bass, Piney Brown, and Earl Washington, was also recorded. It is on the EP *Raised on Rock/For Ol' Times Sake*.

JULY 23: At the Stax Studios, Elvis completed "For Ol' Times Sake" by Tony Joe White, which peaked at No. 41 on *Billboard*'s Top 100 chart during a nine-week stay (RCA APBO-0088). Its flip side was Mark James's "Raised on Rock," which had a nine-week run on the Top 100 chart peaking at No. 41 and hit No. 27 in seven weeks on the Easy-Listening chart (RCA APBO-0088).

JULY 24: Elvis recorded "Girl of Mine" by Barry Mason and Les Reed at Stax Studios.

JULY 25: The instrumentals were recorded at Stax Studios for "The Wonders You Perform," written by Jerry Chestnut. Elvis was scheduled to sing the song, but to date no recording has surfaced.

AUG. 1: Elvis and his staff flew to Las Vegas to rehearse for Elvis's next concert opening there.

AUG. 6: Elvis was exhausted when he began a series of fifty-nine concerts at the Las Vegas Hilton Hotel. Elvis had become a man whom few insiders wanted to be near. If he wasn't sleepwalking, he was sneaking junk food or popping pills. He still talked about killing Mike Stone, and no one trusted what Elvis would do after concerts ended.

MID-AUG.: Elvis took some karate lessons from Bill "Sugarfoot" Wallace. It did not help Elvis's karate very much because Elvis trained in boots, sunglasses, and other nonkarate paraphernalia. Wallace, however, was an excellent martial artist.

SEPT.: Elvis drove a gold-trimmed 1973 Stutz through Memphis.

SEPT. 3: Elvis finished his contracted concerts at the Las Vegas Hilton, having missed two due to illness. Elvis's longtime companion Gordon Stoker of the Jordanaires understood the singer's internal plight. Remembering Elvis in Nevada, Stoker said in a *Beacon Journal* article (May 3, 1991): "Vegas is what brought an end to the good years. . . . [It] was just too much. . . . I don't think it was much more than a year or two later we all started to see a decline in Elvis. . . . He . . . felt like a piece of meat being carved up for everybody else's benefit. Eventually, it just took its toll. He got tired and . . . sort of gave up, I reckon. Worst part is, he never really knew, either. I think it was all just a blur to him."

After the crowds dispersed and the performances were over, Elvis was lonely and felt empty inside. He was a superstar loved by millions with no one to love, respect, or trust, with no one who loved him enough to help him seek competent professional help.

SEPT. 24: At his home in Palm Springs, Elvis recorded Wayne P. Walker's "Are You Sincere" with Voice on backup vocals (RCA PB-11533). It peaked on the Top 100 chart at No. 10 during a twelve-week run. Its flip side was "Solitaire." He also recorded "I Miss You" with backups by Donnie Summer (who wrote the song), Sherrill Neilsen, and Tim Baty. No single was released. Elvis also recorded "Sweet Angeline" by Chris Arnold, Geoffrey Morrow, and Dave Martin with Voice as backup vocalists, using the instrumentals that were recorded on July 25, 1973, at Stax Studios in Memphis. "Sweet Angeline" is on the EP *Raised on Rock/For Ol' Times Sake*.

OCT. 9: Elvis and Priscilla's divorce was finalized and granted in Santa Monica, California. Priscilla's emancipation came with a lucrative divorce settlement. Priscilla soon opened her own boutique, which she named Bix and Beau's, in Los Angeles. She seemed happy with Mike Stone, but she made it clear she would not marry anyone.

OCT. 15: It was reported Elvis's two-week stay in Baptist Memorial Hospital was complicated by pneumonia, but he was also there due to severe depression. The divorce wounded him badly, not because he loved Priscilla, but because she was the first woman to leave him (without his permission) for someone else. Linda Thompson, his live-in girlfriend, demanded the hospital give her a cot in Elvis's room, where she slept for two weeks. Some people claimed Thompson stayed in the hospital so that Elvis could not flirt with female nurses.

Elvis's career and life deteriorated after his divorce from Priscilla. Although Elvis was not a responsible father, he grieved because Priscilla got sole custody of Lisa Marie.

NOV.: *Movie World* disclosed to the public that "Elvis Collapses After Divorce" and featured Elvis and Priscilla on the cover.

NOV. 10–16: *TV Guide* featured Elvis and other stars.

NOV. 14: "Elvis: Aloha From Hawaii" was rebroadcast at eight-thirty P.M. on NBC-TV.

NOV. 16: Elvis was sickly, melancholy, and close to violent. He had lost everyone whom he considered "close." He was tired of the rat race. He felt he had nothing to live for, and worse, he trusted no one.

NOV. 20: Colonel Parker told Elvis to get his act together and act like a man, or his career would go down the tubes and he would truly have nothing to live for.

NOV. 25: Elvis promised the Colonel he would soon record in Memphis and that Parker could start planning another concert tour.

DEC. 10: At Memphis's Stax Studios, Elvis recorded Dennis Linde's "I Got a Feelin' in My Body" with Linde on guitar. The singled peak at No. 6 on *Billboard*'s Country chart during a thirteen-week stay (RCA PB-11679). Its flip side was "There's a Honky Tonk Angel." Elvis also recorded "It's Midnight," written by Billy Edd Wheeler and Jerry Chestnut, which hit No. 9 on *Billboard*'s Country chart and No. 8 on the Easy-Listening chart (RCA PB 10074, released in October 1974). Its flip side was "Promised Land."

DEC. 11: At Memphis's Stax Studios, Elvis completed "If You Talk in Your Sleep" by Red West and Johnny Christopher (who played guitar). It reached No. 17 on *Billboard*'s Top 100 chart during a thirteen-week stay, and it was No. 6 on both the R&B and Country charts (RCA APBO-0280). Its flip side was "Help Me." Elvis also recorded "You Asked Me," written by Billy Joe Shaver, but it was not released until March 1981, after Felton Jarvis overdubbed tracks. Felton's "fix" became a single and peaked at No. 8 during a fifteen-week stay on *Billboard*'s Country chart (RCA PB-12205, with the flip side "Lovin' Arms"). It was also released on the LPs *Guitar Man* and *Promised Land.*

DEC. 12: Chris Christian's "Love Song of the Year" was recorded by Elvis at Stax Studios. It is heard only on the LP *Promised Land.* He also recorded "My Boy," which was released as a single in 1975 with the flip side "Thinking About You" (RCA PB-10191, released in January 1975) and with "Lovin' Arms" (RCA PB-12205, released in April 1975). "My Boy" peaked on the Top 100 chart at No. 20 and at No. 14 on the Country chart. "Mr. Songman," written by Donnie Summer, was released on the LP *Promised Land* and as an uncharted single (RCA PB-10278, released in April 1975, with the flipside "T-R-O-U-B-L-E"). Elvis's uncharted single "Thinking About You" by Tim Baty was released in January 1975, with the flip side "My Boy" (RCA PB-10191).

Elvis recorded "Help Me," a country spiritual previously recorded on two other albums. This was the last religious piece he recorded.

DEC. 13: "Good Time Charlie's Got the Blues" by Danny O'Keefe was recorded by Elvis at Stax Studios, Memphis. It is heard on the LP *Good Times* and on two bootleg LPs. He also recorded Tom Jans's "Lovin' Arms," but it wasn't released until Felton Jarvis redid the instrumental tracks at Young'Un Sound in Nashville in 1981. With "My Boy" as its flip side, "Lovin' Arms" peaked on *Billboard*'s Country chart at No. 8 (RCA PB-12205, released in April 1981).

DEC. 14: Elvis recorded "Talk About the Good Times" by Jerry Reed at Stax Studios. It is heard on the LP *Good Times* (RCA CPL1-0475).

DEC. 15: "There's a Honky Tonk Angel (Who Will Take Me Back In)" by Danny Rice and Troy Seals was recorded by Elvis at the Stax Studios, Memphis (RCA PB-11679, released in August 1979). It reached No. 6 on *Billboard*'s Country chart during a thirteen-week stay. Also recorded was Chuck Berry's "Promised Land" with tambourines by David Briggs overdubbed at a later time. The song

◄ Priscilla and Elvis leave the Superior Court in Santa Monica, California, after he was granted a divorce on grounds of irreconcilable differences, October 10, 1973. *Courtesy of AP/Wide World Photos.*

peaked at No. 14 during a thirteen-week stay on *Billboard*'s Hot 100 chart, and it was up to No. 11 during an eight-week stay on the Easy-Listening chart (RCA PB-10074). Its flip side was "It's Midnight."

DEC. 16: "If That Isn't Love" by Dottie Rambo, "She Wears My Ring" by Boudleaux and Felice Bryant, and "Spanish Eyes" by Bert Kaempfert were recorded by Elvis for the LP *Good Times* at the Stax Studios.

DEC. 18: Singer Bobby Darin died during heart surgery at the Cedars of Leb-anon Hospital in Los Angeles. Darin was one of Elvis's favorite singers. Elvis introduced him in Las Vegas when Darin was in the audience at the International Hilton. Elvis often sang Darin's hit song "Until It's Time for You to Go" and recorded Darin's "I'll Be There" in February 1969.

DEC. 25: Elvis sent Lisa Marie a teddy bear for Christmas, while Linda Thompson received expensive jewelry and a white Maltese dog named Fox-hugh. Those closest to the star claim Elvis gave Thompson over a million dollars' worth of jewels during their courtship.

1974

In 1974, Elvis tried to find new songs that might appeal to Las Vegas crowds, but he was dissatisfied with most of them. He attended every home game of the Memphis Southmen, World Football League; watched *Godfather, Part II* and *Chinatown* over and over again; and all the while pretended everything in life was fine. But it was not.

JAN.: Colonel Parker and Elvis established Boxcar Enterprises to handle merchandising of Elvis-related products that were unrelated to movies and records. Reported distributions were 40 percent to Parker, 15 percent to Tom Diskin, 15 percent to George Parkhill, 15 percent to Freddy Bienstock, and only 15 percent to Elvis! In 1974, Parker received $27,650 from Boxcar and Elvis was paid $2,750 (only 10 percent)! Boxcar Records was also created by Elvis and the Colonel. Its first released record was *Having Fun With Elvis on Stage*, which RCA distributed. Distributions for Boxcar Records were 56 percent to the Colonel, 22 percent to Tom Diskin, and 22 percent to Elvis.

JAN. 8: Elvis Presley Day was proclaimed in Georgia by Gov. Jimmy Carter.

Traveling with fifty singers and musicians, Elvis appeared in over forty cities to give 152 concerts in 1974 (he missed one show in September due to

illness) and earned $7 million. Meanwhile, scandal sheets went wild spreading gossip about him, but few knew he underwent a face-lift in Memphis, had severe physical ailments, and was unable to cope with his life.

Elvis gave producer George Waite financial backing to make a karate documentary titled *The New Gladiators*, but it was never finished or released. Allegedly, Elvis narrated the documentary.

JAN. 24: During a rehearsal for his Las Vegas grand opening, a huge audience watched as Elvis knelt down in the audience and sang to comedian Marty Allen part of "The Most Beautiful Girl." It has not appeared on any release.

JAN. 26: Elvis began twenty-nine shows at the Las Vegas Hilton Hotel, and every show had been sold-out for weeks in advance. Scalpers reportedly received as much as $500 a ticket to any performance.

FEB.: In 1974, Elvis bought a black Story & Clark grand piano for Graceland's music room.

FEB. 2–8: RCA brought a portable studio to Graceland so Elvis could record there.

FEB. 9: Elvis finished his Las Vegas concert commitment.

MAR.: Gov. George Wallace declared one week in March as Elvis Presley Week.

MAR.: Although the tabloids wrote about Elvis's great love for his daughter, Lisa Marie, he rarely saw her, and when they were together, he scarcely spent more than a few minutes with her. He thought being a good father meant spoiling the child with too many possessions. During those brief encounters he would play the piano and sing gospel music and watch her ride a bicycle or horse cart around Graceland.

MAR.: Elvis was on the cover of *Silver Screen*, and an article rumored he would marry Linda Thompson.

MAR. 1–2: Elvis performed at Oral Roberts University in Tulsa, Oklahoma.

MAR. 3: Two sold-out concerts broke new attendance records at the Astrodome in Houston, Texas.

MAR. 4: Elvis performed at the Civic Center in Monroe, Louisiana.

MAR. 5: Elvis performed at the University Memorial Coliseum in Auburn, Alabama.

MAR. 6: Elvis performed at the Garrett Coliseum in Montgomery, Alabama, and he may have visited Gov. George Wallace.

MAR. 7–8: Elvis gave an exhausting show at the Civic Center in Monroe, Louisiana.

MAR. 9: Elvis performed two shows at the Coliseum in Charlotte, North Carolina.

MAR. 10: Elvis appeared at the Roanoke Civic Center in Roanoke, Virginia. He complained his heart was beating "weirdly," but no one took him seriously.

MAR. 11: Elvis performed at the Coliseum, Hampton Roads, Virginia.

MAR. 12: Elvis gave a three-hour show at the Coliseum in Richmond, Virginia.

MAR. 13: Elvis performed at the Coliseum in Greensboro, North Carolina.

◀ Vernon and Elvis enjoying a happy moment. *Courtesy of AP/Wide World Photos.*

MAR. 14:   Elvis performed at the Murphy Athletic Center in Murfreesboro, Tennessee. He was beginning to feel the strain of his overscheduled days and nights. The only peace he had now was inside his hotel rooms.

MAR. 15:   Elvis gave two shows at Stokely Athletic Center in Knoxville, Tennessee, where audiences went berserk.

MAR. 16–17:   Elvis's four performances were played to standing-room-only crowds at the Mid-South Coliseum in Memphis.

MAR. 18:   Elvis performed at the Coliseum in Richmond, Virginia.

MAR. 19:   Elvis gave a thrilling performance at the Murphy Athletic Center in Murfreesboro, Tennessee.

MAR. 20:   Elvis performed at the Mid-South Coliseum in Memphis.

In the morning, and after the concert at Mid-South, Elvis recorded for *Elvis Recorded Live on Stage in Memphis* the gospel song "How Great Thou Art," as well as "I Got a Woman," John Rostill's "Let Me Be There," and "See See Rider." "Let Me Be There" was released by the song's publisher (Al Gallico Music Corp.) as a single demo tape to disc jockeys (RCA JH-10951) in June 1974, but RCA never made a single to distribute to the public. It appears on the Al Gallico release with "Why Me, Lord?" written by Kris Kristofferson, and on the LPs *Elvis Aron Presley* (Dallas, June 6, 1975), *Moody Blue*, and *Elvis Recorded Live on Stage in Memphis*. "Your Mama Don't Dance," written by Kenny Loggins and Jim Messina in 1972, is on the LP *Elvis Recorded Live on Stage in Memphis* with a medley that included "Long Tall Sally," "Whole Lotta Shakin' Goin' On," "Flip, Flop and Fly," "Jailhouse Rock," and "Hound Dog." The medley was also recorded at the Nashville concert

on July 1, 1973, and in Las Vegas on September 3, 1973.

MAR. 28:   Arthur "Big Boy" Crudup died of a stroke. Elvis mourned the passing of the composer of "That's All Right, Mama" and one of the major influences of his life.

APR.:   Although he was married to Dee Stanley Presley, it was rumored Vernon was having an affair with a nurse named Sandy Miller. The rumor turned out to be a fact. Marian Cocke and Kathy Seamon were live-in nurses at Graceland, too, that year. (See *Elvis, My Brother* by Billy Stanley.)

APR. 11:   *Rolling Stone* featured an article entitled "Elvis Anthology: From Memphis to Myth" by Jim Miller.

MAY 10:   Elvis performed at Swing Auditorium in San Bernardino, California, and proved, once again, he was the ultimate rock 'n' roller.

MAY 11:   Elvis gave two sell-out shows at the Forum in Los Angeles, California.

MAY 12:   Elvis performed at Selland Arena in Fresno, California.

MAY 13:   Elvis performed at Swing Auditorium, San Bernardino, California. Late that night, he and his crew flew to Stateline, Nevada.

MAY 14:   Elvis walked through a dress rehearsal for his Stateline show with backup singers, an orchestra, and over one hundred staffers. It was a wild scene because he was too tired to think.

MAY 16:   Elvis began another twenty-two shows for the Sahara Tahoe Hotel in Stateline, Nevada.

MAY 20: A fan named Edward L. Ashley alleged Elvis's bodyguards had beaten him up at the Sahara Tahoe Hotel, after Ashley admitted turning off the circuit breakers on Elvis's floor of the hotel because Ashley wasn't allowed to attend one of Elvis's after-hours parties.

MAY 26: Elvis completed his Nevada concerts. He was not content. Life had lost its glitter and excitement. He was primarily a prisoner of his career, stuck in hotel rooms and rushed on and off stages across America by a troop of bodyguards. He no longer could do *any*thing independently.

MAY 27: Elvis left Nevada for Graceland, where he organized his staff, listened to Vernon's many complaints about his marriage to Dee, tried to please his overanxious stepbrothers, and had to contend with pretending "love" with Linda Thompson (who, much to Elvis's displeasure, had redecorated Graceland).

JUNE 15–16: Elvis gave two shows daily at the Tarrant County Convention Center in Fort Worth, Texas.

JUNE 17–18: Elvis gave two performances at the University of Louisiana Assembly Center in Baton Rouge.

JUNE 19: Elvis was cheered by a sell-out crowd as he performed at the Civic Center in Amarillo, Texas.

JUNE 20: Elvis performed at the Veterans Memorial Auditorium, Des Moines, Iowa.

JUNE 21: Elvis performed at Cleveland, Ohio's Convention Center.

JUNE 22: Elvis put on two shows at the Civic Center in Providence, Rhode Island.

JUNE 23: Elvis gave two shows at the Spectrum in Philadelphia, Pennsylvania.

JUNE 24: Elvis gave two shows at the International Convention Center in Niagara Falls, New York.

JUNE 25: Elvis performed at St. John's Arena in Columbus, Ohio.

JUNE 26: Elvis performed at Freedom Hall in Louisville, Kentucky.

JUNE 27: Elvis gave a concert at the Assembly Hall in Bloomington, Indiana.

JUNE 28: Elvis performed at the Milwaukee Arena in Milwaukee, Wisconsin, before a capacity crowd.

JUNE 29: During his two shows at the Municipal Auditorium in Kansas City, Missouri, the strain of Elvis's schedule began to show again. He looked tired. He was exhausted.

JUNE 30–JULY 1: Elvis gave three shows at the Civic Auditorium in Omaha, Nebraska.

JULY 2: Elvis performed at the Salt Palace, Salt Lake City. Directly after his concert, he flew home to Graceland.

JULY 4: Elvis demonstrated karate at the Tennessee Karate Institute, where Red West, Sonny West, and Charlie Hodge participated. With members of his staff he lit firecrackers on the lawn of Graceland until dawn.

Elvis practiced martial arts with Bill Wallace and Dave Hebler (blinded in his right eye from a BB shot). Hebler owned a karate studio on Alsta Avenue in Glendora, California. Hebler became a member of the Memphis Mafia and traveled as Elvis's bodyguard.

AUG. 15: Elvis and his crew flew to Las Vegas to rehearse Elvis's next run of shows in the neon city.

AUG. 19: Barbra Streisand discussed with Elvis at the Hilton Hotel the possibility of Elvis costarring with her in the movie *A Star Is Born*. Although Elvis wanted to work with Streisand on the project, the Colonel said no. Parker did not want Elvis to play a drugged-out singer in any movie—it was too close to home.

AUG. 19–SEPT. 2: Elvis gave twenty-seven out of twenty-nine scheduled shows at the Hilton Hotel in Las Vegas. He was fatigued and ill almost every night. Parker and the hotel management sold "Souvenir Folio Concert Edition" booklets.

AUG. 19: The first time Elvis was recorded live in concert singing "If You Love Me (Let Me Know)" by John Rostill was at this Las Vegas concert. This version is heard on the bootleg LP *Big Boss Man*. During the concert Elvis sang "When the Snow Is on the Roses," which is on the bootleg LP *Special Delivery From Elvis Presley*.

AUG. 21: At his Las Vegas concert Elvis sang "Take These Chains From My Heart" and it may have been recorded, but it has never been released.

SEPT.: Rona Barrett's *Gossip* featured Elvis, Linda Thompson, and Priscilla on the cover with the inside story titled, "Elvis to Marry Linda Thompson—What Does He See in Her?"

SEPT. 2: Through sweat and tears, Elvis waved good-bye to the standing, cheering audience in Las Vegas. He had completed his obligations and planned to return to Memphis on September 5.

SEPT. 4: Elvis visited friend and fellow singer Vikki Carr before and after her opening performance at the Tropicana Hotel in Las Vegas. Sheila Ryan was Elvis's date for the evening, while Linda Thompson was safely tucked away at Graceland.

SEPT. 23: Elvis bought every available Lincoln Continental Mark IV in stock from Memphis's Shilling Lincoln-Mercury and then gave every car away.

SEPT. 27–28: Elvis performed at Maryland Fieldhouse at College Park, Maryland, to sell-out crowds.

SEPT. 29: Elvis performed at the Olympian Stadium in Detroit, Michigan, and local papers raved about his performance.

OCT.: Elvis appeared on the cover of *Pageant* for an article entitled "Elvis at 40."

OCT. 1: Elvis performed at the Notre Dame Athletic & Convention center, in South Bend, Indiana. He used *Playboy* publisher Hugh Hefner's black DC-9 jet to fly to and from concerts, and he was well acquainted with many of Hefner's "bunnies."

OCT 2–3: Elvis performed at the Civic Center in St. Paul, Minnesota, to sold-out crowds, who adored him.

OCT. 4: Elvis performed at Olympian Stadium in Dayton, Ohio.

OCT. 5: Elvis gave two shows at the Expo Convention Center in Indianapolis, Indiana, to standing room only.

OCT. 6: Elvis gave two shows at the University of Dayton Arena in Dayton, Ohio.

OCT. 7: Elvis performed at the Henry Levitt Arena in Wichita, Kansas, and complained to associates he did not feel well.

OCT. 8: Elvis performed at the Convention Center in San Antonio, Texas. The strain from his tour began to show.

OCT. 9: Elvis performed at the Abilene Expo Center in Abilene, Texas. Fans lined the streets for blocks.

OCT. 11: Edward L. Ashley filed a $6.3-million lawsuit against Elvis for the May 20, 1974, fighting incident at the Sahara Tahoe Hotel. It was later dismissed by the court.

OCT. 11–14: Elvis gave eight shows at the Sahara Tahoe Hotel in Stateline, Nevada, to capacity crowds, even though his appearance was changing— his face had become puffy, his belly was getting larger, and he sermonized more than usual.

OCT 29–31: RCA brought its portable studio equipment to Graceland so Elvis could record in private.

NOV.: *Rolling Stone* reported Elvis was still a superstar and a true American artist.

Elvis won a Grammy for Best Inspirational Performance from a track taken from the LP *Elvis Recorded Live* (in Memphis) with "How Great Thou Art."

DEC.: Elvis tried to reorganize his life and career while he recuperated from various ailments at Graceland. Vernon and the Colonel suspected that members of the Memphis Mafia were planning either to leave Elvis or to tell the whole truth about him, but they only hinted of this to Elvis. The King was already despondent and down. Although he had made hundreds of millions of dollars, there did not seem to be any money in most of his accounts, and worse, he couldn't remember

where he had spent millions of dollars. In bad health, and with Dr. George Nichopoulos prescribing as many prescription drugs for Elvis as he could swallow, it is a wonder the King could remember anything.

A December issue of *Celebrity* reported: "Elvis Presley was hospitalized for a 'recurrent ailment.' . . . The disturbing rumor persisted that the life of the King of Rock 'n' Roll, one of the greatest single music personalities of all time, was in grave danger. It was terribly ironic—even grotesque—that at the youthful age of forty, with every financial aid at his command, Elvis Presley, who throughout his spectacular career never smoked nor drank nor used any drugs because of his sound religious upbringing, should succumb to some mysterious weakness of the flesh that neither medical science nor clean living could conquer." Elvis's devoted fans refused to believe their idol was only human, and the magazine received stacks of negative mail.

▶ A cigar-toting Elvis exits an airplane in Charleston, North Carolina, July 11, 1975. *Courtesy of AP/Wide World Photos.*

1975

While rock bands battled heavy metal groups for record sales and concert attendance, Michael Jackson signed a solo contract with Epic, Billy Joel burst upon the music scene with "Piano Man," "Killer Queen" became Queen's first U.S. hit, the Who toured the States, Aerosmith's "Toys in the Attic" charted for a year, and Bruce Springsteen, Steely Dan, and David Bowie gained in popularity.

JAN. 1:   The criterion for determining gold-record status changed from five hundred thousand to 1 million copies sold.

JAN. 8:   Liberace sent Elvis (among other gifts) his cookbook as a fortieth birthday gift. Elvis was discouraged because he felt "over the hill." At midnight Elvis was rushed to the Baptist Memorial Hospital with severe stomach pains.

JAN. 9:   Elvis was admitted to Baptist Memorial Hospital in Memphis, but moved to Mid-South Hospital, suffering from an impacted colon and hypertension.

JAN. 9:   Rumors spread Elvis had had another face-lift to remove bags under his eyes, but no cosmetic surgery could reverse rapidly and dramatically advancing middle age, which had been enhanced by a dangerous potpourri of addictive prescription drugs, greasy junk food, and a grueling schedule. The Cat's stay at Mid-South Hospital was hush-hush. Medications caused his face and body to bloat.

Vernon Presley (having had a heart attack) entered the hospital on January 9 and roomed near Elvis. While Elvis was hospitalized, he put a $75,000 deposit on Robert L. Vesco's Boeing 707 jet. Elvis soon withdrew from the sale because Vesco was entangled in legal

problems and the FBI questioned Elvis about Vesco. Elvis worried he had indirectly ruined his chances to be given an undercover assignment from the FBI.

JAN 13:   Elvis was on the cover of *People*. The magazine announced, "Elvis is forty," which annoyed him no end. Fans still saw Elvis as the nineteen-year-old rebel rocker of their youth.

CA. JAN. 30:   Elvis was released from the hospital.

During the seventies, fans were told Elvis had been hospitalized for obesity, the flu, respiratory ailments, and bowel problems, but on many occasions he nearly died from drug overdoses. Vernon Presley gave him artificial respiration one time after a near-fatal drug overdose. Sonny West told how drugs altered Elvis's equilibrium: "Even his much vaulted [*sic*] karate seems to have been a myth fostered by the ever-present flatterers. . . . He was blocked out of his mind and very out of condition . . . opponents would let him win, and allow him to go on believing that he could whip all comers. In fact, most of the time, the downers made his coordination so bad that he was as much a danger to himself as to his sparring partner." (See *Elvis, the Illustrated Record.*) As a world-champion martial artist, Billy Blanks of Los Angeles told this author, "The most dangerous person in a sparring ring is someone who does not know how to fight in a controlled manner, or who is too out of it to understand what he or she is doing." Martial-arts champion Dale Kirby of Nashville confirmed, "Elvis was not a true black belt. People humored him, that's all. He was a big star. Those around him did all they could to keep him happy, so they managed to get him black belts whenever he wanted one. Elvis couldn't fight his way out of a paper bag against a true martial artist."

CA. FEB: Elvis was asked to star as Rudolph Valentino in the musical *Ciao Rudy* at Radio City Music Hall. Although Elvis was enthusiastic about the show, the Colonel ruined the deal by asking an absurd $2.5 million for Elvis's participation.

FEB. 1: Elton John joined Elvis at Graceland to celebrate Lisa Marie's birthday. Elton John was the child's favorite singer.

MAR.: The *Pure Gold* LP was released with Elvis in a gold suit on the cover (RCA ANL1-097[e]).

MAR. 10: At RCA's Hollywood studio, Elvis sang "Fairytale" by Anita and Bonnie Pointer. At concerts he told audiences, "The words are the story of my life."

MAR. 11: At RCA's Hollywood studio "And I Love You So" by Don McLean was recorded by Elvis. It was not made into a single, but it appears on four LPs and five bootleg albums. Bill Swan's arrangement of the Kris Kristofferson–Rita Coolidge song "I Can Help" was completed during that session. It was not released as a single.

Elvis had become excited about Tom Jones's version of "Green, Green Grass of Home." Elvis recorded the Claude "Curly" Putnam, Jr., song on March 11, while Marty Lacker and George Klein watched from a distance.

MAR. 12: "Bringing it Back" by Jimmy Gordon was recorded by Elvis at RCA's Hollywood studios, and it reached No. 65 on *Billboard*'s Top 100 during a five-week stay on the chart. Its flip side was "Pieces of My Life" (RCA PB-0401). Elvis also recorded Jerry Chesnut's "T-R-O-U-B-L-E," which reached No. 35 during its nine-week run on *Billboard*'s Hot 100 chart and No. 11 on the Country chart (RCA PB-10278, released in April 1975 with the flip side "Mr. Songman"). Elvis re-

corded "Shake a Hand," written by Joe Morris, and "Woman Without Love," written by Jerry Chesnut, which appears on the LPs *Elvis Aron Presley— Forever* and *Elvis Today*.

MAR. 13: "Pieces of My Life" by Troy Seals was recorded by Elvis at RCA's Hollywood studios. It reached No. 33 on *Billboard*'s Top 100 chart during a ten-week stay (RCA PB-10401).

MAR. 14: Elvis and his group flew to Las Vegas to rehearse for Elvis's opening in that city.

MAR. 18: Elvis, scheduled to perform twenty-nine shows, opened to packed houses at the Hilton Hotel in Las Vegas.

MAR. 22: For the bootleg LP *Long Lost Songs*, the Al Byron–Paul Evans song "Roses Are Red" and "You're the Reason I'm Living" by Bobby Darin were recorded from Elvis's live performance in Las Vegas. (Both were in a medley with "I'll Be There.")

MAR. 25–29: During the day, Elvis slept as much as he could. His hotel room was tomblike, with the windows covered to keep out sunlight. Without advance notice, the Colonel would periodically show up to inspect the situation and make sure Elvis was all right.

APR. 1: Elvis sang "How Great Thou Art" and "If You Love Me (Let Me Know)" at this Vegas concert, which are heard on the bootleg LP *Rockin' With Elvis April Fools' Day* (*Las Vegas, April 1, 1975*). This was the last night of the tour in Las Vegas.

APR. 2–7: Elvis stayed in a private home in Las Vegas and visited celebrity friends, while the Colonel gambled in casinos and drummed up new business deals.

APR. 24:   Elvis performed at the Coliseum in Macon, Georgia.

APR. 25:   Elvis performed at the Veterans Memorial Coliseum in Jacksonville, Florida, before a packed house. Fans became angry when he left the stage too soon and did not return for a finale. What they didn't realize was that their idol was throwing up in a backstage bathroom.

APR. 26:   Elvis gave two shows at the Curtis Hixson Hall in Tampa, while the Colonel reportedly brown-bagged cash selling photos, records, booklets, and other Elvis-related items.

APR. 27–28:   Elvis performed three shows at the Lakeland Civic Center in Lakeland, Florida.

APR. 29:   Elvis performed at the Murphy Athletic Center in Murfreesboro, Tennessee.

APR. 30–MAY 2:   Elvis gave three shows at the Omni in Atlanta, Georgia.

MAY 3:   Elvis was exhausted after giving two shows at the Civic Center in Monroe, Louisiana.

MAY 4:   Elvis gave two shows at the Civic Center in Lake Charles, Louisiana.

MAY 5:   Elvis gave a benefit concert for hurricane victims in McComb, Mississippi, at the State Fair Coliseum in Jackson, Mississippi. The event raised $108,000 for the survivors.

MAY 6–7:   Elvis performed at the Murphy Athletic Center in Murfreesboro, Tennessee. During these concerts, he told fans that a catastrophe can befall any person and sadly related the stories he had heard about the hurricane victims in McComb.

MAY 8–12:   Elvis looked over new singing material but found nothing he wanted to record immediately. He rested at Graceland, played gospel music at his piano day and night, and dealt with many difficulties within the Memphis Mafia.

MAY 28:   Elvis gave an electrifying performance at the Philadelphia Spectrum where Bruce Springsteen was in the audience.

MAY 29:   Elvis and Linda Thompson argued about everything, which infuriated him.

MAY 30–JUNE 1:   Elvis gave three dynamic performances at the Von Braun Civic Center in Huntsville, Alabama.

MAY–JUNE: Elvis sang "Jambalaya" at his concert in Louisiana where it was recorded live. It is on the bootleg LP *Eternal Elvis.*

CA. JUNE: Elvis and Linda Thompson's relationship was ending. He tired of the way she spent his money. At first, she refused to leave Graceland and managed to hang on much longer.

JUNE 3:   Elvis performed two shows at the Municipal Auditorium in Mobile, Alabama.

JUNE 4–5:   Elvis performed at the Hofheinz Pavilion in Houston, Texas, and allowed a myriad of female fans into his dressing room. He no longer wanted people to think he and Linda Thompson were lovers, so he let loose.

JUNE 5:   The press reported that the Colonel forced Elvis to turn down $3.5 million to do one concert for a promoter in London named Arthur Howes. The price may or may not have been true, but the concert opportunity was rejected.

JUNE 6: At Elvis's concert at the Convention Center in Dallas, Elvis sang a few lines from "School Day," written by Chuck Berry, and "I Got a Woman," both of which were recorded for the CD *Elvis Aron Presley (Dallas, June 6, 1975*, RCA PCD2-1185).

JUNE 7: Yet another live performance of "See See Rider" and "Tiger Man" were recorded during Elvis's concert in the Hirsch Coliseum in Shreveport, Louisiana. They are included on the CD *Elvis Aron Presley (Dallas, June 6, 1975)*.

JUNE 8–9: During Elvis's three shows at the State Fair Coliseum in Jackson, Mississippi, he enthusiastically sang "The American Trilogy," talked to the audience about his religious beliefs, and sang "Lawdy Miss Clawdy," "Blue Suede Shoes," and "I Got a Woman."

JUNE 10: Elvis performed at the Mid-South Coliseum in Memphis, and security was at an all-time high. Elvis was secretly rushed on and off the stage before fans could rip him to shreds. He still had sex appeal, or so it seemed to onlookers, despite his increased weight and sagging features.

JULY 8: During Elvis's performance at the Myriad Convention Center in Oklahoma City, Oklahoma, his hair dye began to stream down his face. In the dressing room after the concert, he ranted and raved about his hair's condition and said he was going to let his gray hair grow out. The Colonel forbid it, so Elvis was forced to redye his hair jet-black, which looked fake and tended to make his already pale face look more gaunt.

JULY 9: Elvis performed at the Hulman Civic Center in Terre Haute, Indiana.

JULY 10: Elvis performed at the Cleveland Coliseum in Cleveland, Ohio, and

some people complained that Elvis always sang the same songs. They wanted to hear new rock material.

JULY 11–12: Elvis performed at the Civic Center in Charleston, West Virginia, before a capacity crowd.

JULY 13: Elvis gave two shows at the International Convention Center in Niagara Falls, New York.

JULY 14–15: Elvis performed at the Civic Center in Springfield, Massachusetts, before a capacity crowd.

JULY 16–17: Elvis appeared at the Veterans Memorial Coliseum in New Haven, Connecticut.

JULY 17: Columnist Maggie Daly announced that Elvis was going to play the silent-screen star Rudolph Valentino (for $2.5 million) in a Broadway play titled *Ciao Rudy*, then star in a film of the same title.

JULY 18: Elvis performed at the Cleveland Coliseum in Cleveland, Ohio.

JULY 19: Elvis played a piano at a concert at the Nassau Coliseum in Uniondale, New York, and he sang an emotional, tear-jerking rendition of "You'll Never Walk Alone." He was also recorded singing "If You Love Me (Let Me Know)" and the gospel song "You Better Run" with Charlie Hodge on lead, which appear on the bootleg LP *America's Own*.

JULY 20: During one of his two concerts in Norfolk, Virginia, Elvis insulted Kathy Westmoreland and two members of the Sweet Inspirations and they walked off the stage. Myrna Smith remained, and Elvis presented her with a ring she refused to accept. Presents were not going to solve his abuse of females in his troupe. He later apologized to the "Sweets" and each lady received a $5,000 ring.

JULY 21: Elvis performed in Greensboro, North Carolina.

JULY 23–24: Elvis gave audience members over $220,000 worth of jewelry during his concerts in Asheville, North Carolina. Because fans heard of his generosity, scalpers knew they could ask almost *any* price for a ticket to the second night's show.

JULY 25: Elvis flew back to Graceland with his crew. Linda Thompson had allegedly overcharged his credit cards, but the Cat did nothing more than complain.

JULY 27: Elvis bought and gave away fourteen Cadillac Eldorados.

AUG.: Mike Stone and Priscilla Presley no longer lived together. Stone moved to Las Vegas, where he worked in a casino, and Priscilla pursued an acting career. For a fleeting moment, Elvis thought he would try to regain Priscilla's affection, but it was only an idea. He did nothing to pursue that goal.

AUG. 1–16: Elvis battled various illnesses and became emotionally distraught. He was becoming obese and appeared to be a gigantic, tragic figure.

AUG. 16: Elvis flew to Las Vegas with his crew.

AUG. 18–20: Scheduled to perform for three weeks, Elvis was forced to cancel most of his Las Vegas concerts at the Hilton Hotel due to illness. Elvis sang "Happy Birthday to You" to his guitarist James Burton during one Las Vegas concert. He often sang the song and it appears on four bootleg LPs including *Cadillac Elvis* and *The Legend Lives On*.

AUG. 21–SEPT. ?: Elvis was admitted to the Baptist Memorial Hospital in Memphis, where he remained for two weeks. His staff told reporters he suffered from exhaustion. Linda Thompson visited him almost every day.

AUG. 31: Elvis donated $5,000 to the Jerry Lewis Muscular Dystrophy Association's telethon. Frank Sinatra announced Elvis's generous gift to TV listeners.

SEPT.: The September issue of *Movie Stars* shows Elvis with Barbra Streisand and the claim "A 'Honeymoon' for Barbra and Elvis!" The Colonel had forced Elvis to turn down the lead in *A Star Is Born*, and the two stars had little to do with one another after that. Elvis admired Streisand's talent but felt she would probably have overshadowed him if they sang together.

SEPT. 1: Elvis was sworn as an honorary Shelby County deputy sheriff in Tennessee.

SEPT. 18: Elvis renewed his Tennessee driver's license, number 2571459.

SEPT. 29: Singer Jackie Wilson ("the black Elvis") was paralyzed and in a coma. Elvis sent money to his family.

OCT.: Elvis suffered from some undisclosed disorder and was very ill.

NOV.: Elvis purchased the *Lisa Marie* Convair 880 jet (N8800EP) for $1.2 million.

NOV.: Elvis appeared on the cover of *Country Music*.

NOV. 1–20: The Cat stayed inside and hid from the public. Rumors spread that he almost overdosed. During this period, he was demanding, rude, and impossible to please. If anyone gave him *real* concern, he threw him out of Graceland.

NOV. 28: Elvis flew to Las Vegas to set up his concerts at the Hilton Hotel and to rehearse. Linda Thompson accompanied Elvis to Vegas, but left after a few nights of hell.

DEC. 2: Elvis began seventeen shows at the Hilton Hotel in Las Vegas. Of course, the Colonel had been in Vegas for weeks, pumping enthusiasm. He knew "his boy" was no longer young, good-looking, or at peak performance, so Parker flooded the city with pictures, posters, and bulletins about Elvis's charismatic concerts. Every night's seats were sold out.

DEC. 10: Elvis became distraught during his concert on December 10. He began to preach seriously about the dangers of drugs, disloyal lovers, and sinfulness. People squirmed in their seats in discomfort. Some members of the Memphis Mafia claimed the Cat believed he was the second coming of Jesus Christ and that he thought he had been sent to earth to change people.

DEC. 13: "Softly, As I Leave You" was recorded in concert at the Hilton Hotel (RCA PB-11212, 1978). "America the Beautiful" was sung at concerts by Elvis from 1975 to his death. On December 13, it was recorded live at his midnight performance from the Las Vegas Hilton Hotel. It appeared first on a single with the flip side "My Way" (RCA PB-11165) in 1977. Failing to chart, it was later released on a CD.

DEC. 14: Private investigator John O'Grady suggested to Vernon Presley, the Colonel, and to Elvis that Red West, Sonny West, and Dave Hebler be fired from the Memphis Mafia. O'Grady accused these men of supplying drugs

to Elvis. Parker told Vernon to fire them. It was also rumored the boys were thinking of backstabbing Elvis with a tell-all book about his secret, private life.

DEC. 15: Elvis ended his Las Vegas concert series in an emotional, enthralling last half hour, filled with gospel songs and other old favorites.

DEC. 18: Dave Hebler and Sonny and Red West had problems dealing with an oversedated Elvis, and they often fought with the Cat and his father. The semblance of order within the Memphis Mafia had deteriorated, and all hell was breaking loose. No one seemed to know how to cope with Elvis's many physical and mental disabilities.

Elvis had become obsessed with the supernatural and the occult. He was also worried about becoming impotent and not being able to lose weight. He was a physical and mental wreck.

DEC. 25: Elvis gave the Colonel a Falcon jet for Christmas, which allegedly cost over $1 million. The Colonel predictably sold the airplane and kept the money.

DEC. 30: Elvis was on the cover of *Faces*, in an article entitled "Elvis Presley, the King Comes Back" (wearing glasses).

DEC. 31: Elvis's New Year's Eve performance broke concert receipt records in Pontiac, Michigan ($816,000). He accidentally tore his pants onstage and the Sweet Inspirations quickly took front and center stage to sing "Sweet, Sweet Spirit." Some 62,500 people were in the audience. The press had a heyday with the torn-pants episode. Elvis was so humiliated he considered not reappearing onstage, but he came back to a standing ovation.

Elvis was on the cover of *Celebrity* with an article titled, "Elvis, the Myth and the Malady." The press talked for months about the gifts that Elvis lavishly gave to friends, relatives, and strangers, especially at Christmas. The one that caught the most attention was a diamond medallion cross he gave five-year-old Rhonda Boler during a concert while he sang "Can't Help Falling in Love." He told the girl no one could take it from her. The scene was reenacted in the 1979 TV movie *Elvis*.

1976

Nineteen seventy-six marked America's bicentennial, and millions of citizens took to the streets to celebrate. Jimmy Carter was elected president, and eccentric billionaire Howard Hughes died. The most popular movies were *Rocky*, *All the President's Men*, and *Network*.

In 1976, a fat, sluggish Elvis could barely stand during a rigorous touring schedule that took him to ninety concert halls to complete 130 performances. His battle of the bulge was obvious when, bending down one night, he ripped his pants for the second time. Audiences were beginning to feel sorry for the Cat, and many people came to see if he would pass out or really let it *all* hang out!

JAN 7–14: Elvis bought five cars for $70,000 from the Kumpf Lincoln-Mercury dealership in Denver for police captain Jerry Kennedy, police doctor Gerald Starkey, and several Denver police officers while he vacationed in Vail, Colorado, with the boys.

JAN. 8: Author Bernard Benson sent Elvis a white, leather-bound $250 copy of his book *The Minstrel* as a birthday gift while Elvis vacationed in Vail, Colorado.

FEB.: An issue of *Movie Stars*, with Linda Thompson and Elvis on the cover, reported Elvis told Lisa Marie she would have a new mother. The truth was, all Elvis and Linda Thompson did was argue. She had become his lady-in-waiting, a servant who did everything he wanted her to do.

Elvis was on the cover of *Women's Weekly* in Australia, with an article, "Elvis: At 41, Still the King."

Serious talks between Arthur Fiedler, Elvis, and RCA to have Fiedler and Elvis do a record never led to anything, unfortunately.

FEB. 1: Dave Hebler maintained Elvis intended to wipe out with firearms every drug pusher in the Memphis area, but associates dissuaded him. Elvis's motivation may have been to show critics he was not hooked on drugs. To vent his many frustrations, target practice on recording equipment was common, and shooting TV sets became a form of entertainment.

Rev. David Cummins, pastor of the Christian Church adjoining Graceland, admitted in the *Midnight Globe* (Sept. 20, 1977) that Elvis was kept isolated and reclusive. Dave Hebler conceded,

▲ Elvis and Earl Malone (of the Spirit of Memphis gospel group). *Photograph by Ernest C. Withers. Copyright © 1994 Mimosa Records Productions, Inc.*

"Elvis hasn't had contact with the outside world for years."

FEB. 1: After they played pool and discussed law enforcement in the Jungle Room at Graceland, Elvis, Denver police captain Jerry Kennedy and Ron Pietrafeso of Colorado's Strike Force Against Crime were flown by pilots Milo High and Elwood Davis in the *Lisa Marie* from Memphis to Denver's Stapleton Airport (arrival time one-forty A.M.). There they ate Fool's Gold Loafs (huge sandwiches made with one pound of bacon, butter, Smucker's grape jelly, and Skippy peanut butter packed in a hollowed-out Italian-bread loaf and fried, at a cost of $49.95 each). Elvis drank Perrier water while his friends drank champagne. The group headed back to Memphis at five A.M.

FEB. 2–3: Elvis recorded at Graceland Larry Gatlin's "Bigger They Are, Harder They Fall" and "The Last Farewell" by Roger Whittaker and R. A. Webster. He was feuding with members of the "Memphis Mafia" at the time and trying to get rid of Linda Thompson. "She Thinks I Still Care," written by Dickie Lee, became a single with the flip side "Moody Blue" (RCA PB-10857, released in December 1976). The pair of songs peaked at No. 31 during a thirteen-week stay on *Billboard*'s Hot 100 chart, but "She Thinks I Still Care" was No. 1 within a week on the Country chart. The LP *Guitar Man* includes the song with a different instrumental track, added in October 1980 by Felton Jarvis at Young'Un Sound.

CA. FEB. 2–4: Elvis attempted to record "Running Scared," written by Roy Orbison and Joe Melson, at Graceland, but he was not pleased with any take. To date, the song has not been released.

FEB. 3–4: At his home studio at Grace-

land, Elvis recorded Neil Sedaka and Phil Cody's song "Solitaire." During twelve weeks on the Country chart, it peaked at No. 10 (RCA PB-11533). Its flip side was "Are You Sincere."

FEB. 4–5: At the end of the night on February 4, Elvis recorded at Graceland "I'll Never Fall in Love Again" by Jim Currie and Lonnie Donegan, and Mark James's "Moody Blue." The overdubbing of strings and instrumentals was done at a later date. "Moody Blue" was released in December 1976 and peaked at No. 31 on *Billboard*'s Hot 100 chart, at No. 1 on the Country chart, and No. 2 on the Easy-Listening chart (RCA PB-10857 with the flip side "She Thinks I Still Care"). Songs for the LP *From Elvis Presley Boulevard, Memphis, Tennessee*, were completed during these Graceland sessions (RCA ALP-1506).

FEB. 5–6: "Danny Boy" was recorded by Elvis during an evening session at Graceland. Elvis was also recorded singing the song in the Army, ca. 1959 (recently discovered). "Love Coming Down" by Jerry Chesnut was recorded that night, and it appears with "Danny Boy" on the LP *From Elvis Presley Boulevard, Memphis, Tennessee*. "For the Heart" by Dennis Linde (who played bass for the recording, which was overdubbed at a later date) peaked at No. 28 on *Billboard*'s Top 100 chart during an eleven-week run and No. 6 on the Country chart because of the popularity of its flip side, "Hurt," by Al Jacobs and Jimmie Craine.

FEB. 6–7: Elvis recorded at Graceland "Never Again," written by Jerry Chesnut and Billy Ed Wheeler, which can be heard on the LPs *From Elvis Presley Boulevard, Memphis, Tennessee* and *Our Memories of Elvis*, Vol. 1.

FEB. 8: At Graceland, Elvis recorded

Leon Rose's "Blue Eyes Crying in the Rain," which had been a 1975 hit for Willie Nelson. It is heard only on Elvis's LP *From Elvis Presley Boulevard, Memphis, Tennessee.*

MAR. 3: It has been alleged Elvis signed a thirteen-page last will and testament, which was witnessed by Ginger Alden, Charlie Hodge, and Ann Dewey Smith (wife of the attorney) on March 3, 1976. Elvis's entire estate was to go to his daughter, Lisa Marie, under trustee protection, and the will provided for the health, education, support, maintenance, and welfare of Lisa Marie, her great grandmother (Minnie Mae Presley), Vernon Presley, and any other relatives living at the time of Elvis's death.

The date of the will is March 3, 1976, but news accounts indicate that Elvis met Ginger Alden after *September* 1976. Linda Thompson was still living at Graceland in March 1976! It appears likely from all reliable period documentation that Elvis had not yet met, nor did anyone else at Graceland know well, Ginger Alden at the time of the will's signing. This is most problematic and points to a possible *invalid* last will and testament. Did those who signed the document make a mistake? Did they mean to date the will March 3, *1977?* The signatures on the document are, first, Ginger Alden, 4152 Royal Crest Place; Charles F. Hodge, 3764 Elvis Presley Boulevard, and Ann Dewey Smith, 2237 Court Avenue. The notary public was Drayton Beecher Smith II.

Elvis's will was admitted to probate and ordered recorded on August 22, *1977*. It appears in the record/file in Will Book 209, page 266, and was registered on August 24, 1977. Although leading books, such as *Elvis: His Life From A to Z*, state the will was dated March 3, *1977*, that is *not* correct. It was dated March 3, *1976*, and it was *not* formally recorded *any*where until after the singer's death. The year "1976" is printed four times in the will. No one corrected that to "1977."

Elvis's signature on the will is shaky and unsure. Because Elvis signed very few documents himself in his lifetime (others on his staff customarily forged everything with Elvis's signature), it is possible someone else signed his last will and testament and Elvis knew nothing about it. Could the document have been created at the last minute to avoid estate complications? If that is the case the incorrect date was, in haste, overlooked. One thing is certain: Elvis did not make good his promises to the many people he vowed he would remember. Vernon, who was named executor trustee, knew nothing of this will until after his son's death.

MAR.: A widow named Iladean Tribble announced in an Athens, Alabama, newspaper that she and Elvis were to be married on April 17. Five hundred people arrived for the ceremony—all except the King, who knew nothing about it.

MAR. 17–19: Elvis performed at Freedom Hall in Johnson City, Tennessee, giving two performances a night.

MAR. 20: Elvis gave two shows at the Coliseum in Charlotte, North Carolina.

MAR. 21: Elvis gave two shows at Riverfront Stadium in Cincinnati, Ohio.

MAR. 22: Elvis performed at the Kiel Auditorium in St. Louis, Missouri, before capacity crowds.

APR. 1: Priscilla sold her boutique Bis and Beau's, located at 9650 Santa Monica Boulevard in Los Angeles

APR. 20: Elvis borrowed $700,000 from the National Bank of Commerce to help finance a company called the Presley Center Courts, Inc., which opened a racquet-ball club with that name. Dr. George Nichopoulos was named president and Joe Esposito was vice president (Esposito's mother mortgaged her home to help finance the deal). Michael McMahon (a real estate developer) was also a partner. As chairman of the board, Elvis was responsible and liable for 25 percent of the venture, which ended up costing $1.3 million.

APR. 21: Elvis performed at the Kemper Arena in Kansas City, Missouri.

APR. 22: Elvis performed at the Civic Auditorium in Omaha, Nebraska, to a standing-room-only crowd.

APR. 23: Elvis performed at the McNichols Arena in Denver, Colorado.

APR. 24: At his San Diego concert at the Sports Arena, Elvis sang "My Woman, My Wife," written by Marty Robbins. It has not been released, even though it was recorded.

APR. 25: Elvis gave two shows at the Long Beach Arena in Long Beach, California.

APR. 26–27: Elvis performed at the Coliseum in Seattle, Washington, giving two shows a night to capacity crowds.

APR. 28: Elvis flew with his crew to Nevada to rehearse.

APR. 30: Elvis began fifteen shows at the Sahara Tahoe Hotel in Stateline, Nevada.

MAY 6: At the Sahara Tahoe, Elvis invited impressionist Douglas Roy to come onstage.

MAY 9: Elvis's Sahara Hotel concerts ended with the ailing singer giving his best to audiences.

MAY 27: Elvis, exhausted and frustrated with Memphis Mafia members'

continual complaining, performed at the Assembly Hall, Bloomington, Indiana.

MAY 28: Elvis performed at the Hilton Coliseum in Ames, Iowa.

MAY 29: Elvis's performance at the Myriad Convention Center in Oklahoma City was greeted with thunderous applause all night.

MAY 30: At his concert in the Ector County Coliseum in Odessa, Texas, Elvis was in a playful mood and sang to a fan "Young and Beautiful," "Happy Birthday," and "The Mickey Mouse Club March." These songs are heard on one bootleg LP, *Cadillac Elvis*.

MAY 31: Elvis performed at the Municipal Coliseum in Lubbock, Texas, and reminisced with his friends about the "good old days" when he, Buddy Holly, Johnny Cash, Scotty Moore, Bill Black, and others would jam in that town.

JUNE 1: Elvis performed at the Community Center Arena in Tucson, Arizona.

JUNE 2: Elvis performed at the Civic Center in El Paso, Texas.

JUNE 3: A wild, loud crowd greeted Elvis at the airport before his concert at the Tarrant County Convention Center in Fort Worth, Texas.

JUNE 4–6: Elvis gave four shows at the Omni in Atlanta, Georgia.

JUNE 8: Elvis and Linda Thompson did nothing but fight. She wanted Elvis to stop eating so much, stop pill-popping, and become responsible in their relationship. She only succeeded in infuriating Elvis.

JUNE 19: At his concert in Omaha, Nebraska, "How Great Thou Art" was taped for the LP *Elvis in Concert* (RCA CPL2-2587).

JUNE 25: Elvis performed at the Memorial Auditorium in Buffalo, New York, to a packed house.

JUNE 26: Two sell-out shows at the Civic Center in Providence, Rhode Island, pleased Elvis and his crew.

JUNE 27: Elvis gave two shows at the Capital Centre in Largo, Maryland.

JUNE 28: During a performance at the Spectrum in Philadelphia, Elvis took out a Bible and read from the Scriptures. He had taken on the role of "mentor to the masses," but his fans did not like it.

JUNE 29: Knowing he was losing steam and burning out again, Elvis performed energetically at the Coliseum in Richmond, Virginia, but collapsed in an airplane headed for North Carolina.

JUNE 30: Tired and irritable, Elvis nevertheless performed well to capacity crowds at the Coliseum in Greensboro, North Carolina. With increasing headaches, stomach pains, an aching back, and tired eyes, the Cat was beginning to believe the end was near. He obsessed about death, the hereafter, and heaven.

JULY: Elvis made the cover of *National Lampoon*, which poked fun at his age and weight. The July cover of *TV Picture Life* featured Elvis, Lisa Marie, and Priscilla in an article titled "My Daddy's Home Again."

JULY 1: Elvis performed at the Hirsch Coliseum in Shreveport, Louisiana, where throngs of people showed up to wish him well.

JULY 2: Elvis performed at the Assembly Center, Baton Rouge, Louisiana.

JULY 3: Elvis performed at the Tarrant County Convention Center in Fort Worth, Texas.

JULY 4: A very fat Elvis appeared in an Uncle Sam costume for a Fourth of July performance at Oral Roberts University in Tulsa, Oklahoma. The audience laughed along with Elvis, but it was not one of his best moments. Unfortunately, many photographs were taken of him during this show.

JULY 5: Elvis performed at the Mid-South Coliseum in Memphis, and there was a near riot to buy tickets to the concert. Police lined the streets, the auditorium, and backstage areas.

JULY 7: Elvis was upset when he heard the leading role for the movie *The Legend* (about the life of James Dean) was going to be played by Stephen McHattie. No one considered Elvis for the role because his looks had deteriorated and he was too fat. He blamed everyone around him for letting him become "ugly" and grotesque.

JULY 13: Sparks flew when Vernon Presley fired Dave Hebler and Sonny and Red West from Elvis's employ. Vernon had swiftly eliminated most of Elvis's close male companions, and now no one knew how to handle Elvis's mood swings. Elvis felt alone because he *was* alone.

Weighing close to 250 pounds, he still refused to believe his physical problems could not be "cured" with pills. He had an enlarged heart, glaucoma, persistent hypoglycemia, hypertension, a damaged kidney, a twisted colon, and a prescription-drug addiction. He was a physical wreck and feared he was going blind or dying of cancer. Popping quaaludes and Amytal worsened his condition.

Dr. Nichopoulos prescribed additional pills, professing he was attempting to "wean" his patient off drugs, but his advice made matters worse. Elvis swallowed handfuls of Percodan, Demerol, and Dilaudid pills to kill pain. He switched to downers, tranquilizers, quaaludes, and Valium whenever he needed a "fix."

Sadly, no one seemed to care enough about the man to force him to enter a drug rehab program or hire someone to help Elvis deal with his problem. They allowed him to die slowly in misery and anguishing pain.

CA. JULY 22: Elvis allegedly hired private investigator John O'Grady to throw Linda Thompson out of Graceland. She had lived with Elvis over four years. Why Elvis could not accomplish this task by himself is curious. Again, he had someone do the "dirty work" for him.

O'Grady (whom the King called "Reverend") had been hired earlier by Elvis to investigate charges against Elvis in a paternity suit. O'Grady was instrumental in getting Elvis a narcotics badge because O'Grady was in charge of the Narcotics Division of the Los Angeles Police Department. In 1973, Colonel Parker and Vernon Presley asked O'Grady to go secretly behind Elvis's back and find out who was supplying Elvis with drugs. O'Grady also alleged that Hebler and Sonny and Red West were to blame because they were irresponsible.

JULY 23: Elvis flew to Louisville, Kentucky, without his usual entourage, where he performed to a capacity audience at Freedom Hall. Colonel Parker made certain enough bodyguards and staffers were around Elvis so he would not harm himself or "get lost." Charlie Hodge loyally stayed by Elvis.

JULY 24: Elvis completed two shows at the Civic Center in Charleston, West Virginia.

JULY 25: Elvis performed at the Onondaga War Memorial Auditorium in Syracuse, New York.

JULY 26: Elvis performed at the Community War Memorial Auditorium in Rochester, New York.

JULY 27: Linda Thompson told reporters and friends that Elvis was self-destructive and she could no longer stand to see him hurt himself, nor could she continue to "baby-sit" Elvis. Thus, she moved out of Graceland. She lamented he could have died many times because he took too many sleeping pills.

CA. JULY: Elvis briefly dated Ann Pennington and Sheila Ryan.

JULY 27: Elvis performed again at the Onondaga War Memorial Auditorium in Syracuse, New York.

JULY 28: Elvis performed at the Civic Center in Hartford, Connecticut.

JULY 29: Elvis appeared at the Civic Center in Springfield, Massachusetts.

JULY 30: Elvis performed at Veterans Memorial Coliseum in New Haven, Connecticut.

JULY 31–AUG. 1: Elvis sold out every performance at the Coliseum in Hampton Roads, Virginia.

AUG. 2: Elvis performed at the Civic Center in Roanoke, Virginia.

AUG. 3–5: Elvis tirelessly performed at the Cumberland County Memorial Auditorium in Fayetteville, North Carolina. He became ill after his last performance and was rushed to a hotel suite where he was sedated. The next morning he was flown to Graceland to recuperate.

AUG. 5–26: Elvis was despondent and miserable. Colonel Parker was busy setting up more concert dates and filling in the holes left by Hebler and the Wests. But Elvis was becoming extremely paranoid. He thought things were missing and believed his bank accounts were short of funds. No one seemed to give a damn about his deteriorating health. His life had become a disaster.

AUG. 27: Elvis performed at the Convention Center in San Antonio, Texas. Fans were thrilled to see him back onstage.

AUG. 28: Elvis performed at the Hofheinz Pavilion in Houston, Texas, to an audience of cheering fans.

AUG. 29: Elvis gave a concert at the Municipal Auditorium, Mobile, Alabama.

AUG. 30: Elvis performed at the Memorial Coliseum in Tuscaloosa, Alabama, to capacity crowds.

AUG. 31: Elvis performed at the Coliseum in Macon, Georgia.

SEPT.: The last car Elvis purchased was a 1976 Cadillac Eldorado, equipped with a TV, telephone, bar, and CB radio. He bought over 270 cars in his life, most of which he gave to strangers or friends.

An issue of *TV Star Parade* featured Priscilla and Elvis on the cover and hinted they were to reunite.

SEPT. 1: Elvis performed at the Veterans Memorial Coliseum in Jacksonville, Florida, and many fans were shocked to see how fat he had become.

SEPT. 2: Elvis performed at the Curtis Hixson Hall in Tampa, Florida to an older, less enthusiastic crowd.

SEPT. 3: Elvis performed at the St. Petersburg Bay Front Center, Florida, to a sold-out crowd.

SEPT. 4: Elvis gave two shows at the Civic Center in Lakeland, Florida, and stayed up all night reading the Bible to female fans.

SEPT. 5: Elvis performed at the State Fair Civic Center in Lakeland, Florida, to a capacity crowd.

SEPT. 6: Elvis performed at the Von Braun Civic Center in Huntsville, Alabama, where he sang "The American Trilogy," "In the Ghetto," and "Heartbreak Hotel."

SEPT. 7: The *Memphis Press-Scimitar* ran an article titled "Fat and Forty—But Also Sold-Out." This kind of publicity enraged the Cat.

SEPT. 7–8: Elvis performed at the Convention Center in Pine Bluff, Arkansas, giving two performances a night.

END OF SEPT.: Elvis was hospitalized for hypertension at Baptist Memorial Hospital in Memphis.

CA. OCT.: Elvis met and dated former beauty queen Ginger Alden after asking George Klein to set up a meeting with Ginger's sister, Terry (who was Miss Tennessee). Ginger came with Terry, and Elvis's interest switched to Ginger. He had gone from being almost pathologically promiscuous to impotent, but Alden soon contended she and Elvis were to become engaged.

Elvis fantasized about rekindling his relationship with Priscilla after their divorce. Ex-girlfriend Linda Thompson claimed Elvis had no intention of marrying Ginger Alden. (See *Midnight Globe*, Sept. 29, 1977.) Thompson's brother, Sam, was Elvis's bodyguard during this period. Sam, Vernon Presley, and Bill E. Burk claimed Elvis had no plans to marry Alden.

In Harry McCarthy's article "Elvis Never Planned to Wed Ginger," the author stated that Elvis sent Alden home when he went on tour so he could date backup singer Kathy Westmoreland, and Linda Thompson confirmed the statement.

Elvis gave J. D. Sumner of the Stamps a white, 1976 Lincoln Continental, a $40,000 diamond ring, and a $4,000 watch.

OCT. 14–15: Elvis performed at the Civic Center in Chicago to screaming, wild audiences.

OCT. 16: Elvis performed in Duluth, Minnesota, and his hands were dripping with jewels. Although many fans hoped Elvis would toss them their way, he did not.

OCT. 17: Elvis performed at the Metropolitan Sports Center in Minneapolis, Minnesota, to a sold-out house.

OCT. 18: Elvis gave an energetic performance at the Arena in Sioux Falls, South Dakota.

OCT. 19: Elvis performed at the Dane County Coliseum in Madison, Wisconsin. The mayor proclaimed it Elvis Presley Day in Madison.

OCT. 20: Elvis performed at the Notre Dame University Athletic and Convention Center in South Bend, Indiana.

OCT. 21: Elvis performed at the Wings Stadium in Kalamazoo, Michigan.

OCT. 22: Elvis appeared at the Assembly Hall in Champaign, Illinois. He threw teddy bears and scarves into the exuberant audience.

OCT. 23: Elvis performed at the Cleveland Coliseum in Cleveland, Ohio, and gave tear-jerking renditions of "The American Trilogy" and "Suspicious Minds."

OCT. 24: Elvis performed at Roberts Memorial Stadium in Evansville, Indiana, while the Colonel's staffers sold out of Elvis memorabilia.

OCT. 25: Elvis gave a concert at Memorial Coliseum, Fort Wayne, Indiana.

OCT. 26: Elvis's emotionally charged performance at the University of Dayton Arena in Dayton, Ohio, was overwhelmingly successful, although some critics felt Elvis was too overweight to be seductive. He was a *fat* Cat.

OCT. 27: Elvis performed at the South Illinois University Arena in Carbondale, Illinois. Becoming fatigued, he went directly to his hotel after the concert and told staffers to leave him alone. No longer were the Memphis Mafia members there to soothe him or keep his secrets. Almost everyone had disappeared. Now, his three stepbrothers and Charlie Hodge were doing what Red West, Sonny West, Dave Hebler, and others had done so proficiently. The stepbrothers appeared more interested in acquiring drugs, women, and having a good time than they were in tending to Elvis's every whim. The boys were young and had rarely traveled. It was an adventure for them to see the music world from the inside.

OCT. 29–30: During October and November, Elvis slept only during the day and recorded and read at night. At Graceland he recorded "It's Easy for You" by Andrew Lloyd Webber and

Tim Rice, which was later overdubbed at Young'Un Sound in Nashville in April 1977. The song appears on the LP *Moody Blue*. Elvis completed "Pledging My Love" by Ferdinand Washington and Don Robey, then recorded "Way Down," written by Layng Martine, Jr., with J. D. Sumner as a bass vocal backup. "Way Down"/"Pledging My Love" hit *Billboard*'s No. 1 spot in August 1977, during a seventeen-week stay on the Country chart (RCA PB-10998, released in July 1977). During "Way Down"'s twenty-one weeks on the Top 100 chart, it peaked at No. 18, while it reached No. 14 on the Easy-Listening chart. As Elvis's seventeenth No. 1 record in England, it tied Elvis with the Beatles for the most No. 1 records there. Elvis finished "There's a Fire Down Below," by Elvis's bass player Jerry Scheff, but only the instrumental for the song has surfaced.

OCT. 31–NOV. 1: "He'll Have to Go" by Joe Allison was recorded by Elvis at Graceland. It is on the *Moody Blue* LP.

NOV.: When Elvis heard that Red West, Sonny West, and Dave Hebler had hired Australian columnist Steve Dunleavy to write a book about his private life, he allegedly offered each of them $50,000 not to do it. They turned him down. No longer were they under Elvis's control. They had been kicked out of his life. They needed money and they wanted their own shot at fame. The first printings of four hundred thousand and two hundred thousand copies sold out the next year. When Elvis realized they were going to tell it like it was, he went into the deepest depression of his life. It was completely downhill after that.

NOV. 1: The last song to be recorded at Graceland by Elvis was "Feelings" by Morris Albert. Although several takes were tried, it remained incomplete.

NOV. 2: Elvis bought Ginger Alden a

white Lincoln Continental Mark V and many other gifts.

CA. NOV. 10: The president's brother, Billy Carter, and his wife visited Elvis at Graceland and exclaimed, "You're guarded better than the president!" but Elvis felt as if he had no guards left.

NOV. 23: Jerry Lee Lewis was arrested for making threats outside Graceland. Elvis was not at home.

NOV. 24: Elvis performed at the Centennial Coliseum in Reno, Nevada.

NOV. 25: Elvis performed at the McArthur Court in Eugene, Oregon.

NOV. 26: Elvis performed at the Memorial Coliseum in Portland, Oregon, to enthusiastic crowds.

NOV. 27: Elvis again performed at the McArthur Court in Eugene.

NOV. 28–29: Elvis gave inspired performances at the Cow Palace in San Francisco, but it was obvious to his fans that something was drastically wrong and that he had physical problems that he could no longer hide. The curious bought tickets to Elvis's concerts to gawk at him, but Elvis tried not to let his physical problems alter his performance. He truly was the consummate entertainer. He did the best he knew how to do, regardless of how sick he felt.

NOV. 30: Elvis performed at the Anaheim Convention Center in Anaheim, California. After this performance, he may have gone to see Priscilla and Lisa Marie.

DEC. 2: Elvis began what would be his last performances in Las Vegas, at the Hilton Hotel.
At one performance Elvis ranted

and raved about the evils of drugs. He bellowed, "The other night I had the flu real bad. Someone started the report that I was strung out. If I ever find out who started that, I'll knock their goddamn head off. I've never been strung out in my life." (See *Elvis, The Illustrated Record.*) Colonel Parker was horrified when Elvis swore onstage. He had been swearing a lot lately, and his language was slipping back to that of a Southern hillbilly. The hotel management was upset and told the Colonel to control the Cat.

DEC. 7: A note Elvis wrote on December 7, in a Vegas penthouse suite best explains the desperate mental state that possessed him for years: "I feel so alone sometimes. The night is quiet for me. I would love to be able to sleep. I am glad everyone is gone now. I will probably not rest tonight. I have no need for all of this. Help me, Lord." This note was found by a cleaning person in a wastepaper basket inside Elvis's master bedroom. (It was auctioned at Sotheby's on June 22, 1991.) The letter shows how despondent Elvis had become. He weighed close to 235 pounds and was bloated. Many people found his appearance offensive, and most of those around him accused him of being addicted to hard drugs. He was dejected, gloomy, continuously drugged, and his career had taken a turn for the worse. The handwriting was not only on Elvis's note, it was on the wall.

DEC. 8: Rev. Rex Emanuel Humbard hosted a religious TV show called "Cathedral of Tomorrow" from Akron, Ohio. He claimed Elvis summoned him to the Hilton Hotel to admit his life was coming to an end and asked, "Christ is gonna come real soon, isn't he?" A Los Angeles reporter wrote of that meeting after Elvis had died: "For thirty minutes . . . Elvis talked of nothing but the Scriptures. He quoted the Old Testament of the Bible . . . [and

asked] 'We don't have long then, do we?' and Humbard replied, 'No, we don't.' Elvis shook and trembled. It was an emotional hour of urgency. Elvis sensed he would die soon. Lisa Marie ran into the room and asked why Elvis was crying. Humbard said, 'I think it was a premonition of something. He was reaching for something spiritual, and I think he found some of what he was looking for.' " (*Los Angeles Times*, AP report, "Elvis Felt Second Coming . . . ," Aug. 30, 1977.) It is not confirmed that Lisa Marie was in Las Vegas during this period. If she had been there, it would have been exceedingly painful for the child to see her father in the mental and physical state he was in.

DEC. 9: Despite his many aches and pains, and his heavy reliance on various medications, Elvis did not end up in a hospital during this last Las Vegas concert booking, nor did he miss one performance. Each show opened with blaring horns, and before Elvis's entrance a comedian, gospel group, and a trio warmed up audiences. Although his energy level dropped, he still caused fans to rise in standing ovations night after night. Two-hour concerts never satisfied them.

DEC. 9–10: Ginger Alden and her family visited Elvis in Las Vegas. Elvis was the consummate host to the Aldens, although he was miserable and in pain. He lavished gifts on them all.

DEC. 11: At his concert at the Las Vegas Hilton, Elvis and the Stamps sang a few lines of the gospel song "When God Calls Me Home." It is not on any release. During the concerts on December 11, Elvis threw karate moves into his act, read from the Bible, and told the audience of the lies being written and spoken about him.

DEC. 12: Elvis completed his fifteen shows at the Las Vegas Hilton, ending with "Suspicious Minds," "My Way," and "The American Trilogy," which caused many members of the audience to cry. When Elvis waved to the audience on December 12, it was the last time he would say good-bye onstage to an adoring Las Vegas crowd, but no one knew it at the time.

His love affair with Vegas would never be forgotten or equaled. He was the most popular draw the city had ever known. And that pleased Elvis, because when he first gave a concert there, he was nearly booed offstage. Vowing he would come back and make a difference, for certain, he did it *his way*.

CA. DEC. 24:   Elvis refused to give his three partners any more money to develop their racquet-ball club venture. It had become a financial disaster, and Elvis believed he had been bilked out of hundreds of thousands of dollars.

DEC. 25:   Elvis donated $1,000 to policeman Kelly Lange, gave cars to strangers and friends, and contributed $52,000 to charity.

DEC. 27:   Elvis performed at the Henry Levitt Arena in Wichita, Kansas.

DEC. 28:   Elvis, in the Christmas spirit, sang many religious songs during his concert at the Memorial Auditorium in Dallas, Texas.

DEC. 29:   Elvis performed at the Civic Center in Birmingham, Alabama, before a crowd of cheering fans.

DEC. 30:   Elvis performed at the Omni in Atlanta, Georgia.

DEC. 31:   Elvis's flamboyant, glittering costumes and energetic New Year's performance at the Civic Center Arena in Pittsburgh, Pennsylvania, were warmly received. At this concert, Elvis sang an emotional "Auld Lang Syne" after "Funny How Time Slips Away."

◀ A bloated Elvis singing before 14,000 fans in Providence, Rhode Island, May 23, 1977. *Courtesy of AP/Wide World Photos.*

1977

In 1977, President Jimmy Carter pardoned all Vietnam draft evaders, ending the U.S. monopoly of the Panama Canal, and called the energy crisis the "moral equivalent of war." Eighty million viewers watched Alex Haley's *Roots* on ABC-TV, and the most popular movies of the year were *Star Wars, Pumping Iron, Close Encounters of the Third Kind,* and *Saturday Night Fever.*

In August 1977, the world's greatest rock 'n' roller died in his home, a few miles from the studio where he first recorded a song. After climbing out of poverty and despair to the very pinnacle of success, fame, and fortune, Elvis met his end on a bathroom floor in Graceland, a bloated shell of the sexy, sneering rock 'n' roll idol he once was. A stunned world was moved to tears as it mourned the death of the King.

JAN.   *TV Star Parade* showed Priscilla and Elvis on the cover with a rumored story, "Secret Marriage for Priscilla and Elvis."

Elvis gave money to several people to write a screenplay titled *Billy Easter*, which was to be a nonsinging film role for him. It was never finished.

JAN. 1:   Colonel Parker booked the ailing Elvis in fifty-five concert locations.

JAN. 8:   Elvis spent his birthday with his daughter in California. Priscilla couldn't help but notice that her ex-husband had deteriorated since their last visit.

JAN. 26:   Ginger Alden claimed Elvis proposed to her in the bathroom adjacent to his bedroom. And although he bought her an 11.5-carat diamond ring, it was not intended as an engagement ring. Although it was never announced they were to be married, Alden con-

tended it was to be made public on Christmas day.

FEB. 2:   Elvis did not appear in Nashville for a scheduled recording session. He stayed in his hotel with Ginger Alden and complained about acquaintances and assassins wanting to kill him. When Elvis was high, he often ordered his bodyguards to "rip the eyeballs out" of any assailant before an attacker could be brought to trial. Knowing politicians and stars were targets of overzealous or insane fanatics, Elvis obsessed about being assassinated. Fearing he would be shot during a performance, he often wore a heavy bulletproof vest. Taking diet pills by the handful, his physical appearance deteriorated and his mental haze led to erratic behavior and unpredictable demands.

FEB. 12:   Elvis performed at the Sportatorium in Hollywood, Florida.

FEB. 13:   Elvis performed at the Civic Auditorium in West Palm Beach, Florida, surrounded by bodyguards.

FEB. 14:   For Valentine's Day, Elvis gave a loving, long concert at the St. Petersburg Bay Front Center in Florida. Ginger Alden attended the concert, after which Elvis went into the bathroom for several hours. He was anything but romantic.

FEB. 15:   Elvis performed at the Sports Stadium in Orlando, Florida.

FEB. 16:   Elvis and his entourage flew to Alabama, where he performed at the Garrett Coliseum in Montgomery.

FEB. 17:   Elvis performed to a full

house at the Savannah Civic Center in Georgia.

FEB. 18:   Elvis appeared at the Carolina Coliseum in Columbia, South Carolina.

FEB. 19:   Elvis performed at Freedom Hall in Johnson City, Tennessee, to an overcapacity, frantic crowd.

FEB. 20–21:   Elvis performed at the Coliseum in Charlotte, North Carolina. During his concert on February 20, he introduced Miss Tennessee to the audience. She went onstage to play a classical piano number, which the audience did not appreciate.

MAR. 3:   The date that some people allege Elvis's last will and testament was signed.

MAR. 23:   Elvis performed at the Arizona State University Athletic Center in Tempe, Arizona.

MAR. 24:   Elvis performed at the Civic Center in Amarillo, Texas.

MAR. 25–26:   Elvis performed at the Lloyd Noble Center in Norman, Oklahoma.

MAR. 27:   Elvis appeared at Taylor County Coliseum in Abilene, Texas.

MAR. 28:   Elvis performed at the Municipal Auditorium in Austin, Texas.

MAR. 29–30:   Elvis flew to Louisiana and performed at Rapides Parish Coliseum in Alexandria. Directly after the concert he was rushed by plane to Memphis. He was an exhausted and depressed man.

APR. 1:   Elvis entered Baptist Memorial Hospital in Memphis, critically ill. It was reported he suffered from intestinal flu and fatigue. Prescription drugs

and a junk-food diet helped to destroy his body by draining his system of nutrients and energy. He often binged on doughnuts for weeks at a time, then switched to ice cream and greasy cheeseburgers. When he was forced to lose weight in order to perform, he went on crash diets, became weak and irritable, and dropped up to fifty pounds in a month. It is understandable how he became a physical wreck. The more people complained about his appearance or weight, the worse the situation became.

Many people suspected drugs were ravaging Elvis's physical and mental stability. Drugs killed Hank Williams, Jim Morrison, Janis Joplin, Jimi Hendrix, and many other members of the music community. Elvis didn't drink liquor or smoke cigarettes but consumed every prescribed barbiturate and amphetamine he could con his doctor to order for him, while he publicly denounced junkies.

APR. 5:   Telling reporters he had intestinal flu, Elvis left Baptist Memorial Hospital, after canceling a concert that was to be given at the Louisiana State University Assembly Center.

APR. 6:   As he attempted to recuperate at Graceland, no one knew what to do to cheer the ailing Elvis.

APR. 6–18:   Throngs of fans waited outside Graceland's gates. People worried the King was dying. He was rarely seen in public now. His stepbrothers admittedly brought him as many prescription drugs as he wanted.

APR. 21:   Elvis performed at the Coliseum in Greensboro, North Carolina.

APR. 22:   Elvis performed at the Olympia Stadium in Detroit, Michigan.

APR. 23:   Elvis performed at the University of Toledo Centennial Hall in Toledo, Ohio.

APR. 24: At his April 24 concert at the Crisler Arena in Ann Arbor, Michigan, RCA recorded Elvis singing "Unchained Melody." He played the piano with no band accompaniment. RCA overdubbed percussion, bass, and organ instrumentations and released this performance on the LP *Moody Blue*. It later appeared on *Great Performances* and in other mixes in 1978 and 1980.

APR. 25: Elvis performed at the Saginaw Civic Center in Saginaw, Michigan. At this concert, Elvis was recorded singing Maurice Williams's "Little Darlin'." As a single, it did not chart (RCA 50476, released in October 1978, with the flip side "I'm Movin' On"). The LP *Elvis—A Canadian Tribute* includes songs performed at the Saginaw concert.

APR. 26: Elvis performed at the Wings Stadium in Kalamazoo, Michigan.

APR. 27: Elvis gave a concert at the Milwaukee Arena in Milwaukee, Wisconsin.

APR. 28: Elvis performed at the Brown County Veterans Memorial Coliseum in Green Bay, Wisconsin, to a capacity crowd.

APR. 29: Elvis gave an emotionally charged concert at the Arena in Duluth, Minnesota.

APR. 30: Elvis performed at the Civic Center in St. Paul, Minnesota, to a full house.

MAY: One of the only things Vernon Presley ever did that pleased Elvis was the day in May he filed for divorce from Dee Stanley Presley. Dee had accused Elvis of instigating and encouraging her three sons' bouts with hard drugs and alcohol. She alleged that Graceland was filled with intrigue, sickness, dissent, paranoia, vast greed, and loneliness.

MAY 1–2: Elvis performed at the Chicago Stadium in Chicago, Illinois, to an exhilarated audience.

MAY 3: Elvis was becoming tired again. The schedule Colonel Parker had arranged was too much for any person to handle without the use of uppers and downers. Yet, Elvis performed almost flawlessly at the Saginaw Civic Center in Saginaw, Michigan. He never wanted to let down an audience. He realized many people had to sacrifice to purchase tickets to see him perform and well remembered the time when his mother could not afford the price of an admission ticket to the Mississippi-Alabama Fair.

MAY 4: Elvis flew home to Memphis. Everyone around him was complaining about something. It was a nightmare.

MAY 19: Joe Esposito, Dr. Nichopoulos, and Michael McMahon sued Elvis for $150,000. They claimed he had not kept promises made in regard to the Presley Courts and insisted Elvis had agreed to give them continuous financial help to run their jointly owned racquet-ball club. Elvis refused to be sucked in any further. The business deal was a financial catastrophe, and Elvis owed the bank $700,000 plus interest on the loan he had taken out to start the club.

MAY 20: Elvis performed at the Stokely Athletic Center in Knoxville, Tennessee.

MAY 21: Elvis performed at Freedom Hall in Louisville, Kentucky.

MAY 22: Elvis performed at Capital Center in Landover, Maryland.

MAY 23: Elvis appeared at the Civic Center in Providence, Rhode Island.

MAY 24: Elvis performed at the Civic Center in Augusta, Maine.

MAY 25: Elvis gave a concert at the Community War Memorial Auditorium in Rochester, New York.

MAY 26–27: Elvis performed in Binghamton, New York.

MAY 27: Elvis binged on food and then decided to go on another diet. Because he was hungry all the time, he nervously bit his nails.

MAY 28: Elvis performed at the Spectrum in Philadelphia before a wild group of teenagers and young adults. Near the end of the concert, he drank so much soda the band thought he would not be able to finish the concert.

MAY 29: Elvis left the Civic Center stage in Baltimore due to illness, but returned to finish the set.

MAY 30: Psychic Gloria James made headlines when she predicted Elvis would soon die. Her views were aired on WMEX, a Boston radio station. Because of her predictions, security guards surrounded Elvis day and night. During a concert at the Veterans Memorial Coliseum in Jacksonville, Florida, Elvis spoke to fans about his many problems.

JUNE 1: Elvis performed at the Coliseum in Macon, Georgia.

JUNE 2: Elvis performed at the Municipal Auditorium in Mobile, Alabama, to a huge crowd, which was shocked to see what horrible shape Elvis was in.

JUNE 3: Elvis went back to Memphis to rest.

JUNE 17: Elvis performed at the Hammons Center in Springfield, Missouri.

JUNE 18: Elvis won two *Photoplay* Gold Medal Awards (Favorite Variety Star and Favorite Rock Music Star), which were the last two awards he received during his life.

JUNE 18: Elvis performed at the Kemper Arena in Kansas City, Missouri, and was energetic, humorous, and emotional.

JUNE 19: CBS-TV filmed "Elvis in Concert" at the Omaha Civic Auditorium in Omaha, Nebraska. (Aired posthumously, October 3, 1977, by CBS-TV, a one-hour special ending with a few words from Vernon Presley.) A haggard, yet pleasant-mannered Elvis appeared to be uncomfortable and in pain, but his performance was enthusiastically delivered. He belonged to the audience, no matter what. He loved them and they knew it.

JUNE 20: Elvis performed at Pershing Municipal Auditorium in Lincoln, Nebraska. He was exhausted and looked terrible and asked a CBS-TV film crew not to film his concert that night.

JUNE 21: CBS-TV filmed scenes for its upcoming "Elvis in Concert" at the Rushmore Plaza Civic Center in Rapid City, South Dakota. Elvis only seemed satisfied when he sat at a piano to play "Unchained Melody." As perspiration dripped from his long, dyed-black hair and down his haggard-looking, puffy face, he occasionally smiled at his crew and sipped a Coke. He put every ounce of energy he had left into that concert.

As he performed in Rapid City, Elvis was recorded singing "See See Rider" (on the LP *Elvis in Concert*) and gave an impassioned rendering of "My Way." This recording was released in November 1977, and peaked at No. 6 on *Billboard*'s Easy-Listening chart and No. 22 during a twelve-week stay on the Hot 100 chart (RCA PB-11165, with the flip side "America the Beautiful").

RCA recorded "Unchained Melody" and released it as a single with the flip side "Softly As I Leave You." "Unchained Melody" reached No. 6 during an eleven-week stay on *Billboard*'s Country chart (RCA PB-11212, released in March 1978).

JUNE 22: Elvis performed at the Arena in Sioux Falls, South Dakota, before a huge crowd.

JUNE 23: Elvis performed at the Veterans Memorial Auditorium in Des Moines, Iowa.

JUNE 24: Before a concert at Dane County Coliseum in Madison, Wisconsin, Elvis complained of stomach pains. Yet, he gave his all when he was onstage and nearly passed out after the show.

JUNE 25: Elvis performed at Riverfront Stadium in Cincinnati, Ohio. Although Elvis was in severe pain, his fans were not cheated out of a decent performance.

JUNE 26: Elvis gave his last public performance at Market Square Arena in Indianapolis, Indiana. By this date, he had completed fifty-six concert obligations in 1977. Due to severe head, stomach, and muscle pain, continuous diarrhea, and bouts with vomiting, Elvis had previously been forced to cancel shows in Baton Rouge, Louisiana (for March 31, 1977); Mobile, Alabama (for April 1); Macon, Georgia (on April 2); and Jacksonville, Florida (for April 3). Elvis rescheduled each of these canceled concerts because he did not want any fan to lose money. The public worried the King was dying. Tickets to any canceled concert would be kept as a part of a long legacy of memories that Elvis had given to fans.

Elvis and several band members became ill in Indianapolis, and they were all hospitalized overnight.

JUNE 27: Elvis recuperated in Memphis and fans flocked to Graceland's gates, fearing the worst might come to pass, but Elvis acted as if nothing were wrong and told those who were concerned that he planned to start a new concert tour in Portland, Maine, on August 17.

JUNE 28: Fans surrounded Graceland while Elvis stayed in bed with "the flu."

JULY: Eva-Tone produced "The Elvis Presley Story," a 33⅓-rpm sampler soundsheet for RCA Record Club, which was a promotional tool for Candlelite Music's *The Elvis Presley Story*, a boxed set (Eva-Tone 726771XS). They were never distributed or sold extensively, but collectors were offered the set (which included eleven already-released hits by Elvis).

JULY 1–18: Elvis was extremely ill. He slept up to fifteen hours a day. If he got out of bed, it was to go to the bathroom or play gospel music at his piano in the music room. Visitors came and left, many never seeing the King.

JULY 19: On Los Angeles' "Nine in the Morning Show" (KHJ-TV), psychic Jacqueline Eastland predicted that Elvis was about to die. His body was swollen. He suffered from countless physical ailments. He was emotionally depressed and dependent on pills (and many sources wrongfully claimed he had become addicted to cocaine and heroin as well). Little gratification was left in his life, and he felt he had nothing to live for. Nevertheless, the Colonel told the Cat he should prepare for another singing tour of New England.

CA. AUG.: To stimulate interest in the boxed set *Elvis Presley's Greatest Hits*, a 33⅓-rpm sampler with music and interviews by Elvis was distributed by *Reader's Digest*.

AUG. 1: It didn't take a psychic to realize Elvis was not in good health, but Philadelphia papers ran psychic Marc Salem's prophecy that Elvis would soon be dead, and on that same day the explosive book *Elvis: What Happened?* written by Steve Dunleavy (as told to him by three ex-members of the Memphis Mafia—Red West, Sonny West, and Dave Hebler) was released, causing Elvis to sink into deeper heartbreak, despair, and rage. He felt betrayed.

The book revealed the bizarre private and professional world of Elvis Presley. The cover stated Elvis was "brooding. Violent. Obsessed with death. Strung out. Sexually driven. This is the other side of Elvis—according to the three men who lived with him through it all—a man who . . . charms a beautiful young fan into joining him—on a drug binge for two that nearly kills her. . . . Has for years leaned heavily on uppers, downers. . . . Dunleavy has woven together the experiences of three Presley bodyguards who were there partying with him, womanizing with him, worrying with him—tasting the pleasure and the pains of life with the most fabulous star in showbiz history!"

Loading his guns, Elvis vowed to Vernon Presley he would kill anyone who was quoted in the book. He was disgusted and humiliated and felt the whole world had turned against him. Eventually, in a *National Enquirer* five-part series, Elvis's stepmother, Dee Stanley, supported claims that Elvis was destroyed by drugs: "Elvis' skid into the hell of drugs shattered his body beyond repair—even stealing his sex drive and forcing him to wear diapers. . . . He had blue marks on his arms and the backs of his hands from needles."

AUG. 8: Elvis rented Libertyland amusement park for $2,500 from one-fifteen A.M. until dawn as a present for Lisa Marie. He was incoherent most of the night.

AUG. 10: Elvis rented the United Artists Southbrook four-theater complex to see the James Bond movie *The Spy Who Loved Me.* He carried a PK Walther pistol to the movie.

AUG. 10–16: Elvis attempted to diet because he weighed over 260.

AUG. 11: The Colonel called Elvis and told him to get ready for his next concert tour, and the Cat complained about the tell-all book his ex-bodyguards had written. Parker told him to ignore the book. It was publicity. It would sell tickets.

AUG. 12–15: Jack Kirsch, a pharmacist at the Prescription House located at 1247 Madison Avenue in Memphis, filled all of Dr. George Nichopoulos's prescriptions for Elvis. During a seven-month period, 5,684 pills were sold to Elvis. No one reported Kirsch or Dr. Nichopoulos's actions until it was too late.

AUG. 14: Fans across the U.S. attempted to call Graceland to console Elvis and reassure him they didn't believe anything in *Elvis: What Happened?* After its release, the King fell apart emotionally and lost his passion for life.

AUG. 14–15: Elvis played with Lisa Marie a few minutes each day, put up with his aunt's and Ginger Alden's disapproval of his habits, and played short games of racquet ball.

CA. AUG. 15: Dave Hebler accused Elvis of trying to commit slow suicide by deliberately setting out to destroy himself. "It seems he is bent on death," Hebler told *Daily Mail* reporters. Yet Colonel Parker scoffed at Elvis's worrying about breathing problems during concert tours. The Colonel claimed he thought Elvis was "playing games," but he knew Elvis was an addict and was suffering.

In an interview the day before Elvis died, Red West divulged Elvis was hooked on so many medications, for so many reasons, it was inevitable he would die of an overdose: "Elvis was on pills all day long. He would give himself shots in the arm or leg. He would ask us to give him shots in the rear end. . . . He takes every possible pill you can think of. . . . He takes Demerol and morphine shots for downs. He takes a very strong painkiller that is intended for terminally ill cancer patients. He says it just gives him a high." (*London Evening News*, Aug. 17, 1977.)

AUG. 15:   Elvis's stepbrother, Rick Stanley, said he delivered drugs to Elvis the day he died and confessed at a much later date, "It was either him or me [to die]." (On *A Current Affair*, the show entitled, "Elvis, the Final 24 Hours," April 27, 1992.)

Elvis was last photographed by a fan, Robert Call, at 12:28 A.M., as he drove into Graceland. The photograph appeared in the *National Enquirer* on September 20, 1977.

Colonel Parker was busy in Portland, Maine, setting up promotional materials and booths to sell souvenirs. Elvis was scheduled to appear in concert with a gala opening on August 17. He was to sing two nights in Portland.

Elvis had a cavity filled at Lester Hoffman's Memphis dental office. He tried unsuccessfully to obtain a copy of the movie *Star Wars* for Lisa Marie, who was staying with him. In the afternoon he played with Lisa Marie and sang a few songs at the upright piano downstairs. At four A.M. Pauline Nicholson, the cook, served Elvis ice cream and cookies. He then challenged Jo and Billy Smith to a racquet-ball contest at Graceland, which lasted until six A.M. It is likely Ginger Alden, who was allegedly staying in the house, had gone to bed much earlier.

The last pieces Elvis played on the upright piano were "Blue Eyes Crying in the Rain" and "Unchained Melody."

When everyone in the household went to bed, Elvis stayed up. Ginger Alden claimed the last thing she said to Elvis as he walked into the bathroom was, "Don't fall asleep." He said he wouldn't.

AUG. 16:   Going into a bathroom off his bedroom on the second floor of Graceland at approximately six A.M., Elvis reportedly carried with him *The Search for the Face of Jesus* (about the Holy Shroud of Turin), which was allegedly clutched in his hand at the time of his death. (Most people who knew Elvis claimed comic books provided bathroom entertainment.)

It was common for Elvis to stay in the bathroom for hours. He had a twisted colon, which had not been operated upon, and he had difficulty with bowel movements and had to withstand the pain from bleeding hemorrhoids. Poor eating habits made things worse, either constipating him or causing his stomach to erupt.

In the early morning Elvis called Pauline Nicholson, refused her offer of a snack, and requested his Aunt Delta bring three packets of sleeping medications (Demerol, Amytal, codeine, Valmid, Aventyl, Nembutal, Elavil) to his room. Aunt Delta did as she was told.

At around two-fifteen P.M., Elvis was allegedly found by either Joe Esposito or Ginger Alden on the bathroom floor with his green pajama bottoms around his ankles, facedown on a red shag rug in front of the toilet.

One Philadelphia paper stated he died from "laxative abuse"; in *Elvis, the King*, the author claimed Elvis "was found fully dressed"; the *London Daily Mail* stated he was fully dressed "on his bed"; the *London Daily Express* said he died in the hospital and was a heavy cocaine user; while London's *Evening News* lamented Elvis's "Tragic Drug Secret" and implied he was a drug addict. The gossip and rumors were endless and continue to this day.

Ginger Alden claimed she found Elvis's body and summoned Joe Esposito, Al Strada (a bodyguard), and Dr. Nichopoulos, all of whom said they tried unsuccessfully to revive him. The *Daily Mirror* stated Esposito found Elvis and tried to resuscitate him, but doctors said Elvis "could have been dead for five hours," and if that was the case, rigor mortis would have begun to set in. Thus, claims to resuscitate him were probably devised to reassure the public that all appropriate actions were taken to keep Elvis alive.

In the *Memphis Press-Scimitar* an article by Ron Harris and Tom Schick ("Elvis Dies Quickly at Graceland After Suffering Heart Failure") claimed Al Strada found Elvis's body and that he summoned Joe Esposito. The reporters said Ginger Alden had left the mansion at nine A.M.

Elvis had probably been dead for many hours by the time he was found. He had not gone to bed at his customary time, between six and seven A.M. Whenever he could, he slept all day and stayed up all night. His biological clock had been screwed up for years.

Many have speculated Elvis committed suicide. However, his daughter was in the house. He claimed to adore Lisa Marie, and he would never have wanted her to find him dead on the bathroom floor with his pants down. Reports stated Lisa Marie was confused and upset to learn her "daddy was asleep and won't wake up." Although signs showed Elvis had given up his will to live, he probably had no intention of dying when he did.

At approximately two thirty-five P.M., the Memphis Fire Department's paramedic rescue unit No. 6 arrived at Graceland. Unit No. 6 drove the body seven miles up Route 51 to Baptist Memorial Hospital. Elvis was pronounced "dead on arrival" after an alleged thirty-minute attempted cardiopulmonary resuscitation. He was pronounced clinically dead at three-thirty P.M. by his personal physician, Dr. George C. Nichopoulos.

Dr. Jerry Francisco, chief medical examiner of Shelby County, conducted a three-hour autopsy on Elvis, upon Vernon Presley's request. Dr. Francisco ruled Elvis died as a result of coronary arrhythmia, an irregular beating of the heart resulting from hypertensive heart disease or myocardial infarction.

Supporting the autopsy opinion was Dr. George Nichopoulos, who may earlier have tried to protect himself by telling Charlie Hodge, Larry Geller, and Kathy Westmoreland that Elvis suffered from near-fatal heart attacks on many occasions.

Dan Sears of Memphis's WMPS radio made the first official announcement of Elvis's death. Memphis's Jack Chestnut of WHBQ-TV (Channel 13, an ABC affiliate) broke the news at 3:32 P.M. on August 16 by somberly telling listeners, "Ladies and gentlemen, Eyewitness News interrupts regular programming. We have just learned through reliable sources that Elvis Presley has been pronounced dead at Baptist Hospital."

The world stood still when it heard the dreadful news. It was hard to believe, because a part of us died with Elvis, and we hadn't given him permission to take that part of us with him. When Elvis died, so did our youth.

A huge throng of sobbing, hysterical followers and an international press core descended upon Memphis like a swarm of locusts. ABC, NBC, and CBS news stations saluted Elvis's contributions and achievements in the music world and American culture. Because of a convention in town, the media could not find lodging, so they camped outside Graceland. Pat Boone said, "There's no way to measure his impact on society or the void that he leaves. He will always be the King of Rock and Roll."

By five-thirty P.M., the first announcement of his passing from "cardiac arrhythmia" was heard on radio, and within hours it seemed everyone knew Elvis was dead at the age of forty-two.

Maurice Eliot, a spokesperson for Baptist Memorial Hospital, held a news conference regarding Elvis's death, and

▶ Elvis in better days at Madison Square Garden in New York City, June 9, 1973. *Courtesy of AP/Wide World Photos.*

thousands of fans lined Memphis streets in panicky hysteria.

Remarkably, no drug abuse was determined by the Shelby County medical examiner's preliminary autopsy, yet rumors circulated about Elvis's use of cocaine and heroin (see *New York Daily Mirror*, Aug. 17, 1977); some felt the real facts about his death had been suppressed, while others believed Elvis had been murdered, and many fans assumed they had lost another rock star to a drug overdose.

Elvis's body was prepared for burial at the Memphis Funeral Home, at 1177 Union Avenue (where Elvis had often made late-night visits to study dead bodies).

Elvis was the embodiment of rock 'n' roll's sins and virtues: grand and vulgar, rude and eloquent, absurdly simple and incredibly complex. He became the most revered superstar of the twentieth century because he combined a rebel's image with that of a lovable choirboy. While he stole the hearts and minds of many fans, he gave back as much as he could to society through his music, generosity, humor, and compassion. He was and will remain the innovative and ultimate King of rock 'n' roll. He set the standards and paved the way for all those who followed.

Robert Wilson, critic for the *Memphis Press-Scimitar* proclaimed: "The King will live forever as the legend of rock 'n' roll. Men die, but the legends they create are immortal. . . . He will be remembered as nothing short of a modern god."

The day Elvis died, Colonel Parker was busy at the Dunfet Sheraton Hotel in Portland, Maine, preparing for Elvis to sing at the Cumberland County Civic Center beginning on August 17. Elvis's crew had his monogrammed "E.P." clothing ready and the windows to his hotel room covered with aluminum foil to block out light and fans' curiosity. The concerts were sold out, as usual.

When the Colonel heard the news of Elvis's passing, he dropped his head and muttered, "Oh, dear God," but within minutes he was blueprinting strategies on how to convince Vernon Presley to sign over the rights to merchandise products related to Elvis. Within hours, he was on a plane to Memphis.

Parker told Lamar Fike that Elvis's death didn't change anything as far as he was concerned. Money could still be made from his talent and his name. In 1973, the Colonel had already sold RCA the rights to all of Elvis's master tapes and took 50 percent of $15 million. In 1974, Boxcar Enterprises had successfully achieved the goal of controlling all but 15 percent of Elvis's merchandising royalties. It seemed the Colonel had covered himself on all counts just in case he ever lost his prize possession. Now he planned to capture more of the take.

Frank Sinatra told an audience at the Alpine Valley Music Theater in Wisconsin that in Elvis's death he lost a

"dear friend" and a "tremendous asset" to the music business.

At his death, Elvis's aunt Delta Biggs and other family members lived on the property, and his father paid himself $75,000 a year to "keep finances straight." Members of the Presley family would remain at Graceland. Elvis's will provided for their care for the rest of their lives.

"Pledging My Love" was No. 1 on the Country charts the day Elvis died.

AUG. 17: Singer James Brown was the first celebrity to fly into Memphis to attend Elvis's funeral.

Ardent fans were infuriated when Australia's *The Sun* quoted Priscilla Presley as saying: "It is better that he died now. If he continued at the pace he was going, I'm sure he would have ended up being nothing more than a vegetable."

Louis Couttelene of RCA lamented the loss of RCA's 500-million-record-selling artist and conceded, "He was the greatest legend of the modern entertainment world." (*New York Daily Mirror.*)

Thousands called the White House and demanded Pres. Jimmy Carter authorize a national holiday in Elvis's honor. President Carter's gracious eulogy came on August 17: "Elvis Presley's death deprives our country of a part of itself. He was unique and irreplaceable. More than twenty years ago, he burst upon the scene with an impact that was unprecedented and will probably never be equaled. His music and his personality, fusing the styles of white country and black rhythm and blues, permanently changed the face of American popular culture. His following was immense, and he was a symbol to people the world over of the vitality, rebelliousness, and good humor of his country."

The rock 'n' roll world was in limbo, jolted with disbelief when Elvis died. Mick Fleetwood of the rock group Fleetwood Mac remembers: "The news came over like a ton of bricks. I was driving back from the mountains and I

had the radio on. They were playing an Elvis medley and I thought, 'Great.' And then they came back with the news." Bruce Springsteen said: "He was so incredibly important to me. . . . When I heard the news, it was like somebody took a piece out of me. . . . To me, he's as big . . . as the whole dream . . . he was in mortal combat with the thing. . . . Nothing will ever take the place of that guy. . . . There have been a lot of contenders. But there is only one king." (Quoted in the *Florence* (TN) *Daily News*, Oct. 5, 1977.)

Rumors ran rampant—it was a conspiracy concocted by the FBI so Elvis could do undercover work; it was a publicity stunt to recharge a flagging career; Elvis had gone into hiding to escape the public. It was inconceivable that the man who embodied youth and energy and an impassioned zest for life was gone.

Elvis's interest-free checking-account balance at the National Bank of Commerce at the time of his death was $1,055,173.69.

As Elvis's body laid in state, disc jockeys from Hawaii to Luxembourg played his records day and night, and some stations stopped all advertising out of respect for the King of Rock 'n' Roll (and to keep listeners tuned in). Every TV broadcast showed thousands of mourners weeping or standing silently in vigil outside Graceland. TV stations aired special programs about Elvis. Telephone lines to Memphis were jammed for days. Tennessee florists barely filled the demand for the 3,116 bouquet tributes. Airlines were deluged with calls for tickets to Memphis, and all seats were booked within hours. Musicians and fans alike sobbed in public or traveled down miles of crowded highway toward Graceland to pay their last respects. It was hard to believe he was gone. He never even said "Good-bye."

Thousands of fans congregated outside Graceland hoping to file past the open coffin to get one last glimpse of their idol, who wore a plain white suit, a blue shirt, a silver tie, and the eleven-carat diamond TCB ring.

The Presley family feared the thousand of fans at Graceland would prevent a peaceful funeral ceremony. They also worried the overemotional crowds might create an unsafe situation. Thus, a private funeral at Graceland and a simple ceremony at Forest Hill Cemetery were planned, while hundreds of armed police officers held back mourners at the Graceland gates.

During the wake, Colonel Parker convinced Vernon Presley to sign papers that permitted Factors, Etc., Inc. to control the merchandising of Elvis-related products. The courts later ruled that Parker had no legal rights or interest in the Presley estate. By 1982, Parker would be forced to abdicate all connections to the Elvis Presley name, once and for all.

The *Memphis Commercial Appeal* reported Elvis's heart was enlarged; his liver contained fatty globules; he suffered from hardening in two main arteries leading to the heart; suffered from hypertension; atherosclerosis; coronary artery disease; an ulcerated larynx; and that cotton was stuck in both ears, one of which was filled with pus from an ear infection.

AUG. 18: Elvis's funeral at Graceland was followed by a ceremony and burial at Forest Hill Cemetery. His hearse was driven by Trent Webb. The officiating minister was the Reverend C. W. Bradley, pastor of the Woodvale Church of Christ in Memphis, who said Elvis "dared to be different," "had risen from obscurity to world fame," and "had never forgotten his humble beginnings and never lost contact with humanity." A brief speech was delivered by evangelist Rex Emanuel Humbard, pastor of the Cathedral of Tomorrow of Akron, Ohio.

Those attending the funeral included Priscilla, Lisa Marie, Vernon and Minnie Mae Presley; Colonel Parker; Chet Atkins; Caroline Kennedy (who represented *Rolling Stone*); Ann-Margret and her husband, Roger Smith; James Brown; Charlie Hodge; George Hamilton; Ginger Alden; Linda Thompson; Sammy Davis, Jr.; some members of the Memphis Mafia; and Gov. Raymond Blanton of Tennessee, who ordered all state flags be flown at half-mast on that statewide day of mourning.

Governor Blanton considered Elvis a majestic talent and said he deserved to be hailed for his significant impact on the culture and consciousness of America. For certain, Elvis was (and still is) a gigantic economic boost for the state of Tennessee.

At the funeral services, Jake Hess and the Statesmen sang "Known Only to Him"; James Blackwood and the Stamps sang "How Great Thou Art"; the Stamps gave a melodious rendition of "Sweet, Sweet Spirit" and "His Hand in Mine"; Bill Baize of the Stamps sang "When It's My Turn"; and Kathy Westmoreland emoted a tearful "My Heavenly Father Watches Over Me."

The eulogy was given by comedian Jackie Kahane. Pallbearers included Joe Esposito, Lamar Fike, disc jockey George Klein, guitarist Charlie Hodge, cousin Billy Smith, Jerry Schilling (who had become the Beach Boys' manager), and ironically, Elvis's personal physician, Dr. George C. Nichopoulos. Producer Felton Jarvis was to be the sixth pallbearer, but he was unable to attend the funeral.

A motorcade of fourteen (some sources say eleven) white and cream-colored Cadillacs, lined with motorcycle outriders, accompanied the white Cadillac hearse (license plate 1-CF652) from Graceland to Forest Hill Cemetery.

Elvis was laid to rest in a mausoleum alongside his mother, Gladys. Under heavy guard, a simple, reverent ceremony was conducted. The funeral and burial cost the Presley family $23,789.73.

The Colonel irreverently wore a colorful blue shirt, no tie, and a baseball cap to the wake and funeral. It was in the poorest taste, and onlookers were shocked and puzzled at his choice of dress for the man Parker had called "son."

Elvis had impacted the lives of the eighty thousand mourners who stood in hot, humid Memphis weather, crushed together (many fainting and in need of medical attention) for a chance to pass Elvis's open coffin. People remembered Buddy Holly's words: "Without Elvis none of us could have made it." Elvis's close friend, James Brown, rejoiced in the Cat's achievement when he noted, "Elvis taught white America to get down." Rock singer Bruce Springsteen agreed with *Rolling Stone*'s assessment that Elvis had passed from elusive legend to myth and was the spiritual headquarters for rock 'n' roll.

After James Blackwood heard the news of Elvis's passing, he said if Elvis "had gone into gospel [as his only career], he would still be alive." (*Early Elvis, the Humes Years.*) It is interesting to note Blackwood and his quartet shunned Elvis in the fifties, telling him he couldn't make it as singer of gospel.

Unable to attend Elvis's funeral, Liberace sent a huge guitar-shaped floral arrangement to Graceland. For twenty-one years Elvis had called "Lee" for advice or to talk business and sent him birthday presents and opening-night floral guitars. Liberace, older and wiser than his younger counterpart, strived to help Elvis find inner solace, and he encouraged Elvis to retain that rich, vigorous, kick-ass sound that had horrified the staid, uptight Las Vegas audiences in 1956. That was the true Elvis sound. When the Cat lost that edge, it truly distressed Liberace.

The two men remained close friends until Elvis's untimely death. Grieving over the loss of Elvis, Liberace hoped the lonely, nervous young man had finally found peace. Liberace was saddened that Elvis had been unable to accept or identify fully with the responsibilities and the burdens attached to being named the King of rock 'n' roll.

To appease fans for placing the Panama Canal before a mention of Elvis's death on the news the evening of August 16, CBS saluted the King's achievements in a documentary.

Memphis's *Commercial Appeal* said Priscilla Presley was "really broken up" by Elvis's death and reported Elvis was "an American cultural phenomenon . . . a part of the 'American Dream.' . . . He gave dignity and respect to the pubescent girl or boy who was frightened of growing up, unsure of being loved, afraid of acting natural. . . . He was the entertainer who magnetized the nerve system of the young. . . . His generosity was as much a legend as his career."

As sobbing crowds stood along Elvis Presley Boulevard outside Graceland's gates, their anguish was interrupted by another tragic event. Drunk driver Treatise Wheeler III of Memphis, going 55 mph in a 40-mph zone, intentionally drove his 1963 white Ford Fairlane into the grieving crowd. The vehicle struck Tammy Baiter (who had been born on Elvis's birthday) of St. Clair, Missouri, splintering her pelvis in four places. Alice Hovatar and Juanita Joan Johnson, both from Monroe, Louisiana, were killed instantly. As fans in the crowd stood stunned, the driver backed up, turned, and fled the scene of the crime.

Wheeler was captured and charged with drunk driving, two counts of second-degree murder, leaving the scene of an accident, public drunkenness, and reckless driving. He would serve only a five-year sentence before his 1983 release from prison.

AUG. 19: A spokesperson at the Baptist Memorial Hospital said Elvis "had the arteries of an eighty-year-old man. His body was just worn-out. His arteries and veins were terribly corroded."

Few people believed Elvis died as it was reported. His death was taking on aspects of a cloak-and-dagger murder mystery, with the idea of a possible cover-up to hide certain unsavory facts. Reports varied widely, and journalists went crazy trying to find the truth amidst the gossip and rumors.

All the reports, notes, and photographs of Elvis's autopsy *disappeared* by August 19, and have never been found. Even more suspicious was the fact that before the contents of Elvis's stomach were analyzed thoroughly, they were destroyed and thrown out. The loss of Elvis's body tissue conveniently erased the possibility of conducting a truthful examination to determine the real cause of his death.

Investigative reporter Geraldo Rivera accused the Presleys of conspiring with Shelby County health officials to cover up the fact Elvis overdosed. Rivera stated that to validate that truth might ruin the legend of Elvis and destroy the local tourist trade. Both Dr. Eric Muirhead (Baptist Memorial Hospital's chief of pathology) and Dr. Noel Floredo (present at the autopsy) admitted Elvis's death was due to an interaction of several drugs.

AUG. 20: Little Richard flippantly remarked about Elvis's death, "He was a rocker. I was a rocker. I'm not rockin' anymore and he's not rockin' anymore." However, Bruce Springsteen, blown away by Elvis's passing, revealed his compassionate understanding of the King of rock 'n' roll and comprehended his plight: "I just couldn't believe how someone whose music came in and took away so many people's loneliness, and gave so many people a reason and a sense of all the possibilities of living, could have in the end died so tragically. I guess when you're alone, you ain't nothing but alone." (Quoted from "Elvis" in *Nine-O-Nine* by Nancy Randall.)

The K Mart chain ordered an unprecedented 2 million copies of *Elvis: What Happened?* The book was serialized in *The Star* and nicknamed "The Bodyguard Book."

AUG. 21: RCA reported it had sold over 8 million Elvis records in a six-day period.

AUG. 24: Elvis's will appeared on file in the State of Tennessee, Shelby County Will Book 209, page 266. It was witnessed by Margaret Hare. When its contents were revealed, many people questioned its authenticity, but they were allegedly "silenced" by those in charge.

After Elvis died, it was revealed that 22 percent of Boxcar Enterprises was owned by Elvis and Colonel Parker owned 56 percent. The remaining 22 percent belonged to various parties. Boxcar owned all commercial and merchandising rights to Elvis. On August 24, the Colonel had Vernon Presley sign a contract agreement for all rights to royalties and profits: 25 percent to the Colonel, 25 percent to the estate, and 50 percent to Boxcar Enterprises. Since Colonel Parker owned 56 percent of Boxcar, he would earn over 50 percent of future Elvis-related income. The Colonel also had Vernon sign an agreement that gave Factors Etc., Inc. of Delaware the right to distribute all Elvis-related items (but not films or music). Factors gave the Colonel a $15,000 advance and 5 percent of their total sales. When Vernon died, Priscilla, Joe Hanks, and the National Bank of Commerce became coexecutors of Elvis's estate. Parker earned over $6.5 million from the estate in a two-year period (1977–79). The estate filed a suit against Parker in 1982. He had to relinquish all his rights, but he was paid $2 million to settle.

Attorney Blanchard Tual reported to the court that Parker never registered Elvis with Broadcast Music, Inc. (BMI) or the American Society of Composers, Artists and Publishers (ASCAP). He also revealed that Elvis did not receive any writer's royalties and that Parker received RCA payments when Elvis did not. Parker had also made a deal with the International Hotel (Las Vegas) for a *gratis* year-round hotel suite, food, drinks, transportation, and gambling privileges for himself. Tual went on to report that Parker turned down all tours abroad (up to $1 million for Elvis a night) because Parker had no passport and that Elvis most likely lost millions of dollars due to the Colonel's negligence and greed.

AUG. 26:   South Carolina's *Daily Item* applauded: "He was the king. Those who saw him in person remained convinced that he was the greatest entertainer in the history of show business. . . . He came from a humble background, was poorly educated but uniquely talented. . . . He became a victim of his success. . . . He was unique, an original, and he could sing and entertain with astonishing ability and charisma. Indeed he was the king."

The *Los Angeles Times* confirmed Elvis was a true artist and the "inventor of rock 'n' roll" who "stirred emotions and inspired a new direction in music and a host of gyrating imitators."

The *Tampa Tribune* noted: "The life of Elvis Presley has ended and so has an American era. . . . The rock 'n' roll era he cemented into the nation's culture . . . his throaty baritone changed the country more than it altered him."

AUG. 29:   After Elvis was laid to rest in a crypt alongside his mother's coffin, Ronnie Lee Adkins, Raymond Green, and Bruce Nelson went to Forest Hill Cemetery wearing dark jumpsuits, bulletproof vests, and carrying an M1 carbine, handguns, and grenades. They allegedly attempted to steal Elvis's body from its casket for a multimillion-dollar ransom. It was rumored each man was to be paid $40,000 by an unnamed, outside party to deliver Elvis's body. After their arrest, charges for trespassing were dismissed on October 5 because a court believed their defense was plausible: they claimed their purpose was to prove Elvis's crypt was *empty*. The men said they felt the King of rock 'n' roll was still alive, and that the funeral was a hoax.

SEPT.:   Paul Gambaccini wrote in *Memorial Album* about Elvis: "It wasn't he died when he did that was so hard to take, it was that he could die at all. That such a giant could be only one of the local yokels in Memphis, unable to resist stuffing himself with ludicrous junk food and appalling drugs, was a more painful revelation than the tip-off that Santa Claus is only a state of mind. All fifties rockers had to face . . . the incontrovertible evidence that their youth was a matter of history. The death of Elvis Presley hit adults where they live, in their memories. What sweet memories they are: of permission to dress and groom differently, a transformation of popular music and radio, a liberation from slow dancing. A worldwide youth movement felt a spirit of brotherhood no authority could discourage or deny, and Elvis Presley, that simple Southern boy, was its symbol."

◀ Elvis and his manager Colonel Tom Parker in an RCA office, January 20, 1957. *Courtesy of AP/Wide World Photos.*

Ronnie McDowell's 1977 hit, "The King Is Gone," reached No. 13 on *Billboard*'s Top 100 chart. McDowell did the vocals for the 1979 TV movie *Elvis*, the 1981 TV movie *Elvis and the Beauty Queen*, and the vocals for the 1988 TV miniseries *Elvis and Me*.

Canadian disc jockey Red Robinson released *Elvis—A Canadian Tribute— The Elvis Tapes*.

SEPT. 1: Graceland was valued at $500,000. Its annual upkeep was close to that figure. The staff remained at Graceland to protect the property from vandals and to serve the living members of the Presley family.

At the time of his death, Elvis's trophy room's glass cabinets contained sixty-three gold records (singles); twenty-six platinum (albums); thirty-seven gold (albums); and many citations, awards, and honors.

J. D. Sumner of the Stamps Quartet rented to fans (for $2,000 a day) the Mark IV Elvis had bought him. Sumner claims he turned down one million dollars for the car. (10/8/77 UPI story, Nashville.)

After Elvis died, fans frequented his favorite shops in Memphis and business boomed: Burke's Florist; clubs and restaurants along Beale Street; Goldsmith's Department Store; Lowell Hayes (jewelry); Lanksy Brothers (clothing); Poplar Times (records); the Gridiron restaurant; and Blue Light Studios (where Elvis's first publicity shots were taken; it is no longer in business). Sun Records became a popular spot for many fans.

A Swedish film titled *Elvis! Elvis!* was released in Europe in September. It is the true story of a boy named Elvis Karlsson (named after Elvis Presley) as he struggled through boyhood.

SEPT. 6: For a reported $75,000 fee from the *National Enquirer*, Elvis's cousin Bobby Mann is said to have secretly photographed Elvis in his coffin. The shocking photo appeared on the cover of the *Enquirer* and led to a record-setting sale of 6.5 million copies for the issue. Many questioned the authenticity of Mann's photograph, which seemed to show a much younger and thinner Elvis.

In *New Musical Express*, a member of the Jordanaires contended Mann cruelly capitalized on Elvis's death and claimed the photo was a superimposed image of Elvis in the nine-hundred-pound casket. "Everyone who was at the funeral knows that it was a one hundred percent fake photo," he said. Larry Geller, who allegedly dyed Elvis's hair black and dressed him for burial, had no comment.

SEPT. 7: A sixty-minute version of the ninety-three-minute documentary *Elvis on Tour* aired on NBC-TV and received top ratings.

SEPT. 12: "Way Down" received a gold certificate from the RIAA as a million seller, with the "producer" Elvis Presley and the "executive producer" Felton Jarvis (RCA PB-10998).

SEPT. 13: After appearing on many television shows, Patricia Ann Emanuele and other fans marched to Washington in a campaign to secure an Elvis Presley Day. Maryland congresswoman Barbara Mikulski introduced a bill in Congress to declare January 8 a national holiday. It was voted down.

OCT. 2: An autopsy team concluded that Elvis's death was "polypharmacy" or drug-related. Yet, Dr. Francisco said the cause of death was from hypertensive heart disease with coronary-artery heart disease as a contributing factor. He ruled out drugs as a cause of death. (See "Medical Examiner Rules Out Drugs as Causing Elvis Presley's Death" in the *Memphis Press-Scimitar*, Oct. 2, 1977.)

Because of the bizarre August 29 "break in" to steal Elvis's body, during the evening of October 2 Elvis's and his mother's bodies were removed from their original places of burial and reburied side by side in the grounds of Graceland in an area Elvis had named the Meditation Garden. Vernon Presley's words were inscribed on Elvis's grave at the Meditation Garden:

He was a precious gift from God
We cherished and loved dearly.
He had a God-given talent that he shared
    with the world. And without a doubt,
He became the most widely acclaimed;
    capturing the hearts of young and old
    alike.
He was admired not only as an enter-
    tainer
But as the great humanitarian that he
    was;
For his generosity, and his kind feelings
For his fellow man.
He revolutionized the field of music and
Received its highest awards.
He became a living legend in his own
    time,
Earning the respect and love of millions.
God saw that he needed some rest and
Called him home to be with Him.
We miss you, Son and Daddy. I thank
    God that he gave us you as our son.

There was also an eternal flame at Elvis's grave and its memorial reads: "To Elvis in Memoriam. You gave yourself to each of us in some manner. You were wrapped in thoughtfulness and tied with love. May this flame reflect our never-ending respect and love for you. May it serve as a constant reminder to each of us of your eternal-presence."

J. D. Sumner recorded the tribute album *Elvis Has Left the Building*.

OCT. 3:   CBS posthumously aired "Elvis in Concert," which RCA and CBS-TV rushed to finish. The one-hour special had been shot in June. Vernon Presley said a few words at the end of the program in a gentle eulogy for his son. Songs on the program: "Also Sprach

Zarathustra" (with the Joe Guercio Orchestra), "See See Rider," "That's All Right, Mama," "Teddy Bear"/"Don't Be Cruel," "You Gave Me a Mountain," "Jailhouse Rock," "How Great Thou Art," "I Really Don't Want to Know," "Hurt," "Hound Dog," "My Way," "Early Morning Rain," and "Can't Help Falling in Love."

NOV.:   Dr. Nichopoulos was under suspicion for malpractice (among other things), and he was soon charged by the Tennessee state board of health with illegally prescribing more than 5,300 Schedule 2 drugs to Elvis in a seven-month period. He allowed Elvis to consume over twenty-five pills a day (it was probably more like one hundred to two hundred), and the doctor's last prescription, on August 16, for 680 tablets of the powerful painkiller Dilaudid, had the potential of killing a stable of horses! The *Memphis Press-Scimitar* quoted Nichopoulos on August 17: "He was getting over an eye infection and sore throat, but overall he was a healthy man."

Dr. Raymond Kelly of Los Angeles' Bio Science Laboratories analyzed some of Elvis's body tissue and determined Elvis's body contained many depressant drugs at the time of his death: Valium, Valmid, morphine, pentobarbital, butabarbital, codeine, quaalude, and Placidyl. Red West contended Dr. Nichopoulos filled Elvis's smallest request for drugs and stated Elvis was a "walking drugstore. He was drugged to the limit." (AP Chicago review, Aug. 17, 1977.) But Memphis Mafia member Marty Lacker asserted Elvis was a pill freak, not a drug abuser.

NOV.:   For insertion into *Billboard* magazine, Eva-Tone produced a soundsheet to promote two Chicago radio shows. Short excerpts from the shows were used as a promotional gimmick to stimulate interest in two radio shows titled "Jamboree USA" and

"Elvis: Six-Hour Special" (Eva-Tone 10287733BX). It was a reissue of Eva-Tone's 1956 Lynchburg Audio sound-sheet (Eva-Tone EL-38713T).

CA. NOV.: *Elvis Lives* was a Broadway show, which won the *New York Evening Standard* Award for Best Musical of the Year. It starred Elvis impersonator Larry Seth.

NOV. 15: Dee and Vernon Presley attained a Dominican Republic divorce.

NOV. 20: "Memories of Elvis," hosted by Ann-Margret, was a three-hour (eight to eleven P.M.) NBC telecast that showed footage of the 1968 TV comeback special "Elvis" and clips from the 1973 NBC version of "Elvis: Aloha From Hawaii."

NOV. 27: The Meditation Garden at Graceland was opened to the public, and thousands of fans paid their last respects to the King.

DEC.: Rob-Rich Films bought the theatrical rights to eight of Elvis's films and with Sidney Ginsberg put the movies together as a long program to be shown once a week. The grouping of films opened in New York City at the Beacon Theatre on December 26, 1977, then moved to Memphis, Dallas, and Oklahoma City.

The chairman of Factors, Etc., Inc., Harry Geissler, who had bought from Vernon Presley and the Colonel the right to distribute Elvis-related merchandise, publicly announced he would challenge in court anyone who refuted his license to produce and sell Elvis memorabilia.

Memphis attorney Blanchard Tual was appointed Lisa Marie's guardian ad litem (protector of legal interests) until her eighteenth birthday. Tual became instrumental in removing Colonel Tom Parker from Elvis's estate, its earnings, and royalty incomes.

Felton Jarvis accepted for Elvis the Hall of Fame Award at Don Kirschner's Third Annual Rock Music Awards. The Beatles and Chuck Berry were previous recipients.

DEC. 15: Shelby Singleton had bought ten thousand hours of taped Sun sessions from Sam Phillips in 1969, and announced he was going to release a five-volume set of the Million Dollar Quartet session from December 4, 1956. RCA stopped Singleton with a court injunction. When Carl Perkins and Johnny Cash heard Singleton planned to overdub the sessions, they sued Singleton. A bootleg version of the sessions was released in November 1980, at $16.95 (OMD 001), which infuriated RCA. In 1981, Charly Records made another bootleg (Sun 1006), and in 1987, yet another, with an additional twenty-two tracks added to the original seventeen.

DEC. 31: "Always Elvis," a ten-day convention ($150 per ticket), was set up by Colonel Parker with Vernon, Priscilla, Henri Lewin (president of the Hilton Hotel chain), and Conrad Hilton (owner of the chain). It was scheduled to open early in 1978. No impersonators would be allowed. An unveiling of a huge bronze statue of the King was being planned for the Hilton.

Tommy Durden, who cowrote "Heartbreak Hotel," recorded a tribute record, "Elvis" (Westbound 55405).

Elvis's star on Hollywood's Walk of Fame is at 6777 Hollywood Boulevard near Highland Avenue, Hollywood, California.

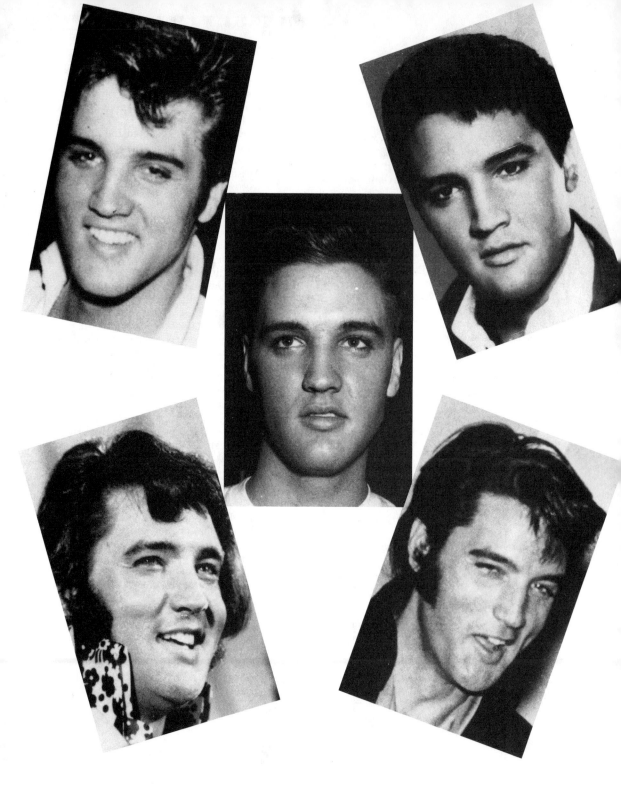

▲ The King of Rock 'n' Roll through the years (from left to right: 1957, 1958, 1962, 1974, 1977). *Courtesy of AP/Wide World Photos.*

PART II

Posthumous
Chronology Related
to Elvis,
1978–93

▲ The U.S. Postal Service's ballot for the Elvis stamp. *Courtesy of the Accord Park, Hingham, Massachusetts, post office.*

POSTHUMOUS CHRONOLOGY RELATED TO ELVIS, 1978–93

1978

Producer Shelby Singleton was ordered by a court to give RCA all of the tapes on which Elvis was heard, tapes Singleton had acquired from Sun Records in 1969. RCA had previously bought those rights from Sun in 1955. Sam Phillips mistakenly sold the same rights twice!

JAN.: Mike Stone was employed as a dealer in a Las Vegas club and moonlighted as a bodyguard for various producers. His trainer, Ed Parker, wrote the book *Inside Elvis*.

Vernon Presley signed a contract with the William Morris Agency and demanded a $25,000 fee for any interview. There were no takers. If he had been willing to be candid and informative, without wanting to be paid a top star's fee, the world may have found out a great deal more about Elvis. Almost everyone who had known the Cat demanded high fees in exchange for their knowledge of him.

JAN. 8: NBC-TV paid tribute to the King with the ninety-minute special "Nashville Remembers Elvis on His Birthday." Guest stars who sang on the program included Jerry Lee Lewis ("You Win Again"); Merle Haggard ("Love Me Tender"); Ronnie McDowell ("The King Is Gone"); Dottie West ("An American Trilogy"); Carl Perkins ("E.P. Express"); Charlie Rich ("Lonely Weekends"); Larry Gatlin ("Help Me"). Elvis was recollected by host Jimmy Dean, Jack Albertson, Nancy Sinatra,

Stella Stevens, Bill Bixby, and Mary Ann Mobley.

FEB.: Ginger Alden's mother sued the Presley estate for $39,587. She alleged Elvis promised to pay off her entire mortgage, but he died before he fulfilled his obligation to her. The case was eventually dismissed.

FEB. 1: Elvis was inducted into *Playboy* magazine's Music Hall of Fame.

FEB. 18: The National Bank of Commerce of Memphis sued the Presley estate for three notes owed to it in the amount of $1,434,536.69. Memphisites wanted to know (along with fans) *where* the $200 million plus he had earned had disappeared. For certain, the Cadillacs and jewelry Elvis bought didn't come to one-twentieth of that amount.

MAR. 23: *Rolling Stone* stated Elvis would be honored and amused to see his "life" after death doing so well via impersonators.

APR.: Inside the magazine *Elvis! Collector's Issue!* Eva-Tone put a plastic soundsheet, published by Green Valley Record Store. It included Elvis's February 25, 1961, press conference at the Claridge Hotel in Memphis (Eva-Tone 1037710A&BX).

APR. 7: Vernon Presley sold Elvis's airplanes to Omni Aircraft Sales of Washington.

MAY: For a scheduled radio special for Universal Sounds Limited, Eva-Tone made a soundsheet on yellow plastic titled "The King Is Dead/Long Live the King" (EVA-Tone 52578X).

MAY 13: *Saturday Review* published an article about Elvis's image being exploited titled "Nights of the Living Dead—Cashing in on Rock and Roll Heaven."

MAY 16: The *National Enquirer* printed a story that claimed Ginger Alden communicated with Elvis's spirit in psychic dreams. Alden's sister, Rosemary, and her mother, Jo, asserted they had seen Elvis's ghost!

SUMMER: The Elvis Presley Youth Foundation in Tupelo was remodeled. It is located behind the home in which Elvis was born.

A life-size statue on Beale Street's Elvis Presley Plaza was commissioned from artist Eric Parks.

Priscilla Presley met model/actor Michael Edwards at a party in Beverly Hills. They dated for over seven years. It was Edwards who introduced Priscilla to the Church of Scientology.

JUNE 1: Elmer and Debra Flint were the first couple to be married inside the Old Saltillo Road home, where Elvis was born, in East Tupelo, Mississippi.

AUG.: Jimmy Velvet auctioned off eighteen items he claimed were once owned by Elvis. Vernon Presley insisted none of the items were Elvis's and that he would "shoot Velvet if he came near the Graceland front gate." (*Washington Post, Aug. 6, 1978.*)

J. D. Sumner and the Stamps' tribute album, *Memories of Our Friend Elvis* (Blue Mark 373), sold well.

AUG. 16–18: Thousands of fans gathered at Graceland to commemorate the first anniversary of Elvis's death.

AUG. 21: *People* magazine ran "The Elvis Legend One Year Later," and Rona Barrett's *Hollywood* told the story of how fans remained close to their idol in an article titled, "Elvis: Gone for a Year but It Still Hurts!"

AUG. 29: A rebroadcast of NBC-TV's "Memories of Elvis" (originally aired on Nov. 20, 1977) hosted by Ann-Margret was shown nationwide.

SEPT.: Priscilla enrolled Lisa Marie in the Church of Scientology in Los Angeles.

SEPT. 1–10: The first annual Elvis Presley Convention was held at the Hilton Hotel in Las Vegas. The convention became a yearly event at which Elvis impersonators met, entertained one another, and voted on the best Elvis impersonator of the year.

SEPT. 8: The Las Vegas Hilton Hotel featured a four-hundred-pound bronze statue of Elvis in its lobby. Part of its inscription reads: "Memories of Elvis will always be with us. None of us really, totally, know how great a performer he was." Priscilla and Vernon Presley were at the presentation ceremonies (see illustration). Carl Romanelli sculpted the 6-foot-tall bronze statue of Elvis, which had been commissioned by Colonel Parker for $150,000.

OCT. 10: *People* magazine recognized Elvismania was charging full steam ahead. Its front cover read, "Remembering Elvis—Imitators, fans and rip-offs launch a billion dollar industry." Everything from $1 bills with Elvis's image to toilet seats were being made and sold rapidly.

▶ Barron Hilton, Priscilla Presley, and Vernon Presley at the Hilton Hotel, Las Vegas, September 8, 1978. *Courtesy of John Reible, Las Vegas News Bureau, Las Vegas, Nevada.*

DEC. 1: Psychic David Behr alleged to have made contact with Elvis in a taped séance. He sold the two-way conversation for $9.95 (sixty-five questions were "answered").

Eva-Tone gave away an eight-inch soundsheet (through the Thompson Company) that included Elvis's "You Don't Have to Say You Love Me," which he had recorded in June 1970 (Eva-Tone 12-27785).

DEC. 18: Impersonator (and foundry worker) Herbert Baer changed his name to Elvis Presley in Manitowoc, Wisconsin.

1979

JAN.: It was discovered that Elvis was not a member of Broadcast Music, Inc. (BMI) and therefore he had not collected royalties on songs that list him as a cocomposer. Because his manager, Colonel Parker, ill-advised him, the Cat probably lost millions of dollars throughout the years in royalties.

Dee Presley collaborated with her sons to write *Elvis, We Love You Tender* and with David Wimbish on *Life With Elvis.* She began lecturing about her life with the singer. In 1992, she was writing another book about Elvis's "sex and drug problems."

Priscilla Presley made her TV debut as a guest on Tony Orlando's NBC special. Later, she became a cohost of the TV series "Those Amazing Animals."

JAN. 8: Groundbreaking began for the Elvis Presley Chapel in Elvis Presley Park, Tupelo, Mississippi, created through the efforts of a Tupelo bookkeeper, Janelle McCombe, who claimed she had asked Elvis before he died how best he could be honored and he replied, "Why not build a chapel to God in my name."

A celebration of the anniversary of Elvis's birth took place in Memphis and in Tupelo, which would become an annual event.

JAN. 27: The Presley family accountant Joseph A. Hanks, the National Bank of Commerce, Memphis, and Priscilla were named to oversee the management of Lisa Marie's inheritance from her father. Priscilla was shocked to discover the estate was close to penniless. She knew she had to do something about the situation in order to protect her daughter's interests.

FEB.: *Record Digest* offered the book *Our Best to You* to six-hundred patrons; in it was a red vinyl 33⅓ rpm soundsheet of "The Graceland Tour" (Record Digest 25794).

FEB. 11: Dick Clark Motion Pictures, Inc. aired *Elvis* on ABC-TV from eight to eleven P.M. It was in production from August 4 to December 14, 1978. The film starred Kurt Russell as Elvis (nominated for an Emmy Award) and Shelley Winters as Gladys Presley. In the film, produced by Dick Clark and directed by John Carpenter, the Elvis vocals were sung by Ronnie McDowell and produced by Felton Jarvis. Musical consultants included the Jordanaires, Kathy Westmoreland, Billy Smith, Marty Lacker, and Sam Phillips. Twenty-five songs were in the film. *Elvis* rated higher than *Gone With the Wind* and *One Flew Over the Cuckoo's Nest* (which both also aired that night) with a Nielsen rating of 27.3.

APR.: Charlie Hodge and Dick Grob started a newsletter about Elvis called *Reflections*.

APR. 17: Colonel Parker wrote to Liberace from his home in Madison, Tennessee: "Friend Lee . . . I know if Elvis were here with me, he would join me with best wishes for the opening of your museum, which will bring much

pleasure to many people. I had two of the large Elvis Hound Dogs left, and I would like for you to have one, with my compliments. It has been many years since we met in Florida when I was with Eddy Arnold. The Best Ever, the Colonel." (Courtesy the Liberace Museum, Las Vegas, Nevada.)

CA. MAY: Bill Carwile purchased from Forest Hill Cemetery two tons of gray marble from Elvis's first tomb. He carved the marble into 44,000 chunks and sold each piece for $80 each (two inches by one inch in size). He also bought the tomb that Gladys had been buried in before being moved to Graceland.

JUNE: Jimmy Velvet opened the Elvis Presley Museum at 3350 Elvis Presley Boulevard across from Graceland. During an auction, over a million dollars' worth of items not belonging to Elvis were allegedly sold. Velvet would run another Elvis auction in 1991. Mike L. Moon opened an Elvis Presley Museum in Pigeon Forge, Tennessee, with a display of items that included Elvis's TCB ring, his automobiles, and costumes. Again, Vernon Presley contended that the items had not belonged to Elvis.

Grenada, a Caribbean island, was the first country to honor Elvis with a stamp.

JUNE 26: Vernon Presley died at nine-twenty A.M. of heart failure at the age of sixty-three. His last girlfriend, Sandy Miller, along with Dee Presley, Priscilla, Lisa Marie, Linda Thompson, Joe Esposito, and the Colonel attended his funeral in Memphis.

His estate was sued for unpaid funeral and hospital bills after he died. He was to be buried next to Elvis, Jesse, and Gladys in Graceland's Meditation Garden.

JUNE 28: Vernon Presley was laid to rest in the Meditation Garden at Graceland. Reverend C. W. Buddy and M. H.

Kennedy officiated at his funeral. Songs by Elvis were played over a loudspeaker, one of which was "Peace in the Valley."

AUG. 14: The unveiling of Elvis Presley Plaza, south of downtown Memphis near Beale Street, included a display of a statue of Elvis by Eric Parks. Hundreds of fans were present at a short ceremony to honor the Cat.

AUG. 17: The Elvis Presley Chapel was dedicated at the thirteen-and-a-half-acre Elvis Presley Park in Tupelo, Mississippi. It cost $800,000. Police officer Larry Montgomery sang three songs.

AUG. 17: Old Saltillo Road in Tupelo became Elvis Presley Boulevard to mark Elvis's birthplace. The area in which he was born was named Elvis Presley Heights (previously East Heights).

SEPT. 13: "The Elvis Cover-Up" was aired on ABC-TV's "20/20," which discussed Elvis's alleged drug addictions and a possible cover-up of facts revolving around his death.

OCT.: Priscilla sold the rights to home movies of the Presleys for $250,000 and signed a three-year contract with Wella Corporation (Wella Balsam) to be a spokesmodel in their hair-product commercials (the first one aired on October 31).

WINTER: An avid Elvis fan attempted to kill Dr. George C. Nichopoulos. Dr. Jerry Francisco held a news conference affirming he had not covered up the facts, nor had he been involved in a cover-up.

In 1979, "CBS-FM Remembers Elvis" was produced, narrated by Jack Miller. *Billboard* ranked it the Top Special Program in a Major Market for the year.

Vernon Presley and the Colonel's photo appeared on the album cover of the 1979 release *Our Memories of Elvis*, Vol. I.

1980

Associated Broadcast, Inc. produced a three-hour radio show titled "The Legend of the King."

FEB. 8: A rebroadcast (shortened to sixty minutes) of NBC-TV's "Nashville Remembers Elvis on His Birthday" (which first aired Jan. 8, 1978) was retitled "Elvis Remembered: Nashville to Hollywood."

FEB. 9: Rep. Barbara A. Mikulski (Dem., MD) again introduced a bill to honor January 8 as national Elvis Presley Day. It did not pass.

MAY 8: Elvis's paternal grandmother, Minnie Mae Presley, died in Memphis at the age of eighty-six.

JUNE 3: Mike Stone submitted material for an article titled "My Secret Love Affair With Priscilla," which appeared in a three-part series in the *Star*. Stone said he had contacted a professional hit man, who agreed to murder Elvis if Elvis ever followed through with his threats to kill Stone.

JUNE 24: In the Frankfurt, Germany, *Globe*, singer Margot Heine Kuzma alleged her son Leroy (b. 12/23/60) was

Elvis's child. Kuzma claimed that in 1959, she dated Elvis in West Germany.

AUG. 24: Priscilla Presley cohosted with Jim Stafford and Burgess Meredith the ABC-TV series "Those Amazing Animals" (through Aug. 23, 1981).

The British album *Elvis Sings Leiber and Stoller* was released in 1980. Leiber and Stoller wrote the liner notes.

SEPT.: Lisa Marie was having trouble in junior high school.

OCT. 6: Felton Jarvis redid many instrumental and backup vocal tracks on Elvis's songs at Young'Un Sound in Nashville. The songs can be heard on the LP *Guitar Man* (remixed version with longer vocals).

BY THE END OF 1980: The movie *Living Legend* was released and was rumored to be a biography of Elvis. Ginger Alden played the part of Jeannie Loring (lover of the Elvis character, named Eli Canfield). Roy Orbison sang the sound track. Earl Owensby, who played the Elvis clone in the movie, lip-synched Elvis's songs.

The 1979 book by Lena Canada, *To Elvis, With Love*, about a cerebral palsy patient's pen-pal relationship with Elvis, was made into a TV movie in 1980 and titled *Touched by Love*. It is not certain if Elvis wrote letters to the child or if his staff members did. Clips from the "Ed Sullivan Show" of Elvis singing "Love Me Tender" and "Reddy Teddy" are also in the film. An Elvis impersonator sang five other songs.

1981

Todd Slaughter, of the British Elvis Presley fan club, released the posthumous album *Inspirations*, which contained previously released religious songs by Elvis. It was advertised as one of Elvis's best gospel albums, earned platinum status, and hit the Top 5 on music charts.

It is ironic (and perhaps unjust) that Elvis won no major awards for his rockabilly or rock 'n' roll achievements. Elvis's only three Grammys were won for his gospel music.

Memphis disc jockey George Klein coproduced the syndicated special "Elvis Memories" for television. Elvis's singing voice was dubbed by Bill Haney. The show consisted primarily of interviews and film clips, with a short clip of Elvis on Wink Martindale's June 20, 1956, show "Dance Party."

JAN.: W. Whit Wells named a small red rose hybrid "Elvis."

JAN. 5: Linda Thompson married Bruce Jenner. They were divorced in 1987.

JAN. 8: Fans flocked to Graceland to celebrate Elvis's birthday.

MAR. 1: A film clip of Elvis singing "Love Me Tender" was shown at the Academy Awards ceremonies in California.

MAR. 1: *Elvis and the Beauty Queen* was aired on NBC-TV from nine to eleven P.M. It tells the story of Elvis's life with Linda Thompson. Don Johnson (who gained forty pounds to play Elvis) and Stephanie Zimbalist (as Linda Thompson) were the leads.

MAR.: Elvis's ex-yacht, the *Potomac* (previously owned by Pres. Franklin D.

Roosevelt, which Elvis gave to the St. Jude's Children's Hospital in Long Beach, California), sank at Treasure Island off San Francisco. After the *Potomac* was seized in a drug raid, the ship was towed to the island in 1980.

APR. 3: The Warner Brothers documentary *This Is Elvis* premiered in Memphis. Forty-seven Elvis songs are heard. Sam Phillips was played by his son, Knox Phillips. It's worth watching.

APR. 4: The world premier of *This Is Elvis* was held at the USA Film Festival in Dallas, Texas.

APR. 10: *This Is Elvis* was released throughout the U.S.

JULY: A court decision barred Factors, Etc., Inc. from any rights to distribute Elvis-related merchandise.

JULY 1–AUG. 28: "Elvis, An American Musical" was performed in Las Vegas at the Hilton Hotel.

In 1981, Steven C. Chanze's book *Is Elvis Alive?* claimed Elvis's death was a hoax organized by his lifelong friend Charlie Hodge, who placed a look-alike in the casket. Hodge filed a milliondollar libel suit against Chanze in 1982.

Platinum ran the story "Elvis Cover-up," but other tabloids had picked up the possible conspiracy story as early as 1977 or 1978.

In 1981, the IRS claimed Elvis's estate owed $14.6 million in inheritance taxes. The Department of Revenue added $2.3 million in tax interest due. In order to secure her daughter's financial future and keep Elvis's memory alive, Priscilla planned to open Graceland to the public. In defense of her marriage, divorce, and business ventures, Priscilla told *Woman's Day*, "We were just two people. We weren't trying to live up to a myth."

In 1981, Colonel Parker allegedly lost most of his money defending himself against various lawsuits, which stemmed from his business relationship with Elvis. The William Morris Agency volunteered to help support the Colonel through the rough times.

AUG. 15–21: *TV Guide* featured a portrait of Elvis on its cover with an article titled "How TV Reacted the Day Elvis Died."

SEPT. 15: At the Hollywood Palladium, some of the contents of Elvis's Beverly Hills home were auctioned by Don B. Smith. Bids came to a disappointing $50,000.

In 1981, Lisa Marie dropped out of high school. She soon became a drug addict, which caused friction between mother and daughter.

1982

Jack Soden was hired by Priscilla Presley in 1982, for $60,000 a year (plus bonuses) to run Graceland. He is still director. Soden is from Kansas City and is a former stockbroker/investment banker.

JUNE 7: Priscilla Presley opened Graceland to the public, charging $5 for admission. The upstairs, where Elvis's bedroom and private chambers are, has never been open to the public. The decoration of other rooms has been changed several times. Many of Elvis's possessions were taken by friends, stolen, sold, or kept in the mansion. In 1990, the inside of the mansion looked shabby, unkempt, and dirty. In 1991, the famous 1928 gold-leaf Kimball grand piano was sold and removed from the music room (where it had been since 1982). It was replaced by a black grand piano, which Linda Thomspon allegedly purchased. In 1992, Graceland was given a face-lift in order to prepare for yet another TV special.

The effect of Elvis and his music is hard to estimate, but it is fitting that Graceland honors his achievement-filled life with a Hall of Gold, in which his gold and platinum RIAA records and awards are displayed, alongside other trophies and presentations. Elvis said, "Long after I'm gone, what I did today will be heard by someone. I just want them to get the best of what I had." (See *Elvis, Images of a Legend.*)

OCT.:   RCA released *The Elvis Medley* of six songs: "Jailhouse Rock," "Teddy Bear," "Hound Dog," "Don't be Cruel," "Burning Love," and "Suspicious Minds" (RCA PB-13351). The medley had a nine-week stay on *Billboard*'s Top LPs chart.

1983

JAN. 8:   Vince Everett opened an Elvis Presley Museum in London.

New York CPA Joseph F. Rascoff managed Elvis Presley Enterprises and Elvis's trust. Rascoff compared Elvis to Mickey Mouse in popularity and marketing appeal.

Colonel Parker was paid $2 million by RCA to relinquish his rights to any and all of Elvis's record royalties. Factors, Etc., Inc. had previously bought Elvis's merchandising rights, and Parker legally agreed not to use or mention Elvis's name again.

APR.:   Priscilla Presley made her TV-movie acting debut with a leading role (as a scuba teacher) in the movie *Love Is Forever* starring Michael Landon. Soon after, she appeared on the popular TV series "Dallas," as "Jenna Wade."

1984

"Disciples of Elvis," produced by Thomas Corby and released by Monticello Productions, also known as "Mondo Elvis," is a disturbing look at the bizarre and often obsessive world of Elvis fans.

AUG.:   *Life* ran "The King's Ransom," an article that stated: "Elvis Presley is worth more dead than alive—his memory earning ten times as much as he made in his forty-two years, and that was $100 million."

1985

JAN. 5: "Elvis: One Night With You" showed the complete six P.M. performance from June 27, 1968 (of a taping of the comeback "Elvis"). The television special was made for Home Box Office cable TV. It was rerun repeatedly during the month.

JAN. 8: The video *Elvis Presley's Graceland*, narrated by Priscilla Presley, features the interior of Graceland. This tour of Elvis's mansion was on Showtime cable-TV network throughout the month and was produced by Steve Binder. It was filmed from August to November 1984, with an $800,000 budget. (Note: The first filmed glimpse of Elvis's 1928 Kimball gold-leaf grand piano is in this video. The piano is now owned by The 148 Investment Group of Akron, Ohio, and it is on display at the Country Music Hall of Fame.)

Priscilla tells fans of Elvis: "He was the King of rock 'n' roll, but he was more than that. He was a very special human being who touched our lives, our consciousness . . . as few men have ever done. There's no doubt that we all miss Elvis. . . . All the charm, the tal-

ent, the magic, the indefinable gift that made him such an important part of our lives, but we're very grateful for all the memories he's left us."

AUG.: A sixty-minute syndicated TV special titled "Elvis: The Echo Will Never Die" featured locals who knew or worked with Elvis. It was hosted by Kasey Kasem. Celebrities interviewed included Tom Jones, B. B. King, Ursula Andress, and Sammy Davis, Jr.

CA. AUG.: Paul Simon recorded the album *Graceland* in honor of Elvis. It won the 1986 Album of the Year Grammy Award, and the song "Graceland" received a 1987 Grammy for Record of the Year.

By the end of 1985, Priscilla Presley stopped dating model/actor Michael Edwards. For a short period she dated hairdresser Ellie Ezerzer.

Priscilla Presley (with Sandra Harmon) wrote *Elvis and Me*, a best-selling book (which became a 1988 TV miniseries).

Lee Cotton wrote the book *All Shook Up*.

1986

Paul McCartney hosted *The Real Buddy Holly Story* on British television, the BBC, in which color film footage of Elvis performing in Lubbock, Texas (ca. 1953–55) was shown. The box for the videocassette stated the footage of Elvis is the earliest known, which is correct.

FEB.: Elvis was posthumously inducted into the Rock and Roll Hall of Fame in Cleveland, Ohio, with its other first ten inductees: Chuck Berry, Little Richard, the Everly Brothers, James Brown, Sam Cook, Buddy Holly, Ray Charles, Fats Domino, and Jerry Lee Lewis.

SEPT. 22: "The Twilight Zone" featured an episode called "The Once and Future King," about an Elvis impersonator (played by Jeff Yagher) who mistakenly kills the man he imitates. Red West played a bit part.

► Jerry Lee Lewis at the Silverbird in Las Vegas. *Courtesy of John Reible, Las Vegas News Bureau, Las Vegas, Nevada.*

1987

The Jordanaires recorded and released the LP *A Tribute to Elvis' Favorite Spirituals*. The songs included were "Didn't It Rain," "Peace in the Valley," "Joshua Fit de Battle," "Search Me, Lord," "Dig a Little Deeper," "You Better Run," "Let Us Break Bread Together," "Wonderful Time Up There," "How Great Thou Art," "I'm a Rollin'," "Dip Your Fingers in Some Water," "Roll Jordan Roll," "One of These Mornings," and "Onward Christian Soldiers."

FEB. 8: In "Liberace on Living in the Limelight" (*San Antonio Light*, 2/8/87) the pianist talked of Elvis and his tragic ending. Liberace stated, "I remember going to see Elvis in 1969, in Las Vegas, when he made his so-called comeback. He was thrilling . . . electric. When I went to see him a few years later, he was just going through the motions. I sat there and cried because I knew how great he'd been capable of being, and how he just sort of threw it away. . . . I was very flattered that he considered me a friend, but I've more or less come to the conclusion that it's a lot easier to become famous than to remain famous. . . . You have to work at it."

MAR. 1: Priscilla Presley gave birth to a son, Navarone. The father is Brazilian writer-director Marco Garibaldi, with whom Priscilla lives. They are not married.

AUG.: *USA Today* named Fred L. Worth and Steve D. Tamerius's 1981 book, *All About Elvis*, one of five best books on the superstar. *USA Today* conducted a telephone call-in for fans to vote on their favorite Elvis song. With almost 31 percent of the votes "Suspicious Minds" came in No. 1 and "Love Me Tender" was No. 2 with 24 percent of the vote.

AUG. 16: Cinemax cable TV aired "Elvis '56," on August 16 at nine P.M. It was rerun throughout the month. This is a *must see* for those who know and love the early photography of Alfred Wertheimer, who took many vintage fifties shots. Period home movies are also included. "Elvis '56" is narrated by Levon Helm. Of particular interest to those enthralled with Elvis's early rock hits are glimpses of the "Hound Dog" and "Don't Be Cruel" recording sessions.

WINTER: *Florida Close-up* featured Jay B. Leviton's photos of the private Elvis of the fifties.

Elvis's 1957 recording of "I'll Be Home For Christmas" was used during the closing credits of *Lethal Weapon*.

1988

JAN.: The top money-earning dead artists in the music industry were named: No. 1, Elvis; No. 2, John Lennon of the Beatles; No. 3, Jimi Hendrix; and No. 4, Jim Morrison of the Doors.

A Dr. John Presley alleged he is the secret brother of Elvis and that Gladys and Vernon put him in an orphanage. There is no proof of this.

FEB. 7–8: The ABC-TV miniseries *Elvis and Me* was aired from nine to eleven P.M. over two nights. It is the story of Priscilla's life with Elvis, based on the book written by Priscilla Presley and Sandra Harmon. Dale Midkiff portrays Elvis and Susan Walters plays Priscilla. Over 63 million people watched the two nights' broadcast. It was the highest-rated TV movie of the 1987–88 season.

SUMMER: The summer issue of *Rejoice* printed a comprehensive overview of Elvis's gospel music. Photographs showed Elvis at a piano at Graceland with the Sunshine Boys, Eddie Wallace, Lamar Fike, Fred

Daniels, Ace Richman, and Burl Strevel.

SEPT.: *Memphis* magazine's "Dead Reckoning" scrutinized the Shelby County Medical Examiner's Officer in regard to the causes of Elvis's death.

Elvis, His Life From A to Z by Fred Worth and Steve Tamerius was published. It is a fine source for information and history related to Elvis.

The video release of *Elvis '56* (originally aired on Cinemax, August 16, 1987) made the top of *Billboard*'s Top Music Videocassette chart. If you only want to see *one* Elvis video, this is it.

OCT. 3: In *Forbes*'s "Elvis Presley Died in 1977. Guess How Much He Will Earn This Year?" the merchandising of Elvis was scrutinized.

OCT. 4: The National Enquirer's cover story was titled "Elvis Is Alive" and showed photographs taken in September 1988 that were said to be of Elvis Presley.

1989

In 1989, Mel Bergman acquired the rights to a taped version of the book *Is Elvis Alive?* and Bill Stanley wrote in his book *Elvis, My Brother*, "Weeks before Elvis' death the will was changed," but no proof of this has surfaced.

The video *Elvis: Comeback '68* was aired on NBC-TV. It would never have occurred to the jittery, nervous Elvis in 1968, that a 1989 *TV Guide* might name

his NBC-TV appearance the best rock performance ever to air on television. He had retained his crown and this would have pleased him.

Lisa Marie Presley and her husband, Daniel Keough, proudly announced the birth of their first child, Danielle. Keough's father was a religious leader at a Church of Scientology branch when the couple met.

1990

END OF MAY: At the first Elvis Awards ceremony held in New York City's Armory, the Rolling Stones' Keith Richards presented the blues guitarist Eric Clapton the award for Best Rock Guitarist (a trophy with Elvis singing at a microphone).

NOV. 27: "Priscilla Presley, How to Live with a Legend" was written by Leonora Langley for *Woman's Day.* Langley quoted a revealing statement made by Priscilla: "Being married implies ownership. . . . All of a sudden, one owns the other and the respect is lost."

During 1990, Graceland made millions of dollars from admission tickets and souvenirs.

The ABC-TV docu-series "Elvis: Good Rockin' Tonight" premiered featuring Michael St. Gerard as Elvis. Gerard also played Elvis in *Heart of Dixie* and *Great Balls of Fire!*

1991

JAN. 8: Many people, such as Iva Finkenbiner of Conway, South Carolina, celebrated Elvis's birthday every January 8. To mark the event in 1991, Iva baked a guitar-shaped cake and sold handmade blue suede shoes and hound dogs from her shop, Craft Patch.

Lisa Marie and Priscilla Presley promoted Oldsmobiles in a national TV ad campaign. Priscilla also ran full-page ads for her perfume, "Moments," which stated, "A Single Moment Can Change Your Life."

MAY: It was announced that Lisa Marie would not do anything with her inheritance until she turned thirty, not twenty-five. Tickets to Graceland currently cost $15.95 (more than triple the original price tag; tours include a small museum, Elvis's airplane and tour bus, and shops.)

MID-MAY: Priscilla and Lisa Marie have been criticized by fans for being members of the Church of Scientology.

Elvis fans were upset by rumors that Lisa Marie and Priscilla had willed (or given) Graceland and/or Elvis's assets from royalties to the Church of Scientology. Elvis Presley Enterprises, Inc., has kept Priscilla and Lisa Marie's plans for their assets from Elvis's estate a secret. One thing is for sure: money that Lisa Marie receives from Elvis's royalties and estate goes in part, via donations, to the Church of Scientology.

JULY 8: Russian leader Boris Yeltsin admitted one of his favorite Elvis songs is "Are You Lonesome Tonight." (*Boston Herald,* 7/8/91).

AUG. 13: *Weekly World News'* story "Elvis Photo Taken Just Days Ago . . . By a St. Louis Housewife" refueled fans' hopes that the King was still alive.

SEPT. 23: Kelly Wadsworth made the news when she claimed she had seen Elvis in a diner in Clyde, Ohio. Elvis "sightings" are numerous and frequent. Someone calling himself Jon Burrows (one of Elvis's code names) and using Elvis's social security number was transacting financial deals through December 1991. The identity of this mysterious Mr. Burrows has yet to be uncovered.

NOV. 1–2: *USA Today* ran a short article "What's Next? Elvis: Still Dead? The Latest Word . . ."

NOV. 10: Bono of the rock group U2 said, "Elvis Presley could say more in *somebody else's* song than Albert Goldman could say in any book." (*Cleveland Plain Dealer*, Nov. 10, 1991.) Goldman had been universally criticized for his book, *Elvis*, published by McGraw-Hill, which paints an unflattering picture of the King.

NOV. 14: *Rolling Stone* featured Elvis's gold-lame jacket, and the issue included *Elvis Presley, RCA, 1956*, and the album cover for *50,000,000 Elvis Fans Can't Be Wrong*.

DEC.: *Art and Antiques* featured Elvis's first performance guitar to be auctioned (with an estimated value of $350,000–400,000) at Red Baron Antiques in Atlanta, Georgia (which had reportedly sold Elvis records from 1954–56 for $198,000).

The funniest chronicle of Elvis's "afterlife" is Greil Marcus's *Dead Elvis*. "Elvis continues to fascinate because he remains an enigma," says Marcus. The *Sun* illustrated the absurdity of it all with its article "Statue of Elvis Found on Mars."

ABC-TV went to court to make Elvis's autopsy public.

Graceland's income from Elvis is estimated to be as high as $50 million a year. In any normal month, Graceland has receipts of approximately $20,000 a day from the sale of house-tour tickets alone.

Elvis Presley Enterprises oversees licensing of Elvis-related business deals and merchandising. Graceland is a subsidiary of Elvis Presley Enterprises. Music royalties go to the estate, not EPE (approximately $1.5 million yearly).

1992

JAN.: After years of fans' campaigning for an Elvis Presley stamp, the U.S. Postal Service issued a 1993 commemorative stamp to honor him as the King of rock 'n' roll, in a fourteen-part Legends of American Music stamp series. The date of its release was to be January 8, 1993, the King's fifty-eighth birthday.

Elvis supporters have a seventy-one-year-old grandmother, Pat Geiger of Vermont, to thank for spearheading the Elvis stamp drive since 1984. As "20/20" revealed (June 6, 1992), the Elvis Presley estate paid Pat Geiger's way to Memphis to witness the winner of the Elvis-stamp image when it was unveiled. With the help of William D. Lorge (a Republican state representative from Bear Creek, Wisconsin) a thirteen-member Citizens' Stamp Advisory Committee was convinced to "immortalize" Elvis by allowing him to be the first music personality to appear in the 1993 Legend series.

Predicting the stamp would be the most popular in U.S. postal history, the Postal Service pleased millions of devotees when it took an unprecedented step: the public was asked to vote on a U.S. stamp's image. Would it be the Hillbilly Cat, that pubescent Elvis of the fifties, or would they prefer the older, overweight Elvis of the seventies? In 1991, the U.S. Postal Service cleared $175 million selling specialty stamps. Ballots for the "image election" would be printed on postcards.

JAN. 22: *The Elvis Conspiracy—The Elvis Files*, a two-hour special, was aired on TV, hosted by Bill Bixby. Seventy-nine percent of the viewing audience believed Elvis was alive and in hiding. The program alleged that after Nixon and Elvis met in 1970, Elvis may have become a secret FBI agent in the government protection program and he may now live in Eerie, Indiana. Author Gail Brewer-Giorgio of Las Vegas professed the "FBI has declassified over thirty thousand documents related to Elvis" (which is close to accurate). She also alleged she can document that Elvis attempted to work for the FBI from 1971 to 1974 in a sting operation against organized crime and drugs. Mel Bergman concluded, "He did not die, but merely dropped out."

During the TV show, Joe Esposito recoiled, saying, "Elvis is dead. I was there! . . . He's definitely not an agent for any law enforcement agency." Charlie Hodge and Larry Geller also saw Elvis's body after he died.

The FBI scrutinized Elvis for years. When he first hit the national scene, FBI agents watched the Cat because Hoover suspected he would try to overthrow the government. In the sixties, he was stalked because he was considered a possible drug dealer. When the FBI was alerted to Elvis's insistence on obtaining a narcotics badge (which he received from Pres. Richard M. Nixon in 1970), the Bureau thought Elvis meant to use the badge to buy and sell contraband. In the seventies, the FBI conjectured that Elvis wanted to purchase Robert Vesco's airplane for drug trafficking.

JAN. 27: An article titled "No One Wants to Remember the Fat Elvis" appeared in the *Cleveland Plan Dealer* regarding which stamp would win the U.S. Postal Service's contest. Two images of Elvis were selected from sixty-five paintings by eight artists—a young Elvis and the "Las Vegas" Elvis of the seventies.

Many Elvis fans did not appreciate the younger image's conservative-looking, slick hairstyle or the tie around his neck. A younger, sneering Elvis was the image that people remembered and the one that would most accurately portray the rock 'n' roll rebel.

The older Elvis showed the King with sideburns, his gem-studded collar up, and an intensely emotional expression. Unlike the younger image, the seventies' view shows Elvis as he was, sweating during an impassioned performance. While it represented a time when a tiring schedule, loneliness, and illness dominated his life, it also symbolized the lasting power and influence of the man. In many ways, the older image was more appropriate than the younger image.

JAN. 27: The Postmaster General affirmed in *People* that the Postal Service was promoting the "Love Me Slender" look and was trying to "avoid the word *bloated*."

FEB. 17: On "Geraldo," a fan in the audience told Dee Stanley Presley (after she accused Elvis of many indiscreet acts), *"You'll never tarnish gold!"* The audience became close to violent in its defense of Elvis's reputation. Dee responded, "Everyone around Elvis lived a lie," which was, in part, true, but no one wanted to hear it. Janelle McCombe, Joe Esposito, and J. D. Sumner denied Dee's various and scandalous claims, which included Elvis having sex with Gladys, the possibility he was gay, that he was a hard-drug user, and many more accusations.

FEB. 18: Dee Presley wrote a five-part series in the *National Enquirer*. Headlines read: "Elvis and His Mom Were Lovers/Forbidden Love Led to Her Death/Suicide Note Proves He Killed Himself/The Horrifying Night He Raped Priscilla/His Secret Gay Life." Sensationalizing almost every aspect of Elvis's life, Dee revealed her "information" fifteen years after the singer's death.

FEB. 24: On the TV show "Geraldo," Elvis's cook for eleven years, Mary Jenkins, denied she told Dee Presley facts about Presley family incest, called Dee Presley "a liar," and claimed she was unaware Elvis had a drug problem!

Elvis's stepbrother Billy Stanley claimed in *Elvis, My Brother* that the Cat consumed "nine packs" of drugs the night he died. He also asserted Aunt Delta brought Elvis drugs hours before his death.

FEB. 24: Dan Rather announced on the nightly news that Elvis was "wanted dead or alive." Dan Rather then decreed "ballot" postcards would be released on April 6, so the public could vote for the Elvis stamp portrait of their choice. Rather suggested the Elvis stamp election might be more spirited than the forthcoming presidential election in November.

MAR. 4: Priscilla Presley was named one of the 50 Most Beautiful People in the World, 1992, in *People*. The issue showed Priscilla with red hair. She was 46. The article alleged Elvis's estate was worth $50 million.

MAR. 19: Michael Goldbert wrote of the Elvis stamp in *Rolling Stone:* "Elvis' fans have been pushing for a stamp to memorialize Elvis since just a few years after his death. . . . What we've done is translate this push for an Elvis stamp into a whole series."

MAR. 23–24: The State of Tennessee brought five new charges against Dr. George C. Nichopoulos for having overprescribed drugs to Elvis and others. The State Department of Health planned to suspend and revoke permanently Nichopoulos's medical license. (Reported in the *Patriot Ledger*, Brockton, MA, Mar. 24, 1992.)

MAR. 20: CBS-TV filmed Hank Williams, Jr., at Elvis's gold-leaf 1928 Kimball grand piano for the "Country Music Hall of Fame's Twenty-fifth Anniversary Celebration." The TV special was later aired to a national audience.

APR. 5: Disc jockey Jay Gordon (who runs a sixty-minute show of Elvis oldies on Boston's WODS-FM 103.3 every Sunday at eight A.M.) gave nineteen-cent stamps to anyone who promised to place one on a postcard, vote for his or her favorite Elvis stamp image, and mail it to the U.S. Postal Service.

APR. 6: April 6 was the first day the public could vote on which Elvis image it wanted on the stamp. The 5 million postcard ballots distributed to post offices vanished within hours, while "Entertainment Tonight" and CNN asked people to call in votes to their affiliate stations (at a cost of up to ninety cents per call). Everyone seemed to be jumping on the lucrative bandwagon. Attentive viewers called in their votes to TV stations, and the masses listened the next night to learn which stamp image was ahead in the polls. The younger Elvis was leading.

APR. 17: *National Enquirer* writer Mike Wallace said on "A Current Affair" that Lisa Marie claimed to have had "an out-of-body experience." He also said that Lisa Marie's second birthday party for her daughter Danielle was nothing like the kind of party Elvis would have thrown for his granddaughter.

APRIL 18: Jim and Judith Kelley of Rockland, Massachusetts, were married à la Elvis. Guests danced as two Elvis impersonators (Doug McIntyre and Ron Allsop) sang Elvis hits in rhinestone-studded costumes. An impressive ice sculpture of Elvis graced the main table, while Elvis stamp ballots were at each place setting. (See photograph on page 324.)

APR. 24: Even though ABC News announced that Ralph Nader opposed the Elvis stamp, Postmaster General Anthony M. Frank decided to run the issue.

"A Current Affair" asked Elvis's stepbrother Rick Stanley about Elvis's death (Rick is now a minister who preaches against drug abuse) and Dr. Nichopoulos, who shook his head and said, "I couldn't believe he had died." Vester Presley claimed, "Elvis had bone cancer. . . . He was takin' drugs."

APR. 24: The deadline for sending in a postcard to the U.S. Postal Service to vote for the Elvis stamp was midnight. The Postal Service had impersonators of Elvis in over fifty locations to remind people to vote.

APR. 27: "Don't Be Cruel" was the background music honoring Democratic presidential hopeful Bill Clinton during a Boston fund-raiser.

MAY: "Hard Copy" aired "I, Elvis—The Last Moments in the Life of the King" and advertised the show in many national magazines: "From rising star to fallen idol. Never before heard eyewitness accounts. The raw Elvis. The rare Elvis. The real Elvis. A "Hard Copy" exclusive. Three consecutive nights. Don't miss a single moment. AN EXCLUSIVE REPORT." *Nothing* new was revealed.

MAY 1: Cybill Shepherd asserted on Sally Jessie Raphael's TV show that she met Elvis at Graceland in 1972, and had to bring a girlfriend with her for protection. However, she dated Elvis on the sly in 1966, and showed *no* fear of him then.

MAY 6: Elvis's 1928 gold-leaf Kimball grand piano was shown by CBS-TV's Mark McEwen, who incorrectly said Elvis bought the piano as a gift for his mother. Priscilla Presley has told fans for years that she bought it for Elvis for their first wedding anniversary.

JUNE 4: The winning image for the Elvis stamp was announced at Graceland at 7:36 A.M. by Priscilla Presley who revealed the winning image to be the young Elvis of the fifties. Postmaster General Anthony Frank told the audience it had received 851,000 votes, while the older likeness of Elvis lost with 277,000.

Wisconsin Senate candidate Russell Feingold had "Elvis" endorse him in a 1992 ad, while presidential hopeful Bill Clinton played "Heartbreak Hotel" on a sax on the Arsenio Hall show before a national TV audience.

Is it any wonder Elvis appeared in Democratic Party literature as the convention's "entertainment coordinator"? During his campaign for president, Gov. Bill Clinton napped on a plane listening to Elvis tapes and kept the King's photographs by his side. (See *Life*, November 1992.) In December 1992, Clinton received from DJ Jay Gordon (WODS, Boston, "Elvis Only" program) three Elvis CDs and "The Cards of His Life," for which president-elect Clinton wrote a thank-you note stating, "I'm looking forward to listening to the CDs. The cards will make a great addition to my Elvis memorabilia."

JUNE 15: *U.S. News & World Report* noted the Postal Service's stamp election cost $300,000, but revenues from the Elvis commemorative stamp were

▲ Elvis impersonators Ron Allsop (left) and Doug MacIntyre (right) at the wedding celebration of Mr. and Mrs. Jim Kelley of Rockland, Massachusetts, 1992. *Courtesy of Mr. and Mrs. Jim Kelley.*

expected to reach $20 million. (See *People*, June 15, 1992.)

JUNE 23: RCA released a boxed set of 140 tracks (14 previously unreleased) titled *The King of Rock 'n' Roll: The Complete '50s Masters. Rolling Stone* gave it a "classic" rating on August 6. The limited-edition, numbered set of digitally remastered five CDs (or five tapes) came with a ninety-two-page booklet on the recording history of Elvis in the fifties, and a page of thirty-six Elvis "stamps" illustrating Elvis's fifties' RCA record covers. Price for the CD box set, $75 (found in discount stores for as little as $48). The RCA collection covers original RCA Record Label and Sun masters. By November 20, the set reached platinum in the U.S. and gold in the rest of the world. It was the 111th RIAA platinum or gold certification earned for an Elvis recording.

JULY: Publishers Clearing House of Port Washington, New York, sold a limited-edition series of nine genuine Elvis Presley postage stamps from around the world. A 45-rpm "record sleeve" listed titles of Elvis's greatest hits. The package cost $10.95.

In October 1992, U.A.V. Apparels offered through Home Shopping Club (HSC) for $19.95 (plus $3.95 for shipping and handling and state tax) a 100 percent cotton Elvis Presley nightshirt, adorned with a large color image of

ROCK & ROLL SINGER, 1935-1977

29 USA ELVIS

the "winning Elvis stamp." By the end of the year, the winning image would appear on over a hundred different marketed items.

JULY: WRMR-AM 850 deejay/lawyer Bill Randle (of Lakewood, OH) sold the rights to some of the earliest film footage of Elvis in concert (shot by cameraman Jack Barnett) to the London-based Merlin Group for a reported $1 million. The Merlin Group turned a quick profit and sold the film to PolyGram International for a rumored $2.2 million. PolyGram planned to air the footage on U.S. television in 1993, and release it in video form.

The eighteen minutes of film shows Elvis, Scotty Moore, and Bill Black on October 20, 1955, performing five songs at Brooklyn High School in Cleveland, when the "hillbillies" opened for Bill Haley & the Comets, Pat Boone, and the Four Lads. On October 19 of that year, deejay Tommy Edwards (WERE) put Elvis on the air at the old Circle Theater at E. Tenth Street, and eighteen days later, Colonel Parker entered the picture and became Elvis's manager.

Randle claims he had a contract to manage Elvis dated November 3, 1955, which he never signed, but was given to him by publishers Jean and Julian Aberback of Hill and Range.

The newly found 1955 footage, considered "lost" for thirty-seven years, was discovered in a vault at Universal Studios in Los Angeles. Originally titled *The Pied Piper of Cleveland*, it was shot for Universal to honor country music's top deejay in 1955, Bill Randle. When Universal did not release the film, Randle bought the Elvis sections. Randle showed the film on WEWS Channel 5 and at the Euclid Shore Junior High School in 1956. *Note:* Randle was the first disc jockey to play Presley records above the Mason-Dixon Line. Randle will not discuss the price he received for the footage.

The Merlin Group is rumored to have found 150 letters allegedly written by Elvis to an elderly female confidant

▲ The winning Elvis stamp. *Courtesy of the Accord Park, Hingham, Massachusetts, post office.*

in Germany. The last letter is rumored to have been written the day before he died. The Group is working on a documentary that will highlight the last five years of Elvis's life.

AUG.: In August of 1992, Revolutionary Comics issued the first in a series called "The Elvis Presley Experience" by Herb Shapiro, Patrick McCray, and Aaron Sowd, and "Elvis Shrugged" (July 1992) by McCray/Crompton, which are both "unauthorized and proud of it." Fox Comics Legend Series published "The Unauthorized Biography of Elvis," and Jam Press began a ten-part comic-book series in black-and-white titled "Elvis, His Life & Afterlife" in August 1992. Jam Press also offered Elvis T-shirts for $15 with limited-edition prints for $70 and posters of Elvis for $15.

AUG.: The film *Honeymoon in Vegas* featured thirteen Elvis impersonators. Crammed full of Elvis hits, the PG-13 flick was a box-office smash.

One hundred feet from Elvis's birthplace in Tupelo, the dedication of another Elvis Presley Museum drew national attention, and throngs of visitors waited patiently to view the small museum's displays. All the memorabilia in the museum was donated by Janelle McCombe, chairwoman of the Elvis Presley Memorial Foundation.

AUG. 12: The television show "48 Hours" focused on Elvis mania. Dan Rather stated that "Forty-four percent of all Americans are Elvis fans." Calling Elvis "an original artist" who earned more than 110 gold/platinum records (which far exceeds the total for any other artist), Rather noted fanatics "love Elvis." Singer Joan Jett admitted, if there had been no Elvis, there would be no rock 'n' roll as we know it.

AUG. 16: Over twenty-five thousand devoted fans flocked to Graceland to

be a part of an annual candlelight vigil to honor Elvis's memory.

Since his death, the myths surrounding Elvis have grown out of proportion. The most popular T-shirt sold on Elvis Presley Boulevard shows various locations of "Elvis sightings" in the last few years, from the local greasy spoon to a K Mart in Chicago. Elvis's legacy continues to grow, and the fact that many people still insist he is alive and well only proves he is growing in prominence, not diminishing into obscurity.

Mori Yasumasa from Japan won the 1992 Elvis impersonator contest in Memphis and was awarded $500.

AUG. 17–20: "I saw Elvis at the Republican National Convention, Houston, TX, Aug. 17–20, 1992" buttons were sold at the Republican Convention. The Democrats had a similar button that sold out in New York City.

AUG. 20: At the Republican Convention, Pres. George Bush referred to Elvis twice during his acceptance speech for the Republican nomination. Democratic presidential hopeful Gov. Bill Clinton of Arkansas had previously announced his adoration for Elvis and had campaigned for the young-Elvis stamp image.

Crown published the humorous book *Elvis for President (by the Committee to Elect the King)*.

AUG. 20: The Japanese contemplated creating their own version of Graceland.

AUG. 28: The Toronto Institute for Elvis Presley Studies was directed by Kevin Quain, author of *The Elvis Reader*.

OCT. 15: In this issue of *Rolling Stone*, Ray Charles stated that Elvis learned to shake his hips "on Beale Street in Memphis. That's where he saw the *black* people doin' that. Ain't no way they'd let anybody like us get on TV and do that, but *he* could 'cause he's white." In that same issue, Bruce Springsteen was asked if he was ever a victim of "the Elvis Presley syndrome." Springsteen responded, "The type of fame that Elvis had . . . the pressure of it and the isolation that it seems to require has gotta be really painful. I wasn't gonna let that happen to me."

Sloane Gallery in Denver, Colorado, featured a painted wooden sculpture by Leonid Sokov titled *Elvis and Lenin*. The Elvis image was taken directly from the movie *Jailhouse Rock*. (See *Art News*, October 1992, for a color reproduction.)

In 1992, an Elvis cookbook was published. If you are a junk-food junkie, this is the book you've been looking for!

The first of 660 Elvis Celebrity Cards (the size of baseball cards) were released by the River Group, P.O. Box 2149, Westport, CT 06880. A set of four cards went on sale in Boston for $12. Selling at first for $1.50 a packet, the price climbed to $15 in some locales. At $3 per card, the 660 cards will cost collectors an astounding $1,980. Series I, II, and III each contained 220 cards and were sold individually or in twelve-card packs. No complete set was sold as a unit, therefore collectors were forced to buy many more cards to complete a set. No pack had the same cards in them. The 660 cards complete fourteen Elvis Collection subsets, which have some exclusive photos. For $9.95, a fifty-card set commemorating Elvis's platinum and gold records became available. An album with ten protective sheets, subset dividers, and two five-by-seven "King" cards were on sale for $19.95. The River Group also promoted an Elvis watch, an Elvis T-shirt, two videos, and other Elvis-related items.

The TV film *Elvis and the Colonel: The Untold Story* began production in October. Beau Bridges played Colonel Parker and Bob Youngblood portrayed Elvis. (Aired Jan. 10, 1993, on NBC.)

OCT. 24: CNN announced the birth of Lisa Marie's second child, a seven-pound-eight-ounce boy, named Benjamin Storm, born in Tampa Bay, Florida.

NOV.: A Postal Service promotion of memorabilia associated with the Elvis stamp was sent to stamp-poll participants. "In January the King will Rule . . . own a piece of rock 'n' roll history" was printed on a brochure telling of items for sale: an Elvis Stamp Sleeve and Sheet of Stamps ($11.60); the Elvis Commemorative Album with a block of four mint stamps ($19.95); the Elvis Limited-Edition Print ($14.95); the Exclusive "First Day" Ceremony Program, with an Elvis stamp and Graceland cancellation ($5.95)—the lot for $44.95. Millions of enthusiasts called 1-800-STAMP-24.

Rolling Stone featured Alfred Wertheimer's June 30, 1956, photo of Elvis kissing a young actress backstage during the rehearsals for "Baby, Let's Play House." Other photos and stories of Wertheimer's exclusive photo sessions with Elvis are in the same issue.

NOV. 3: Bill Clinton, an avid Elvis fan, was elected the forty-second president of the United States.

An eighty-page copy of Elvis's estate inventory became available to fans on November 3. For a copy, send $15.95 to Enterprise, 20-04 Utopia Parkway, Suite 211, Whitestone, NY 11357.

Unseen Elvis was a compilation of candid shots from the collection of Jim Curlin, published by Bullfinch Press with Little, Brown & Company at $29.95.

Timothy Frew published a book titled *Elvis*.

NOV. 19: Elvis music was played daily on Prague's radio station Prognosis. One Prague disc jockey announced in November that Elvis had been seen in the square. The story was covered on "Prime Time Live," November 19.

DEC. 1: *Life*'s special issue of rock 'n' roll reported, "Elvis Presley, a regular at the all-you-can-eat pharmaceutical buffet, was found dead (on the throne, in a matter of speaking) in his lavish Graceland bedroom. . . ." (p. 54)

DEC. 10: The U.S. Postal Service announced the Elvis stamp was "selling out" its unprecedented 300-million issue (nearly double all others) before its release date of January 8, 1993. It would make philatelic history as the best-selling stamp in U.S. history. By the end of December a 500-million issue was printed to fill fans' demands.

Postal Service Presley paraphernalia licensed and sold (with the approval of the Presley estate) included everything from coffee mugs and puzzles to pot holders and skirts. The Postal Service was delighted with advance orders for four sold-out limited-edition Elvis philatelic collectibles ($5.95–19.95).

DEC. 10–24: *Rolling Stone* paid tribute to eight artists, one of whom was Elvis.

DEC. 22: What would Christmas be without Elvis? The Hanover Mall in Hanover, Massachusetts, sold silk ties of Elvis and framed 3-D pictures of the Cat that lit up and played "Viva Las Vegas." If a fan didn't like those gift ideas, Hallmark produced a full-length-figure, brass-plated Elvis Keepsake Ornament, and the U.S. Postal Service sold Elvis-stamp Christmas ornament balls. Springbok distributed a thousand-piece "Elvis, the King" puzzle for $15.95. The Bradford Exchange advertised the Delphi release (endorsed and authorized by the estate of Elvis Presley) of three limited-edition collector porcelain plates in the "Elvis Presley Hit Parade" series (each eight and one-quarter inches across, full color, with twenty-two-karat gold borders, $29.75) featuring Elvis Presley in *Loving You*, "Heartbreak Hotel," and "Blue Suede Shoes" (to order call 1-800-541-8811). The Bradford Exchange had previously issued a "Looking at the Legend Series," which included Elvis's performance on the USS *Arizona* with his mother, and in *Viva Las Vegas.*

1993

JAN. 1: The *Boston Globe* announced the youthful image of Elvis and his stamp were "in" for 1993 trends, while the chunky Elvis was "out."

JAN. 8: At 12:01 A.M. from Graceland, 500 million U.S. postal stamps with Elvis's image were released to the public for sale. Jack Soden (chief executive officer of Elvis Presley Enterprises, Inc.) made a few remarks, followed by Marvin Runyon (Postmaster General and chief executive officer of the U.S. Postal Service) with a dedication. Mark Stutzman of Mountain Lake, Maryland, was honored for having designed the winning stamp's image. (The older image of Elvis had been designed by John Berkey of Excelsior, Minnesota.)

The first issue was "stamped" with the musical gates of Graceland adorning a postcard. The Postal Service published a large booklet titled *Elvis Presley*, the first of the U.S. Postal Service Commemorative Edition (copyright 1992). In it was written: "Elvis Presley changed the world with his music. Almost single-handedly he launched the musical movement that became the Age of Rock & Roll."

The release of the postage stamp coincided with Graceland's three-day birthday bash, beginning at midnight on January 7.

At 12:01 A.M., January 8, Elvis Presley Day was proclaimed in Memphis, and fifteen hundred fans stood in the rain for hours for tickets to join in the celebration. Graceland restaurants and shops were open twenty-four hours, there was a dinner party with a lavish birthday cake, and a dance gala featured Elvis music. An estimated $3 million in tickets to the party and in souvenirs were sold in Memphis.

The celebration ended on January 9, with the annual Elvis Fan Club Presidents' luncheon at the Heartbreak Hotel Restaurant, followed by the Memphis Symphony's final salute to the King. For those who couldn't be in Memphis, TNT's week-long "Elvis Lives" TV series featured a two-part miniseries during a festival of Elvis films.

Advertisements stated that upcoming Memphis postmarks of the Elvis stamp would feature the gates of Graceland, and a variety of envelopes bearing the first-day issues, cover, and cancellations would be available to anyone who appeared at designated postal offices.

But . . . *did* Graceland *really* issue the "first-day" stamps? Actually, the Postal Service had mistakenly shipped thousands of Elvis commemorative stamps to the Amarillo, Texas, post office approximately twelve days before they were to be officially released. Therefore the Amarillo post office *sold all their stamps in December 1992!* So if you didn't buy stamps from Amarillo, you don't have the *premiere* "first-day" issues!

JAN.: Elvis dressed in his gold-lamé suit is the image on a rare hologram promo card distributed by International, Inc.

JAN. 9: It seems even presidents know a good thing when they see it. Following President Clinton's fondness for Elvis, the Richard Nixon Presidential Library in California sold Nixon/Elvis White House wristwatches for $45, and an oversize postcard showing Nixon and Elvis at the White House from 1970, in honor of both Nixon's eightieth birthday on January 9 and Elvis's fifty-eighth birthday on January 8. Two life-size cutouts of President Nixon and Elvis were also available for photo shoots.

JAN. 12: The *National Enquirer* reported that Lisa Marie claimed to have spoken to Elvis and that he recently instructed her to write, sing, and act in movies. Jerry Schilling (once a member of the Memphis Mafia) is her manager. The article also claimed Lisa Marie plans "to become the new Elvis."

The *National Examiner* advertised five different envelopes featuring the Elvis stamp. At $2 each or $8 for a set of five, each envelope had the official first-day postmark of January 8, 1993. Fleetwood First Day Covers were certified by the Official First Day of Issue postmark of Memphis, Tennessee, and were painted by artist Tom McNeely in full color. The images included Elvis as a Young Rocker, as a Teen Idol, as a GI, in Hollywood, and in Vegas.

Everyone wanted to ride atop the Elvis stamp bandwagon. By 1991, twelve countries had issued Elvis stamps. (See *U.S. News & World Report*, 12/28–1/4, 1992.) Six months before the U.S. Postal Service's release, the tiny island of St. Vincent, British West Indies, was busily printing nine different stamps presenting various stages of the singer's career. Jeffrey Franz of the International Collectors Society, Baltimore, MD (1-800-333-5116, ext. 9) distributed the oversized $1 stamps in the U.S. for $9 a sheet (plus $3 postage). Limit: six sheets per customer. Each sheet was accompanied by "99 Little Known Facts About Elvis Presley" (many of which are incorrect).

JAN. 16: It seems everyone "cared" about Elvis after it was too late. "Dick Clark Ripped Elvis' Manager" appeared in the *Beacon Journal* of Akron, Ohio.

While he toured to promote the American Music Awards in Los Angeles, Clark talked about Colonel Parker's "horrendous mismanagement" of Elvis. "Mr. Showbiz, who bit his tongue for years, insists Parker was despicable." Clark alleged the reports of Elvis's manager taking 50 percent of his client's earnings were way too low: "Parker also took exorbitant agent's fees for cutting deals off the top," Clark admitted. "The Colonel made more money than his act. . . . He kept him [Elvis] in a cage like an animal. He trotted him out like a trained bear." Clark went on to say: "It's my contention that had Elvis been handled properly and had loved ones around him who really cared, who weren't just sucking his blood dry, he might be alive today."

JAN. 20: The *Boston Globe* listed Elvis first in a list of "favorite music" for Bill and Hillary Clinton and noted one of President Clinton's political nicknames was "Elvis."

JAN. 21: The Elvis stamp created a new kind of problem for the U.S. Postal Service: thousands of ardent Elvis fans affixed the stamp to envelopes sent to fictitious names and addresses hoping the envelopes would come back stamped "Return to Sender—Address Unknown".

FEB. 2: Many newspapers ran the story of Lisa Marie's decision *not* to sell her father's estate, as provided in his will. Lisa turned the magical age of twenty-five on February 1, the date upon which she could legally take charge of her inheritance from Elvis. Lisa Marie decided to leave the management of Graceland and every aspect of Elvis's multimillion-dollar estate, to Jack Soden, head of Elvis Presley Enterprises. Inc., for no less than five more years. Lisa Marie serves on the board and now has control of the estate. Up until February 1, 1993, the estate was managed under a trust. Elvis's estate is cur-

rently estimated to be worth between $60 and $100 million.

MAR. 1: *People* magazine ran a front page cover story about Lisa Marie titled "Elvis' Baby Girl . . ." and noted her dad's estate is now hers and is worth close to $100 million.

MAR. 5: Jack Soden, chief executive officer of Elvis Presley Enterprises, is a savvy businessman hired by Priscilla Presley. EPE signed a contract with RCA giving the Presley estate a royalty for every sale of Elvis material. Since 1983 (when the Tennessee legislature guaranteed commercial rights to the name and image of a deceased celebrity would pass to his or her heirs) anyone wanting to obtain a license to create and sell Elvis-related objects must pay a hefty licensing fee to EPE and pay an *advance* royalty to EPE, calculated upon expected sales of said item(s). It is rumored companies have paid in excess of $1 million to create and sell Elvis-related commodities.

MAY 14: Elvis's Martin D-18 sold in London at Christie's South Kensington for $152,000.

MAY 15: At the Classic American Guitar Show at Five Towns College in Dix Hills, New York, dealer Stanley Jay of Mandolin Brothers Ltd. of Staten Island asked $75,000 for a 1958 Gibson LG-1 guitar that he claims Elvis gave to Anita Wood as a Christmas present that year. It is inscribed "To Little, From EP" ("Little" was a nickname for Wood). (See *Maine Antique Digest*, August 1993.)

MAR. 17: The acoustic guitar Elvis strummed while serenading Ann-Margret in the 1964 film *Viva Las Vegas* sold for $22,000 at Richard Wolfer's rock memorabilia auction in San Francisco. It was featured in *Art and Auction*, May 1993.

APR.:   The Republic of the Marshall Islands announced the issue of a $5 commemorative coin (with protective case) honoring the fortieth anniversary of Elvis's first recording. The cupronickel coin is sold through Fleetwood (1-800-443-3233) for $5 each plus a $1.50 handling charge, limited to five coins per person.

APR. 19:   Unicover World Trade Corporation, by authority of the government of the Republic of the Marshall Islands, offered a commemorative coin set (boxed with a certificate of authenticity) for $71, which included a $50 silver coin (one full troy ounce of .999 pure silver), a $10 commemorative coin of solid brass with a decagonal border, and a $5 round commemorative coin of cupronickel. Minted in 1993, limited edition (1-800-443-3232).

APR. 26:   While the Elvis Presley Museum on Tour traveled through Boston, Massachusetts, the *Boston Globe* featured impersonator Lee Blaze of Danvers, Massachusetts, appearing as the King of Suffolk Downs. Elvis impersonators participated in karaoke contests and received free admission to the traveling exhibition of Elvis's furniture, artwork, and personal items.

MAY: Fleetwood issued a limited-edition Proofcard first edition of the first Elvis stamp, certified by the Official First Day of Issue postmark of Memphis, Tennessee, in a deluxe collector's album. Original artwork by Tom McNeely. Size: six by nine inches. Available for $10 (plus shipping and handling). Call 1-800-443-3232.

The Ashton-Drake Galleries of Niles, Illinois, offered for sale (one to a customer) a sixteen-inch Elvis doll dressed in a white jumpsuit named "Elvis—the King of Las Vegas" from the Elvis: Lifetime of a Legend Series ($99.96 plus $5.88 shipping and handling; $149 each in Canada). Hand-painted porcelain, premiere grade. The company boasts that its 1992 "Elvis at

Ascot" doll, which originally sold for $125, is now worth $211 (advertised in *USA Weekend*, May 2, 1993).

The Franklin Mint of Franklin Center, Pennsylvania, together with Graceland offered for sale "the First Hand-Signed Limited Edition Art Print of its King" by Nate Giorgio, measuring twenty-two and a half by twenty-eight and a half inches, matted in blue suede, with a twenty-four-karat-gold-coated coin bearing the seal of Graceland and framed under glass for $19 plus $3 shipping and handling.

The Bradford Exchange of Niles, Illinois, offered for sale Plate No. 1, "The Rock and Roll Legend," in the Commemorating the King series of limited-edition eight-and-a-quarter-inch plates. The first plate features the Elvis stamp (at the right of the plate) with a blown-up version of the King holding a microphone. Bradex #84-D19-23-1; $29.75 each plus shipping and handling.

The Ardleigh-Elliott Company of Niles, Illinois, with Graceland issued a limited-edition music box that played "Heartbreak Hotel" under the name of '68 Comeback Special. The music box is an original issue in the Elvis' Greatest Hits! Music Box Collection. Approximately three inches in diameter, it features the King in black leather as he sang before an international TV audience in 1968 ($34.95 plus shipping and handling).

The Washington Mint of Weston, Connecticut, offered for sale the first strike of the Official Elvis Presley One Pound Silver Proof coin for $319. Its sixteen troy ounces (497.65 grams) of silver measures three and a half inches in diameter. Elvis's portrait is on one side and Graceland is on the reverse. Each is numbered and registered on its edge. Limited edition of ten thousand (1-800-926-MINT).

MAY 3:   Andy Warhol's 1963 silkscreen and painting on canvas entitled *Double Elvis* was estimated to bring $700,000–900,000 at Sotheby's Contemporary Art Sale on May 3. *Double Elvis* was based on a studio photo still from the 1960

film *Flaming Star* and portrays Elvis in a cowboy outfit holding a pistol. Warhol's *Elvis, 21 Times* (1962) was estimated to bring $400,000–600,000 at the same sale. It represents Warhol's earliest efforts at serial imagery. (See *Antiques and Art Weekly*, Apr. 23, 1993.)

MAY 14: At Christie's auction house in South Kensington, England, the Martin D-18 guitar that Elvis used to record "That's All Right, Mama" and "Blue Moon of Kentucky" for Sun in 1954, was estimated to bring over $150,000. In 1956, Elvis traded the guitar at O.K. Houck Piano Company in Memphis for a white baby grand piano with gold-leaf trim. Within hours, a fan bought the guitar. From 1974 to 1991, it was on loan to the Country Music Hall of Fame. It was then sold by auction to a British collector in 1991, for $214,500. Christie's considers the guitar the most important modern guitar ever to be sold at auction. (See *Maine Antique Digest*, May 1993.)

JUNE: Current, Inc. of Colorado Springs, Colorado, offered four youthful images of Elvis on bank checks. They are available in packets of 200 for $9.95 or 150 colorless duplicate style checks for $12.50. (Call 1-800-533-3973.)

The island nations of St. Thomas and Principe issued a legal-tender Elvis Presley five-hundred-dobras coin. U.S. citizens can purchase the coins (#35281) for $19.95 each through PCS of Minneapolis, Minnesota.

Sotheby's estimated Elvis's jumpsuit, cape, and belt (ca. 1972) to bring $15,000–20,000 in its Collector's Carousel sale in New York.

JUNE 1: The Bradford Exchange issued its seventh painted porcelain plate "Always on My Mind," by artist Nate Giorgio, in the twelve-plate series Elvis Presley Hit Parade ($29.75 each plus shipping and handling).

Value Fair offered RCA's *Elvis 50 Years 50 Hits* (two double-length cassettes for $19.95 or two long-playing CDs for $25.95) with a free copy of RCA's "Love Me Tender." Add $4.50 for shipping and handling. (Call 1-800-578-2386.)

JUNE 14: "Elvis" was printed on the first U.S. postal stamp of the rock star. "Elvis Presley" is the only differing aspect of the second Elvis stamp issued on June 14. It can be purchased by itself or in a booklet of "The Legends of Rock 'n' Roll" (including stamps of Bill Haley, Buddy Holly, Ritchie Valens, Otis Redding, Clyde McPhatter, and Dinah Washington).

Warner Custom Music jumped on the lucrative Elvis bandwagon and distributed a double-length CD or cassette, a twenty-four-page "Collector's Booklet," twenty Rock 'n' Roll/Rhythm 'n' Blues stamps, and a limited-edition fourteen-by-twenty-one-inch *Legends* poster (free while supplies lasted in June), all for $32.90. "Return to Sender" is featured on the *Legends* album. (Call 1-800-872-4487.)

Fleetwood of Cheyenne, Wyoming, offered $50, $10, and $5 coins (legal tender of the Republic of the Marshall Islands) with the second Elvis Presley stamp on First Day Cover envelopes ($66, $22, and $16.50 respectively. Call 1-800-443-3232).

Fleetwood's Elvis stamp promo envelope stated "Long Live the King! An outstanding collection honoring the immortal Elvis Presley!" Offerings included a set of five First Day Covers of the second Elvis Presley stamp with fifteen mint twenty-nine-cent rock 'n' roll stamps ($12.35 each set); five First Day covers of the first Elvis stamp ($8 each); an Elvis Presley combination First Day Cover with the first and second stamps ($7.50 each); a deluxe collector's album for the sets ($7 each); and a proofcard first edition of the first stamp ($8.50 each). A free first-day-issue postcard was included with every $25 purchase (while supplies lasted.)

Preferred Customer Service's *Coin Line* promotional flyer offered for sale "the most dramatic error of the year!

Unknown to government inspectors—the Elvis stamp that Rocked and Rolled," an *error* stamp with four colors "shifted" out of place. "It's almost as if the spirit of Elvis were alive," the brochure boasts, pricing each error stamp at $149. Twenty-two available; probably no more than 150 mistakenly overlooked by postal inspectors. Item #34974. (Call 1-800-777-6468.)

JUNE 16:   The U.S. Postal Service released Legends of American Music's Rock and Roll, Rhythm & Blues stamps at twenty-nine cents each, $5.80 per packet of twenty stamps, and sheets of thirty-five stamps, which include the second Elvis stamp, Bill Haley, Clyde McPhatter, Ritchie Valens, Otis Redding, Buddy Holly, and Dinah Washington.

JUNE 22:   Sotheby's in New York City auctioned off Elvis's sunglasses for $1,200 and his 1972 rhinestone-studded jumpsuit for $17,250 in its Collector's Carousel sale. Other items owned by Elvis included a 1969, silver, four-door Mercedes limousine 600 sedan (ID #600 001 321), bought by the King in 1970, as a Christmas present to himself; a platinum 45 single's RIAA Award for "Burning Love" and another for the album *Elvis in Concert;* Elvis's lapis lazuli fourteen-karat gold ring (nugget style); a pair of aviator sunglasses; a cream cotton jumpsuit from Nudie's Rodeo Tailors; a pair of gold cuff links engraved "EP"; a "gold" key for Elvis's Rolls-Royce; a champagne glass from the Presley wedding; signed movie scripts; a souvenir photo album dated August 5, 1956; and a Guitarra Clásica de España Estrella acoustic guitar covered in "gold" and inscribed "Elvis."

JUNE 24:   The Associated Press announced Elvis's autopsy notes will be reexamined by a forensic pathologist to settle disputes about the actual cause of death. Many people (including Dr. Eric Muirhead, a Memphis pathologist who was present at the Presley

autopsy) question Dr. Jerry Francisco's original findings, which stated Elvis died of heart disease and not from drug abuse. In May 1993, the Shelby County Commission filed a lawsuit to force the State of Tennessee to reopen an investigation into the singer's 1977 death.

JULY: The Bradford Exchange offered for $37.74 a porcelain plate titled "Mystery Train," No. 8 in the Elvis Presley Hit Parade Series. (Limited edition. Bradex No. 84-D19-14.8.) Bradford/Delphi offered a limited-edition porcelain plate, No. 2 in its Commemorating the King series, titled "Las Vegas, Live" for $32.74. (Bradex No. 84-D19-23.2), and plate No. 6 in the Elvis Presley on the Big Screen series, which shows Elvis in *Spinout*, for $37.74 (Bradex No. 84-D19-15.6).

Ardleigh-Elliott of Niles, Illinois, offered a porcelain music box of Elvis at the January 14, 1973, "Aloha From Hawaii" concert, wearing his American-eagle jumpsuit. The box plays "Blue Suede Shoes." Priced at $38.29, including shipping and handling.

Hammacher Schlemmer offered seven limited-edition, numbered, gold-plated 45-rpm Elvis records with a reproduction of the original album jacket, framed and matted with certification of authenticity, priced from $99.95 to $129.95. Record displays include "Blue Suede Shoes," "Return to Sender," "If I Can Dream," "Hound Dog/Don't Be Cruel," "Are You Lonesome Tonight," "Love Me Tender," and "Heartbreak Hotel." The company also sells The King commemorative plates, authorized by Graceland and the U.S. Postal Service for $29.75 (plus shipping and handling).

Elvis Silver Stamp Proofs, authorized by Graceland and the U.S. Postal Service, offered a half-pound (248.82 grams) of .999 pure silver rectangular Commemorative Stamp Proof with an eleven-and-a-quarter-inch circumference (2.48 by 3.15 inches) for sale to the public for $154 (plus shipping and handling. Call 1-800-777-MINT).

JULY 5: Elvis was the No. 1 record seller "beyond the grave" for the first half of 1993 with fans buying 750,000 CDs and cassettes. (See *Newsweek*, "Rock and Roll Forever," July 5.)

JULY 31: The *Sun News* of Myrtle Beach, South Carolina announced that Texas rock promoter and producer Bill Smith is suing Graceland for $50,000 because it has spread the false rumor Elvis is dead. Smith adamantly believes the King faked his death and that Graceland has been "supplementing Elvis's finances ever since."

AUG.: *Reader's Digest* featured Elvis and an article titled "Where Elvis Lives."

Life magazine's cover headline announced, "Exclusive: Lost Snapshots From His Army Years—Elvis Young and Innocent." Readers learn about Elvis memorabilia collector Andreas Schroer's obsession with the King of rock 'n' roll, and of his latest book, *Private Presley*, which has 231 previously unpublished photographs of Elvis.

AUG.: The Bradford Exchange offered for sale Bruce Emmett's painted plate "The King of Creole" from the Elvis on the Big Screen series (Bradex no. 01531 for $29.95, plus shipping and handling); Nate Giorgio's painted plate "Blue Moon of Kentucky," plate No. 9 in the Elvis Presley Hit Parade series (Bradex No. 84-D19-14.9 for $37.74); and David Zwierz's painted plate "Love Me Tender," plate No. 1, and "Are Your Lonesome Tonight," plate No. 2, both from the Portraits of the King series (Bradex No. 84-D19-11.1 and 84-D19-11.2, each $30.94).

SEPT. 28: RCA Records released five CDs and five cassettes in numbered boxed sets titled *Elvis From Nashville to Memphis—The Essential 60's Masters I*. The digitally remastered music includes 130 tracks with nineteen previously unreleased songs. A ninety-four-page booklet with liner notes, record-session data, a discology of sixties music, and a stamp sheet of Elvis's sixties record covers are included in each set. Priced in stores from $74–54.99.

DEC. 10: Music producer Ike Turner claimed on the "Jerry Springer" show that he *hid* Elvis behind a piano in an all-black club on Eleventh Street in West Memphis as early as 1951, so that Elvis could listen to black rhythm and blues.

▲ Elvis and the Wilburn Brothers (Teddy and Doyle), Nashville, Tennessee. *Courtesy of the Country Music Foundation Library and Media Center, Nashville, Tennessee.*

The Future

Elvis is a media sensation with no obvious saturation level. No singer or performer to date has eclipsed his popularity and staying power. It is unfortunate that Elvis became a prisoner of stardom and the puppet of merchandisers. As the old saying goes, "it's not how much you throw up on the wall, it's how much you make *stick* that counts." In death, Elvis joined the greatest legends in the annals of rock 'n' roll, who often outrank their living counterparts.

Elvis's persona lives in music and in the memories of his fans. Those who never had the privilege to see Elvis perform live, or who were born after he died, often ask, "Why are we still talking about Elvis Presley?" Those of us who watched his career from beginning to end admit you had to *be* there to comprehend fully the dynamics of Elvis's actions. Through his music, he challenged everyone to be a little freer, more accepting, and a lot more creative. He made a distinctive difference in the lives of millions of people. He was not merely a singer or a movie star. His message and his presence made people *re*think what they believed in. He moved society, and people took him into their hearts and homes. He changed the way people thought and the way music sounded. Elvis seduced the nation and the world. Elvis was, in the truest sense, loved because, as *Rolling Stone* put it, "he was the spiritual headquarters for rock 'n' roll."

Elvis may be physically dead, but he's alive in people's memories and in every act that goes against a one-sided government, a narrow-sighted parent, a hypocritical minister, an uninformed teacher, a slandering member of the press, a person who feels alone, or anyone who shows prejudice against any person or race. Elvis is there when a person of poverty or color decides to make a difference and move on. Elvis is there whenever a teenager feels down and out because his appreciation of them and his message to them lifts their spirits and gives them a reason for being alive. Elvis is there whenever an individual or group challenges the First Amendment. Elvis is there whenever the next innovative musician, composer, dancer, poet, or writer decides it's all right to be different and stands for beliefs that may go against the norm.

Although he passed away in 1977, Elvis remains one of the top money earners in the music world. He's legend grown to myth; a rock icon; a celebrated rebel; and a working-class American hero who found comfort and salvation in music.

Fans pushed Elvis to the top and turned him into a fabled figure of pop culture. The only victim of the journey was the King of rock 'n' roll himself. The rest of us became hostages of his continuing, magnetic presence and original message.

Elvis's Statistics

Male Caucasian

Height: 6'1"

Weight: 180 (He weighed 5 pounds at birth and more than 255 at the time of his death.)

Hair: light blondish brown (He dyed his hair black.)

Eyes: blue (scar under left eye)

Chest: 39–40"

Waist: 32" (in the fifties; over 44" in the seventies)

Hips: 41"

Shirt: 15½–17 neck, 35" arm

Shoe size: 11D; combat-boot size 12

Blood type: O

Social security number: 409-52-2002

Selective Service number: 40-86-35-16

Army serial number: 53310761 (draft number)

Registration number for his Convair 880 Jet: N880EP

Registration number for his Jet Commander airplane: N777EP

National Bank of Commerce checking account number: 011-143875 (He signed all checks "E. A. Presley.")

Alias Names: Jon Burrows, Dr. John Carpenter

Guitars: Martin D-28 and Gibson J-200

Favorite piano: a 1928 gold-leaf Kimball grand

Favorite flower: jasmine

Favorite dinner plates: Noritake's Buckingham pattern

Favorite bacon: King Cotton

Favorite bread: Wonder enriched

Favorite board games: Scrabble and Monopoly

Favorite sports: karate, racquet ball, football

Favorite magazine: *Mad*

Favorite restaurants: Gridiron at 4101 Elvis Presley Blvd., Route 51, Memphis; Tiny Naylor's and Hamburger Heaven, Los Angeles

Favorite meal: pork chops with brown gravy and apple pie for dessert—served with Pepsi

Favorite movie: *The Party* with Peter Sellers

Elvis's boots were by Vedi or San Remos (patent leather).

Elvis's bed was King-size, of course.

Elvis's bedroom at Graceland was once predominantly black and crimson. Photographs of Jesus and Gladys Presley were at his bedside, alongside a ceramic tiger.

Elvis carried a library of records with him on tour, which include Billy Eckstine, Arthur Crudup, Roy Hamilton, Hank Williams, Golden Gate Quartet, Mario Lanza, the Harmonizing Four, the Soul Stirrers, Mahalia Jackson, Arthur Prysock, the Blackwood Brothers, Brook Benton, and B. B. King.

Favorite book (other than the Bible): Kahlil Gibran's *The Prophet*

Favorite comic-book series: *Captain Marvel*

Favorite actors: James Dean, Marlon Brando, Dean Martin, Rudolph Valentino

Favorite wild animal: tigers

Favorite make of car: Cadillac

Favorite gemstone: diamond

Favorite home: Graceland

Favorite colors: blue, black, white, gold

Favorite comedians: Monty Python and Peter Sellers

Favorite Biblical Quotes

I Corinthians 13:1: "Though I speak with the tongues of men and of angels, and have not charity, I am become as sounding brass or a tinkling cymbal."

Matthew 19:24: "It is easier for a camel to go through the eye of a needle, than for a rich man to enter into the kingdom of God." This is one of Gladys's and Elvis's most quoted passages, and its words haunted the King at the end of his life.

Psalms 101:1: "I will sing of mercy and judgment: unto thee, O Lord, will I sing."

Martial Arts

Although people claimed he earned an eighth-degree black belt, Elvis was *not* a black-belt master. He "earned" (gratis) his first degree in 1960, and second degree in 1963, from Kang Rhee. He skipped his third and fourth degrees, which is not possible in a real karate master's program. Kang Rhee conferred his fifth, sixth, and seventh degrees, and Ed Parker presented Elvis with an eighth-degree black belt (master of the art, which Elvis had not earned). The so-called "karate" he used in movies (*G.I. Blues, Wild in the Country, Follow That Dream, Blue Hawaii, Harum Scarum, Roustabout, Kid Galahad)* was nothing more than an imitation of martial-arts fighting techniques. No master of tae kwon do spars in dojos wearing leather boots, jewelry, sunglasses, or long capes.

Elvis's karate name in tae kwon do was Tiger. Elvis picked that name because he felt tigers were the most proficient animals on earth. They were swift, powerful, beautiful, and agile. They could come and go without being detected. To be tigerlike was to be kinglike. Elvis identified with their mystery and their splendor. He had various images of tigers in Graceland (ceramic, painted, and bronze tigers) at the time of his death.

WOMEN IN ELVIS'S LIFE

In the fifties, Elvis's swiveling hips and sneering lips enticed women worldwide. Worried parents and religious, political, and educational leaders tried futilely to veil the rocker's sexual potency, but the more critics ranted, the deeper fans' passion grew.

Hedda Hopper (Hollywood gossip columnist) complained, "I don't like Elvis Presley because I consider him a menace to young girls!" Hopper accused Elvis of being "the most obscene, vulgar influence on young America today." Nevertheless, Elvis was adored and idealized by millions of women, both young and old. And while Las Vegas showgirls and eager, beautiful Hollywood starlets often flung themselves at him, Elvis was not seriously swayed by many women, as hard as they tried to please him both in and out of bed. But they continued to flock to him, to adore him, to worship him, and always, to love him.

Alden, Ginger met Elvis after disc jockey George Klein arranged for Elvis to meet her more famous sister, Terry (Miss Tennessee), in 1976. Attracted to both sisters, Elvis preferred Ginger (nicknamed "Gingerbread") and they began dating. Ironically, Ginger's father, Walter Alden, inducted Elvis into the Army on March 24, 1958, but Elvis did not meet Walter's daughters until the end of 1976. Ginger is a beauty queen, having won the titles of Miss Traffic Safety (Memphis) and Miss Mid-South. She was first runner-up for Miss Tennessee University (1976).

Lavishing Ginger with gifts, which included a white Lincoln Continental Mark V, Ginger alleged Elvis proposed marriage on January 26, 1977, in the bathroom adjoining his bedroom at Graceland, and that he gave her an 11.5-carat diamond engagement ring.

Elvis bought Ginger a home at 4152 Royal Crest Place. Ginger claims the two were to be married at the Memphis Greek Orthodox Church, Christmas Day, 1977. After Elvis died, Ginger Alden took up a career in acting.

Although first reports asserted that Joe Esposito found Elvis dead, Ginger claims she found him in the bathroom the day he died.

Ginger and her mother, Jo Laverne, told the *National Enquirer* (May 16, 1978) they communicate with the spirit of Elvis and have seen his ghost. After Elvis died, Jo sued the Presley estate professing Elvis promised to pay off Jo's mortgage, home improvements, and legal fees that had been accumulated during Jo's divorce.

Allen, Patricia is the only female pianist to record with Elvis. She can be heard on the June 1966 recording session for the film *Double Trouble*.

Andress, Ursula costarred with Elvis in the 1963 Hal B. Wallis film *Fun in Acapulco*. Although Andress was married to actor John Derek at the time, the press claimed she and Elvis were having an affair. Elvis said publicly Andress had broader shoulders than he did and *that* embarrassed him.

Ann-Margret was called the "female Elvis Presley" after she worked in Las Vegas with George Burns's comedy act. She was a dancer and singer on various television shows and starred in *Pocketful of Miracles* (1961) and *Bye Bye Birdie* (1963). She costarred with Elvis in *Viva Las Vegas* (1964). Because Priscilla lived at Graceland, whenever Ann-Margret called Elvis at the house, she used the nicknames Bunny, Thumper, and Scoobie. Memphis Mafia members called her Rusty Amo, taken from her role in *Viva Las Vegas*. Elvis and Ann-Margret lunched together every day during his filming of *Girl Happy* (1965). The press immediately linked the two romantically because they not only rode motorcycles together but stayed in the same hotels, and most importantly, she told the press she and Elvis were engaged to be married. Elvis denied any marriage plans, but the two remained close friends even after Ann-Margret married actor Roger Smith. Elvis gave Ann-Margret a round, pink bed and sent guitar-shaped floral arrangements to Ann-Margret's openings until he died. She and her husband attended Elvis's funeral.

Ballard, Caroline at age nine was Elvis's first girlfriend in Tupelo. Her father, James Ballard, was a minister at the Presleys' East Tupelo First Assembly of God Church.

Beaulieu, Priscilla Ann was the only wife of Elvis Presley and the mother of his only legitimate child, Lisa Marie. Her stepfather, an Air Force captain, was transferred to Weisbaden, Germany, where Elvis was stationed nearby. She met Elvis in 1959, at the age of fourteen, at a party in Germany, wearing a blue-and-white sailor dress and white socks. Some references claim Priscilla planned the meeting while others say it was Elvis who saw her first and asked U.S. airman Currie Grant to make an introduction. Grant affirms it was Priscilla who pursued Elvis. The Cat soon nicknamed her Cilla. She first visited and then moved to Graceland, and her presence was kept a secret. She soon discovered Elvis had many romantic affairs.

The couple was married in Las Vegas on May 1, 1967, and they became parents of Lisa Marie nine months later. They were divorced in 1973. In 1972, she became romantically involved with Mike Stone; then actor/model Michael Edwards from 1978–85;

Ellie Ezerzer in 1986; and on March 1, 1987, she gave birth to Brazilian director-writer-producer Marco Garibaldi's son, Navarone. The couple remains unmarried and Priscilla works in movies, commercials, and modeling.

To Priscilla's credit, she has established a career that is separate from the world of Elvis and has helped turn a close-to-bankrupt estate into a fortune that is worth close to $100 million. Despite the pain, loneliness, and anguish she suffered while living with Elvis, she has tried to build and maintain a strong, positive, and uplifting image of her ex-husband in order to keep his legend alive. Standing five foot three inches, this caring, savvy, gray-eyed beauty is not only a devoted and loving mother *and* grandmother, but someone who has created for herself a meaningful and successful career out from under the powerful shadow of her ex-husband.

The Presley wedding, which took eight minutes, was presided over by Nevada Supreme Court justice David Zenoff and was conducted in a private ceremony in Milton Prell's suite at the Aladdin Hotel, Las Vegas. Prell owned

▲ Priscilla Presley. *Private collection.*

the hotel and was a close friend of Colonel Tom Parker's. Priscilla's thirteen-year-old sister, Michelle, was the maid of honor. Best men were Joe Esposito and Marty Lacker. Guests included jeweler Harry Levitch and his wife, Francis; George Klein and his wife, Barbara Little; Colonel Tom Parker; Vernon Presley and his second wife, Dee; Donald Beaulieu, Priscilla's brother; Major and Mrs. Joseph P. Beaulieu, the bride's parents; and Patsy Presley Gambill (Elvis's cousin) and her husband, Gee Gee (Elvis's chauffeur). Priscilla's gown was silk organza, trimmed with seed pearls, with a six-foot train. A rhinestone tiara held a three-quarter-length tulle veil. Her three-carat diamond engagement ring, surrounded with twenty smaller diamonds, was allegedly lost at their Circle G Ranch in Mississippi. Some sources claim Elvis lost his gold band as well. Their unusual wedding breakfast consisted of suckling pig, fried chicken, oysters Rockefeller, and champagne. A six-tier wedding cake was studded with tiny pearls and red/pink hearts. Comedian Redd Foxx attended the breakfast and a band played "Love Me Tender." A second reception was held at Graceland.

Bedford, Eloise was Elvis's "girlfriend" in the fifth grade at the East Tupelo Consolidated School.

Biggs, Delta Mae Presley was Elvis's favorite aunt and sister to his father, Vernon. Having no children of her own, she adored and pampered Elvis. When Delta's husband, Pat Biggs, died in 1966, Elvis sent some of his pals to take care of the funeral arrangements and to bring his aunt back to Memphis. He put her on the Graceland payroll as a companion and housekeeper. Minnie Mae Presley, her mother, also lived in the mansion. After Gladys Presley died, Minnie Mae and Delta moved into Gladys's room at Graceland. Defiant, opinionated, and overprotective of Elvis, Delta was known to go head-to-head with members of the Memphis Mafia.

Blackman, Joan costarred with Elvis in *Blue Hawaii* (1961) and *Kid Galahad* (1962).

Blackwood, Malessa dated Elvis in 1976, and held the beauty title Miss Memphis Southmen (queen of the city's franchise in the World Football League). On their first date, Elvis bought her a Pontiac Grand Prix and nicknamed her Brown Eyes. He asked her to move to Graceland, but she did not like the idea—she believed in marriage. Elvis stopped dating her when he heard that!

Boyd, Patricia was a secretary at Graceland who married Red West in 1961. She retired when she became pregnant in 1963.

Bradshaw, Joan briefly dated Elvis in Hollywood in 1957.

Buergin, Margrit was a beautiful, blond, sixteen-year-old German stenographer whom Elvis dated in West Germany. He nicknamed her Little Puppy, but decided not to extend their relationship because she could not speak English.

Carr, Vikki introduced Elvis to a good Los Angeles diet doctor, and in return he bought her a diamond ring. Carr was a singer who charted "It Must Be Him" in 1967 (Liberty 55986). Elvis attended her opening in Las Vegas' Tropicana Hotel on September 4, 1974.

Carter, Anita was a love interest in 1955. As entertainers, they toured together that year, and Elvis was so crazy about Anita he pretended he was sick and had to go to the hospital just to get her attention.

Clarke, Jane dated Elvis secretly after they met in Paris in 1959, at the Lido club, and later in Las Vegas when she was performing at the Tropicana Hotel in 1963.

Cocke, Marion J. was Elvis's personal nurse after 1975, at the Baptist Memorial Hospital. Calling her his "security blanket," he showered her with a fur, jewelry, and a car, and they were close friends. She authored a 1979 book about Elvis titled *I Called Him Babe*.

Connors, Carol was a studio musician who claimed in *People* magazine that Elvis was the first man with whom she made love. In 1958, she sang the hit "To Know Him Is to Love Him." They dated for ten months. Carol Connors cowrote the theme song "Gonna Fly Now" for *Rocky* and other hits.

deBarbin, Lucy claimed to have known Elvis in Monroe, Louisiana, in 1953, and alleges to have given birth to his daughter, Desiree, on August 23, 1958. She coauthored the book *Are You Lonesome Tonight?* which asserts she had a twenty-four-year affair with Elvis. In 1987, Geraldo Rivera called deBarbin's book "Elvisgate." DeBarbin claims never to have told Elvis they had a daughter because she feared the wrath of her ex-husband and did not want to harm the superstar's reputation.

Dors, Diana claimed in the newspaper *Midnight Globe* (Sept. 20, 1977) she and Elvis had a torrid affair while she was married to Dennis Hamilton. Elvis met Dors in 1956 at a Hollywood party. She stated that they secretly stayed together in Mexico, that she saw Elvis smoke pot, and that he bought her a pink Cadillac. Dewey Phillips and others kept secret this relationship.

Evans, Marilyn was the Las Vegas showgirl who went with Elvis in 1956 to Sun Records, the day of the now-famous Million Dollar Quartet session. Evans and Elvis met at the New Frontier in Las Vegas and they dated for a short period.

Fabares, Shelley costarred with Elvis in *Girl Happy* (1964), *Spinout* (1966), and *Clambake* (1967) and they dated briefly. Shelley's single "Johnny Angel" was knocked out of the first-place spot on the popular charts by Elvis's "Good Luck Charm." In *Spinout*, after the director screamed "Cut!" during a kiss between Elvis and Shelley, the two-some continued to kiss for several minutes. Shelley was his favorite costar. Shelley Fabares appeared on TV in "The Donna Reed Show" and now co-stars in ABC's "Coach."

Farrell, Ann claims she married Elvis in 1957, in Alabama, but she is unable to produce documentation. She alleges she refused to sleep with Elvis unless they were man and wife.

Fuller, Candy Jo is a country-western singer who claims to be the illegitimate daughter of Elvis. She maintains her mother, Terry Taylor, and Elvis were lovers in the fifties and that Elvis sent her money for years.

Goodman, Diana dated Elvis briefly in the seventies. She was Miss Georgia in 1975. Linda Thompson accompanied them on many of their dates, and later Linda became his major love interest.

Harris, Zelda alleged that after one date with Elvis after an Alabama concert in 1960, they were married.

Hart, Dolores played opposite Elvis in 1957's *Loving You* and was the romantic lead in 1958's *King Creole*. Elvis nicknamed her Whistle Britches. In 1959, she wrote for *Photoplay*, "What It's Like to Kiss Elvis." She said Elvis loved people a lot but that he was a lonely man. Hart confessed to insiders she was in love with Elvis. In 1970, she became a Catholic nun and today is mother superior at the Convent of Regina Laudis in Bethlehem, Connecticut.

Hearn, Barbara dated Elvis for years in the fifties and early sixties. In 1957, she played a bit part in the movie *Loving You*. She visited Elvis and Gladys at the Audubon house almost daily, and rumors spread Barbara Hearn and Elvis were to marry.

Holman, Alberta was the loyal maid who started working for Elvis in 1956, while the family lived on Audubon Drive, and she was still with him at his death. Elvis nicknamed her "Alberta VO-5" and "05." She also cared for Dee Stanley's boys when they lived at the mansion. Alberta was accused by Dee of knowing "all about the skeletons in the family closet." (See *National Enquirer*, Feb. 18, 1992.) Dee asserted on television that Alberta told her of Elvis and his mother's incest, of drug abuse, and of Elvis's suicide attempts.

Hugueny, Sharon was an actress Elvis dated in 1963, after Priscilla came to live with him at Graceland.

Jackson, Mahalia was the most influential and gifted gospel singer to come from the Baptist and Sanctified churches. Dee Stanley, Elvis's stepmother, told this author in 1991, "Elvis listened to Jackson, his favorite blues artist, for hours every day. . . . He adored her." Jackson's music vastly influenced Elvis. The twosome met in Hollywood, which was a big thrill for both of them. Jackson died in 1972.

Jenkins, Mary was the cook at Graceland (1963–77), whom Elvis adored. Elvis bought Jenkins six cars and a home. She played herself in the 1981 movie *This Is Elvis*. In 1984, Beth Pease wrote her story in *Elvis, The Way I Knew Him*.

Juanico, June a receptionist, dated Elvis from 1955 to 1956. They met at his Biloxi, Mississippi concert.

Keisker, Marion was Sam Phillips's insightful and aggressive secretary who made certain Elvis Presley was heard and taken seriously at Sun Records. Without Keisker's insistence that Sam hear the "new sound" of Elvis, the singer may not have made it to stardom. Keisker had previously been a talk-show host for the Memphis station WHER and was nicknamed Miss Radio of Memphis. In September 1957,

Keisker left Sun Records and became a captain in the U.S. Air Force. She later met Elvis in West Germany while she worked with the Armed Forces Television Network. The two remained friends.

Kirkham, Mildred (Millie) was a backup singer for many Elvis recordings and live performances from 1955 through the 1970s. She sang for a short period with the Jordanaires.

Lewis, Barbara Jean sang jingles in Charlotte, North Carolina, and met Elvis in June 1954. She claims they dated for one year and alleges she gave birth in Jackson, Mississippi, to Elvis's daughter, Deborah Delaine Presley in June 1955. Deborah, a movie extra and a law clerk, denounced as a hoax Lucy deBarbin's claim that deBarbin's daughter, Desiree, is Elvis's daughter. In 1988, Deborah filed a suit against the Presley estate claiming her "fair share." She has yet to prove her claims.

Lime, Yvonne dated Elvis briefly in 1956 and in 1957, while they filmed *Loving You*.

Locke, Dixie was a high school sweetheart of Elvis's who accompanied him to First Assembly of God rallies. They met in 1953, at the Rainbow Rollerdome and dated steadily until 1955. They attended Southside High School's prom together, and in 1954 Elvis went with Dixie to her prom. They were photographed together frequently, and Elvis gave her his class ring. When he was on the road, he called her almost daily, and she became the president of one of the first Elvis Presley fan clubs. Many people contend Elvis wanted to marry Dixie, but she left him in the summer of 1955, because his tour schedule kept him so far away from her. Dixie soon met someone else and was married. Losing Dixie devastated Elvis, who had assumed she would always wait for him. Dixie is portrayed in the 1979 TV movie *Elvis* as a girl named "Bonnie."

McMann, Betty claims to be Elvis's first girlfriend and says she taught him how to dance.

Mobley, Mary Ann costarred with Elvis in *Girl Happy* (1965) and *Harum Scarum* (1965). Mobley was Miss Mississippi and Miss America. She is married to talk-show host Gary Collins.

Moore, Mary Tyler costarred with Elvis in 1969's *Change of Habit*, and despite rumors of their romance, they were just good friends.

Moreno, Rita dated Elvis in 1957, during the shooting of *Loving You*. She is best known for her 1961 Oscar-winning performance in *West Side Story*.

Newton, Billie Joe alleges she was married to Elvis and gave birth to his three children—the first when she was nine years old! She insists they were divorced in 1956, because Colonel Parker demanded it. Her published story in the *Globe*, March 17, 1981, states all the documentation regarding the marriage, divorce, and the births were "destroyed." According to the same article, two other women claimed to be married to Elvis: Ann Farrell in 1957, in Russellville, Alabama, and Zelda Harris in 1960. There is no proof or validity to any of the I-was-married-to-Elvis stories, which have periodically appeared in many of the tabloids. All of these so-called "wives of Elvis Presley" claim documentation of their marriages has been conveniently "lost" or "destroyed."

Nicholson, Pauline was a maid and cook at Graceland (1963–77) devoted to Elvis. He gave her a Buick LeSabre in 1964. She portrays herself in the 1981 movie *This Is Elvis*.

O'Neal, Doris was a secretary at Graceland.

Paget, Debra was a starlet whom Elvis could not openly date because she was romantically involved with Howard Hughes during the filming of 1956's *Love Me Tender*. Elvis convinced Priscilla to dye her hair to look more like Paget's. Elvis and Paget remained friends for years.

Parker, Patricia Ann was a Hollywood waitress who brought a paternity suit against Elvis in Los Angeles, August 21, 1970. She alleged her son Jason, born in Presbyterian Hospital, Hollywood, California, on October 19, 1970, is the singer's son. The suit was dropped after Elvis passed a lie detector test and a blood test proving that Jason was not his son.

Pearl, Minnie was a close friend and colleague of Elvis's. Pearl was a featured performer in 1945, when Elvis sang "Old Shep" at the Mississippi-Alabama Fair. Pearl accompanied Elvis on tour to Hawaii in the sixties and performed with him on the USS *Arizona* for a memorial benefit in March 1961. They remained friends until his death. Minnie Pearl is a member of the Country Music Hall of Fame and was a regular on the TV series "Hee Haw."

Peters, Vicki dated Elvis in 1971, and told the *National Insider* (Oct. 24, 1971) Elvis had a drug problem. He never spoke to her again.

Pittman, Barbara was a singer who recorded for the Sun label and dated Elvis in the mid-1950s.

Portnoy, Lillian received her fifteen minutes of fame when she became known as the "last woman to kiss Elvis" before he boarded the USS *General Randall* on September 22, 1958, and sailed for Europe with the U.S. Army. Lillian gave him a boxed cheesecake and kissed him good-bye.

Presley, Davada (Dee) Elliot Stanley was the second wife of Vernon Presley, the mother of Billy, David, and Rick

Stanley, and the stepmother of Elvis. On July 3, 1960, in Huntsville, Alabama, without Elvis present, she became Vernon's wife. The couple met in West Germany in 1959 during Elvis's Army stint. Dee was divorcing her husband of ten years, Army sergeant William Stanley. Elvis disapproved strongly of his father's dating and then marrying anyone so soon after Gladys's death. The couple lived at Graceland with Dee's three sons, and then they moved nearby to Dolan Drive. Dee became pregnant and had a miscarriage. Vernon filed for divorce on May 5, 1977. On November 15, 1977, it was reported Dee obtained a Dominican Republic divorce. She then married Lewis Tucker. In 1979, she and her sons published a book called *Elvis, We Loved You Tender*, which accused Elvis of (among other things) drug abuse, rape, incest, and suicide.

Presley, Gladys Love Smith was the beloved mother of Elvis and wife of Vernon Presley. Gladys was born in Pontotoc County, Mississippi, the daughter of Robert Lee Smith and Doll Mansell Smith. Twenty-one-year-old Gladys married seventeen-year-old Vernon Presley in Pontotoc County, June 17, 1933. Elvis was born January 8, 1935, and was the Presleys' only child. Elvis's twin brother, Jesse Garon, was stillborn. In 1942, Gladys had another miscarriage. Elvis called her Sattnin, a name he also used for Priscilla later in life.

With Elvis's fame came Gladys's dependence on vodka and diet pills. She lost her lust for life, became ill and despondent, and died a lonely, detached, suffering soul. In a September 1956 interview, Gladys told reporters one of her favorite songs was "Don't Be Cruel." On August 14, 1958, at three A.M. Gladys died of a heart attack, complicated by acute hepatitis at the Methodist Hospital in Memphis. Elvis would not allow an autopsy. She was buried at Forest Hill Cemetery. After Elvis died, Gladys's body was moved next to his at the Meditation Garden at Graceland. Gladys's tombstone reads: "She was the sunshine of our home."

Shelley Winters portrayed Gladys in the 1979 TV movie *Elvis*. In 1981, she was portrayed by Debbie Edge and Virginia Kiser in *This Is Elvis*. Red River Dave recorded "New Angel Tonight (A Tribute to Elvis' Mother)" for Marathon Records.

Gladys was the central figure in her son's life and vice versa. After Elvis became famous and "left the nest," Gladys could not live without him. Elvis was distraught knowing he had not made her happy. When she died, Elvis was beside himself with guilt and spent the rest of his life saying he was "sorry" for not fulfilling the one woman he vowed he would always love.

Presley, Lisa Marie is the legitimate daughter of Priscilla and Elvis Presley, born exactly nine months after they were married, on February 1, 1968. Charlie Hodge drove the couple to the Memphis Baptist Hospital in a new Cadillac. Joe Esposito followed, serving as a backup car in case of an emergency. Lisa Marie was born at 5:01 P.M., delivered by Dr. T. A. Turman. She weighed six pounds fifteen ounces and measured twenty inches. An entourage of friends and police officers waited outside her hospital room. Elvis admitted he was "a little shaky" becoming a father.

Lisa Marie's middle name was in honor of Colonel Parker's wife, Marie. As a child inside Graceland, she led a sheltered, highly protected, isolated life. Her father lavished extravagant presents on her, while her mother tried to keep a semblance of order and sanity in her life.

After Priscilla and Elvis were divorced, Priscilla retained full custody of Lisa Marie. Elvis had visiting rights. Lisa Marie was at Graceland the day Elvis died. Priscilla refused to allow the press to take photographs of Lisa, and to some extent she led a "normal" life after 1977. In 1978, Priscilla enrolled Lisa Marie in the Church of Scientology in Los Angeles. In 1980, Lisa Marie dropped out of school and never returned. She flirted with drugs and alcohol, which must have infuriated and depressed her mother. In 1984, Lisa Marie met guitar player Danny Keough through the church, and in October 1988, the couple married.

On May 29, 1989, Lisa Marie gave birth to Danielle at eight-fifteen P.M. at St. John's Hospital in Santa Monica, California. Their baby weighed seven pounds two ounces and was the only grandchild of Priscilla until the birth of Benjamin Storm in 1992.

As the sole heir to her father's estate (which has been protected and well supervised by her mother since 1981), Lisa Marie will take custody of Graceland and the royalties from her famous father's legendary life when she is thirty. Estimates of that inheritance are close to $100 million. *People* magazine ran an article in March 1993 regarding that inheritance, and claimed Lisa Marie's plans to become a singer. Her current manager is ex–Memphis Mafia member Jerry Schilling.

Presley, Minnie Mae Hood was Elvis's paternal grandmother, whom he nicknamed the Dodger. Minnie Mae lived with Vernon and Gladys beginning in Tupelo, and ending at Graceland. When Elvis went to Germany with the Army, she and Vernon resided at 14 Goethestrasse, Bad Nauheim, West Germany. Minnie Mae had a feisty temper, used snuff, and wore sunglasses twenty-four hours a day. She was a great comfort to Elvis after Gladys died. Minnie Mae passed away on May 8, 1980, after a two-month illness. She is buried in the Meditation Garden with Gladys, Vernon, and Elvis at Graceland.

Prowse, Juliet costarred with Elvis in *G.I. Blues.* Prowse's dancing ability, personality, and figure intrigued Elvis. Although the press linked them romantically, she was dating Frank Sinatra at the time and became Sinatra's fiancée.

Elvis is quoted to have said, "She has a body which would make a bishop stamp his foot through a stained-glass window." When asked why she didn't date Elvis, she told the press his fame got in the way. The press also accused Elvis of openly competing for Prowse in order to rile Sinatra.

"Robertson, Jane," is a pseudonym for a girl who had her stomach pumped after she nearly overdosed on the prescription drug Hycodan, which she and Elvis were taking at Graceland in 1971. Red and Sonny West talk about the incident in *Elvis: What Happened?*

Rooks, Nancy W. was a maid hired by Dee. She worked at Graceland for eleven years. Elvis bought her a 1974 Pontiac Ventura. She coauthored with Vester Presley *The Presley Family Cookbook* in 1980, and *The Maid, the Man, and the Fans: Elvis Is the Man* with Mae Gutter. In the 1981 movie *This Is Elvis* she portrays herself.

Ryan, Sheila was a beautiful *Playboy* playmate who dated and traveled with Elvis in 1974 and 1975. Joe Esposito introduced her to Elvis after Elvis's breakup with Linda Thompson, and prior to Ginger Alden. Sheila married actor James Caan in January 1976.

Scrivener, Mildred was Elvis's Humes High School homeroom teacher and one of the first to encourage him to perform. He sang "Keep Them Cold Icy Fingers off of Me" in her minstrel show, April 9, 1953.

Seamon, Kathy was a private nurse at Graceland, 1975.

Sharp, Nancy dated Elvis in 1960, after they met on the set of *Flaming Star.* She was engaged to singer Tommy Sands and was a wardrobe assistant in Hollywood.

Shepherd, Cybill, the beautiful blond model turned actress, allegedly took four days off from filming *The Last*

Picture Show to be with Elvis. They dated secretly in 1966 and again in 1970 (prior to the Presleys' divorce). Shepherd starred in the TV series "Moonlighting" and has three children.

Sinatra, Nancy, daughter of Frank and Nancy Sinatra, was a confidant and friend of Elvis's. In 1960, Nancy met Elvis at the airport on his return from Germany, and rumors spread of a romance between them. Subsequently, they appeared on her father's TV special, and Priscilla feared Nancy and Elvis were in love at the time (see *Elvis and Me.*) In 1968, Nancy played opposite Elvis in the film *Speedway*. Nancy gave Priscilla a baby shower. Nancy was married at one time to Elvis "imitator" Tommy Sands. In 1970, Elvis, Priscilla, and other family members attended Nancy's Las Vegas International opening.

Smith, Lillian was Gladys Presley's sister. From 1960 to 1962, she was employed at Graceland as a secretary to answer fan mail.

Spreckles, Judy Powell was the heiress to the Spreckles sugar dynasty who was romantically linked to Elvis in 1958. Judy accompanied him to his Army induction and also gave Elvis a stunning four-star black sapphire ring in Las Vegas.

Stefaniak, Elisabeth Claudia was secretary to Elvis in Bad Nauheim, after she briefly dated him in West Germany. She lived with the Presley family at 14 Goethestrasse and earned $35 a week. In 1960, Elisabeth married Rex Mansfield, a friend of Elvis's. The Mansfields wrote *Elvis the Soldier*.

Stevens, Connie dated Elvis briefly in 1961. Expecting to have an intimate dinner alone with Elvis one night, she was shocked when Joe Esposito picked her up and brought her to the singer's Bel Air mansion, where a group of people had gathered. Stevens was furious and demanded to be taken home. They never dated again.

Stevenson, Venetia was an actress who dated Elvis in 1957 and 1958. She flew to West Germany and lived with Elvis for a short period during his Army tour, which upset Elisabeth Stefaniak. In 1962, Stevenson married Don Everly of the Everly Brothers.

Storm, Tempest was a stripper who was romantically involved with Elvis for a few days in 1957. She wrote about their whirlwind love affair in the 1987 book *Tempest Storm: The Lady Is a Vamp*. She states she last saw Elvis in 1970, and that he visited her during her performance in Las Vegas. She alleges Elvis climbed into her room and stayed until three A.M. Elvis was married to Priscilla at the time.

Streisand, Barbra was the first major performer to appear at Las Vegas' International Hotel; Elvis was the second. Streisand offered Elvis the male lead in *A Star Is Born* which Colonel Parker turned down. Priscilla and Elvis visited Streisand in Vegas, 1970. In 1978, at the Riviera Hotel in Vegas, Streisand broke Elvis's record for being the highest-paid Las Vegas performer. Streisand is one of the only young singers or actresses in Elvis's life with whom he didn't have an affair.

Sullivan, Virginia claims to have had a secret fourteen-year love affair with Elvis from 1963 to 1977. She alleges they met at the Club Creole in Mobile, Alabama, in 1955. She claims that she and Elvis registered as Mr. and Mrs. Frank Thompson at a Holiday Inn, but has no proof to support her claims.

Sweet Inspirations was Elvis's black, female backup singing group, which sang with him in concerts and on a few recordings for eight years. Members included **Emily Cissy Houston** (mother of Whitney Houston), **Myrna Smith, Estelle Brown,** and **Sylvia Shenwell.** When Elvis heard "Sweet Inspiration," a 1968 Atlantic release by the group, he asked the women to join his organization and tour with him. They appear in the 1979 TV movie *Elvis* and in the 1980 movie *The Idolmaker.* Elvis insulted two members of the group in 1975, and they marched off the stage. Elvis presented Myrna Smith, who remained onstage, with a ring as an apology. Afterward, he gave each member of the group a ring and apologized for his chauvinistic remarks. Elvis recorded the Sweet Inspirations' songs "Unchained Melody" (1968) and "Let It Be Me" (1967). Elvis affectionately nicknamed the women the Sweets.

Taylor Terri (aka Gloria Stiles), was a singer who claimed she met Elvis in Bossier City, Louisiana, in 1955, and later gave birth to his child, Candy Jo, on December 22, 1957, at Lincoln, Nebraska's St. Elizabeth's Hospital. She stated Elvis often called her and sent her money, and they remained good friends through both of her marriages. She has not proved her claims.

Thompson, Linda Diane began dating Elvis during the breakup of his marriage to Priscilla. She was Miss Tennessee at the time. They stayed together four years. An English major at Memphis State University, she dropped out of college after three and a half years to be with Elvis. Elvis gave her an American Express card, furs, hundreds of thousands of dollars' worth of jewelry, a car, and homes for Linda, her parents, and her brother. She lived at Graceland from 1972 to 1976, and redecorated most of the mansion. Thompson allegedly charged over $29,000 on Elvis's credit cards before their final breakup. In October 1973, she stayed by Elvis's bedside when he was admitted to the Baptist Memorial Hospital. They broke up in 1976 because of Elvis's drug problem. Elvis and Thompson remained friends until his death. She has kept in touch with Lisa Marie. In 1981, Thompson married Olympic athlete Bruce Jenner, and they separated six years later. She has recorded a few singles and has appeared on many TV shows since the death of Elvis.

Thornton, Willie Mae was the blues artist who originally recorded "Hound Dog" in August 1952. She accused Elvis of stealing the song from her and blamed Elvis for exploiting black artists. The Cat said none of her comments were true.

Tribble, Iladean alleged she and Elvis were to be married in Athens, Alabama, April 17, 1976. In April, she put a wedding announcement in a local paper, and hundreds of fans showed up for the Tribble/Presley wedding!

Tschechowa, Vera was a young German actress who occasionally dated Elvis from 1958 to 1960, while he was stationed in West Germany.

Van Doren, Mamie dated Elvis in 1957, while she was married to Ray Anthony. She often performed at the Riviera Hotel.

Wardlow, Billy dated Elvis after Betty McMann. Elvis considered marrying Wardlow.

Watts, Debbie alleged she was the secret lover of Elvis from 1972 to 1977 (see *Star* article, Sept. 20, 1977).

West, Pat Boyd was a secretary at Graceland who helped Elvis with various chores. In 1961, she married Red West, one of the Memphis Mafia.

Westmoreland, Kathy was a singer/actress who toured with Elvis during 1970–77 concerts. Elvis told audiences she was the "beautiful little girl with the high voice." They dated off and on during that seven-year period. Elvis bought Westmoreland many cars and gifts. She wrote an autobiography, *Elvis and Kathy*, in which she claims to have slept with and fallen in love with Elvis. Elvis often made chauvinistic and rude remarks onstage to Westmoreland, stating she slept with his band members and so forth. In 1975, she and the Sweet Inspirations walked off the stage. With Larry Geller and Charlie Hodge, Westmoreland maintains that Dr. George Nichopoulos said that Elvis took drugs to ease the pain of bone cancer. She sang "My Heavenly Father Watches Over Me" at Elvis's funeral. In 1978, she starred in the Broadway show *The Legend Lives*, and in the 1979 TV movie *Elvis* she sang on the sound track.

Wheeler, Kate dated Elvis on and off in 1956.

Wilbank, June dated Elvis several times in 1958.

Wiley, Sharon dated Elvis in the fifties. Rumors flew they had a passionate, serious relationship.

Wood, Anita was one of the first women Elvis wanted to marry. She was a radio and television personality known for her charm, wit, and beauty. Cliff Greaves introduced the blonde to Elvis

in 1957. Elvis nicknamed her Little Beadie, and their love affair seemed serious. Little Bit was a poodle he gave her on Christmas, 1958. They often stayed at Eddie Fadal's Waco, Texas, home together while Elvis was stationed at Fort Hood. The bootleg recording *Forever Young, Forever Beautiful* features Wood, Fadal, and Elvis. A Memphis newspaper reported Wood and Elvis were to marry before he left for Germany, but Colonel Tom Parker stopped all plans because he feared it would harm the star's popularity with female fans. Wood married Johnny Brewer and they had three children. In 1972, she filed a suit against a Memphis paper for romantically linking her to Elvis after she was married. The paper claimed she met Elvis in Vegas and wanted to rekindle their romance. She was awarded a $240,000 settlement.

Wood, Natalie dated Elvis in 1956, after being introduced to him by actor Nick Adams. Movie magazines and tabloids said they were to marry. Wood, Elvis, Gladys, and Vernon spent a weekend together at Graceland. Wood claimed negative publicity was ruining their friendship and that they were not in love. Shelley Winters, however, told the press they were in love. Wood died on November 28, 1981, in a drowning accident.

Yancey, Becky was a fan who became a secretary at Graceland from 1962 to 1974. She coauthored a 1977 book titled *My Life with Elvis*, which tells of her years at Graceland. Along with Bonya McGarrity and Pat Boyd, Yancey signed Elvis's name to photographs and to fan-mail responses.

Young, Barbara claimed she had a love affair with Elvis that resulted in their daughter's birth (Deborah Presley) on March 4, 1956. In 1987, she filed a $125-million lawsuit against the Presley estate. Young claims to have been singing in Charlotte, North Carolina, when she met Elvis. She divorced her husband on the day Elvis died, August 16, 1977.

Young, Tammy played pool with Elvis during his high school years. On occasion, they would roller-skate or go to the movies together.

Zancan, Sandra dated Elvis in 1972, after he and Priscilla filed for divorce. She was a showgirl in Vegas.

Zehetbauer, Anjelika was a nightclub dancer who dated Elvis while he was in Germany. He called her his "German fräulein."

Many actresses, dancers, singers, and fans claim to have been loved by Elvis or say they made love with him. For certain, he was not monogamous or loyal to any one female, and his reputation as a great lover was mostly fantasy on the part of the women who desired him. From almost every account, as a lover Elvis is portrayed as a man incapable of being romantic. His mind continuously wandered to the next day, the next tour, the next song, the next woman.

Girls were passed around and shared among Elvis and the Memphis Mafia like party favors. The men who traveled with Elvis did nothing to encourage him to remain faithful to his wife or to himself, and vowed to keep secret his behavior. Therefore, Elvis did whatever he wanted to do—with whomever he wished or whoever allowed it. Everyone knew the rules, and if Elvis could not control those around him, the Colonel did. That is until the 1977 release of *Elvis: What Happened?*—which blew the lid off of everything he had kept concealed.

As he continuously searched for happiness, the more women he dated, the more insecure and lonelier Elvis became. His is the lamentable story of a world-famous superstar torn emotionally and physically to shreds by those who professed to adore him, and by his inability to handle grief, abuse, and negative publicity. In the final analysis, Elvis trusted *no* one after Gladys Presley died. She remained his *only* true confidant, even though he abandoned her for his career at the end of her life. No matter how many friends or lovers he had, no relationship paralleled that of Elvis with his mother. She was truly the only woman in his life.

Girlfriends and Dates

Elvis gave girlfriends, wives of friends, casual acquaintances, and female strangers "Tender Loving Care" (TLC) fourteen-karat-gold necklaces with a lightning bolt through the letters. He often gave girlfriends, dates, wives of friends, fans, and strangers expensive diamond rings and other costly gifts, including homes and cars.

In recent years, many women have come forward with claims that Elvis fathered their children or that they secretly dated the King. The women Elvis took out as friends and those he dated romantically include:

1. Alden, Ginger ("Gingerbread" and "Chicken Neck," 1976–77)
2. Andress, Ursula (code name "Alan" at Graceland)
3. Ann-Margret (code names "Thumper" and "Bunny," 1964–65)
4. Ballard, Caroline (his first girlfriend, age nine, the minister's daughter at East Tupelo First Assembly of God Church)
5. Beaulieu, Priscilla Ann (met 1959; married 5/1/67; separated from 2/23/72; divorce filed 8/18/72; divorce final 10/9/73)

6. Bedford, Eloise (fifth grade, at East Tupelo Consolidated School)
7. Blackwood, Malessa (nineteen years old, a beauty queen, 1976)
8. Bonner, Barbara (dated Elvis in the sixties)
9. Bradley, Arlene (alleges she dated Elvis from 1957 to 1963)
10. Bradshaw, Joan (in Hollywood, 1957)
11. Buergin, Margrit (sixteen-year-old German stenographer, 1958)
12. Carter, Anita (singer who toured with Elvis in 1955)
13. Clarke, Jane (allegedly dated Elvis in 1959 at the Lido; also claims to have dated him in Vegas in 1963)
14. Connors, Carol (singer/writer who dated Elvis, 1959–60)
15. deBarbin, Lucy (alleges she dated Elvis in 1957—and then John Wayne in 1958!—and claims her child Desiree is Elvis's).
16. Deshannon, Jackie (singer-composer, dated Elvis for six months in the midsixties; doubled-dated with Jimmy O'Neill, the host of ABC-TV's "Shindig")
17. Dolan, Kitty (singer at the Tropicana, 1956 for several months)
18. Dors, Diana (wrote "Elvis Was My Love" for the *London Sunday Mirror* and alleges dating him 1956–57)
19. Duncan, Sandra (mistaken for Elvis's girlfriend in November 1972 issue of *TV Radio Show*)
20. Evans, Marilyn (a dancer, 1956)
21. Fabares, Shelley (actress, dated Elvis in midsixties)
22. Sandy Ferra (singer who dated Elvis in 1960; married Wink Martindale)
23. Gabriel, Kathy (Vegas showgirl, 1956)
24. Gentry, Bobbie (singer; in the late fifties)
25. Goodman, Diana (Miss Georgia; dated Elvis in the seventies)
26. Harmony, Dottie (dated in 1957, Memphis)
27. Hart, Dolores (dated Elvis in 1958)
28. Hearn, Barbara (school chum he dated during the fifties and sixties)
29. Holdridge, Cheryl (actress, dated Elvis in 1962)
30. Hugueny, Sharon (actress, dated Elvis in 1963)
31. Hyman, B. D. (daughter of Bette Davis; actress who saw a lot of Elvis in 1961, but it's questionable if they dated)
32. Juanico, June (receptionist in Biloxi, MS, 1955)
33. Lewis, Barbara Jean (allegedly dated Elvis 1954–55 and maintains Elvis is the father of her daughter Deborah)
34. Lime, Yvonne (during *Loving You* filming, 1957, Hollywood)
35. Lipton, Peggy (alleges to have dated Elvis)
36. Locke, Dixie (girlfriend at Humes High School, 1953–55)
37. McMann, Betty (may have been Elvis's first girlfriend, 1950–51)
38. Miller, Mindy (dated Elvis in 1976, after Linda Thompson)
39. Moreno, Rita (actress; dated Elvis in 1957, during *Loving You*)
40. Newton, Billy Joe (alleges she was married to Elvis in 1956, gave birth to three of his children and divorced him.)
41. Parker, Patricia Ann (alleged she had an affair with Elvis from 1969 to 1970, and that her child, Jason, was his son)
42. Pennington, Ann (dated after Linda Thompson, 1976)
43. Peters, Vicki (dated Elvis in 1971)
44. Pittman, Barbara (singer; dated in the fifties)

45. Preston, Sandy (Elvis took her to the Sahara Hotel in 1956 to see Edgar Bergen)
46. Ryan, Sheila (*Playboy* pinup dated Elvis from September 4, 1974 to 1975)
47. Sharp, Nancy (wardrobe assistant Elvis dated in 1960)
48. Shepherd, Cybill (actress, dated Elvis in 1966 and 1970)
49. Sinatra, Nancy (met Elvis at McGuire Air Force Base on March 3, 1960, and they were linked romantically via the press)
50. Spreckles, Judy Powell (heiress who dated Elvis in 1958)
51. Stefaniak, Elisabeth (briefly dated in West Germany)
52. Stevens, Connie (actress, dated Elvis in 1961)
53. Stevenson, Venetia (actress, dated Elvis, 1957–58)
54. Storm, Tempest (stripper in Las Vegas, dated Elvis in 1957)
55. Sullivan, Virginia (alleges to have dated Elvis secretly from 1963 to 1977)
56. Taylor, Terri (alleges she dated Elvis and had his child)
57. Thompson, Linda (1972–76, nicknamed Precious and Adiadne)
58. Tribble, Iladen (alleged she was to marry Elvis in 1976)
59. Tschechowa, Vera (German actress, dated Elvis from 1958 to 1960)
60. Van Doren, Mamie (actress, who dated Elvis and Burt Reynolds in 1957, while she was married to musician Ray Anthony)
61. Vaughn, Regis (Wilson) was Elvis's senior-prom date at the Peabody Hotel
62. Wardlow, Billy (dated Elvis after he left Betty McMann in 1951)
63. Watts, Debbie (alleges she secretly dated Elvis from 1972 to 1977)
64. Westmoreland, Kathy (singer who dated Elvis from 1970 to 1977)
65. Wheeler, Kate (dated Elvis in 1956)
66. Wilbank, June (dated Elvis in 1958)
67. Wiley, Sharon (seriously dated Elvis in the midfifties)
68. Wood, Anita (disc jockey for Memphis radio WHHM; singer; nicknamed Little Beadie; dated seriously from 1957 to 1959. Elvis wanted to marry her)
69. Wood, Natalie (actress, dated Elvis in 1956)
70. Young, Barbara (alleges she dated Elvis, 1954–56, which resulted in a daughter, Deborah Presley, born on March 4, 1956)
71. Young, Tammy ("dated" Elvis in high school)
72. Zancan, Sandra (Vegas showgirl who dated Elvis in 1972)
73. Zehetbauer, Anjelika (German dancer, dated Elvis in 1958)

MEN IN ELVIS'S LIFE—"MAFIA" AND MISERY

If Elvis ever had deep, positive feelings for *any* man, he did not openly admit it or show it. The only man he was loyal to was his manager, Colonel Parker, but the reasons for Elvis's dedication remain debatable.

The men who created support groups around Elvis fed his ego, took care of his needs, kept his secrets, and pampered, guarded, and assisted him on tours, movie sets, or at Graceland. They bowed to his every demand because they were paid to do so. Because it was almost impossible for Elvis to return devotion, respect, or even loyalty, most of these men felt little more for Elvis than employee to employer. Nevertheless, here are the men in Elvis's life:

Aberbach, Jean and **Julian** (brothers) were the owners of Hill and Range, country-music publishers. Good friends of Colonel Parker since 1944, at the Colonel's request they became the publishers of Elvis's entire repertoire of recorded music (with Elvis Presley Publishing Co. and Gladys Music). Elvis's inside man at Hill and Range was Memphis Mafia member Lamar Fike. Hill and Range paid $15,000 for their rights to Elvis and became a part of the complicated deal RCA made with Sun Records. Colonel Parker negotiated the size of everyone's share of the pie.

Ackerman, Paul was the first national magazine editor/reporter to appreciate the talent of Elvis. In the midfifties Ackerman was the music editor for *Billboard* magazine, and Elvis received a lot of recognition via that source.

Sam Phillips gave Ackerman his eulogy in 1977.

Adams, Jack sold Elvis the 163-acre De-Soto County, Mississippi, Twinkletown Ranch (later named the Circle G Ranch by Elvis, the *G* standing for Graceland) on February 9, 1967, for $300,000 (using Graceland as collateral). A fifty-foot, white cross on the property inspired Elvis to buy it. The property had a small house, but Elvis and Priscilla lived outside it, in a three-bedroom trailer! Elvis stocked a lake on the property with fish, bought a fleet of twenty-five Ford trucks for his staff, and maintained a stable of horses.

Adams, Nick was a Hollywood actor who became close friends with James Dean when the two men did a Pepsi-Cola ad in 1951. He chose another "rebel" as a friend, Elvis Presley, when Elvis filmed *Love Me Tender*. Eventually, Adams starred in a TV series called "The Rebel." Adams and Elvis liked to dress in black leather and drive Harley-Davidsons together and party in hotel rooms until dawn. Elvis tried to get Adams cast in *Love Me Tender*, but the producers claimed he was too young. Adams was married to Carol Nugent and had two children. He committed suicide with a drug overdose, February 17, 1968.

Alden, Walter was the father of Elvis's last girlfriend, Ginger Alden, and the officer who inducted Elvis into the Army on March 24, 1958.

Allen, Steve featured Elvis on his TV show, "The Steve Allen Show," in 1956. In one infamous segment, Allen introduced "the new Elvis" in a tuxedo and made him sing "Hound Dog" to a pathetic-looking dog. The next day after this embarrassing moment for Elvis, his fans picketed the studio with signs that read "Give Us the Real Elvis."

Atkins, Chet is a master guitarist/engineer who helped create "the Nashville sound." Hired by Steve Sholes, Atkins produced many Presley recordings at RCA's Nashville studios (1956–58). Felton Jarvis later took his place as producer for RCA materials related to Elvis, which helped boost the Cat's career. Atkins had become too concerned with RCA's management, and Elvis's music suffered because of it. Atkins was a session musician (guitar) for many of Elvis's tracks as well as Hank Williams, the Everly Brothers, and many other greats. In 1973, Atkins was inducted into the Country Music Hall of Fame. He stated he didn't think anyone as powerful and original as Elvis would come along again in his lifetime. Atkins was honored with the Lifetime Achievement Grammy Award in February 1993.

Auberback, Larry worked for the William Morris Agency in Los Angeles and acted as an agent for Elvis with the Colonel's consent.

Ausborn, Carbel Lee. See **Mississippi Slim.**

Ausborn, James is the younger brother of country-western singer Mississippi Slim (born Carvel Ausborn). James was a pal of Elvis's when, as a novice, Elvis listened to Slim at the Tupelo radio station. James and Elvis were in the same school for a short time and hid behind black blues clubs to listen to jiving musicians play R&B. James was present at the "Black and White Jamboree" (WELO radio) in 1944, when Elvis sang "Old Shep" with Mississippi Slim accompanying on guitar.

Ayers, Rick was one of Elvis's many hairdressers. Elvis and Ayers were also workout partners at Graceland.

Baer, Max, Jr., was a companion of Elvis's in California, where the two would play football, party, or go to clubs. He played Jethro Bodine on TV's "The Beverly Hillbillies" (1962–71). Baer is an actor/director.

Baize, Bill was a tenor with J. D. Sumner and the Stamps, whom Elvis admired greatly. He sang "When It's My Turn" at Elvis's funeral.

Barris, George and his wife, Shirley, were friends of Priscilla and Elvis in California. George was a car customizer, and because of their mutual love for automobiles, Elvis and George became close buddies. George customized the "solid-gold" Cadillac (actually white with imitation-gold touches inside) that is at the Country Music Hall of Fame, and also Elvis's Greyhound tour bus.

Beinstock, Freddie worked for Hill and Range and selected the songs from which Elvis would choose to record. Beinstock's selections lessened the quality of Elvis's work.

Below, Bill custom-made Elvis's jumpsuits and capes (1968–77). In 1968, he designed Elvis's black leather outfit for the television special.

Bennett, Roy C. composed forty-three songs that Elvis sang in films.

Berle, Milton showcased Elvis on his variety show on April 3 and June 5, 1956. The TV exposure boosted Elvis's popularity, but critics tore Elvis apart for being "vulgar." Elvis denied he was doing anything wrong.

Bernero, Johnny was the original drummer on Elvis's Sun Record sessions prior to 1955 and is so credited by J. D. Fontana.

Berry, Chuck is more than a witty bluesman or a flamboyant rock artist. Like Elvis, Chuck Berry took blues to rock 'n' roll. Both men admired (with caution) the other. Elvis sang or recorded many of Berry's songs including "Memphis, Tennessee," "Merry Christmas, Baby," "Brown-Eyed Handsome Man," "Too Much Monkey Business," "School Day," "Promised Land," and "Johnny B. Goode."

Berry's hits include "Maybellene," "School Day" (1957), "Rock and Roll Music" (1957), "Sweet Little Sixteen" (1958), and "Johnny B. Goode" (1958), and he appeared in such films as *Rock, Rock, Rock* (1956), *Rock and Roll* (1957), and *Go, Johnny, Go.* (1958).

Berry was inducted into the Rock 'n' Roll Hall of Fame with Elvis.

Biggs, Patrick was a favorite uncle and husband to Delta Mae Presley (Vernon's sister). When Biggs wanted to buy a nightclub, Elvis financed it. Biggs was a caretaker at times at the ranch and at Graceland.

Binder, Steve was the insightful and inspired TV producer who went to NBC-TV with the idea for the December 3, 1968, Elvis "Comeback Special" Christmas show, which gave Elvis the opportunity to perform live after years of being absent. Although Colonel Parker had another idea for the show, Binder overpowered the Colonel and presented Elvis as a sexy, raw rebel. When Elvis appeared on TV wearing black leather and singing "Tiger Man," he reestablished his roll as the King of Rock. Elvis got along with Binder and appreciated his intuition and wisdom. In 1980, Binder produced the Graceland TV special that is narrated by Priscilla Presley.

Black, Bill was a bassist who first joined the Starlight Wranglers with Doug Poindexter and Scotty Moore, and then in 1955, the Blue Moon Boys with Scotty Moore and Elvis, managed by Bob Neal. (Today his bass is owned by Paul McCartney.) Earlier, Bill and Johnny Black jammed with Elvis in the Lauderdale Courts, and the boys' mothers were close friends. In the book *Gladys and Elvis*, the author states Black's father, Louis, encouraged Elvis to cut an acetate as early as 1952. Sam Phillips of Sun Records encouraged Black and Moore to join with Elvis. In March 1955, Black and Moore went to New York City with Elvis to audition for (and be rejected by) the "Arthur Godfrey's Talent Scouts." They performed together at the "Louisiana Hayride" and did gigs across the South, and "Blackie" became well-known for riding his bass across the stage like a horse. In 1957, he played Eddy the bassist in *Loving You* and in *Jailhouse Rock*. Scotty Moore and Black left Elvis on September 21, 1957, because while they were each making only $100–200 a week (and were expected to pay for their own touring expenses), Elvis was earning millions. It was an insult to Moore and Black, who were instrumental in creating Elvis's sound. Black played three more sessions with Elvis, only to be replaced by Bob Moore. With Scotty Moore, Black started the Bill Black Combo in 1957. He died of a brain tumor October 21, 1965, at the Baptist Memorial Hospital, Memphis. Elvis did not attend his funeral.

Blackwell, Otis was a prolific black songwriter whose works have been recorded by many great entertainers including Jerry Lee Lewis and Elvis. His most famous songs are "Fever," "Breathless," "Great Balls of Fire," "Don't Be Cruel," and "All Shook Up." Although the Colonel, Hill and Range publishers, and others listed Elvis as a cowriter of many Blackwell songs, the two men never met. The only reason Blackwell allowed his name to be linked with Elvis's as coauthor was because Blackwell wanted Elvis to sing "Don't Be Cruel," "All Shook Up," and "Paralyzed."

Blackwood Brothers was a gospel singing group that (in the fifties) included R. W. Blackwood, James "Mr. Gospel Music" Blackwood, Bill Lyles, and Bill Shaw. Other members included Cecil Blackwood, Pat Hoffmaster, Tommy Fairchild, Ken Turner, and William Snow. The Presleys belonged to the same Assembly of God Church the Blackwood Brothers attended. Their previous gospel group was called the Songfellows, and Elvis wanted to be a member. Cecil Blackwood left the Songfellows to join the Blackwoods. Prior to Cecil's departure, the Songfellows had rejected Elvis from their group because they said he couldn't "hear" harmonies. The Blackwood Brothers won many Grammy Awards and cut over 120 albums. On August 16, 1958, they sang at Gladys's funeral, and in 1977, at Elvis's.

Bland, Bobby "Blue" was photographed with Elvis in 1956, with Little Junior Parker (1927–71) and other singers and musicians on Beale Street. Bland was a patriarch of soul singing whose grainy vocal style drew from gospel and blues. First working as B. B. King's chauffeur, Bland informally sang with the Beale Streeters, who included King, Roscoe Gordon, Willie Nix, and Johnny Ace. His big break came in 1955 with his first single, "It's My Life, Baby," for Duke Records. Elvis knew Bland and liked his arrogant soul and rhythm and blues style.

Bobo, F. L. sold Elvis's first guitar to the Presleys in 1945, instead of the rifle and bicycle he allegedly wanted.

Bond, Eddie toured with Elvis in September 1955 as a fellow rockabilly artist. He had a band called the Stompers with which Conway Twitty once sang. Elvis may have performed with the Stompers in gigs around Memphis in

1953. Bond told *Goldmine* magazine he fired Elvis from a gig in 1954 at the Hi Hat Club.

Boone, Pat is the all-American, clean-cut singer who had a love/hate relationship with Elvis because while Boone admired his competitor's talent, he detested rock 'n' roll. The duo first met when Boone's smooth, sweet, comfortable singing was accepted and Elvis was rejected on "Arthur Godfrey's Talent Scouts." In October 1955, they sang on the same stage in Cleveland, Ohio. In 1956, Elvis sang Boone's "Don't Forbid Me" (Dot 15521) during the Million Dollar Quartet session. In 1957, Elvis stated Boone was "undoubtedly the finest voice out now" (August 31 interview with Red Robinson). Boone lived down the street from Elvis and Priscilla in Beverly Hills.

Bradley, Gen. Omar Nelson whom Elvis admired as a hero, was a U.S. Army general and chairman of the Joint Chiefs of Staff (1949–50). Elvis gave Bradley a TCB gold emblem and chain at the general's home.

Bradley, Rev. C. W. officiated Elvis's fu-

▲ Elvis with Nappy Brown, "Little Junior" Parker, and Bobby "Blue" Bland in Memphis, Tennessee. *Photograph by Ernest C. Withers. Copyright © 1989 Mimosa Records Productions, Inc.*

neral ceremony at Graceland, August 18, 1977, at two P.M. He was pastor of the Memphis Woodvale Church of Christ.

Bragg, Johnny was a black lead singer with the Prisonaires (inmates at the Tennessee State Prison) who alleged Elvis visited him in prison. He also claimed that his group sang backup with Elvis at a charity benefit in Nashville.

Brando, Marlon is an Academy Award–winning actor whose vulnerable sneer and rebellious nature in *The Wild One* intrigued Elvis so much he took on his look and attitude. Elvis's 1960 role in *Flaming Star* had been written for Brando. The producer of the Dorsey brothers' "Stage Show" said Elvis was "the guitar-playing Marlon Brando." Milton Berle called Elvis "the Marlon Brando of rock."

Brown, James, "The Godfather of Soul," met Elvis in Hollywood at the Hyatt Continental Hotel. Becoming lifelong friends and admirers, the two men enjoyed singing gospel music together. Elvis wanted to sing and record with Brown's band, the Famous Flames, but for some unfortunate reason, the Colonel forbid it. Brown flew to Memphis to be with the family when Elvis died and was one of the few people to attend the private ceremonies in 1977.

Brown, Tony was the drummer who replaced Glen D. Hardin in Elvis's touring TCB band (1974–77).

Burnette, Johnny was born in Memphis and was a popular rockabilly singer when Elvis hit the scene. Burnette, Red West, and Elvis attended Humes High School together. On weekends, Burnette and Elvis went to Beale Street to hear black bluesman B. B. King. In 1954, Elvis backed Burnette in a casual gig at Airways Used Cars in Memphis. Burnette organized a rockabilly band in 1958 with Johnny Dorsey and Paul Burlinson (all Golden Gloves fighters).

Elvis dubbed Burnette's group the Dalton Gang. They recorded (but were not released) on the Sun label and appeared on Ted Macks' "Original Amateur Hour." Burnette drowned August 1, 1964, in Clear Lake, California, during a fishing trip.

"Burrows, Jon" ("Colonel" or "Dr.") was the code name used by Elvis to screen or receive mail and personal phone calls. He also used the name when he traveled to Washington, DC, to talk with President Nixon. When he wrote Nixon on American Airlines stationery, he told Nixon his code name was Jon Burrows.

Burton, James earned $5,000 a week playing in Elvis's TCB band as the lead guitarist (1969–77), and he recorded some sessions (including "Merry Christmas Baby") with Elvis. At Hollywood's A&M Records, Elvis paid $6,000 for an instrumental album of Burton's music to be recorded.

"Carpenter, Dr. John" was an alias Elvis used to elude fans when he stayed in hotels or traveled by air. John Carpenter was also Elvis's character's name in *Change of Habit* (1969).

Carter, Billy, Pres. Jimmy Carter's brother, said upon visiting Elvis in Memphis that the rock star was guarded better than the president.

Carter, Jimmy, thirty-ninth president of the United States, was an avid fan of Elvis's and said his death resulted in the country losing a part of itself and that Elvis "permanently changed the face" of American pop culture. As governor, he named a day Elvis Presley Day.

Cash, Johnny began rockabilly singing at the Sun label after Elvis was a star in 1955. He and Elvis sang at the Overton Park Shell, Memphis, on August 5, 1955. Together with Carl Perkins, Cash and Elvis toured together from

Abilene, Texas, to St. Louis on the Jamboree circuit, October 1955. Cash is part of the Million Dollar Quartet session and sued to prohibit its over-dubbed release. He left Sun in 1958 for Columbia Records. In Las Vegas in August 1969, Elvis introduced himself as Johnny Cash and then sang "I Walk the Line" and "Folsom Prison Blues." Cash, nicknamed the Man in Black, is an inductee in the Country Music Hall of Fame.

Childress, Hubert was Elvis's army captain/company commander in West Germany.

Church, Charles R. owned Memphis's Indoor Shooting Center, where Elvis purchased police accessories and TV equipment. He installed closed-circuit-TV systems in Graceland, which were controlled from Elvis's bedroom.

Clark, Albert, Jr., worked as a grounds-keeper and handyman at Graceland for twelve years.

Clark, Dick is the disc jockey dubbed the world's oldest teenager and host of the long-running TV dance program "American Bandstand." During Elvis's Army tour, Clark interviewed him by phone (January 8, 1959) and later produced the TV movie *Elvis*. As an avid fan of Elvis's, Clark was in the audience at Elvis's Las Vegas premiere, July 31, 1969, at the International Hotel, and he often defended Elvis against the cunning tactics of Colonel Parker.

Clement, Jack was a Memphis bandleader, violinist, and composer whom Elvis often met at Taylor's Cafe. Clement appeared with Elvis as "Cowboy Jack" at Memphis's Eagle's Nest, ca. 1953–54, where Elvis earned $10 to sing between Clement's band and Johnny Burnette.

Coffman, Richard J. was platoon leader of Elvis's Army group in West Germany. He was a first lieutenant from Nevada, Missouri.

Cole, J. D. was the Lawhon Grammar School principal in Tupelo who entered Elvis in the 1945 Mississippi-Alabama Fair and Dairy Show, where Elvis won second prize singing "Old Shep."

Coley, Henry was the six-foot-three-inch, robust master sergeant at Fort Hood, Texas, who watched over Elvis's platoon.

Covington, Pappy booked Elvis on the "Louisiana Hayride" and set up his 1955 tour through Arkansas, Louisiana, and Texas. During these gigs, Elvis received wide recognition and was called "the Hillbilly Cat" and "the King of Western Bop." It was also during this tour Scotty Moore, Bill Black, and Elvis were dubbed "the Blue Moon Boys."

Cramer, Floyd backed Elvis on Nashville recording sessions (1956–68) and was a talented piano player who became famous for his slip-note style. He and Elvis played the "Louisiana Hayride" at the same time and were on the same program during the Jamboree tour, October 1955.

Creel, Tom W. was stationed with Elvis in West Germany and later became his stand-in in movies.

Crudup, Arthur "Big Boy" was the R&B singer/composer/guitarist who had a major influence on Elvis's singing style. Crudup recorded with RCA from 1941–54, and Elvis financed Crudup's recording sessions at Fire Records in the fifties. Elvis was a huge fan of the legendary bluesman, who wrote "That's All Right, Mama," the first hit Elvis recorded, "My Baby Left Me" and "So Glad You're Mine" (both sung by Elvis), and "Father of Rock 'n' Roll." In 1974, Crudup died of a stroke in Nassawadox, Virginia, at the age of sixty-eight.

Curtis, Tony was Elvis's favorite actor in the early fifties, before he discovered James Dean and Marlon Brando. Some people say Elvis changed his hair color and style to emulate Tony Curtis.

The 1949 movie *City Across the River* first caught Elvis's attention. It dealt with tough inner-city life in the Brooklyn slums, and Curtis's handsome, somewhat defiant nature came across as something to copy. Curtis's role in *Son of Ali Baba* (1952), his title role in *Houdini* (1953), and his sexy, athletic performance in *Trapeze* (1956) inspired Elvis as well.

Darin, Bobby was a pop star and actor during Elvis's reign as King of Rock. Elvis said he liked Darin's voice a great deal, and Elvis introduced him to audiences in Las Vegas. The two men admired each other and spent time together when they could. When Elvis turned down a part in *Too Late Blues*, Darin got the role.

David, Elwood piloted Elvis's Corvair 880 jet, the *Lisa Marie*.

Davis, Oscar ("The Baron") was impressed with Elvis's performances at Memphis's Eagle's Nest and was instrumental in arranging for Colonel Parker to meet and hear Elvis in 1954. The rest is history. He assisted Parker with Elvis's career for a short period and later managed Jerry Lee Lewis.

Davis, Richard was valet to Elvis in 1962, after the two men played touch football together in Memphis. Vernon fired him in 1969 to save money.

Davis, Sammy, Jr., was the dancer/ singer who performed with Elvis in 1960 on ABC-TV's "Frank Sinatra Special." Elvis went to Davis's performances and Davis often was in the audience when Elvis performed. Davis can be seen in 1970's *Elvis—That's the Way It Is*. Some reports say Davis and Elvis danced down the aisle at a Chuck Berry concert. Because of their deep friendship, Elvis gave Davis a 157-carat black sapphire ring. "In the Ghetto" was first offered to Davis, who couldn't sing it properly, so Elvis was given the chance to do it right. Sammy Davis, Jr., attended Elvis's funeral.

Dean, James was the sexy, rebellious movie star who became Elvis's idol after Elvis saw him in *East of Eden*. Elvis was influenced by Dean's pout and sulking mannerisms. Referring to Elvis as the "musical James Dean" after Dean's untimely death, many felt Elvis would take his place in the film world. Their mutual friend was Nick Adams, and Elvis and Dean each allegedly dated Ursula Andress. Elvis was such a fan of *Rebel Without a Cause* that he memorized the entire script and watched it over one hundred times. In 1956, a magazine titled *Elvis and Jimmy* hit the stands and sold out. When David Weisbart announced he would make a documentary movie on Dean's life, Elvis asked to play Dean. That film was never produced. Elvis accurately called Dean a "genius" and held him in the highest esteem. Dean died in a car accident in 1955.

Diddley, Bo was an R&B singer whom Elvis saw at the Apollo Theatre in New York in 1956. Bo Diddley and many other people accused Elvis of imitating Bo's hip movements onstage, but that was not true—Elvis was known for gyrating hips as early as 1942, in church revivals, and he became noted for it at his 1954 Overton Park Shell concert. Elvis didn't see Bo Diddley perform until 1956. Bo Diddley's hits included "You Can't Judge a Book by Its Cover," "I'm a Man," "Sweet Little Rock 'n' Roller," "Memphis," "Bo Diddley," and "Say, Man."

Diskin, Tom was the brother-in-law and yes-man to Colonel Parker, who nicknamed him Penguin. Writer Jerry Hopkins claimed Diskin turned down the chance to manage Elvis prior to the Colonel's meeting Elvis.

Dvorin, Al produced the 1961 Hawaiian benefit gig for the USS *Arizona* and was the master of ceremonies. As a bandleader, he played many sessions and shows with Elvis and was the announcer for *Elvis Recorded Live on Stage in Memphis* (1974).

Dwyer, Ronald is the attorney who defended Elvis and the Memphis Mafia in court, February 19, 1973, when a $4-million suit was issued against them for bodily harm and harassment in Las Vegas. It was dismissed.

Ellington, Buford was governor of Tennessee. He declared Elvis Presley Day on September 19, 1967, and gave the King the title "colonel" before the General Assembly of the State Legislature on March 8, 1961. Now both Elvis and Tom Parker had honorary "colonel" bestowed upon them. Ellington admired Elvis and knew how much his reputation and stardom helped the state of Tennessee. He lowered the flags throughout the state the day Elvis died.

Esposito, Joe, nicknamed Diamond Joe and the Lion, was Elvis's closest male friend and a member of the Memphis Mafia, who remains loyal to Elvis to this day. The two men met in the Army in West Germany (not in Fort Hood as some claim), and with Marty Lacker, Esposito was best man at the Presleys' wedding in 1967. Esposito's wife was matron of honor. Joe Esposito did almost anything Elvis asked him to do and was at his side almost continuously. He was Elvis's highest-paid employee. At various times he was a bookkeeper, bodyguard, and road manger for Elvis. For a few years he acted as Elvis's accountant. Esposito is heard playing guitar and percussion instruments on two 1971 Nashville recordings with Elvis, and later on a recording made at the Stax Studio in July 1973. When Elvis found out that Joe told the Colonel about some of Elvis's drug habits, Elvis fired Joe and then rehired him. In May 1977, a few months before Elvis died, Esposito, Dr. Nichopoulos, and Mike McMahon sued Elvis for $150,000, but Esposito continued working for Elvis. It was Esposito

who informed Priscilla by phone that Elvis had died.

In 1977, Esposito sued the Presley estate for the rights to publish and distribute a home video he claims he shot of Elvis at the Circle G Ranch. He is currently writing a book about Elvis and the Memphis Mafia.

Fabian was a pop singer and actor whom Elvis met in Hollywood. The two young stars became friends, and in December 1960, Fabian visited Graceland. During one of Elvis's karate demos, the King tore his pants, so Fabian took his off and gave them to Elvis. Fabian kept the torn pants as a souvenir.

Fadal, Edward E. met Elvis on October 12, 1956, at Waco, Texas, at the Heart o' Texas Coliseum, and the two remained lifelong friends. Fadal was a disc jockey for KRLD in Dallas, and a theater manager. When Elvis was stationed at Fort Hood, Fadal built a special room onto his home and put a piano in it for Elvis's use. The bootleg tape *Forever Young—Forever Beautiful* has Fadal's tapes of those days at the house (August 1977, Memphis Flash Records). Fadal is the president of the Elvis Memorial Club and is writing a book about the singer. Elvis appreciated Fadal because he allowed the King to do whatever he wanted to do without pressure or prejudice. Fadal's home is set up as a small museum to honor Elvis and is open by appointment to fans and tourists.

Feathers, Charles may have produced some of Elvis's earliest recordings on the Sun label, without getting credit for doing so. He made demos and recorded for Sun, Meteor Records, and other companies using the names Jess Hooper and Charlie Morgan. In Bob Neal's August 5, 1955, 8th Anniversary Jamboree at Overton Park Shell, Feathers and Elvis performed.

Fike, Lamar (nicknamed Great Speckled Bird and Buddha) loitered outside of Graceland so much that Elvis finally invited him in and he eventually became a member of the Memphis Mafia. The 350-pound Fike served as Elvis's bodyguard, lighting system's operator in Vegas, and tour organizer for many trips. Fike tried to enlist in the Army when Elvis was drafted and was turned down due to his weight; however, he flew to West Germany and traveled with the boys to Paris. Elvis, Red West, and Fike often got in fights at the Gruenwald Hotel in Germany. West and Fike also hung out at Beck's Beer Bar and were known for rowdy behavior. In 1962, Fike left Elvis to manage Brenda Lee, only to return a few years later. He also helped Albert Goldman write his scathing biography about Elvis. He was "Neham Ewing" in *This Is Elvis* (1981).

Finlator, John refused to give Elvis a narcotics-agent badge from the Narcotics Bureau in Washington, DC (of which Finlator was director), even after Elvis offered him a contribution of $50,000. Elvis then went to President Nixon, who gave him the honor.

Foley, Clyde Julian "Red" was a veteran at the Grand Ole Opry, hosted the TV show "Ozark Jubilee," and was inducted into the Country Music Hall of Fame in 1967. Foley met Elvis and Charlie Hodge in 1956. Elvis recorded many Foley songs and was highly influenced by his style and talent. In the movie *Jailhouse Rock*, a picture of Red Foley can be seen hanging in Elvis's prison cell. He was also a favorite of Gladys Presley's.

Fontana, D. J. was Elvis's drummer on forty-six recording sessions (1955–69) after the two met on "Louisiana Hayride," October 16, 1954. Contrary to rumor, Fontana says he did not play for any of Elvis's Sun Records pieces. Johnny Bernero was the Sun drummer. Fontana has cameos in the films *Loving You* and *Jailhouse Rock*, and in the 1975 movie *Nashville*. In 1969, Fontana left Elvis to work as a session player in Nashville, and he authored

D. J. Fontana Remembers Elvis. Like Scotty Moore and Bill Black, he was grossly underpaid by Elvis when he worked for him.

Ford, Benjamin Francis "Whitey" convinced Colonel Parker to sign Elvis and persuaded Gladys and Vernon Presley to allow their son to work for Parker. The Presleys did not trust or like the Colonel.

Fortas, Alan (nicknamed Hog Ears) was an all-Memphis football hero who joined Elvis in 1958, and became a somewhat feared (by the press) Memphis Mafia member because of his size and strength. He was Elvis's bodyguard during the shooting of *King Creole* and later managed the Circle G Ranch. A tambourine player, he played in the June 1968 NBC-TV special. Elvis was generous with Fortas and bought him many expensive gifts, which included a motorcycle, a car, and rings. In 1987, Fortas wrote *My Friend Elvis*. He is presently a businessman in Memphis.

Foxx, Redd was the only entertainer to attend the Presley wedding in 1967. Elvis adored his off-color sense of humor.

Freed, Alan was a disc jockey for WINS-NY radio who has been credited for having coined the phrase *rock and roll* and who first played Elvis's "Heartbreak Hotel" over New York radio. His career was destroyed during the payola scandals in the music world in the fifties.

Gambill, Marvin, Jr., nicknamed Gee Gee, was a member of the Memphis Mafia and served as a chauffeur and valet to Elvis. He married Elvis's cousin Patsy Presley (who was a secretary at Graceland), and Elvis often called him "my cousin." He and Patsy attended the Presleys wedding. Elvis often bought the couple gifts, which included cars, a horse, and jewelry.

Gardner, "Brother" Dave was the comedian who helped warm up audiences before Elvis appeared onstage.

Gardner, Hy was a *New York Herald Tribune* columnist who interviewed Elvis on July 1, 1956, for the "Hy Gardner Calling" show, a WRCA Channel 4 TV broadcast in the New York area. That interview can be heard on the 1971 bootleg album *TV Guide Presents Elvis.*

Garland, Hank "Sugarfoot" replaced Scotty Moore on guitar and played with Elvis on recordings and on tour from 1958 to 1961, and earned the reputation of being one of the best guitarists in Nashville.

Geller, Larry was Elvis's hairstylist and "religious adviser" from April 30, 1964, through the seventies. He became exceedingly close to Elvis after he told him about the occult, parapsychology, the supernatural, and world religions. Geller put together a religious library for Elvis (which Priscilla and the Colonel detested) and highly influenced Elvis regarding philosophical and religious matters after 1965. Whenever Geller cut Elvis's hair, Parker, who did not trust Geller, demanded someone else be in the room. When Parker succeeded in ruining their relationship, the Colonel made certain the occult/religious library was burned. Geller styled Elvis's hair for his funeral. Geller portrayed himself in the 1979 TV movie *Elvis* and cowrote with Jess Stearn *The Truth About Elvis* (1980). He authored *Elvis's Spiritual Journey* (1983). In 1989, his book *Elvis Speaks* attacked members of the Memphis Mafia, and Geller claimed it was the book Elvis had planned to write.

Gilliland, Homer was another hairstylist for Elvis from 1967 to 1977. His main job was to keep Elvis's hair dyed jet-black. Elvis gave Gillilant his gold-lamé suit.

Gleason, Jackie was the famous TV/movie comedian who supervised Elvis's first appearances on the Dorsey brothers' "Stage Show" in 1956, and then said Elvis would not last.

Gleaves, Cliff was a rockabilly singer who accompanied Elvis to Hollywood as a gofer in 1956, while Elvis filmed *Love Me Tender*. He was present at the Million Dollar Quartet session in December 1956, and on January 4, 1957, drove Elvis to his physical for the Army. From 1958 to 1959, Gleaves stayed with Elvis in West Germany.

Golden, George decorated Graceland in 1957.

Grant, Currie introduced Priscilla Beaulieu to Elvis in 1959. Grant, a clerk for Air Force intelligence at Schierstein, was involved with the Air Force variety show. Grant has publicly stated Priscilla sought him out and asked him to introduce her to Elvis, while Priscilla has said Grant approached her and asked if she wanted to meet Elvis.

Grant, Marshall was a pianist who played backup for Elvis in 1955.

Greene, Shecky was a comedian who worked Las Vegas with Elvis at the New Frontier Hotel, April 23–May 6, 1956. Greene turned down the Colonel's offer to tour with Elvis.

Greenwood, Earl was an Army pal at Fort Hood, Texas, and later served as Elvis's publicist.

Grob, Dick was security chief at Graceland for more than seven years and was a member of the Memphis Mafia. He served as a fighter pilot in the U.S. Air Force and was a sergeant in the Palm Springs, California, Police Department. Grob introduced Elvis to many law enforcement officers.

Groom, Arthur fired Elvis in May 1952 at Loew's State Theater, Memphis, for hitting another usher. Both boys were let go.

Haley, Bill placed the first rock 'n' roll hit on the charts in 1953 with "Crazy, Man, Crazy" (Essex 321). He met Elvis at Cleveland's Brooklyn High School, October 20, 1955. In that same year, his music drew worldwide attention in the movie *Blackboard Jungle*, which featured the hit "Shake, Rattle and Roll."

Hamill, Rev. James E. tried to discourage Elvis from going into music. He felt Elvis couldn't sing, after Elvis tried out for a gospel quartet at the First Assembly of God Church in 1953. Hamill eulogized Gladys at her funeral in August 1958.

Hand, Albert was the first publisher/founder (1959) of the newsletter *Elvis Monthly*. He visited Elvis on the set of *Roustabout* in 1964.

Hardin, Glen D. was a pianist for Elvis, 1970–76, who also arranged/wrote Elvis's version of "Bridge Over Troubled Waters."

Harmon, Murray "Buddy" was a percussion player for Elvis, 1958–68. He also played bongos and drums and appeared on nine Elvis film tracks.

Hays, Lowell was the Memphis jeweler who designed Elvis's 11.5-carat $55,000 diamond ring and who sold Elvis approximately $880–900,000 worth of jewelry (most of which he gave away).

Hebler, Dave was a bodyguard/martial-artist friend of Elvis's from 1974 to 1976. The two men met in 1972 at Hebler's California karate dojo. Hebler coauthored *Elvis: What Happened?* Many people believe the book was written in anger because Red and Sonny West and Hebler were fired without warning by Vernon Presley.

Henry, Robert (known as Mr. Beale Street) is quoted in *Look* (May 5, 1971): "Elvis used to come down to a colored place on Hernando and watch black performers. . . . I met him

through Dewey Phillips [the disc jockey]." Through Robert Henry, Elvis had many introductions to black musicians and singers from 1950 to 1955.

Hess, Jake was the gospel singer from whom people believed Elvis stole his singing style. Hess was a member of the Imperials, a group that sang with Elvis until 1971, when Colonel Parker replaced them with J. D. Sumner and the Stamps. Hess was also a member of the gospel group the Statesmen Quartet, who sang "Known Only to Him" at Elvis's funeral.

Hill, Ed was a singer with the Four Stamps, which backed Elvis from 1971 to 1977. He authored the 1979 book *Where Is Elvis?*

Hodge, Charlie (nicknamed Slewfoot and Waterhead) met Elvis in 1956, and became a singer/guitarist/aide to Elvis. He lived in a converted apartment behind Graceland for seventeen years and supported Elvis in everything he did. At five feet three inches, Hodge was one of the shortest members of the Memphis Mafia, so he wore lifts in his shoes. Elvis and Hodge were also stationed together in West Germany. Hodge sang a duet with Elvis on "I Will Be Home Again" (which they recorded in 1960). Hodge managed Elvis's personal life and much of his music schedule and drove Priscilla and Elvis to the hospital the day Lisa Marie was born. Hodge allegedly witnessed Elvis's will and wrote with Elvis and Red West "You'll Be Gone." He played cameo parts in *Charro!* and *Clambake*, portrayed himself in *Elvis* in 1979, and was a feature character in the 1988 TV drama *Elvis and Me*. If anyone was Elvis's enduring friend, it was Charlie Hodge, who stayed with Elvis until he died.

Hoffman, Dr. Lester is the Memphis dentist whom Elvis visited the day he died.

Holly, Buddy was a rockabilly singer

who met Elvis at the Cotton Club in Lubbock, Texas, October 15, 1955, and who is quoted as having said, "None of us would have made it without Elvis." Elvis promised to get Holly and his pal Bob Montgomery on "Louisiana Hayride," but when they showed up, Elvis was absent. Buddy Holly, Ritchie Valens, and Jiles Perry Richardson died in a plane crash on February 3, 1959. After the accident, Elvis refused to fly unless absolutely necessary.

Hookstratten, E. Gregory was the lawyer who represented Elvis during his divorce proceedings in Los Angeles.

Hunt, Dr. William R. was the doctor who signed the birth certificate and delivered Elvis and his stillborn brother, Jesse Garon on January 8, 1935, at the Presleys' home on Old Saltillo Road, for a $15 fee, which the Presleys did not pay. Most likely, the correct birth certificate is the one signed by Dr. Hunt, not the one signed by Vernon, who was actually absent at the birth.

Jarrett, Hugh was a member of the Jordanaires, whose specialty was blues mixed with gospel barbershop. He and Elvis often sang gospel music at the Ellis Auditorium's piano after concerts.

Jarvis, Felton became Elvis's producer at RCA in 1966, and had always held Elvis in the deepest regard. With Steve Sholes, he helped revitalize Elvis's diminishing career. Jarvis left RCA in 1970, to devote full-time attention to the King's recordings and performances, and he remained loyal to Elvis until Elvis's death. When Jarvis needed a kidney operation, Elvis paid all costs, and remained a close and supportive friend. After Elvis's death, at the 1977 Rock Music Awards, Jarvis accepted on Elvis's behalf the Hall of Fame award. RCA released a limited-production LP in 1977, *Felton Jarvis Talks About Elvis*. Jarvis died of a stroke in 1981.

John, Elton, the rock 'n' roll superstar, once offered to write Elvis a song. Elvis arranged to have Elton John visit Lisa Marie on her birthday on February 1, 1975, because he was her favorite singer.

Jones, Tom, the sexy pop singer and entertainer, met Priscilla and Elvis at the Ilikai Hotel in Hawaii. Jones was one singer Elvis worried might threaten his own popularity. Elvis gave Jones a TCB medallion and the two men became friends. In 1969, rumors spread they would make a movie together, but it did not materialize. Elvis recorded two of Jones's hits, "I'll Never Fall in Love Again" and "Without Love."

Kahane, Jackie was a comedian who frequently opened for Elvis. Once he was booed off the Madison Square Garden stage because fans only wanted to see Elvis. Kahane delivered the eulogy at Elvis's funeral and recorded the tribute record "Requiem for Elvis" (Raintree 2206).

Kennedy, Jerry was a police captain in Denver, Colorado, who served as Elvis's Denver security guard. He received a $13,000 Lincoln Continental Mark IV from Elvis on January 14, 1976. Elvis later gave Kennedy's wife a car.

Kerkorian, Kirk was the owner of the International Hotel in Las Vegas and a close friend of Colonel Parker's. He lent his DC-9 jet to Elvis so he could travel in comfort.

Kesler, Stanley A. wrote five songs that Elvis recorded. As a steel guitarist/bass player/engineer, Kesler toured with the King from 1954 to 1955.

King, B. B., the legendary "King of the Blues" (also a disc jockey for WDIA), first influenced Elvis on Beale Street, when Elvis would sneak in to hear Lucille (King's guitar) explode with R&B magic. As a singer for the Sun label prior to Elvis's recording there, King admits he knew Elvis before Elvis recorded. King and Elvis appeared together on WDIA's "Goodwill Review" in December 1956. Elvis deeply respected King for his talent and kindness.

Kingsley, James was a *Memphis Commercial Appeal* reporter who was close to Elvis. The reporter gave Elvis a lot of publicity in the Memphis paper, which caused near riots in the area whenever Elvis was in town to sing live. Kingsley often visited Graceland.

Kingsley, James was a member of the Memphis Mafia and worked as Elvis's bodyguard before he went to Hollywood and became a stuntman. He committed suicide in 1989.

Kirsch, Jack was the pharmacist who filled Dr. Nichopoulos's prescriptions for Elvis and gave him 5,684 pills in a seven-month period. He lost his pharmacist's license in April 1980.

Klein, George was the disc jockey and program director for the Memphis radio station WHBQ. Klein attended Humes High School with Elvis, where he claims he protected Elvis from class bullies. Klein worked at WKEM in 1953, when he allegedly asked Elvis to perform "Keep Them Cold Icy Fingers off of Me." Klein was a member of the Memphis Mafia, and in the sixties, Elvis paid for plastic surgery on Klein's nose. Klein had cameo roles in *Frankie and Johnny* (1966) and *Double Trouble* (1967). His voice is heard on the 1972 documentary *Elvis on Tour*. With his wife, Barbara, Klein attended the Presley wedding, and Elvis was best man at their wedding. Klein introduced Elvis to Dr. Nichopoulos and later, to Linda Thompson. In 1977, Elvis tried to convince Pres. Jimmy Carter to suspend charges against Klein for mail fraud. Carter refused to get involved and Klein was found guilty. Klein wrote *The King of Rock 'n' Roll*, a film that has not yet been produced. Today Klein hosts a radio show from Beale Street, on WEZI-AM in Memphis, which is primarily devoted to Elvis.

Lacker, Marty was a member of the Memphis Mafia (1960–67) who served as Elvis's bookkeeper/secretary in 1964. The two men went to Humes High School. With Joe Esposito, he was a best man at the Presley wedding, and both signed the marriage certificate. He and his wife, Patsy, coauthored the book *Elvis, Portrait of a Friend* in 1979, in which Patsy accused Elvis of introducing her husband to drugs.

Lansky, Bernard and **Guy** owned Peak Records of Memphis and ran Lansky's Clothing Emporium at 126 Beale Street, where Elvis shopped. In 1956, Elvis traded a Messerschmitt auto for clothing! The Lansky brothers provided the pallbearers outfits at both Elvis's and Vernon's funerals. It was in the Lanskys' shop that Elvis and fellow musicians met to gossip and discuss music.

Lastfogel, Abe was Elvis's personal agent at the William Morris Agency in Los Angeles.

Leaptrot, Bill was a schoolmate of Elvis's at Humes and was with Elvis when Elvis left the Army. He became a *Press-Scimitar* photographer and wrote the article "The Kid From the North Side."

Leech, Mike was a bass guitarist who worked with Elvis at the American Sound Studios in 1969. He also backed Elvis in sessions during March 1975.

Leiber, Jerry was the prolific songwriter who (with Mike Stoller) wrote twenty-three songs for Elvis. A 1980 British LP, *Elvis Presley Sings Leiber and Stoller*, shows the trio on the album cover. Leiber, a student of the blues, admitted Elvis knew more about black music and traditions than he did.

Lennon, John of the Beatles visited Elvis

at Bel Air on August 27, 1965. Lennon said, "Before Elvis there was nothing," and, "If there hadn't been Elvis, there would not have been the Beatles." The Beatles were highly inspired by Elvis's early career, but they would later denounce his seventies music as insipid.

Lepley, Sleepy-Eyed John was the Memphis WHHM disc jockey working at the Eagle's Nest in 1954, where Elvis performed for $10 a night.

Levitch, Harry was the local Memphis jeweler (159 Union Street) who sold Elvis Priscilla's wedding ring in 1967 for $4,000. He and his wife attended the wedding after delivering the ring to Elvis in Las Vegas.

Lewis, Jerry Lee, nicknamed the Killer, was one of the most talented, electrifying singers/pianists in the rockabilly movement. Famous for his heavy-pounding piano techniques and wild performances, Lewis first recorded with Sun in 1956, after Elvis was a big hit. By 1958, Lewis's hits included "Whole Lot of Shakin' Going On," "Great Balls of Fire," and "Breathless." He was a tremendously energetic artist who ruined his career when he married a thirteen-year-old cousin, Myra Gale Brown, in 1958. When Lewis was kept from seeing Elvis in November of 1976, he shot a gun at Graceland and was arrested. Judge Albert Boyd found him not guilty.

Elvis and Lewis shared similar backgrounds and respected each other, but they were also competitors. Lewis remains one of the original rock 'n' roll heroes.

Lewis, Sammy signed Elvis to perform at the New Frontier Hotel, Las Vegas, April 23–May 6, 1956.

Liberace was the flamboyant pianist most admired by Elvis. Like Elvis, Liberace loved black music and fraternized with many black musicians and singers.

In 1956, Elvis met Liberace and his brother, George. Liberace and Elvis shared a love for the piano, gospel music, gold (they both owned gold pianos and wore gold lamé), cars, flash, and glitter. Dewey Phillips called Elvis "the poor man's Liberace" at the Eagle's Nest, October 1953. By the sixties, Lee's rhinestone jackets weighed up to forty pounds, and his fur capes pulled sixteen-foot trains! He toured with fifty-four trunks of costumes; Elvis had twenty by 1968. Elvis sent Liberace guitar-shaped flower arrangements for each of his openings. The pianist died in 1987.

Little Richard is a black rock 'n' roll singer whose outlandish style and frantic performances exemplify the heart of rock 'n' roll.

Like Elvis, Little Richard sang gospel and learned to play the piano at church. His hits include "Get Rich Quick," "Tutti Frutti," "Long Tall Sally," and "Good Golly, Miss Molly."

Elvis covered "Rip It Up" and "Ready Teddy," two of Little Richard's songs. In 1969, Elvis told Little Richard he was "the greatest" and that he "inspired" him. Little Richard sarcastically told *Rolling Stone*, "I thank God for Elvis Presley. I thank the Lord for sending Elvis to open the doors so I could walk down the road." Little Richard became one of the most unique musicians to emerge from the fifties rock scene. He received a Grammy for Lifetime Achievement in 1993.

Long, Shorty was an RCA pianist who played on many of Elvis's hit songs, including "Tutti Frutti," "Don't Be Cruel," and "Blue Suede Shoes."

Lord, Jack was an actor who starred in "Hawaii Five-O," to whom Elvis gave many gifts (among them a solid-gold gun). The two men were close friends, and Lord saw Elvis perform in Las Vegas six times.

Loyd, Harold was a cousin of Elvis's who served as a night-shift gate guard at Graceland. He founded the Graceland Fan Club of Memphis and in 1979, he cowrote with George Baugh *The Gates of Graceland*. He also wrote the 1979 tribute song "A Prayer for Elvis."

Loyd, Robert, Harold's son, was a security guard at Graceland. It was Harold who called the police on November 23, 1976, when Jerry Lee Lewis was causing a commotion outside Graceland with a .38 derringer.

Mansfield, Donald was one of twelve soldiers who went with Elvis from Memphis to Fort Chaffee, Arkansas. He also traveled to West Germany with Elvis and together they practiced karate. He married Elvis's secretary, Elisabeth Stefaniak, who lived with Elvis in West Germany. In 1983, Mansfield and his wife coauthored *Elvis in Deutschland* and *Elvis the Soldier* (in which Mansfield states he gave Elvis amphetamine pills in January 1959, and that Elvis bought drugs from another soldier).

Martin, Dean was the singer/actor who influenced Elvis's early career. The two men recorded "I Don't Care If the Sun Don't Shine," and in 1970, Elvis sang in Las Vegas (with Martin in the audience) Martin's "Everybody Loves Somebody" at the International Hotel.

Martin, Freddy was a popular Las Vegas bandleader who headlined with Elvis at the New Frontier Hotel, 1956.

Martin, Grady was a guitarist who played for Elvis and Hank Williams. He backed Elvis in March of 1962 and February 1965.

Martindale, Wink met Elvis the evening of July 10, 1954, after Dewey Phillips played Elvis's records on WHBQ radio in Memphis. Martindale hosted KLAC-TV's "Dance Party" and interviewed Elvis in 1956.

Matthews, Neal, a tenor with the Jordanaires, said Elvis was the most dynamic artist ever to step on the stage.

McCartney, Paul of the Beatles was, like John Lennon, mesmerized by Elvis's singing. With Lennon he cowrote two songs Elvis recorded: "Hey Jude" and "Yesterday." He visited Elvis in Bel Air in 1965.

McClellan, Lou bought the Circle G Ranch with a note carried by Elvis in May 1969. When he could not make the payments or get a gun permit to run a shooting range on the property, Elvis bought it back and resold it.

McMahon, Mike played racquet ball with Elvis at Graceland and got him involved in a shaky investment deal, the Presley Center Courts, Inc. at Popular Avenue in 1975. Dr. Nichopoulos was president of the group they called Racquet Ball of Memphis, Inc. Elvis was chairman of the board, and Joe Esposito was VP. Elvis did not have $700,000 to invest so he borrowed it from the National Bank of Commerce, Memphis. When the company started to go under in 1976, Elvis left the investment enterprise. When he refused to invest more money, Esposito and Nichopoulos sued him for $150,000, claiming Elvis had promised to lend money to the corporation whenever it was needed.

McPhatter, Clyde was a singer and soldier who served in West Germany with Elvis. Elvis told Sam Phillips, "If I had a voice like that man, I'd never want for another thing." From 1950 to 1953, McPhatter was with Billy Ward and the Dominoes and was replaced by Jackie Wilson of the Drifters.

Meyer, Dr. David was a Memphis ophthalmologist who treated Elvis's glaucoma in the seventies.

Miller, Mitch turned Elvis down as a recording artist for Columbia because Bob Neal asked $18,000 for the Cat's contract from Sun. Miller claimed no one was worth that much money.

Milsap, Ronnie was the blind country

singer who sang a duet with Elvis during "Don't Cry, Daddy." Milsap and his Short Kids entertained Elvis and his guests on New Year's Eve, 1968. He also sang and played piano for Elvis at American Sound Studio in 1969.

Mississippi Slim (Carbel Lee Ausborn) was a country singer who befriended the young Elvis and inspired his singing. The famous Mississippi Slim accompanied nine-year-old Elvis when Elvis sang "Old Shep" for WELO's "Black and White Jamboree." Slim had his own radio show on WELO on Saturday, and Elvis often visited him there. His brother, James Ausborn, was a grammar-school chum. Through Mississippi Slim, Elvis gained a sense of what the music world was about and looked upon Slim as a father figure.

Moman, Chips influenced Elvis's "new" sound in 1969 at the American Sound Studios, Memphis, where he was a producer.

Moore, Scotty was lead guitarist for Elvis from the first Sun recording in July 1954 to June 1968. He and Bill Black established "the Elvis sound," and by 1955, Moore, Elvis, and Black became known as the Blue Moon Boys. After an initial meeting on June 27, 1954 (requested by Sam Phillips), Black, Moore, and Elvis recorded "That's All Right, Mama," and by July 12, Moore became Elvis's first manager, though he eventually allowed Elvis to cancel the contract and sign with Bob Neal. In September 1957, Bill and Scotty left Elvis over a salary dispute but soon returned. The Colonel and Elvis never gave them royalties, nor did they receive praise and credit for their work. Scotty rejoined Elvis from 1960 to 1968 to record, but Black did not return. Scotty's 1968 NBC-TV gig with Elvis was the last time he saw the King. Elton John once said it was Scotty's guitar riffs on "The Steve Allen Show" that inspired John to go into music. Today Scotty Moore is a proficient studio musician in Nashville, Tennessee.

Morris, Bill frequently accompanied Elvis to the Ellis Auditorium and Beale Street gigs. He became mayor of Shelby County. He wrote "Remembering the Good Times with Elvis" in which he says Elvis's favorite music was gospel and "when he finished singing . . . Elvis would do a little preaching."

Morris, Bobby convinced Elvis to sing "Suspicious Minds." He was the musical conductor at Las Vegas' International Hotel and was a close friend of Colonel Parker's.

Morris, William L. gave Elvis a permit to carry firearms and took him through FBI headquarters in Washington, DC, on December 30, 1970. Elvis gave Morris a Mercedes five days prior to going to Washington.

Neal, Bob managed Elvis, Bill Black, and Scotty Moore from 1954 to 1955, before Parker took Elvis for himself. Elvis signed with Parker, August 15, 1955, but still paid Neal his 15 percent. Neal helped Elvis finance his first car, a four-year-old Lincoln Continental. Unlike Parker, who never helped finance anything for his clients, Neal was a helpful, compassionate person, who played the ukulele and had a wonderful sense of humor.

Nelson, Ricky had become famous as the son of Ozzie and Harriet on his family's TV series, on which he made his music debut. After Nelson's girlfriend heard Elvis on the radio it inspired Nelson to compete for the applause. His first recording was Fats Domino's "I'm Walkin' " (Verve 10047). Nelson nervously met his idol at a Hollywood party, and Elvis made him feel comfortable by asking him questions about the "Ozzie & Harriet" show. On December 31, 1985, Nelson and his band were killed in a plane crash in Texas.

Newton, Wayne and Elvis joked about their performances, and each imitated the other. Newton bought Elvis's Jet

Commander for $300,000. Newton was grief-stricken when Elvis died.

Nichopoulos, Dean (son of George Nichopoulos) played various sports at Graceland with the King, took care of his wardrobe, and occasionally helped with tour plans. Elvis practiced faith healing on Dean.

Nichopoulos, Dr. George C. was the infamous doctor who prescribed pills for Elvis, Jerry Lee Lewis, and Marty Lacker. Owing Elvis over $300,000 in loans, the doctor kept in close contact with him. Elvis filled eight prescriptions the day before he died, and during the last months of his life the doctor prescribed almost six thousand narcotic and amphetamine pills for Elvis. Ironically, the doctor served as a pallbearer at Elvis's funeral. In September 1979, the Tennessee Board of Medical Examiners charged Nichopoulos with "indiscriminately prescribing 5,300 pills and vials for Elvis in the seven months before his death," and in January 1980, his medical license was suspended for three months. He was acquitted of overprescribing addictive drugs to ten patients and found not guilty of malpractice and unethical conduct.

Nixon, Richard Milhous met Elvis at the White House, December 21, 1970. Elvis arrived without an appointment, wearing sunglasses and a cape. He received a Narcotics Bureau badge from the president, and Elvis gave Nixon a commemorative World War II Colt .45 pistol. Jerry Schilling and Sonny West also met the president. Nixon asked Elvis to sing at the White House, but the Colonel's $25,000 fee was turned down. No one is paid to entertain at the White House! In January 1993, the Nixon Presidential Library celebrated the birthdays of Nixon (Jan. 9) and Elvis (Jan. 8) and sold memorabilia of the two men marking their 1970 meeting.

Norris, Chuck is a world-champion mar-

tial artist and film star who once owned the now-defunct karate dojo where Priscilla was instructed by Mike Stone in the seventies.

O'Grady, John (nicknamed "Reverend" by Elvis) was a private investigator who helped Elvis win a paternity suit. His badge collection inspired Elvis to also collect them. He was hired by Elvis's lawyer Ed Hookstratten to find out who was selling Elvis drugs—three doctors and one dentist were uncovered. Allegedly, O'Grady told Elvis to fire Dave Hebler and Red and Sonny West.

Orbison, Roy was a classic country and rock star who went to Sun studios after being inspired by Elvis's sound. He interviewed Elvis on his TV program in the fifties, and the two singers respected and admired one another.

"Mean Woman Blues" and "Candy Man" were Elvis's favorite songs by Orbison, but Elvis thought Orbison lowered his standards when he toured with the Beatles in 1963 (he had previously toured with Elvis). He died of a heart attack in December 1988.

Parker, Ed (nicknamed "Kahuna" by Elvis) was a bodyguard and karate instructor. In 1971 or 1972, Parker invited Elvis to a California karate tournament. When Elvis noticed a huge sign advertising he would be at the event, he became furious and did not speak to Parker for over a year. Parker (probably as a gesture to get Elvis into his life again) gave Elvis an eighth-degree black belt. In 1978, Parker wrote *Inside Elvis*.

Parker, Little Junior was a black R&B musician/singer who wrote Elvis's 1955 hit "Mystery Train." On his early up tempo records, a compelling rhythm with distorted solo guitar sections caught Elvis's attention.

Parker, "Colonel" Tom was Elvis's manager and promoter, and he became *the* most important man in Elvis's life.

He was born Andreas Cornelius van Kuijk in Breda, Holland, on June 26, 1909, and he entered (possibly illegally) the U.S. in 1929. *Variety* (June 8, 1983) quotes Parker confessing that he is not an American citizen. When the Presley estate attempted to sue Parker in the Manhattan Federal Court, he declared, "I am a man without a country" and claimed he could not be sued under federal law. *Variety* asserted Parker's 1929 "illegal entry" into the U.S. was the reason for the outside settlement between the Colonel and the Presleys. When Elvis wanted to tour Europe, Parker gave the excuse he couldn't travel abroad because as a foreigner, he could not obtain a passport back into the U.S.

Although stories about Parker's origins differ, some believe he was born in 1910. By 1920, he was orphaned and lived with a man whom he called "uncle," who ran the Great Parker Pony Circus. By 1927, Parker hit the "bottle-cap circuit," performing with a monkey and a pony. He then managed a pie car on a train that transported members of the Royal American carnival from city to city, and he professed to be a psychic palm reader and an artist. (He caught sparrows, painted them yellow, and sold them as canaries!)

Always traveling with one show or another, the cigar-smoking Parker was usually on the edge of poverty with a "great idea to make millions" up his worn sleeves. Through the forties and early fifties he entered many arenas, including the music world.

During the Depression, Parker became a convincing press agent for showboats, circuses, carnivals, and freak shows. In Nashville, Parker met Eddy Arnold and signed him to a management contract, but the most profitable contract of Parker's career was when he signed Elvis Presley in 1955. The Colonel and Elvis established Boxcar Enterprises, which oversaw Elvis-related products, Gladys Music, and Boxcar Records.

Throughout Elvis's film and recording careers, Parker profited more from Elvis's work than Elvis did. By April 1965, Parker told reporters Elvis had earned $150 million on recordings and $125 million in movies. Whatever the real figures were, it is a fact Elvis's estate nearly went bankrupt and that Parker made more than the King earned.

The Colonel attended Elvis's funeral in a colorful shirt and baseball cap, which seemed to show a lack of respect for the man who made Parker rich and famous. By the day after the funeral, Parker had secured Vernon's signature on papers that allowed Parker's company, Factors, Etc., Inc. to handle all Elvis-related items/products. The courts later ruled Parker had no rights to any Elvis materials or his name. Parker told the courts that because he was not an American citizen, he could not be sued in an American court. In 1981, he said that he owned as much of Elvis dead as he did when Elvis was alive (*This Is Elvis*).

Colonel Parker's aggressive, innovative tactics enabled Elvis's career to skyrocket to unimaginable heights. Parker had contacts that most people envied, and by the time he met Elvis, he had networked with important music and film executors from around the country. For whatever reasons, few people said no to this inventive promoter. As Hal Wallis said, to negotiate with the shrewd manager was comparable to making a deal with the devil.

▲ Colonel Tom Parker. *Courtesy of private collector.*

For whatever reasons, Elvis allowed Parker to control and run his life, obeying the Colonel's orders and following his demands without protest.

Now in his eighty-fourth year, Colonel Parker is probably pleased to see that all the work he did for his "boy" is still paying off. Elvis is bigger now than he was in his lifetime. By court order, Colonel Parker is not allowed to work or deal with anything related to Elvis. The old Colonel believes he has been mistreated and misunderstood by everyone.

Pepper, Gary was a cerebral palsy victim to whom Elvis sent $400 a month until Elvis died. Vernon stopped the payments in October 1977. At Graceland, Pepper helped write to fans, clubs, and organizations in response to their letters about Elvis, he started one of the first Elvis Presley fan clubs, and he tried to have the Mid-South Coliseum's name changed to the Elvis Presley Coliseum. Pepper died in 1980.

Perkins, Carl Lee was a rockabilly guitarist/singer and contemporary of Elvis's who met the Cat in 1954. Perkins's hit "Blue Suede Shoes" was recorded on December 19, 1955. (Sun 234). In 1974, the two appeared together for a Memphis concert.

Phillips, Dewey Mills was a WHBQ disc jockey who played Elvis's record fourteen times in a row on July 7, 1954. Later that night, Phillips gave Elvis his first radio interview. Some sources claim Dewey Phillips provided drugs to Jerry Lee Lewis and Elvis in the early fifties. He was one of the first disc jockeys to use the term *rockabilly* on the air, and the first person to play Jerry Lee Lewis (1956). Elvis and Phillips had many arguments and feuds, particularly the time Elvis took him to Hollywood and Phillips proceeded to prove to the show biz city how crude Southerners could be. At Phillips's 1968 funeral, Elvis giggled continuously.

Phillips, Judd was Sam Phillips's brother, a former Army chaplain. He also promoted Roy Acuff and Jimmy Durante and was a past associate of Colonel Parker's. He co-owned Sun Records with Sam (1953). He has worked in various record companies and was an executive with Mercury Records. He says he first encouraged Elvis to go into Sun and cut an acetate, which cannot be verified. Countless other people have made that claim.

Phillips, Sam grew up on a farm, where he first heard black music from an old, blind sharecropper named Uncle Silas Payne. Phillips appreciated "race music" and black musicians and realized there was money to be made from their sound.

Plans to become a criminal defense lawyer fell through when Phillips was a teenager and his father died suddenly. Having to support his family, he got a job as a disc jockey on WLAY in Muscle Shoals, Alabama, where he earned a radio engineering certification. By 1944, Phillips transferred to Nashville, where he broadcast over WLAC radio, and then on WREC, a Memphis station.

With little money and some help from his brother, Judd (a radio announcer), Phillips converted a radiator shop on Union Avenue into what was

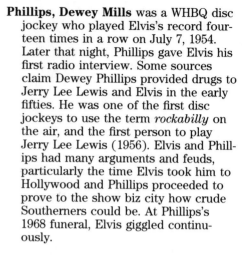

◄Guitarist Carl Perkins. *Courtesy of private collector.*

eventually to become Sun Records. The quarters were so tiny, business deals and music discussions were held next door at Taylor's Cafe. Sun's table was the third booth from the windows. It was Phillips's intention to find "boys from the farms and backwoods" who were loaded with "potential" and record them.

In 1952, Judd and Sam Phillips actively started to look for a white singer with a black, up-tempo, hep style and sound. Scotty Moore and Bill Black were asked to join in the search, and auditions were held from 1952 to 1954 to find Phillips's "wonder boy." No one was found until Marion Keisker insisted Phillips listen to Elvis.

Phillips was the genius who recognized the talent of Elvis, Jerry Lee Lewis, Johnny Cash, Roy Orbison, Conway Twitty, and many other rockabilly singers. Phillips's dilemma was that in order to promote new artists, he often sold the rights to his greatest talents to pay for lesser ones. A case in point is Elvis. In 1969, Phillips sold Sun Records and almost all its rights to Shelby Singleton (including the Million Dollar Quartet sessions, which a court later ruled illegal because Phillips had previously sold those rights to RCA). He recognized and rewarded avant-garde talent in an era when few people would take a chance and spend money on newcomers with innovative sound. He gave Elvis his beginning and never regretted selling his contract. Phillips still lives in Memphis.

Pomus, Doc was a songwriter who never met Elvis. He wrote fifteen songs that Elvis recorded.

Presley, Jesse Garon was Elvis's stillborn twin brother, born on January 8, 1935, and delivered approximately thirty to thirty-five minutes before Elvis. Elvis obsessed about Jesse's death and often talked to him as if he were alive. At Graceland's Meditation Garden his name is incorrectly spelled "Jessie" in the ground plaque. His body was buried in an unmarked grave the day he died and has not been moved.

Presley, Jessie D. McClowell was Vernon's father, who refused to post bail when Vernon was put in jail for forgery in 1937. Jessie crushed Elvis by telling him there was no Santa Claus. Jessie recorded on Legacy Park (2000) *The Roots of Elvis.*

Presley, Vernon Elvis was the father of Elvis Presley and husband of Gladys Love Smith. He was the brother of Vester, Delta Mae, Nashville, Lorene, and Gladys. As an eighth-grade dropout, Vernon worked as a truck driver, farmhand, field picker, and housepainter. At one time Vernon was sentenced to three years at the Parchman penitentiary for forgery. In 1948, he moved his family from Tupelo to Memphis. After Gladys's death in 1958, Vernon married "Dee" Stanley in 1960, and with her three sons lived at Graceland. Elvis was offended when his father remarried so soon after Gladys's death and did not attend the wedding. Vernon's family soon moved to Hermitage Street adjacent to Graceland. Dee and Vernon divorced in November 1977. As financial adviser to his son (1958–77), Vernon was incapable of doing a good job. At Elvis's death he earned $75,000 a year. He appeared in two Elvis films and was portrayed in three TV movies. Vernon died June 26, 1979.

Presley, Vester was the brother of Vernon and uncle to Elvis. Vester still works at Graceland as a gatekeeper. Vester allegedly gave Elvis guitar lessons in 1946. He cowrote *A Presley Speaks* and *The Presley Family Cookbook.* In 1979, he recorded "A Message to Elvis Fans and Friends" (Ves Pres 1) and portrayed himself in the 1981 movie *This Is Elvis.*

Pusser, Buford was the sheriff of McNairy County, Tennessee, whom Elvis admired for his fight against organized crime. When Buford's home burned down in a mysterious fire, Elvis anonymously sent him a sizable check to cover expenses. Buford died in a car accident, August 24, 1974.

Randi, Don played keyboard for Elvis's 1968 movie *Speedway* sound track and the piano/organ for Elvis's 1968 NBC-TV special.

Randle, Bill was one of the first disc jockeys outside the South to play Elvis's records regularly and help bring him to national attention. On October 20, 1955, the Blue Moon Boys opened at Cleveland's Brooklyn High School (fee $350) with headliners Pat Boone, Bill Haley & the Comets, and others. Randle was the event's promoter, and he asked a camera crew from Universal to film Elvis in performance, to become a part of *The Pied Piper of Cleveland: A Day in the Life of a Famous Disc Jockey.* It is the earliest known footage of Elvis, and in 1992, after securing the rights for the film, Randle sold the footage (sight unseen) for a reported $1.9 million. It was then sold for $2.2 million to PolyGram (which plans a documentary). Today, Bill Randle hosts a radio music-talk show in Cleveland, Ohio.

Reed, Jerry was a composer/singer/guitarist who met Elvis at Graceland and called him "the prettiest man I ever seen." He wrote and played guitar on Elvis's recordings of "Guitar Man" (1967) and "U.S. Male" (1968).

Reeves, Jim was a fifties country singer and minor-league baseball player who appeared on "Louisiana Hayride." Reeves and Elvis recorded for RCA and were friends. They may have done gigs in some of the same local clubs from 1954 to 1955.

Rhee, Kang was the owner of the Kang Rhee Institute of Self Defense, Inc., in Memphis, who became an instructor/friend of Elvis in 1970. Elvis allegedly gave Rhee $50,000 to build a new tae kwon do dojo.

Rivera, Geraldo is the television host and investigative reporter who emceed Elvis's June 9, 1971, press conference at the Las Vegas Hilton Hotel. Geraldo has been fascinated with the Elvis phenomenon for decades. On September 13, 1979, during an edition of "20/20," he reported "The Elvis Cover-Up," which revealed Elvis's drug problem and a possible cover-up of the circumstances of his death. In 1977, Rivera told Steve Dunleavy (author of *Elvis: What Happened?*) he did not believe Elvis was addicted to any hard drugs ("Good Morning America"). In 1987, Rivera refuted facts in DeBarbin's book *Are You Lonesome Tonight?* In 1992, Geraldo interviewed Davada "Dee" Stanley, Joe Esposito, and others in a discussion that revolved around Dee's allegations about Elvis that were published in the *National Enquirer.*

Robbins, Marty was the songwriter/country singer who toured with Elvis, 1955–56. He was one of the first singers to "cover" an Elvis tune, "That's All Right, Mama," December 7, 1954.

Russell, Nipsey is the black comedian who opened many of Elvis's Las Vegas acts.

Sands, Tommy claims to have introduced Elvis to the Colonel, who managed Sands from 1949 to 1952. Sands and Elvis were on "Louisiana Hayride" and traveled through Texas together in 1955.

Saperstein, Hank was an associate of the Colonel's. He handled the promotion, distribution, and sales of Elvis-related products.

Scheff, Jerry was a session musician and a member of Elvis's TCB Band from 1969 to 1976. He played on the sound track of *Easy Come, Easy Go* and was formerly a member of Jim Morrison's group, the Doors.

Schilling, Jerry, nicknamed "the Cougar" by Elvis, was a member of the

Memphis Mafia (1964–76) who met Elvis playing touch football. He became a manager for the Sweet Inspirations and the Beach Boys. Elvis paid for Schilling's first wedding. He accompanied Elvis to the 1970 White House meeting with President Nixon and was a pallbearer at Elvis's funeral. He also serves as the creative affairs director for the Presley estate. He co-produced the TV series "Elvis: Good Rocking Tonight" and is now managing Elvis's daughter's career.

Shapiro, Dr. Max was a dentist who gave Elvis medication in Bel Air. He claimed Elvis's estate owed him $14,000 for dental work he did on some of Elvis's friends. Elvis agreed to pay their bills.

Shaw, Arnold was a music producer who promoted Elvis's music. He worked for Hill and Range and helped Elvis sign with RCA after he arranged for WERE in Cleveland to play Elvis's music. He is a professor of music at the University of Nevada, Reno, and has authored many music-related books.

Sheppard, T. G. may have introduced Elvis to Linda Thompson. Elvis gave him a GMC customized bus in 1975. Sheppard played backup for the Beach Boys and became a country singer. He met Elvis roller-skating at the Rainbow Rollerdome in Memphis after two of the Memphis Mafia knocked him to the ground.

Sholes, Steve was an RCA Victor executive who was instrumental in signing Elvis with RCA. Sholes gave Elvis free reign in his song selection and performance style and has been credited for bringing out the creative side of Elvis. In 1967, Sholes became a member of the Country Music Hall of Fame. He died in 1968.

Shook, Jerry was a bassist in Elvis's TCB band.

Sinatra, Frank is the famous singer/actor who featured Elvis in the May 12, 1960, special, "Welcome Home, Elvis." When it was rumored Elvis was dating Sinatra's fiancée, Juliet Prowse, Elvis's costar in *G. I. Blues*, Sinatra visited Elvis in his dressing room. What was said is unknown, but Elvis did not date Prowse after that. Elvis often saw Sinatra's daughter, Nancy (who met Elvis at the airport when he returned from West Germany), in Las Vegas. Throughout their careers Frank Sinatra and Elvis were linked by the press as major competitors. During Elvis's seventies tours, Sinatra loaned the Cat his jet, and it was in Sinatra's jet that Priscilla and Elvis flew from Las Vegas to Palm Springs.

"Sivle Yelserp" (*Elvis Presley* spelled backward) was the name given by Chet Atkins to keep the press from knowing Elvis was recording in Nashville, March 1960.

Smith, Billy was Elvis's first cousin. Billy worked at Graceland and served as Elvis's companion for over twenty years.

Smith, Carrol "Junior" was a cousin who traveled with Elvis in the fifties and accompanied him to New York City to be on Steve Allen's show. Wounded in Korea, he died in 1958.

Smith, Gene was a cousin, a Memphis Mafia member, and Elvis's chauffeur for ten years. Together the boys worked at Precision Tool Company in Memphis and double-dated in the fifties. To stop Elvis from sleepwalking, Smith often slept in Elvis's room. Smith, who lived at Graceland for many years, looked after Elvis's wardrobe in Hollywood.

Smith, John was an uncle who worked as a gate guard at Graceland until his death in 1968. He claimed to have taught Elvis to play the guitar, which was not true.

Smith, Travis was a gate guard and relative of Elvis's. He died in 1966.

Smith, William "Billy" was the cousin closest to Elvis and a protected member of the Memphis Mafia who served as Elvis's valet and wardrobe man. He and his wife lived behind Graceland in a trailer, and Smith often played racquet ball with Elvis (as he did the day Elvis died).

Snow, Hank was a country singer who became associated with Parker in 1954. In 1955, during his tours with Parker, Parker signed a contract with Elvis. In 1961, Snow sued Parker for signing Elvis without his okay—Snow claimed *he* discovered Elvis and attempted to get Steve Sholes to buy Elvis's contract for $10,000 from Sam Phillips.

Spector, Phil produced records for Elvis and the Beatles. He claimed the Colonel hypnotized Elvis. Spector's bodyguard was Mike Stone, who stole Priscilla from Elvis.

Speer, William took the first publicity shots of Elvis in Memphis at the Blue Light Studio, 1954–55.

Stanley, David is Elvis's stepbrother by his mother Dee's marriage to Vernon Presley. When Elvis died, David was a security guard at Graceland. In *Life with Elvis*, Stanley claimed he had a problem with drugs and that Elvis took prescription cocaine (a fact denied by most others). He coauthored *Elvis, We Loved You Tender* and *Life with Elvis*. Today he is a minister.

Stanley, Richard Earl "Rick," another stepbrother of Elvis's by Dee's marriage to Vernon Presley, was working at Graceland the night Elvis died. With his wife, Angela, Stanley toured in the seventies with Elvis and bought Elvis drugs from the Methodist Hospital Pharmacy with forged prescriptions (for which he was arrested in 1975). Elvis fired Rick when he allegedly slandered Linda Thompson, who was Elvis's girl at the time. Elvis rehired him after Linda left. Rick coauthoried *Elvis, We Loved You Tender* with his

brothers David and William. Rick is a minister today and claims Elvis's death saved him from continuing drug abuse.

Stanley, William "Billy" Job, Jr., Elvis's stepbrother by his mother's marriage to Vernon Presley, was nicknamed Charles Manson because Elvis thought he resembled the mass murderer. He was on the Graceland payroll and did odd jobs and errands. In the book he coauthored, *Elvis, We Loved You Tender*, he claimed after Elvis had an affair with Billy's wife, Anne, he divorced her. He is the author of the 1977 book *Elvis: His Last Tour*.

Stoker, Gordon was a pianist/singer and a member of the Jordanaires, who sang backup for Elvis for thirteen years.

Stone, Mike was the black-belt karate instructor who taught Priscilla Presley tae kwon do and gained her confidence and short-lived love. After his wife divorced him and retained custody of their two children, Stone moved in with Priscilla in an apartment in Huntington Beach, California. In 1973, Elvis allegedly threatened Stone's life. In an article called "My Secret Love Affair with Priscilla," Stone claimed if Elvis had killed him, Stone's underworld connections would have killed Elvis. Stone and Priscilla separated after 1975. He moved to Las Vegas and now works in a casino.

Strada, Al, a member of the Memphis Mafia, was in charge of Elvis's wardrobe from 1972, and traveled with him on tour.

Sullivan, Ed was the host of "The Ed Sullivan Show," TV's highest-rated variety show. Elvis appeared three times on the show for a total fee of $50,000. On August 6, 1956, Sullivan was in an auto accident and thus missed Elvis's first appearance on September 9. On October 28, 1956, and January 6, 1957, Elvis's appearances took top ratings, and the once skeptical Sullivan thanked Elvis for being on his show.

On the January 6 show the cameras showed Elvis only from the waist up.

Sumner, Donnie was a backup and duet vocalist with Elvis and son of J. D. Sumner of the Stamps Quartet. He wrote two songs Elvis recorded.

Sumner, J. D. was a six-foot-five-inch bass singer with the Sunshine Boys and the Blackwood Brothers (1954–65). From 1972 to 1977, his group, the Stamps, backed Elvis on recordings and in concerts. Sumner often sang gospel duets with Elvis onstage. The Stamps included J. D. Sumner (leader), Donnie Sumner, Bill Blaize, Ed Knoch, Richard Staborn, and Ed Wideman. Among other things, Elvis gave Sumner a $55,000 Lincoln stretch limo. In 1971, Sumner wrote *Gospel Music Is My Life*, and the Stamps sang two tribute LPs to Elvis: *Elvis' Favorite Gospel Songs* (QCA 362) and *Memories of Our Friend Elvis* (Blue Mark 373), 1978. In 1972, the Stamps toured with Elvis and backed him until he died. After Elvis's death, Sumner opened a business in Memphis on Music Row.

Taurog, Norman directed nine of Elvis's films. Elvis bought him many gifts and liked to work with him. Taurog felt Elvis was not given good enough scripts and therefore his talent was not fully explored on film.

Thomas, Rufus was the first black disc jockey to play Elvis records (WDIA, Memphis). He claimed Elvis gave "an injection to black music that no black artist had ever done" and was instrumental in helping Elvis meet and jam with black artists along Beale Street.

Thompson, Sam was a bodyguard for Elvis and a Graceland gate guard in the seventies. He was Linda Thompson's brother, and he allegedly delivered Linda's note to the King, telling Elvis of her decision to end their relationship.

"Tiger" was Elvis's martial-arts name. Elvis told people he had an eighth-degree black belt in tae kwon do (the eighth degree represents "master of the art"), but it is debatable whether he actually earned the highly regarded title. Dale Kirby, champion tae kwon do artist of esteem says, "People felt obligated to *give* him degrees, but he did *not* earn them. That takes years and thousands of hours of training. He was a celebrity and those around him wanted to please him. It was a macho thing. He was no true black belt." Elvis did not know or use proper form, and no black belt wears boots to perform, nor do they wear dark sunglasses and huge pieces of jewelry, which can get tangled in a fight (or hurt someone). Tae kwon do world champion, Bill Wallace worked out with Elvis during photo shoots, but if Elvis *really* fought Wallace, Elvis would have been beaten severely in a matter of seconds. He trained minimally with Ed Parker at Kang Rhee's studios, where Elvis broke a wrist in September 1974. Elvis's karate was actually at a white to blue belt beginner's level. Priscilla earned a green belt from Mike Stone at Chuck Norris's studio.

Elvis's inability to manage his health and life goes against everything that a black-belt degree symbolizes—discipline, control, self-respect, and concern for others. His haphazard, dangerous use of guns shows just how far off course Elvis was from those values. A stray bullet from one of his tantrums struck Dr. Nichopoulos and almost landed in Vernon Presley's head. In 1974, Elvis shot out a light switch in Las Vegas. The bullet went through a wall and almost hit Linda Thompson. Elvis shot twelve bullets into a Ferrari, and he made a habit of shooting out TV sets (especially when Robert Goulet or Mel Torme appeared on TV). He shot a chandelier and blew out a restaurant ceiling at the Las Vegas Hilton. In 1972, it took his entourage to stop Elvis from killing Mike Stone. Elvis's stepbrother David Stanley said Elvis actually flew to California to kill Red and Sonny West after *Elvis: What Happened?* was released in 1977. When he died, Elvis owned over thirty guns, including a sawed-off shotgun, machine guns, M16s, and derringers.

Tomlin, Don met Elvis through J. D. Sumner and became his black-belt bodyguard.

Tubb, Ernest put Elvis on his radio program, "Midnight Jamboree," October 2, 1954. His son, Justin, toured with Elvis from January to April 1956.

Vanderhoof, Bruce was a gutsy disc jockey for KYA in San Francisco who was fired after he continuously played "Love Me Tender" after the station banned Elvis in 1957.

Velvet, Jimmy was a recording artist who charted two songs in the sixties. The King gave Velvet, a devoted Elvis fan, a Mercedes 600 limo in 1974. After Elvis died, Velvet opened Elvis Presley museums across from Graceland and in Nashville. Vernon Presley accused Velvet of lying about what was authentic Elvis memorabilia and threatened to sue Velvet. Jimmy Velvet lives in the Nashville area and is still an avid Elvis devotee.

Wallace, Bill "Sugarfoot" was Elvis's bodyguard and occasional karate instructor (1974).

Wallis, Hal B. was the producer of many of Elvis's films for Paramount Pictures in Hollywood. Wallis felt Elvis was talented and offered him roles that were far superior to the ones he took. Colonel Parker often turned down parts if the salary was not high enough—much to the dismay of Wallis. Five days after Elvis's screen test, Wallis signed him to a seven-year, $450,000 contract with Paramount Pictures for three movies. The contract was later renegotiated for much more money. Wallis was instrumental in making Elvis a movie star and won many Academy Awards, but none for Elvis's films.

Warhol, Andy was an avant-garde pop artist who painted the 1956 *Shoe Portrait* of Elvis and in 1963 created a huge silk screen of multiple images of Elvis with a pistol in his hand.

Waters, Muddy introduced the electric guitar to Delta blues in 1944. Muddy Waters's first single on the Chess label was "Rollin' Stone," a phenomenal blues hit from which the Rolling Stones took their name.

Waters was an essential contributor to the early careers of Howlin' Wolf and Chuck Berry, and an inspiration and influence on Elvis's early years as a singer and musician.

Wayne, Sid composed thirty-two songs that Elvis sang in movies.

Weisman, Ben composed with Fred Wise thirty-four songs that Elvis sang in movies.

Wertheimer, Alfred is the photographer who took approximately 3,800 photographs of Elvis from 1956 to 1958. Wer-

theimer told this author, "Elvis made the girls cry. He touched emotion. He was a natural, but Colonel Parker ruined photographic opportunities when he took control in April 1956." Wertheimer's 1979 book, *Elvis '56: In the Beginning*, features many of his photographs and was the basis for the 1987 Cinemax special "Elvis '56." Wertheimer lives in New York City.

West, Delbert "Sonny," also nicknamed the Eagle in karate by Elvis, was a member of the Memphis Mafia and lived in an apartment behind Graceland for years, taking care of the fleet of vehicles Elvis owned. He is the cousin of Red West. Elvis and Priscilla were in West's wedding party, December 28, 1971. He was fired by Vernon, July 13, 1976. West appeared in several of Elvis's movies and was his friend and protector for years.

West, Robert Gene "Red," also called the Dragon in karate, was a devoted member of the Memphis Mafia and close associate of Elvis's since their high school days. In 1960, West became Elvis's bodyguard. He was a stuntman in fourteen of Elvis's films, traveled extensively with Elvis throughout the U.S., and eventually married Elvis's secretary Pat Boyd on July 1, 1961. West was fired by Vernon with Sonny West and Dave Hebler on July 13, 1976.

In 1975 a private investigator blew the lid off the drugs being carted in and out of Graceland when he told Colonel Parker and Vernon Presley that he suspected Hebler and the Wests of supplying Elvis with drugs. In 1977, West participated in writing the explosive book *Elvis: What Happened?*

In 1989, West had a small role in Patrick Swayze's movie *Road House.*

White, Bukka (Booker T. Washington White) was born on November 12, 1906, in Houston, Mississippi. He recorded his first blues hit, "Shake 'Em on Down," in 1937. His sound and technical ability intrigued Elvis, and the two met often to discuss the blues. White died of cancer in Memphis on February 26, 1977.

Wilson, Jackie was a favorite artist of Elvis's and was nicknamed the Black Elvis. Wilson replaced Clyde McPhatter to become a member of Billy Ward and His Dominoes. In 1975, Elvis sent Wilson's wife a $30,000 check after Wilson suffered a stroke. Wilson was in a coma from September 29, 1975, until his death on January 21, 1984.

Wise, Fred was a songwriter who cowrote approximately thirty of Elvis's songs (mostly for movies).

Wolf, Howlin' was a master bluesman whose deep, untamed voice probably did more to shape rock 'n' roll than any other blues artist's before or after him. Influencing the progression of black-oriented music, this Delta bluesman's electric Chicago sound inspired Elvis.

Howlin' Wolf influenced a generation of stars including Elvis, Eric Clapton, and the Rolling Stones.

Wolfman Jack is a disc jockey who played most of Elvis's fifties songs. Wolfman Jack stated after Elvis died that he would be remembered for two thousand years.

Zenoff, Judge David performed Elvis and Priscilla's wedding ceremony on May 1, 1967, at the Aladdin Hotel in Las Vegas. He was a justice of the Nevada State Supreme Court.

◀ Film producer Hal B. Wallis. *Courtesy of private collector.*

The Memphis Mafia ("El's Angels")

Late in 1959, the press began to notice a protective "mafia" of bodyguards always seemed to surround Elvis. By 1960, Elvis's close male companions (who included relatives, employees, and associates) were dubbed the Memphis Mafia by the media.

These were the men who tended to the "care" and feeding of Elvis Presley. No matter how ridiculous the request or how impossible (or dangerous) the demand, it was their job to fulfill it.

Bodyguard, confidant, baby-sitter, gofer, yes-man, pusher, or pimp—no matter what their role, the goal remained the same: keep Elvis happy. The consequences of anything less could have meant the loss of their much-prized and sought-after jobs.

Salary for each man in the fifties and sixties was a low $250 a week; in the seventies it was raised to $425 a week. While perks included everything from down payments on homes to cars, women, and jewelry, none of the Memphis Mafia members received vacations or pensions. In order to be at Elvis's beck and call at any hour of the day or night, many lived in trailers or mobile homes behind Graceland or on other Presley properties. (Elvis purchased eight mobile homes on credit and placed them at the Circle G Ranch for members of the Memphis Mafia.)

In December 1969, each member received a fourteen-karat-gold "TCB" necklace. Everyone in the entourage acted in a security capacity at one time, and many carried .38-caliber pistols, which Elvis supplied.

Elvis *never* stepped outside of Graceland without one of his "boys" at his side. As one movie director astutely observed, they were his "fart catchers"—there to serve the master.

After Elvis's death, many of the members of the Memphis Mafia found a new kind of fame as they cashed in on the Elvis Presley phenomenon through books, television, and lectures as they told the world about their relationships with the King of rock 'n' roll.

Memphis Mafia Members

1. "Hamburger" James Caughley (gofer in the 1970s in Las Vegas)
2. Richard Davis (Elvis's valet, 1962–69, at Bel Air home)
3. Joe Esposito ("Diamond Joe," number one aide to Elvis, 1960–76)
4. Lamar Fike ("Bull"; lighting engineer, bodyguard, 1958–62)
5. Alan Fortas (bodyguard, managed Circle G Ranch, 1958–77)
6. Marvin "Gee Gee" Gamble (chauffeur, 1967–69)
7. Larry Geller (hairdresser Elvis's "spiritual adviser," 1964–67)
8. Cliff Gleaves (chauffeur, bodyguard, 1956–59)
9. Dick Grob (security chief, bodyguard, 1969–76)
10. Louis Harris (bodyguard and general aide)
11. Dave Hebler (karate devotee, bodyguard, 1974–76)
12. Charlie Hodge ("Slewfoot," "Waterhead"; singer/guitarist/personal aide, seventeen years)

13. Jimmy Kingsley (bodyguard)
14. George Klein (companion, disc jockey, 1953–77)
15. Marty Lacker (bookkeeper, secretary, 1960–67)
16. Elisha Matthew "Bitsy" Mott (traveling aide, 1955–56)
17. Jerry Schilling (bodyguard, Bel Air security man, 1964–76)
18. Raymond Sitton (280-pound bodyguard, 1965–?)
19. Billy Smith (general aide to his cousin Elvis, 1956–77)
20. Carol "Junior" Smith (bodyguard, general aide, 1955–58)
21. Gene Smith (Elvis's cousin, chauffeur, aide, wardrobe man)
22. Al Strada (bodyguard in the seventies until Elvis's death)
23. Don Tomlin (bodyguard who was a black belt in karate)
24. Delbert "Sonny" West ("the Eagle"; vehicle maintenance, bodyguard, 1957–76)
25. Red West ("the Dragon"; bodyguard, composer, actor, 1960–1976)

ELVIS'S TELEVISION APPEARANCES

MAR. 5, 1955: The audition for the "Louisiana Hayride," a regional telecast of KWKH-TV. Elvis appeared fifty times on the "Louisiana Hayride" from October 16, 1954 (in which Elvis was interviewed by Frank Page during the "Lucky Strike Guest Time" segment, which promoted new artists) until December 15, 1956 (a benefit for the Shreveport YMCA). Over 190 CBS radio stations carried the program. Elvis broadcast other "Louisiana Hayride" shows from Gladewater and Waco, Texas.

MAR. 14, 1955: "Town and Country Jubilee," an interview with Jimmy Dean.

MAR. 19, 1955: "Grand Prize Saturday Night Jamboree," telecast live from Houston's Eagle's Nest.

MAY 31, 1955: "The Roy Orbison Show" from Odessa, Texas; an interview with Roy Orbison. Johnny Cash was also on the show.

JAN. 28, 1956: "Stage Show" with Tommy and Jimmy Dorsey, a CBS-TV variety show. In December 1955, Elvis signed a contract for four appearances at $1,250 a show. Other appearances were on February 4, 11, and 18, 1956. He signed for another two shows, which aired on March 17, 1956 and March 24, 1956.

APR. 3, 1956: "The Milton Berle Show" (broadcast from the deck of the USS *Hancock*, San Diego) and June 5, 1956 (with Debra Paget). The June 5 show was Berle's last show.

JUNE 20, 1956: "Dance Party" on Memphis's KLAC-TV with deejay Wink Martindale.

JULY 1, 1956: "The Steve Allen Show" (in which Elvis dressed in a tuxedo and sang "Hound Dog" to a sleepy-eyed hound.)

JULY 1, 1956: "Hy Gardner Calling," a split-screen remote broadcast with interviewer Hy Gardner. The show was shown on the New York station WABD, March 30, 1958.

SEPT. 9, 1956: "The Ed Sullivan Show." CBS-TV signed Elvis to a $50,000 three-appearance contract. He also appeared on October 28, 1956, and January 6, 1957.

DEC. 31, 1956: "Holiday Hop," KLAC-TV, Memphis, interviewed by Wink Martindale.

JAN. 8, 1959: A telephone interview with Dick Clark on "American Bandstand." Elvis had been voted Best Singer of the Year, and "King Creole" was voted Best Song of the Year. The program was dedicated to Elvis's twenty-fourth birthday.

MAY 12, 1960: "Welcome Home, Elvis," the fourth and final Sinatra-Timex special of the 1959–60 season, on ABC-TV, taped in Miami Beach at the Fontainebleau Hotel's Grand Ballroom, March 26, 1960. Elvis's salary: a cool $125,000 for a six-minute appearance.

DEC. 3, 1968: "Elvis" (known as his "comeback") aired at nine P.M., sponsored by the Singer Company. Elvis rehearsed the show June 17–19; music tracks were laid down June 21–22. Elvis taped on June 27 at Studio 4, NBC, Burbank, California; by June 29,

four tapes were completed. Taping for final production took place on June 30. Bob Finkel won a Peabody Award for producing the show. The show was rerun on August 22, 1969; it was aired on Britain's BBC-2 on December 31, 1968.

JAN. 14, 1973: "Elvis: Aloha From Hawaii" was a benefit concert for the Kuio-kalani Lee Cancer Fund and had a $2.5-million budget. It was first aired on January 14, 1973, and seen by approximately one *billion* people worldwide. Elvis's dress rehearsal on January 12 was performed before more than six thousand fans inside the Honolulu International Center Arena. It was beamed on January 14 by satellite to Australia, Japan, New Zealand, South Vietnam, South Korea, the Philippines, Thailand, and other countries, including small sections of China. On January 15, it was telecast to twenty-eight European nations. After the audience departed, Elvis recorded five songs for a U.S. edition of the concert. The ninety-minute special was broadcast on April 4, 1973, NBC, at eight-thirty P.M. and rerun on November 14, 1973, at eight-thirty P.M. Twenty-nine songs were sung for a world audience and ratings were high.

OCT. 3, 1977: "Elvis in Concert" was the King's last TV appearance. It was recorded and filmed at the Omaha Civic Auditorium in Nebraska on June 19, 1977, and the Rushmore Plaza Civic Center, Rapid City, South Dakota, on June 21. It was rushed by RCA and CBS producers to stations as a one-hour special after Elvis died. Fourteen songs were sung.

Television Specials Dedicated to Elvis

"Memories of Elvis" was a three-hour broadcast hosted by Ann-Margret on NBC on November 20, 1977. It was rerun on August 29, 1978, due to popular demand.

"Nashville Remembers Elvis on His Birthday" aired January 8, 1978, on NBC-TV. Hosted by Jimmy Dean, this ninety-minute special was rerun as an hour show on February 8, 1980, and retitled "Elvis Remembered: Nashville to Hollywood."

A 1981 syndicated special coproduced by George Klein was called "Elvis Memories." Some of Elvis's songs were dubbed by Bill Haney.

"Disciples of Elvis" was a 1984 syndicated Monticello Productions special, which featured fans and impersonators of the King. One segment showed two women who claimed they were Elvis's daughters.

"Elvis: One Night With You" aired January 5, 1985, on Home Box Office cable TV and was a taping originally made for the June 27, 1968, "Elvis" TV special. There were several reruns of the fifty-three-minute show during January 1985.

Elvis Presley's Graceland, hosted by Priscilla Presley, took viewers on a tour through the King's home. A Showtime cable TV broadcast, it was produced/directed by Steve Binder and filmed from August to November 1984. It aired repeatedly during January 1985. Available on videocassette.

"Elvis: The Echo Will Never Die" was hosted by Kasey Kasem and aired in August 1985. This hour-long syndicated special featured tributes to Elvis by friends and colleagues (B. B. King, Sammy Davis, Jr., Tom Jones, Ursula Andress).

"Elvis '56," narrated by Levon Helm, was a Cinemax cable TV production based upon a book and photographs by Alfred Wertheimer. It is a good look at Elvis's early years. First shown on August 16, 1987, it was rerun during that month. Available on videocassette since 1988 (hitting the *Billboard* charts). Highly recommended.

Elvis is mentioned and/or honored on many television stations on the anniversary of his birth and/or death each year. In 1991 to 1993 many tabloid-type TV programs had shows dedicated to the discussion of various scandalous events and/or myths regarding Elvis, which included the mysteries surrounding his death, his drug abuse, and love affairs. Throughout January to March 1992, the U.S. stamp honoring Elvis was the topic of numerous talk shows and news telecasts. It seems that the public and the media can't get enough of the man!

ELVIS'S RADIO SHOWS

OCT. or NOV. 1944: WELO, "Black and White Jamboree," Tupelo, MS

OCT. 3, 1945: WELO, "Mississippi-Alabama Fair & Dairy Show," Tupelo, MS

1953: WKEM, George Klein interview, Memphis

JULY 7, 1954: WHBQ, Dewey Phillip's "Red Hot & Blue," Memphis

OCT. 2, 1954: WSM, two shows in Nashville, "Grand Ole Opry" and "Ernest Tubb's Midnight Jamboree"

OCT. ?, 1954: KNUZ, "The Old Texas Corral," Houston, and KSIG in Gladewater, TX

OCT. 22, 1954: "The Old Barn Dance," New Orleans, LA

DEC. 11, 1954: KWKH, "Red River Roundup," Shreveport, LA

JAN. 1, 1955: KNUZ, "Grand Prize Saturday Night Jamboree," Houston, TX

JAN. 16, 1955: WBIP, Booneville, MS, and that same month for WMPS, Memphis, "Milkman's Jamboree"

JAN. 29, 1955: KNUZ, "Grand Prize Saturday Night Jamboree," Houston, TX

FEB. 26, 1955: WERE, "Circle Theatre Jamboree," Cleveland, OH

MAR. 19, 1955: KNUZ, "Grand Prize Saturday Night Jamboree," Houston, TX

MAR. 28, 1955: WERE, "Circle Theatre Jamboree," Cleveland, OH

APR. 16, 1955: KRLD, "Big D Jamboree," Dallas, TX

CA. MAY 27, 1955: KOCA, Kilgore, TX

MAY 28, 1955: KRLD, "Big D Jamboree," Dallas, TX

JUNE 18, 1955: KRLD, "Big D Jamboree," Dallas, TX

JULY 2, 1955: KEYS, Corpus Christi, TX

JULY 23, 1955: KRLD, "Big D Jamboree," Dallas, TX; KECK, "Pioneer Jamboree," Odessa, TX (with Lee Anderson)

AUG. 8, 1955: KSIG, Gladewater, TX

AUG. 31, 1955: WMPS, Memphis

SEPT. 3, 1955: KRLD, "Big D Jamboree," Dallas, TX

SEPT. 11, 1955: WCMS, Norfolk, VA

SEPT. 20, 1955: WRVA, "Old Dominion Barn Dance," Richmond, VA

DEC. 3, 1955: WBAM, "Talent Search of the Deep South," Montgomery, AL

APR. 13, 1956:   KSTB from Breckenridge, TX, airs a taped interview by Jay Thompson with Elvis from Wichita, KS

APR. 15 or 22, 1956:   WMAC interview with Charlie Walker, San Antonio, TX

JULY 1956:   Two WNOE shows in New Orleans, LA

OCT. 31, 1956:   WMPS in Memphis

Courtesy of the Country Music Foundation Library and Media Center, Nashville, Tennessee.

DEC. 22, 1956:   "Goodwill Review," WDIA, Memphis

OCT. 23, 1957:   Elvis's last radio show, aired over WHBQ, was an interview with George Klein in Memphis.

After 1957, Colonel Tom Parker did not find it financially rewarding to have Elvis do radio shows. The Colonel's demand of $10–25,000 per broadcast was more than any station in America could afford!

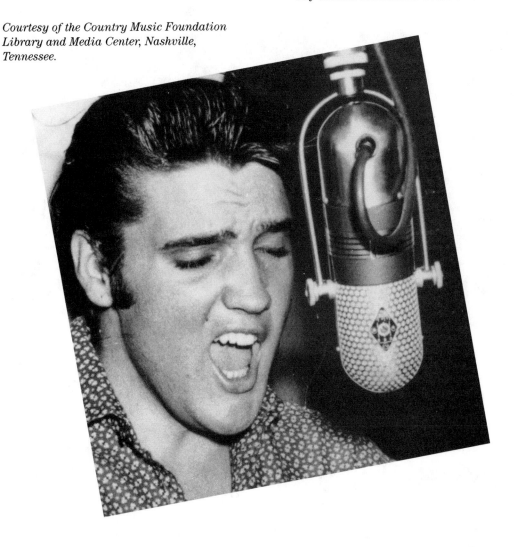

▲ The poster for *G.I. Blues*, 1960. *Courtesy of Paramount Pictures.*

PART III

Movie Data

*Courtesy of the James Agency and
the Liberace Foundation.*

MOVIE DATA

Elvis's Films in Chronological Order

1. *Love Me Tender* (1956)
2. *Loving You* (1957)
3. *Jailhouse Rock* (1957)
4. *King Creole* (1958)
5. *G.I. Blues* (1960)
6. *Flaming Star* (1960)
7. *Wild in the Country* (1961)
8. *Blue Hawaii* (1961)
9. *Follow That Dream* (1962)
10. *Kid Galahad* (1962)
11. *Girls! Girls! Girls!* (1962)
12. *It Happened at the World's Fair* (1963)
13. *Fun in Acapulco* (1963)
14. *Kissin' Cousins* (1964)
15. *Viva Las Vegas* (1964)
16. *Roustabout* (1964)
17. *Girl Happy* (1965)
18. *Tickle Me* (1965)
19. *Harum Scarum* (1965)
20. *Frankie and Johnny* (1966)
21. *Paradise, Hawaiian Style* (1966)
22. *Spinout* (1966)
23. *Easy Come, Easy Go* (1967)
24. *Double Trouble* (1967)
25. *Clambake* (1967)
26. *Stay Away, Joe* (1968)
27. *Speedway* (1968)
28. *Live a Little, Love a Little* (1968)
29. *Charro!* (1969)
30. *The Trouble With Girls* (1969)
31. *Change of Habit* (1969)
32. *Elvis—That's the Way It Is* (1970)
33. *Elvis on Tour* (1972)

Movies in Which Elvis Sang a Duet

1. *King Creole:* "Crawfish" with Kitty White.
2. *Wild in the Country:* "Husky Dusky Day" with Hope Lange.
3. *It Happened at the World's Fair:* "How Would You Like to Be" with Vicki Tiu; "Happy Ending" with Joan O'Brien.
4. *Girls! Girls! Girls!:* "Earth Boy" with Ginny and Elizabeth Tiu.
5. *Fun in Acapulco:* "Mexico" with Larry Domasin.
6. *Viva Las Vegas:* "The Lady Loves Me" with Ann-Margret.
7. *Frankie and Johnny:* "Petunia, the Gardener's Daughter," lip-synched by Donna Douglas,

dubbed by Eileen Wilson.
8. *Paradise, Hawaiian Style:* "Scratch My Back, Then I'll Scratch Yours" with Marianna Hill; "Queenie Wahine's Papaya" and "Datin' " with Donna Butterworth.
9. *Easy Come, Easy Go:* "Yoga Is As Yoga Does" with Elsa Lanchester.

10. *Clambake:* "Who Needs Money," lipsynched by Will Hutchins, dubbed by Ray Walker.
11. *The Trouble With Girls:* "Signs of the Zodiac" with Marilyn Mason.
12. *Speedway:* "There Ain't Nothing Like a Song" with Nancy Sinatra.

Actors, Actresses, Backup Vocals, Bit Parts, Advisers

Ed Asner played Frank Gerson in *Kid Galahad* (1962) (his film debut) and Lieutenant Moretti in *Change of Habit* (1969).

Ken Becker appeared in four of Elvis's films: as Wayne in *Loving You* (1957); as Mac in *G.I. Blues* (1960); a drunk in *Girls! Girls! Girls!* (1962); as Greg in *Roustabout* (1964).

Bill Belew was Elvis's wardrobe designer for *Elvis—That's the Way It Is* (1970) and *Elvis on Tour* (1972).

Bill Bixby played James J. Jameson, III in *Clambake* (1967) and Kenny Donford in *Speedway* (1968).

Bill Black appeared in *Loving You* (1957) as Eddie (a bass player) and in *Jailhouse Rock* as a bass player (1957).

George Ciser appeared in four of Elvis's films: as Jake the bartender, *Jailhouse Rock* (1957); as a crapshooter in *It Happened at the World's Fair* (1963); as the manager at Swinger's in *Viva Las Vegas* (1964); and as a bald man in *Speedway* (1968).

Joe Esposito appeared as a carnival man in *It Happened at the World's Fair* (1963); *Kissin' Cousins* (1964) as

Mike; as a member of Shorty's pit crew in *Spinout* (1966); a bit part in *Clambake* (1967); a workman in *Stay Away, Joe* (1968); as a gambler in *The Trouble With Girls* (1969). He was also a "technical assistant" for *Elvis—That's the Way It Is* (1970) and was an "assistant to Elvis" for *Elvis on Tour* (1972). After Elvis died, Esposito was a consultant for the Warner Brothers movie *This Is Elvis* (1981).

Shelley Fabares costarred in *Girl Happy* (1965), *Spinout* (1966), and *Clambake* (1967).

D. J. Fontana appeared in *Loving You* (1957) as a musician (drummer); as a drummer in *Jailhouse Rock* (1957); and as a musician in *G.I. Blues* (1960).

Edith Head was costume designer for the following Elvis films: *Loving You* (1957), *King Creole* (1958), *G.I. Blues* (1960), *Blue Hawaii* (1961), *Girls! Girls! Girls!* (1962), *Fun in Acapulco* (1963), *Roustabout* (1964), *Paradise, Hawaiian Style* (1966), and *Easy Come, Easy Go* (1967).

Charlie Hodge had a bit part in *Clambake* (1967); was a guitarist in *Speedway* (1968); and Mexican peon in *Charro!* (1969). He was a "technical assistant" for *Elvis—That's the Way It Is* (1970) and was a musician for *Elvis on Tour* (1972). After Elvis's death, Hodge played himself in the 1979 TV movie *Elvis* and acted as a consultant.

The Jordanaires appeared as themselves in 1957's *Loving You*, and received credit for vocal accompaniment, as well as in *King Creole* (1958); *G.I. Blues* (1960); *Flaming Star* (1960); *Blue Hawaii* (1961); *Girls! Girls! Girls!* (1962); *It Happened at the World's Fair* (1963); *Fun in Acapulco* (1963) with the Four Amigos; *Roustabout* (1964); *Happy Girl* (1965); *Tickle Me* (1965); *Harum Scarum* (1965); *Frankie and Johnny* (1966); *Paradise, Hawaiian Style* (1966); *Spinout* (1966); *Easy Come, Easy Go* (1967); *Clambake* (1967); *Stay Away, Joe* (1968); *Speedway* (1968); and *The Trouble With Girls* (1969). After Elvis died, the Jordanaires were consultants on the film *Elvis* (1979).

Hal Kanter wrote and directed *Loving You* (1957) and cowrote (with Herbert Baker) *Blue Hawaii* (1961).

George Klein had a bit part in *Frankie and Johnny* (1966) and *Double Trouble* (1967).

Douglas Laurence produced *Stay Away, Joe* (1968), *Speedway* (1968), *Live a Little, Love a Little* (1968). After Elvis died, Laurence wrote the screenplay for and produced *Elvis*, a Dick Clark Motion Pictures, Inc. film that aired on ABC-TV February 11, 1979.

Jana Lund gave Elvis his first on-screen kiss in *Loving You* (1957).

Scotty Moore appeared in *Loving You* (1957) as a guitar player; *Jailhouse Rock* (1957) as a guitar player; and in *G.I. Blues* (1960) as a musician.

Debra Paget appeared with Elvis on "The Milton Berle Show," June 5, 1956, and costarred with him in *Love Me Tender* (1956).

Colonel Tom Parker received credit as technical adviser (for which most sources claim he did nothing but collect an extra salary on top of his 50 percent of Elvis's take) in *Loving You* (1957); *Jailhouse Rock* (1957); *King Creole* (1958); *G.I. Blues* (1960); *Flaming Star* (1960); *Blue Hawaii* (1961); *Follow That Dream* (1962); *Kid Galahad* (1962); *Girls! Girls! Girls!* (1962); *It Happened at the World's Fair* (1963); *Fun in Acapulco* (1963); *Kissin' Cousins* (1964); *Roustabout* (1964); *Girl Happy* (1965); *Tickle Me* (1965); *Harum Scarum* (1965); *Paradise, Hawaiian Style* (1966); *Spinout* (1966); *Easy Come, Easy Go* (1967); *Double Trouble* (1967); *Clambake* (1967); *Elvis—That's the Way It Is* (1970); *Elvis on Tour* (1972); and in the Warner Brothers movie *This Is Elvis*.

Gladys Presley appeared in *Loving You* (1957).

Vernon Presley appeared in *Loving You* (1957), *Live a Little, Love a Little* (1968), and was an assistant to Elvis for *Elvis on Tour* (1972).

Richard J. Reeves appeared in five Elvis movies: as a harmonica-playing convict in *Blue Hawaii* (1961); as Officer Wilkins in *Girl Happy* (1965); as a bartender named Jim in *Tickle Me* (1965); as a bedouin in *Harum Scarum* (1965); and in *Frankie and Johnny* (1966).

Jerry Schilling played a bit part as the deputy sheriff in *The Trouble With Girls* (1969) and was an "assistant to Elvis" for *Elvis on Tour* (1972). Schilling acted as a consultant on the Warner Brothers release *This Is Elvis* (1981) and was technical adviser for New World Television's production *Elvis and Me* (1988), shown on ABC-TV February 7–8, 1988.

Mike Stoller appeared as a pianist in *Jailhouse Rock* (1957).

The Sweet Inspirations were backup vocalists in *Elvis—That's the Way It Is* (1970) and in *Elvis on Tour* (1972).

Norman Taurog directed Elvis in *G.I. Blues* (1960); *Blue Hawaii* (1961); *Girls! Girls! Girls!* (1962); *It Happened at the World's Fair* (1963); *Tickle Me* (1965); *Spinout* (1966); *Double Trouble* (1967); *Speedway* (1968); and *Live a Little, Love a Little* (1968).

Hal B. Wallis produced *Loving You* (1957); *King Creole* (1958); *G.I. Blues* (1960); *Blue Hawaii* (1961); *Girls! Girls! Girls!* (1962); *Fun in Acapulco* (1963); *Roustabout* (1964); *Paradise, Hawaiian Style* (1966); and *Easy Come, Easy Go* (1967).

David Weisbart produced *Love Me Tender* (1956), *Flaming Star* (1960), *Follow That Dream* (1962), and *Kid Galahad* (1962).

Allan Weiss wrote the story for *Girls! Girls! Girls!* (1962) and its screenplay with Edward Anhalt; *Fun in Acapulco* (1963); the story for *Roustabout* (1964) and the screenplay with Anthony Laurence; the story for *Paradise, Hawaiian Style* (1966) and the screenplay with Anthony Laurence; and *Easy Come, Easy Go* (1967) and the screenplay with Anthony Laurence.

Del "Sonny" West had a bit part in *Kid Galahad* (1962); was Jackson He-Crow in *Stay Away, Joe* (1968); was a technical assistant for *Elvis—That's the Way It Is* (1970); and is listed as an "assistant to Elvis" in *Elvis on Tour* (1972).

Red West appeared as an Indian in *Flaming Star* (1960); as Hank Tyler in *Wild in the Country* (1961); as a bank guard in *Follow That Dream* (1962); as a bongo-playing member of a tuna-boat crew in *Girls! Girls! Girls!* (1962); Fred in *It Happened at the World's Fair* (1963); a poolside guest in *Fun in Acapulco* (1963); was one of the "Sons of the Lone Star State" in *Viva Las Vegas* (1964); as a carnival worker in *Roustabout* (1964); an extra in the Kit Kat Club, *Girl Happy* (1965); as a bully in a bar in *Tickle Me* (1965); an assassin in *Harum Scarum* (1965); as Rusty, a man who fights with Elvis, in *Paradise, Hawaiian Style* (1966); as a member of Shorty's pit crew in *Spinout* (1966); a bit part in *Clambake* (1967); as a newspaper worker in *Live a Little, Love a Little* (1968); and is listed as an "assistant to Elvis" for *Elvis on Tour* (1972).

Debut Performances in Elvis's Films

In *Loving You:* Bill Black, D. J. Fontana, Dolores Hart, the Jordanaires, Scotty Moore, Gladys Presley, Vernon Presley. In *Jailhouse Rock:* Jennifer Holden. In *G.I. Blues:* Kerry Charles, Donald Clark, Sigrid Maier, David Paul, Donald James Rankin, Terry Earl Ray, Leticia Roman, Priscilla Taurog, David Clark Wise. In *Wild in the Country:* Christina Crawford. In *Blue Hawaii:* Flora K. Hayes. In *Follow That Dream:* Gavin Koon, Robin Koon. In *Kid Galahad:* Ed Asner, Orlando de la Fuente. In *Girls!*

Girls! Girls!: Laurel Goodwin. In *It Happened at the World's Fair:* Vicky Tiu. In *Roustabout:* Racquel Welch. In *Frankie and Johnny:* George Klein. In *Double Trouble:* Annette Day. In *Clambake:* Charlie Hodge. In *Stay Away, Joe:* Susan Trustman. In *Speedway:* Ross Hagen, Patti Jean Keith. In *Live a Little, Love a Little:* Ursula Menzel. In *Charro!:* Lynn Kellogg. In *The Trouble With Girls:* Pepe Brown, Nicole Jaffe, Anissa Jones, Marlyn Mason, Jerry Schilling. In *Change of Habit:* Jane Elliot.

Last Performances in Elvis's Films

Jailhouse Rock: Judy Tyler

G.I. Blues: Ludwig Stossel

Wild in the Country: Jason Robards, Sr.

Harum Scarum: Philip Reed

Spinout: Carl Betz, Una Merkel, Frederick Worlock

Easy Come, Easy Go: Frank McHugh

Clambake: Hal Peary

Change of Habit: Richard Carlson, Ruth McDevitt, Elvis.

Film Production Companies

Allied Artists: *Tickle Me* (1965, a Ben Schwalb Production).

MGM: *Jailhouse Rock* (1957, an Avon Production); *It Happened at the*

World's Fair (1963, a Ted Richmond Production); *Kissin' Cousins* (1964, a Four Leaf Production); *Viva Las Vegas* (1964, a Jack Cummings–George Sidney Production); *Girl Happy* (1964, a

◄Elvis in *Easy Come, Easy Go. Courtesy of Paramount Pictures. Copyright © 1994 by Paramount Pictures. All Rights Reserved.*

391

Euterpe Production); *Harum Scarum* (1965, a Four Leaf Production); *Spinout* (1966, a Joe Pasternack Production); *Double Trouble* (1967, a B.C.W. Production); *Stay Away, Joe* (1968, a Douglas Laurence Production); *Speedway* (1968, a Douglas Laurence Production); *Live a Little, Love a Little* (1968, a Douglas Laurence Production); *The Trouble With Girls* (1969, a Lester Welch Production); *Elvis—That's the Way It Is* (1970, a Herbert F. Soklow Production); *Elvis on Tour* (1972, a Cinema Associates Production).

MGM gave Elvis two Culver City dressing rooms, one of which was Clark Gable's.

National General Pictures: *Charro!* (1969, a Harry Caplan Production).

Paramount Pictures (all Hal B. Wallis Productions): *Loving You* (1957);

King Creole (1958); *G.I. Blues* (1960); *Blue Hawaii* (1961); *Girls! Girls! Girls!* (1962); *Fun in Acapulco* (1963); *Roustabout* (1964); *Paradise, Hawaiian Style* (1966); *Easy Come, Easy Go* (1967).

Twentieth Century-Fox: *Love Me Tender* (1956, a David Weisbart Production); *Flaming Star* (1960, a David Weisbart Production); *Wild in the Country* (1961, a Company of Artists, Inc. Production).

United Artists: *Follow That Dream* (1962, a Mirisch Company Production); *Frankie and Johnny* (1966, an Edward Small Production); and *Clambake* (1967, a Levy-Gardner-Laven Production).

Universal: *Change of Habit* (1969, a Universal Pictures and NBC Production).

More Movie Trivia

Black-and-white films: *Love Me Tender, Jailhouse Rock,* and *King Creole.*

In two films Elvis's costars lost their bikini tops as they swam: Joan Blackman in *Blue Hawaii* and Shelley Fabares in *Clambake.*

Hawaii was the setting for: *Blue Hawaii, Girls! Girls! Girls!* and *Paradise, Hawaiian Style.*

Six films (in which Elvis does not appear) have Elvis music in the tracks: *Touched by Love* (1980); *Diner*

(1982); *Heaven Help Us* (1985); *Mischief* (1985); *Lethal Weapon* (1987); *Tin Men* (1987). *Dudes* (1987) includes an Elvis impersonator. *Honeymoon in Vegas* (1992) features Elvis impersonators, including twelve skydiving Elvis's.

The top five rental videos: *Viva Las Vegas; Blue Hawaii; Love Me Tender; G.I. Blues;* and *Jailhouse Rock.*

(For information regarding LPs/singles/ CDs/videos of recorded music from sound tracks see "Records, CDs, and Videos.")

PART IV

People in Elvis's Life

▲ Elvis at the Ellis Auditorium piano, Memphis, Tennessee. *Courtesy of John Reible, Las Vegas News Bureau, Las Vegas, Nevada.*

PEOPLE IN ELVIS'S LIFE

Studio Musicians and Band Members

1. Patricia Allen (pianist), *Double Trouble*, 1967.
2. Chet Atkins (guitarist) at Nashville recording sessions 1/10–11/56, 4/11/56, 6/10–11/58; A&R man for RCA, 1960–68.
3. Johnny Bernero (drummer) at some Sun sessions, but often not credited; he was credited for "I Forgot to Remember to Forget," 1955.
4. Bill Black was Elvis's bassist. He toured with the Blue Moon Boys and appears on many recordings.
5. Hal Blaine (drummer) in sessions for *Blue Hawaii*, March 1961, and the 1968 NBC-TV special.
6. Blue Moon Boys: Bill Black (bassist) with Scotty Moore (lead guitarist) played with Elvis at the "Louisiana Hayride" and at clubs from 1954 to 1958, and in sessions dating 1/15–16/58, 1/23/58, 2/2/58 (Black's bass is now owned by Paul McCartney). They played the original backup instruments at Sun studios. They often appeared with Elvis after 1958, but not as the Blue Moon Boys. D. J. Fontana joined the group as its drummer in 1956.
7. Eddie Bond backed Elvis at the Hi Hat Club, 1954.
8. Harold Bradley played guitar for "Snowbird," September 1970.
9. David Briggs played guitar from 1963–67 and for the recording session for "Snowbird," September, 1970.
10. Dudley Alonzo Brooks (pianist) at sessions from 1956 to 1964; he also played piano on "All Shook Up" on January 12, 1956, at Radio Recorders, but Mike Stoller is also heard.
11. Tony Brown (pianist) toured with Elvis's TCB Band, 1974–77.
12. James Burton (lead guitarist) joined Elvis from 1957 to 1972 as a session player.
13. Jerry Byrd played steel guitar, August 1968, on "Beyond the Reef," and he often sang minor backup vocals.
14. Gene Chrisman was a drummer who played for Elvis at the American Sound Studios.
15. Charlie Christopher on guitar, December 11, 1973.
16. Merry Clayton occasionally sang in backup sessions or kept time with a tambourine.
17. Tommy Cogbill was a studio musician who recorded with Elvis at the American Sound Studios, Memphis.
18. Floyd Cramer (pianist) played for "Louisiana Hayride" performances and recording sessions from January 1956 to January 1968.
19. "Billy" Black Cunningham (uncredited) on bongos and on a

cardboard box for "I Don't
Care If the Sun Don't Shine"
and "Blue Moon," Sun sessions.

20. Ken Darby Trio provided
backup vocals for the sound
track of *Love Me Tender*, and
Darby was the film's musical
director.

21. Jimmy Day played steel guitar
for Elvis during the fifties and
at "Louisiana Hayride" performances.

22. Tim Dixon and his band occasionally backed Elvis at the
Eagle's Nest, Memphis,
September–October 1954.

23. Peter Drake (steel guitarist)
backed Elvis from 1966 to 1968
for "Guitar Man," "Big Boss
Man," "You'll Never Walk
Alone."

24. Donald (Duck) Dunn played
bass at the Stax Studios sessions July 21–25, 1973.

25. Al Dvorin and his twenty-piece
orchestra backed Elvis in 1961
at the benefit concert in Hawaii
for the USS *Arizona* and for
other concerts in the sixties.

26. Bobby Emmons was an organist at the American Sound Studios in Memphis who recorded
with Elvis.

27. Joe Esposito (guitarist) for the
May 15–21 and June 8–9, 1971
recordings, and at Stax Studios,
July 1973.

28. D. J. Fontana (drums) for sessions from 1956 to 1968. Fontana claims he did not play for
any of the Sun sessions.

29. Alan Fortas ("Hog Ears")
played tambourine for the TV
special in June 1968.

30. Hank "Sugarfoot" Garland (guitarist) backed Elvis from 1958
to 1961 and in the March 25,
1961, Pearl Harbor concert.

31. Jimmy Gordon (guitar) on
"Bringing It Back," 1975.

32. Marshall Grant played bass and
Carl Perkins (guitar) for backups in 1955 during the Bob
Neal concert tours for Elvis.

33. Murray "Buddy" Harmon
played percussion for sessions
between 1958 and 1968, and for
nine movie sound tracks.

34. Glen D. Hardin (pianist) played
with Elvis's TCB Band from
1970 to 1976 and wrote the arrangement for "Bridge Over
Troubled Waters."

35. Jimmie Haskell played accordion, April 28, 1960, on
"Wooden Heart."

36. Charlie Hodge (who also sang
three duets with Elvis—"You
Better Run," "I Will Be Home
Again," and "Could I Fall in
Love") played rhythm guitar
from 1960 to 1977.

37. Marvin Hughes played the piano for "I Want You, I Need
You, I Love You," April 11,
1956.

38. John Hughey was a studio guitarist at the American Sound
Studios, Memphis, who recorded with Elvis.

39. Bill Justin played sax on the
sound track of *Kissin' Cousins*, 1963.

40. Jerry Kennedy was a guitarist,
1961–63.

41. Barney Kessel (guitar) for
Girls! Girls! Girls! and *Fun in
Acapulco* sound tracks, and for
sessions on July 26–27 and August 4–5, 1965.

42. Larry Knechtel (bass) on
Speedway sound track and
NBC-TV special, June 27–29,
1968.

43. Ed Kollis played harmonica for
"Gentle on My Mind," January
15, 1969; he was a studio guitarist at American Sound Studios, Memphis.

44. Mike Leech (bass guitar) at
American Sound Studios,
January–February 1969, and
overdub bass for Elvis's March
10–13, 1975, session.

45. Dennis Linde provided the
overdubbing at Graceland for
February 2–8, 1976, and April
24–25, 1977, sessions and

played guitar for "Burning Love," March 1972, and "I Got a Feelin' in My Body," December 10, 1973.

46. Shorty Long played piano on "One-Sided Love Affair," "Hound Dog," "Don't Be Cruel," "Any Way You Want Me," "My Baby Left Me," "Blue Suede Shoes," and "Tutti Frutti."

47. Grady Martin played guitar at the March 1962, February 1965, and March 20, 1967, recording sessions.

48. Charlie McCoy (harmonica and bass) played on sound tracks for *Frankie and Johnny; Easy Come, Easy Go; Harum Scarum;* and *Paradise, Hawaiian Style.*

49. Ronnie Milsap played piano on many recordings, including "Gentle on My Mind," January 15, 1969.

50. Hugo Montenegro's Orchestra backed "Charro," October 1968.

51. Bill Moore (guitarist and session player) replaced Bill Black, 1958–66.

52. Bob Moore (bass guitarist) played at Nashville sessions in 1958 and 1966.

53. Scotty Moore (lead guitarist with a Gibson) backed Elvis with Bill Black as the Blue Moon Boys from 1954 to 1958, and rejoined him from 1960 to 1968. His last gig with Elvis was the NBC-TV special, which was the last time Moore saw Elvis.

54. Joe Moscheo (pianist and a member of the Imperials Quartet) played at the RCA studio session in Nashville, May 15–21, 1971.

55. Jimmy Mulidore played a flute solo during the February 17, 1972, live recording of "American Trilogy" from Vegas.

56. Carl "Cubby" O'Brien (drums) recorded *Charro!* sound tracks

October 1968 and *Change of Habit*, March 5–6, 1969.

57. Carl Perkins (guitar) played backup for early 1955 Jamboree concerts with Elvis.

58. Luther Perkins played live in one appearance during the 1955 tour.

59. Norbert Putnam played bass at RCA's Nashville studio, 1971. He also played bass on "Beyond the Reef," August 1968.

60. Don Randi played keyboard, piano, and organ on the 1968 NBC-TV special, and piano for the *Speedway* sound track in June 1967.

61. Boots Randolph played sax and vibes on April 3, 1960, and for twenty sessions between January 15 and 17, 1968.

62. Jerry Reed played lead guitar and wrote "U.S. Male," "Guitar Man," and "Too Much Monkey Business," 1968.

63. Don Robertson, piano, "A World of Our Own," September 1962.

64. Leon Russell played piano for several movie sound tracks.

65. Jerry Scheff played bass on the sound track of *Easy Come, Easy Go.*

66. Henry Slaughter played piano/organ for RCA Nashville sessions, May 25–28 and June 10, 1966.

67. Glenn Spreen (saxophonist) overdubbed the sound track of *The Trouble With Girls*, 1968, and two sessions at the American Sound Studios in 1969.

68. Ray Stevens played trumpet for May 26–28, 1966, recording sessions.

69. Gordon Stoker played the organ for "Peace in the Valley," January 13, 1956, at Radio Recorders and backed Elvis with piano for thirteen years. He also played accordion, October 15, 1961.

70. Mike Stoller played backup piano for the recorded version of

"Baby, I Don't Care," 1957.
71. Billy Strange was musical director for *Roustabout; Live a Little, Love a Little;* and *The Trouble With Girls* and played guitar for *Viva Las Vegas.*
72. Henry Strzelecki played bass for May 26–28, 1966, recording sessions.
73. "Tiny," H. J. Timbrell played guitar for the Radio Recorders in Hollywood at Elvis sound track sessions from 1957 to 1966.

74. Bergin White did the overdubbing of instrumentals for Elvis's "Moody Blue" single in 1976.
75. Bobby Wood was a studio musician at American Sound Studios, Memphis.
76. Chip Young was a guitarist for 1966–67 recording sessions.
77. Reggie Young played electric sitar on "Stranger in My Own Home Town," February 1969 and was a studio guitarist at American Sound Studios in Memphis.

Elvis's TCB Band Members (1969–76)

Pat Houson (trumpet); Glen D. Hardin (piano); Ronnie Tutt (drums); Hal Blaine (drums); Jerry Scheff (bass/guitar); James Burton (lead guitar); John Wilkenson (rhythm guitar); Joe Osborne (bass); Marty Harrell (trombone); Jerry Shook (bass); Tony Brown (drums).

Backup Singers— Individuals/Groups

1. The Amigos (Jose Vadiz, Miguel Alcaide, Pedro Berrior, and German Vega) sang with the Jordanaires at the January 22–23, 1963, Radio Recorders sessions for the *Fun in Acapulco* sound track.
2. Joe Babcock sang backup vocals May 26–27, 1963, at RCA studios in Nashville and provided backups Feb. 17–22, 1969, at the American Sound Studios, Memphis.
3. Tim Baty did backup vocals for "I Miss You," September 24, 1973, in Palm Springs.
4. The Lea Jan Beriniti Singers worked with Elvis in the sixties.
5. The Blossoms (Jean King, Fanita James, Darlene Love) backed Elvis in the 1968 NBC-TV special and were singing "neighbors" in *Change of Habit.*
6. The Blue Moon Boys (Scotty Moore and Bill Black used the name in 1954 to 1955) later did

backups through 1968.

7. Jerry Byrd played steel guitar, August 1968, for "Beyond the Reef" and often sang minor backup vocals.

8. The Cherokee Cowboys with Ray Noble Price backed Elvis on the "Louisiana Hayride," April 30, 1955, performance.

9. Merry Clayton was a session backup singer for three years.

10. Al Dvorkin and his orchestra backed Elvis from 1961.

11. Ray Edenton played second guitar for "Beyond the Reef," August 1968. He was at various sound-track sessions.

12. Mary and Ginger Halladay and Jeannie Green (the Halladay Sisters) sang backup during six recording sessions in Nashville, Memphis, and Hollywood, 1969–75.

13. Buddy Harman played drums, August 1968, "Beyond the Reef," and he occasionally added "sound" to backup vocals.

14. The Imperial Quartet (Jack Hess, Jim Murray, Gary McSpadden, and Armand Morales in 1969; later included Terry Blackwood, Joe Moscheo, and Sherrill Nielsen) backed Elvis from 1969 to 1971.

15. The Jordanaires (originally with Bill Matthews, Cully Holt, Bob Hubbard, and Monty Matthews). Those who backed Elvis were Gordon Stoker, Neal Matthews, Hoyt Hawkins, and Hugh Jarrett. The Jordanaires sang at the September 26, 1956, concert in Tupelo (first released in 1985 by RCA in the *Golden Celebration* set), and they first recorded a session with Elvis on July 3, 1956. Some of the members of the Jordanaires did a New York City recording session on June 10–11, 1958 (Ray Walter replaced Hugh Jarrett) for four

Elvis songs. They sang backups for many movies including *Loving You*, *King Creole*, and *G.I. Blues*.

16. Anita Kerr singers (also called Little Dippers) overdubbed the backup vocals for RCA for Elvis's 1955 "Tomorrow Night" on March 18, 1965.

17. Mildred (Millie) Kirkham sang on *Elvis' Christmas Album*, September 5–7, 1957, and sang for Elvis on and off for fifteen years. She was often backed by June Page, Dolores Edgin and Sandy Posey.

18. The Carole Lombard Quartet and the Jubilee Four sang on the sound track of *Viva Las Vegas*, 1963.

19. The Carole Lombard Trio with the Jubilee Four and the Jordanaires sang backups for *Girl Happy*, July 1964.

20. The Mellow Men backed Elvis in 1963 for "One Broken Heart for Sale" and "They Remind Me Too Much of You," and for the sound track of *It Happened at the World's Fair*, 1962.

21. Ronnie Milsap sang and played backup at American Sound Studios recordings in January 1969, and sang a duet with Elvis, "Don't Cry Daddy" (he may have sung the high notes on "Kentucky Rain").

22. The Bobby Morris Orchestra backed Elvis on July 4, 1956, at Russwood Park, Memphis.

23. The Nashville Edition recorded Nashville sessions on March 15, 1970, June 5–8, 1970, and March 15, 1971.

24. Sherrill Nielsen sang backup vocals for "I Miss You" in Palm Springs, September 24, 1973.

25. Doug Poindexter and the Starlight Wranglers backed Elvis in Memphis clubs, 1953–55.

26. Sandy Posey sang backup vocals with Elvis, 1968–70.

27. Chuck Prescott, John Dodson, and Red Robinson sang backup vocals for "Love Me Tender," 1956. They were a trio.

28. Ray Price and the Cherokee Cowboys backed Elvis on "Louisiana Hayride," 1954.

29. Temple Riser sang a duet with Elvis on March 15, 1971, and for "The First Time Ever I Saw Your Face" in Nashville.

30. Dave Rowland (of the Stamps Quartet) sang backups for Elvis.

31. Leon Russell backed Elvis on piano for many movie sound tracks and often sang backups.

32. Ben and Brock Speer often sang backup vocals with Gordon Stoker for Elvis in the fifties.

33. The Stamps (or the Stamps Quartet) (J. D. Sumner, Ed Enoch, Ed Hill, Donnie Sumner, Bill Blaize, Larry Strickland, Buck Buckles, and Richard Sterban) backed Elvis on albums from 1972 to 1977.

34. Gordon Stoker sang backup with the Jordanaires and Elvis for thirteen years.

35. Gordon Stoker, Brock Speer, and Ben Speer backed the RCA session in Nashville for "Heartbreak Hotel" (the Jordanaires did *not* back "I Was the One," "I Want You, I Need You, I Love You," or "Heartbreak Hotel") and three other early sessions.

36. J. D. Sumner was a bass singer first with the Sunshine Boys, then with the Blackwood Brothers (1954–65), and then organized his own group, the Stamps. J. D. Sumner sang duets with Elvis during concerts with the tunes "Why Me Lord" and "Help Me."

37. The Sweet Inspirations (with Emily Cissy Houston, Estelle Brown, Sylvia Shenwell, and Myrna Smith) backed Elvis in the movie *Change of Habit* in 1969, and sang backups for Elvis and warmed up audiences at concerts, 1968–77.

38. Donnie Summer sang backup vocals on September 24, 1973, during the recording session of "I Miss You."

39. The Surfers (with Patrick Sylvia, Bernard Ching, Clayton Naluai, and Alan Naluai) sang backup at Radio Recorders, Hollywood, March 21–23, 1961, and for the sound track of the movie *Blue Hawaii*.

40. Voice (with Sherrill Nielsen, who was also with the Imperials, guitarist John Rich, bassist Tommy Hensley, and pianist Tony Brown) backed Elvis in live concerts from 1973 to 1975.

41. Bass singer Ray Walker (of the Jordanaires) sang backup for "A Fool Such as I" at RCA's Nashville studio, June 1958.

42. Kathy Westmoreland (who replaced Mildred Kirkham) sang backups from 1970–77.

43. Kitty White sang "Crawfish" in a duet with Elvis for the sound track of *King Creole*. It was Elvis's first duet.

44. At the American Studios the following singers backed Elvis during sessions: Joe Babcock, Dolores Edgin, Mary Greene, Charlie Hodge, Mary Holladay, Millie Kirkham, Sonja Montgomery, Susan Pilikington, Sandy Posey, Donna Thatchet, and Hurshel Wiginton.

People and Companies Who Worked for Elvis

1. Aberbach, Jean and Julian, music publishers, Hill and Range, with two subsidiary companies: Elvis Presley Music and Gladys Music
2. Alberta, maid, 1956–72
3. Auberback, Larry, Elvis's agent at William Morris Agency
4. Ayers, Rick, hairdresser from 1971; practiced karate with Elvis
5. Baugh, George, security guard, Graceland
6. Belew, Bill, tailor/designer of Elvis's costumes from 1968
7. Bell, Howard, made and sold Elvis-related products through Special Products, Inc. with Hank Saperstein
8. Bienstock, Freddie, manager of Hill and Range Music Publishers, later an A&R man for RCA; received 15 percent of Boxcar Enterprises royalties
9. Boucher, Jack, caretaker of the Circle G Ranch
10. Bouchere, Carol, stewardess on Elvis's Convair 880 jet, 1975
11. Boyd, Patricia, secretary at Graceland who had the authority to sign Elvis's name to fan mail; married to Red West
12. Caughley, Hamburger James, valet at Graceland
13. Church, Charles R., TV-system installer/repair person
14. Clark, Albert, Jr., grounds-keeper/handyman, Graceland
15. Cocke, Marian J., personal nurse from 1975 until his death
16. Coleman, George, electrician at Graceland
17. Covington, Pappy, "Louisiana Hayride" booking agent, 1955–56
18. David, Elwood, pilot of Elvis's Convair 880 jet
19. Davis, Oscar "the Baron," introduced Colonel Parker to Elvis and was indirectly involved with Elvis promotions and tours
20. Davis, Richard, valet and wardrobe man, 1962–69
21. Deary, Joan, in charge of Elvis's RCA catalog through 1973
22. DeVore, Sy, designed Elvis's $9,000 1962 wardrobe
23. Diskin, Tom, brother-in-law of the Colonel, who received 15 percent of Boxcar Enterprises royalties and 22 percent of Boxcar Record royalties from Elvis's work
24. Doors, Inc. at 911 Rayner St., Memphis, built the now-famous Music Gates for Graceland, 1957
25. Dunavant, Robert, probate-court clerk who handled Elvis's will
26. Dwyer, Donald, attorney
27. Esposito, Joe, bodyguard, chauffeur, bookkeeper, road manager, 1960–77
28. Fain, Harry M., attorney who handled a 1970–71 paternity suit
29. Fike, Lamar, operated lighting systems at concerts, body-guard, 1958–62
30. Fortas, Alan, worked at Grace-land/Circle G Ranch

31. Gambill, Marvin "Gee Gee," Jr., valet/chauffeur, 1967–69
32. Geller, Larry, hairdresser, religious "guru" until 1967
33. Gerson, Pat Parry, beautician who styled Elvis's hair and allegedly gave him Frank Adams's book the *Shroud of Turin*, which some claim Elvis had with him when he died
34. Ghanem, Dr. Elias, treated Elvis in the seventies in Vegas
35. Gibson, Henrietta, nursemaid to Lisa Marie at Graceland
36. Gilliland, Homer "Gil," hairdresser, 1967–77
37. Gleaves, Cliff, salaried employee, 1956–57
38. Golden, George, decorator at Graceland, 1957
39. Goldsmith's Department Store, provided Graceland's furnishings
40. Greenwood, Earl, publicist/press agent for Elvis
41. Grob, Dick, security chief of Graceland, 1969–76
42. Guercio, Joe, Elvis's musical arranger in Vegas, 1967–76
43. Hays, Lowell, Elvis's jeweler
44. Henley, Tish, Elvis's private nurse during concert tours
45. Hodge, Charlie, rhythm guitarist who was Elvis's daily aide; supervisor of Elvis's daily routine for seventeen years
46. Hoffman, Dr. Lester, dentist
47. Hookstratten, E. Gregory, attorney
48. Hooten, Arthur, aide at Graceland around 1959
49. Hulett, Thomas, booking agent with Concerts West
50. I.C. Costume Company, supplied Vegas costumes to Elvis
51. Ivy, Troy, gardener at Graceland until September 1967
52. Jackson, Pee Wee, gardener at Graceland
53. Jarvis, Felton, Elvis's producer at RCA, 1966–70, full-time with Elvis, 1970–77
54. Jenkins, Mary/Mary Flemings, cook at Graceland, 1963–77
55. Kantor, Dr. Edward, eye, ear, nose, and throat specialist in Beverly Hills who was Elvis's doctor from 1958 to 1970
56. Keaton, Mike, general maintenance, Graceland, 1964
57. Kennedy, Jerry, policeman who served as a security guard, 1976
58. Kerkorian, Kirk, signed Elvis in Vegas, 1959, and lent him a jet
59. Kingsley, James, bodyguard for Elvis who became a stuntman
60. Kirsch, Jack, pharmacist, Prescription House, Memphis, who in 1977 gave Elvis 5,684 pills in a seven-month period
61. Klein, George, general aide, introduced Dr. Nichopoulos, Linda Thompson, and others to Elvis
62. Lacker, Marty, bookkeeper/secretary, 1960–67
63. Lastfogel, Abe, nicknamed the Little Square Man, as president of the William Morris Agency personally served as Elvis's agent
64. Leiber, Jerry, with Mike Stoller, one of the best songwriters and moral supports Elvis ever had
65. Levitch, Harry, Memphis jeweler who sold Elvis Priscilla's engagement ring and other jewelry
66. Lewis, George, guard at Graceland
67. Lewis, Paulette Shafer, secretary at Graceland
68. Loyd, Harold, night-shift gateman, Graceland
69. Loyd, Robert, security guard, Graceland
70. Madison Cadillac, dealership that sold/serviced Elvis's Cadillacs, 1957–77
71. Manning, Jim, flight engineer on Elvis's Convair 880 jet, 1975–77
72. McGarrity, Bonya, secretary at Graceland from 1962 to 1975

who signed Elvis's name to fan mail

73. McGregor, Mike, grounds-keeper/handyman at Graceland
74. Memphis Pool and Landscaping Co., took care of Elvis's pool
75. Meyer, Dr. David, eye doctor, Memphis
76. Minor, Wilma, Los Angeles nutritionist
77. Neal, Bob, music manager/booking agent, 1955–56
78. Nichols, C. W., housepainter who did Graceland
79. Nicholson, Pauline, cook and maid at Graceland, 1963–77
80. Nichopoulos, Dean, worked with Elvis's wardrobe in Vegas
81. Nichopoulos, Dr. George C., the physician who prescribed Elvis's pills, medications, and "treatments" until Elvis died
82. Nudie's Rodeo Tailors, created Elvis's gold-lamé outfits
83. O'Grady, John, private investigator who suggested Elvis fire Red and Sonny West and Dave Hebler
84. O'Neal, Doris, a secretary at Graceland
85. Pachucki, Al, an engineer who worked with Elvis at RCA's Nashville Studios, 1970
86. Parker, Ed, bodyguard, personal karate trainer, 1972
87. Parker, Pamela, secretary who answered fan mail
88. Parker, Colonel Tom, manager/promoter/agent, 1955–77
89. Parkhill, George, received 15 percent of Boxcar Enterprises royalties and worked for the Colonel on Elvis's projects
90. Pepper, Gary, mailroom worker, who helped answer fan mail
91. Pepper, Sterling, gate guard at Graceland
92. Peters, Gerald, chauffeur in Beverly Hills
93. Phillips, Judd, helped produce Elvis's Sun records

94. Phillips, Sam, "discovered" Elvis and cut his first records
95. Presley, Delta Mae, Elvis's aunt, and housekeeper from 1967–77
96. Presley, Patsy, secretary at Graceland, replacing Patricia Boyd
97. Presley, Vernon, bookkeeper, caretaker of estate
98. Presley, Vester, head gate guard, Graceland, 1957 to the present
99. Pritchett, Uncle William Earl, cared for eighteen horses at the Circle G Ranch and was head groundskeeper at Graceland
100. Proby, P. J., sung demos from which Elvis would select songs
101. Rhee, Kang, martial arts instructor, 1970
102. Robbins, Dennis, Elvis's Vegas optician
103. Rooks, Nancy W., a Graceland maid
104. Roy, Alvena, housekeeper and cook at Graceland, six years
105. Saperstein, Hank, merchandised/exploited Elvis-related products with the Colonel after 1956; established Factors, Etc., Inc.; sold items through Special Projects, Inc.
106. Seamon, Kathy, private nurse at Graceland, 1975
107. Shafer, Paul, supplied Elvis with movies from Malco Theaters
108. Shapiro, Dr. Max, Beverly Hills dentist
109. Shaver, Sean, official photographer who took almost eighty thousand photos of Elvis
110. Shaw, Arnold, music publisher/A&R man for Elvis in fifties
111. Sholes, Steve, signed Elvis with RCA
112. Smith, Gene, chauffeur and maternal cousin of Elvis's,

cared for Elvis's wardrobe in Hollywood

113. Smith, John, uncle to Elvis and a gate guard at Graceland
114. Smith, Lillian, secretary at Graceland from 1960–62
115. Smith, Travis, gate guard at Graceland through 1965
116. Smith, William "Billy," close cousin of Elvis's; wardrobe caretaker, valet, general aide until Elvis's death
117. Spector, Phil, singer/composer/producer who introduced Elvis to Mike Stone
118. Speer, William, photographer of Elvis, 1954–55
119. Stanley, David, stepbrother, security guard at Graceland from 1970 until Elvis's death
120. Stanley, Rick, stepbrother who took Richard Davis's place as Elvis's valet, 1969–77
121. Stanley, William "Billy" Job, aide to Elvis, ca. 1967–75
122. Stefaniak, Elisabeth, secretary to Elvis in West Germany
123. Stole, Fred, gatekeeper at Graceland for fourteen years
124. Stoller, Mike, one of the best songwriters for Elvis
125. Strada, Al, wardrobe man at Graceland and also a guard
126. Strauss, Ron, copilot for Elvis's Convair 880 jet, 1975–77

127. Swan, Billy, gate guard at Graceland
128. Thompson, Sam, bodyguard/security guard, the seventies
129. Weintraub, Jerry, booking agent for Concerts West
130. Wertheimer, Alfred, photographer who snapped over 3,800 candids of Elvis, 1956–58
131. White, Carrie, cut Elvis's hair in Beverly Hills
132. Williams, Ernestine, maid at Graceland for five years
133. Winfield, Nigel, found all of Elvis's airplanes for purchase
134. Yancey, Becky, secretary at Graceland from 1962 to 1972
135. Original session engineers included Jim Malloy (May 25–27, 1966, June 10, 1966, and September 10–11, 1967 Nashville); Bill Porter (March 1960 to May 28, 1963, Nashville); Al Puchucki (May 28, 1966, January 15, 1968, Nashville, January 13, 1969, to February 22, 1969, Memphis); Roy Shockley (assistant engineer, January 13, 1969, to February 22, 1969, Memphis); Ron Steele (January 12, 1964, Nashville); and Bill Vandervort (January 17, 1968, Nashville)

Fellow Army Recruits and Servicemen

Recruits who traveled from Memphis to Fort Chaffee, Arkanas, by bus, March 24, 1958, and were then shipped to Fort Hood, Texas, March 28, 1958:

Timothy Christopher, Jr. (US 53310768)
Daniel Gilmore (US 53319768)
R. Guy Farley (US 53310763)
Louis C. Hern (US 53310761)

Wallace J. Hoover (US 24887433)
Robert T. Maharrey (US 53310765)
Donald R. Mansfield (US 25255673)
William C. Montague (US 53310767)
Alex E. Moore (US 53310760)
William R. Norvell (US 25347005)
James Payne, Jr. (US 53310766)
Elvis A. Presley (US 53310761)
Nathanial Wiggison (US 53310764)

Tom W. Creel was stationed with Elvis in Germany and was hired as Elvis's double in several movies. The motto of the U.S. Army Second Armored Tank Division was "Hell on Wheels." While in Friedberg, Elvis's main duty was as scout jeep driver to platoon sergeant M. S. Ira Jones. Elvis took karate lessons in West Germany from Jurgen Seydel and Hank Slemansky (who was later killed in Vietnam).

Elvis was awarded two marksmanship medals: one for rifle and pistol shooting, and one for sharpshooting with a carbine.

"Operation Elvis" was an official group/program to handle the fans and other Elvis phenomena while he served in the Army, from March 24, 1958 to March 5, 1960. A special truck was designated to pick up and deliver thousands of pieces of mail to Elvis each day.

Participants in and Places of <u>Football Games</u>

Max Baer, Jr. (director and actor), was on Elvis's Bel Air football team, which played at De Neve Park. Also, singer Ricky Nelson, Jack Lord, Dean Torrence, Ty Hardin, Lee Majors, Michael Parks, actor Gary Lockwood, Dell Dean, and actor Robert Conrad played on Sundays in Bel Air. Richard Davis played in Memphis. Others included James Elam, Gene Smith, Charles McSwain, Kent McCord, Pat Boone (in Bel Air), Charlie Hodge, Freddie Vincent, Donald "Rex" Mansfield (1950s), Sonny and Red West, Jim Kingsley, Wilroy McElhaney, Jerry Baxter, Billy Dodds, Dick Grob, Larry Bell, Alan Fortas, Jack Counce, Glen D. Hardin, Pretty Boy Moore, Jerry Ellis, Ron Heller (in Bel Air), George Klein, Bitsy Mott, and Jerry Schilling.

Elvis may or may not have played football at Humes High School for a few months. On August 31, 1957, Elvis told interviewer Red Robinson his favorite team was the Cleveland Browns and he knew all the major pro players. In Germany, Elvis broke a finger during a touch football game with Red West and several GIs. At Graceland and during breaks from movie shoots, Elvis hired referees for games where he and his friends would play for hours. Elvis Presley Enterprises sponsored a local football team in 1963, with which Elvis played occasionally (Oct.–Nov. 1963). Elvis often rented the Whitehaven High School football field and stadium, hired a professional referee, and played end during games between him, with members of the Memphis Mafia, and opposing local, amateur teams.

ELVIS PRESLEY DAYS, OFFICIALLY RECOGNIZED

1. Sept. 26, 1956, at the Mississippi-Alabama Fair and Dairy Show. Elvis gave the city of Tupelo $10,000 from his concert's proceeds.
2. Feb. 25, 1961, State of Tennessee.
3. Sept. 29, 1967, State of Tennessee.
4. Nov. 11, 1970, State of Oregon.
5. Jan. 13, 1973, celebrated in Honolulu, Hawaii, by the city's mayor.
6. Jan. 8, 1974, proclaimed by Gov. Jimmy Carter, Georgia.
7. Oct. 19, 1976, State of Wisconsin.
8. Jan. 8, 1981, State of South Carolina.
9. Jan. 8, 1981, State of Alabama.
10. Jan. 8, 1981, State of Florida.
11. Jan. 8, 1981, State of Illinois.
12. Jan. 8, 1981, State of Georgia.
13. Jan. 8, 1981, State of Kansas.
14. Jan. 8, 1981, State of North Carolina.
15. Jan. 8, 1981, State of Pennsylvania (letter of recognition)
16. Jan. 8, 1981, State of Virginia (letter of recognition)
17. Jan. 8, 1982, State of Tennessee.
18. Jan. 8, 1992, State of Tennessee.
19. Alabama governor George Wallace declared a week in March 1974 as "Elvis Presley Week."

▶ Bud Abbot, Barbara Stanwyck, and Elvis when the Cat donated $50,000 to the Motion Picture Relief Fund, June 10, 1965. *Courtesy of AP/Wide World Photos.*

ELVIS IMPERSONATORS

Since Elvis's death, thousands of impersonators have made full-time careers imitating the King. They appear throughout the world at concert openings, parties, parades, book and record shops, weddings, bachelor parties, and elsewhere. On July 4, 1968, over two hundred Elvis impersonators appeared at a birthday party for the Statue of Liberty in New York City. They were also at the 1988 Olympics in Seoul and can always be found in celebrations commemorating Elvis's birthday and death in Memphis each year.

On January 8, 1993—to celebrate what would have been Elvis's fifty-eighth birthday and the release of the Elvis stamp in Memphis—over twelve hundred Elvis imitators surfaced in fifty states. "Elvis sightings" occurred throughout the world. Not only did the King of rock 'n' roll come back—he had multiplied! Was it newsworthy? You bet it was. Every local and national television station carried the remarkable birthday bash/stamp story.

For a reference to leading Elvis impersonators see *I Am Elvis* (American Graphic Systems, Inc., Pocket Books, 1991).

An Elvis Impersonator Hall of Fame meeting and the Elvis Impersonator Convention are held annually in Las Vegas. The Hall of Fame inductee for 1992 was forty-two-year-old Ryder Preston, an Elvis impersonator for twenty-six years.

Here is a list of the most well-known impersonators:

Perry Adelson (Las Vegas)
Mike Albert (Ohio)
Ron Allsop (Bellingham, MA)
Rick Ardisano (River Grove, IL)
Sammy Stone Atchison (Port Arthur, TX)
Morris Bates (Tennessee)
Marvin Benefield ("Vince Everett" after *Jailhouse Rock* role)

Clayton Benke-Smith (Battle Ground, WA)
Randy Black (Melrose Park, IL)
Larry Blong (home unknown)
Tessie Blue (home unknown)
Bruce Borders (Jasonville, IN)
Michael Bozzo (Sharon, PA)
Elvis Bobby Bradshaw (Round Lake Beach, IL)
Jimmy Breedlove (black Elvis impersonator)
Gary Wayne Bridges (great resemblance, Little Ferry, NJ)
Barry Brunnel (Tennessee)
Louis Michael Bunch, Jr./Louis Michael (Springfield, MO)
Angelo "Elvis" Campo (Chicago, IL)
Julian "Elvis" Campo (Chicago, IL)
Dave Carlson (Oak Forest, IL)
David Carrol (Minnesota)
Bubba Cauldron (home unknown)
Frankee Cee (San Jose)
Paul Chan (London)
Andy Childs (Memphis)
Bill Cochran (Wheeling, IL)
Dorol Conrad (the West Coast)
Jamie Coyne (Columbus, OH)
Johnny Cramier (Knoxville, TN)
Rusty Dee (St. Petersburg, FL)
Terry Dene (Great Britain)
Pat Disimine ("Elvis Little," Ontario, Canada)
Matt Dollar (Bristol, TN)
Eric "Elvis" Domino (Chicago Ridge, IL)
Rick Dunham (Dawson, IL)
Rob "Elvis" Dye (Chesthill, IL)
Ron Dye (Wilmington, IL)
Joe "Elvis" Earl (Lake City, FL)
Johnny Earl (Middlesex, England)
El-Ray-Vis (Indiana)
Raymond El-Royus (New York)
El Vez ("The Mexican Elvis," Los Angeles)

Lee Elvis (Brooklyn, NY)
Bob Erickson ("Bobby E," Prior Lake, MN)
Vince Everett (London)
Roger Franke (Blue Springs, MO)
Ron Furrer (St. Louis)
Kenny G. (Hampshire, England)
Tony Galvan (San Francisco)
Kim Garner (Tallahassee, FL)
Ron George (Todd Productions, Nut Tree, CA)
Clarence Giddens ("Black Elvis," Nassawadox, VA)
Les Grey ("Tulsa McLean" after *G.I. Blues* role, Oklahoma)
Nick Guerrero (Graceland Chapel, Las Vegas)
Robby Guterro (New York)
Jim Gutierrez (Vacaville, CA)
Ed Hamilton (Steamwood, IL)
Bill Haney (W. Memphis, AR)
Johnny Harra (home unknown)
Connie Hartman (Warren, OH)
Bert Hathaway (Moses Lake, WA)
Corey Heichel (Westerville, OH)
Tim Hilliard (Chicago)
Russ Howe (Absecon, NJ)
Ron Hutchinson (Cheshire, England)
Frank Iannaggi (Cleveland, OH)
Kiyoshi Ito (Tokyo)
Donn Jett (Florida)
Storey Jones (female)
Janice K ("The Lady Elvis," Exeter, NB)
Ray Kajkowski (Gobles, MI)
E. P. King (Las Vegas)
Richard Larsen (Noah, UT)
Johnny Lawson (Graceland Chapel, Las Vegas)
Little El/Marcel Forestieri (New Castle, DE)
Rich Lockname (Carlsbad, NM)
Steve Long (Tennessee)
Bobbie Lord (Miami)
Craig MacIntosh (Detroit, MI)
Doug McIntyre (Rockland, MA)
Mike Malone (Parin, NJ)
Rick Marino (Jacksonville, FL)
Jerome Marion (Manteno, IL)
Jeffrey Marn (W. Newton, PA)
Shane Martin (S. Jordon, UT)
James Meis ("Little Jimmy," Winfield, KS)

Alan Meyer (considered the number one Vegas Elvis impersonator)
Michael and Blue Suede (San Francisco)
Gary Michaels (Glenview, IL)
Kevin Mills (Delran, NJ)
Mike Moat (Secaucus, NJ)
David "Elvis" Orton (Clearlake, CA)
Joseph Dale Paige ("Joe Elvis")
Jerry Papp (Jerry "El," Kendall Park, NJ)
Dena Kay Patterson (Edgerton, KS)
Nick Paulichenko (Hamilton, Ontario)
Jerry Presley (Tennessee)
Richard "Duke" Presley (Tennessee)
Terry Presley (Tennessee)
Tony Presley (Tony Smith)
Ryder Preston (South Carolina)
Andrew Priest (home unknown)
Miguel Quintana ("Little Elvis," Englewood, CO)
Darrin Race ("Darrin," Columbia, SC)
Charles Randall (Fort Worth, TX)
Gary Raye (East Peoria, IL)
Johnny Risk (home unknown)
Deke Rivers (named after Elvis's role in *Loving You*)
Gil Rogers (Gloucester, MA)
John Paul Rossi (Wood Dale, IL)
Douglas Roy (Canada; shared a stage with Elvis, 5/6/76)
Johnny Rusk (Seattle, WA)
Rick Saladan (Philadelphia, PA)
Bud Sanders (El Paso, TX)
Richard Satana (California)
Rick Saucedo (Chicago, IL)
Nazar Sayegh (New York City)
Richard Sellers (New York)
Larry Seth/Big El (Blackwood, NJ)
Bob Shane (early impersonator in Hawaii)
Gene Shaw (W. Monroe, LA)
Peter Singh (London)
Freddy Starr (appears in Memphis)
Robert Stefano (appears in Tennessee)
Ron Stein (Chino, CA)
Dimitri Theodosis (San Saba, TX)

Joseph Tirrito ("Joe Elvis," Country-side, IL)
Danny Vann (Canton, MI)
Hans Vige (Jacksonville, FL)
Jonathan Von Brana (Honolu-lu, HI)
Elvis Wade (Wade Cummings, Tennessee)
James Wallace (San Jose, CA)
David Wayne (appears in Tennessee)
Ken Welsh ("Elvis Eagle," Melbourne, Victoria, Australia)

Julian Whitaker (Beltsville, MD)
Jim White (Manchester, England)
Robert Whitesfield (England)
Peter Wilcox (Laurel Canyon, CA)
John Wilson (Nashville, TN)
Dennis Wise (Joplin, MO)
Bobby Wiserman (New York)
Mori Yasumasa (Japan)
Eddie Youngblood (Kogarah, NSW, Australia)
Jeff Zandberg (Studio City, CA)

ELVIS'S TELEPHONE NUMBERS AND ADDRESSES

Telephone Numbers

(There were no area codes.)

Memphis: 397-4427
398-4882
398-9722
870-0370 (the Colonel)

Beverly Hills: 278-3496
278-5935
274-8498 (the Colonel)

Palm Springs: 325-3241
325-4781 (the Colonel)

Addresses

Tupelo, Mississippi

1. 306 Old Saltillo Road, Elvis's birthplace, is now 306 Elvis Presley Drive. The two-room wood-frame house that Vernon built for $180 was designated a state historical site by the Mississippi Department of Archives and History on January 8, 1978.
2. Reese Street, where the Pres-leys stayed with Vester and Clettes Presley and their daughter Patsy, 1940–41.
3. Kelly Street, a rented, small apartment, 1942.
4. Vernon paid $200 down on the house on Berry Street on August 8, 1945. He was forced to sell it on July 18, 1946. "Doll" Smith lived here with the Pres-

leys, and then Minnie Mae Presley moved in.

5. Commerce Street, a rental, in 1946 (now a shopping mall).
6. 510½ Maple Street, South Tupelo, where the Presleys lived with Gladys's cousin Frank Richards and his wife, Leona.
7. Mulberry Alley, a low-income rental near the city dump and railroad tracks.
8. 1010 North Green Street, in the Shakerag section of Tupelo.

Memphis, Tennessee

9. 572 Poplar Avenue (Sept. 12, 1948–Sept. 20, 1949) was a crowded boardinghouse of sixteen families. The Presleys shared a bath and kitchen with other families. Their first-floor apartment was rented for $35 a month. The house has been demolished and the property is now an empty lot.
10. 185 Winchester Street, a two-bedroom apartment (number 328), on the first floor, was rented by the Presleys from September 20, 1949 to January 7, 1953. It was located in the federally funded 433-unit Lauderdale Courts. The Presleys were evicted.
11. 398 Cypress Street (rented from January 7 to April 1953 for $50 a month).
12. For a few weeks, the Presleys may have lived at 698 Saffarans, before moving to a duplex at 462 Alabama Street (rented from April 1953 to the end of 1954). Bill Black's mother lived in the same complex, and a rabbi and his wife—who had a phonograph and a telephone—lived upstairs. It was demolished and paved over for a ramp to I-40.
13. 2414 Lamar Avenue (rented from end of 1954 to mid-1955).

It is now the location for the Tiny Tot Nursery School.

14. 1414 Getwell Street (rented from mid-1955 to May 11, 1956).
15. 1034 Audubon Drive, where Elvis bought a three-bedroom home in April 1956 for $40,000. The family lived here from May 11, 1956 to March 1957. Elvis allegedly sold the house for $55,000. It had an iron fence, which still exists at the property. The Audubon Drive neighbors hated the Presleys and the commotion caused by fans. A neighborhood group asked the Presleys to leave.
16. 3764 Elvis Presley Boulevard (in a suburb of Memphis called Whitehaven) is where Graceland sits. Elvis purchased the house for over $100,000 and lived there until his death. It is now a memorial and tourist attraction run by Elvis Presley Enterprises.

Southern California

17. Elvis stayed at the Knickerbocker Hotel on Ivar Avenue, on the eleventh floor with the Memphis Mafia, Gladys, and Vernon, during the filming of *Loving You*. He then stayed at the Beverly Wilshire Hotel and eventually moved to the Regent Beverly Wilshire, at 9500 Wilshire Boulevard.
18. 565 Perugia Way, Bel Air (a rental, 1960–63; moved back into the home, 1963–65), where the Beatles met Elvis. The home was adjacent to the Bel Air Country Club and was designed by Frank Lloyd Wright. Pat Boone lived down the street.
19. 1059 Bellagio Road, Bel Air, was a rental that had a bowling

alley. Elvis lived here briefly in 1963 and 1965.

20. 10550 Rocco Place, Bel Air (a rental from late 1965 to May 7, 1967). The former one-story ranch house is now a two-story Tudor with a tennis court.

21. 1174 Hillcrest, a three-bedroom home in the Trousdale Estates, was purchased on May 7, 1967, for approximately $400,000. When Elvis and Priscilla divorced, Elvis and his entourage stayed here. It was surrounded by a wall. Danny Thomas lived down the street.

22. 144 Monovale, in the Holmby Hills, Los Angeles, was once owned by actor Robert Montgomery. Priscilla stayed here during divorce proceedings. This home was sold to Telly Savalas for $650,000 in 1975.

23. 825 Chino Canyon Road was a vacation home in Palm Springs. Elvis built this white stucco, single-story, fifteen-room ranch for $85,000 and willed it to Lisa Marie. In 1979, it was sold to Frankie Valli for $385,000.

24. 1350 Leadera Circle, was in Palm Springs. Elvis rented the five thousand-square-foot home in April 1970. Elvis and Priscilla had spent their wedding night here with members of the Memphis Mafia.

Other Homes

25. 906 Oak Hill Drive in Killeen, Texas. Elvis rented the four-bedroom house for members of the Memphis Mafia and his parents in May 1958, until his Army unit left Fort Hood for Germany. On weekends, Elvis stayed in a Quality Inn in Fort Worth, Texas.

26. 14 Goethestrasse was in Bad Nauheim, West Germany. For $800 a month, Elvis rented a five-bedroom, white stucco house at this location, from October 1958 to the end of 1959, while he served in the Army.

27. 4152 Royal Crest Place in Memphis was the home Elvis bought and gave as a gift to Ginger Alden. It was one block from Graceland.

28. The Circle G Ranch was located on 163 acres off Rt. 301, in DeSoto County Near Walls, Mississippi. While driving with Jerry Schilling and Alan Fortas, Elvis spotted this huge spread and bought it on February 9, 1967. It was sold on May 21, 1969, to a gun club. When the gun club could not obtain a shooting permit, Elvis bought the ranch again and resold it in 1973. While he owed the property, he installed mobile homes for his crew and bought Ford Ranchero trucks for Memphis Mafia members. He kept nine to twelve ranch hands at the location to tend a stable of horses and care for the property, but it proved to be too extravagant a hobby for Elvis to maintain. It had a main house, a gatehouse, a surrounding wall, and expansive pastures.

ELVIS'S NICKNAMES AND CODE NAMES

Elvy; Mama's Boy; E; El; Big E; Big El; the Cat; Elvis the Pelvis; the Hillbilly Cat; the King; the King of Rock 'n' Roll; the King of Pop Rock; the King of Swoon; the King of Love; the King of Hearts; Hillbilly Frank Sinatra; Alan (code name at Graceland); Jon Burrows; the Chief; Crazy Cat; Crazy; the Country Cat; Fire Eyes; the King of Country; the King of Western Bop; Wiggle Hips; Tiger Man; Buttons; Bunting; Mr. Dynamite; Memphis Flash; E.P.; Mr. Rhythm; Sir Swivel Hips; Pelvie; Pelvis Elvis; Tiger (karate name); Elvis Pretzel; Mr. Safety; the Atomic Powered Singer; "my boy" and "son" (used by the Colonel); Hillbilly Bopper; Mr. Obscene; Mr. Wiggle and Shake; Poor Man's Liberace; Whirling Dervish of Sex.

ELVIS'S PETS

Baba, a collie; Bear, a prize-winning Tennessee walking horse; Boy, his first mongrel dog; Domino, a quarter horse; Edmund, a Pomeranian with Elvis when he died; several peacocks; Fluff, a cat Elvis gave to Lisa Marie; Foxhugh, a Maltese terrier given to Linda Thompson; Getlo, a chow; Honey, a puppy Elvis gave Priscilla for Christmas 1962; a mynah bird that said, "Elvis, go to hell!"; Mare Ingram, a horse at the Circle G; Muffin, a great Pyrenees dog; Puff, Lisa Marie's cat at Graceland; Rising Sun, a $3,500 palomino horse, the favorite of his pets; Scatter, a chimpanzee; Sherlock, a basset hound; Snoopy, a Great Dane; Stuff, a black poodle; Sweet Pea, a dog Elvis gave Gladys in 1956; Teddy Bear of Zixi Pom-Pom, a poodle given to Elvis in Germany, 1960; and a stable of seventeen horses.

PART V

Collecting Elvis

*Courtesy of the Country Music
Foundation Library and Media
Center, Nashville, Tennessee.*

COLLECTING ELVIS

Elvis and the Beatles are the most collected and collectible entertainers in the history of music. Their songs and their personalities captivate the imaginations, dreams, and pocketbooks of fans worldwide. Elvis is more popular today than he was when he was alive. As one fan aptly put it recently, "I don't love him like a lover or husband. I love him like a brother. He's *family*. He's a part of all of us. Just because he died doesn't mean I don't love him." Because millions feel the same way, whenever a new product becomes available, devotees rush to purchase it because it reminds them of the Cat, or the years in which they were part of this new phenomenon called rock 'n' roll.

Memorabilia

Elvis Presley advertising, promotion, and merchandising has been growing since Colonel Parker first developed an item with Elvis's image on it in the fifties. The brilliant retailing genius of Parker and his crew should not be underestimated. In 1956, Parker hired a Beverly Hill's firm, Special Products, Inc. (owned by Hank Saperstein and Howard Bell) to promote and exploit Elvis's image. In the early fifties, Parker also arranged with New York City–based Hill and Range Music Company to set up two subsidiary companies, Gladys Music and Elvis Presley Music, and partial royalties from songwriters who worked for Hill and Range were filtered into Elvis's and Colonel Parker's accounts. In 1974, Parker founded Boxcar Records, from which Parker took 56 percent of the profits and Tom Diskin and Elvis each got 22 percent. At the same time, Parker formed Boxcar Enterprises with Tom Diskin, George Parkhill, and Freddie Bienstock. This company oversaw the making, merchandising, and distribution of Elvis-related products. Elvis netted a mere 15 percent from all sales. No "perfect" bookkeeping was kept, thus the Cat could not have successfully audited these men, nor could anyone else. For the most part, Elvis did not care about that kind of issue. He trusted those who worked with him, which is unfortunate. People abused the honor.

It would take hundreds of pages to list all of the Elvis-related items that have been created and sold. Several books are tremendous sources for memorabilia: *Elvis Collectibles* (Johnson City, TN: Overmountain Press); Jerry Osborne, Perry Cox, and Joe Lindsay's *Memorabilia of Elvis Presley and the Beatles* (New York: House of Collectibles, 1988); Jerry Osborne's *The Official Price Guide to Records* is somewhat outdated; *The Elvis Catalogue: Memorabilia, Icons and Collectibles* by Lee Cotton (a Dolphin/Doubleday Book, 1987) is a good source.

On October 10, 1978, *People* magazine realized that Elvis mania was charging full steam ahead. Their front cover read, "Remembering Elvis—Imitators, fans and rip-offs launch a billion dollar industry." Everything from $1 bills with Elvis's image to toilet seats with his likeness were being made.

On May 13, 1978, *Saturday Review* in "Nights of the Living Dead, Cashing in on Rock and Roll Heaven" talked of clever merchandising of Elvis after death. *Life* ran "The King's Ransom" in August 1984, which stated, "Elvis Presley is worth more dead than alive—his memory earning ten times as much as he made in his forty-two years, and that was $100 million."

As the legendary status of Elvis grows, so do the prices for his autograph, but remember, Elvis had a staff of people who signed his name to photographs, books, and other items. It's difficult to authenticate a *real* Elvis Presley signature. Signatures by his staff are numerous and are often thought to be from the King's hand. *Buyer beware!* Memorabilia

in pristine condition can bring megabucks, while torn, soiled, or tattered items bring considerably less. Period pieces from 1948 to 1977 are the most desirable collectibles, and one of the most sought after items is Elvis wine (even though he did not drink liquor). Nineteen ninety-two and nineteen ninety-three were banner years for the production of Elvis items, and these will go up in value as they are sold out (especially limited-editions).

The Earliest Memorabilia (from 1954)

Colonel Tom Parker produced a veritable gold mine of Elvis-related items that fans snapped up as fast as they came off the assembly lines. Elvis had little or no say in what was made in his name or image.

Not including records, Elvis-related memorabilia included: anklets attached to Elvis cards; Elvis rubber dolls; glass ashtrays; autograph books; belts of plastic or leather; belt buckles; billfolds; *Love Me Tender* zipper binders, flasher key chains, buttons, heart-shaped necklaces in silver or gold tone, bracelets, earrings, pillows, shifts, wrapped candies, framed photos, tour books, perfume, lipstick, shoes, and sneakers; *Hound Dog* stuffed animals, lipstick, charms, necklaces, pillows, bolo ties, and bookends; original 1956 magazine articles; Browser Box made by RCA Victor; 1956 "Elvis Presley National Fan Club, I like Elvis & his RCA Records" buttons; fan-club membership cards; Elvis scrapbooks, diaries, photo albums, record cases with Elvis holding a guitar and a sad-looking dog; bubblegum cards and gum wrappers; Elvis cake decorations, 1956; sixty-six bubblegum cards by Topp Gum Company, sold in lots of five for five

cents or one cent each, with the set offered in two parts: "Ask Elvis" (cards 1–46) and *Love Me Tender* (cards 47–66); 1956 *Loving You* charm bracelets, and a regular charm bracelet; "Elvis for President" buttons (for the song by that title by "campaign manager" Lou Monte, 1956); earrings with Elvis photos; Elvis carrying cases; six-inch-square ceramic Elvis tiles; charm bracelets with continuing updated charms; coasters; coin purses with key chains; concert placards; 1956 coaster ashtrays; Elvis pens and pencils; various tour books, 1956–59; The Elvis Presley Show posters (1956), announcements, napkins, photos, and show cards; Elvis Presley one-year diary; fan-club packet and membership cards; gum-ball-machine pins (round) with "Don't Be Cruel," "You're Nothin' but a Hound Dog," "Love Me Tender," "I Like Elvis" (one plain; one with photo of Elvis), and "Always Yours Elvis"; original unopened record albums; round pins; celluloid pins; "Rock and Roll Stars" arcade cards (Elvis's card is numbers thirty-seven of sixty-six); individual round, gold Elvis charms; adjustable finger rings with Elvis's head; 1956 black-and-white postcards; "The Elvis Presley Game—A Party Game for the Young at Heart"; drinking glasses with Elvis's portrait; guitar with carrying case, 1956–57; songbook "For Emenee Guitar Including Elvis Presley Song Hits," 1956; early promo photo cards stating, "Elvis Presley, Exclusive RCA Victor Recording Artist"; Elvis Presley felt skirts; handbags (clutch); handkerchiefs; gabardine hats with magnets or tags (about five different designs); "Elvis Presley Jeans" with tag; flasher key chains; key chain/coin purses; lipstick by Teenager Lipstick Corp. (with card); medallion with "I Want You, I Need You, I Love You," "Don't Be Cruel," "Hound Dog," and "Heartbreak Hotel" printed on it; Elvis mittens; heart-shaped necklace with an engraving of Elvis; pajamas; prenumbered, paint-by-numbers Elvis paint sets; patches with cards, ribbons, bows attached; Elvis Presley pencils, dozen a pack (also with a "signed" binder); pencil sharpeners; phonographs, including a portable "autographed" model with a manual and printed instructions from RCA Victor; Elvis photo albums ("In Person—Elvis Presley, Country Music's Mr. Rhythm"; "Elvis Presley—Mr. Dynamite"; "Souvenir Photo Album—Elvis Presley"); Hound Dog aftershave; Elvis pillows, featuring photos from various movies; pins with Elvis's photo attached to a guitar; pin (flashers); twelve-inch platter plate of Elvis; record cases; rings with color pictures of Elvis; scarves with two drawings of Elvis with a guitar; sheet music; stick-on sideburns; lapel insignias; song folio, magazines, and books of sheet music ("Elvis Presley Album of Jukebox Favorites"); "Love Me Tender Song Folio With Pictures"; bobby socks attached to an Elvis card; an eight-inch bronze statuette; shirt tags with Elvis and his guitar; tickets to Elvis shows; title strips on discs; wallets with coin purse and key chain; wallet (French purse); wallet for photos; "Souvenir Picture Album," sold Jan.–Apr. 1956; "Elvis Presley Souvenir Photo Album," 1956; wooden and Plexiglas double-card plaque with logo Elvis Presley "The King"; Elvis Presley Dog Tag sweater clips, 1958–60; dog-tag bracelets, anklets, necklaces; Elvis Presley Christmas postcards or regular Christmas cards; Elvis party invitation; Hit Stars bubble-gum cards (Elvis is card number fifty-nine), 1957; 1960 paper Army cap; "the Elvis Pocket Handbook," published in England by Albert Hand in 1961; 1962 *Follow That Dream* medallion on bracelet; the Memphis Charity Show Committee program, "In Person, Memphis' own Elvis and his show"; 1963 calendars of Elvis; 1965 *Girl Happy* photo on pocket watch; Elvis fabric, thirty inches wide, sold by the yard at $25; Elvis (*Elvin*) shirt imprinted with various records and Elvis's image; *Blue Hawaii* lei necklace with round medallion of Elvis, Hawaiian shirts, skirts, ties, hats, bracelet charms, rings, necklaces; Elvis's "Gold Car" tour cards or ads; 1962 coloring contest sheet for free tickets to *Girls! Girls! Girls!*; a sixteen-by-twenty poster by June Kelly published by RCA; two original 1966 romance comics featuring Elvis; "Elvis, the Swingin' Kid," 1962, published in London; "Elvis," a full-color folio, published by RCA Victor, sixteen pages, 1963; a line of Easter postcards, 1969; *Tickle Me* feathered pens; Las Vegas "Elvis" matchbooks, ticket stubs, table cards, letters, advertisements.

Collectible magazines with Elvis on the cover include: *Teenage Rock and Roll Review*, October 1956; *Dig*, November 1956; *Dig*, January 1957; *Rock 'n' Roll Jamboree*, Fall 1956; *Rock 'n' Roll Stars*, 1956, 1957 (nos. 2 and 3); *Rock and Roll Roundup*, April 1957; *Elvis Presley, Pat Boone, Billy Haley—Rock 'n' Roll Battlers*, 1956; *Elvis vs. the Beatles*, 1956; *Elvis and Jimmy*, 1956 (James Dean); *Cool*, 1957, vol. 1, no. 1; *Hep Cats Review*, Feb. and Dec. 1957; *Elvis, Pat, Tab and Belafonte*, July 1957; *Cool and Hep Cats*, 1958; *Who's Who in Rock 'n' Roll*, 1958; *Elvis and Tom (Jones)*, 1969; in *Superstars*, "Glenn Campbell/Elvis Presley," 1970; from England, two magazines were printed ca. 1955–57 *Elvis Presley and . . .* and *The Amazing Elvis Presley* (featured on both covers); *The Official Elvis Presley Fan Club of Great Britain Monthly*, 1957, vol. 1, no. 1 (reprinted in 1977); 1962, 1963, 1966, 1970–72, 1977–80 pocket calendars; "Meet Elvis," Star Special #1,

1962, published by Albert Hand, followed by "Elvis Special" booklets 1963–82; period Las Vegas postcards, ads, booklets, programs, Hilton Hotel publication "A Guide to What's Happening Now" with Elvis on the cover; Las Vegas menus with Elvis's photo on the cover, 1969–75; August 1966 "Films and Filming" with Elvis and a child on cover; 1968 radio and TV specials promo booklets; photo souvenir folios of concerts; "Pageant," August 1973 and March 1974; *Look*, May 4, 1971; *People*, Jan. 13, 1975, *Country Music Magazine*, November 1975; *Preview*, February 1977; the only two issues printed of *Elvis* magazine (1976 and 1977) by Ideal Publishing Company; "the Elvis Years," a pinup special by "Circus," 1975; *Faces*, Dec. 20, 1975; *Elvis Mania*, published in England, 1975; *Elvis, the Trials and Triumphs of the Legendary King of Rock & Roll*, May 1976; Elvis complimentary gift bags (plastic); Elvis summer-festival pennants from the Hilton and International Hotels, Las Vegas; RCA promotional foldout folders; 1971 Elvis Presley wristwatch; the 1966 Boxcar Enterprises Elvis cards; Elvis cards from 1978 (sixty-six cards); bandanas; tote bags with Elvis playing the piano; 1970s Elvis scarf; 1978 Budweiser-beer promo LP "Michelob presents 'Elvis Memories' "; pewter figures, limited edition of three from Perth Pewter, 1977, by Ron Spicel; a gold-record plaque with Elvis in bell-bottom jumpsuit by Mark Freed, A&A Specialties, Boxcar/Factors license; *Graceland* magazine, 1979–, published by an Elvis fan club (Elvis Presley Geselleschaft e.v., Postfach 1264, D-8430 Neumarket 1, Germany); Always Elvis Festival souvenir program, Las Vegas Hilton, September 1978; Elvis tribute radio show five-inch reel-to-reel tapes, 1978/1981; paper organizers with four different covers, $2–5; Elvis puzzles; Elvis plaster busts from Mexico; Elvis styrenes plastic "bronzed" seven-by-seventeen-inch wall plaque with acrylic lacquer; Elvis Presley plate from a lithograph by Adler, from Limoges, France, one-hundred-inch diameter, ten thousand made in 1977; Sun label coasters, three and three-quarters-inches wide, sets of eight; Sun label buttons, two and one-quarter-inches wide;

Elvis clear bottle banks; "J.S.N.Y." marked musical standing figure, ca. 1978–80; The Elvis paperdoll book with a cardboard cutout, 1983; Elvis Presley *auto shade*, $5.99; three bisque Royal Orleans collector's plates and three ten-inch figurines, each a limited edition of twenty thousand (Live in Las Vegas, Aloha From Hawaii, The Mississippi Benefit Concert); Elvis bumper stickers and baseball caps manufactured by Richards and Southern; Elvis Presley wine, one hundred thousand cases of Blanc D'Oro named Always Elvis, an import from Italy by Frontenac Vineyards, $4 a bottle, 1979; a sixteen-by-twenty-inch foil poster by F. J. Warren Limited of England, $24; King of Rock board game, 1979; sepia prints of the King, Ludlow Sales, Inc., $13–15 each; five Elvis Presley limited-edition dolls by World Doll, each created by Joyce Christopher, each twenty-nine inches tall, $100 each; Elvis radio, from Hong Kong, 1977, $20; four collector's mugs of "Hound Dog," "Lonesome Tonight," "Teddy Bear," "Don't Be Cruel"; 1978 bubblegum cards, Topps Gum Company, set of sixty-six (fifteen cents per pack of four); Elvis playing cards, $3–6 per pack, by various makers; commemorative plate by Bill Jacobson, twenty-five thousand, limited edition, $45, with four images of Elvis; 1977 concert photo album of tours, authenticated by Vernon Presley, Fan Club of Great Britain; three wall clocks, an alarm clock, two wristwatches (created 1978–79); "Elvis and Hound Dog" decanters, McCormick Distilling Company, $199.95; Elvis blankets, fifty by sixty or sixty by eighty inches, $30–40, TAC Industries, 1978–80; wooden plaque with clock by Venson & Company, ten by twelve and nineteen by forty inches, $10.95–64.95; hand-painted, porcelain "talking" Elvis figurine, Nostalgia Collectibles, limited edition of twenty-five thousand, $99; a series of Elvis postcards from American Postcard Company, also a line of postcards from Athena International; postcards made by Graceland; Hallmark Cards, Inc., produced a line of Elvis greeting cards, calendars; California Gold Record Company, limited-edition gold-plated record collection series, $89 each;

eight pins and six key chains, Gift Creations; wall paneling by Welsh Forest Products in Memories of Elvis series, four-by-eight-foot and sixteen-by-twenty-four-foot panels, $9.95–20; hand-tinted Elvis Presley Fan Club stationery note cards, ninety-five cents each. In Graceland shops three hundred $2,500 Elvis dolls (originally made in 1982), a $80 vinyl doll, and a $3,000 Elvis grandfather clock sold out. Trinket-type souvenirs and

the more expensive items are all hot sellers.

An Andy Warhol original painting or lithograph of Elvis (1956/1963) is worth several million dollars today; other valuable items include signed contracts by Elvis or the Colonel; signed letters by Elvis, Priscilla, Gladys Presley, or the Colonel; original costumes, clothing, instruments, jewelry, and any other personal items once owned by the King.

Latest Memorabilia (from 1990)

Millions of fans still flock to purchase items made with Elvis's image or name on them. The singer's estate is making millions of dollars annually from the sale and royalty/licensing fees for Elvis products.

With the production and promotion of the U.S. Postal Service's commemorative stamp of Elvis, issued on January 8, 1993, many manufacturing companies jumped on the King's bandwagon, and hundreds of items were created, marketed, and sold during the 1992–93 season. Memorabilia items included a porcelain bust eight and three-quarter inches tall by Goebels, West Germany, 1977 (bisque); three bronze sculptures of Elvis (bronze I, titled "Journey Into Graceland," by Bill Rains, 42 castings, forty-one-inches high, sold for $25,000; bronze II is eighteen inches high, 142 castings, $5,000; and Bronze III is twelve inches tall, 1042 castings, $1,500); limited edition posters of Bill Rains's bronzes of Elvis. In October 1992, the first of 660 Elvis Celebrity Cards (the size of baseball cards) were released by The River Group, P.O. Box 2149, Westport, CT 06880. A set of four cards was on sale in Boston for $12. At a minimum of $3 each in the "hot" market, the 660 cards will

cost collectors an astounding $1,980 and up! Series I, II, and III each contain 220 cards and are sold individually or in twelve-card packs. The 660 cards will complete the fourteen Elvis Collection subsets with some exclusive photos. For $9.95, a fifty-card set commemorating Elvis's platinum and gold records are also available. An album with ten protective sheets, subset dividers, and two five-by-seven King cards on sale for $19.95. The River Group also sold life-size Elvis series I and II posters, full color, at $19.95 each; a limited-edition watch for $19.95; the First Day Cover/Commemorative Medallion set at $24.95; a Deluxe Elvis Collection Album Kit (to protect three-inch cards) for $19.95; "King"-size five-by-seven-inch postcards, a set of twenty-five for $14.95; a special set of fifty cards commemorating Elvis's greatest gold and platinum singles and LPs, $9.95; the Elvis stamp as a 3½-by-½-inch image backed with gold foil, in a Plexiglas case for $5.95; twenty-five Quotable Elvis cards with a Plexiglas card holder, $14.95; and a cotton-polyester-blend T-shirt with Elvis portrait and the gates of Graceland, $12,95. In December a popular item was a

Christmas ornament with the Elvis stamp embossed on it; Elvis silk shirts and blouses; Elvis silk ties in two designs ($20–50); a Find Elvis magic wand, with sparkles, stars, musical notes, and a tiny image of Elvis inside. The Ashton-Drake Galleries of Niles, Illinois, offered in 1993 an "Elvis the '68 Comeback Special" porcelain doll, by artist Lia DiLeo, $99.95; neon 3-D photographs of the King; Elvis glowing pens and pencils; bronze Hallmark full-figure ornaments; Elvis ceramic heads with glowing eyes and fake black hair; Elvis trading stamps (which were included in CDs, LPs, books, ads); Elvis Presley nylons, hand-painted by SoHo (NYC) artists and sold in the streets for $22–44 a pair; ceramic masks, clay art; Halloween costumes; a *Collegeville flag*; umbrellas; handmade ceramic hotels with Elvis's image inside and a placard asking, "Are you lonely tonight?"; stuffed hound dogs with Elvis dog tags; Elvis teddy bears; latex balloons, life-size posters, and Mylar balloons; belt buckles; Avon Products, Inc., porcelain figures; squeaking Elvis seat cushions; plastic cups, figurines, guitars, pianos, and plates; handmade Elvis dolls that range in price from $150 to $2,500; the list goes on and on.

Most of the items listed above were available in 1993. New items of the year included a Commemorative Stamp Watch for $39.99, Fingerhut, St. Cloud, MN, or American Family, Huntington Station, NY 11746; a framed gold replica of the "Love Me Tender" single, $135; ceramic Elvis stein with gold accents illustrating the commemorative stamp, $69.95; a cotton afghan decorated with Elvis images, $49.95; Find Elvis wand filled with liquid in which images float, $7.49; Elvis-stamp desk clock, $49.95; Elvis trading cards, twelve-pack (supposed to retail at $1.49 each but have gone as high as $10 per pack); Elvis glass with the Cat playing a piano; Elvis standing clock; Elvis glow-in-the-dark lamp; Elvis-stamp earrings and

tie tack, $3.99 each; small Elvis jigsaw puzzles, $2.99; hand-painted Elvis shirts and hats (SoHo); ceramic pink Cadillacs; ceramic Elvis figurines; mirrors with Elvis glowing out of them; Elvis etchings and drawings; Elvis hearts; Elvis and teddy bears on posters, ceramic plates, cups; a jigsaw puzzle with various images, $9.95 each; prints, posters, postcards, ranging from $1.20–400; Elvis plate with stamp's image, $29.95; afghans, $9.95–150; from the Washington Mint, Alexandria, VA, a one-ounce Elvis/Graceland silver proof coin, "First Day of Issue" stamped card with postmark with certificate and display case at $29.95 (plus $2.50 postage), offered in February 1993; from the Washington Mint, a registered fourteen-karat-gold edition coin of Elvis/Graceland and the First Day Cover of the postcard with stamp, at $175 (plus $5 postage); from the Washington Mint, a matched set of one silver and one fourteen-karat-gold Elvis/Graceland coin with First Day Cover of the stamp, $195 (no postage). The Bradford Exchange (1-708-966-2770, Niles, Chicago, Illinois) has created exquisite, limited-edition porcelain plates. Each plate is either eight and one-quarter or eight and a half inches in diameter. Edition sizes are usually limited to 150 firing days. Since 1988, five series have been produced and distributed: 1988, "Elvis Presley: Looking at a Legend" (sixteen plates); 1990, "Elvis Presley: In Performance" (twelve plates), "Portraits of the King" (eight plates); 1992, "The Elvis Presley Hit Parade" (six plates), "Elvis Presley on the Big Screen" (six plates). To order available plates call 1-800-323-5577 (the Bradford Exchange's Client Services Department). For current prices of sold-out plates and their availability call the Bradford Exchange's Trading Floor at 1-800-323-8078. When first issued, each plate retails from $24.95–34.75. They go up in value with demand and availability and are well worth the investment.

Movie Memorabilia

To promote Elvis's movies, various companies made items to encourage audiences to rush to theaters to purchase tickets. After Elvis filmed each movie, the masses were showered with Presley gimmickry. The most common items included:

Movie *posters:* three-sheet (42×81 inches), six-sheet (81 inches square), twenty-four-sheet (108×162) inches); *stills* are studio 8×10-inch prints illustrating scenes from a film (black-and-white; some in color); *lobby cards* are 11×14 inches and were made in sets of eight, featuring different film scenes in full color; *window cards* are 14×22 inches; *insert cards* are 14×36 inches; *lobby photos* are 22×28 inches.

BLUE HAWAII (1961): insert card; lobby card; lobby photo; one-sheet; still; window card; and tiki mug.

CHANGE OF HABIT (1969): insert card; lobby card; lobby photo; one-sheet; still; window card.

CHARRO! (1969): insert card; lobby card; lobby photo; one-sheet; still; window card.

CLAMBAKE (1967): insert card; lobby card; lobby photo; one-sheet; still; window card.

DOUBLE TROUBLE (1967): insert card; lobby card; lobby photo; one-sheet; still; window card.

EASY COME, EASY GO (1967): insert card; lobby card; lobby photo; one-sheet; still; window card.

ELVIS ON TOUR (1972): insert card; lobby card; lobby photo; one-sheet; still; window card.

ELVIS, THAT'S THE WAY IT IS (1970): insert card; lobby card; lobby photo; one-sheet; still; window card.

FLAMING STAR (1960): insert card; lobby card; lobby photo; one-sheet; still; window card.

FOLLOW THAT DREAM (1962): insert card; lobby card; lobby photo; one-sheet; still; window card.

FRANKIE AND JOHNNY (1966): insert card; lobby card; lobby photo; one-sheet; still; window card.

FUN IN ACAPULCO (1963): insert card; lobby card; lobby photo; one-sheet; still; window card.

FUN IN ACAPULCO/GIRLS! GIRLS! GIRLS! (a double-bill release in 1966): insert card; lobby card; lobby photo; one-sheet; still; window card.

G.I. BLUES (1960): insert card; lobby card; lobby photo; one-sheet; still; window card; a glass mug with signatures of Elvis and Juliet Prowse.

GIRLS! GIRLS! GIRLS! (1962): insert card; lobby card; lobby photo; one-sheet; still; window card.

GIRL HAPPY (1965): insert card; lobby card; lobby photos; one-sheet; still; window card.

HARUM SCARUM (1965): insert card; lobby card; lobby photo; one-sheet; still; window card.

IT HAPPENED AT THE WORLD'S FAIR (1963): insert card; lobby card; lobby photo; one-sheet; still; window card.

JAILHOUSE ROCK (1957): insert card; lobby card; lobby photo; one-sheet; still; window card. (One of the most desired film collectibles.)

KID GALAHAD (1962): insert card; lobby card; lobby photo; one-sheet; still; window card.

KING CREOLE (1958; and a second run while Elvis was in Germany, 1959): insert card; lobby card; lobby photo; one-sheet; still; window card. (One of the most desired film collectibles.)

KISSIN' COUSINS (1964): insert card; lobby card; lobby photo; one-sheet; still; window card; button that reads, "I'm A Kissin' Cousin."

LIVE A LITTLE, LOVE A LITTLE (1968): insert card; lobby card; lobby photo; one-sheet; still; window card.

LOVE ME TENDER (1956): insert card; lobby card; lobby photo; one-sheet; still; window card; *Theatre Pictorial* (magazine).

LOVING YOU (1957): insert card; lobby card; lobby photo; one-sheet; still; window card.

PARADISE HAWAIIAN STYLE (1966): insert card; lobby card; lobby photo; one-sheet; still; window card.

ROUSTABOUT (1964): insert card; lobby card; lobby photo; one-sheet; still; window card.

SPEEDWAY (1968): insert card; lobby card; lobby photo; one-sheet; still; window card.

SPINOUT (1966): insert card; lobby card; lobby photo; one-sheet; still; window card.

STAY AWAY, JOE (1968): insert card; lobby card; lobby photo; one-sheet; still; window card.

TICKLE ME (1965): insert card; lobby card; lobby photo; one-sheet; still; window card; feather-ended pen; press pack with feathers inside and a list of song titles from the film.

TROUBLE WITH GIRLS (1969): insert card; lobby card; lobby photo; one-sheet; still; window card.

VIVA LAS VEGAS (1964): insert card; lobby card; lobby photo; one-sheet; still; window card.

WILD IN THE COUNTRY (1961): insert card; lobby card; lobby photo; one-sheet; still; window card.

Elvis's rarest placard is from the seventies: "Elvis—Extra Special Show by Popular Demand, Sunday Morning, Sept. 2nd, at 3:00 A.M., a Las Vegas Hilton show." Note the time. Fifty were printed.

Leading Buyers and Sellers of Elvis Memorabilia

Ableser's Fine Jewelers (sells TCB products), 251 N. Beverly Dr., Beverly Hills, CA 90213, (213) 275-3088

Always Elvis, P.O. 528, Dearborn Heights, MI 48127

ARC Promotions, (317) 646-5305

B's Wax, P.O. Box 1803, Greenville, NC 27835-1803

Dave Bushey, 103 Arkansas, Box 473, Hoffman, MN 56339

Erik Christensen, Ved Egedam 13,89- 3400 Hilleroed. Denmark

Collector's Corner, 3521 Walker, Memphis, TN 38111

Colleen's Collectibles, 1482 Oakland Park, Columbus, OH 43224; (614) 261-1585

CVC Collectibles, 12228 Venice Blvd., #219, Los Angeles, CA 90066

Lloyd Davis, P.O. Box 1305, Ashland, OR 97520

Discoveries, P.O. Box 255, Port Townsend, WA 98368

Elvis International, 1000 Quayside, #1910, Miami, FL 33138

Elvis Internat'l Forum, P.O. Box 11203, Burbank, CA 91510

Elvis Memories, 11 St. Matthew's Close, Naburn Village, York YO1 4RT, England

Elvis Presley Enterprises, 3764 Elvis Presley Boulevard, Memphis, TN 38101

Elvis Specialties, Box 504, Pasadena, MD 21122

Elvis World, P.O. Box 388, Bound Brook, NJ 08805

Elvis World, Box 16792, Memphis, TN 38186

Goldmine, Dept. BGD, 700 E. State St., Iola, WI 54990

Graceland, Box 16508, Memphis, TN 38116; (901) 332-3322

Graceland Records, Joe Carter, 209 Main St., Marlborough, MA 01752

Jean Haffner, 5840 Hampton St., St. Louis, MO 63109

Imaine, Suite 168, 30 Jericho Turnpike, Commack, NY 11725

Jerryroll Productions (Elvis books), Box 255, Port Townsend, WA 98363

Linda Jones, 1302 Oak Shadows, Austin, TX 78756

Bob Livingston, Box 140, Vergennes, VT 05491

Nicholas Mele, 168 Jefferson Ave., Harbor Isle, NY 11558

Memories Unlimited, Charles A. Wathen, P.O. Box 2046, Everett, WA 98203

Memory Lane (out-of-print records) 1940 E. University Dr., Tempe, AZ 85281

Metro Music, P.O. Box 10004, Silver Spring, MD 20904-0004

Midnight Records, P.O. Box 390, New York, NY 10011

Orbis, P.O. Box 1, Porishead Bristol BS 20 9EG, England

Walter Piotrowski, 2210 Nightingale, Deerborn, MI 48128

Positively 4th Street, 208 W. Fourth Ave., Olympia, WA 98501

Princeton Record Exchange, 20 S. Tulane St., Princeton, NJ 08542

Helmut Rauch, 1702 W. Belle Plaine, Chicago, IL 60613

Record & Tape Traders, 736 Dulaney Valley Crt., Towson, MD 21204

Rockaway Records, 2390 N. Glendale Blvd., Los Angeles, CA 90039

Rockhouse, Nieuwveenseweg 23, 2421 La Nieuwkoop, Holland; tel: 01725-7132; fax: 73202

Rockin' Robin, 1657 S. Wooster St., Los Angeles, CA 90035

Rock Island, 114 W. Fletcher Ave., Tampa, FL 33612

Rowe's Rare Records, 54 W. Santa Clara

St., San Jose, CA 95113

Dave Slobodian, 4533 Napier St., Burnaby, BC, Canada V5C 3H4; (604) 299-7902

Darryl Stolper, 950 Kagawa St., Pacific Palisades, CA 90272

This Old House, P.O. Box 468, Almont, MI 48003

Times Square Records, P.O. Box 391, Knightsbridge Station, Bronx, NY 10463

Used But Not Abused Records, Box 2456,

Russellville, AR 72801

Vinyl Vendors, 1800 S. Robertson Blvd., #279, Los Angeles, CA 90035

Jack Wolak's Rare Necessities, P.O. Box 88, N. Syracuse, NY 13212

Wooden Indian, The, Graceland Crossing, 3727 Elvis Presley Blvd., Memphis, TN 38116

Worldwide Elvis, Box 10, Brooklandville, MD 21022

Fan Clubs

All for the Love of Elvis, c/o Ilse Oulette, 31 Sheppard St., Fort Leonard-wood, MD 25473

Association of Elvis Presley Fan Clubs, Joyce and Donna Gentry, 5320 53rd Avenue E., Lot Q-47, Bradenton, FL 34203

Because of Elvis Fan Club, 6833 S. Gessner, Box 153, Houston, TX 77035, or 8880 Bellaire, Box 359, Houston, TX 77036

Blueberry Hill Remembers Elvis, 6504 Delmar, St. Louis, MO 63130 (president Joe Edwards)

Blue Hawaiians for Elvis Fan Club, Sue Wiegert, Box 69834, Los Angeles, CA 90069

Burning Love Fan Club, 1904 Williams-burg Dr., Streamwood, IL 60107 (Bill DeNight)

Elvis Always Fan Club, c/o Ann C. Morrison, Route 3, Box 1200, Folkston, GA 31537

Elvis & Friends, 333 W. State, Trenton, NJ 08618

Elvis and Friends, 4017 Route 413, Levittown, PA 19056

Elvis Arkansas-Style Fan Club, c/o Beverly Rook, 11300 Donnie Dr., Mabelvale, AR 72103

Elvis, California Fans, 5 Nona Ave., Freedom, CA 95019 (president—Terry Marcos)

Elvis Chicago Style, Mike Keating, Box 388554, Chicago, IL 60638

Elvis Collector, The, c/o Earl Shilton, P.O. Box 10, Leicester LE9 7FD, England

Elvis Country Fan Club of Texas, 4912 W. Park Dr., Austin, TX 78731-5536 (or Box 9113, Austin, TX 78766)

Elvis Dixieland Fan Club, 1306 Rosedale Dr., Demopolis, AL 36732

Elvis Echoes of Love, 5930 Montibello, Imperial, MO 63052

Elvis Fan Club, Box 4537, Corpus Christie, TX 78469

Elvis Fans from Hoosierland, c/o Sharon Ott, 37 S. Lynhurst, Indianapolis, IN 46241

Elvis Fans United, 110 Graston Ave., Syracuse, NY 13219 (Pat Schwald)

Elvis Fever Fan Club: c/o Anna Mae Meyers, 4014 Keeners Rd., Baltimore, MD 21220

Elvis Forever TCB, P.O., Box 10676, Pinellas Park, FL 34665

Elvis Friends Are the Best Friendship Circle, 3007 Southpoet Ave., Chesapeake, VA 23324; also at 1924 S. Philadelphia St., Amarillo, TX 79103 (Sandy Warehime)

Elvis Friendship Circle, 2908 Juen Lane, Bossier City, LA 71112

Elvis, Heart of Gold Fan Club, P.O. Box 126, Kahoka, MO 63445 (president—Jean Brewer)

Elvis in Canada, c/o Fran Roberts, P.O. Box 6065, Station F, Hamilton, Ontario, Canada L9C 5S2

Elvis International Forum, Box 8383, Van

Nuys, CA 91409

Elvis Is King Fan Club, c/o David Trotter, 59 Cambridge Rd., New Silksworth, Sunderland SR3 2DQ, England

Elvis List (to have your name included in Elvis mailings to and from various fan clubs), P.O. Box 306, Oshkosh, WI 54902

Elvis Lives On, 270 Bronson Way NE, Renton, WA 98056

Elvis Lives On Campaign, Alice Schlichte, P.O. Box 20720, Hennerray Road P.O., Wanchai, Hong Kong; also at 13658 SE 192nd Street, Renton, WA 98058

Elvis Love's Burning, Box 7462, Shreveport, LA 71107

Elvisly Yours, c/o Sid Shaw, P.O. Box 315, London NW10, England

Elvis Memorial Club of Texas, Eddie Fadal, Box 3194, Waco, TX 76707

Elvis Memorial Fan Club of Hawaii, Charlie Ross, Box 15120, Honolulu, HI 96815

Elvis Memorial Society of Syracuse, Sue Fetcho, 411 Mallard Dr., Camillus, NY 13031

Elvis Memories, Box 2401, Livermore, CA 94550

Elvis Memphis Style, P.O. Box 16143, Memphis, TN 38186-0143 (president— Cyndi Sylvia)

Elvis Now Fan Club, The, c/o Sue McCasland, P.O. Box 6581, San Jose, CA 95150

Elvis Now or Never, 123 Ford Street, Boonville, NY 13309 (Kay Brown)

Elvis Place, Box 9, Benton, LA 71006-0009

Elvis Presley Circle City Fan Club; Velda Griner, 2550 Mars Hill St., Indianapolis, IN 46241

Elvis Presley Continentals of Florida: c/o Shirley Schwebs, P.O. Box 1571, Kissimmee, FL 32741

Elvis Presley Fan Club, 25 Ave. Berchem, 1231, Howald, Luxembourg, West Germany

Elvis Presley Fan Club of Australia, c/o Wayne Hawthrone, P.O. Box 82, Elsternwick, Victoria 3185, Australia

Elvis Presley Fan Club of Florida, John

Beach, 2202 James Rd., Jacksonville, FL 32210

Elvis Presley Fan Club of Great Britain: c/o Todd Slaughter, P.O. Box 4, Leicester, England

Elvis Presley Fan Club of Queensland, c/o Katrina Searle, P.O. Box 151, Chermaide, Queensland 4032, Australia

Elvis Presley Fan Club of Rochester, New York, 127 Duxbury Road, Rochester, NY 14626

Elvis Presley Fan Club of Tasmania, c/o Elaine Green, P.O. Box 165, Sorrell 7172, Tasmania, Australia

Elvis Presley Fan Club of the Capital District, Box 265, RD #3, Schenectady, NY 12306

Elvis Presley Fan Club of the Hudson Valley, Betty Stokes, 260 Elvis Presley Blvd., Stone Ridge, NY 12482

Elvis Presley Fan Club of Tokyo, P.O. Box 5, Kasai, Tokyo 134, Japan

Elvis Presley Foundation, Box 1352, Norfolk, VA 23501

Elvis Presley Foundation of NY, Alaine T. Silverman, 130 Jerusalem Ave., Apt. 321, Hempstead, NY 11550

Elvis Presley Gesellschaft e.v., Postfach 1264, D-8430, Neumarkt 1, Germany

Elvis Presley Gesellschaft e.v., Postfach 1929, W-4770, Soest, Germany (Peter Kranzler)

Elvis Presley Home Town Fan Club, c/o Sandra Cottrell, Tupelo, MS 38801

Elvis Presley King "O" Mania Fan Club, c/o Mario Grenier, 552 Croteau Quest, Thetford Mines, Quebec, Canada G6G 6W7

Elvis Presley Memorial Center of Texas, P.O. Box 3194, Waco, TX 76707

Elvis Presley TCB Fan Club of Chicago, c/o Jeanne Kalweit, 4939 Spring Rd., Oak Lawn, IL 60453

Elvis Special, The, Box 1457, Pacifica, CA 94044

Elvis Teddy Bears, The, 744 Caliente Dr., Brandon, FL 33551

Elvis, Thanks for the Memories Fan Club, 228 E. 9 South, Salt Lake City, UT (president—Sylvia Wade)

Elvis, That's the Way It Is Fan Club of Chicago, P.O. Box 189, Franklin Park, IL 60131 (president—Carol Hopp)

Elvis the King Fan Club, 4714 Dundee Dr., Jacksonville, FL 32210

Elvis, This One's for You, c/o Casey Korenek, 11400 February Dr., Austin, TX 78753

Elvis Till We Meet Again Fan Club, c/o Doreen Oldroyd, 124 Rankin Rd., Sault Ste. Marie, Ontario, Canada P6A 4R8

Elvis Today, 8534 S. Keeler Ave., Chicago, IL 60652 (president—Bryan R. Gruszka)

Elvis—Today, Tomorrow & Forever Fan Club, c/o Ray and Diana Hill, P.O. Box 41, Gloucester GL1 2LN, England

Elvis World, Bill Burk, Box 16792, Memphis, TN 38186

Elvis World, Box 388, Bound Brook, NJ 08805

Elvis Worldwide Fan Club, Box 53, Romulus, MI 48174

Elvis Worldwide Memorial Fan Club, 3081 Sunrise, Memphis, TN 38127 (Will McDaniel)

E.P. Continentals, Box 42571, Kissimmee, FL 34742-1571

Eternally Elvis TCB, Inc., 2251 NW Ninety-third Ave., Pembroke Pines, FL 33024 (June Poalillo)

Exclusive Elvis Presley Fan Club, The, Tony and Pearl Cattemull, 30 Addison Rd., Teddington, Middlesex TW11 9EX, England

For the Heart Fan Club, 5004 Lyngail Dr., Huntsville, AL 35810 (president—Steve Camp)

Graceland Express, Box 16508, Memphis, TN 38186

Graceland News, Beth Pease and Josh Cooke, Box 161431, Memphis, TN 38186

Having Fun with Elvis, Judy Dial, 5310 Binz-Engleman Rd., San Antonio, TX 78219

Having Fun with Elvis Fan Club, 5206 Tom Stafford, San Antonio, TX 78219

If I Can Dream Elvis Presley Fan Club, P.O. Box 1032, Cotuit, MA 02635; 13 Artisan Way, Forestdale, MA 02544 (Carol Cabral)

It's Elvis Time, Postbus 27015, 3003 LA, Rotterdam, Holland (Peter Haan)

It's Only Love Elvis Presley Fan Club,

Jack Myers, 266 Harmony Grove Rd., Liburn, GA 30247

Jailhouse Rockers, P.O. Box 570817, Tarzana, CA 91357-0817 (president— Sandy Huszar)

King of Our Hearts, c/o Rosemary Lucci, 6117 Silberman Dr., San Jose, CA 95120; or Irene Maleti, 2445 Fernwood Ave., San Jose, CA 905128

Lawton Fans for Elvis, P.O. Box 1201, Lawton, OK 73502 (president—Todd Padgett)

Let's Be Friends With Elvis, Thaddaeus-Robl-Strasse 9a, 8000 Munich 45, Germany (Sabina and Michael Witzel)

Los Angeles Fans for Elvis, 8806 Villanova Ave., Los Angeles, CA 90045 (president—Sandra Bray)

Love 4 Elvis Fan Club, Fran Colvin, Box 2271, Clifton, NJ 07011- 2271 (president—Fran Colvin)

Memories of Elvis Fan Club, c/o Betty Roloson, 302 Whitman Court, Glen Burnie, MD 210861

Mile High on Elvis Fan Club, Box 2332, Arvada, CO 80001

New Jersey State Association for Elvis, The, c/o Robert Job, 304 Carlton Ave., Piscataway, NJ 08854

New Pen Pal Fan Club, P.O. Box 4236, Bellflower, CA 90706

Official Elvis Presley Fan Club, Western Branch, The, 1220 W. Parkway Ave., W. Valley City, Utah 84119 (president—Randy Knox)

Official Elvis Presley Fan Club Worldwide, c/o Todd Slaughter, P.O. Box 4, Leicester, England (founded in 1956 by Jeannie Seward)

Oklahoma Fans for Elvis, c/o Keith Mitchell, 302 S. Eleventh St., Frederick, OK 73542

Oklahoma Fans for Elvis, c/o Bill and Judy Wilson, 421 W. Sixth St., Bristow, OK 74101

W. Olkowski, Molndalsvagen 27/196, 41263 Göteborg, Sweden

Operation Critters, P.O. Box 543, Mendocino, CA 95460 (president—Mary Etta Duncan)

Presley-Ites Fan Club, The, c/o Kathy Ferguson, 6010 Eighteenth St., Zephyrhills, FL 33540

Presley Nation Fan Club, The, 2941 Sunflower Circle E., Palm Springs, CA 92262

Press'ley Press, The, Box 15230, Milwaukee, WS 53215

Reflections of Elvis, 14210 Schwartz Rd., Grabill, IN 46741

Remembering Elvis Fan Club of Ohio, P.O. Box 674, Arlington, OH 45814 (president—Rita Rund)

Remembering Elvis with TLC in Alabama, 725 Cherokee Trail, Anniston, AL 36206

Return to Sender, 2501 Barclay Ave., Portsmouth, VA 23702

Return to Sender Fan Club, 3446 Dandelion Crescent, Virginia Beach, VA 23456

Suspicious Minds Fan Club, c/o Julie Banhard, 4610 Owen St., Memphis, TN 38122

Taking Care of Business: c/o Gloria Johnson, P.O. Box 1158, Glen Allen, VA 23060

TCB, Box 1925, Pittsfield, MA 01202

TCB Elvis Presley Fan Club of Virginia, Box 1158, Glen Allen, VA 23060

TCB Fan Club, 2103 W. Fiftieth St., Chicago, IL 60609

TCB for Elvis Fan Club, P.O. Box 2655, Gastonia, NC 28053 (president—Joanne Young)

TCB for Elvis in Fans, P.O. Box 2655, Gastonia, NC 28053

TCB for Elvis Presley in Kentucky, c/o Linda Derositt, P.O. Box 21754, Lexington, KY 40522

TCB in South Georgia, 1220 N. Hutchinson Ave., Adel, GA 31620

TCB in West Georgia, 105 S. Meadowcliff Circle, Carrollton, GA 30117 (Kim Outlawa, editor)

Then, Now and Forever, Box 161130, Memphis, TN 38116 (president—Betty Hicks)

Tidskriften Elvis, Box 4506, S-175 04 Jarfalla, Sweden (contact: Ake Flodin)

True Fans for Elvis, 62 Lowell St., S. Portland, ME 04106

True Fans for Elvis Fan Club, c/o Carol Brocher, P.O. Box 681, Saco, ME 04072

Welcome to Our Elvis World, 5648 Arnhem Road, Baltimore, MD 21206 (Pat Carr)

Welcome to Our Elvis World Fan Club, c/o Karen Oberender, 5708 Van Dyke Rd., Baltimore, MD 21206

We Remember Elvis Fan Club, c/o P. Parker, 1215 Tennessee Ave., Pittsburgh, PA 15216

Wonder of You, The, c/o Dorothy Kimes, 277 Magothy Blvd., Pasadena, MD 21122

Young and Beautiful Friends of Elvis, The, Bayonne, NJ 07002 (president—Megan Murphy)

Licensed Manufacturers Authorized by Elvis Presley Enterprises

Advanced Graphics, Pacheco, CA (posters)

S. Alden, Inc., Kansas City, MO (board/trivia games)

Americana Art China Co., Sebring, OH (stein)

American M.W., Inc., Lawndale, CA (greeting card with musical T-shirt)

American Postcard Co., NYC (postcards, paper fans)

Angel Gifts, Fairfield, IA (poster)

Antique Company, Thousand Oaks, CA (prints)

Art One Images, Monterey, CA (poster)

Ashton-Drake Galleries, Niles, IL (porcelain doll)

Athena International, England (posters, postcards, greeting cards)

Avon Products, Inc., NYC (porcelain figurine)

Award Design Metals, Noble, OK (belt buckle)

Azhari Trading Co., NYC (tapestry)

Bradford Exchange, Niles, IL (porcelain plates)

Bradley Time, NYC (wristwatch, alarm clock, wall clock, clock radio with cassette)

Button Up Co., Troy, MI (buttons)

California Gold Record Co., Tustin, CA (gold-plated record)

Celebrity Shade, Long Beach, CA (automobile sunshade)

Clay Art, San Francisco, CA (ceramic masks)

Collegeville Flag, Collegeville, PA (Halloween costumes)

Comptoir Murino, France (umbrellas)

Container Tech, Inc., Barrington, IL (life-size posters, latex balloons, Mylar balloons)

Creative Accessories, Ltd., Bellmore, NY (mirrored acrylic)

Custom Images, Inc., St. Charles, IL (silk-screened mirror and glass)

D&G Philatelic, Inc., W. Hempstead, NY (commemorative stamp)

Danbury Mint, Norwalk, CT (porcelain doll)

Danilo Promotions, London, England (calendar)

Delphi, Niles, IL (porcelain plates)

Dixie Seal and Stamp Co., Atlanta, GA (signs, license plate)

W. J. Duncan, LTD, Victoria, Australia (miscellaneous items)

Elvis, West Haven, CN (life-size posters, cards sets, watches)

Elvis Presley Museum, Franklin, TN (museum, traveling exhibit)

Ernst, Escondido, CA (collector plates)

Eugene Doll and Novelty, Brooklyn, NY (vinyl, porcelain, and plastic dolls)

Sally Evans Collection, Crown Point, NJ (prints painted)

G&E Distributing, Inc. (dba Elvis Gold Limited) Knoxville, TN (framed 45-rpm gold record)

Gift Creations, N. Hollywood, CA (key chains, pins)

Glen Gary Associates, Newbury Park, CA (postcards, photographs, posters)

Great American Gift Co., New Rochelle, NY (glassware, money clip, weather thermometer, glassware)

Hallmark Cards, Inc., Kansas City, MO (satin pillow, posters, puzzle, campaign buttons, greeting cards, calendars, postcards)

Shelley Husta, Evanston, IL (museum, original artifacts)

Ideal Decor, Zurich, Switzerland (poster)

International Custom Design, Denver, CO (T-shirts)

JKA Specialties, Vincetown, NJ (celluloid picture buttons)

K&M, Inc., Memphis, TN (souvenir items)

Landmark General, Novato, CA (calendar)

Lapin Products, Asbury Park, NJ (toy 1950 pink Cadillac, toy touring van, three different toy guitars)

Legends in Concert, Las Vegas, NV (concert re-creation)

Lenan Company, Hollywood, FL (suede ribbons, T-shirts, posters, Tribute in Blue program)

Ludlow Sales, NYC (postcards, sepia framed prints)

Marketcom, Inc., St. Louis, MO (posters)

McCormick Distilling Co., Weston, MO (ceramic decanters)

Paul Miller Commemoratives, Marietta, GA (prints)

Mobile Merchandising, LTD, London, England (T-shirts)

Modern Crafts Marketing, Ogallala, NE (latch-hook wall covering, latch-hook pillow)

Movie Ad Corp., Coral Springs, FL (stationery, envelopes, note cards, greeting cards, stick-on seals, memo sheets, sepia art prints)

Nardico Western Sculpture, Garland, TX (carved Italian terra stone)

Nathan, NYC (character puzzle)

National Historic Mint, Westbury, NY (commemorative medallion, belt buckle)

Natural Choice Industries, Westlake Village, CA (body and hair care products)

New Lugene's Inc., Branson, MS (beer

mugs, old-fashioned glasses, shot glasses)

Nexu, Wabash, NJ (sweat and T-shirts)

Nostalgia Collectibles, Northbrook, IL (electronic "talkie" plates, mugs)

Nugeron, Perret, France (postcards, novelty boxes, miniposters)

Omni Group Cruises, Hollywood, CA (cruise-ship package)

On-The-Road, Tarzana, CA (replica street sign)

Orbis, London, England (musical pop-up book)

Orion Press, Tokyo, Japan (cardboard prints)

Pearl Enterprises, Memphis, TN (retail and mail-order fiftieth-anniversary commemorative grandfather clocks, two versions)

PM & Company, San Bernardino, CA (art enamel pins)

Portal Publications, Corte Madera, CA (posters, note cards)

Bill Rains Productions, Billings, MT (bronze statue, porcelain statue, postcards, poster)

Ramallah Wholesale, Brisbane, CA 94005

Rauch Industries, Inc., Gastonia, NC (Christmas ornament)

R.B.S., North Brunswick, NJ (framed prints, satin jackets)

Reed Productions, San Francisco, CA (spiral pad, pocket covers, postcards)

Reflex Marketing, Herts, England (laminated prints)

Richards and Southern, Goodlettsville, TN (pens, pencils, datebook, place mats, postcards, baseball cap, bumper sticker)

Ricordi, Milano, Italy (postcards, posters, note cards)

The River Group, Westport, CT (limited-edition fifty-card set, card album, post-ers, watch, protective sheets for cards, life-size poster, five-by-seven-inch King cards, etc.)

Royal Orleans, New Orleans, LA (limited-edition lithograph, Christmas ornaments, porcelain plate and figurines)

Scandecor International, Uppala, Sweden (posters)

Schylling, Ipswich, MA (Elvis magic wand)

Starr Associates, NYC (doll)

TAC Industries, NYC (blankets)

Tomy Corporation, Carson, CA (figural mugs)

Topperscot, Inc., Denver, CO (Christmas ornament)

Unique Plastics Co., Portland, OR (decoupage plaques and clocks)

United States Postal Service (commemorative stamp; Elvis limited-edition print; first-day-ceremony program; Elvis commemorative album; stamp sheet and stamp saver; watch; afghan; porcelain stein; throw, fifty by sixty-seven inches; first-day postcards)

USA Corp., Old Hickory, TN (plastic jet)

Venson and Company, Santa Cruz, CA (*decoupage* clocks and plaques)

Verkerke, Rigi, Switzerland (posters, pennant posters)

Walker-McNeil, Marlborough, CT (music box)

F. J. Warren, Hertfordshire, England (gold record)

Washington Mint, Alexandria, VA (first-day-issue commemorative stamp with a silver/gold proof set)

Welsh Forest Products, Memphis, TN (wood paneling)

Yorkshire Company, Glen Ellyn, IL (plush hound dog)

Zippo Manufacturing Company, Bradford, PA (commemorative lighter)

Elvis-Related Sights for Fans and Tourists

1. Alfred's, 197 Beale St., features Elvis memorabilia, gold records, and a model of Graceland.
2. Baptist Memorial Hospital, 899 Madison Ave., Memphis, TN.
3. Barris Kustom Industries, where Elvis's custom Cadillac was created. Located at 10811 Riverside Dr., N. Hollywood, CA. (213) 877-2352.
4. Bits and Beau's Boutique, once owned and managed by Priscilla Presley, was located at 9650 Santa Monica Blvd. in Los Angeles, CA. Giannino's Italian fast-food restaurant is now at the location.
5. Boomland, run by Wallace Reeves, at I-57, exit 10, Charleston, MO, has some of Elvis's cars on display and other memorabilia. (314) 683-6108).
6. Buford Pusser Home & Museum has a lot of Elvis memorabilia. Pusser St., Adamsville, TN. (901) 632-4080.
7. Celebrity Room, run by Gus Serafim in his restaurant, features a fifty-seat room filled with Elvis memorabilia (photos, shirts, albums), 7515 Brook Rd., Richmond, VA. (804) 266-3328.
8. Chiska (Chickasaw) Hotel, where Dewey Phillips broadcast "Red, Hot and Blue" from the mezzanine, 272 S. Main St., Memphis, TN.
9. Church of Elvis, a twenty-four-hour coin-operated establishment, which is a part of an art gallery called "Where's the Art"; some inventive images of the King are enticing and fun; 219 SW Ankeny St., Portland, OR. Run by Stephanie Pierce.
10. Circle G Ranch, which Elvis owned (renamed Flying Circle G), 163 acres in Walls, MS. (601) 781-1411.
11. Eddie Fadal's home (an Elvis mini-museum) at 2807 Lasker Ave., off I-35, Waco, TX. (817) 776-5388. The house is open for tours by appointment and features a huge brightly colored stained-glass window.
12. Elvis, Elvis, Elvis, the All Elvis Shop, International Marketplace, 2330 Kalakaua, HI. (808) 923-5847. Some items are not for sale (such as the four bottles of Always Elvis wine!), but most items can be purchased.
13. *Tupelo, Mississippi.* Elvis Presley birthplace, 306 Elvis Presley Dr. (it was 306 Old Saltillo); 9–5:30 P.M., Monday–Saturday, May–Sept., alongside the Elvis Presley Memorial Chapel with stained-glass panel, the Elvis Presley (Youth) Center, and Elvis Presley Park. Admission: $1 adults; fifty cents under twelve. Also see other local Elvis attractions including the fairgrounds; WELO radio station; the Lawhon Elementary School (140 Lake St., E. Tupelo); the Milam Junior High School (720 West Jefferson, corner of Gloster); the First Assembly of God Church, 206 Adams St. (now the First Apostolic Church of Jesus Christ); the Lyric Theater at N. Broadway and Court streets (the Strand Theater is no longer in existence); Leake and Goodlett lumberyard, 105 E. Main St.; Long's Cleaners, 130 E. Main St.; Tupelo Garment Company; the Elvis McDonald's, 372 S. Gloser, south of Main St.; Elvis Presley Lake and Campground, five miles north of his birthplace, off Canal Extended, north of New Highway 78 (admission $1, campsites are $5–10 a night); Roy Martin's Groceries, Lake Street at Highway 78 and N. Saltillo Rd.; Priceville Cemetery, where Jesse Ga-

ron is buried, on Feemster Lake Rd.; Tupelo Hardware, 114 W. Main at N. Front St.; Tupelo Museum, Ballard Park, off Highway 6, west of town, (601) 841-6438.

14. Elvis Presley Impersonators International Association Convention. For information on times, dates, locations, call (708) 297-1234.

15. Elvis Presley Memorial Trauma Center, 877 Jefferson Ave., Memphis, TN 38130. (901) 575-8372.

16. Elvis Presley Museum, 5700 Highway 192, Kissimmee, FL; two and a half miles east of Disney World in the Old Town Mall. Open ten A.M. to ten P.M. daily; admission, $4 adults, $3 children. Run by Jimmy Velvet. (407) 396-8594.

17. Elvis Presley Museum, run by Mike Moon in Ontario, Canada, opened in 1979. It has Priscilla and Elvis's honeymoon Cadillac, X rays of Elvis's hands, and other interesting items. Located at Maple Leaf Village Mall, off Clifton Hill. (416) 357-0008.

18. Elvis Presley Museum, run by Mike Moon, Highway 441 on the parkway, one block south of Ogle's Water Park, Pigeon Forge, TN. Many interesting items shown. Nine A.M. to ten P.M. daily. (615) 453-6499.

19. The Elvis Presley Museum, opened by impersonator Vince Everett, is in London, England, near Rising Sun Pub at 46 Tottenham Court. Sundays feature Elvis music. Paul Chan, a Chinese Elvis impersonator, does his act at two Graceland Palace restaurants in London.

20. Elvis Presley Museum in Munkerdale, Sweden (opened in 1984), on the E-6, on the route to Oslo, Norway.

21. Elvis Presley Plaza, Beale Street, Memphis, TN. (901) 526-0110

22. Germany. 14 Goethestrasse is where the Presleys stayed during Elvis's Army stint. A doctor now lives in the five-bedroom, stucco home in Bad Neuheim. In Friedberg, Elvis's hair and the comb the barber used to cut

his million-dollar locks are still on display at Ray Barracks.

23. *Graceland.* 3764 Elvis Presley Blvd., Memphis, TN. Elvis Presley's cherished home, which features some of the original furnishings (although most of the furniture has been changed numerous times since his death); plus his recording studio; trophy room; racquetball courts; and Meditation Garden; as well as costume and memorabilia displays; cars; garages; pool; and movie scripts. Daily tours are given every ten minutes. Packages are available for all the sights at $15.95 (adults), $14.35 (Seniors), $10.95 (children); Graceland only costs $7.95/$7.20/$4.75. (Directed by Mr. Jack Soden.)

Other Graceland attractions:

The Elvis Presley Automobile Museum at Highway 51 Drive-In features a ten-minute film by Steve Binder; $4.50/$4.05/$2.50.

The *Lisa Marie*, a Convair 880 jet, made in December 1958, features original furnishings and the famous TCB logo; self-guided tour; $4.25/$3.80/$2.75.

The Tour Bus, refurbished by George Barris. Complete with pillows and bed. Owned by Jim Sturm, on loan to Graceland, $1 admission for all.

The Elvis Up-Close Museum is behind glass and offers some furnishings, a gold-plated telephone, videotapes, and miscellaneous memorabilia. $1.75 each (not worth it).

If I Can Dream film clips, $1.50 each ticket.

For information call (800) 238-2000 or (901) 332-3322. Write P.O. Box 16508, 3734 Elvis Presley Blvd., Memphis, TN 38116-0508. Hours: June–August, 8 A.M.–7 or 8 P.M., September–April, 9 A.M.–6 P.M.; May, 8 A.M.–6 P.M. Closed on Thanksgiving, Christmas, New Year's Day, and Tuesdays from November to February. Elvis's birthday is celebrated January 8 each year, and a vigil in memory of Elvis takes place on August 16.

The Best Graceland Gift Shops:
EP's LPs
The 880 Echo Papa Gift Shop
The 50% Off Gift Shop
The Gotta Get to Memphis Gift
    Shop
The Graceland Gift Shop
The Graceland Photo Shop
The Relive and Magic Museum and
    Gift Shop

24. Grand Guitar Museum, 535 New Kingsport Highway, Nashville, TN. (615) 968-1719.
25. Guinness World Records Exhibition Center, on Highway 441 in Gatlinburg, TN, features two Elvis photos, and TCB touring jackets, (615) 436-9100. The World of Illusions, on Highway 441, Gatlinburg, TN, has an illusion of Elvis singing (615) 436-9701; Stars Over Gatlinburg at Reagan Terrace Mall, on Highway 441, Gatlinburg, TN, has wax figures of Elvis.
26. **Hollywood, California.**
     Next to the Bel Air Country Club, at 565 Perugia Way, stood the home that Elvis rented, and where he entertained the Beatles in 1965. The original house Elvis rented has been demolished.
     Residences at 1059 Bellagio Rd. (difficult to find) and 10550 Rocca Place are not worth seeking out. The first home Elvis bought in California is located in Trousdale Estates, at 1174 Hillcrest Rd. With its original iron gate, the property is difficult to see beyond the walls. Eventually, this home was where Elvis stayed while Priscilla roomed at 144 Monovale Rd. in Holmby Hills (during the Presleys' divorce). The Hillcrest Rd. home was sold in 1975 to Telly Savalas, who put a tennis court in the front yard.
     CBS Television City, where "The Ed Sullivan Show" was filmed, is located at Fairfax Ave. and Beverly Blvd., Los Angeles.
     Paramount Studios, where Elvis began his film career, is located at 5451 Marathon St., Hollywood, CA.
     NBC Studios, where Elvis performed his Christmas special in 1968, is at 3000 West Alameda Ave., Burbank, CA.
     Radio Recorders is now where Studio 56 Productions is located, at 7000 Santa Monica Blvd.
     Elvis's star (actually a record) is at 6777 Hollywood Blvd., east of Highland Ave.
     Hollywood's Wax Museum at 6767 Hollywood Blvd. has a wax figure of the King in a pink jumpsuit.
27. The home in which Elvis recorded in September 1973, was willed to Lisa Marie, who sold it to Frankie Valli for $385,000. It is located at 825 Chino Canyon Rd., Palm Springs, CA. At 1350 Leaders Circle is the home where Elvis and Priscilla "honeymooned." Colonel Parker's home was located nearby at 116 Vista Verpera Dr.
28. Elvis and his family lived in apartment 328 on the first floor of Lauderdale Courts, 185 Winchester St., east of Third Ave., Memphis, TN. (See list of addresses for other residence locations.)
29. L.C. Humes High School, 659 North

Manassas Ave., features an Elvis Presley room with a golden bust of Elvis. Call Loretta Griffin at (901) 543-6700, ext. 6695, for appointment.

30. Lansky's Clothier to the King, 126 Beale St., Memphis, TN; call for appointment (901) 525-1521.

31. *Las Vegas, Nevada.*

The Presleys' wedding ceremony was held at the Aladdin Hotel in the second-floor suite of Milton Prell, who owned the hotel (now co-owned by Wayne Newton), at 3667 Las Vegas Blvd. South. The room can be rented, but no one is certain *which* room it is! Figure that one out! For appointment and reservations call (800) 634-3424.

The New Frontier Hotel (where Elvis debuted in April 1956) is now called the Frontier. There is no longer a Venus Room (where Elvis performed), and the hotel has been completely redecorated. Located at 3120 Las Vegas Blvd. South, (800) 643-6966.

The Flamingo Hotel, where *Viva Las Vegas* scenes were shot with Elvis and Ann-Margret, is located at 3555 Las Vegas Blvd. South. The Tropicana, at 3801 Las Vegas Blvd. South was another luxury hotel that Elvis frequented.

The Las Vegas Hilton (formerly the International until 1971) was where Elvis made his flamboyant comeback. The documentary film *Elvis, That's the Way It Is* was filmed here, and Priscilla said "so long" to Elvis at this hotel. Elvis stayed on the thirtieth floor in the Imperial Suite (renamed the Elvis Presley Suite). The room is available only to celebrities. A large bronze statue of Elvis by Carlo Romanelli and a bronze guitar are located at the Hilton. Address: 3000 Paradise Rd. For reservations and information call (800) 732-7117. This is *not* the Flamingo Hilton on Las Vegas Blvd. Don't get the two hotels confused.

Elvis and his crew stayed on the top floor of the Sahara Hotel, at 2535 Las Vegas Blvd. South, (800) 634-6666.

Jon Bon Jovi, an avid Elvis fan, was married at the Graceland Wedding Chapel in 1989. For a $150 fee, any couple can be married in the chapel and hear a half hour of singing by an Elvis impersonator (Johnny Lawson or Nick Guerrero). Elvis and Priscilla's wedding license is displayed. Located at 619 Las Vegas Blvd. South. To reserve a date and time for a ceremony call (702) 382-0091.

If you want to see Elvis impersonators at their best (and hear a variety), go to Vegas World at 2000 Las Vegas Blvd., (702) 383-5264, or the Imperial Palace, located at 3535 Las Vegas Blvd. (across from Casears Palace). Phone for reservations (800) 634-6441.

32. Libertyland, off Eastern Parkway, between Central and Southern avenues, Memphis, TN, features Elvis impersonators. Hours vary; (901) 274-1776.

33. London Wax Museum, 5505 Gulf Blvd., St. Petersburg Beach, FL, (813) 360-6985, has a wax figure of Elvis on display.

34. *Memphis locations where Elvis sang:*

Bon Air Club, 1850 S. Bellevue Blvd.
Eagle's Nest (no longer exists, Highway 78)
Katz Drug Store, 2256 Lamar Ave. (now an American Thrift Store)
Overton Park Shell, N. Parkway and E. Parkway
Ellis Auditorium, Main St. and Exchange
Stax recording studio, 625 E. McLemore Ave. (demolished in 1991)
Mid-South Coliseum, in the fairgrounds, next to Libertyland, northeast of the intersection of Southern Ave. and E. Parkway.

◄ Elvis registering at the Sahara Hotel in Las Vegas. *Courtesy of John Reible, Las Vegas News Bureau, Las Vegas, Nevada.*

Places Elvis worked in Memphis:

Crown Electric Company (was at 353 Poplar Ave.)

Loew's State Theater, 152 S. Main

Marl Metal Manufacturing Company, 208 Georgia Ave.

Upholsteries Specialties Co., 210 W. Georgia Ave.

M. B. Parker Machinists Shop, 1449 Thomas

Precision Tool, 1132 Kansas St.

35. Memphis Memories, an all-Elvis shop in Levittown, PA. Contact Ron and Linda Cade, 4017 Route 413, Levittown, PA 19056. (215) 943-4089. Hours vary. Mail-order catalog, $2.

36. The Memphis Police Museum, 159 Beale St., Memphis, TN, features some memorabilia. No admission.

37. Memphis Recording Services/Sun Studio, 706 Union St., Memphis, TN 38103. (901) 521-0664. Tours are $4, adults; $3, children; 9 A.M.–7 P.M. daily.

38. Murdo Pioneer Auto Museum, 503 Fifth St., Murdo, SD. (605) 669-2691. Elvis's auto and Harley motorcycle are on display. Run by Dave Geisler.

39. **Nashville, Tennessee.**

The Car Collector's Hall of Fame has Elvis's Eldorado from 1976. Located at 1534 Demonbreun St., on Music Row. (615) 255-6804.

The Country Music Hall of Fame features Elvis's 1928 gold-leaf Kimball grand piano and Organ system, Elvis's gold-white Fleetwood Cadillac, Elvis's gold-lamé jacket, and other memorabilia. At 4 Music Square, (615) 256-1639; open June–August from 8 A.M.–8 P.M.; September–May, 9 A.M.–5 P.M. $6 admission, subject to change. This is a *definite* must for collectors, fans, historians, or the curious. The Country Music Hall of Fame has many interesting displays. Visit their large country-music shop.

Country Music Wax Museum & Shopping Mall, with a figure of Elvis, 118 Sixteenth Ave. South; $4 adults;

$1.75 children.

Elvis Museum and Gift Shop, run by Jimmy Velvet, 1520 Demonbreun St., on Music Row, (615) 256-8311. Hours, 8 A.M.–10 P.M. daily. Very small and extremely commercial, but the people are pleasant and friendly. (*Note:* The museum that Jimmy Velvet runs in Nashville is not a museum. It is a one-room shop where memorabilia is sold.)

Music Valley Wax Museum of the Stars, off Briley Parkway at 2515 McGavock Pike; $3.50 adults; $1.50 children.

RCA's Studio B, at Roy Acuff Place and Music Square West (formerly Hawkins St. at Seventeenth Ave.). Admission is free with ticket proof from the Country Music Hall of Fame.

Ryman Auditorium, Fifth Ave. North, (615) 254-1445. Admission is $2 for adults; $1 for children.

Television News Archives, Vanderbilt University Library, contains network news coverage of Elvis from 1955 to 1977. West End Ave., north off of I-440. For an appointment call (615) 322-2927.

40. The Willie Nelson Showcase, with displays of Elvis and J. D. Sumner memorabilia. Music Village Blvd., Twitty City, TN. (615) 882-1800.

41. Nudie's Rodeo Tailors, where Elvis's gold-lamé outfit from RCA was made, located at 5015 Lankershim Blvd. N. Hollywood, CA. For appointment call (213) 877-9505.

42. Paradise Gardens, run by Rev. Howard Finster, in Summerville, GA, east off Highway 27. Features Elvis folk art.

43. Sam Phillips Recording Service, Inc., 639 Madison Ave., Memphis, TN.

44. Pigeon Forge, TN, "A Salute to Elvis," Memories Theater, Parkway, Highway 441. (615) 428-7852.

45. RCA Studios at 155 E. Twenty-fourth St., New York City, is where Elvis recorded "Don't Be Cruel" and "Hound Dog" in 1956.

46. Sierra 76 Truck Shop, 200 N. McCarran Blvd., I-80, exit 19, Sparks, NV, has a large collection of Elvis jewelry, handguns, and photos.
47. Taylor's Restaurant, 710 Union Ave., Memphis, TN (next to Sun studios), is now named Sun Studio Cafe.
48. The Fantastic Museum in Redmond, Oregon, owns Elvis's first guitar (so advertised). For an appointment call (503) 923-0000.
49. University of Mississippi Blues Archives, in Oxford, MS, (601) 232-7753. Room 340, Farley Hall, Mon.–Fri., 8:30–5:00.
50. Warwick Hotel (where Elvis stayed in room 527 in 1956) is located at 65 West Fifty-fourth St., New York City. For appointment or reservations call (212) 247-2700. Elvis's room is $160–200 a night.
51. WMPS, where Bob Neal broadcast, is at 112 Union St., Memphis, TN.
52. World Tattoo Gallery at 1255 S. Wabash St., Chicago, IL. For an appointment call (312) 939-2222. They hold an Elvis-oriented tattoo art exhibit every December.

Courtesy of the Country Music Foundation Library and Media Center, Nashville, Tennessee.

PART VI

Records, CDs, and Videos

◄Elvis with Bonita Cole and B. B. King. *Photograph by Ernest C. Withers.*
Copyright © 1994 Mimosa Productions, Inc.

▲ Elvis surrounded by teenage fans at the Ellis Auditorium in Memphis, Tennessee. *Photograph by Ernest C. Withers. Copyright © 1994 Mimosa Records Productions, Inc.*

RECORDS, CDs, AND VIDEOS

Elvis's songs have been on *Billboard*'s Top 100, Rhythm & Blues (R&B), Country, Easy-Listening, and Best-Selling charts. During his life, 114 of Elvis's songs were listed in the Top 40; 40 were Top 10; 18 were No. 1 with a total of eighty weeks in that position; and 90 albums hit the charts (not including bootlegs). Over *1.5 billion* of his records have been sold to date.

Gold records: Singles and extended-play albums must sell more than 1 million units in order to qualify as a gold record; long-playing albums must sell more than $1 million worth of records to qualify (through December 31, 1974). After January 1, 1975, a gold LP CD was required to sell over five hundred thousand units.

Note: RIAA is an abbreviation for Recording Industry Association of America.

Posthumous RIAA Awards for U.S. LPs

Elvis in Concert, released 10/77, Platinum Award

He Walks Beside Me, Favorite Songs of Faith and Inspiration, released 2/78, Gold Award

Elvis: A Legendary Performer, Vol. 3, released 11/78, Gold Award

Memories of Christmas, released 8/82, Gold Award

The Number One Hits, released 6/87, Gold Award

The Top Ten Hits, released 6/87, Gold Award

The King of Rock-n-Roll, released 6/92, Gold Award

Gold Record Singles

(years given are date recorded)

1956:
"Heartbreak Hotel"
"I Was the One"
"I Want You, I Need You, I Love You"
"Don't Be Cruel"
"Hound Dog"

"Any Way You Want Me"
"Love Me Tender"

1957:
"Too Much"
"Playing for Keeps"
"All Shook Up"
"Treat Me Nice"
"Don't"

"Teddy Bear"
"Loving You"
"Jailhouse Rock"
"That's When Your Heartaches Begin"
"I Beg of You"

1958:

"One Night"
"Wear My Ring Around Your Neck"
"Hard Headed Woman"
"I Got Stung"

1959:

"I Need Your Love Tonight"
"A Big Hunk o' Love"
"(Now and Then There's) A Fool Such As I"

1960:

"It's Now or Never"
"A Mess of Blues"
"Stuck on You"
"Are You Lonesome Tonight?"
"Wooden Heart"
"I Gotta Know"

1961:

"I Feel So Bad"
"Little Sister"
"Can't Help Falling in Love"
"Surrender"
"(Marie's the Name) His Latest Flame"
"Rock-A-Hula-Baby"

1962:

"Where Do You Come From?"
"Anything That's a Part of You"
"She's Not You"
"Return to Sender"
"Good Luck Charm"
"I Feel So Bad"

1963:

"Bossa Nova Baby"
"One Broken Heart for Sale"
"(You're the) Devil in Disguise"

1964:

"Kissin' Cousins"
"Ain't That Loving You Baby"
"Blue Christmas"
"Viva Las Vegas"

1965:

"Crying in the Chapel"
"Puppet on a String"
"I'm Yours"

1966:

"Frankie and Johnny"

"Love Letters"
"Spinout"
"Tell Me Why"
"All That I Am"
"If Every Day Was Like Christmas"

1967:

"Indescribably Blue"
"Big Boss Man"

1968:

"Stay Away"
"Let Yourself Go"
"If I Can Dream"
"Guitar Man"
"We Call on Him"
"Almost in Love"

1969:

"His Hand in Mine"
"Charro"
"In the Ghetto"
"Suspicious Minds"
"Don't Cry, Daddy"
"Clean Up Your Own Back Yard"

1970:

"The Wonder of You"
"Mama Likes the Roses"
"You Don't Have to Say You Love Me"
"Kentucky Rain"
"I've Lost You"
"Patch It Up"
"I Really Don't Want to Know"

1971:

"Where Did They Go, Lord"
"Only Believe"
"I'm Leavin' "
"It's Only Love"

1972:

"Burning Love"
"Separate Ways"
"American Trilogy"

1973:

"Raised on Rock"

1974:

"It's Midnight"
"Take Good Care of Her"

1975:

"T-R-O-U-B-L-E"
"My Boy"

1976:

"Hurt"

1977:

"Way Down"
"My Way"

Single Top 10 Hits During Elvis's Life

Note: Although Elvis is listed as a contributing writer on various songs, it is doubtful he actually wrote any song. His name was added to songs by Colonel Tom Parker in order to make Elvis more viable as a "musician" and to tie up royalty rights.

Songs are listed by date of chart debut.

Abbreviations used: RD (recording date); CD (chart debut); PCP (peak chart position); Gold or Platinum, as certified by RIAA.

"Heartbreak Hotel": RD 1-10-56; CD 3-3-56; PCP No. 1 (Mae Axton, Tommy Durden, Elvis Presley); Platinum. It took ten weeks to hit No. 1.

"I Want You, I Need You, I Love You": RD 4-11-56; CD 5-26-56; PCP No. 1 (Maurice Mysels, Ira Kosloff); Platinum

"Hound Dog": RD 7-2-56; CD 8-4-56; PCP No. 1 (Jerry Leiber, Mike Stoller); 3x Platinum

"Don't Be Cruel": RD 7-2-56; CD 8-4-56; PCP No. 1 (Otis Blackwell; Elvis Presley); 3x Platinum

"Love Me Tender": RD 8-2-56 or 9-24-56; CD 10-20-56; PCP No. 1 (composed by Ken Darby, but credited to Elvis and Darby's wife, Vera Matson) 2x Platinum

"Love Me": RD 9-1-56; CD 11-17-56; PCP No. 2 (Jerry Leiber; Mike Stoller); Platinum

"Too Much": RD 9-2-56; CD 1-26-57; PCP No. 1 (Lee Rosenberg, Bernard Weinman); Platinum

"All Shook Up": RD 1-12-57; CD 4-6-57; PCP No. 1 (Otis Blackwell; Elvis Presley); 2x Platinum. It reached No. 1 in three weeks and went from No. 6 to No. 1 in one week.

"Teddy Bear": RD 1-24-57; CD 4-6-57; PCP No. 1 (Kal Mann, Bernie Lowe); Platinum

"Jailhouse Rock": RD 4-30-57; CD 10-14-57; PCP No. 1 (Jerry Leiber, Mike Stoller); 2x Platinum

"Don't": RD 9-6-57; CD 1-27-58; PCP No. 1 (Jerry Leiber, Mike Stoller); Platinum

"I Beg of You": RD 2-23-57; CD 1-27-58; PCP No. 8 (Rose Marie McCoy, Kelly Owens); Platinum

"Wear My Ring Around Your Neck": RD 2-1-58; CD 4-21-58; PCP No. 2 (Bert Carroll, Russell Moody); Platinum. *Note:* "Wear My Ring Around Your Neck" entered *Billboard*'s Top 100 chart at No. 7, stayed on the chart for fifteen weeks, but never reached the No. 1 position.)

"Hard Headed Woman": RD 1-15-58; CD 6-30-58; PCP No. 1 (Claude DeMetrius); Platinum

"One Night": RD 2-23-57; CD 11-3-58; PCP No. 1 (Dave Bartholomew, Pearl King); Platinum

"I Got Stung": RD 6-11-58; CD 11-3-58; PCP No. 8 (Aaron Schroeder, David Hill); Platinum

"A Fool Such As I": RD 6-10-58; CD 3-23-59; PCP No. 2 (Bill Trader); Platinum

"I Need Your Love Tonight": RD 6-10-58; CD 3-30-59; PCP No. 4 (Sid Wayne, Bix Reichner); Platinum

"A Big Hunk o' Love": RD 6-10-58; CD 7-6-59; PCP No. 1 (Aaron Schroeder, Sid Wyche); Gold

"Stuck on You": RD 3-21-60; CD 4-4-60; PCP No. 1 (Aaron Schroeder, J. Leslie McFarland); Platinum. The song leaped from No. 6 to No. 1 in one week.

"It's Now or Never": RD 4-3-60; CD 7-18-60; PCP No. 1 (Aaron Schroeder, Wally Gold; based on the Italian song " 'O Sole Mio" written in 1901 by G. Capurro and Eduardo Di Capua); Platinum

"Are You Lonesome Tonight?": RD 4-4-60; CD 11-14-60; PCP No. 1 (Roy Turk, Lou Handman, 1926); 2x Platinum.

It took three weeks to reach No. 1, but it leaped from No. 35 to No. 2 within eight days.

"Surrender": RD 10-30-60; CD 2-20-61; PCP No. 1 (Doc Pomus, Mort Shuman); Platinum

"I Feel So Bad": RD 3-12-61; CD 5-15-61; PCP No. 5 (Chuck Willis); Gold

"Little Sister": RD 6-26-61; CD 8-21-61; PCP No. 5 (Doc Pomus, Mort Shuman); Gold

"His Latest Flame": RD 6-26-61; CD 8-28-61; PCP No. 4 (Doc Pomus, Mort Shuman); Gold

"Can't Help Falling in Love": RD 3-23-61; CD 12-4-61; PCP No. 2 (George Weiss, Hugo Peretti, Luigi Creatore); Platinum

"Good Luck Charm": RD 10-15-61; CD 3-17-62; PCP No. 1 (Aaron Shroeder, Wally Gold); Platinum

"She's Not You": RD 3-19-61; CD 8-4-62; PCP No. 5 (Doc Pomus, Jerry Leiber, Mike Stoller); Gold

"Return to Sender": RD 3-7-62; CD 10-20-62; PCP No. 2. On *Billboard*'s Hot 100 chart for sixteen weeks and No. 2 for five weeks. (Otis Blackwell, Winfield Scott); Platinum

"One Broken Heart for Sale": RD 9-62; CD 3-63; PCP No. 11 (Otis Blackwell, Winfield Scott); Platinum

"Devil in Disguise": RD 5-16-63; CD 6-29-63; PCP No. 3 (B. Giant, B. Baum, F. Kaye); Gold

"Bossa Nova Baby": RD 1-22-63; CD 10-19-63; PCP No. 8 (Jerry Leiber, Mike Stoller); Gold

"Kissin' Cousins": RD 10-63; CD 12-63; PCP No. 11 (Fred Wise, Randy Starr); Gold

"Viva Las Vegas": RD 7-63; CD 4-64; PCP No. 29 (Doc Pomus, Mort Shuman); Gold

"Ain't That Loving You Baby": RD 6-10-58; CD 9-64; PCP No. 16 (Clyde Otis, Ivory Joe Hunter); Gold

"Crying in the Chapel": RD 10-31-60; CD 4-24-65; PCP No. 3 (Artie Glenn); Platinum

"I'm Yours": RD 6-26-61; CD 8-65; PCP No. 11 (Don Robertson, Hal Blair); Gold

"Puppet on a String": RD 6-7/64; CD 10-65; PCP No. 3 (Sid Tepper, Roy C. Bennett); Gold

"Blue Christmas": RD 9-5-57; CD 11-65; PCP No. 1 (Billy Hayes, Jay Johnson); Gold

"Tell Me Why": RD 1-12-57; CD 1-66; PCP No. 33 (Titus Turner); Gold

"Frankie and Johnny": RD 5-65; CD 3-66; PCP No. 25 (Hughie Cannon, 1904 as "He Done Me Wrong"; Elvis sang an arrangement by Alex Gottlieb, Fred Karger, Ben Weisman); Gold

"If I Can Dream": RD 6-29-68; CD 10-68; PCP No. 12 (W. Earl Brown); Gold

"In the Ghetto": RD 1-21-69; CD 5-3-69; PCP No. 3 (Mac Davis); RIAA Platinum

"Clean Up Your Own Backyard": RD 8-23-68; CD 6-69; PCP No. 35 (Billy Strange; Mac Davis); Gold. It made three charts.

"Suspicious Minds": RD 1-23-69; CD 9-13-69; PCP No. 1 (Mark James); Platinum

"Don't Cry, Daddy": RD 1-15-69; CD 11-29-69; PCP No. 6 (Mac Davis); Platinum

"The Wonder of You": RD 2-19-70; CD 5-16-70; PCP No. 9 (Barker Knight); Gold

"I've Lost You": RD 6-4-70; CD 8-70; PCP No. 5 (Ken Howard, Alan Blaikley); Gold

"You Don't Have to Say You Love Me": RD 6-6-70; CD 11-70; PCP No. 4 (V. Pallavicini, P. Donaggio); Gold

"I Really Don't Want to Know": RD 6-7-70; CD 12-70; PCP No. 21 (Don

Robertson, Howard Barnes); Gold
"Burning Love":   RD 3-28-72; CD 8-19-72; PCP No. 2 (Dennis Linde); Platinum
"Separate Ways":   RD 3-27-72; CD 11-

72; PCP No. 3 (Red West, Richard Mainegra); Gold
"Way Down":   RD 10-29-76; CD 6-77; PCP No. 14 (Layng Martine, Jr.); Platinum

American EPs With RIAA Certificates During Elvis's Life

Platinum:

Loving You, Vol. 1
King Creole, Vol. 1 and Vol. 2
Elvis Sings Christmas
The Real Elvis
Follow That Dream
Love Me Tender
Peace in the Valley

2x Platinum:

Elvis, Vol. 1
Jailhouse Rock

LPs on *Billboard's* Top 10 Chart

1. *Blue Hawaii* (No. 1 for twenty weeks)
2. *Elvis Presley* (No. 1 for twenty weeks)
3. *Loving You* (No. 1 for ten weeks)
4. *G.I. Blues* (No. 1 for ten weeks)
5. *Elvis* (No. 1 for five weeks)
6. *Elvis's Christmas Album* (No. 1 for four weeks)
7. *Something for Everybody* (No. 1 for three weeks)
8. *Roustabout* (No. 1 for one week)
9. *Aloha From Hawaii via Satellite* (No. 1 for one week)
10. *King Creole* (No. 2 for two weeks)
11. *Elvis Is Back* (No. 2 for three weeks)
12. *Elvis's Golden Records* (No. 3 for one week)
13. *Girls! Girls! Girls!* (No. 3 for one week)
14. *Elvis's Golden Records*, Vol. 3 (No. 3 for two weeks)
15. *Fun in Acapulco* (No. 3 for one week)
16. *Peace in the Valley*, the EP (No. 3 for one week)
17. *Moody Blue* (No. 3 for one week)
18. *Pot Luck* (No. 4 for one week)
19. *It Happened at the World's Fair*

(No. 4 for one week)
20. *Elvis in Concert* (No. 5 for one week)
21. *Kissin' Cousins* (No. 6 for one week)
22. *Girl Happy* (No. 8 for one week)

23. *Harum Scarum* (No. 8 for one week)
24. *Elvis—TV Special* (No. 8 for one week)
25. *Elvis for Everyone* (No. 10 for one week)

LPs on the Charts for More Than One Year

1. *G.I. Blues* (111 weeks—over two years!)
2. *Blue Hawaii* (79 weeks)

3. *Elvis Is Back* (56 weeks)
4. *Aloha From Hawaii via Satellite* (52 weeks)

Grammy Awards Won by Elvis

1. Best Sacred Performance, *How Great Thou Art*, 1967 (his twelfth nomination for a Grammy)
2. Best Inspirational Performance, *He Touched Me*, 1972 (his thirteenth nomination for a Grammy)

3. Best Inspirational Performance, "How Great Thou Art" (from the LP *Elvis as Recorded Live on Stage in Memphis*, June 1974, RCA DJLI-0606), 1974 (his fourteenth nomination)

Grammy Award Nominations

1. 1959: Record of the Year, "A Fool Such As I" (Bobby Darin's "Mack the Knife" won)
2. 1959: Best Performance by a Top 40 Artist, "A Big Hunk o' Love" (Nat King Cole's "Midnight Flyer" won)
3. 1959: Best Rhythm & Blues Performance, "A Big Hunk o' Love" (Dinah Washington's "What a Difference a Day Makes" won)
4. 1960: Record of the Year, "Are You Lonesome Tonight?" (Percy Faith's "Theme From 'A Summer Place' " won)

5. 1960: Best Vocal Performance, Male, "Are You Lonesome Tonight?" (Ray Charles's "Georgia on My Mind" won)
6. 1960: Best Performance by a Pop Singles' Artist, "Are You Lonesome Tonight?" (Ray Charles's "Georgia on My Mind" won)
7. 1960: Best Vocal Performance on an Album, Male, *G.I. Blues* (Ray Charles's *Genius of Ray Charles* won).
8. 1960: Best Soundtrack Album or Recording of Original Cast from a Motion Picture or Television, *G.I. Blues*

lost to *Can-Can*

9. 1961: Best Soundtrack Album or Recording of an Original Cast from a Motion Picture or Television, *Blue Hawaii* lost to *West Side Story*.

10. 1968: Best Sacred Performance,

You'll Never Walk Alone (Jack Hess's *Beautiful Isle of Somewhere* won)

11. (*Posthumous*) 1978: Best Country Vocal Performance, Male, "Softly, As I Leave You" ("Georgia on My Mind" by Willie Nelson won)

Other Grammy Award Nominations for Elvis's Albums

1. 1959: Best Album Cover, *For LP Fans Only* (lost to *Shostakovich: Symphony #5*)
2. (*Posthumous*) 1980: Best Album

Notes, *Elvis Aron Presley* (Frank Sinatra's *Trilogy: Past, Present and Future* won)

No. 1 Singles on *Billboard's* Top 100 Chart

"All Shook Up" (8 wks); "Heartbreak Hotel" (7 wks); "Don't Be Cruel" (7 wks); "Teddy Bear" (7 wks); "Jailhouse Rock" (6 wks); "Are You Lonesome Tonight?" (6 wks); "It's Now or Never" (5 wks); "Love Me Tender" (4 wks); "Stuck on You" (4 wks); "A Big Hunk o' Love" (2 wks); "Good Luck Charm" (2 wks); "Surrender" (2 wks); "Don't" (1 wk); "Suspicious Minds" (1 wk)

No. 1 Singles on *Billboard's* Juke Box and Best Seller Charts

"Hard Headed Woman" (No. 1 on the Juke Box and Best Seller charts, No. 2 on Top 100); "I Want You, I Need You, I Love You" (No. 1 on Best Seller chart; No. 3 on Top 100 chart); "Too Much" (No. 1 on Juke Box and Best Seller charts; No. 2 on the Top 100 chart); "Hound Dog" (No. 1 on Juke Box and Best Seller charts; No. 2 on Top 100 chart)

No. 1 Singles on *Billboard's* Rhythm and Blues Chart

"Treat Me Nice" (5 wks); "Jailhouse Rock" (5 wks); "All Shook Up" (4 wks); and for one week "Teddy Bear," "Loving You," "Hound Dog," and "Don't Be Cruel"

No. 1 Singles on *Billboard's* Country Chart

"Heartbreak Hotel" (17 wks); "I Was the One" (17 wks); "Don't Be Cruel" (5 wks); "Hound Dog" (5 wks); "I Forgot to Remember to Forget" (2 wks); and for 1 week "Guitar Man," "She Thinks I Still Care," "Mystery Train" "Treat Me Nice," "Teddy Bear," "Loving You," "Jailhouse Rock," "Way Down," "Pledging My Love," and "Moody Blue"

No. 1 Singles on *Billboard's* Easy-Listening Chart

"Crying in the Chapel" (7 wks); "Can't Help Falling in Love" (6 wks); "I'm Yours" (3 wks); "Such an Easy Question" (2 wks); and for one week "The Wonder of You," "My Boy," and "You Don't Have to Say You Love Me"

No. 1 Albums on *Billboard's* Extended-Play Chart

King Creole, Vol. 1 (29 wks); *Jailhouse Rock* (28 wks); *Loving You*, Vol. 1 (5 wks); *Elvis*, Vol. 1 (2 wks); *Elvis Sings Christmas Songs* (2 wks); *King Creole*, Vol. 2 (1 wk)

446

No. 1 Records on British Charts

"It's Now or Never" (8 wks); "All Shook Up" (7 wks); "Wooden Heart" (6 wks); "The Wonder of You" (6 wks); "A Fool Such As I" (5 wks); "Way Down" (5 wks); "Good Luck Charm" (5 wks); "I Need Your Love Tonight" (5 wks); "Rock-A-Hula-Baby" (4 wks); "Surrender" (4 wks); "Are You Lonesome Tonight?" (4 wks); "Can't Help Falling in Love" (4 wks); "(Marie's the Name) His Latest Flame" (4 wks); "I Got Stung" (3 wks); "Jailhouse Rock" (3 wks); "One Night (3 wks); "She's Not You" (3 wks); "Return to Sender" (3 wks); "Crying in the Chapel" (2 wks); "You're the Devil in Disguise" (1 wk)

British Top 100/Hot 100 Chart for Twenty Weeks or Over

"All Shook Up" (30 wks); "Hound Dog' (28 wks); "Don't Be Cruel," "Heartbreak Hotel," "Jailhouse Rock" (27 wks); "Teddy Bear" (25 wks); "I Want You, I Need You, I Love You" (24 wks); "Love Me Tender" (23 wks); "Loving You" (22 wks); "Way Down" (21 wks); "Don't" (20 wks); "It's Now or Never" (20 wks)

"Bubbling Under" Recordings (Songs that didn't make the Top 100 on *Billboard*'s charts)

1. "Come What May," released in June 1966
2. "Edge of Reality," released in November 1968
3. "Fools Fall in Love," released in January 1967
4. "Little Darlin'," released in October 1978
5. "Never Ending," released in July 1964
6. "Softly, As I Leave You," released in March 1978
7. "Suspicion," released in April 1964
8. "We Call on Him," released in April 1968
9. "Wooden Heart," released in November 1964
10. "Wooden Heart," reissued in October 1965
11. "You'll Be Gone," released in February 1965

Gospel Recordings, Singles

"Amazing Grace" (recorded, March 15, 1971)
"Amen" (April 9, 1972)
"Bosom of Abraham" (June 9 or 10, 1971)
"By and By" (May 27, 1966)
"Crying in the Chapel" (October 31, 1960)
"Down by the Riverside" (December 4, 1956)
"An Evening Prayer" (May 18, 1971)
"God Calls Me Home" (date uncertain)
"He Touched Me" (May 18, 1971/album—Grammy Award, 1972)
"He's Only a Prayer Away" (ca. 1958–60)
"His Hand in Mine" (October 30, 1960)
"How Great Thou Art" (two Grammy Awards: May 25, 1967, album, and a live session from 1974 single)
"I Believe" (January 12, 1957)
"I Hear a Sweet Voice Calling" (December 5, 1956)
"I John" (June 9, 1971/and April 1972)
"If the Lord Wasn't Walking by My Side" (May 28, 1966)
"In the Garden" (May 27, 1966)
"Jesus Knows What I Need" (October 30, 1960)
"Joshua Fit the Battle" (October 31, 1960)
"Known Only to Him" (October 31, 1960)
"Lead Me, Guide Me" (May 17, 1971)
"Let Us Pray" (September 22, 1969)
"Miracle of the Rosary" (May 5, 1971)
"On the Jericho Road" (December 4, 1956)

"Padre" (May 15, 1971)
"Peace in the Valley" (December 4, 1956)
"Promised Land" (December 15, 1973)
"Put Your Hand in the Hand" (June 8, 1971)
"Reach Out to Jesus" (June 8, 1971)
"Seeing Is Believing" (May 19, 1971)
"So High" (May 27, 1966)
"Softly and Tenderly" (December 4, 1956)
"Somebody Bigger Than You and I" (May 17, 1966)
"Stand by Me" (May 26, 1966)
"Swing Low, Sweet Chariot" (October 31, 1960)
"Take My Hand, Precious Lord" (January 13, 1957)
"That Lonesome Valley" (December 4, 1956)
"We Call on Him" (September 11, 1967)
"When God Calls Me Home" (December 11, 1976, four lines)
"When God Dips His Love in My Heart" (December 4, 1956)
"When the Saints Go Marching In" (December 4, 1956)
"Where Could I Go but to the Lord" (May 28, 1966)
"Where No One Stands Alone" (May 26, 1966)
"Who Am I?" (February 22, 1969)
"Why Me, Lord" (March 20, 1974)
"Without Him" (March 27, 1966)

Recordings With Elvis on Piano

1. The Million Dollar Quartet sessions, first issue (S 5001); RCA/BMG Records, USA (2023-2-R; *The Complete Sun Sessions* from Sun jam sessions [RCA 6414, USA]).

2. "How the Web Was Woven," in re-

hearsal July 1970, at MGM studios and show, in the 1970 documentary *Elvis*, and on the sound-track recording from RCA, Nashville, June 5, 1970. Also on bootleg LPs *The King: From the Dark to Light* (sound track) and *That's the Way It Is* (sound track).

3. "I'll Take You Home Again, Kathleen," "It's Still Here," and "I Will Be True" recorded May 19, 1971, RCA Studios, Nashville; released June 1973 on *Elvis* (RCA APL 1-0283).

4. Elvis played the piano with overdubbing on RCA's *Elvis Aron [sic] Presley* from the New Frontier Hotel, Las Vegas, May 6, 1956; released in 1980 (RCA CPLS-3699).

5. "My Heart Cried for You," "Write to Me From Naples," and "Suppose" recorded at Graceland, released October 1984 in RCA's boxed set *A Golden Celebration* (RCA CPM6-5172).

6. "One Night of Sin," recorded on January 24, 1957 at Radio Recorders. The raunchier version was released in 1983 on *Elvis—A Legendary Performer*, Vol. 4 (RCA CPL1-4848).

7. "I'll Hold You in My Heart," recorded on January 23, 1969, at the American Sound Studios and released on *From Elvis in Memphis* (1970, RCA AFLI-1506, new number RCA LSP-4155) and *The Memphis Record* (June 1987, RCA 6221-1-R).

8. "As Long As I Have You" at Radio Recorders, November 16, 1958. "Beyond the Reef," May 27, 1966.

9. "When the Snow Is on the Roses," in Las Vegas. Elvis sang and played the piano alone, August 24, 1970.

10. "Trying to Get to You" at Sun Records, July 11, 1955.

11. "Old Shep," played on September 2, 1956 (take No. 5) at Radio Recorders, Hollywood, released on EP *Elvis*, Vol. 2 (RCA EPA-993) and a blank promotional disk that is exceedingly rare (RCA PRO-12, Dec. 1956); British LP *Elvis Presley No. 2* (take No. 1, HMV-CLP-1105); LPs *Double Dynamite* (Pickwick DL2-5001, Dec. 1975); *Elvis* (RCA LPM-1382, Oct. 19, 1956); *Elvis Sings for Children and Grownups Too!* (RCA CPL1-2901, July 1978), and *Separate Ways* (RCA Camden CAS 2611, January 1973). Bootleg LPs *Eternal Elvis* (take No. 1, no record label, 1978) and *The Rocking Rebel*, Vol. 3 (take No. 3, Golden Archives Records GA 350, 1979).

12. "I Understand," "Happy, Happy Birthday, Baby," "I Can't Help It," "Who's Sorry Now?" and "Just a Closer Walk With Thee" were recorded at the Fadals' home in Waco, Texas, 1958; all were released on the Paul Lichter bootleg LP *Forever Young, Forever Beautiful* (Memphis Flash Records JL 92447, 1978). These songs were "a home recording" of Elvis, who sang with records and played around on the piano. "Just a Closer Walk With Thee" is the clearest song with his accompaniment.

13. "He's Only a Prayer Away" was recorded in West Germany on a piano in Elvis's rented house. It was released in 1984 on RCA's CPM6-5172 LP *A Golden Celebration* (*West Germany, 1958–1960*).

14. "Unchained Melody" recorded April 24, 1977, from the Crisler Arena, Ann Arbor, Michigan, during a live concert (album); the single's release was recorded at the Rushmore Civic Center, Rapid City, South Dakota, June 21, 1977. (Singles: RCA PB-11212, March 1978; RCA JH-11212, March 1978, a DJ promotional disk; RCA GB-11988, May 1980. LPs: *Always on My Mind* (RCA 6985-1-R, May 1988), *Elvis Aron [sic] Presley* (RCA CPL8-3699, July 1980), *Moody Blue* (RCA AFL1-2428, July 1977) bootleg two-record LP *Rocking With Elvis New Year's Eve, Pittsburgh, PA, Dec. 31, 1976* (Spirit of America Records HNY 7677, 1972).

Songs Listing Elvis as Composer, Adapter, or Arranger

1. "All Shook Up," cowritten with Otis Blackwell
2. "Aloha Oe," adapted and arranged
3. "Amazing Grace," adapted
4. "America the Beautiful," adapted
5. "By and By," adapted
6. "Don't Be Cruel," cowritten with Otis Blackwell
7. "Farther Along," arranged and adapted
8. "The First Noel," arranged and adapted
9. "I Was Born About Ten Thousand Years Ago," adapted
10. "I'll Take You Home Again Kathleen," adapted
11. "I'm Gonna Walk Dem Gold Stairs," adapted
12. "Joshua Fit the Battle," arranged and adapted
13. "Let Me," cowritten with Vera Matson
14. "Love Me Tender," cowritten with Vera Matson
15. "Milky White Way," arranged and adapted
16. "O Come, All Ye Faithful," arranged and adapted
17. "Oh Little Town of Bethlehem," arranged
18. "Paralyzed," cowritten with Otis Blackwell
19. "Poor Boy," cowritten with Vera Matson
20. "Run On," arranged and adapted
21. "Santa Lucia," arranged
22. "So High," arranged
23. "Stand by Me," arranged
24. "Swing Down, Sweet Chariot," arranged
25. "That's Someone You Never Forget," cowritten with Red West
26. "We're Gonna Move," cowritten with Vera Matson
27. "You'll Be Gone," cowritten with Red West and Charlie Hodge

Unreleased Recorded Songs by Elvis

1. "Alfie" (he sang one line in Las Vegas, February 20, 1973)
2. "Also Sprach Zarathustra" (he sang from 1972–1977 in concerts)
3. "The Big Hurt" (recorded at Graceland in the 1960s)
4. "Bill Bailey, Won't You Please Come Home" (in the 1960s)
5. "Bivouac" (for *Spinout* in 1966, but no tape has surfaced)
6. "Blue Guitar" (at "Louisiana Hayride" and perhaps at Sun)
7. "Blues Stay Away From Me" (in the background at Sun, 1954)

8. "Bourbon Street" (for *King Creole*)
9. "Breathless" (in the late 1950s or early 1960s)
10. "Candy Kisses" (for *Loving You*)
11. "Chautauqua" (at United Recorders, ca. August 23–26, 1968)
12. "Come Out, Come Out (Wherever You Are)" (perhaps at American Sound Studio, ca. January 1969)
13. "Comin' Home Baby" (the song Elvis played when he introduced members of the TCB Band to audiences in the 1970s)
14. "Cryin' Heart Blues" (at "Louisiana Hayride"; Sun Records)
15. "Crying" (at Graceland in 1976)
16. "Dancing on a Dare" (for *Loving You*, mentioned in *TV Guide*)
17. "Dark as a Dungeon" (perhaps at Sun Records)
18. "Detour" (rumored he recorded it for *Loving You*)
19. "Down the Line" (he sang it with Buddy Holly in jam sessions and perhaps at Sun Records, ca. 1955)
20. "Fabulous" (rumored to have been recorded at Sun Records)
21. "Fool, Fool, Fool" (rumored to have been recorded at Sun)
22. "Funky Fingers" (recorded, perhaps, on June 6, 1970)
23. "Give Me More, More, More (of Your Kisses)" (He sang it at "Louisiana Hayride" and perhaps at Sun.)
24. "Gone" (at "Louisiana Hayride" and perhaps at Sun)
25. "Hawaiian Sunrise" (for *Blue Hawaii*, 1961)
26. "I Apologize" (rumored he recorded it at Sun)
27. "I Don't Hurt Anymore" (rumored he recorded it at Sun)
28. "I Never Had It So Good" (for *Roustabout*, February–March 1964)
29. "I Played the Fool" (rumored he recorded it at Sun)
30. "It'll Be Me" (rumored to have recorded it for RCA)
31. "Juanita" (sang it on tour, 1953–56, and may have recorded it at Sun)
32. "Little Girl" (reported to have recorded it for RCA)
33. "Lonely Avenue" (rumored to have recorded it for RCA)
34. "Long Journey" (may have recorded it for RCA)
35. "Love Will Keep Up Together" (at Graceland, ca. 1976–77)
36. "Lovebug Itch" (rumored to have recorded it)
37. "Merry Christmas, Darlin' " (may have recorded it at RCA)
38. "Mexican Joe" (rumored to have recorded it at Sun)
39. "Muskrat Ramble" (perhaps for *King Creole*)
40. "Night Train to Memphis" (perhaps recorded at Sun)
41. "Nine Pound Hammer" (rumored to have recorded it for Sun)
42. "No Particular Place to Go" (recorded by Felton Jarvis)
43. "Noah" (rumored he recorded it in the 1950s)
44. "Now Is the Hour" (for *Paradise, Hawaiian Style*, 1965)
45. "Oakie Boogie" (rumored to have been recorded at Sun)
46. "On Wisconsin" (Elvis may have recorded a few lines for the movie *The Trouble With Girls*, 1969)
47. "Over the Line" (may have been recorded in the 1960s)
48. "Play a Simple Melody" (may have been recorded at Sun)
49. "Ready for Love" (rumored he recorded it)
50. "Rock and Roll Music" (a jam recorded by Felton Jarvis)
51. "Rockin' Little Sally" (rumored to have been recorded)
52. "Satisfy Me" (rumored to have been recorded in the 1960s)
53. "Stormy Monday Blues" (for RCA in the 1960s, maybe)
54. "Sunshine" (perhaps recorded at Sun in 1955)
55. "Tennessee Dancin' Doll" (perhaps in the 1950s)
56. "That's the Stuff You Gotta Watch" (perhaps at Sun)
57. "Too Late to Worry, Too Blue to Cry" (rumored to have been recorded in the 1960s)

58. "Tupelo, Mississippi Flash" (perhaps self-recorded)
59. "Twenty Flight Rock" (perhaps recorded in the 1960s)
60. "Wabash Cannonball" (perhaps recorded)
61. "We're Gonna Live It Up" (for *Loving You*, 1957)
62. "What a Friend We Have in Jesus" (one line was recorded in the 1970s for *This Is Elvis*)

63. "Yeah, Yeah, Yeah" (for *Viva Las Vegas*, July 1963)
64. "You Are My Sunshine" (at Sun Records)
65. "You Can't Blame a Guy for Trying" (for a movie, 1960s)
66. "You Can't Say No in Acapulco" (for *Fun in Acapulco*, 1963)
67. "You Turned the Tables on Me" (studio recording, 1950s)

Songs Elvis Sang with No Known Recording

1. "All I Really Want to Do" (in Las Vegas in the 1970s)
2. "Along Came Jones" (He sang one line to Tom Jones at the International Hotel, Las Vegas, August 21, 1970.)
3. "Always Late (With Your Kisses)" (sung at "Louisiana Hayride" gigs and perhaps at clubs, 1954–56)
4. "Aubrey" in Las Vegas in the 1970s
5. "Bad Moon Rising" (in Las Vegas in the 1970s)
6. "Blowin' in the Wind" (in Las Vegas in the 1960s)
7. "Book of Happiness" (perhaps recorded at Graceland)
8. "Born to Lose" (in Las Vegas in the 1970s)
9. "Breakin' the Rules" (while on tour, 1954–55)
10. "By the Time I Get to Phoenix" (Las Vegas, the 1970s)
11. "The Cattle Call" (in concerts in the 1950s)
12. "Chain Gang" (in Las Vegas, the 1970s)
13. "Diana" (at concerts in the 1970s)
14. "El Paso" (at concerts in the 1970s)
15. "Get Rhythm" (Johnny Cash wrote it for Elvis, but it's not believed he recorded it.)
16. "God Bless My Daddy" (reportedly

he sang it at Lawhon Elementary School)
17. "Goodnight, My Love" (in concerts in the 1970s)
18. "The Great Pretender" (in concerts in the 1950s)
19. "Happy Birthday to You" (many concerts, 1955–77)
20. "House of the Rising Sun" (concerts in the 1970s)
21. "I Can See Clearly Now" (concerts in the 1970s)
22. "I Want It That Way" (in an occasional concert)
23. "I Write the Songs" (in concerts in the 1970s)
24. "It Ain't Me Babe" (in concerts in the 1970s)
25. "It's Over" (in concerts and other events)
26. "Jingle Bells" (in concerts in the 1960s and 1970s)
27. "Joy" (sung on occasion and may have recorded ca. 1968–70)
28. "Lodi" (sung in concerts in the 1970s)
29. "Mr. Tambourine Man" (in concerts in the 1970s)
30. "She Belongs to Me" (in concerts in the 1970s)
31. "Susie Q" (in Las Vegas concerts in the 1970s)

32. "Take Your Finger out of It, It Don't Belong to Me" (allegedly in a Memphis shopping center, ca. 1953–54)
33. "Talkin' 'Bout Your Birthday Cake" (in a Memphis shopping center, 1953–54)
34. "That's Amore" (in gigs and concerts from 1953)
35. " 'Till I Waltz Again With You" (at Humes High School, 1953)
36. "Turn Around, Look at Me" (in Las Vegas concerts, the 1970s)
37. "Turn Me Loose" (perhaps in West Germany, late 1959)
38. "When the Swallows Come Back to Capistrano" (in concerts during the 1960s and 1970s on occasion)

Boxed Sets

1. *15 Golden Records—30 Golden Hits* (RCA PP-11301, released in October 1977). Fifteen singles, each separately packed in a color photo sleeve.
2. *20 Golden Hits in Full Color Sleeves* (RCA PP-11340, released in December 1977). All of these hits were released in the October issue (RCA PP-11301).
3. *Elvis' Greatest Hits—Golden Singles*, Vol. 1 (RCA PP-13897, released in October 1984). Six singles pressed on gold vinyl with a special gold "50th" anniversary label to commemorate the fiftieth anniversary of Elvis's birth. A new photograph was on each sleeve.
4. *Elvis' Greatest Hits—Golden Singles*, Vol. 2 (RCA PP-13989, released in October 1984). With the same gold "50th" anniversary label, each record was pressed in gold vinyl and each sleeve had a new photograph of Elvis.
5. *Elvis, the King of Rock 'n' Roll—The Complete 50's Masters* (RCA 07863, released in July 1992). A boxed set of five cassettes or CDs with a sheet of thirty-six colored stamps of Elvis's album covers and a large booklet scanning the history of the 1950s work recorded by Elvis. In the March 4, 1993, issue of *Rolling Stone* the album was given the Critics' 1993 Music Award for the Best Reissue Album of the year.

6. *Elvis From Nashville to Memphis—The Essential 60s Masters* (RCA 66160-2 07863), released on September 28, 1993, limited edition, numbered boxed sets). A five-CD or five-cassette boxed set with 130 digitally remastered tracks that cover nineteen previously unreleased songs. Included are a ninety-four-page booklet with liner notes by Peter Guralnick, record-session data, a discology of sixties music (recorded prior to 1972), and a stamp sheet of Elvis's sixties record covers. Compilation produced by Ernst Mikael Jorgensen and Roger Semon. Executive produced by Paul Williams. Digitally remastered by Dick Baxter at BMG Recording Studios, New York City. Audio restoration by Bill Lacey. Priced from $74–$54.99.

1 "Make Me Know It," "Soldier Boy," Stuck on You," "Fame and Fortune," "A Mess of Blues," "It Feels So Right," "Fever," "Like a Baby," "It's Now or Never," "The Girl of My Best Friend," "Dirty, Dirty Feeling," "Thrill of Your Love," "I Gotta Know," "Such a Night," "Are You Lonesome Tonight?" "Girl Next Door Went A'Walking," "I Will Be Home

Again," "Reconsider Baby," "Surrender," "I'm Comin' Home," "Gently," "In Your Arms," "Give Me the Right," "I Feel So Bad," "It's a Sin," "I Want You With Me," "There's Always Me."

2 "Starting Today," "Sentimental Me," "Judy," "Put the Blame on Me," "Kiss Me Quick," "That's Someone You Never Forget," "I'm Yours," "His Latest Flame," "Little Sister," "For the Millionth and the Last Time," "Good Luck Charm," "Anything That's Part of You," "I Met Her Today," "Night Rider," "Something Blue," "Gonna Get Back Home Somehow," "(Such an) Easy Question," "Fountain of Love," "Just for Old Time's Sake," "You'll Be Gone," "I Feel That I've Known You Forever," "Just Tell Her Jim Said Hello," "Suspicion," "She's Not You," "Echoes of Love," "Please Don't Drag That String Around," "(You're the) Devil in Disguise," "Never Ending," "What Now, What Next, Where To," "Witchcraft," "Finder's Keepers, Losers Weepers," "Love Me Tonight."

3 "(It's a) Long Lonely Highway," "Western Union," "Slowly but Surely," "Blue River," "Memphis, Tennessee," "Ask Me," "It Hurts Me," "Down in the Alley," "Tomorrow Is a Long Time," "Love Letters," "Beyond the Reef" (previously unreleased; original undubbed master), "Come What May" (alternative take 7), "Fools Fall in Love," "Indescribably Blue," "I'll Remember You" (original unedited master), "If Every Day Was Like Christmas," "Suppose" (master), "Guitar Man/What'd I Say" (original unedited master), "Big Boss Man," "Mine," "Just Call Me Lonesome," "Hi-Heel Sneakers"

(original unedited master), "You Don't Know Me," "Singing Tree," "Too Much Monkey Business," "U.S. Male."

4 "Long Black Limousine," "This Is the Story," "Wearin' That Loved On Look," "You'll Think of Me," "A Little Bit of Green," "Gentle on My Mind," "I'm Movin' On," "Don't Cry Daddy," "Inherit the Wind," "Mama Liked the Roses," "My Little Friend," "In the Ghetto," "Rubberneckin'," "From a Jack to a King," "Hey Jude," "Without Love (There Is Nothing)," "I'll Hold You in My Heart ('Til I Can Hold You in My Arms)," "I'll Be There," "Suspicious Minds," "True Love Travels on a Gravel Road," "Stranger in My Own Home Town," "And the Grass Won't Pay No Mind," "Power of My Love."

5 "After Loving You," "Do You Know Who I Am," "Kentucky Rain," "Only the Strong Survive," "It Keeps Right On A-Hurtin'," "Any Day Now," "If I'm a Fool (for Loving You)," "The Fair is Moving On," "Who Am I?," "This Time/I Can't Stop Loving You" (informal recording), "In the Ghetto" (alternative take 4), "Suspicious Minds" (alternative take 6), "Kentucky Rain" (alternative take 9), "Big Boss Man" (alternative take 2), "Down in the Alley" (alternative take 1), "Memphis, Tennessee" (alternative take 1 from the 1963 session), "I'm Yours" (alternative take 1 from an undubbed version), "His Latest Flame" (alternative take 4), "That's Someone You Never Forget" (alternative take 1), "Surrender" (alternative take 1), "It's Now or Never" (original undubbed master), "Love Me Tender/Witchcraft" (from "The Frank Sinatra Timex Special").

CD Discography

Compact discs with studio-quality sound were introduced to the mass market by CBS/Sony in 1983. Fans were appalled to read, "Stereo effect reprocessed from monophonic," on the cover of the first Elvis 1985 CD, *Elvis' Golden Records* (PCD1-1707), which had been poorly remastered by RCA from original monaural masters. Unfortunately, RCA destroyed the Sun label's sound on the CD *The Complete Sun Sessions* (RCA Victor 6414-2) by repeating their 1985 mistake! Elvis CDs include:

Aloha From Hawaii via Satellite, RCA Victor CD07863-5262-3
Alternate Aloha, RCA Victor CD 6985-2-R
Always on My Mind, 6/85, RCA Victor PCD1-5430

Best of Christmas, RCA CD 7013-2-R
Billboard *Greatest Christmas Hits, 1955–Present*, CD R21K-70636
Billboard *Top Rock 'n' Roll Hits, 1956*, CD R21K-70599
Billboard *Top Rock 'n' Roll Hits, 1957*, CD R21K-70618
Billboard *Top Rock 'n' Roll Hits, 1958*, CD R21K-70619
Billboard *Top Rock 'n' Roll Hits, 1959*, CD R21K-70620
Blue Hawaii, 4/88, RCA Victor CD 3683-2-R
Burning Love (and Hits From His Movies), Vol. 2, 12/87, RCA/Camden CADI-2595

Complete Sun Sessions, The, 7/87, RCA Victor 6414-2

Double Dynamite, 1987, Pair PDC2-1010

Elvis, 11/84, RCA Victor PCD1-5199
Elvis—A Valentine Gift for You, RCA Victor, PCD1 5353

Elvis Aron Presley Forever, 3/88, Pair PDC2-1185 (*Note:* His middle name is misspelled.)
Elvis' Christmas Album, 10/87, RCA/Camden CAD1-2428
Elvis' Christmas Album, 8/85, RCA Victor, PCD1-5486
Elvis' Christmas Classic, RCA Victor, CD9801-2-8
Elvis Collector's Gold, BMG Music, CD3114-2-R
Elvis Country, 3/88, RCA Victor 6330-2
Elvis for Everyone, RCA Victor CD 3450-2-R
Elvis' Golden Records, 5/84, RCA Victor PCD1-1707
Elvis' Golden Records, Vol. 1, RCA Victor, PCD1-5296
Elvis' Golden Records, Vol. 2, 11/84, RCA Victor, PCD1-5297
Elvis' Golden Records, Vol. 3, RCA Victor, CD 2765-2-R
Elvis' Golden Records, Vol. 4, RCA Victor, CD 1297-2-R
Elvis' Golden Records, Vol. 5, 11/84, RCA Victor, PCD1-4941
Elvis Presley, 11/84, RCA Victor PCD1-5198
Elvis Presley, RCA Victor CD 07863-52587-2
Elvis Presley, As Recorded at Madison Square Garden, RCA Victor CD 7863-54776-2
Elvis Presley—Elvis Is Back, RCA Victor, CD 2231-2-R
Elvis Presley—His Hand in Mine, RCA Victor CD 1319-2-8
Elvis Presley Story, The (extremely rare, never distributed; ten compact discs written by Jerry Hopkins, originally broadcast in 1975; thirteen-hour biography)
Elvis Sings Leiber and Stroller, RCA Victor CD 3026-2-R

Sheet Music

Collectors seek the oddest and most popular examples of Elvis's repertoire, especially any sheet music that was signed or inscribed by the King. The rarest and most desirable:

"Who Needs Money"
"Smorgasbord"
"Yoga Is As Yoga Does"
"I Beg of You"
"A Dog's Life"
"I Got Stung"
"Animal Instinct"
"Golden Coins"
"Catchin' On Fast"
"El Toro"
"Ito Eats"
"Have a Happy"
"Petunia, the Gardener's Daughter"
"Shake That Tambourine"

The first song folio (pink-bordered) published by Hill and Range was 1955's "The Elvis Presley Album of Juke Box Favorites, No. 1," which pictured Elvis in his now-famous pigeon-toed position, holding his guitar. It cost $1. This issue had four unreleased songs: "Rag Mop," "I Almost Lost My Mind," "Cryin' Heart Blues," and "I Need You So." The $1.50, 1956 reissue excluded those four songs and replaced them with "Heartbreak Hotel," "I Was the One," "Blue Suede Shoes," and "Mystery Train." Other sheet music followed: "Heartbreak Hotel"; "Hound Dog"; "Don't Be Cruel"; "My Baby Left Me"; "That's When Your Heartaches Begin"; "Too Much"; "All Shook Up"; "Jailhouse Rock"; "(Let Me Be Your) Teddy Bear"; "One Night"; "Love Me Tender"; "I Don't Care If the Sun Don't Shine"; "Stuck on You" (with Eddie Fadal's photo of Elvis on the cover); "Roustabout"; "Can't Help Falling in Love"; "You're the Devil in Disguise"; "Ask Me"; "Ain't That Loving You, Baby"; "A Little Less Conversation"; "We Call on Him" song folio, 1968; "In the Ghetto"; "You Don't Have to Say You Love Me"; "Life"; "Burning Love"; "Until It's Time for You to Go"; "It's a Matter of Time"; "Separate Ways"; "Moody Blue"; "Way Down" (with color cover); and "My Way" (1973 and 1976).

Best-Known Songs Elvis "Reinvented"

1. Creedence Clearwater Revival's classic "Proud Mary"
2. Mickey Newberry's "American Trilogy," which includes "Dixie," "All My Trials," and "The Battle Hymn of the Republic"
3. Marty Robbins's "You Gave Me a Mountain"
4. Simon & Garfunkel's "Bridge Over Troubled Water"
5. James Taylor's "Steamroller"

Long-Playing Standard Album Releases

(*Note:* An asterisk denotes an album produced in Elvis's lifetime.)

*__Almost in Love__ (RCA Camden CAS-2440, released in November 1970) featured six songs from Elvis's films (some alternative takes) and peaked at No. 65 on *Billboard*'s Top LP chart during an eighteen-week stay. In 1973, "Stay Away, Joe" was replaced by "Stay Away" in the album's reissue. *Songs:* "Almost in Love"; "Long Legged Girl (With the Short Dress On)"; "Edge of Reality"; "My Little Friend"; "A Little Less Conversation"; "Rubberneckin' "; "Clean Up Your Own Backyard"; "U.S. Male"; "Charro"; "Stay Away, Joe." *Almost in Love* (Pickwick CAS-2440, released in December 1975). Same songs as RCA Camden CAS-2440.

*__Aloha From Hawaii Via Satellite__ (RCA VPSX-6089, released in February 1973), a two-record sound track of the TV special "Elvis: Aloha From Hawaii," was a quadradisc album, and the first to go gold (certified on February 12, 1973) in the record industry. Within a week it was No. 1 on *Billboard*'s Top LP chart during a fifty-two-week run. *Songs:* introduction, "Also Sprach Zarathustra"; "See See Rider"; "Burning Love"; "Something"; "You Gave Me a Mountain"; "Steamroller Blues"; "My Way"; "Love Me"; "Johnny B. Goode"; "It's Over"; "Blue Suede Shoes"; "I'm So Lonesome I Could Cry"; "I Can't Stop Loving You"; "Hound Dog"; "What Now, My Love"; "Fever"; "Welcome to My World"; "Suspicious Minds"; introductions by Elvis; "I'll Remember You"; "Long Tall Sally"; "Whole Lotta Shakin' Goin' On"; "An American Trilogy"; "A Big Hunk o' Love"; "Can't Help Falling in Love." RIAA's two-time Platinum Award winner.

*__Aloha From Hawaii via Satellite__ (RCA CPDA-2642, released in February 1977) was a new album number for RCA VPSX-6089; RCA R-213736 was released in February 1973, through the RCA Record Club in stereo.

__Alternate Aloha, The__ (RCA 6985-1-R, released in May 1988) featured recordings from the rehearsal of the TV special "Elvis: Aloha From Hawaii," January 12, 1973, excluding "Hound Dog," which was replaced by "Blue Hawaii" (recorded on January 14). *Songs:* "Also Sprach Zarathustra"; "See See Rider"; "Burning Love"; "Something"; "You Gave Me a Mountain"; "Steamroller Blues"; "My Way"; "Love Me"; "It's Over"; "Blue Suede Shoes"; "I'm So Lonesome I Could Cry"; "What Now, My Love"; "Fever"; "Welcome to My World"; "Suspicious Minds"; introductions by Elvis; "I'll Remember You"; "An American Trilogy"; "A Big Hunk o' Love"; "Can't Help Falling in Love"; "Blue Hawaii."

__Always on My Mind__ (RCA AFL1-5430, released in May 1985) was a purple vinyl record, with a gold anniversary label, recorded in celebration of Elvis's birthday. *Songs:* "Separate Ways"; "Don't Cry, Daddy"; "My Boy"; "Solitaire"; "Bigger They Are, Harder They Fall"; "Hurt"; "Pieces of My Life"; "I Miss You"; "It's Midnight"; "I've Lost You"; "You Gave Me a Mountain"; "Unchained Melody"; "Always on My Mind."

__Audio Self-Portrait, An__ (RCA DJMI-0835, released in 1985) is a disc jockey promo release of interviews with Elvis and includes a *TV Guide* interview from September 26, 1956, and 1960–61 interviews. Informative and personable.

*__Back in Memphis__ (RCA LSP-4429, released in November 1970) contained sides three and four of the LP *From Memphis to Vegas/From Vegas to Memphis* (RCA LSP 6020), all recorded at American Sound Studios, Memphis on January 13–26, 1969, and February 17–22, 1969. The album was on *Billboard*'s Top LP chart for three weeks and reached No. 183. *Songs:* "Inherit the Wind"; "This Is the Story"; "Stranger in My Home Town"; "A Little Bit of Green"; "And the Grass Won't Pay No Mind"; "Do You Know Who I Am"; "From a Jack to King"; "The Fair Is Moving On"; "You'll Think of Me"; "Without Love (There Is Nothing)."
*__Back in Memphis__ (RCA AFL1-4429, released in January 1977, a reissue of RCA LSP-4429).

__Beginning Years, The__ (Louisiana Hayride, LH-3601, released in January 1985) with a twenty-page photo booklet, "D. J. Fontana Remembers Elvis. "Louisiana Hayride" performances by Elvis from the 1950s are featured as well as some dialogue and remarks by Frank Page and an Elvis interview with Horace Logan. *Songs:* "That's All Right, Mama"; "Blue Moon of Kentucky"; "Good Rockin' Tonight"; "I Got a Woman"; "Tweedlee Dee"; "Baby, Let's Play House"; "Maybellene"; "That's All Right Mama" (on both sides of the record); "Hound Dog."

*__Blue Hawaii__ (RCA LPM-2426, released in October 1961). This million-copy seller includes songs from Elvis's movie *Blue Hawaii;* gold RIAA certification, December 21, 1961. Disc jockeys named it their second-favorite album of 1961, and it sold over 5 million copies within fourteen months. It remained No. 1 for eight weeks out of seventy-nine on *Billboard*'s Top LP chart. *Songs:* "Blue Hawaii"; "Almost Always True"; "Aloha One"; "No More"; "Can't Help Falling in Love"; "Rock-A-Hula-Baby"; "Moonlight Swim"; "KU-U-I-P-O"; "Ito Eats"; "Slicin' Sand"; "Hawaiian Sunset"; "Beach Boy Blues"; "Island of Love (Kauai)"; "Hawaiian Wedding Song." *__Blue Hawaii__ (RCA LSP-2426, released in October 1961 as a stereo version of RCA LPM-2426). The stereo version was the first of Elvis's stereo albums to reach No. 1 (for four weeks) and No. 2 (for twelve weeks) on *Billboard*'s Top LP chart. Same songs as RCA LPM-2426. RIAA's two-time Platinum Award winner.
Blue Hawaii (RCA AFL1-2426 released in September 1977) is simply a new number for RCA LSP-2426.
Blue Hawaii (RCA AYLI-3683, released in May 1980) is simply a new number for RCA AFL1-2426.

*__Burning Love and Hits from His Movies,__ Vol. 2 (RCA Camden CAS-2595, released in November 1972) with both sides of Elvis's hit single "Burning Love"/"It's a Matter of Time" and eight songs from his films. Bonus color photo included. RIAA cold-certified for a million copies sold. It reached No. 22 on *Billboard*'s Top LP chart during a twenty-five-week run. *Songs:* "Burning Love"; "Tender Feeling"; "Am I Ready"; "Tonight Is So Right for Love"; "Guadalajara"; "It's a Matter of Time"; "No More"; "Santa Lucia"; "We'll Be Together"; "I Love Only One Girl." RIAA's Gold Award.
*__Burning Love and Hits From His Movies__, Vol. 2 (Pickwick CAS-2595, released in December 1975) is exactly the same album as RCA Camden CAS-2595.

*__Clambake__ (RCA LSP-3893, released in November 1967) featured seven songs from Elvis's film *Clambake* and five others. Bonus photo of Elvis and Priscilla's wedding. The album reached No. 14 on *Billboard*'s top LP chart during a fourteen-week stay. *Songs:* "Guitar Man"; "Clambake"; "Who Needs Money"; "A House That Has Everything"; "Confidence"; "Hey, Hey, Hey"; "You Don't Know Me"; "The Girl I Never Loved"; "How Can You Lose What You Never Had?" "Big Boss Man"; "Singing Tree"; "Just Call Me Lonesome." *Clambake* (RCA LSP-3893, released on November 19, 1967) was a stereo version of RCA LPM-3893. The album did not chart. *Clambake* (RCA AFL1-2565, released in September

1977) was simply a new number for RCA LSP-3893.

C'mon Everybody (RCA Camden CAL-2518, released in August 1971) featured songs from Elvis's films *Kid Galahad, Viva Las Vegas, Follow That Dream,* and *Easy Come, Easy Go.* The album was on *Billboard*'s Top LP chart for eleven weeks and reached No. 70. *Songs:* "C'mon Everybody"; "Angel"; "Easy Come, Easy Go"; "A Whistling Tune"; "Follow That Dream"; "King of the Whole Wide World"; "I'll Take Love"; "Today, Tomorrow and Forever"; "I'm Not the Marrying Kind"; "This Is Living." *C'mon Everybody* (Pickwick CAS-2518, released in December 1975 and *not* a stereo album) contains the same songs as RCA Camden CAL-2518.

Complete Sun Sessions, The (RCA 6414-1-R, released in June 1987). A two-record set with sixteen Sun master recordings, twelve alternative takes, and outtakes on six songs. Peter Guralnick contributed extremely well-written and documented liner notes. *Songs:* (master takes) "That's All Right, Mama"; "Blue Moon of Kentucky"; "Good Rockin' Tonight"; "I Don't Care If the Sun Don't Shine"; "Milkcow Blues Boogie"; "You're a Heartbreaker"; "Baby Let's Play House"; "I'm Left, You're Right, She's Gone"; "Mystery Train"; "I Forgot to Remember to Forget"; "I Love You Because"; "Blue Moon"; "Tomorrow Night"; "I'll Never Let You Go (Little Darlin')"; "Just Because"; "Trying to Get to You"; (the outtakes) "Harbor Lights"; "I Love You Because" (takes 1 and 2); "That's All Right, Mama"; "Blue Moon of Kentucky"; "I Don't Care If the Sun Don't Shine"; "I'm Left, You're Right, She's Gone"; ("My Baby's Gone," take 9); "I'll Never Let You Go (Little Darlin')"; "When It Rains It Really Pours"; (the alternative takes) "I Love You Because" (takes 3, 4, 5); "I'm Left, You're Right, She's Gone" ("My Baby's Gone," takes 7, 8, 10, 11, 13, and 12—in that order).

Country Memories (RCA R-244069, released in 1978) was a double LP from RCA's Record Club that featured all previously released songs. *Songs:* "I'll Hold You in My Heart"; "Welcome to My World"; "It Keeps Right On A-Hurtin' "; "Release Me"; "Make the World Go Away"; "Snowbird"; "Early Morning Rain"; "I'm So Lonesome I Could Cry"; "Funny How Time Slips Away"; "I'm Movin' On"; "Help Me Make It Through the Night"; "You Don't Know Me"; "How Great Thou Art"; "I Washed My Hands in Muddy Water"; "I Forgot to Remember to Forget"; "Your Cheatin' Heart"; "Baby, Let's Play House"; "Whole Lotta Shakin' Goin' On"; "Gentle on My Mind"; "For the Good Times."

Country Music (Time-Life, STW-106, released in 1981) sold in grocery stores. Electronically rechanneled to simulate stereo. *Songs:* "Blue Moon of Kentucky"; "Old Shep"; "When My Blue Moon Turns to Gold Again"; "Are You Lonesome Tonight?"; "Your Cheatin' Heart"; "Wooden Heart"; "Suspicious Minds"; "Little Cabin on the Hill"; "U.S. Male."

Date with Elvis, A (RCA LPM-2011, released in September 1959) with double cover. First issued with photos of Elvis leaving America for West Germany and a calendar on the reverse with his return date circled (which was incorrectly marked at March 24; he was discharged on March 5). The album reached No. 32 on *Billboard*'s Top LP chart during an eight-week stay. *Songs:* "Blue Moon of Kentucky"; "Young and Beautiful"; "(You're So Square) Baby, I Don't Care"; "Milkcow Blues Boogie"; "Baby, Let's Play House"; "Good Rockin' Tonight"; "Is It So Strange?"; "We're Gonna Move"; "I Want to Be Free"; "I Forgot to Remember to Forget." *A Date With Elvis* (RCA LSP-2011-e, released in January 1965) was a stereo release of RCA LPM-2011). *A Date With Elvis* (RCA AFL1-2011-e, released in 1977) was simply a new number given to RCA LSP-2011-e).

Double Dynamite (Pickwick DL2-5001, released in December 1975) two records with selections from nine RCA

Camden LPs. *Songs:* "Burning Love"; "I'll Be There (If Ever You Want Me)"; "Fools Fall in Love"; "Follow That Dream"; "You'll Never Walk Alone"; "Flaming Star"; "The Yellow Rose of Texas"/"The Eyes of Texas"; "Old Shep"; "Mama"; "Rubberneckin' "; "U.S. Male"; "Frankie and Johnny"; "If You Think I Don't Need You"; "Easy Come, Easy Go"; "Separate Ways"; "Peace in the Valley"; "Big Boss Man"; "It's a Matter of Time." *Double Dynamite* (RCA PDL2-1010, released in mid-1982) was a reissue of the double LP DL2-5001 with a different cover and without "If You Think I Don't Need You" and "You'll Never Walk Alone."

*Double Trouble (RCA LPM-3787, released in June 1967) has eight songs from Elvis's film *Double Trouble*. A bonus photo was included in the first run and then eliminated. The album reached No. 47 during twenty weeks on *Billboard*'s Top LP chart. *Songs:* "Double Trouble"; "Baby, If You'll Give Me All of Your Love"; "Could I Fall in Love"; "Long Legged Girl (With the Short Dress On)"; "City by Night"; "Old MacDonald"; "I Love Only One Girl"; "There Is So Much World to See"; and bonus songs: "It Won't Be Long"; "Never Ending"; "Blue River"; "What Now, What Next, Where To?" **Double Trouble* (RCA LSP-3787, released in June 1967) was a stereo release on RCA LPM-3787; and RCA AFL1-2564 released in September 1977, was simply a new number given to RCA LSP-3787.

Earth News (EN 8-22-77) was a series of five-minute segments released the week of Elvis's death, August 22–29, 1977, to radio stations that subscribed to Earth News Network's programming. It featured fourteen segments in all from 1956, plus interviews with Elvis, Red West, Willie Mae Thornton, Steve Binder, and the Dick Clark/Elvis phone call "interview."

*Elvis (RCA LPM-1382), Elvis's second album, was released in October 1956. With the exception of "So Glad You're Mine" the album's songs were recorded from September 1–3, 1956, at RCA's Studio B in Hollywood. RIAA gold certification came after 3 million copies were sold. It was No. 1 for five weeks out of thirty-two on *Billboard*'s Top LP chart. *Songs:* "Rip It Up"; "Love Me"; "When My Blue Moon Turns to Gold Again"; "Long Tall Sally"; "First in Line"; "Paralyzed"; "So Glad You're Mine"; "Old Shep"; "Ready Teddy"; "Any Place Is Paradise"; "How's the World Treating You?"; "How Do You Think I Feel." RIAA Gold Award.

*Elvis (RCA LSP-1382-e, released in February 1962) is an electronically reprocessed stereo release. *Elvis* (RCA AFL1-1382-e, released in 1977) is simply a new number for RCA LSP-1382-e. *Elvis* (RCA AFM1-5199, released in 1985) celebrates the fiftieth anniversary of Elvis's birth with a special label and gold paper band around its jacket; digitally remastered in mono.

*Elvis (RCA APL1-0283, released in July 1973) with 1970s recordings from Nashville, Hollywood, and Las Vegas. The album peaked at No. 52 on *Billboard*'s Top LP chart during a thirteen-week stay. *Songs:* "Fool"; "Where Do I Go From Here?"; "Love Me, Love the Life I Lead"; "It's Still Here"; "It's Impossible"; "For Lovin' Me"; "Padre"; "I'll Take You Home Again, Kathleen"; "I Will Be True"; "Don't Think Twice, It's All Right."

*Elvis (RCA DPL2-0056-e, released in August 1973); two records with twenty top hits. The album, sold via TV ads and not in stores, sold 3 million copies and received RIAA certification. *Songs:* "Hound Dog"; "I Want You, I Need You, I Love You"; "All Shook Up"; "Don't"; "I Beg of You"; "A Big Hunk o' Love"; "Love Me"; "Stuck on You"; "Good Luck Charm"; "Return to Sender"; "Don't Be Cruel"; "Loving You"; "Jailhouse Rock"; "Can't Help Falling in Love"; "I Got Stung"; "Teddy Bear"; "Love Me Tender"; "Hard Headed Woman"; "It's Now or Never"; "Surrender."

Elvis—A Canadian Tribute (RCA KKL1-7065, released in October 1978) was first distributed in Canada because of the many Canadian composers on the album. The limited-edition, numbered album sold over six hundred thousand copies for its gold certification, and it reached No. 86 in seven weeks on *Billboard*'s Top LP chart and No. 7 during eighteen weeks on the Hot Country LP chart. *Songs:* introduction, "Jailhouse Rock"; introduction, "Teddy Bear"; "Loving You"; "Until It's Time for You to Go"; "Early Morning Rain"; the 1957 Vancouver press conference with Elvis; "I'm Movin' On"; "Snowbird"; "For Lovin' Me"; "Put Your Hand in the Hand"; "Little Darlin' "; "My Way."

*Elvis—A Collectors' Edition (RCA TB-1, released in 1976) is a boxed set made in Canada and sold via ads on TV. It consists of previously sold songs from other LPs: *Elvis* (RCA DPL2-0056-e, *Elvis Forever*, and *Elvis in Hollywood*. A twenty-page booklet was a bonus with the purchase.

*Elvis—A Legendary Performer, Vol. **1** (RCA CPL1-0341, released in January 1974), with an alternative take of "I Love You Because" and the U.S. release of "Tonight's All Right for Love." RIAA certified the album gold on January 8, 1975. It reached No. 43 during fourteen weeks on *Billboard*'s Top LP chart. By 1978, it recharted at No. 62 during fourteen more weeks on the Top LP chart. *Songs:* "That's All Right Mama"; "I Love You Because"; "Heartbreak Hotel"; "Don't Be Cruel"; "Love Me"; "Trying to Get to You"; "Love Me Tender"; "Peace in the Valley"; "A Fool Such As I"; "Tonight's All Right for Love" (unreleased song from *G.I. Blues*); "Are You Lonesome Tonight? (unreleased live version); "Can't Help Falling in Love;" excerpts from Elvis's live press concert, September 22, 1958. RIAA's Gold Award.

*Elvis—A Legendary Performer, Vol. **2** (RCA CPL1-1349, released in January 1976) included unreleased live versions of "Blue Suede Shoes" and "Baby, What You Want Me to Do" (from "Elvis," the TV special) and an alternative take on "I Want You, I Need You, I Love You" and unreleased versions of "Harbor Lights," "Blue Suede Shoes,"

and "Blue Hawaii." There is also an interview with Jay Thompson from Wichita, Kansas (April 13, 1956) and a press conference aboard the USS *Arizona* from March 25, 1961. A booklet of sixteen pages titled "The Early Years Continued" is included. RIAA gold-certified October 25, 1977, it reached No. 46 in seventeen weeks on *Billboard*'s Top LP chart. *Songs:* "Harbor Lights" (new release); Thompson interview with Elvis; "How Great Thou Art"; "If I Can Dream"; "I Want You, I Need You, I Love You" (alternative take); "Blue Suede Shoes"; "Blue Christmas"; "Jailhouse Rock"; "It's Now or Never"; "Blue Hawaii" (live recording); "Cane and a High Starched Collar" (new release); presentation of awards to Elvis; "Blue Hawaii"; "Such a Night"; "Baby What You Want Me to Do"; "How Great Thou Art"; "If I Can Dream." RIAA's Gold Award.

Elvis—A Legendary Performer, Vol. **3** (RCA CPL1-3078, released in December 1978), included a limited-edition picture disc; same songs as RCA CPL1-3082.

Elvis—A Legendary Performer, Vol. **4** (RCA CPL1-4848, released in November 1983); "Plantation Rock" was released and "Mona Lisa" and "I'm Beginning to Forget You" had recently been found at Graceland. The Ann-Margret–Elvis duet from *Viva Las Vegas*, "The Lady Loves Me," is included as well as an interview with Elvis, and Ray and Norma Pillow. *Songs:* "When It Rains, It Really Pours"; interviews with Ray and Norma Pillow; "One Night"; "I'm Beginning to Forget You"; "Mona Lisa"; "Plantation Rock"; "Swing Down, Sweet Chariot"; "The Lady Loves Me"; "Wooden Heart"; "That's All Right, Mama"; "Are You Lonesome Tonight?"; "Reconsider Baby"; "I'll Remember You."

Elvis Aron Presley (with misspelled middle name; RCA CPL8-3699, released in July 1980), an eight-LP boxed set to celebrate Elvis's twenty-five years with RCA. Seventy-eight songs with sixty-five new releases by RCA. The album reached No. 27 on *Billboard*'s Top LP chart during a fourteen-week stay. It hit No. 8 on the Hot Country LP chart and quickly sold over six hundred thousand copies. An enjoyable overview grouping. *Songs:* (Early Live Performance) "Heartbreak Hotel"; "Long Tall Sally"; "Blue Suede Shoes"; "Money Honey;" an Elvis monologue; (An Early Benefit Performance) "A Fool Such As I"; "I Got a Woman"; "Love Me"; introductions; "Such a Night"; "Reconsider Baby"; "I Need Your Love Tonight"; "That's All Right, Mama"; "Don't Be Cruel"; "One Night"; "Are You Lonesome Tonight?"; "It's Now or Never"; "Swing Down, Sweet Chariot"; "Hound Dog"; (Collector's Gold From the Movie Years) "They Remind Me Too Much of You"; "Tonight Is So Right for Love"; "Follow That Dream"; "Wild in the Country"; "Datin' " Shoppin' Around"; "Can't Help Falling in Love"; "A Dog's Life"; "I'm Falling In Love Tonight"; "Thanks to the Rolling Sea"; (The TV Specials "Elvis: Aloha From Hawaii" and "Elvis in Concert") "Jailhouse Rock"; "Suspicious Minds"; "Lawdy Miss Clawdy"; "Baby What You Want Me to Do"; "Blue Christmas"; "You Gave Me a Mountain"; "Welcome to My World"; "Tryin' to Get to You"; "I'll Remember You"; "My Way"; (The Las Vegas Years) "Polk Salad Annie"; "You've Lost That Lovin' Feelin' "; "Sweet Caroline"; "Kentucky Rain"; "Are You Lonesome Tonight?"; "My Babe"; "In the Ghetto"; "An American Trilogy"; "Little Sister"; "Get Back"; "Yesterday"; (Lost Singles) "I'm Leavin' "; "The First Time Ever I Saw Your Face"; "High Heel Sneakers"; "Softly, As I Leave You"; "Unchained Melody"; "Fool"; "Rags to Riches"; "It's Only Love"; "America the Beautiful"; (Elvis at the Piano) "It's Still Here"; "I'll Take You Home Again, Kathleen"; "Beyond the Reef"; "I Will Be True"; (The Concert Years, Part One) "Also Sprach Zarathustra"; "I Gotta Woman"/"Amen"/"I Gotta Woman"; "Love Me"; "If You Love Me (Let Me Know)"; "Love Me Tender"; "All Shook Up"; "Teddy Bear"/"Don't Be Cruel"; (The Concert Years, Concluded) "Hound Dog"; "The Wonder of You"; "Burning Love"; dialogue/introductions "Johnny B. Goode"; introductions/"Long Live Rock and Roll"; "T-R-O-U-B-L-E"; "Why Me, Lord?"; "How Great Thou Art"; "Let Me Be There"; "An American Trilogy"; "Funny How Time Slips Away"; "Little Darlin' "; "Mystery Train"/"Tiger Man"; "Can't Help Falling in Love."

Elvis Aron Presley—Forever (RCA PDL2-1185, released in March 1988) is a two-record set that did not chart. *Songs:* "Blue Hawaii"; "Hawaiian Wedding Song"; "No More"; "Early Morning Rain"; "Pieces of My Life"; "I Can Help"; "Bringing It Back"; "Green, Green Grass of Home"; "Mean Woman Blues"; "Loving You"; "Got a Lot o' Livin' to Do"; "Blueberry Hill"; "T-R-O-U-B-L-E"; "And I Love You So"; "Woman Without Love"; "Shake a Hand."

*Elvis As Recorded at Madison Square Garden (RCA LSP-4776, released in June 1972). Recorded on June 10, 1972, at the evening concert at Madison Square Garden, New York City. RIAA certification for gold, August 4, 1972. The album reached No. 34 during eleven weeks on *Billboard*'s Top LP chart. *Songs:* Introduction; "Also Sprach Zarathustra"; "That's All Right, Mama"; "Proud Mary"; "Never Been to Spain"; "You Don't Have to Say You Love Me"; "You've Lost That Lovin' Feelin' "; "Polk Salad Annie"; "Love Me"; "All Shook Up"; "Heartbreak Hotel"; "Teddy Bear"/"Don't Be Cruel"; "Love Me Tender"; "The Impossible Dream"; introductions by Elvis; "Hound Dog"; "Suspicious Minds"; "For the Good Times"; "An American Trilogy"; "Funny How Time Slips Away"; "I Can't Stop Loving You"; "Can't Help Falling in Love." RIAA's two-time Platinum Award winner.

Elvis As Recorded at Madison Square Garden (RCA AQL1-4776, released in 1979) is simply a new number for RCA LSP-4776.

*Elvis' Christmas Album (RCA LOC-1035, released in November 1957) with twelve songs, four from his EP *Peace* *in the Valley* and eight recorded in Hollywood's Radio Recorders, September 5–7, 1956. No. 1 for four weeks out of seven on *Billboard*'s Best Selling LP chart, December 1957. *Songs:* "Santa Claus Is Back in Town"; "White Christmas"; "Here Comes Santa Claus"; "I'll Be Home for Christmas"; "Blue Christmas"; "Santa, Bring My Baby Back (to Me)"; "O Little Town of Bethlehem"; "Silent Night"; "Peace in the Valley"; "I Believe"; "Take My Hand, Precious Lord"; "It Is No Secret." RIAA two-time Platinum Award winner.

*Elvis' Christmas Album (RCA LPM-1951, released in November 1958) is simply a new number given to RCA LOC-1035, with a new album cover. The album hit *Billboard*'s Top LP chart at No. 33, January 1961; No. 120 in January 1962; No. 59 in December 1962. **Elvis' Christmas Album* (RCA LSP-1951-e, released in November 1964) is a reissue of LPM-1951 and is an electronically reprocessed stereo album. *Elvis' Christmas Album* (RCA AFM1-5486, released in September 1985) is a digitally remastered mono reissue of RCA LPM-1951. Made of green vinyl, it hit No. 178 during two weeks on *Billboard*'s Top LP chart.

*Elvis' Christmas Album (RCA Camden CAL-2428, released in November 1970) with "Mama Liked the Roses" and a completely new collection of Christmas tunes. *Songs:* "Blue Christmas"; "Silent Night"; "White Christmas"; "Santa Claus Is Back in Town"; "I'll Be Home for Christmas"; "If Every Day Was Like Christmas"; "Here Comes Santa Claus"; "O Little Town of Bethlehem"; "Santa, Bring My Baby Back (to Me)"; "Mama Liked the Roses." *Elvis' Christmas Album* (RCA CAS-2428, released in December 1975) is a reissue of RCA Camden CAL-2428; cover change; monaural. RIAA's Platinum Award winner.

*Elvis Country (RCA LSP-4460, released in January 1971) with songs recorded at RCA's Nashville studios, all sung in 1970. RIAA gold certification, December 1, 1977. The album reached No. 12 in a twenty-one-week stay on *Bill-*

board's Top LP chart and No. 6 on Hot Country LPs in a twenty-six-week stay. The eight-track cartridge set hit No. 12 on *Billboard*'s Best-Selling cartridges chart. *Songs:* "Snowbird"; "Tomorrow Never Comes"; "Little Cabin on the Hill"; "Whole Lotta Shakin' Goin' On"; "Funny How Time Slips Away"; "I Really Don't Want to Know"; "There Goes My Everything"; "It's Your Baby, You Rock It"; "The Fool"; "Faded Love"; "I Washed My Hands in Muddy Water"; "Make the World Go Away"; "I Was Born About Ten Thousand Years Ago." *Elvis Country* (RCA AFL1-4460, released in 1977 was simply a new number for RCA LSP-4460.) *Elvis Country* (RCA AYMI-3956, released in May 1981) was a new number given to RCA AFL1-4460, and it's an LP in the Best Buy series of RCA records.

Elvis Country (RCA DPL1-0647, released in 1984) is from the Dominion Music Corporation, distributed to discount stores on the ERA Records (BU 3930). *Songs:* "Are You Lonesome Tonight?"; "Suspicion"; "Your Cheatin' Heart"; "Blue Moon of Kentucky"; "Don't"; "I Forgot to Remember to Forget"; "Help Me Make It Through the Night"; "Kentucky Rain"; "I Really Don't Want to Know"; "Hurt"; "There's a Honky Tonk Angel (Who Will Take Me Back In)"; "Always on My Mind"; "Green, Green Grass of Home."

*Elvis for Everyone (RCA LPM-3450, released in June 1965) with unreleased 1957 recordings. It reached No. 10 on *Billboard*'s Top LP chart during a twenty-seven-week stay. The cover showed Elvis in a record store, behind the counter, with five other albums showing. *Songs:* "Your Cheatin' Heart"; "Summer Kisses, Winter Tears"; "Finders Keepers, Losers Weepers"; "In My Way"; "Tomorrow Night"; "Memphis, Tennessee"; "For the Millionth and Last Time"; "Forget Me Never"; "Sound Advice"; "Santa Lucia"; "I Met Her Today"; "When It Rains, It Really Pours." **Elvis for Everyone* (RCA LSP-3450, released in July 1965) is in stereo. *Elvis for Everyone* (RCA AFL1-3450) was released in 1977 and is simply a

new number for RCA LSP-3450). *Elvis for Everyone* (RCA AYM1-4332) was released in February 1982 and is a new number for RCA AFL1-3450. It is now a Best Buy LP.)

Elvis Forever (RCA KSL2-7031, released in February 1974), is a Canadian release sold in the U.S. via TV ads; two-records. *Songs:* "Treat Me Nice"; "I Need Your Love Tonight"; "That's When Your Heartaches Begin"; "G.I. Blues"; "Blue Hawaii"; "Easy Come, Easy Go"; "Suspicion"; "Puppet on a String"; "Heartbreak Hotel"; "One Night"; "Memories"; "Blue Suede Shoes"; "Are You Lonesome Tonight?"; "High Heel Sneakers"; "Old Shep"; "Rip It Up"; "Such a Night"; "A Fool Such as I"; "Tutti Frutti"; "In the Ghetto"; "Wear My Ring Around Your Neck"; "Wooden Heart"; "Crying in the Chapel"; "Don't Cry, Daddy."

Elvis' Gold Records, Vol. 4 (RCA LPM-3921, released in February 1968), with million sellers. This was the last of the monaural albums. A seven-by-nine-inch photo of Elvis was included. The album hit No. 33 in a twenty-two-week stay on *Billboard*'s Top LP chart. *Songs:* "Love Letters"; "Witchcraft"; "It Hurts Me"; "What'd I Say"; "Please Don't Drag That String Around"; "Indescribably Blue"; "(You're the) Devil in Disguise"; "Lonely Man"; "A Mess of Blues"; "Ask Me"; "Ain't That Loving You, Baby?"; "Just Tell Her Jim Said Hello." *Elvis' Gold Records*, Vol. 4 (RCA LSP-3921, released in February 1968) is in stereo. *Elvis' Gold Records*, Vol. 4 (RCA AFL1-3921, released in 1977 is a new number given to RCA LSP-3921). RIAA's Gold Award.

Elvis' Gold Records, Vol. 5 (RCA AFL1-4941, released in March 1984), included ten million-sellers. *Songs:* "Suspicious Minds"; "Kentucky Rain"; "In the Ghetto"; "Clean Up Your Own Back Yard"; "If I Can Dream"; "Burning Love"; "If You Talk in Your Sleep"; "For the Heart"; "Moody Blue"; "Way Down."

Elvis' Golden Records (RCA LPM-1707, released in April 1958) contained fourteen gold records. There are many mistakes on the liner notes of the album. The album received its RIAA gold certification on October 17, 1961. It reached No. 3 on *Billboard*'s Best-Selling LP chart during a forty-week stay. In 1978, it recharted at No. 63 during twenty-three weeks on the chart. In London, the album was on a red label (RCA RB-16069). *Songs:* "Hound Dog"; "Loving You"; "All Shook Up"; "Heartbreak Hotel"; "Jailhouse Rock"; "Love Me"; "Too Much"; "Don't Be Cruel"; "That's When Your Heartbreaks Begin"; "Teddy Bear"; "Love Me Tender"; "Treat Me Nice"; "Any Way You Want Me"; "I Want You, I Need You, I Love You." *Elvis' Golden Records* (RCA LSP-1707-e, released in February 1962) was an electronically reprocessed stereo album. *Elvis' Golden Records* (RCA AFL1-1707-e, released in 1977) was a new number for RCA LSP-1707-e. *Elvis' Golden Records* (RCA AQL1-1707-e, released in 1979) was a new number for RCA AFL1-1707-e. *Elvis' Golden Records* (RCA AFM1-5196, released in 1985) featured all tracks digitally remastered and restored, monaural sound, a gold band around the album, and a fiftieth "Anniversary" label. RIAA's five-time Platinum Award winner.

Elvis' Golden Records, Vol. 3 (RCA LPM-2765, released in September 1963) included all million sellers, and an eight-by-ten-inch color photo booklet. The album received its RIAA gold certification on November 1, 1966. It reached No. 3 during a forty-week stay on *Billboard*'s Top LP chart. After Elvis died, it reentered the chart and reached No. 64. *Songs:* "It's Now or Never"; "Stuck on You"; "Fame and Fortune"; "I Gotta Know"; "Surrender"; "I Feel So Bad"; "Are You Lonesome Tonight?"; "Good Luck Charm"; "Anything That's Part of You"; "She's Not You." *Elvis' Golden Records*, Vol. 3 (RCA LSP-2765) was a stereo release, September 1963). *Elvis' Golden Records*, Vol. 3 (RCA AFL1-2765, released in 1977) was a new number for RCA LSP-2765). RIAA's Platinum Award.

Elvis! His Greatest Hits (RCA RDA-0101A, released in 1979) was a seven-LP boxed set from *Reader's Digest* with a booklet of liner notes and a bonus LP, *Elvis Sings Inspirational Favorites.* Eighty-four songs are included, previously listed and recorded many times.

Elvis: His Songs of Inspiration (RCA DML1-0264, released in 1977) was supplied by Candlelite Music to people who bought the five-LP boxed set *The Elvis Presley Story.* Songs: "Crying in the Chapel"; "Put Your Hand in the Hand"; "I Believe"; "How Great Thou Art"; "If I Can Dream"; "Peace in the Valley"; "Amazing Grace"; "An American Trilogy"; "Follow That Dream"; "You'll Never Walk Alone."

Elvis in Concert (RCA APL2-2587, released in October 1977) features songs from Elvis's concerts in Omaha, Nebraska, on June 19, 1977, and Rapid City, South Dakota, on June 21, 1977. The album went platinum within seven days, receiving certification on October 14, 1977. It reached No. 5 in a seventeen-week stay on *Billboard*'s Top LP chart. It was Elvis's last recorded LP to chart. *Songs:* comments from fans with an opening riff: "Also Sparch Zarathustra" opening riff; "See See Rider"; "That's All Right, Mama"; "Are You Lonesome Tonight?"; "Teddy Bear"; "Don't Be Cruel"; comments from fans; "You Gave Me a Mountain"; "Jailhouse Rock"; fans' comments; "How Great Thou Art"; fans' comments; "I Really Don't Want to Know"; Elvis introduces Vernon Presley; "Hound Dog"; "My Way"; "Can't Help Falling in Love"; closing riff and message from Vernon Presley; "I Got a Woman"; "Amen"; Elvis talks; "Love Me"; "O Sole Mio" (Sherrill Neilsen); "It's Now or Never"; "Tryin' to Get to You"; "Hawaiian Wedding Song"; "Fairytale"; "Little Sister"; "Early Morning Rain"; "What'd I Say"; "Johnny B. Goode"; "And I Love You So." *Elvis in Concert* (RCA CPL2-2587, released in 1982) was a new number for RCA APL2-2587).

Elvis in Demand (RCA PL42003, released in 1977) came out in honor of the twenty-first year of the Official Elvis Presley Fan Club of Great Britain. Its members selected their favorite songs for the album. *Songs:* "Suspicion"; "High Heel Sneakers"; "Got a Lot o' Livin' to Do"; "Have I Told You Lately That I Love You?"; "Please Don't Drag That String Around"; "It's Only Love"; "The Sound of Your Cry"; "Viva Las Vegas"; "Do Not Disturb"; "Tomorrow Is a Long Time"; "(It's a) Long Lonely Highway"; "Puppet on a String"; "The First Time Ever I Saw Your Face"; "Summer Kisses, Winter Tears"; "It Hurts Me"; "Let It Be Me."

*Elvis in Hollywood (RCA DPL2-0168, released in January 1976) was two records, sold only from TV ads. Except for three songs, all are movie-title songs. A twenty-three-page booklet is included. *Songs:* "Jailhouse Rock"; "Rock-A-Hula-Baby"; "G.I. Blues"; "Kissin' Cousins"; "Wild in the Country"; "King Creole"; "Blue Hawaii"; "Fun in Acapulco"; "Follow That Dream"; "Girls! Girls! Girls!"; "Viva Las Vegas"; "Bossa Nova Baby"; "Flaming Star"; "Girl Happy"; "Frankie and Johnny"; "Roustabout"; "Spinout"; "Double Trouble"; "Charro"; "They Remind Me Too Much of You."

*Elvis in Person at the International Hotel, Las Vegas, Nevada (RCA LSP-4428, released in November 1970) features selections from the *From Memphis to Vegas/From Vegas to Memphis* LP, recorded live in concert, August 22 and 26, 1969. *Songs:* "Blue Suede Shoes"; "Johnny B. Goode"; "All Shook Up"; "Are You Lonesome Tonight?"; "Hound Dog"; "I Can't Stop Loving You"; "My Babe"; "Mystery Train"; "Tiger Man"; "Words"; "In the Ghetto"; "Suspicious Minds"; "Can't Help Falling in Love." *Elvis in Person at the International Hotel, Las Vegas, Nevada* (RCA AFL1-4428, released in 1977) was a new number for RCA LSP-4428; and RCA AYL1-3892, released in February 1981, was a new number for RCA ALF1-4428, which is now an RCA LP Best Buy.

*Elvis Is Back (RCA LPM-2231, released

in April 1960) has songs from 1960, recorded at RCA's Nashville studios. Bonus photos included in an album booklet. It was No. 2 for three out of fifty-six weeks on *Billboard*'s Best-Selling LP chart. *Songs:* "Make Me Know It"; "Fever"; "The Girl of My Best Friend"; "I Will Be Home Again"; "Dirty Feeling"; "Thrill of Your Love"; "Soldier Boy"; "Such a Night"; "It Feels So Right"; "The Girl Next Door Went A-Walking"; "Like a Baby"; "Reconsider Baby." *Elvis Is Back* (RCA LSP-2231, released in April 1960) was a stereo release and reached No. 9 during fourteen weeks on *Billboard*'s Best-Selling Stereophonic LP chart). *Elvis Is Back* (RCA AFL1-2231, released in 1977) was a new number for RCA LSP-2231).

Elvis Love Songs (K-Tel NU-9900, released in October 1981) was sold through The K-Tel Company via TV ads and then in record stores. *Songs:* "Suspicious Minds"; "She's Not You"; "The Wonder of You"; "Love Letters"; "Wooden Heart"; "I Want You, I Need You, I Love You"; "Memories"; "Kentucky Rain"; "Love Me Tender"; "It's Now or Never"; "Are You Lonesome Tonight?"; "You Don't Have to Say You Love Me"; "I Just Can't Help Believin' "; "Can't Help Falling in Love"; "Surrender"; "Loving You."

The Elvis Medley (RCA AHL1-4530, released in November 1982) it reached No. 133 during a nine-week stay on *Billboard*'s Top LP Chart. *Songs:* "Jailhouse Rock"/"Teddy Bear"/"Hound Dog"/"Don't Be Cruel"/"Burning Love"/ "Suspicious Minds" (medley); "Jailhouse Rock"; "Teddy Bear"; "Hound Dog"; "Don't Be Cruel"; "Burning Love"; "Suspicious Minds"; "Always on My Mind"; "Heartbreak Hotel"; "Hard Headed Woman."

Elvis Memories (ABC Radio ASP-1003, released in December 1978) was a three-LP boxed set produced by ABC Radio. The three-hour program aired on January 7, 1979, and scanned Elvis's career and featured all previously released hits.

Elvis Now (RCA LSP-4671, released in February 1972). All songs were re-corded at RCA's Nashville studios in 1970 and 1971, except for "Hey Jude" (American Sound Studios, January 1969). The album reached No. 43 in nineteen weeks on *Billboard*'s Top LP chart. *Songs:* "Help Me Make It Through the Night"; "Miracle of the Rosary"; "Hey Jude"; "Put Your Hand in the Hand"; "Until It's Time for You to Go"; "We Can Make the Morning"; "Early Morning Rain"; "Sylvia"; "Fools Rush In"; "I Was Born About Ten Thousand Years Ago." *Elvis Now* (RCA AFL1-4671, released in 1977) was a new number for RCA LSP-4671. RIAA's Gold Award.

Elvis Presley (RCA LPM-1254, released in March 1956) was Elvis's first album, with five songs from Sun Records and seven from January 1956. (New York City and Nashville studios, RCA.) Gold RIAA certification was received on November 1, 1966. The album peaked at No. 1 for ten weeks out of forty-nine on *Billboard*'s Best-Selling Pop Albums chart. *Songs:* "Blue Suede Shoes"; "I'm Counting on You"; "I Got a Woman"; "One-Sided Love Affair"; "I Love You Because"; "Just Because"; "Tutti Frutti"; "Tryin' to Get to You"; "I'm Gonna Sit Right Down and Cry (Over You)"; "I'll Never Let You Go (Little Darlin')"; "Blue Moon"; "Money Honey." *Elvis Presley* (RCA LSP-1254-e, released in February 1962) is an electronically reprocessed stereo album. *Elvis Presley* (RCA AFL1-1254-e, released in 1977) is a new number for RCA LSP-1254-e. *Elvis Presley* (RCA AFM1-5198, released in 1985) celebrated the fiftieth year of Elvis's birth, with digitally remastered songs in monaural sound.

Elvis Presley Collection, The Vol. 1 (RCA Camden PDA-009, released in 1976), contained two LPs, *You'll Never Walk Alone* and *Elvis Sings Hits From His Movies*, Vol. 1.

Elvis Presley Collection, The Vol. 2 (RCA Camden PDA-042, released in 1979) was a two-record import from Great Britain and contained the LP *Separate Ways* and selections from other LPs previously released on Camden.

Elvis Presley Story, The (RCA DML5-0263, released in July 1977) was a special five-LP boxed set by Candlelite Music, sold on TV and in advertisements, featuring all previously released works of Elvis's entire career.

Elvis Presley Story, The (Watermark EPS 1A-13B, released in 1975) aired in 1970 as a twelve-hour radio show. In 1975, it was expanded to thirteen hours on thirteen LPs. Consists of all previously released music, plus interviews with Elvis as well as other singers.

Elvis Presley Story, The (Watermark EPS 1A-13B, released in 1977) is a thirteen-LP boxed set identical to the EPS 1A-13B first released, except for a few minor changes on sides one and twenty-six due to Elvis's death.

Elvis Recorded Live on Stage in Memphis (RCA CPL1-0606, released in June 1974) was recorded on March 20, 1974, at the Mid-South Coliseum in Memphis. Elvis is listed as executive producer and Al Dvorin is featured as the master of ceremonies. The album reached No. 33 in a thirteen-week stay on *Billboard*'s Top LP chart. *Songs:* "See See Rider"; "I Got a Woman"; "Love Me"; "Tryin' to Get to You"; "Long Tall Sally"; "Whole Lotta Shakin' Goin' On"/"Your Mama Don't Dance"/ "Flip, Flop, and Fly"; "Jailhouse Rock"/ "Hound Dog"; "Why Me, Lord?"; "How Great Thou Art"; "Blueberry Hill"/"I Can't Stop Loving You"; "Help Me"; "An American Trilogy"; "Let Me Be There"; "My Baby Left Me"; "Lawdy Miss Clawdy"; "Can't Stop Loving You." *Elvis Recorded Live on Stage in Memphis* (RCA APD1-0606, released in June 1974) was a quadradisc release. RCA AFL1-0606 was a new number for RCA CPL1-0606, released in 1977. RCA AQL1-4776, released in 1979, was a new number for RCA AFL1-0606.

Elvis Remembered (Creative Radio, CRS 1A-3B, released in 1978). Creative Radio Shows of Berkeley, California, produced this three-LP overview of Elvis's career. Cue sheets are included, plus live versions of five songs.

Elvis Sings Flaming Star (RCA Camden CAS-2304, released in April 1969) was Elvis's first Camden release. The album peaked at No. 96 during a sixteen-week stay on *Billboard*'s Top LP chart. *Songs:* "Flaming Star"; "Wonderful World"; "Night Life"; "All I Needed Was the Rain"; "Too Much Monkey Business"; "The Yellow Rose of Texas"/"The Eyes of Texas"; "She's a Machine"; "Do the Vega"; "Tiger Man." *Elvis Sings Flaming Star* (Pickwick CAS-2304, released in December 1975) was a reissue of RCA Camden CAS-2304).

Elvis Sings for Children and Grown-ups Too (RCA CPL1-2901, released in July 1978) contains all old releases except for "Big Boots" (an alternate take). A greeting card was attached to the album. During an eleven-week stay on *Billboard*'s Top LP chart, the album reached No. 130. In six weeks it peaked at No. 5 on the Country LP chart. *Songs:* "Teddy Bear"; "Wooden Heart"; "Five Sleepy Heads"; "Puppet on a String"; "Angel"; "Old MacDonald"; "How Would You Like to Be?"; "Cotton Candy Land"; "Old Shep"; "Big Boots"; "Have a Happy."

Elvis Sings Hits From His Movies, Vol. 1 (RCA Camden CAS-2567, released in June 1967). "Guitar Man" and "Big Boss Man" were not from any of his movies, despite the album's title. During a fifteen-week stay on *Billboard*'s Top LP chart, it hit No. 87. *Songs:* "Down by the Riverside"/"When the Saints Go Marching In"; "They Remind Me Too Much of You"; "Confidence"; "Frankie and Johnny"; "Guitar Man"; "Long Legged Girl (With the Short Dress On)"; "You Don't Know Me"; "How Would You Like to Be?"; "Big Boss Man"; "Old MacDonald." *Elvis Sings Hits From His Movies*, Vol. 1 (Pickwick CAS-2567, released in December 1975) is a reissue of Camden CAS-2567.

Elvis Sings the Wonderful World of Christmas (RCA LSP-4579, released in October 1971). The album's eleven songs were recorded at RCA's Nashville studios in May 1971. A five-by-seven-inch color postcard was inside the album jacket. *Songs:* "O Come, All Ye Faithful"; "The First Noel"; "On a Snowy Christmas Night"; "Winter Wonderland"; "The Wonderful World of Christmas"; "It Won't Seem Like Christmas (Without You)"; "I'll Be Home on Christmas Day"; "If I Get Home on Christmas"; "Holly Leaves and Christmas Trees"; "Merry Christmas, Baby"; "Silver Bells." **Elvis Sings the Wonderful World of Christmas* (RCA ANL1-1936, released in 1973) was a new number for RCA LSP-4579, and a Pure Gold series album. It received its RIAA gold certification on November 4, 1977, and in December it went platinum. It received two Platinum Awards.

Elvis Speaks to You (Green Valley Record Store GV-2001/2003, released in April 1978) contains previously released interviews from the LPs *Exclusive Live Press Conference* and *The King Speaks*. Two songs by the Jordanaires, plus a conversation with the Jordanaires about Elvis's life, and a Houston, Texas, interview are included, as well as a February 25, 1961, Memphis interview.

Elvis Talks Back (Flashback Records, released in 1979) features the Vancouver news conference with Peter Noone interview, a telephone conversation between Canadian disc jockey Red Robinson and Colonel Tom Parker in August 1965, and talks on the set of *Charro!* with Charles Warren (producer-director) and two actresses, August 1968.

Elvis Talks!—The Elvis Presley Interview Record (RCA 6313-1-R, released in 1987) was a reissue by a disc jockey promo record called *An Audio Self-Portrait*. This LP was only available via mail order for $12.48 via USA Fulfillment, P.O. Box 1065, Church Hill, Maryland 21690 or via 1-800-872-0728, ext. 722. Included the *TV Guide* interview from September 26, 1956, and interviews from 1960 to 1961.

The Elvis Tapes (Great Northwest Music Company, GNW-4005, released in December 1977) with the August 31, 1957, Vancouver press conference at Empire Stadium right before Elvis's concert performance. The tapes were released on Polydor Records (Polydor 2912-021).

Elvis: The First Live Recordings (Music Works PB-3601, released in February 1984). A five-record set featuring "Louisiana Hayride" performances from the fifties. It peaked at No. 163 during four weeks on *Billboard*'s Top LP chart. *Songs:* "introduction, Horace Logan and Elvis; "Baby, Let's Play House"; "Maybellene, Tweedlee Dee"; "That's All Right, Mama"; comments from Frank Page; "Hound Dog."

Elvis, the Hillbilly Cat (Music Works PB-3602, released in July 1984) contains the first "Louisiana Hayride" performance and "I Got a Woman" and "Good Rockin' Tonight" from a Houston Eagle's Nest performance on March 19, 1955. *Songs:* "introduction with Elvis and Horace Logan; "That's All Right, Mama"; Elvis talking to Horace Logan; "Blue Moon of Kentucky"; thoughts from Frank Page; "Good Rockin' Tonight"; "I Got a Woman."

*Elvis: The Other Sides—Worldwide Gold Award Hits, Vol. 2 (RCA LPM-6402, released in August 1971). A four-record boxed set of gold million sellers. Included are a piece of cloth supposedly from Elvis's white suit in the movie *Clambake* and a color photo of the King. In the album's seven-week stay on *Billboard*'s Top LP chart, it hit No. 120. *Songs:* "Puppet on a String"; "Witchcraft"; "Trouble"; "Poor Boy"; "I Want to Be Free"; "Doncha' Think It's Time"; "Young Dreams"; "The Next Step Is Love"; "You Don't Have to Say You Love Me"; "Paralyzed"; "My Wish Came True"; "When My Blue Moon Turns to Gold"; "Lonesome Cowboy"; "My Baby Left Me"; "It Hurts Me"; "I Need Your Love Tonight"; "Tell Me Why"; "Please Don't Drag That String Around"; "Young and Beautiful"; "Hot Dog"; "New Orleans"; "We're Gonna

Move"; "Crawfish"; "King Creole"; "I
Believe in the Man in the Sky"; "Dix-
ieland Rock"; "The Wonder of You";
"They Remind Me Too Much of You";
"Mean Woman Blues"; "Lonely Man";
"Any Day Now"; "Don't Ask Me Why";
"Marie's the Name—His Latest Flame";
"I Really Don't Want to Know";
"(You're So Square) Baby, I Don't
Care"; "I've Lost You"; "Let Me"; "Love
Me"; "Got a Lot o' Livin' to Do"; "Fame
and Fortune"; "Rip It Up"; "There Goes
My Everything"; "Lover Doll"; "One
Night"; "Just Tell Her Jim Said Hello";
"Ask Me"; "Patch It Up"; "As Long As I
Have You"; "You'll Think of Me"; "Wild
in the Country."

Elvis Today (RCA APL1-1039, released
in May 1975) contains songs recorded
in Hollywood, March 10–13, 1975. The
album hit No. 57 during its thirteen
weeks on *Billboard*'s Top LP chart.
Songs: "T-R-O-U-B-L-E"; "And I Love
You So"; "Susan When She Tried";
"Woman Without Love"; "Shake a
Hand"; "Pieces of My Life"; "Fairytale";
"I Can Help"; "Bringing It Back";
"Green, Green Grass of Home." *Elvis
Today* (RCA APD1-1039, released in
May 1975) was a quadradisc release.
Elvis Today (RCA AFL1-1039, released
in 1977) was a new number for RCA
APL1-1039.

Elvis—TV Special (RCA LPM-4088,
released in November 1968). Al of
these songs were recorded in June
1968 at Western Recorders of Hollywood and NBC-TV's Burbank Studios
for the 1968 TV special. A few takes
are in stereo. On August 27, 1969, the
album received gold certification. The
album reached No. 8 during a thirty-
two-week stay on *Billboard*'s Top LP
chart. *Songs:* "Trouble"/"Guitar Man";
"Lawdy Miss Clawdy"/"Baby What You
Want Me to Do"; dialogue; "Heartbreak
Hotel"/"Hound Dog"/"All Shook Up"/
"Can't Help Falling in Love"/"Jailhouse
Rock"; dialogue; "Love Me Tender";
dialogue; "Where Could I Go But to the
Lord?"/"Up Above My Head"/"Saved";
dialogue; "Blue Christmas"; dialogue;
"One Night"; "Memories"; "Nothings-
ville"; dialogue; "Big Boss Man"/"Guitar

Man"; "Little Egypt"/"Trouble"/"Guitar
Man"/"If I Can Dream." *Elvis—TV Special* (RCA AFM1-4088, released in
1977) was a new number for RCA
LPM-4088. *Elvis—TV Special* (RCA
AYM1-3894, released in February 1981)
was a new number for RCA AFM1-
4088. It is a Best Buy LP.

*Elvis: Worldwide 50 Gold Award
Hits,* **Vol. 1** (RCA LPM-6401, released
in August 1970). A four-record, boxed
set containing fifty gold-record hits. A
twenty-page booklet was included. The
album was certified gold on February
13, 1973, and eventually went platinum.
It reached No. 45 during a twenty-two-
week stay on *Billboard*'s Top LP chart
and reached No. 25 on the Country LP
chart. In 1978, it reentered the Top LP
chart and reached No. 83 during a
fourteen-week stay. *Songs:* "Heartbreak
Hotel"; "I was the One"; "I Want You, I
Need You, I Love You"; "Don't Be
Cruel"; "Hound Dog"; "Love Me Ten-
der"; "Any Way You Want Me"; "Too
Much"; "Playing for Keeps"; "All Shook
Up"; "That's When Your Heartaches
Begin"; "Loving You"; "Teddy Bear";
"Jailhouse Rock"; "Treat Me Nice"; "I
Beg of You"; "Don't"; "Wear My Ring
Around Your Neck"; "Hard Headed
Woman"; "I Got Stung"; "(Now and
Then There's) A Fool Such As I"; "A
Big Hunk o' Love"; "Stuck on You"; "A
Mess of Blues"; "It's Now or Never"; "I
Gotta Know"; "Are You Lonesome To-
night?"; "Surrender"; "I Feel So Bad";
"Little Sister"; "Can't Help Falling in
Love"; "Rock-A-Hula-Baby"; "Anything
That's Part of You"; "Good Luck
Charm"; "She's Not You"; "Return to
Sender"; "Where Do You Come
From?"; "One Broken Heart for Sale";
"(You're the) Devil in Disguise";
"Bossa Nova Baby"; "Kissin' Cousins";
"Viva Las Vegas"; "Ain't That Loving
You, Baby"; "Wooden Heart"; "Crying
in the Chapel"; "If I Can Dream"; "In
the Ghetto"; "Suspicious Minds";
"Don't Cry, Daddy"; "Kentucky Rain";
excerpts from the EP *Elvis Sails.*

Essential Elvis—The First Movies
(RCA 6738-1-R, released in January
1988) with twelve new releases in a

seventeen-song album, three of which were from movies. *Songs:* "Love Me Tender"; "Let Me"; "Poor Boy We're Gonna Move"; "Loving You"; "Party"; "Hot Dog"; "Teddy Bear"; "Loving You"; "Mean Woman Blues"; "Got a Lot o' Livin' to Do"; "Loving You"; "Party"; "Lonesome Cowboy"; "Jailhouse Rock"; "Treat Me Nice"; "Young and Beautiful"; "Don't Leave Me Now"; "I Want to Be Free"; "You're So Square Baby I Don't Care"; "Jailhouse Rock"; "Got a Lot o' Livin' to Do"; "Love Me Tender." (Repeats are different/alternative takes.)

Exclusive Live Press Conference (Green Valley Record Store, GV-2001, released in October 1977) featured the press conference with Elvis held in Memphis at the Claridge Hotel Empire Room, February 25, 1961.

***50,000,000 Elvis Fans Can't Be Wrong—Elvis's Gold Records,* Vol. 2** (RCA LPM-2075, released in December 1959). This album features ten songs that sold over a million copies and was the second in the Gold Record LP series. The cover showed Elvis in his gold-lamé RCA suit. The album was certified gold and reached No. 2 in a six-week stay on *Billboard*'s Top LP chart. *Songs:* "I Need Your Love Tonight"; "Don't"; "Wear My Ring Around Your Neck"; "My Wish Came True"; "I Got Stung"; "One Night"; "A Big Hunk o' Love"; "I Beg of You"; "A Fool Such As I"; "Doncha' Think It's Time."

RCA LSP-2075-e with the same title was an electronically reprocessed stereo album released in February 1962. RCA AFL1-2075-e with the same title, released in 1977, was a new number assigned to RCA LSP-2075-e. RCA AFM1-5197, released in 1985, was with restored tracks and digitally remastered. RIAA's Platinum Award.

Fifty Years, Fifty Hits (RCA SVL3-0710, released in 1985) was a three-LP set available first through TV advertising and then sold via magazine ads and contained previously released songs.

For LP Fans Only (RCA LPM-1990, released in February 1959) was the first record album in history not to mention the artist's name. The back of the album showed Elvis "the soldier" in uniform. The album reached No. 19 on *Billboard*'s Top LP chart in an eight-week run. *Songs:* "That's All Right, Mama"; "Lawdy Miss Clawdy"; "Mystery Train"; "Playing for Keeps"; "Poor Boy"; "My Baby Left Me"; "I Was the One"; "Shake, Rattle and Roll"; "I'm Left, You're Right, She's Gone"; "You're a Heartbreaker." *For LP Fans Only* (RCA LSP-1990-e, released in January 1965) was an electronically reprocessed stereo album. RCA AFL1-1900-e, with the same title, released in 1977, was a new number given to RCA LSP-1900-e.

Frankie and Johnny (RCA LPM-3553, released in April 1966) was the sound track from the movie *Frankie and Johnny;* a twelve-inch-square color photo was included as well as twelve songs from the movie. The album reached No. 19 during nineteen weeks on *Billboard*'s Top LP chart. *Songs:* "Frankie and Johnny"; "Come Along"; " Petunia, the Gardener's Daughter"; " Chesay"; "What Every Woman Lives For"; "Look Out, Broadway"; "Beginner's Luck"; "Down by the Riverside"; "When the Saints Go Marching In"; "Shout It Out"; "Hard Luck"; "Please Don't Stop Loving Me"; "Everybody Come Aboard." Other albums with the same title: RCA LSP-3553, released in April 1966, was a stereo release; RCA APL1-2559, released in September 1977, was a reissue of RCA LSP-3553; Pickwick ACL-7007, released in November 1976, had a different order of songs and took out three songs: "Chesay"; "Look Out, Broadway"; "Everybody Come Aboard." The album covers were also different. *Songs:* "Frankie and Johnny"; "Come Along"; "What Every Woman Lives For"; "Hard Luck"; "Please Don't Stop Loving Me"; "Down by the Riverside"; "When the Saints Go Marching In"; "Petunia, the Gardener's Daughter"; "Beginner's Luck"; "Shout It Out."

From Elvis in Memphis (RCA LSP-4155, released in June 1969) included songs recorded in January–February 1969 at American Sound Studios, Memphis. An eighty-by-ten photo from Elvis's 1968 TV special was a bonus with the album. The LP was certified gold by RIAA on January 28, 1970. It hit No. 13 during a twenty-four-week stay on *Billboard*'s Top LP chart, and it reached No. 2 on the Country chart during thirty-four weeks. *Songs:* "Wearin' That Loved On Look"; "Only the Strong Survive"; "I'll Hold You in My Heart ('Till I Can Hold You in My Arms)"; "Long Black Limousine"; "It Keeps Right On A-Hurtin' "; "I'm Movin' On"; "Power of My Love"; "Gentle on My Mind"; "After Loving You"; "True Love Travels on a Gravel Road"; "Any Day Now"; "In the Ghetto." RCA AFL1-4155, with the same title, released in 1977, was simply a new number given to the 1969 release RCA LSP-4155. *From Elvis in Memphis* (MFSL-1-059, released in 1982) was by Mobile Fidelity Sound Laboratories. Recorded at half speed, the songs are the same as *From Elvis in Memphis* (RCA LSP-4155).

From Elvis Presley Boulevard, Memphis, Tennessee (RCA APL1-1506, released in May 1976) featured ten songs recorded at Graceland, February 2–8, 1976. RIAA gold certification was given for the album on October 7, 1977 (for over five hundred thousand copies sold). The album charted at No. 41 in seventeen weeks on *Billboard*'s Top LP chart, and during a six-week stay on the Country chart it peaked at No. 1. *Songs:* "Hurt"; "Never Again"; "Blue Eyes Crying in the Rain"; "Danny Boy"; "The Last Farewell"; "For the Heart"; "Bitter They Are, Harder They Fall"; "Solitaire"; "Love Coming Down"; "I'll Never Fall in Love Again." RCA APD1-1506, released in 1976 with the same title, was a quadradisc release. RCA AFL1-1506, released in 1977, was a new number given to RCA APL1-1506.

From Elvis With Love (RCA R-234340, released in 1978) was a two-record RCA Record Club album of twenty songs. *Songs:* "Love Me Tender"; "Can't Help Falling in Love"; "The Next

Step Is Love"; "I Need Your Love Tonight"; "I Can't Stop Loving You"; "I Want You, I Need You, I Love You"; "I Love You Because"; "Love Letters"; "A Thing Called Love"; "A Big Hunk o' Love"; "Love Me"; "Without Love (There Is Nothing)"; "Faded Love" (unreleased version, side three); "Loving You"; "You've Lost That Lovin' Feeling"; "Have I Told You Lately That I Love You"; "You Don't have to Say You Love Me"; "True Love"; "Ain't That Loving You Baby"; "Please Don't Stop Loving Me."

From Memphis to Vegas/From Vegas to Memphis (RCA LSP-6020, released in November 1969) was Elvis's first double LP. Sides one and two were recorded at Las Vegas's International Hotel in August 1969. Sides three and four were recorded from January to February 1969 at the American Sound Studios in Memphis. As a bonus, two eight-by-ten-inch photographs of Elvis from the 1968 TV special were included. It sold a million dollars' worth of records within a month and received its gold-record certification on December 12, 1969. The album reached No. 12 during twenty-four weeks on *Billboard*'s Top LP chart and was No. 5 on the Country chart. In November 1970, RCA released the same records individually. Sides one and two were released as ***Elvis in Person at the International Hotel, Las Vegas, Nevada*** and sides three and four were released as the LP ***Back in Memphis***. *Songs:* sides one and two: "Blue Suede Shoes"; "Johnny B. Goode"; "All Shook Up"; "Are You Lonesome Tonight?"; "Hound Dog"; "I Can't Stop Loving You"; "My Babe"; "Mystery Train"; "Tiger Man"; "Words"; "In the Ghetto"; "Suspicious Minds"; "Can't Help Falling in Love." Sides three and four: "Inherit the Wind"; "This is the Story"; "Stranger in My Own Home Town"; "A Little Bit of Green"; "And the Grass Won't Pay No Mind"; "Do You Know Who I Am?"; "From a Jack to a King"; "The Fair Is Moving On"; "You'll Think of Me"; "Without Love (There Is Nothing)."

Fun In Acapulco (RCA LPM-2576, released in December 1963) contained eleven songs from the film/sound-track, plus two bonus songs. The album peaked on *Billboard*'s Top LP chart at No. 3 during a twenty-four-week stay. *Songs:* "Fun in Acapulco"; "Vino, Dinero y Amor"; "Mexico"; "El Toro"; "Marguerita"; "The Bullfighter Was a Lady"; "(There's) No Room to Rhumba in a Sports Car"; "I Think I'm Gonna Like It Here"; "Bossa Nova Baby"; "You Can't Say No in Acapulco"; "Guadalajara"; "Love Me Tonight" (bonus); "Slowly But Surely" (bonus). (RCA LSP-2576, released in December 1963) was a stereo release, same songs. RCA AFL1-2576, released in 1977, was a new number given to RCA LSP-2576. RIAA's Gold Award.

G. I. Blues (RCA LPM-2256, released in October 1960) was the sound track from the movie, with the special inner sleeve "Elvis Is Back" included. RIAA gold certification was granted in March 1963 (but over 3 million copies were sold). The album peaked at No. 1 (for ten weeks) and stayed on *Billboard*'s Top LP chart for 111 weeks! *Songs:* "Tonight Is So Right for Love"; "What's She Really Like?"; "Frankfurt Special"; "Wooden Heart"; "G. I. Blues"; "Pocketful of Rainbows"; "Shoppin' Around"; "Big Boots"; "Didja Ever"; "Blue Suede Shoes"; "Doin' the Best I Can." *G. I. Blues* (RCA LSP-2256, released in October 1960) was a stereo album that reached No. 2 on the Stereo LP chart during a forty-seven-week stay; RCA AFL1-2256, released in 1977, was a new number for RCA LSP-2256; RCA AYL1-3735, released in 1980, was a new number for RCA AFL1-2256.

Girl Happy (RCA LPM-3338, released in April 1965) had eleven songs from the 1965 film *Girl Happy* (a film Elvis did not like) and one bonus song, "You'll Be Gone." The album was gold certified and reached No. 8 in thirty-one weeks on *Billboard*'s Top LP chart. *Songs:* "Girl Happy"; "Spring Fever"; "Fort Lauderdale Chamber of Commerce"; "Startin' Tonight"; "Wolf Call"; "Do Not Disturb"; "Cross My Heart and Hope to Die"; "The Meanest Girl in Town"; "Do the Clam"; "Puppet on a String"; "I've Got to Find My Baby"; "You'll Be Gone." *Girl Happy* (RCA LSP-3338, released in April 1985) was a stereo release with the same songs; RCA AFL1-3338 was a new number for RCA LSP-3338.

Girls! Girls! Girls! (RCA LPM-2621, released in November 1962) was the sound-track LP for the 1962 movie by that title. The album was No. 3 during its thirty-two-week stay on *Billboard*'s Top LP chart. *Songs:* "Girls! Girls! Girls!"; "I Don't Wanna Be Tied"; " Where Do You Come From?"; "I Don't Want To"; "We'll Be Together"; "A Boy Like Me, a Girl Like You"; "Earth Boy"; " Return to Sender"; "Because of Love"; "Thanks to the Rolling Sea"; "Song of the Shrimp"; "The Walls Have Ears"; "We're Coming In Loaded." RCA LSP-2621, released in November 1962 with the same title, was a stereo album that hit No. 5 on the Stereo LP chart during twenty weeks. RCA AFL1-2621, released in 1977, was a new number given to RCA LSP-2621. RIAA's Gold Award.

Golden Celebration, A (RCA CPM6-5172, released in October 1984) celebrated the fiftieth anniversary of Elvis's birth. This six-record set included the Sun sessions, full "Stage Show" performances, Milton Berle and the Steve Allen show performances, the Mississippi-Alabama Fair and Dairy Show performance on September 26, 1956, full Ed Sullivan appearances, recordings from the TV special "Elvis" on June 27, 1968, and nine newly discovered songs that were recorded at Graceland. The set hit No. 80 on *Billboard*'s Top LP chart during a nineteen-week stay and reached No. 55 in seven weeks on the Country chart. *Songs:* (the Sun sessions) "Harbor Lights"; "That's All Right, Mama"; "Blue Moon of Kentucky"; "I Don't Care If the Sun Don't Shine"; "I'm Left, You're Right, She's Gone"; "I'll Never Let You Go (Little Darlin')"; "When It Rains, It Really Pours"; (the "Stage Show" performances) "Shake, Rattle

and Roll"/"Flip, Flop and Fly"; "I Got a
Woman"; "Baby, Let's Play House";
"Tutti Frutti"; "Blue Suede Shoes";
"Heartbreak Hotel"; "Tutti Frutti"; "I
Was the One"; "Blue Suede Shoes";
"Heartbreak Hotel"; "Money Honey";
"Heartbreak Hotel"; (the Milton Berle
shows) "Heartbreak Hotel"; "Blue
Suede Shoes"; dialogue; "Blue Suede
Shoes"; "Hound Dog"; dialogue; "I
Want You, I Need You, I Love You";
introductions; "Hound Dog"; (the
Mississippi-Alabama Fair and Dairy
Show) "Heartbreak Hotel"; "Long Tall
Sally"; introductions/presentations; "I
Was the One"; "I Want You, I Need
You, I Love You"; "I Got a Woman";
"Don't Be Cruel"; "Ready Teddy";
"Love Me Tender"; "Hound Dog"; inter-
views with Gladys and Vernon Presley,
Nick Adams, a fan, and Elvis; "Love
Me Tender"; "I Was the One"; "I Got a
Woman"; "Don't Be Cruel"; "Blue
Suede Shoes"; "Baby, Let's Play
House"; "Hound Dog"; announcements;
(from the Ed Sullivan show) "Don't Be
Cruel"; "Love Me Tender"; "Ready
Teddy"; "Hound Dog"; "Don't Be
Cruel"; "Love Me Tender"; "Love Me
Tender"; "Hound Dog"; "Hound Dog";
"Love Me Tender"; "Heartbreak Hotel";
"Don't Be Cruel"; "Too Much"; "When
My Blue Moon Turns to Gold Again";
"Peace in the Valley"; (Elvis at home
in Graceland) "Danny Boy"; "Soldier
Boy"; "The Fool"; "Earth Angel"; "He's
Only a Prayer Away"; (collector's trea-
sures) parts of an interview for *TV
Guide;* "My Heart Cries for You";
"Dark Moon"; "Write to Me From Na-
ples"; "Suppose"; (Elvis's 1968 TV spe-
cial) "Blue Suede Shoes"; "Tiger Man";
"That's All Right, Mama"; "Lawdy Miss
Clawdy"; "Baby, What You Want Me to
Do"; monologue; "Love Me"; "Are You
Lonesome Tonight?"; "Baby, What You
Want Me to Do"; monologue; "Blue
Christmas"; monologue; "One Night";
"Trying to Get to You."
Good Rockin' Tonight (RCA 130.252,
released in 1956) was a French ten-
inch LP with four original Sun Records
songs; no echo. *Songs:* "Good Rockin'
Tonight"; "I Don't Care If the Sun

Don't Shine"; "That's All Right, Mama";
"Blue Moon of Kentucky"; "Baby, Let's
Play House"; "I'm Left, You're Right,
She's Gone"; "Milkcow Blues Boogie";
"You're a Heartbreaker."
Good Times (RCA CPL1-0475, released
in March 1974) contained songs re-
corded in December and July 1973 at
Stax Studios, Memphis. The album
reached No. 90 during an eight-week
stay on *Billboard*'s Top LP chart.
Songs: "Take Good Care of Her";
"Lovin' Arms"; "I Got a Feelin' in My
Body"; "If That Isn't Love"; "She Wears
My Ring"; "I've Got a Thing About You,
Baby"; "My Boy"; "Spanish Eyes";
"Talk About the Good Times"; "Good
Time Charlie's Got the Blues." *Good
Times* (RCA AFL1-0475, released in
1977) was a new number for RCA
CPL1-0475).
Greatest Hits, Vol. 1 (RCA AHL1-2347,
released in November 1981) with "Sus-
picious Minds" and "The Sound of
Your Cry" in stereo for the first time
and live versions of four songs. *Songs:*
"The Wonder of You"; "A Big Hunk o'
Love"; "There Goes My Everything";
"Suspicious Minds"; "What'd I Say?";
"Don't Cry, Daddy"; "Steamroller
Blues"; "The Sound of Your Cry";
"Burning Love"; "You'll Never Walk
Alone."
Greatest Show on Earth, The (RCA
DML1-0348, released in 1978 by Can-
dlelite Music). Distributed as a bonus
for anyone who purchased the five-LP
boxed set *Memories of Elvis. Songs:*
"True Love"; "Sweet Caroline"; "Har-
bor Lights"; "Gentle on My Mind"; "It's
Impossible"; "What Now, My Love";
"Until It's Time for You to Go"; "Early
Morning Rain"; "Something"; "The First
Time I Saw Your Face"; "The Impossible Dream."
Guitar Man (RCA AAL1-3917, released
in January 1981), produced by Felton
Jarvis, included new back tracks. An
ad regarding the release of the 1981
documentary *This Is Elvis* was inserted. The LP reached No. 49 in
twelve weeks on *Billboard*'s Top LP
chart and No. 6 on the Hot Country LP
chart during a thirty-one-week stay.

Songs: "Guitar Man"; "After Loving You"; "Too Much Monkey Business"; "Just Call Me Lonesome"; "Lovin' Arms"; "You Asked Me To"; "Clean Up Your Own Back Yard"; "She Thinks I Still Care"; "Faded Love"; "I'm Movin' On."

Harum Scarum (RCA LPM-3468, released in October 1965). The sound track for the movie of the same title with two bonus songs. A twelve-inch-square photo of Elvis was included. The LP reached No. 8 during twenty-three weeks on *Billboard*'s Top LP chart. *Songs:* "Harem Holiday"; "My Desert Serenade"; "Go East, Young Man"; "Mirage"; "Kismet"; "Shake That Tambourine"; "Hey, Little Girl"; "Golden Coins"; "So Close, Yet So Far (From Paradise)"; "Animal Instinct" (bonus); "Wisdom of the Ages" (bonus). *Harum Scarum* (RCA LSP-3468) was a stereo release, distributed in October 1965. RCA AFL1-2558, released in September 1977, was a new number given to RCA LSP-3468.

Having Fun With Elvis on Stage (Boxcar Records, released in 1974). There are no songs or music on this album, which features Elvis talking to an audience. Boxcar Records was owned by Colonel Tom Parker and Elvis. The album was sold by the Colonel outside concert halls. *Having Fun With Elvis on Stage* (RCA CPM1-0818, released in October 1974) was a reissue of the Boxcar original. No songs. This record made *Billboard*'s Top LP chart for seven weeks, hitting No. 130. RCA AFM1-0818, released in 1977, was a new number given to RCA CPM1-0818.

He Touched Me (RCA LSP-4690, released in April 1972) included twelve gospel songs. The album won Elvis his second Grammy Award for Best Inspirational Performance of the Year and RIAA's Gold Award. The LP reached No. 79 on *Billboard*'s Top LP chart during a ten-week run. *Songs:* "He Touched Me"; "I've Got Confidence"; "Amazing Grace"; "Seeing Is Believing"; "He is My Everything"; "Bosom of Abraham"; "An Evening Prayer"; "Lead Me, Guide Me"; "There Is No God but God"; "A Thing Called Love"; "I, John"; "Reach Out to Jesus." *He Touched Me* (RCA AFL1-4690, released in 1977) was a new number for RCA LSP-4690.

He Walks Beside Me (RCA AFL1-2772, released in April 1978) with a twenty-page pamphlet of color photographs. "The Impossible Dream" and "If I Can Dream" were alternative takes, unreleased until this album. The LP hit No. 113 during eight weeks on *Billboard*'s Top LP chart and No. 6 during a twenty-week stay on the Country chart. *Songs:* "He Is My Everything"; "Miracle of the Rosary"; "Where Did They Go, Lord?"; "Somebody Bigger Than You and I"; "An Evening Prayer"; "The Impossible Dream"; "If I Can Dream"; "Padre"; "Known Only to Him"; "Who Am I?"; "How Great Thou Art."

His Hand in Mine (RCA LPM-2328, released in December 1960). This million seller, Elvis's first gospel album, reached No. 13 during a twenty-week stay on *Billboard*'s Top LP chart. In April 1969, it was certified gold and received its Platinum Award soon after. The cover shows Elvis at the piano. *Songs:* "His Hand in Mine"; "I'm Gonna Walk Dem Golden Stairs"; "In My Father's House"; "Milky White Way"; "Known Only to Him"; "I Believe in the Man in the Sky"; "Joshua Fit the Battle"; "He Knows Just What I Need"; "Swing Down, Sweet Chariot"; "Mansion Over the Hilltop"; "If We Never Meet Again"; "Working on the Building." *His Hand in Mine* (RCA LSP-2328, released in December 1960) was a stereo release. RCA ANL1-1319, released in March 1976, was a reissue of RCA LSP-2328. In the Pure Gold series, it contained the same songs with a new album cover. On December 1, 1977, it received its second gold certification. RCA AYM1-3935, released in May 1981, was a new number for RCA ANL1-1319.

How Great Thou Art (RCA LPM-3758, released in March 1967) was the LP for which Elvis won his first Grammy Award for Best Sacred Performance. The cover featured Elvis at the left in front of a country church. The LP was gold certified on February 16, 1968, and eventually received two Platinum Awards. It reached No. 18 during twenty-nine weeks on *Billboard*'s Top LP chart. *Songs:* "How Great Thou Art"; "In the Garden"; "Somebody Bigger Than You and I"; "Farther Along"; "Stand by Me"; "Without Him"; "So High"; "Where Could I Go but to the Lord?"; "By and By"; "If the Lord Wasn't Walking by My Side"; "Run On"; "Where No One Stands Alone"; "Crying in the Chapel." *How Great Thou Art* (RCA LSP-3758, released in March 1967) was a stereo album. RCA AFL1-3758, released in 1977, was a new number given to RCA LSP-3758. RCA AQL1-3758 was released in 1979 and was a new number for RCA AFL1-3758.

I Got Lucky (RCA Camden CAL-2533, released in October 1971) contained nine songs from movies, as well as "Fools Fall in Love." The LP hit No. 104 during an eight-week stay on *Billboard*'s Top LP chart. *Songs:* "I Got Lucky"; "What a Wonderful Life"; "I Need Somebody to Lean On"; "Yoga Is As Yoga Does"; "Riding the Rainbow"; "Fools Fall in Love"; "The Love Machine"; "Home Is Where the Heart Is"; "You Gotta Stop"; "If You Think I Don't Need You." *I Got Lucky* (Pickwick CAS-2433, released in December 1975) was released in monaural, not stereo. Same songs.

I Was the One (RCA AHL1-4678, released in May 1983) with overdubbed tracks by Felton Jarvis. It reached No. 103 during its six weeks on *Billboard*'s Top LP chart and No. 35 during nine weeks on the Country chart. *Songs:* "My Baby Left Me"; "(You're So Square) Baby"; "I Don't Care"; "Little Sister"; "Don't"; "Wear My Ring Around Your Neck"; "Paralyzed"; "Baby, Let's Play House"; "I Was the One"; "Rip It Up"; "Young and Beautiful"; "Ready Teddy."

International Hotel, Las Vegas, Nevada, Presents Elvis—August 1969 (released on August 10, 1969, by RCA). This limited-edition boxed set for guests at Elvis's opening included the LPs *From Elvis in Memphis* and *Elvis—TV Special*, RCA's record and tape catalog of Elvis's releases, a 1969 calendar, a nine-page letter from the Colonel, an eight-by-ten-inch color photo, and two eight-by-ten black-and-white photos of Elvis.

International Hotel, Las Vegas, Nevada, Presents Elvis—1970 (released in February 1970 by RCA as a promotion to those who attended Elvis's opening concert). A limited-edition boxed set with the LP *From Memphis to Vegas/From Vegas to Memphis*. Also included was the single "Kentucky Rain"/"My Little Friend," RCA's tape/record catalog of Elvis's releases, a pocket calendar, one eight-by-ten black-and-white photo of Elvis, a souvenir photograph album, an International Hotel menu, and a note from Colonel Parker and Elvis.

Interviews With Elvis (Starday SD-995, released in 1978) was a reissue of *The Elvis Tapes* (Great Northwest Music Company, GNW-4005).

It Happened at the World's Fair (RCA LPM-2697, released in April 1963) contained ten songs from the movie by the same title. The LP reached No. 4 in twenty-six weeks on *Billboard*'s Top LP chart. It hit No. 15 on the Stereo chart during a seventeen-week stay. *Songs:* "Beyond the Bend"; "Relax"; "Take Me to the Fair"; "They Remind Me Too Much of You"; "One Broken Heart for Sale"; "I'm Falling in Love Tonight"; "Cotton Candy Land"; "A World of Our Own"; "How Would You Like to Be?"; "Happy Ending." *It Happened at the World's Fair* (RCA LSP-2697, released in April 1963) was a stereo album; RCA AFL1-2568, released in September 1977, was a new number for RCA LSP-2697.

King Creole (RCA LPM-1884, released in August 1958) with eleven songs from the movie of that title. Included was an eight-by-ten-inch photograph of Elvis in his Army uniform. The LP reached No. 2 during fifteen weeks on *Billboard*'s Top LP chart. *Songs:* "King Creole"; "As Long As I Have You"; "Hard Headed Woman"; "Trouble";

"Dixieland Rock"; "Don't Ask Me Why"; "Lover Doll"; "Crawfish"; "Young Dreams"; "Steadfast, Loyal and True"; "New Orleans." *King Creole* (RCA LSP-1884-e, released in February 1982) was an electronically reprocessed stereo album; RCA AFL1-1884-e, released in 1977, was a new number for RCA LSP-1884-e. RCA AYL1-3733-e, released in November 1980, was a new number for RCA AFL1-1884-e.

King Speaks, The (Great Northwest Music Company, GNW-4006, released in December 1977) was a reissue of *Exclusive Live Press Conference* (Green Valley Record Store GV-2001) with new opening and closing remarks by Canadian deejay Red Robinson.

Kissin' Cousins (RCA LPM-2894, released in March 1964) was the sound track for the movie of the same title and featured three bonus songs, as well as nine from the movie. A movie photo was included with the album. A million seller, the album was gold certified and reached No. 6 during a thirty-week stay on *Billboard*'s Top LP chart. *Songs:* "Kissin' Cousins" (#2); "Smokey Mountain Boy" (bonus); "There's Gold in the Mountains"; "One Boy, Two Little Girls"; "Catchin' On Fast"; "Tender Feeling"; "Anyone (Could Fall in Love With You)"; "Barefoot Ballad"; "Once Is Enough"; "Kissin' Cousins"; "Echoes of Love" (bonus); "(It's a) Long Lonely Highway" (bonus). *Kissin' Cousins* (RCA LSP-2894, released in March 1964) is a stereo release; RCA AFL1-2894 is a new number for RCA LSP-2894, released in 1977; RCA AYM1-4115, released in September 1981, is a new number for RCA AFL1-2894.

Le Disque D'Or (RCA 6886 807, a French import released in 1978). *Songs:* "C'mon Everybody"; "A Whistling Tune"; "I'll Be There (If Ever You Want Me)"; "I Love Only One Girl"; "Easy Come, Easy Go"; "Santa Lucia"; "Tonight Is So Right for Love"; "Guadalajara"; " Angel"; "A Little Less Conversation"; "Follow That Dream"; "Long Legged Girl (With the Short Dress On)."

Legend of a King, The (ABI-1001, called the first "disc-u-mentary," released in 1980) was a three-hour radio special without songs. From Associated Broadcasting, Inc.

Legendary Concert Performances (RCA R-244047, released in 1978). A two-record set featuring songs from Las Vegas Hilton and International Hotel live concerts and the TV special "Elvis: Aloha From Hawaii." *Songs:* "Blue Suede Shoes"; "Sweet Caroline"; "Burning Love"; "Runaway"; "My Babe"; "Johnny B. Goode"; "Yesterday"; "Mystery Train"/"Tiger Man"; "You Gave Me a Mountain"; "Never Been to Spain"; "See See Rider"; "Words"; "Proud Mary"; "Walk a Mile in My Shoes"; "Steamroller Blues"; "Polk Salad Annie"; "Something"; "Let It Be Me"; "The Impossible Dream"; "My Way."

Legendary Magic of Elvis Presley, The (RCA DVL1-0461, released in September 1980). Candlelite Music distributed this LP to those who had purchased the six-LP boxed set. *The Legendary Performances of Elvis Presley* (RCA DML6-0412). *Songs:* "The Wonder of You"; "(You're So Square) Baby, I Don't Care"; "My Wish Came True"; "Suspicious Minds"; "I Want You, I Need You, I Love You"; "Little Sister"; "It's Now or Never"; "Too Much"; "Are You Lonesome Tonight?"; "Burning Love"; "(Now and Then There's) A Fool Such As I"; "Hard Headed Woman"; "In the Ghetto"; "When My Blue Moon Turns to Gold Again"; "Don't Cry, Daddy"; "Jailhouse Rock"; "(Marie's the Name) His Latest Flame"; "One Night."

Legendary Performances of Elvis Presley, The (RCA DML6-0412, released as a six-LP boxed set, November 1979) sold on television during the 1979 Christmas season. *Songs:* "Take My Hand, Precious Lord"; "Where Could I Go but to the Lord?"; "In the Garden"; "It Is No Secret"; "Stand By Me"; "Mama Liked the Roses"; "Padre"; "All That I Am"; "I'm Leavin' "; "Forget Me Never"; "Frankie and Johnny"; "Down by the Riverside"/"When the

Saints Go Marching In"; "Happy Girl"; "Do the Clam"; "G.I. Blues"; "Also Sprach Zarathustra"/"See See Rider"; "Johnny B. Goode"; "Lawdy Miss Clawdy"/"Baby What You Want Me to Do"; "Whole Lotta Shakin' Goin' On"/"Long Tall Sally"; "It's Over"; "Snowbird"; "I Love You Because"; "Just Because"; "Release Me"; "Mystery Train"; "Blue Moon of Kentucky"; "It Keeps Right on A-Hurtin' "; "I Don't Care If the Sun Don't Shine"; "I'm Movin' On"; "Baby, Let's Play House"; "Shake, Rattle and Roll"; "I Slipped, I Stumbled, I Fell"; "Tutti Fruitti"; "Ain't That Loving You, Baby"; "(Let's Have a) Party"; "Tiger Man"; "Paralyzed"; "High Heel Sneakers"; "I Got a Woman"; "Any Day Now"; "How's the World Treating You?"; "Only the Strong Survive"; "Just for Old Times' Sake"; "You've Lost That Lovin' Feeling"; "They Remind Me Too Much of You"; "Danny"; "Indescribably Blue"; "It Feels So Right"; "Tell Me Why"; "Fools Rush In"; "Please Don't Stop Loving Me"; "Proud Mary"; "Never Been to Spain"; "Don't Think Twice, It's All Right"; "Fools Fall in Love"; "Walk a Mile in My Shoes"; "Blue Moon"; "Witchcraft"; "Runaway."

*Let's Be Friends (RCA Camden CAS-2408, released in April 1970) was recorded all in stereo, except the monaural "Mama." An alternative take is heard in "Almost." The LP hit No. 105 during eleven weeks on Billboard's Top LP chart. Songs: "Stay Away, Joe"; "If I'm a Fool (for Loving You)"; "Let's Be Friends"; "Let's Forget About the Stars"; "Mama"; "I'll Be There (If You Ever Want Me)"; "Almost"; "Change of Habit"; "Have a Happy." Let's Be Friends (Pickwick CAS-2408, released in December 1975) was a reissue of Camden CAS-2408).

*Louisiana Hayride (Louisiana Hayride, NR-8485, released in 1976) and Louisiana Hayride (Louisiana Hayride, NR-8973, released in 1983) with interviews. Songs: "Fancy Pants"; "That's All Right, Mama"/"Blue Moon of Kentucky" (Oct. 16, 1954) and "Tweedlee Dee" (Dec. 18, 1954) with

Jimmy Day (steel guitar), D. J. Fontana, Scotty Moore, Bill Black, and Floyd Cramer (piano); "Baby, Let's Play House"; "Maybellene"; "That's All Right, Mama" (Aug. 1955); "I Was the One"; "Love Me Tender"; "Hound Dog" (Dec. 16, 1956).

Louisiana Hayride Saturday Nite (Louisiana Hayride LP 973, released in January 1985) was recorded by remote from Gladewater, Texas, December 18, 1954.

*Love Letters From Elvis (RCA LSP 4530, released in May 1971) with three photos of Elvis in his white, studded Vegas outfit on the cover. Featured songs from the June 4–8, 1970, RCA Nashville studio sessions. The album reached No. 33 in a fifteen-week stay on Billboard's Top LP chart, and it reached No. 12 during twelve weeks on the Country chart. Songs: "Love Letters"; "When I'm Over You"; "If I Were You"; "Got My Mojo Working"; "Heart of Rome"; "Only Believe"; "This Is Our Dance"; "Cindy, Cindy"; "I'll Never Know"; "It Ain't No Big Thing"; "Life." Love Letters From Elvis (RCA AFL1-4530, released in 1977) was a new number for RCA LSP-4530.

*Loving You (RCA LPM-1515, released in July 1957). One side featured seven songs from the movie Loving You and the other side contained five songs from January to February 1957 Radio Recorders sessions, Hollywood. Gold certified, April 9, 1968. The album stayed No. 1 for ten straight out of twenty-nine weeks. Songs: "Mean Woman Blues"; "(Let Me Be Your) Teddy Bear"; "Loving You"; "Got a Lot of Livin' to Do"; "Lonesome Cowboy"; "Hot Dog"; "Party"; "Blueberry Hill"; "True Love"; "Don't Leave Me Now"; "Have I Told You Lately That I Love You?"; "I Need You So." *Loving You (RCA LSP-1515-e, released in February 1962) was an electronically reprocessed stereo album; RCA AFL1-1515-e, released in 1977, was a new number for RCA LSP-1515-e.

Mahalo From Elvis (Pickwick ACL-7064, released in September 1978) with all songs on side one from the TV special "Elvis: Aloha From Hawaii," even though "No More" was not on the program. Side two songs were from Elvis's movies. *Songs:* "Blue Hawaii"; "Early Morning Rain"; "Hawaiian Wedding Song"; "Ku-U-I-Po"; "No More"; "Relax"; "Baby, If You'll Give Me All of Your Love"; "One Broken Heart for Sale"; "So Close, Yet So Far (From Paradise)"; "Happy Ending."

Memories of Christmas (RCA CPL1-4395, released in August 1982) with an original master of "Merry Christmas, Baby"; calendar included. *Songs:* "O Come, All Ye Faithful"; "Silver Bells"; "I'll Be Home for Christmas"; "Blue Christmas"; "Santa Claus Is Back in Town"; "Merry Christmas, Baby"; "If Every Day Was Like Christmas"; "Silent Night."

Memories of Elvis (RCA DML5-0347, released in 1978). Candlelite Music released the five-LP boxed set with Robert Charles Howe illustrations of Elvis on the cover. A bonus LP, *The Greatest Show on Earth*, and a sixteen-page booklet titled "Musical History's Finest Hour" were included. *Songs:* "One Broken Heart for Sale"; "Young and Beautiful"; "A Mess of Blues"; "The Next Step Is Love"; "I Gotta Know"; "Love Letters"; "When My Blue Moon Turns to Gold Again"; "If Every Day Was Like Christmas"; "Steamroller Blues"; "Any Way You Want Me"; "(Such an) Easy Question"; "That's When Your Heartaches Begin"; "Kentucky Rain"; "Money Honey"; "My Way"; "Girls! Girls! Girls!"; " Lonely Man"; "U.S. Male"; "My Wish Came True"; "Kiss Me Quick"; "As Long As I Have You"; "Bossa Nova Baby"; "I Forgot to Remember to Forget"; "Such a Night"; "I Really Don't Want to Know"; "Doncha' Think It's Time?"; "His Hand in Mine"; "That's All Right, Mama"; "Nothingville"; "(You're So Square) Baby, I Don't Care"; "Playing for Keeps"; "King of the Whole Wide World"; "Don't Ask Me Why"; "Flaming Star"; "I'm Left, You're Right, She's Gone"; "What'd I Say?"; "There Goes My Everything"; "Patch It Up"; "Reconsider Baby";

"Good Rockin' Tonight"; "You Gave Me a Mountain"; "Rock-A-Hula-Baby"; "Mean Woman Blues"; "It Hurts Me"; "Fever"; "I Want to Be Free"; "Viva Las Vegas"; "Old Shep"; "Anything That's Part of You"; "My Baby Left Me"; "Wild in the Country"; "Memphis, Tennessee"; "Don't Leave Me Now"; "I Feel So Bad"; "Separate Ways"; "Polk Salad Annie"; "Fame and Fortune"; "Tryin' to Get to You"; "I've Lost You"; "King Creole."

Memphis Record, The (RCA 6221-1-R, released in June 1987). A two-record set from sessions at the American Sound Studios, Memphis, 1969. *Songs:* "Stranger in My Own Home Town"; "Power of My Love"; "Only the Strong Survive"; "Any Day Now"; "Suspicious Minds"; "Long Black Limousine"; "Wearin' That Loved On Look"; "I'll Hold You in My Heart"; "After Loving You"; "Rubberneckin' "; "I'm Movin' On"; "Gentle on My Mind"; "True Love Travels on a Gravel Road"; "It Keeps Right On A-Hurtin' "; "You'll Think of Me"; "Mama Like the Roses"; "Don't Cry, Daddy"; "In the Ghetto"; "The Fair Is Moving On"; "Inherit the Wind"; "Kentucky Rain"; "Without Love"; "Who Am I?"

Michelob Presents Highlights of Elvis Memories (ABC OCC810, released in December 1978) promoted the radio special "Elvis: Memories . . ." *Songs:* "Memories"; "Heartbreak Hotel"; "Love Me Tender"; "Hound Dog"; "Don't Be Cruel"; "Jailhouse Rock"; "It's Now or Never"; "Viva Las Vegas"; "Separate Ways"; "You Don't Have to Say You Love Me"; "Are You Lonesome Tonight?"; "Can't Help Falling in Love"; "If I Can Dream."

***Moody Blue** (RCA AFL1-2428, released in July 1977). Side one features songs from live concerts; side two are recordings from the Graceland studio. The first release was on translucent blue vinyl. The LP was certified platinum in September 1977, and again in 1979. The album reached No. 3 in a thirty-one-week stay on *Billboard*'s Top LP chart, and it was No. 1 on the Country chart. *Songs:* "Unchained Melody"; "If You Love Me (Let Me Know)"; "Little Darlin' "; "He'll Have to Go"; "Let Me Be There"; "Way Down"; "Pledging My Love"; "Moody Blue"; "She Thinks I Still Care"; "It's Easy for You." *Moody Blue* (RCA-2428, released in August 1977) was a new number for RCA AFL1-2428.

1950's Rock 'n' Roll Music Collection, The—The Elvis Presley Collection (RCA DML3-0632, released in 1983). A three-record set produced, distributed, and promoted by Candlelite Music. *Songs:* "Don't Be Cruel"; "Loving You"; "Trouble"; "I Was the One"; "When My Blue Moon Turns to Gold Again"; "Are You Lonesome Tonight?"; "Hard Headed Woman"; "Don't"; "Little Sister"; "One Night"; "A Big Hunk o' Love"; "(Marie's the Name) His Latest Flame"; "I Got Stung"; "I Want You, I Need You, I Love You"; "Jailhouse Rock"; "The Wonder of You"; "Too Much"; "Love Me"; "All Shook Up"; "Heartbreak Hotel"; "Crying in the Chapel"; "Teddy Bear"; "Can't Help Falling in Love"; "Hound Dog"; "Love Me Tender"; "Return to Sender"; "It's Now or Never."

Number One Hits, The (RCA 6382-1-R, released in June 1987) featured eighteen No. 1 songs in chronological order plus a commemorative poster and inner sleeve. The LP only reached No. 143 during its nine-week stay on *Billboard*'s Top LP chart. *Songs:* "Heartbreak Hotel"; "I Want You, I Need You, I Love You"; "Hound Dog"; "Don't Be Cruel"; "Love Me Tender"; "Too Much"; "All Shook Up"; "Teddy Bear"; "Jailhouse Rock"; "Hard Headed Woman"; "A Big Hunk o' Love"; "Stuck on You"; "It's Now or Never"; "Are You Lonesome Tonight?"; "Surrender"; "Good Luck Charm"; "Suspicious Minds."

***On Stage—February, 1970** (RCA LSP-4362, released in June 1970) contained songs recorded at the International Hotel, Las Vegas, February 17–19, 1970 (except "Yesterday" and "Runaway," August 22 and 26, 1969). The album was gold certified in February 1971. It reached No. 13 during a twenty-week

stay on *Billboard*'s Top LP chart and No. 13 on the Country chart. *Songs:* "See See Rider"; "Release Me"; "Sweet Caroline"; "Runaway"; "The Wonder of You"; "Polk Salad Annie"; "Yesterday"; "Proud Mary"; "Walk a Mile in My Shoes"; "Let It Be Me." *On Stage—February, 1970* (RCA AFL1-4362, released in 1977) was a new number for RCA LSP-4362; RCA AQL1-4362, released in February 1983, was a new number for RCA AFL1-4362).

One Night With You (RCA DVM1-0704, released in January 1985). Released by Home Box Office with its cable TV special "One Night With You" with the same songs as the LP *Elvis—TV Special* (RCA LPM-4088).

Our Memories of Elvis (RCA AQL1-3279, a February 1983 release). The album contains no overdubbing by RCA and features a cover photo of Vernon Presley and Colonel Parker in front of Graceland. The album reached No. 132 during a seven-week stay on *Billboard*'s Top LP chart. It hit No. 6 on the Country chart. *Songs:* "Are You Sincere?"; "It's Midnight"; "My Boy"; "Girl of Mine"; "Take Good Care of Her"; "I'll Never Fall in Love Again"; "Your Love's Been a Long Time Coming"; "Spanish Eyes"; "Never Again"; "She Thinks I Still Care"; "Solitaire."

Our Memories of Elvis, Vol. 2 (RCA AQL1-3448, released in August 1979) featured no overdubbing and songs of Elvis live in the studio. The album reached No. 157 during five weeks on *Billboard*'s Top LP chart and No. 12 on the Country chart. *Songs:* "I Got a Feelin' in My Body"; "Green, Green, Grass of Home"; "For the Heart"; "She Wears My Ring"; "I Can Help"; "There's a Honky Tonk Angel (Who Will Take Me Back In)"; "Find Out What's Happening"; "Thinking About You"; "Don't Think Twice, It's All Right."

Our Memories of Elvis, Vol. 2 (RCA DJL1-3455, released in August 1979). A few hundred copies were distributed to radio disc jockeys. *Songs:* "I Got a Feeling in My Body"; "For the Heart"; "She Wears My Ring"; "Find Out What's Happening." Side two contained the same four songs with no overdubbing.

Paradise, Hawaiian Style (RCA LPM-3643, released in June 1966) contained songs from the sound track of the movie by that title. Included "Sand Castles," which was cut from the movie. It reached No. 15 during a nineteen-week run on *Billboard*'s Top LP chart. *Songs:* "Paradise, Hawaiian Style"; "Queenie Wahine's Papaya"; "Scratch My Back (Then I'll Scratch Yours)"; "Drums of the Islands"; "Datin' "; "A Dog's Life"; "A House of Sand"; "Stop Where You Are"; "This Is My Heaven"; "Sand Castles" (bonus). *Paradise, Hawaiian Style* (RCA LSP-3643, released in June 1966) was a stereo release. RCA AFL1-3643, released in 1977, was a new number for RCA LSP-3643.

Personally Elvis (Silhouette Music 1001/2, released with incorrect dates for interviews given; 1979). A two-record set covering interviews in Memphis with WMPS's Bob Neal, ca. August 26–28, 1955; in San Antonio, Texas, with Charlie Walker, April 15 or 22, 1956; at New York City's Warwick Hotel, March 24, 1956, and a continued interview at the Warwick, March 24, 1956; in San Antonio, October 13, 1956; and in Honolulu with Peter Noone, August 19, 1965.

Pickwick Pack (Pickwick, released in November 1978). A seven-LP boxed set with the albums *Burning Love and Hits From His Movies*, Vol. 2; *Elvis' Christmas Album; Elvis Sings Hits From His Movies*, Vol. 1; *I Got Lucky; Mahalo From Elvis; Separate Ways; You'll Never Walk Alone.*

Pot Luck (RCA LPM-2523, released in June 1962) with eight songs recorded in RCA's Nashville studios, March 18–19, 1962. The LP reached No. 4 during a thirty-one-week stay on *Billboard*'s Top LP chart. *Songs:* "Kiss Me Quick"; "Just for Old Times Sake"; "Gonna Get Back Home Somehow"; "(Such an) Easy Question"; "Steppin' out of Line"; "I'm Yours"; "Something Blue"; "Suspicion"; "I Feel That I've Known You Forever"; "Night Rider"; "Fountain of Love"; "That's Someone You Never Forget." *Pot Luck* (RCA LSP-2523, released in June 1962) was a stereo album that reached No. 8 on *Billboard*'s Stereo LP chart during a seventeen-week stay. RCA AFL1-2523, released in 1977) was a new number for RCA LSP-2523.

Promised Land (RCA APL1-0873, released in January 1975) with songs recorded at Memphis's Stax Studios in December 1973. The album reached No. 47 during a twelve-week stay on *Billboard*'s Top LP chart. *Songs:* "Promised Land"; "There's a Honky Tonk Angel (Who Will Take Me Back In)"; "Help Me"; "Mr. Songman"; "Love Song of the Year"; "It's Midnight"; "Your Love's Been a Long Time Coming"; "If You Talk in Your Sleep"; "Thinking About You"; "You Asked Me to." *Promised Land* (RCA APD1-0873) was a quadradisc released in January 1975. RCA AFL1-0873 was a new number for RCA APD1-0873).

Pure Gold (RCA ANL1-0971-e, released June 1975) compiles hits from RCA's budget line, a Pure Gold series. Album number OPUS 91130625 was for Pure Gold and was distributed in the Eastern-bloc countries. *Songs:* "Kentucky Rain"; "Fever"; "It's Impossible"; "Jailhouse Rock"; "Don't Be Cruel"; "I Got a Woman"; "All Shook Up"; "Loving You"; "In the Ghetto"; "Love Me Tender." RIAA's two-time Platinum Award winner.

Pure Gold (RCA AYL1-3732, released in November 1980) was a new number for RCA ANL1-0971-e).

Raised on Rock/For Ol' Times Sake (RCA APL1-0388, released in November 1973). All but two songs were recorded July 21–25, 1973, at Stax Studios, Memphis. "I Miss You" and "Are You Sincere?" were recorded in Elvis's Palm Springs, California, home, September 24, 1973. The album reached No. 50 in a thirteen-week stay on *Billboard*'s Top LP chart. *Songs:* "Raised on Rock"; "Are You Sincere?"; "Find Out What's Happening"; "I Miss You"; "Girl of Mine"; "For Ol' Times

Sake"; "If You Don't Come Back";
"Just a Little Bit"; "Sweet Angeline";
"Three Corn Patches."

Reconsider Baby (RCA AFL1-5418, re-
leased in April 1985) was a rhythm and
blues album. The original 1955 Sun
take of "Tomorrow Night" is included.
Songs: "Reconsider, Baby"; "Tomorrow
Night"; "So Glad You're Mine"; "One
Night"; "When It Rains, It Really
Pours"; "My Baby Left Me"; "Ain't That
Loving You, Baby?"; "I Feel So Bad";
"Down in the Alley"; "High Heel Sneak-
ers"; "Stranger in My Own Home
Town"; "Merry Christmas, Baby."

Remembering Elvis (RCA PDL2-1037,
released in 1983). A two-record set
that featured tracks all previously released. *Songs:* "Blue Moon of Kentucky"; "Young and Beautiful";
"Milkcow Blues Boogie"; "Baby, Let's
Play House"; "Good Rockin' Tonight";
"We're Gonna Move"; "I Want to Be
Free"; "I Forgot to Remember to Forget"; "Kiss Me Quick"; "Just for Old
Times Sake"; "Gonna Get Back Somehow"; "(Such an) Easy Question";
"Suspicion"; "I Feel That I've Known
You Forever"; "Night Rider"; "Fountain
of Love."

Return of the Rocker (RCA 5600-1-R,
released in March 1986) with hits from
1960 to 1963. *Songs:* "King of the
Whole Wide World"; "(Marie's the
Name) His Latest Flame"; "Little Sis-
ter"; "A Mess of Blues"; "Like a Baby";
"I Want You With Me"; "Stuck on You";
"Return to Sender"; "Make Me Know
It"; "Witchcraft"; "I'm Comin' Home";
"Follow That Dream."

Rocker (RCA AFM1-5182, released in Oc-
tober 1984). This blue vinyl LP com-
memorated the fiftieth anniversary of
Elvis's birth and included a photo of
Elvis on a Harley-Davidson motorcycle
in the fifties. The album hit No. 154
during a four-week stay on *Billboard*'s
Top LP chart. *Songs:* "Jailhouse Rock";
"Blue Suede Shoes"; "Shake, Rattle and
Roll"; "Lawdy Miss Clawdy"; "I Got a
Woman"; "Money Honey"; "Ready
Teddy"; "Rip It Up"; "Shake, Rattle and
Roll"; "Long Tall Sally"; "(You're So

Square) Baby, I Don't Care"; "Hound
Dog."

Rock 'n' Roll Forever (RCA DML1-0437,
released in August 1981) was a Can-
dlelite promotional LP given to those
who bought the five-LP boxed set *Top
100 Rock'n'Roll Hits of All Time* (RCA
DML5-0463). *Songs:* "One Night";
"Teddy Bear"; "Love Me Tender";
"Don't Be Cruel"; "I Want You, I Need
You, I Love You"; "Jailhouse Rock";
"Heartbreak Hotel"; "Blue Suede
Shoes"; "Hound Dog"; "All Shook Up."

*Roustabout (RCA LPM-2999, released
in October 1964) contained eleven
songs from the sound track of *Roustabout.* In January 1965 it was No. 1 on
Billboard's Top LP chart during a
twenty-seven-week stay, and it received RIAA's Gold Award. *Songs:*
"Roustabout"; "Little Egypt"; "Poison
Ivy League"; "Hard Knocks"; "It's a
Wonderful World"; "Big Love, Big
Heartache"; "One-Track Heart"; "It's
Carnival Time"; "Carny Town";
"There's a Brand New Day on the Horizon"; "Wheels on My Heels." **Roustabout* (RCA LSP-2999) was a stereo
album, released in October 1964. RCA
AFK1-2999, released in 1977, was a
new number for RCA LSP-2999.

*Separate Ways (RCA Camden CAS-
2611, released in January 1973) with a
three-by-five-inch color greeting card.
In eighteen weeks on *Billboard*'s Top
LP chart, it peaked at No. 46. *Songs:*
"Separate Ways"; "Sentimental Me"; "In
My Way"; "I Met Her Today"; "What
Now, What Next, Where To?"; "Always
on My Mind"; "I Slipped, I Stumbled, I
Fell"; "Is It So Strange?"; "Forget Me
Never"; "Old Shep." **Separate Ways*
(Pickwick CAS-2611, released in De-
cember 1975) was a Pickwick reissue
of RCA Camden CAS-2611).

***Singer Presents Elvis Singing Flam-
ing Star and Others** (RCA PRS-279,
released in November 1968) with two
studio tracks and eight movie songs.
Available only through Singer Sewing
Centers during the December 3, 1968,
NBC-TV show "Elvis"; a color photo of
the TV special was a bonus with the

album. In 1969, RCA reissued the album as *Elvis Sings Flaming Star. Songs:* "Flaming Star"; "Wonderful World" (from *Live a Little, Love a Little*); "Night Life"; "All I Needed Was the Rain"; "Too Much Monkey Business"; "The Yellow Rose of Texas"/ "The Eyes of Texas"; "She's a Machine"; "Do the Vega"; "Tiger Man" (NBC live recording from 1968 Elvis special).

*Something for Everybody (RCA LPM-2370, released in June 1961). During twenty-five weeks on the Top LP chart, it spent three weeks as No. 1. All songs (except "I Slipped, I Stumbled, I Fell") were recorded in RCA's Nashville studios, March 12–13, 1961. *Songs:* "There's Always Me"; "Give Me the Right"; "It's a Sin"; "Sentimental Me"; "Starting Today"; "Gently"; "I'm Comin' Home"; "In Your Arms"; "Put the Blame on Me"; "Judy"; "I Want You With Me"; "I Slipped, I Stumbled, I Fell" (bonus). **Something for Everybody* (RCA LSP-2370, released in July 1971) was a stereo album. It reached No. 14 during a seventeen-week stay on *Billboard*'s Stereo LP chart. RCA AYM1-4116, released in September 1981, was a new number for *Something for Everybody*, RCA AFL1-2370, released in 1977.

*Special Christmas Programming (RCA UNRM-5697, released in November 1967 to radio stations) was a promo release to enhance the December 3, 1967, radio special "Seasons Greetings from Elvis" (rerun on December 10).

*Special Palm Sunday Programming (RCA SP-33-461, released to radio stations in March 1967) promoted Elvis's Palm Sunday radio program aired on March 19, 1967. *Songs:* "How Great Thou Art"; "In the Garden"; "Somebody Bigger Than You and I"; "Stand by Me"; "Without Him"; "Where Could I Go but to the Lord?"; "Where No One Stands Alone"; "Crying in the Chapel"; "How Great Thou Art" (excerpt).

*Speedway (RCA LPM-3989, released in June 1968). Side one is all from *Speedway* and included the Nancy Sinatra/ Elvis duet "There Ain't Nothing Like a Song"; side two had five bonus songs. An eight-by-ten-inch photo was included with the album, which reached No. 82 on *Billboard*'s Top LP chart in thirteen weeks on the list. The cover showed seven views of Elvis. *Songs:* "Speedway"; "There Ain't Nothing Like a Song"; "Your Time Hasn't Come Yet, Baby"; "Who Are You (Who Am I)?"; "He's Your Uncle, Not Your Dad"; "Let Yourself Go"; "Your Groovy Self" (solo by Nancy Sinatra); "Five Sleepy Heads" (bonus); "Western Union"; "Mine" (bonus); "Goin' Home" (bonus); "Suppose" (bonus). This was the only Presley album that featured another artist's solo. **Speedway* (RCA LSP-3989, released in June 1968) was a stereo album; RCA AFL1-3989 was released in 1977 and was a new number for RCA LSP 3989.

*Spinout (RCA LPM-3702, released in October 1966) with nine songs from the movie *Spinout*. A color photo was a bonus. The LP reached No. 18 during thirty-two weeks on the *Billboard*'s Top LP chart. *Songs:* "Stop, Look and Listen"; "Adam and Evil"; "All That I Am"; "Never Say Yes"; "Am I Ready"; "Beach Shack"; "Spinout"; "Smorgasbord"; "I'll Be Back"; "Tomorrow Is a Long Time" (bonus); "Down in the Alley" (bonus); "I'll Remember You" (bonus). **Spinout* (RCA LSP-3702) was a stereo LP released in October 1966. RCA AFL1-2560, released in September 1977, was a new number for RCA LSP-3702; RCA AYL1-3684, released in May 1980, was a new number for RCA AFL1-2560.

Sun Collection, The (RCA Starcall HY-1001, released in August 1975, an English import) with fifteen songs recorded at Sun Records. Due to worldwide demand, RCA renamed and redistributed the LP as *The Sun Sessions* (RCA APM1-1675).

Sun Sessions, The (RCA APM1-1675, released in April 1975) with fifteen original Sun recordings and an alternative take on "I Love You Because." The

LP hit No. 76 during an eleven-week stay on *Billboard*'s Top LP chart. *Songs:* "That's All Right, Mama"; "Blue Moon of Kentucky"; "I Don't Care If the Sun Don't Shine"; "Good Rockin' Tonight"; "Milkcow Blues Boogie"; "You're a Heartbreaker"; "I'm Left, You're Right, She's Gone"; "Baby, Let's Play House"; "Mystery Train"; "I Forgot to Remember to Forget"; "I'll Never Let You Go (Little Darlin')"; "I Love You Because"; "Tryin' to Get to You"; "Blue Moon"; "Just Because"; "I Love You Because" (take #2).

*That's the Way It Is (RCA LSP-4445, released in December 1970) featured only two songs from the documentary *Elvis—That's the Way It Is*, 1970 ("You Don't Have to Say You Love Me" and "The Next Step Is Love"). The other ten songs were from the International Hotel, Las Vegas, August 13–14, 1970 (four songs), and the June 4–6, 1970, RCA Nashville studio sessions (six songs). On June 28, 1977, the album was certified gold. During twenty-three weeks on *Billboard*'s Top LP chart, it hit No. 21, but it reached No. 8 on the Country chart during seventeen weeks. The eight-track cartridge peaked at No. 21 on the Best-Selling Cartridge chart during a seven-week run. *Songs:* "Just Can't Help Believin' "; "Twenty Days and Twenty Nights"; "How the Web Was Woven"; "Patch It Up"; "Mary in the Morning"; "You Don't Have to Say You Love Me"; "You've Lost That Lovin' Feelin' "; "I've Lost You"; "Just Pretend"; "Stranger in the Crowd"; "The Next Step Is Love"; "Bridge Over Troubled Water." **That's the Way It is* (RCA AFL1-4445, released in 1977) was a new number for RCA LSP-4445; RCA AYM1-4114, released in September 1981, was a new number for RCA AFL1-4445.

This Is Elvis (RCA CPL2-4031, released in March 1981) was a two-record set of the sound track for the 1981 documentary *This Is Elvis*. It had a ten-week run on *Billboard*'s Top LP chart, peaking at a miserable No. 115. Nevertheless, it's a great album. *Songs:* "(Marie's the Name) His Latest Flame"; "Moody Blue"; "That's All Right, Mama"; "Shake, Rattle and Roll"/"Flip, Flop and Fly"; "Heartbreak Hotel"; "Hound Dog"; excerpt by Hy Gardner/ Elvis interview; "My Baby Left Me"; "Merry Christmas, Baby"; "Mean Woman Blues"; "Don't Be Cruel"; "Teddy Bear"; "Jailhouse Rock"; Army swearing in; "G.I. Blues"; excerpt from Elvis's departure-for-Germany press conference and an excerpt from home-from-Germany press conference; "Too Much Monkey Business"; "Love Me Tender"; "I've Got a Thing About You, Baby"; "I Need Your Love Tonight"; "Blue Suede Shoes"; "Viva Las Vegas"; "Suspicious Minds"; excerpt from Jaycees' award of "Top Ten" to Elvis; "Promised Land"; excerpt from Elvis's Madison Square Garden press conference; "Always on My Mind"; "Are You Lonesome Tonight?"; "My Way"; "An American Trilogy"; "Memories."

Top Ten Hits, The (RCA 6383-1-R, released in June 1987). Thirty-eight gold hits in a two-record set with commemorative inner sleeves and a bonus poster. It peaked at No. 117 during eight weeks on *Billboard*'s Top LP chart. *Songs:* "Heartbreak Hotel"; "I Want You, I Need You, I Love You"; "Hound Dog"; "Don't Be Cruel"; "Love Me Tender"; "Love Me"; "Too Much"; "All Shook Up"; "Teddy Bear"; "Jailhouse Rock"; "Don't"; "I Beg You"; "Wear My Ring Around Your Neck"; "Hard Headed Woman"; "One Night"; "I Got Stung"; "(Now and Then There's) A Fool Such As I"; "I Need Your Love Tonight"; "A Big Hunk o' Love"; "Stuck on You"; "It's Now or Never"; "Are You Lonesome Tonight?"; "Surrender"; "I Feel So Bad"; "Little Sister"; "(Marie's the Name) His Latest Flame"; "Can't Help Falling in Love"; "Good Luck Charm"; "She's Not You"; "Return to Sender"; "(You're the) Devil in Disguise"; "Bossa Nova Baby"; "Crying in the Chapel"; "In the Ghetto"; "Suspicious Minds"; "Don't Cry, Daddy"; "The Wonder of You"; "Burning Love."

Valentine Gift for You, A (RCA AFL1-5353, released in January 1985) contained previously released songs and commemorated the fiftieth anniversary of Elvis's birth; pressed on red vinyl. During its short three-week stay on *Billboard*'s Top LP chart, it reached No. 154. *Songs:* "Are You Lonesome Tonight?"; "I Need Somebody to Lean On"; "Young and Beautiful"; "Playing for Keeps"; "Tell Me Why"; "Give Me the Right"; "It Feels So Right"; "I was the One"; "Fever"; "Tomorrow Is a Long Time"; "Love Letters"; "Fame and Fortune"; "Can't Help Falling in Love."

*Welcome to My World (RCA APL1-2274, released in March 1977) was an album of country songs, all previously released (except "I Can't Stop Loving You"). On September 20, 1977, the album was certified gold, and eventually it went platinum. It reached No. 44 during a twenty-five-week run on *Billboard*'s Top LP chart and No. 4 on the Country chart during an eleven-week stay. *Songs:* "Welcome to My World"; "Help Me Make It Through the Night"; "Release Me"; "I Really Don't Want to Know"; "For the Good Times"; "Make the World Go Away"; "Gentle on My Mind"; "I'm So Lonesome I Could Cry"; "Your Cheatin' Heart"; "I Can't Stop Loving You." **Welcome to My World* (RCA AFL1-2274, released in 1977) was a new number given to RCA APL1-2274; RCA AQL1-2274, released in 1977, was a new number given to RCA AFL1-2274.

Worldwide Gold Award Hits, Parts 1 & 2 (RCA R-213690, released in 1974) was a two-record set and an RCA Record Club release with the first four sides from the LP *Elvis: Worldwide 50 Gold Award Hits*, Vol. 1 (RCA LPM-6401).

*Worldwide Gold Award Hits, Parts 3 & 4 (RCA R-214657, released in 1978) was two LPs with sides five, six, seven, and eight from *Elvis: Worldwide 50 Gold Award Hits*, Vol. 1, (RCA LPM-6401).

*You'll Never Walk Alone (RCA Camden CALX-2472, released in March 1971) contained five songs in monaural and four in stereo. In its twelve weeks on *Billboard*'s Top LP chart, it peaked at No. 69 and west gold. *Songs:* "You'll Never Walk Alone"; "Who Am I?"; "Let Us Pray"; "Peace in the Valley"; "We Call on Him"; "I Believe"; "It Is No Secret"; "Sing You Children"; "Take My Hand, Precious Lord." **You'll Never Walk Alone* (RCA CAS-2472, released in December 1975) was a release of RCA Camden CALX-2472.

Extended-Play Albums (EPs)

Aloha From Hawaii via Satellite (RCA DTFO-2006, released in February 1973). A six-track EP for jukeboxes in stereo at 33⅓ rpm.

Any Way You Want Me (RCA EPA-965, released in October 1956). Four songs.

Christmas With Elvis (RCA EPA-4340, released in November 1958) with four tracks—two from each side of the 1957 *Elvis' Christmas Album*.

Clambake (MTR-244, released in 1968). A promo four-track record to promote interest in the film *Clambake*.

Dealer's Prevue (RCA SDS-7-2, released in June 1967). A promotional EP sent to record stores featuring four RCA singers, each with two songs: Elvis, Martha Carson, Lou Monte, and Herb Jeffries.

Dealer's Prevue (RCA SDS-57-39, released in October 1957). A promo record for stores with six recording artists: Elvis, Stuart Hamblen, Statesmen Quartet, Perry Como, Eddie Fisher, and Kathy Barr.

Easy Come, Easy Go (RCA EPA-4387, released on March 24, 1967). A promotion for the film *Easy Come, Easy Go*. The release included other advertising gimmicks.

***Elvis*, Vol. 1** (RCA EPA-992, released on October 19, 1956) and similar to the *Elvis* LP (which was released the same day). The EP hit No. 1 for two weeks on *Billboard*'s EP chart, and it was the first EP in history to sell 1 million copies. A small number of these EPs were distributed with the cover from the EP *Elvis Presley* (RCA EPA-747) while the back of the album told the story of Elvis's appearance on "Stage Show." Four songs.

***Elvis*, Vol. 2** (RCA EPA-993, released in November 1956). Released with the same cover as volume one and the *Elvis* LP. Four songs. "Old Shep" hit the Top 100 chart, topping at No. 47.

Elvis by Request (RCA LPC-128, released in April 1961) featured two songs from *Flaming Star* and two No. 1 hits. This EP was the only 33⅓ rpm released to the public. It sold over 1 million copies. Four songs, one of which ("Flaming Star") reached No. 14 on *Billboard*'s Hot 100 chart.

Elvis/Jaye P. Morgan (RCA EPA-992/ 689, released in December 1956). A promo to dealers with a double-pocket EP set with two records that covered Elvis and Jaye P. Morgan releases.

Elvis Presley (RCA EPA-747, released on March 13, 1956) with four songs from the LP *Elvis Presley*. "Blue Suede Shoes" from the EP hit No. 24 on *Billboard*'s Hot 100 list, and the EP was on the EP chart at No. 10. Several back covers were printed for the EP.

Elvis Presley (RCA EPB-1254, released on March 13, 1956). This double EP had the same cover and four cuts from the LP *Elvis Presley*; in 1957 it hit No. 9 on the EP chart during a three-week stay. Three versions of the EP exist. Eight songs on each.

Elvis Presley (RCA EPA-830, released in September 1956) with four cuts from three single releases from a four-week period. The cover featured Elvis, Bill Black, and Scotty Moore.

Elvis Presley (RCA SPD-22, released in October 1956). A two-record, double-pocket EP; a promotional gimmick to buy a Victrola at $32.95 was included, along with radio advertisements and printed ads. Eight songs.

Elvis Presley (RCA SPD-23, released in October 1956) with Elvis's signature stamped in gold. This was a three-record set with eight songs from the LP *Elvis Presley*, plus four other hits. The EP was given away free to those who bought a Model 7EP45 portable 48-rpm Victrola at $47.95 for $1 down and $1 a week. Twelve records by other artists were also in the package.

Elvis Presley—The Most Talked About New Personality in the Last Ten Years of Recorded Music (RCA EPB-1254, released in March 1956). A two-record promo with twelve songs from the LP *Elvis Presley*.

Elvis Sails (RCA EPA-4325, released in December 1958) with a news "Extra" on the cover from September 22, 1958, and a calendar on the reverse. No music, but three interviews with Elvis before he left for Germany. A hole was punched in the EP so fans could pin it up. The EP hit *Billboard*'s EP chart for twelve weeks, peaking at No. 2.

Elvis Sails (RCA EPA-5157, released in May 1965) was a reissue of EPA-4325, Gold Standard. No calendar on reverse.

Elvis Sings Christmas Songs (RCA EPA-4108, released on November 19, 1957, with *Elvis' Christmas Album*). It was on *Billboard*'s EP chart for seven weeks, hitting No. 2. It was No. 1 for two weeks on the EP chart in 1959.

***EP Collection, The*, Vol. 2** (RCA EP2, released in 1982), boxed. Three records with selections from *A Touch of Gold*, Vol. 2, *G. I. Blues—The Alternative Tapes*, Vol. 2, and *Collector's Gold*. Offered only in Great Britain. Twelve songs.

Extended Play Sampler (RCA SPA-7-61, released in October 1957) was sent only to radio stations to promote interest in other EPs. Featured "Jailhouse Rock"; twelve songs by twelve artists offered.

Follow That Dream (RCA EPA-4368,

released in May 1962). To promote the movie. The title song hit No. 5 on the Easy-Listening chart, and the EP was No. 15 on *Billboard*'s EP chart. Four songs.

Good Rockin' Tonight (Motion Picture Service EP-1206, released in 1956). To promote the hit of the month; one record with four songs.

Great Country/Western Hits (RCA SPD-26, released in November 1956) with ten EPs; four songs by Elvis; sixteen by other artists.

Heartbreak Hotel (RCA EPA-821, released in April 1956). Three previously released songs and "Money Honey". The EP peaked on the *Billboard*'s chart at No. 5 in 1958, with "Money Honey" at No. 76 on the Top 100 chart.

Jailhouse Rock (RCA EPA-4114, released on October 30, 1956) was a promotional EP to disc jockeys (each received three) for the film and the LP. The EP was No. 1 for twenty-two straight weeks on *Billboard*'s EP chart. It dropped to No. 2 for one week, and then climbed back to No. 1 for another six weeks (No. 1 for twenty-eight weeks out of a forty-nine-week run). The million seller was *Billboard*'s EP of 1958. Five songs.

Just for You (RCA EPA-4041, released in September 1957). Contained "Is It So Strange" and three songs from *Loving You*. The EP hit No. 2 on *Billboard*'s EP chart. Four songs.

Kid Galahad (RCA EPA-4371, released in September 1962). To promote the movie. "King of the Whole Wide World" hit *Billboard*'s Hot 100 chart at No. 30. Six songs.

King Creole (RCA EPA-4319, released in July 1958). Four songs from the movie. The million-seller EP had twenty-three consecutive weeks at No. 1 on *Billboard*'s EP chart (it was No. 1 for twenty-nine out of fifty-four weeks).

King Creole (RCA EPA-5122, released in November 1959). A reissue of EPA-4319, Gold Standard.

***King Creole* Vol. 2** (RCA EPA-4321, released in August 1958). During its twenty-two-week stay on *Billboard*'s

EP chart, it was No. 1 for one week and No. 2 for seventeen weeks. Four songs.

Love Me Tender (RCA EPA-4006, released in November 1956). With four songs from the movie, it peaked at No. 2 on the EP chart and "Poor Boy" peaked at No. 35 on the single's chart.

***Loving You*, Vol. 1** (RCA EPA 1-1515, released in June 1957) with four songs from the movie. During the week of September 28, 1957, four of Elvis's EPs charted, this one peaking at No. 1 for five weeks.

***Loving You*, Vol. 2** (RCA EPA 1-1515, released in June 1957). Four songs from the movie. The EP peaked at No. 4 on *Billboard*'s EP chart. Two covers were issued.

Peace in the Valley (RCA EPA-4054, released on March 22, 1957). The first religious EP by Elvis to sell a million copies; it was No. 3 on *Billboard*'s EP chart. This version was distributed in Great Britain and was Elvis's first religious EP. Four songs.

Peace in the Valley (RCA EPA-5121, released in November 1959, Gold Standard series). A reissue of EPA-4054.

Perfect for Parties (RCA SPA-7-37, released on October 25, 1956). Elvis introduced each of six songs from other LPs. Advertised extensively on radio and in magazines. With a clipped ad and twenty-five cents, fans could send for the EP (Dept. 776, RCA Victor, Philadelphia 5, PA). For $1, seven cover reprints would be sent.

Promotion Disc (RCA PRO-12, released in December 1956). Featured "Old Shep"; sent to radio disc jockeys. Featured one song by Elvis and one each by Hank Snow, Eddy Arnold, and Jim Reeves.

RCA Family Record Center (RCA PR-121, released in February 1962). A promotional "Compact 33" EP; sent to record stores only; eight interrupted, incomplete songs.

Real Elvis, The (RCA EPA-940, released in September 1956) with Elvis's first two RCA singles; in *1958*, the EP charted for five weeks and peaked at No. 5. Four songs.

Real Elvis, The (RCA EPA-5120, released in November 1959). A reissue Gold Standard of EPA-940.

Save-On Records (**Bulletin for June 1956**) (RCA SPA-7-27, released in June 1956). Given to those who had RCA Save-On-Record-Coupon-Books. One song each from ten different albums and ten different artists. With a coupon, $1 was discounted on the price of any album the buyer selected. Postage-free from RCA to the buyer. Elvis's selection was "I'm Gonna Sit Right Down and Cry (Over You)."

See the Sea, the Elvis Way (EPA-4386, distributed in May 1964) from New Zealand. RCA-EPAS-4386 was the stereo version. Four songs.

The Sound of Leadership (RCA SPD-19, released in June 1956). A souvenir eight-box set of thirty-two million-sellers (from 1907 to 1956's "Heartbreak Hotel" by Elvis) given to record distributors by RCA reps.

Stay Away (RCA EPA-994, released in January 1957). Both sides of the LP *Elvis* are featured. Four songs.

Tickle Me (RCA EPA-4383, released in June 1965) with five songs from the movie. The EP charted at No. 70 on *Billboard*'s chart. Three covers were issued.

Touch of Gold, A, Vol. 1 (RCA EPA-5088, released in April 1959) with Elvis in his gold lamé suit on the cover and a "fan club card" inside. Gold Standard series; with three RCA hits and one from Sun.

Touch of Gold, A, Vol. 2 (RCA EPA-5101, released in September 1959).

Gold Standard series; three RCA hits and one from Sun; cover featured two photographs of Elvis in gold-lamé.

Touch of Gold, A, Vol. 3 (RCA EPA-5141, released in January 1960) with three RCA hits and one from Sun. Three photographs of Elvis in gold-lamé on the cover. Gold Standard series.

Tupperware's Hit Parade (Tupperware THP-11973, released in January 1973). A promotional from the Tupperware Company, with "All Shook Up" as its feature.

TV Guide Presents Elvis Presley (RCA GB-MW-8705, released in September 1956). A one-sided promo record distributed to radio stations that included parts of an August 6, 1956, interview with Elvis and *TV Guide*'s Paul Wilder, from Lakewood, Florida.

Viva Las Vegas (RCA EPA-4382, released in June 1964) as a promo for the movie. Four songs from the movie.

(No title, RCA SPD-15, released in January 1956.) A ten-EP promotional boxed set with four of Elvis's Sun recordings. This EP is exceedingly valuable if it is in good condition, with its black RCA Victor labels and the paper inserts/box/sleeves.

(No title, RCA DJ-7, released in October 1956.) Sent to disc jockeys only with Elvis's "Love Me Tender"/"Any Way You Want Me (That's How I Will Be)," which was RCA's 47-6643 single release. Two songs by Jean Chapel.

(No title, RCA DJ-56, released in January 1957.) Distributed to disc jockeys only; two tracks by Dinah Shore, and Elvis's RCA 47-6800 ("Too Much" and "Playing for Keeps").

Recommended Records to Understand the Era

Aloha From Hawaii via Satellite (RCA DTFA-2006, an extended-play EP/VPSX 6089, February 1973). The only EP released in stereo format; 33⅓ speed (unusual for Elvis). Made for jukeboxes; good cut of grand performance.

Arthur Crudup: That's All Right, Mama (Relci 7036) shows the similarity of Crudup's style and Elvis's.

B. B. King, Every Day I Have the Blues (Telstar Records TST-3507, 1990) with twelve great hits from the master bluesman including "B.B. Boogie," "The Letter," "The Pawnbroker," "Sweet Sixteen," and "The Other Night Blues."

B. B. King Live at the Apollo (GRP Records, GRD-9637).

B. B. King Live in Cook County Jail (MCA, MCAC-27005).

Best of Muddy Waters (TST/TSD-3504); *The Best of Bo Diddley* (TST/TSD 3506); *The Best of Chuck Berry* (TST/TSD-3508). All are absolute must listening.

Blackwood Brothers, The—Old Time Singing (Hollywood, HT-453, 1991) gives a more modern-day listening experience to the gospel tradition Elvis loved.

Bo Diddley—His Greatest Hits (Chess CHC 9106).

Bob Dylan's Greatest Hits, Vol. 2 (Columbia Records, CGT 31120).

Buddy Holly Story, The (Epic Records/CBS, PET 35412, 1978).

Burbank Sessions, The, Vol. 1 (Audifon AFNS 62768). Bootleg; good moments with the Blue Moon Boys and shorts from the 1968 TV special. Hard to find, but worth the hunt.

Carl Perkins (Dot, MCAC-39035, 1985) and *Carl Perkins Blue Suede Shoes*

(Sun, R4-70342, from earlier sessions, released 1990).

Chester Burnett a.k.a. Howlin' Wolf (Chess 60016, first issue). A double album set of the blues master.

Chuck Berry Golden Hits (Mercury Records, 826 256-4, M-1).

Complete Sun Sessions, The (RCA 6414-1-R). Two-record set, thirty-two songs. Conversation and down-to-earth session playing. Released in 1986. *A must!*

Downhome Rockabilly (Sun 1014) with the fabulous Sleepy Labeef's ""There Is Something on Your Mind." Spirited listening.

Elvis: A Golden Celebration (RCA CPM 6-5172). Six records include all 1956–72 television appearances, and outtakes from the 1968 TV "Comeback Special."

Elvis—A Legendary Performer, Vol. 1 (RCA KSL2-7032). Two-record set, reissue; with unreleased live versions of five songs. January 1974.

Elvis Back in Memphis (RCA LSP-4429, one record, November 1970).

Elvis' Christmas Album (RCA AFK1-5486; a reissue of LPM/LOC-1035). Twelve tunes including "I Believe," "I'll Be Home for Christmas," and "White Christmas" with the Jordanaires, 1957. A good listening experience for the holidays.

Elvis Country (RCA AYL1-3956) shows the earlier influences on Elvis from the Hank Williams/Hank Snow generation, but a rocking "Whole Lotta Shakin' " allows it to kick.

Elvis' Gold Records (RCA AQK1-1707, 1962) with the Jordanaires; thirteen of Elvis's early, great hits. A must for all listeners.

***Elvis Gospel 1957–1971, Known Only
to Him*** (RCA 9586-4-R). Fourteen
songs, well produced by Steve Sholes,
Felton Jarvis, and Chips Momen, 1989.
This is the best overall survey of
Elvis's love for gospel music. An absolute must for all listeners.

***Elvis Greatest Hits—Golden Singles,
Vol. 1*** (RCA PP-13897, boxed set, Oc-
tober 1984, six singles) and Vol. 2
(RCA PP-13898, boxed set, October
1984, six singles). Volume one includes
"In the Ghetto"/"If I Can Dream"; Vol-
ume two includes "Little Sister"/
"(Marie's the Name) His Latest Flame."

***Elvis—He Walks Beside Me, Favorite
Songs of Faith and Inspiration***
(RCA AFK1-2772) with the Imperials
Quartet, the Jordanaires, the Sweet
Inspirations, and J. D. Sumner and the
Stamps, 1978. Eleven songs include
"The Impossible Dream" and "How
Great Thou Art."

Elvis in Hollywood (RCA DPL 2-0168).
Two-record set, September 1976.

Elvis in Memphis (LSP-4155, June
1969). Thirteen songs not as well produced as some of his sixties recordings. Includes not-too-often-heard
"Wearin' That Loved On Look," "Only
the Strong Survive," "Long Black Limousine," "Power of Love," and others.

Elvis in Nashville (RCA 8468-4-R, produced by the Country Music Foundation, 1988) is a good review of the
music Elvis cut in Nashville, 1954–71.
With comments inside the jacket by
Chet Atkins, Gordon Stoker of the Jordanaires, and Jay Orr (CMF). Scans
from 1956 ("I Got a Woman") to June
9, 1971 ("Early Mornin' Rain," "It's Still
Dark," "I, John").

***Elvis in Person at the International
Hotel*** (RCA LSP-4428, one record, November 1970).

Elvis—NBC Special (RCA AYM1-3894)
is a fine accounting of the TV comeback show's variety.

Elvis Presley (RCA EPB-1254, March 13,
1956). Original two-record set with
"Blue Suede Shoes," "Tutti Frutti," etc.
Rather poor recording equipment
makes some of it hard to hear, but a

good way to study the recording disad-
vantages of the fifties.

Elvis Presley (RCA, LPM/LSP-1254, April
1956) contains twelve of the first rock
'n' roll hits from the fifties.

Elvis Presley, C'mon Everybody (RCA/
CAK-2518, 1985). Ten hits from Elvis's
movies, including "Easy Come, Easy
Go," "Follow That Dream," and "King
of the Whole Wide World." Not as
great as his early music, but definitely
emotional and well sung.

Elvis Presley, He Touched Me (RCA
PK-1923/LSP-4690). Award-winning album includes twelve religious songs,
1972.

Elvis Presley, His Hand in Mine (RCA
AYK1-3935 and LPM/LSP-2328, October
1960) contains twelve religious songs
with the Jordanaires and demonstrates
the diversity of Elvis's rocking gospel
music in 1961.

Elvis Presley, How Great Thou Art
(RCA AQK1-3758/LPM/LSP-3758) with
eleven religious songs backed by the
Jordanaires and the Imperials Quartet,
1967. Award-winning achievement.

Elvis Presley, Promised Land (RCA
APK1-0873) with ten religious songs
backed by J. D. Sumner and the
Stamps, 1975.

***Elvis Presley Recorded Live on Stage
in Memphis*** (RCA CPK1-0606). Vocal
accompaniment by Voice, J. D. Sumner
and the Stamps, the Sweet Inspirations,
and Kathy Westmoreland. Executive
producer for the album was Elvis Presley. A diversity of hits and lesser-
known songs by Elvis included
"Blueberry Hill," "American Trilogy,"
"Lawdy Miss Clawdy," "See See Rider,"
"Long Tall Sally," "Mama Don't
Dance." 1974.

***Elvis Presley, The Great Perfor-
mances*** (RCA 2227-4-R, 1990). Accompanied video volumes one and two of
the same title, with brief comments on
the jacket by Andrew Solt and Jerry
Schilling. Narrated (like the videos) by
George Klein.

Elvis Presley—The Number One Hits
(RCA 6382-4-8) contains a good selection of songs. 1988.

Elvis Presley, You'll Never Walk Alone (RCA Special Projects, CAK-2472). A mixture of movie hits and lesser-known hits by Elvis. The title song comes from the movie *Carousel*. 1985.

Elvis Recorded Live at Madison Square Garden (RCA LSP 4776). One record, includes "Also Sprach Zarathustra," "Proud Mary," "Polk Salad Annie," "Exit Music," and others. June 1972.

Elvis Sings the Wonderful World of Christmas (RCA ANKI-1936/LSP-4579) with the Imperials Quartet, 1971. Eleven songs.

Elvis—That's the Way It Is (RCA LSP-4445). One record, includes "You've Lost That Lovin' Feelin'," "I've Lost You," "Just Pretend," "How the Web Was Woven," and other oddities. December 1970.

Father of Rock 'n' Roll, The (RCA LPV 573). A hard-to-find, but must-hear Arthur Crudup record, which includes "That's All Right, Mama." You will hear why Elvis admired Crudup so much.

From Elvis Presley Boulevard, Memphis, Tennessee (APL 1-1506). Includes "Never Again," "Danny Boy," "Blue Eyes Crying in the Rain," "Solitaire," etc. May 1976.

From Memphis to Vegas/Vegas to Memphis (RCA LSP-6020). A double LP, with such oddities as "Johnny B. Goode," "My Babe," "Words," "Inherit the Wind," "A Little Bit of Green," "The Fair Is Moving On," etc. November 1969.

Great Country/Western Hits (RCA SPD-26, November 1956). A ten-EP boxed set with twenty sides of early country music by Elvis.

Hank Williams's 40 Greatest Hits (Polydor 821-233-1). The best overall Williams sessions.

Having Fun With Elvis on Stage (CPM 1-0818). No music, just comments by Elvis to himself, his band, and his audience. A rare spontaneous must-have if you can find it. October 1974.

He Walks Beside Me (RCA Victor AFL1-2772). A posthumous album released in 1978 of eleven religious songs. Easier to find than some of the earlier religious records. Good overall sound quality.

His Songs of Inspiration (RCA DML1-0264). A posthumous album released in 1977. Ten religious songs, the best of his gospel music.

Howlin' Wolf Moanin' in the Moonlight (Chess/MCA CHC-9195). Twelve raw, earthy blues songs from the original 1959 session. Shows the origins of rock 'n' roll.

Jerry Lee Lewis's Greatest Hits (Evergreen 2691714). A must!

Jerry Lee Lewis: The Sun Years (Charly Sun Box 102). An incredible listening experience, showing the dynamic breadth, strength, and spontaneity of one of the best rockabilly artists.

Jordanaires: A Tribute to Elvis' Favorite Spirituals (Step One Records, SOR 0029, 1987). Contains one of his favorite groups' hand-picked religious songs sung in Elvis's honor. Fourteen robust, genuine songs rendered with feeling.

Jordanaires: Elvis Memories (World Wide Music MC 190189) with twelve of Elvis's songs sung by the Jordanaires, with D. J. Fontana (Elvis's original drummer) on drums. A one-page text about Elvis and the Jordanaires is informative. 1989.

Just Keep A Movin' (Detour 33-0004) is Hank Snow at his best. This album celebrates the birth of rock.

Little Richard's Greatest Hits (recorded live, Epic Records/CBS, PET 40389).

Memphis Blues (United 101) with Bobby Bland, Howlin' Wolf, Walter Horton, Junior Parker, and Joe Hill Louis, as recorded by the astute and innovative Sam Phillips in the early fifties.

Million Dollar Quartet, The (Charly CDX 20) with Elvis, Jerry Lee Lewis, Carl Perkins, and perhaps Johnny Cash jamming in 1956 at the Sun studios. They fool around with gospel, country, blues, and rock tunes. Laid-back, inspiring, and fun to listen to. Released on tape (RCA 2023-4-R, 1990).

Moody Blue (RCA AFL1-2428). Elvis's last album; one record of ten songs released in July 1977 (the month he died). Includes "Unchained Melody," "If You Love Me (Let Me Know)," "Little Darlin'," "He'll Have to Go," "Let Me Be There." Side 2: "Way Down," "Pledging My Love," "Moody Blue," "She Thinks I Still Care," "It's Easy For You."

New South, The (Elektra 5E-539) is a fine Hank Williams, Jr., album, showing his diversity and awareness.

1977 Rockabilly (Sun 1004). A poor production of the Sun years, but crucial listening for those who want to hear the raw, casual sessions of Sam Phillips's early discoveries.

Otis Blackwell, 1953–1955 (Interstate Music, Ltd., England). Songs recorded at the Audio-Video Studios, New York City. A fine overview of Blackwell's lesser-known works.

Promised Land (APL1-0873). Songs include "Help Me," "Mr. Songman," "If You Talk in Your Sleep," and other oddities. January 1975.

Reconsider Baby (RCA AFL1-5418). A telltale record of Elvis's blues, 1954–72. A different look at the singer.

Rockabilly '56, '59, Vol. 1 and 2 (Country Music Foundation CMF-014-C, 1988) is a comprehensive survey of the rockabilly singers coming out of the country-western, blues, R&B, and gospel traditions. Volume one features Joe Clay, Ric Cartey, Homer and Jethro, Pee Wee King, through to the melodious vocals of Roy Orbison. Seventeen vocalists in all! Volume two adds David Houston, Tommy Black & the Rhythm Rebels, Martha Carson, Janis Martin, Dave Rich, the Sprouts, Milton Allen, the Morgan Twins, and others to the list. Fifteen artists in all. These are the artists whose careers or recordings flourished after Elvis Presley's popularity skyrocketed. Fine albums.

Rockabilly King (English Polydor 2310 293) with "One Hand Loose," the best of Charlie Feathers, direct, simple, raw, fast.

Rocking Years, The (Charly Sun Box 106). Twelve records, 221 tunes; diverse and a must for historians.

Sun Box, The (Charly Sun Box 100). This three-record set gives a good, overall view of the Sun sessions.

Sun Country Years, The (German Bear Family label, 15211). This ten-record set features an overview of country sessions from Sun's earliest to latest sounds.

Sun Recordings (original): "That's All Right, Mama"/"Blue Moon of Kentucky" (August 1954, Sun 209); "Good Rockin' Tonight"/"You're a Heartbreaker" (October 1954, Sun 215); "Baby, Let's Play House"/"I'm Left, You're Right, She's Gone" (January 1955, Sun 217); "Mystery Train"/"I Forgot to Remember to Forget" (August 1955, Sun 223). A must for every Elvis enthusiast!

Sun Sessions, The (APM1-1675). One record filled with the early great tunes; all reissues. March 1976.

TV Guide Presents Elvis Presley. This promotional record was sent to radio stations and features a rare interview with Elvis at the age of twenty-one. Fewer than twelve copies are known to exist.

Touch of Gold, A Vol. 1 (RCA-EPA-5088), Vol. 2 (RCA EPA-5101), and Vol. 3 (RCA EPA-5141) were released in 1959 and 1960 and give a fine overview of Elvis's early works.

Welcome to My World (APL1-2274) includes a lofty, strong voice singing, "I Really Don't Want to Know," the title song, "Make the World Go Away," "I'm So Lonesome I Could Cry," "Your Cheatin' Heart," "I Can't Stop Loving You." March 1977.

Woke Up Screaming (Ace 41). The gutsy, early Memphis blues sound of Bobby Bland.

Worldwide 50 Gold Award Hits (RCA LPM-6401). A four-record set that contains an incredible collection of Elvis's best songs from all periods of his career. August 1970.

You'll Never Walk Alone (CAS-2472, March 1971). A fine example of Elvis's religious music.

Bootleg Albums

Elvis's bootleg songs and albums are those that were secretly recorded during live performances or rehearsal sessions. Bootleg songs are those that were stolen from Elvis and smuggled to producers who were not connected in any way to Elvis and Colonel Parker. They did not profit from sales of bootleg recordings.

Aloha Rehearsal Show—Kui Lee Cancer Benefit (Amiga Records 5-73-210, released in 1980). One record; features Elvis's rehearsal session for "Elvis: Aloha From Hawaii," taped on January 12, 1973.

America's Own (Geneva, 2LP2001, released in 1979). Two-record set recorded at a live concert at the Nassau Coliseum, Uniondale, NY, July 19, 1975.

Behind Closed Doors (Audifon Records AFNS 66072-4, released in 1979) with takes from various Elvis movies; four records.

Blue Hawaii Box, The (Laurel BPM-501-A, released in 1981) with fourteen songs gleaned from 110 song takes from the movie *Blue Hawaii*. Sold with "A New Era" booklet.

Blue Hawaii Sessions, The (Laurel LPM 2427, released in 1987). Fourteen songs from *Blue Hawaii* (seven alternative takes).

Burbank Sessions, The, Vol. 1 (Audifon Records AFNS 62768, released in 1979). Two records from two performances on June 27, 1968, at the NBC Studios, Burbank, CA, for the TV special "Elvis."

Burbank Sessions, The, Vol. 2 (Audifon Records AFNS 62968, released in 1981). Two records of two performances held on June 29, 1968, for the TV special "Elvis."

Cadillac Elvis (TCB Records 1-8-35, released in 1979). Many cuts from *Elvis—That's the Way It is;* the "Steve Allen Show"; *Elvis on Tour;* and the TV special "Elvis"; plus short interviews with Elvis, Colonel Parker, Peter

Noone; tributes from Sammy Davis, Jr., Ann-Margret, Pat Boone, Jerry Lewis, Steve Allen, Fats Domino, and Murray the K.

Command Performance (ECP 101, released in 1977) with fourteen concert takes, 1970–74, from the Las Vegas Hilton Hotel ("Reconsider Baby" was from Madison Square Garden, New York City, and "Oh, Happy Day" was from the International Hotel, Las Vegas). It's the only live performance of "It's Midnight" released in any form.

Complete Kid Galahad Sessions, The, Vols. 1, 2, and 3 (each produced by TCB Records, 3-30-973, 3-30-974, 3-30-975). One record each, each released in 1987.

Complete Wild in the Country Sessions, The (Laurel LPM-502-D, released in February 1988). From the 1961 movie by that title; two records of five songs.

Dog's Life, A (Audifon Records 67361, released in 1980). All alternative studio takes of twelve songs from the movies *Kid Galahad* and *Paradise, Hawaiian Style.*

Dorsey Brothers (Golden Archives Records 56-GA-100, released in 1976) from Elvis's performances from January 28 to March 24, 1956, on the Dorseys' TV program, "Stage Show." A record of twelve songs.

Elvis (Neuphone Records, released in 1974). One record, German produced, with "Shake, Rattle and Roll" from the Dorsey show on January 28, 1956; cuts from various movies; and the RCA 447-0639 single, "Kiss Me Quick"/"Suspicion."

Elvis' 1961 Hawaii Benefit Concert (Golden Archives Records GA 200, released in 1978). Everything taken from the March 25, 1961, Bloch Arena, Pearl Harbor, concert; one record with fifteen songs.

Elvis on Tour (Amiga Records 2 72 020,

released in 1980). All taken from the documentary *Elvis on Tour;* some songs excluded.

***Elvis Presley Is Alive and Well and Singing in Las Vegas,* Vol. 1** (No Record Label, released in 1975). Mostly taken from the Las Vegas concerts in August 1974 and August 1975. Poor quality.

Elvis Rocks and the Girls Roll (Pink and Black LPM-1510, released in 1986). One record from dressing-room rehearsals for the TV special "Elvis," 1968, and unreleased songs from *Girls! Girls! Girls!*

Elvis Sings Songs From Tickle Me (Audition Supertone US/53310761, released in 1987). One record with alternative takes of songs from *Tickle Me.*

Entertainer, The (Rooster Record Company R LP 501, released in 1978). One record, emphasizing the fifties (side one) and the seventies in Las Vegas (side two).

Eternal Elvis (Eagle Records LPS-685, released in 1979). One record; three duets overdubbed electronically with Elvis and Shirley Bassey, Lloyd Price, and Jerry Lee Lewis, plus talks with Sam Phillips and Chet Atkins and a few top hits.

First Year—Recorded Live, The (Black Belt Records, LP2, released in 1979) with songs from January 29, 1955, at Houston's Eagle's Nest; Jay Thompson's interview with Elvis in Wichita Falls, KS; three "Louisiana Hayride" performances; and a shortened interview with Elvis and Bob Neal of radio WMPS, Memphis.

First Years, The (HALW 00001, released in 1979). An interview with Scotty Moore and the January 29, 1955, Eagle's Nest performance in Houston. One record.

Forever Young, Forever Beautiful (Memphis Flash Records, JL 92447, released in 1978). One record; all recorded at Eddie Fadal's Waco, TX, home during a visit from Anita Wood and Elvis. Elvis sings over other singers' records and plays the piano.

From Hollywood to Vegas (Brookville Records BRLP 301, released in 1974). Movie sound tracks, Las Vegas concerts, and an announcement from November 20, 1972's press conference in Honolulu.

From Las Vegas . . . to Niagara Falls (Live Productions LVLP 1897-98, released in 1974). Two records from the Hilton Hotel's September 3, 1973, concert, Las Vegas, and the evening show in Niagara Falls, June 24, 1974.

From the Beach to the Bayou (Graceland Records GL 1001, released in 1978). One record; alternative studio takes from three movies.

From the Waist Up (Golden Archives 56-57 GA 150, released in 1976). One record with all of Elvis's performances on the Ed Sullivan TV show.

Good Rocking Tonight (Bobcat Records LP 100, released in 1974) with the now-famous conversation between Sam Phillips and Jerry Lee Lewis about rock and roll and religious beliefs and mysteries; also features "Mystery Train," "Good Rocking Tonight," and "Blue Moon of Kentucky."

Got a Lot o' Livin' to Do (Pirate Record PR 101, released in 1976). One record with songs from *Jailhouse Rock;* plus the Dick Clark/Elvis phone interview, and four songs from August 31, 1957, at the Vancouver concert.

Hawaii USA (Laurel LPM-8665, released in 1987). One record; twenty-five unreleased takes from eight songs from *Paradise, Hawaiian Style* sessions.

Hillbilly Cat Live, The (Spring Fever Record Club SFLP-301, released in 1970). Two-record set with Elvis's first two TV performances on the "Ed Sullivan Show" and seven other previously released recordings.

***Hillbilly Cat, 1954–1974, The,* Vol. 1** (Brookville Records BRLP 311, released in 1974). One record with Elvis's first two Ed Sullivan appearances and seven previously released songs.

The King: From the Dark to the Light (Tiger Records, TR 101, released in 1974). One record from the sound tracks of *Elvis on Tour* and *Elvis—That's the Way It Is.*

King Goes Wild, The (Wilde Productions PRP 207, released in 1975). One record of all three Ed Sullivan show performances.

King of Las Vegas Live (Hazbin/Wizardo Records 351, released in 1973). One record; fourteen songs from Vegas as shown in *Elvis—That's the Way It Is.*

Last Farewell, The (E.P. Records PRP 781, released in 1977). Two records: a recording of the King's last live concert performance at Market Square Arena, Indianapolis, eight-thirty P.M., June 26, 1977, with the Joe Guercio Orchestra.

Leavin' It Up to You (Audifon Records AFNS 66173, released in 1980). One record; all from a Las Vegas rehearsal, a rehearsal for "Elvis: Aloha From Hawaii," and studio alternative takes of three songs.

Legend Lives On, The (Presley Collection Series PCS 1001, released in 1976). One record from Las Vegas shows in 1969 and 1972.

Long Lost Songs (Vault Records VAP, 1020, released in 1985). One record. Despite the album's title, these are just old songs from Vegas concerts, except one, "Where No One Stands Alone" (from February 19, 1977, Johnson City, Tennessee), and one unknown bathroom conversation.

Loving You (Gold Suit Productions GSR 10001, released in 1975). One record from four movie sound tracks and two songs from the "Ed Sullivan Show"; plus a March of Dimes message.

Loving You Recording Sessions (Vik EPP 254, a British production, released in 1982) with takes of "Loving You" and "Jailhouse Rock" and two 1956 interviews.

Million Dollar Quartet, The (Million Dollar Records OMD 001, released in 1980) with seventeen songs recorded on December 4, 1956, with Elvis, Jerry Lee Lewis, Carl Perkins, and Johnny Cash at Sun Records. One record. Elvis plays piano and guitar.

Monologue L. P., The (Bullet Records,

released in 1973). One record: songs from July 31, 1969, live performance at the International Hotel in Las Vegas.

One Million Dollar Quartet, The (S Records, S-5001, released in 1987). Two-record set. The entire Million Dollar sessions. First sold in Great Britain and then in the U.S. *The* most important bootleg. There was also a picture disc available.

Plantation Rock (Audifon Records AFNS 67360, released in 1979). One record with songs from *Blue Hawaii*, *Girls! Girls! Girls!*, and "*Elvis: Aloha From Hawaii.*" The title song "Plantation Rock" was unreleased from *Girls! Girls! Girls!*

Please Release Me (1st Records 161, released in 1970). One record; two songs from an Ed Sullivan performance and the rest from "Elvis," the TV special.

Rockin' Rebel, The (Golden Archives Records GA 250, released in 1978). One record with Elvis carrying a guitar over his shoulder and wearing a cowboy outfit. Songs from the Milton Berle show of June 5, 1956; a La Crosse, WS, interview, May 14, 1956; Sun alternative takes; songs from *King Creole*. Volume two featured songs from Eagle's Nest and "Louisiana Hayride" performances (Golden Archives Records GA 300). Volume three has two "Loving You" takes and an alternative take of "Old Shep" and songs from Ed Sullivan and Steve Allen shows; plus two interviews.

Rockin' With Elvis April Fools' Day (Live Stage Productions 72722, released in 1980). One record with songs all taken from *Elvis Recorded Live on Stage in Memphis* (RCA CPL1-0606, 1974) with one exception, "Can't Help Falling in Love."

Rockin' With Elvis New Year's Eve, Pittsburgh, PA, Dec. 31, 1976 (Spirit of American Records HNY 7677, released in 1977). Two-record set; all recorded at Elvis's Pittsburgh concert, December 31, 1976. With Joe Guercio Orchestra.

'68 Comeback, The (Memphis Records

MKS 101, released in 1976). One record; all taken from prerecorded vocals for the TV special "Elvis" on December 3, 1968. Volume two was more of the same, taken from recordings done on June 28 and June 30, 1968. One record, released in 1978 (Amiga Records MKS 192).

Sold Out (E.P. Records PRP 251, released in 1974. One record; songs from an Anaheim, CA, concert; a recording session in Nashville, July 1, 1973; and three songs lifted from *Elvis on Tour*.

Special Delivery From Elvis Presley (Flaming Star Records Co., FSR 3, released in 1979). One record; an electronic duet overdubbed with Linda Ronstadt of "Love Me Tender"; plus movie tracks, studio alternative takes, and a few concert tracks.

Standing Room Only, Vol. 2 (Eagle Records Corp. NOTN 3003, released in 1979). One record mislabeled as "Volume 2." A chronology of songs from 1955 to 1968. Volume three was released in 1980 and features songs from October 1954 to 1968. One record.

Sun Years, The (Sun International Corp., Sun 1001, released in 1977). One record; all incomplete, cut songs from 1955 to 1956, and interviews with Jay Thompson and Charlie Walker.

Superstar Outtakes (E.P. Records PRP 254, released in 1976). One record; songs from "The Steve Allen Show," the TV special "Elvis," and an International Hotel (Las Vegas) concert. Volume two was more of the same, with the concert taken from the Hilton Hotel, 1972. One record released in 1977 (E.P. Records PRP 258).

Susie Q (Astra AST-103, released in 1985). One record with songs from Vegas shows (except "You Don't Know Me," a studio take).

That's All Right (Melodiya 48919 003, released in 1990), a Russian album under the old Soviet record label Melodiya. A single LP compilation of sixteen songs from Sun and RCA; with liner notes by Russian journalist Andrei Gavrilov. *Songs:* "That's All Right, Mama"; "Heartbreak Hotel"; "Blue Suede Shoes"; "I Want You, I Need You, I Love You"; "My Baby Left Me"; "Don't Be Cruel"; "Hound Dog"; "Love Me Tender"; "Love Me"; "All Shook Up"; "That's When Your Heartaches Begin"; "One Night"; "Loving You"; "Teddy Bear"; "I Got Stung"; "Jailhouse Rock."

That's the Way It Is (Amiga Records 2 71 190, released in 1980). One record; all from the sound track of the documentary by the same title.

To Know Him Is to Love Him (Black Belt Records LPI, released in 1978). One record; all songs taken from live concerts at the International Hotel, Las Vegas.

Unfinished Business (Reel to Reel Record Company 3800, released in 1980). One record; all songs are alternative takes, mostly from Elvis's movie sound tracks.

Vegas Years, 1972–1975, The (TAKRL 24913, released in 1976). Two-record set; all songs are from Hilton Hotel performances in Las Vegas, except a version of "Hound Dog" taken from the "Ed Sullivan Show" on October 28, 1956.

Viva Las Vegas! (Lucky Records LR 711, released in 1979). One record; all the songs are from the 1964 movie sound track *Viva Las Vegas*, with Ann-Margret's solo "Appreciation"/"My Rival" and the Elvis/Ann-Margaret duet.

Videos

Elvis (Simitar #2127, approximately 45 minutes, 1990). Mostly already-published newsreel footage, TV appearances on the Dorsey brothers, Milton Berle, and Steve Allen shows, and photos from the Sun sessions through Elvis's film career. Produced by Ray Altherton, Burbank, CA.

Elvis (Passport International Productions, Rathway, NJ, SSS-3P-101, color/black-and-white, 91 minutes, 1991). With segments from Elvis's TV appearances on the Dorsey brothers and Steve Allen shows; many coming-attraction movie trailers; and Elvis in Hollywood. Three cassettes, each approximately thirty minutes in length.

Elvis: Aloha From Hawaii (Lightyear 72259, 75197-3, color, 75 minutes, 1991). Here is the hype before and during Elvis's hottest, electrifying concert in Hawaii. Produced and directed by Marty Pasetta; musical director, Joe Guercio and his orchestra; with the Stamps Quartet, the Sweet Inspirations, Kathy Westmoreland, and Elvis's band. This benefit concert for cancer was an RCA and Elvis Presley production. See Elvis fit, humorous, opulent, and full of energy, as he drips with perspiration, diamond rings, gold jewelry, and a star-studded, bell-bottomed, white jumpsuit adorned with American eagles (and a cape that he throws into the audience). He puts everything he has into this performance. At the end of the concert, an audience member hands him a golden crown. He carries it offstage, waving to the adoring crowd. Thirty-two songs.

Elvis and the Colonel: The Untold Story (NBC-TV movie, January 10, 1993, nine P.M.; starring Beau Bridges as the bartering, carnival huckster Colonel Tom Parker; Elvis is played by Rob Youngblood; two hours). The major "untold" story here is largely incorrect. Although Bridges gives a decent performance, the poorly written Elvis role becomes even more preposterous when the "ghost" of Elvis appears and speaks in the film. *Not recommended.*

Elvis '56 (Music Media 1987, #M470, color/black-and-white, 61 minutes). Produced and directed by Alan Raymond, Susan Raymond; written by Martin Torgoff, Alan Raymond, Susan Raymond; with early, wonderful photography by Alfred Wertheimer; narrated by Levon Helm. *Elvis '56* focuses on the beginning of the rock legend's career, when innocent gyrations and gospel-oriented rockabilly music led to meteoric recognition, wealth, and a whirlwind, jet-set lifestyle. This video is the best view of the King's raw, dynamic, spirited youth and how it took the world by storm.

Elvis Lives (three videotapes; color and black-and-white; 90 minutes; Passport International Productions, Inc., SSS3P-101, 1991). Glimpses of Elvis from clips of movie trailers, TV shows (such as Dorsey and Allen), with some unreleased footage that was held back from movie theaters.

Elvis on Tour (MGM/UA home video, M600153, 93 minutes, 1972). Produced and directed by Pierre Adidge and Robert Abel. This is the best look at the charisma, dynamics, and talent of Elvis as well as an intimate, casual portrait of the public and private Elvis. Twenty-six songs are in *Elvis on Tour*, which was first titled *Standing Room Only*. The opening monologue is by Jackie Kahane. Disc jockey–friend George Klein introduces "Suspicious Minds" during scenes of Graceland. Director Martin Scorsese was montage supervisor. The film grossed $494,270 the first week in 187 theaters. The Hollywood Foreign Press voted the film Best Documentary of 1972.

Elvis, One Night With You (Lightyear 72259-75196-3; 53 minutes; lists for $19.95; first copywritten in 1985/1992).

Produced by Steve Binder and Claude Ravier. The King at his live 1968 return concert.

Elvis Presley—That's The Way It Is (his 1970 tour; thirty songs; 109 minutes). A very fine video and a must-see for anyone who relishes live performances. Casual rehearsal scenes filled with humor at MGM studios (Elvis falls off his chair; a microphone "folds"; he rides a two-seat bicycle with Joe Esposito, later donated to the Great Britain fan-club raffle; and he ad-libs "son of a bitch" and "shocks the hell out of me"). We also see his opening performances at the International Hotel in Las Vegas (with Sammy Davis, Jr., Juliet Prowse, Cary Grant, and other celebrities in the audience). Intermingled between musical sets are scenes of Elvis with his adoring fans, kissing audience members, handing out sweat-soaked scarves, and joking around with his band members and backup singers. His exhausting effort during "Polk Salad Annie" is contrasted by a moving spiritual delivery of "Bridge Over Troubled Water." He *is* the consummate star.

Elvis Presley, the Echo Will Never Die (MAL/recounts his career).

Elvis Presley's Graceland (Congress Video Group 05300, 60 minutes, 1985). Hosted by Priscilla Beaulieu Presley; directed by Steven Binder; producers, Steve Binder and Claude Rauier; executive producer, Joseph F. Rascoff. A guide through Graceland (most of which had been redecorated for this film, and whose decor differs from that shown in *Elvis, the Great Performances* (as aired on CBS-TV, April 24, 1992). The video has segments of interviews, moments at Sun, the Army, a Sullivan show, and Elvis's death. Graceland's Hall of Gold is impressive. The pool room shows the more "native" side of the King!

Elvis '68 Comeback Special (Lightyear 72259-75198-3, color, 76 minutes, from December 3, 1968, twenty-seven hits, 1991). Executive producer, Bob Finkel;

produced and directed by Steve Binder; written by Allan Blye and Chris Beard; music production, Bones Howe. Elvis in black leather is a must-see for his fans. Despite a few tacky production numbers (the whorehouse scene with "Let Yourself Go," which was cut from the actual TV special, is in the video), his rock 'n' roll is flawless. Elvis once again proves he is the original rock 'n' roll rebel.

Elvis, the Great Performances, aired April 24, 1992, on CBS-TV. This two-hour film gives an overview of the "great" performances of Elvis's career (with many deletions) and includes amateur home-movie clips throughout. Hosted by Priscilla Presley from a newly decorated Graceland. Produced by Jerry Schilling; directed and written by Andrew Solt. The video includes "My Happiness" (first recording for Gladys Presley)—the sound is scratchy but it's sung in earnest; January 28, 1956, Dorsey brothers show; early Tupelo outdoor stage show in '56; two uncensored Milton Berle shows, April 3 and June 5, 1956 (Elvis's gyrations during "Hound Dog" infuriated critics, but Milton Berle gets into the act and twists his hips and legs, too, inspiring seven hundred thousand "pan mail" complaints); footage of Elvis singing "Blue Suede Shoes" for a Paramount screen test, April 1, 1956 (still with blond hair and dressed in all black, no tie); "Hy Gardner Calling" segment, revealing a shy, bemused Elvis; "I Want You, I Need You, I Love You," as taped on "Steve Allen Show," July 1, 1956 (in tuxedo); the September 9, 1956, censored Elvis singing "Reddy Teddy" and "Love Me Tender" on the "Ed Sullivan Show"; a WHBQ "Wink Martindale's Dance Party" segment; "from the waist up only" Elvis singing "Don't Be Cruel" on Sullivan's January 6, 1957, show (wearing a lamé vest with a white shirt)—Sullivan verbally supports Elvis at the end of the show; July 9, 1957, footage of *Loving You*; scene of Hollywood party with Dolores Hart, 1957; July 9, 1957, "Teddy Bear" sung in red-

and-white cowboy costume on the film stage; black-and-white footage of "Jailhouse Rock" sung on the film set, and black-and-white footage of "I'm Evil" from *King Creole;* March 24, 1958, Army footage shows how Elvis was accosted by the press; Army return in snow with TV reporters; interview with Elvis in his Graceland office claiming he has "no big romance" with Priscilla in Germany; a May 12, 1960, calm, no-energy imitation of Sinatra by Elvis singing "Fame and Fortune" in the "Welcome Home Elvis" Sinatra special; May 1, 1967, wedding footage; "All Shook Up" and "If I Can Dream," footage from the December 3, 1968, special from Hawaii; personal tour-bus footage; November 11, 1970, Portland, Oregon, act with "Suspicious Minds" with full orchestra; a short clip of the hotel interview in Vegas; an emotional version of "Always on My Mind" in a recording session (after Elvis and Priscilla's separation), January 14, 1973; the "American Trilogy" as sung January 14, 1973, on satellite (a slender, fit Elvis with diamond rings and a white jumpsuit); a short from the 1970 Houston press conference in which Elvis discusses the influences of gospel, country, blues; and the final June 21, 1977, segment, which is painful to watch—a bloated, perspiring, fat Elvis, seated at a piano singing "Unchained Melody" (dressed in a gold-studded, white jumpsuit). Then, it's back to quick clips from 1956, including "Money Honey." Although no new insights or footage is shown, all Presley fanatics will appreciate the video (RCA: BMG Music).

Elvis, the Great Performances, Center Stage, Vol. 1 (color and black-and-white Buena Vista Home Video, #1032, 52 minutes, January 1990). Produced by Jerry Schilling; written and directed by Andrew Solt; executive producer, Andrew Solt; narrated by disc jockey George Klein. A refreshing, in-depth look at the early, sensuous, rebellious Elvis. A ten-page text by Peter Guralnick accompanies the video.

Elvis, the Great Performances, the Man and the Music, Vol. 2 (color and black-and-white, Buena Vista Home Video, #1033, 52 minutes, January 1990). Produced by Jerry Schilling; written, directed, and executive-produced by Andrew Solt; narrated by George Klein. Volume two features the personal sides of Elvis, his charismatic style, and his energetic ability to perform on command. A ten-page text by Peter Guralnick accompanies the video.

Elvis, the Lost Performances (MGM/UA M202759; one hour). A must for anyone who wishes to view Elvis at his best during various stages of his early career.

Movies Elvis's acting roles are chronicled by title and each can be purchased separately. Beware poor copies of bootleg tapes.

This is Elvis (Warner Home Video 1986, #11173, color/black-and-white, 144 minutes). Executive producer, David L. Wolper; written, directed, and produced by Andrew Solt and Malcolm Leo; music score by Walter Scharf; consultants, Jerry Schilling and Joe Esposito. Interviews with family and friends of Elvis's help make this video stand out from many of the others. Documentary footage helps give a good view of the man behind the myth and the footlights.

TV Guide Presents Elvis Presley (RCA GB-MW-8705, September 1956). This hard-to-find film features excerpts from an August 6, 1956, interview with Elvis by Paul Wilder at the Lakewood, Florida, concert.

Young Elvis (Amvest Video, 1989, #VS-016, color/black-and-white, 75 minutes). Not recommended. Poor-quality taping. Crude, overlit, blurry views of Elvis's performances on the Dorseys' "Stage Show" and the Milton Berle show aboard the USS *Hancock;* several renderings of "Blue Suede Shoes." Ironically, *Young Elvis* begins with his funeral.

Courtesy of John Reible,
Las Vegas News Bureau,
Las Vegas, Nevada.

BIBLIOGRAPHY

ABC News. "The Elvis Cover-Up." Transcripts of "20/20," Sept. 13, 1979, Dec. 27, 1979.

————. Discussion of the Elvis stamp. Feb. 24, 1992.

Adams, Nick. "Elvis Wanted to Be Role Model for Teens." In Bill E. Burk's *Elvis World* 13 (1989): 11, 28.

Adler, Bill. *Love Letters to Elvis* (a compilation). Nd.

Adler, David. *The Life & Cuisine of Elvis Presley.* New York: Crown Trade Paperbacks, 1993.

Adler, Davis, and Ernest Andrews. *Elvis My Dad* (unauthorized). New York: St. Martin's Press, 1990.

Adler, Renata. *A Year in the Dark: Journal of a Film Critic 1968–1969.* New York: Random House, 1969.

Alexander, Alice. "He Knew the Private Elvis." *Nashville Tennessean,* Aug. 12, 1977, 6.

Alico, Stella H. *Elvis Presley/The Beatles.* London: Pendulum Press, 1979.

Alternatives ("The Grand Strand's Cultural Periodical," Myrtle Beach, SC, vol. 8, no. 18). "Elvis in Town on January 7," front page; "Elvis, the King to Speak" and "Elvis in Town Jan. 7th Cancelled on Jan. 8th," p. 5. Dec. 21–Jan. 15, 1993.

"Am I the Girl for Elvis?" *Movie Teen Illustrated,* Mar. 1958.

Amazing Elvis Presley (magazine). 1956.

American Graphic Systems. *I Am Elvis.* New York: Pocket Books, 1991. A book about impersonators.

————. "Presley MD Hearing Put Medicine on Trial." Feb. 8, 1980.

————. "Presley's MD Struggles for a New Life." Dec. 11, 1981.

American Pop:
—"Boston DJ Lobbies for Elvis Stamp." No. 18, Sept. 1991, 2.
—Gordon, Jay. "Elvis: The Sixties Years." No. 20, Dec. 1991, 1–2.

Anderson, Nancy. "Elvis, by His Father, Vernon Presley." *Good Housekeeping,* Jan. 1978, 158.

Anderson, Robert, and Gail North. *Gospel Music Encyclopedia* New York: Sterling Publishing Co., Inc., 1979.

Archer, Jules. "Elvis Presley, Stop Hounding Teenagers." Reprinted from 1956 in *True Story*, Nov. 1977.

Armes, Marty. "Presley: The Product Is Sex." *Hi-Fi*, Apr. 1969.

Arnoff, Carol. "Elvis Was My Neighbor." *Modern Screen*, nd.

Aros, Andrew A. *Elvis: His Films and Recordings*. Diamond Bar, CA: Applause Publishers, 1959.

Arrington, Cal. "Fans Squawk and Sales Soar as Albert Goldman Steps on Elvis's Blue Suede Shoes." *People*, Jan. 18, 1982.

Artforum. "The Last Breakfast." Sept. 1985.

———. "Still Dead: Elvis Presley Without Music." Sept. 1990.

———. "A View of Graceland: The Absence of Elvis." Mar. 1984. (As "William Eggleston's View of Graceland . . .")

Atcheson, Richard. "Wild and Crazy Guys." *Lear* 4, no. 3 (May 1991): 69.

Atlanta Journal (newspaper):
   —"Elvis to Rock 'n' Roll Here." June 22, 1956, 34.
   —"Firemen Superior to Elvis as Date, Secretary Says." Sept. 18, 1956, 25.
   —" 'Rose Real Cool' to Presley" (about Elvis's feelings toward Billy Rose, who knocked rock 'n' roll). Sept. 19, 1956.
   —"Teen-age Squeals. Presley Rocks Fans. $15 Shirt Ripped Off." June 23, 1956, 6.

Bangs, Lester. "Death Comes to Elvis Presley." *Village Voice*, Aug. 19, 1977, 1–6.

———. "Where Were You When Elvis Died?" (1977). In *Psychotic Reactions and Carburetor Dung*, edited by Greil Marcus. New York: Knopf, 1987.

Barrett, Rona. "Elvis: Gone for a Year but it Still Hurts." *Hollywood*, Oct. 1978.

———. "Elvis Presley & Lynda Thompson—What Are They 'Engaged' In?" *Gossip*, Sept. 1974.

Barry, Ron. *The Elvis Presley American Discography*. Phillipsburg, NJ: Sports Service Maxigraphics, 1980.

Barson, Michael. *Rip It Up! Postcards from the Heyday of Rock 'n' Roll*. New York: Pantheon, 1989.

Barth, Jack. *Roadside Elvis*. Chicago: Contemporary Books, 1987.

Battalle, Phyllis. "Priscilla Presley: Her Struggle to Raise Elvis's Daughter, and Revelations on the King of Rock 'n' Roll." *Ladies Home Journal*, Feb. 1984.

Baxter, Jerry, and Alan Baster. "Man in the Blue Suede Shoes." *Harper's*, Jan. 1958, 45–47.

Bellis, Terry. "Elvis' Gospel Music." *Elvis*—"the official Elvis Presley Fan Club of Great Britain," June/July 1991, 23–24. (Courtesy, Thomas J. Francis.)

Benson, Bernard. *The Minstrel.* Memphis, TN: Minstrel Publishing Co., 1976. (With comments by Charlie Hodge, Dick Grob.)

Berry, Chuck. *Chuck Berry: The Autobiography.* New York: Harmony Books, 1987.

Best Songs (magazine). June 1956.

"Beware Elvis Presley." *America* 95 (June 23, 1956): 294–95.

Billboard, The:

—"Army to Give Elvis Presley a G.I. Haircut." Oct. 1956, 1.

—"Daily Ain't Hay. Sholes Hay. Sholes Has Last Laugh as Presley Rings Up Sales." Apr. 21, 1956, 27.

—"Gyrations. Presley on Pan but Cash Keeps Rolling." June 1956, 18.

—"Lip Rouge to Rock 'n' Roll." Sept. 19, 1956, 31.

—"Presley Disks Get Canada Sales Marks." Dec. 8, 1956, 24.

—"Presley Gets 3D Gold Disk." Aug. 4, 1956, 18.

—"Presley Juggernaut Rolls. Merchandising Campaign Expected to Top $20 Mil. Sales by Year's End." Sept. 29, 1956, 31, 34.

—"A Winnah, Presley Hot As a $1 Pistol on Victor." March 3, 1956.

Black, Kay Pittman. "FBI Arrests Two, Seeks Four . . . Indictment Claims Six Tried to Defraud Elvis." *Memphis Press-Scimitar*, Oct. 19, 1977.

Blackburn, Richard. "Music and Elvis" (interview). *Crawdaddy*, Feb. 1976.

Blount, Richard. "Elvis!" *Esquire*, Dec. 1983, 172–74.

Booth, Stanley. "A Hound Dog to the Manor Born." *Esquire*, Feb. 1968.

Boston Globe. "Elvis Worship," Aug. 23, 1993, 31; "Getting in Our Licks on Elvis," "Can't Shake His Vote for the Young Elvis" (two parts), Joseph P. Kahn, and "Heavily Favoring the Heavy Elvis," Mark Muro, Living Arts Section, Feb. 26, 1992, 39; adv, Dec. 13, 1992, 19; Dec. 27, 1992, 64; "The President and the King," Dec. 16, 1992, 88. "A Convolution of Resolutions," Bella English, Metro Region, Dec. 30, 1992, 21; "What's In and What's Out," in Living Arts, Jan. 1, 1993, 49.

Bowser, James. *Starring Elvis Presley.* New York: Dell Pub. Co., 1977.

Braden, Betsy. "Memphis Will Honor King Elvis." *Atlanta Journal–Constitution*, Aug. 7, 1983.

Bradford Exchange, The (Morton Grove, IL). Catalogue of commemorative porcelain plates, vol. 1, Jan. 1993, front cover, 11.

Bradford, James. "For Presley the Grass Is Greener." *TV Times*, Mar. 16, 1966.

Bradshaw, J. "Elvis," *Esquire*, Oct. 1977.

Bradshaw, Jon. "Elvis the Man." Reprint in *Reader's Digest*, 1977, from an article in *Esquire*.

Brewer-Giorgio, Gail. *Is Elvis Still Alive?* New York and Los Angeles: Tudor Publishing Co., 1988.

Brixley, Ken, and Twyla Dixon. *Elvis at Graceland* with photos by Wm. Eggelston. Memphis publisher, 1983.

Brown, Colin. "Craze Over Elvis." *Coronet*, Sept. 1956.

Bryant, A. "Elvis Presley and the Uncritical Worship He Engenders." *Illustrated London News*, Feb. 9, 1957.

Buckle, Philip. "All Elvis." A *London Daily Mirror* publication, 1962.

Burk, Bill E. *Dot . . . Dot . . . Dot . . .* Memphis: Shelby House, 1987.

———. *Early Elvis: The Humes Years.* Memphis: Red Oak Press, 1990.

———. "Elvis . . ." *Akron Beacon Journal*, nd, 6.

———. *Elvis: A 30 Year Chronicle.* Osborne Enter., 1980.

———. *Elvis, Rare Images of a Legend.* Memphis: Prowash Pub., 1990.

———. *Elvis Through My Eyes.* Memphis: Burk Enterprises, 1987.

———. "Elvis World." *EW* 13, Burk Enterprises, 1989.

Burnette, Billy Joe. "Welcome Home Elvis." Gusto-Starday, 1977.

"Captain Marvel and the Wonderful Magic Carpet" (Whiz Comics, a Fawcett Publication), vol. 15, no. 88, Aug. 1947.

"Captain Marvel, Jr." (comic book, a Fawcett Publication), vol. 10, no. 60, Apr. 1948.

Carr, Roy, and Mick Farren. *Elvis Presley: The Illustrated Record.* London: Eel Pie Publishers, 1982.

Carson, Johnny. A quote from "The Tonight Show," Oct. 31, 1991, regarding Elvis's staying power.

Carter, Pres. Jimmy. "Death of Elvis Presley," a statement by the president, Aug. 7, 1977. *Public Papers of President Jimmy Carter*, vol. 2, 1977, 1478.

Carter (Jimmy) Library, Atlanta, GA. Letter to the author from James A. Yancey, Jr., archivist. July 15, 1991.

Cash, Johnny. *Man in Black.* Grand Rapids, MI: Zondervan, 1975.

Cash, W. J. *The Mind of the South.* New York: Vintage, 1941; New York: Knopf, 1960. About Southern feudalism and the hillbilly milieu.

Casting Call. "Elvis Presley." Sept. 1, 1977.

Cawthon, Raad. "Elvis Fans Jam Memphis in Homage to 'the King.'" *Atlanta Journal*, section A, Aug. 18, 1984.

CBS-TV. "Elvis, the Great Performances." Hosted by Priscilla Presley, two hours from Graceland; Jerry Schilling, producer; written/directed by Andrew Solt; aired Apr. 24, 1993 (video recording). The music is covered on the LP with the same title and a two-video set with the same title.

————. CBS morning-news coverage of the Country Music Hall of Fame's 25th Anniversary Celebration showed Elvis's gold-leaf Kimball piano, Apr. 29, 1992.

Celebrity Spotlight Series Presents: Elvis, 10th Anniversary Salute. "The Road to Growing Up: As Told by Elvis, June 1953, a Star Is Born and the Legend Begins, a Complete Guide to Every Film Elvis Made, Elvis's Army Days," 1987.

Chapple, Steve, and Reebee Garofalo. *Rock 'n' Roll Is Here to Pay.* Chicago: Nelson-Hall, 1977.

Charlotte News, The (newspaper):

—"In Elvis' Defense. . . ." June 26, 1956, 7A.

—"Our Girls Go Ga-Ga Over Elvis." Feb. 11, 1956, section 2, p. 2.

—"Right for Young Folk: Burl Ives" (who supports Elvis verbally). June 27, 1956, 7A.

—"Singing Star to Appear Here." Feb. 3, 1956, 9A.

Charters, Samuel B. *The Country Blues.* New York: DaCapo Press, 1959.

Christensen, John. "The Legend." *Akron Beacon Journal*, Aug. 1977.

Circus Pinups #3: The Elvis Years (magazine). Aug. 1975.

Claypool, Bob. "Music: Elvis Presley." *Houston Post*, Aug. 29, 1976, section B.

Clayton, R. "Colonel Parker Accused of Ripping Off Elvis." *Rolling Stone*, Sept. 17, 1981, 8–9.

Cocke, Marion J. *I Called Him Babe.* Memphis: Memphis State University Press, 1979.

Cocks, Jay. "Last Stop on the Mystery Train." *Time*, Aug. 29, 1977, 56–59.

Cogan, Arlene, and Charles Goodman. *Elvis, This One's for You.* Castle Books, 1985.

Cohn, Nik. *A WopBopaLooBob a LopBamBoom.* London: Paladin, 1969.

Cohn, Nik, and Guy Peellaert. *Rock Dreams.* New York: Rogner and Bernhard/Random House, 1973.

Collins, Lawrence. *The Elvis Presley Encyclopedia.* Globe Communications Corp., 1981. (Sixty-four pages.)

Coltharp, Russell, Memphis, TN. Correspondence with the author and interviews, June 5, 1991–Aug. 1991.

Commercial Appeal, The (Memphis newspaper):
- —"At Home with Elvis Presley." Mar. 7, 1965, 14–15, 17–19.
- —"Death Captures Crown of Rock and Roll—Elvis Dies Apparently After Heart Attack," Lawrence Buser. Aug. 17, 1977, front page.
- —"Elvis and the Ministers Around Him." Aug. 20, 1977.
- —"Elvis Draws 'Em; So Does 'Giant'. . ." Nov. 24, 1956.
- —"Foe of Presley Punches Himself into Workhouse." Nov. 24, 1956.
- —"Graceland Gallery." Feb. 5, 1985, 14–16.
- —"Memphis Leads World in Mourning for Elvis Presley." Aug. 17, 1977, front page, 8–10.
- "Presley to Sing on Radio Show Saturday Night." Oct. 14, 1954.
- —"Shell Show Friday." July 25, 1954.
- —"Trappings of Fame." Aug. 17, 1977, 50.

Complete TV (magazine). Feb. 1957.

Condon, Evelyn. "What Is an Elvis Presley?" *Cosmopolitan,* Dec. 1956, 54–61.

Confidential (magazine). Cover illustrations of Elvis. 1957.

Connor, A. A. "Elvis: The Mystique." *Reader's Digest,* Jan. 1978, 75–76. (Taken from a Dec. 26, 1976, article in *The Milwaukee Journal.*)

"Conway Store Honors Elvis Presley." *Myrtle Beach (SC) Sun News,* Jan. 9, 1992, 1, 7C.

Cool and Hep Cats (magazine). Oct. 1958.

Cool, Special Issue on Elvis Presley (magazine). Vol. 1, no. 1, 1957.

Corboy, Thomas. *Rock 'n' Roll Disciples.* Monticello Productions, 1985.

Cortez, Diego. *Private Elvis.* Stuttgart, Germany: FEY, 1978. (This book is oddly put together with photos of Elvis with hookers in West Germany during his Army days.)

Cosmopolitan. "What Is an Elvis Presley?" Vol. 141. Dec., 1956. 54–62.

Cotton, Lee. *All Shook Up: Elvis Day-By-Day.* Ann Arbor, MI: Pierian Press, 1985.

———. *The Elvis Catalogue.* New York: Dolphin Books, 1987.

Cotton, Lee, and Howard A. DeWitt. *Jailhouse Rock: The Bootleg Records of Elvis Presley 1970–1983.* Ann Arbor, MI: Pierian Press, 1983.

Coughlin, Ruth Pollack. "Elvis, A to Z." *Detroit News,* Aug. 13, 1987, 3D. (Courtesy William A. Clark.)

Country Song Roundup. The July 1955 issue has a headline that reads, "Elvis Presley—Folk Music Fireball," with story/photo page 14. (This was probably the first national magazine to bring Elvis to public attention on its cover.)

———. Aug. 1956 issue has Carl Perkins and Elvis on the cover.

Court Records: *Tennessee Board of Medical Examiners vs. George C. Nichopoulos, M.D.,* complaint, deposition, proceedings, 1979–80; *State of Tennessee ex. rel. James P. Cole and Charles C. Thompson v. Jerry T. Francisco, Shelby County Medical Examiner, and Hugh W. Stanton, Jr., District Attorney General for 16th Judicial Circuit;* Chancery Court pleadings and depositions; Tennessee Supreme Court, ruling, Tenn. 643 S.W. 2d., 105.

Cowherd, Kevin. "No one wants to remember the fat Elvis." *The Plain Dealer* (Cleveland, OH), Jan. 27, 1992, 42.

Cranor, Rosaline. *Elvis Collectibles.* Johnson City, TX: Overmountain Press, nd.

Crawdaddy (magazine). Nov. 7, 1971; May 28, 1972; Apr. 1973; Dec. 1973; Nov. 1977.

"A Craze Called Elvis." *Coronet* 40 (Sept. 1956): 153–57.

Creem (magazine). Jan. 1972; May 1973; July 1975; Dec. 1977; Apr. 1978; Feb. 1979; Feb. 1980; Jan. 1982; Feb. 1983.

Creem Close Up (magazine). Dec. 1984.

Cris, Henry. "Elvis and the Colonel." *Pix,* June 29, 1963.

Crumbacker, Marge, and Gabe Tucker (an ex-employee of Colonel Tom Parker). *Up and Down with Elvis: The Inside Story.* New York: Putnam, 1981. (Tucker is a friend of the Colonel's and the book takes the Colonel's point of view regarding Elvis.)

Crutchfield, James A. *The Tennessee Almanac.* Nashville, TN: Rutlege Hill Press, 1986.

"Current Affair." Two-part TV segment: "Elvis, the Final 24

Hours" with Maureen O'Brien hosting, interviews with Rick Stanley, Ginger Alden, George Klein, Joe Esposito, Dr. George Nichopoulos, Vester Presley; "Elvis: The Next Generation" with interview from *Enquirer* writer Mike Wallace, showing Lisa Marie, her husband, and two-year-old daughter Danielle at the child's birthday party (at which Wallace sneers).

Dahlin, Robert. "Unique Appeal of Elvis Presley's Music Now Carries Over to Books About Him." *Publisher's Weekly.* Sept. 5, 1977, 34.

Dallas (TX) Morning News (newspaper):
—"Cheers Constant. Presley Thrills Crowd. Oct. 15, 1956.
—"Elvis Presley Disturbance Surely Hit Seismic Scale." Oct. 12, 1956, 106–9.

Dallas Times Herald, The (newspaper):
—"Elvis Presley. What Makes Him Tick?" Sept. 9, 1956.
—"He's Real Cool . . ." Aug. 19, 1956, 1.
—"Plans Kept Secret. Elvis Hush-Hush Irks Eager Fans." Oct. 11, 1956.

Danielson, Sarah Parker. *Elvis: Man and Myth.* Bison Books, 1990.

Daroff, Elizabeth. "Elvis." *McCalls*, July 1980, 98, 141–44.

Dawson, Walter. "Another Elvis Friend Clears the Air." *Memphis Commercial Appeal*, Aug. 12, 1979, 17.

DeBarbin, Lucy, and Dary Matera. *Are You Lonesome Tonight?* New York: Villard Books, 1987. A tale about Lucy DeBarbin's alleged affair with Elvis that produced a child.

"The Debate Over Censorship Goes On." *U.S. News & World Report*, Mar. 16, 1992, 8.

DeGarmo and Key. *Rock Solid . . . The Rock-u-Mentary* (video). Benson Company, 1988.

Dellar, Fred, Roy Thompson, and Douglas Green. *The Illustrated Encyclopedia of Country Music.* New York: Harmony Books, 1977.

"Delphi Presents the Elvis Presley Hit Parade." Letter of four pages regarding first-issue plates of "Heartbreak Hotel" and "Hound Dog," 1992–93, copyright with Elvis Presley, Inc.; two-page color announcement illustrating "Hound Dog" plate, 1992.

Denisoff, R., and R. Peterson, eds. *The Sounds of Social Change.* Chicago: 1972.

Deri, Laura. "Elvis's Longevity." *Pageant*, Dec. 1976, 4–5.

DeVecchi, Peter. *The Sounding Story*. Germany, 1959. May have been the first book written about Elvis.

DeWitt, Howard. *Sun Elvis*. Pierian Press. (Covers to 1956.)

Dig (magazine). Nov. 1956; Jan. 1957; "Elvis Presley Profile," Apr. 1963.

Discoveries (magazine):

—Elvis Presley interviewed. No. 1, Jan/Feb. 1988.

—Early Elvis Presley concert and interview. No. 2, Mar/Apr. 1988.

—Is Elvis Presley alive? A most incredible story, Elvis Presley in print. No. 4, July/Aug. 1988.

—The latest *Jailhouse Rock* discovery. No. 6, Dec. 1988.

—Elvis Presley's first recordings, counting the Elvis Presley cover songs. No. 7, Jan. 1989.

—Elvis Presley meets the Jones brothers. No. 8, Mar. 1989.

—Elvis Presley on TV, Elvis picture discs, Dee Presley's untold story. Aug. 1989.

—Elvis Presley–Joe Esposito interview and collecting Elvis Presley compact discs. Aug. 1990.

Doll, Susan (contributing writer). *Elvis: A Tribute to His Life*. Publications International, 1989. (A good overview.)

———. *The Films of Elvis Presley*. Lincolnville, IL: Publications International, Ltd., 1990.

Doussard, James. "His Movies." *Akron (OH) Beacon Journal*, Aug. 1977.

Downbeat:

—"Elvis Is Awful, but I Love Him." Aug. 22, 1956, 8.

—"Elvis Presley, Can Fifty Million Americans Be Wrong?" Sept. 19, 1956, 41. (Guess where the LP title came from.)

—"Presley Invades H'Wood with Impact of Brando." May 30, 1956, 39.

—"A Psychologist's Viewpoint [on Elvis]," Sept. 19, 1956, 42–43, 46.

—"RCA Excited, a Country & Western Singer . . ." Jan. 25, 1956, 14.

Dundy, Elaine. *Elvis and Gladys*. New York: Dell Publishing, 1985.

Dunleavy, Steve, Red West, Sonny West, Dave Hebler. *Elvis: What Happened?* New York: Ballantine Books, 1977.

East Coast Rocker (magazine). No. 1, 1986; No. 41, 1987.

Edwards, Hank. "Merchandising Elvis." *Hi Fi*, Nov. 1972, 74–76.

Edwards, Michael. *Priscilla, Elvis and Me.* New York: St. Martin's Press, 1988. (Not recommended.)

Egerton, John. "Elvis Lives," *Progressive*, Mar. 1979, 20–23.

Eipper, Laura. "The Legend Lives On." *Nashville Tennessean*, Aug. 16, 1978, Panorama, cols. 1–3, p. 41.

Elliott, Lawrence. "Where Elvis Lives." *Reader's Digest*, Aug. 1993, 47–52.

"Elvis." Memphis, TN: James R. Reid, 1987.

Elvis (magazine, Ideal Publishing Co.):
  —"Yesterday . . . Today." 1975.
  —"Elvis, the Hollywood Years," 1976.

"Elvis." *Rolling Stone* memorial edition, Sept. 22, 1977, 49–52.

"Elvis." *Time*, June 19, 1972, 49–50.

"Elvis." *TV Radio Mirror* special edition, 1956.

"Elvis." *Goldmine: The Collector's Record and Compact Disc Marketplace* 16, no. 16, issue 262 (Aug. 10, 1990):
  —Escott, Colin. "Elvis in the Projects," 17–18.
  —Escott, Colin. "Elvis Presley: Archaeology and Garbology—The Early Days," 20.
  —Haertel, Joe. "Retracing Elvis's Memphis & Tupelo Footsteps," 29–30, 32, 34, 36, 38, 131.
  —Tamarkin, Jeff. "Elvis Book Update," 28.
  —Thompson, David. "The King and Them," 24–25.
  —Umphred, Neal. "The Legend of a King," 22, 25.

Elvis ("The Official Memorial Fan Club Publication"). 1978.

Elvis: A Pictorial History (a poster magazine). 1977.

Elvis: A Tribute to the King. Cousins Publications, 1977. (With a pull-out color poster of Elvis as a GI.)

Elvis Album. Lincolnwood, Il: Publications International, Ltd., 1991.

"Elvis, America and Us." *Country Music* (magazine), Nov. 1975. (Also on cover.)

Elvis and Jimmy (Dean) (double feature; magazine). 1956.

Elvis and Tom (Jones) (magazine). 1969.

Elvis Answers Back (magazine). 1956. (With cardboard 78-rpm record attached to the cover.)

Elvis Aron Presley, 1935–1977, the Memorial Album. Memphis, TN: Wise Publications,1977.

"Elvis at 42, Bit Slower, but He's Still the King." *Atlanta Journal-Constitution*, Jan. 9, 1977.

"Elvis Bookmark." Trivia No. 1–4, distributed by Graceland, 1991.

"Elvis Can Pack a Pistol." *Seattle Post-Intelligencer*, Oct. 23, 1970.

Elvis Classics: R&B Tunes Covered by Elvis Presley. Japan: P-Vine, 1989.

Elvis Confidentially (an LP with five live interviews). London, England: Arena Records Limited, 1987. (ARAD 1008).

"Elvis Conspiracy, The." Aired on Channel 25 in New York City by Geraldo Rivera, Jan. 22, 1992, with Joe Esposito (recorded).

"Elvis Dead." *New York Daily Mirror*, Aug. 17, 1977, 1, 3.

"Elvis Dead." *The Sun* (Sydney, Australia), Aug. 17, 1977, 1, 24, 46.

"Elvis' Fans Besiege the Presley Home/Elvis' Tragic Drugs Secret. *Evening News* (London, England), Aug. 17, 1977, 1–2.

"Elvis Films Features Home Movies." *Knoxville Journal*, Apr. 4, 1981, Focus section.

"Elvis' Grin Enthralls Girl Fans." *Buffalo Courier Express*, Apr. 1, 1957.

"Elvis' Guitar Coming Up at Red Baron, Oct. 5." *Antiques and the Arts Weekly*, Aug. 30, 1991, 29.

"Elvis Had Million-Plus in Check Account." *Knoxville News Sentinel*, Nov. 23, 1977.

Elvis: His Love and Marriage (magazine). 1957.

"Elvis in Concert." Bat Productions, 1987. (Contains thirty-four color pages of Elvis).

Elvis in the Army (magazine). 1959.

Elvis International Forum. Thousand Oaks, CA: Creative Radio Network. Issues from 1988 to 1992, vol. 5, no. 4.

Elvis Is Everywhere. Photos by Rowland Scherman. New York: Clarkson Potter, 1992.

"Elvis, King of Rock, Dies at 42." *Channel Islands Daily Mail*, Aug. 17, 1977, front page, 3.

"Elvis' legacies in Germany dying." *Cleveland Plain Dealer*, Mar. 9, 1992.

Elvis Mania. Published in Great Britain, 1975. (With pull-out photos; thirty-two pages.)

"Elvis May Have Drug Problem, Paper Says." *Knoxville News Sentinel*, Apr. 2, 1977.

"Elvis Memories" (recording). ABC Radio, Aug. 13, 1978. (Director, Warren Summerville; producer, George Michaels.)

Elvis Monthly. Derbyshire, Aug. 1985, no. 307. The *Monthly* began publication in 1955 by Albert Hand for the Official Elvis Presley Fan Club Worldwide, Great Britain.)

"Elvis 1988 Calendar Magazine." Harris Publications, 1988.

"Elvis, 1935–1977." *View* (Tupelo, MS), Aug. 1977. (Newspaper overview on the occasion of Elvis's death.)

Elvis One Year Later. New York: Dell, 1978. (With centerfold poster.)

Elvis, One Year Later (radio programming, promotion). (Two five-inch reel-to-reel tapes.) Nashville Productions, 1978.

Elvis Photo Album (magazine). 1956. (With 125 photos.)

Elvis Pocket Handbook, The. Published in Great Britain by Albert Hand, summer 1961. (One hundred pages.)

Elvis Precious Memories, vol. 2. 1989. L.A.: Blue Hawaiians Fan Club.

"Elvis Presley." *Casting Call* (magazine), Sept. 1, 1977.

"Elvis Presley." *Country Music*, Mar. 1977, 24–25.

"Elvis Presley." *Heavy Metal,"* Oct. 1980.

"Elvis Presley." *Mother Jones*, Aug. 1978, 10.

Elvis Presley and the People Who Have Meant Most in His Life (magazine). Published in Great Britain, ca. 1958, sixty-four pages.

Elvis Presley Anthology, Vol. 2, Milwaukee, Wisconsin: Hal Leonard Pub. Co., 1978.

"Elvis Presley Died in 1977. Guess How Much He Will Earn This Year?" *Forbes*, Oct. 3, 1988.

"Elvis Presley Dies at 42." *New York: Daily News*, Aug. 17, 1977, front page, 2.

"Elvis Presley—Dig the Greatest." *Hep Cat's Review*, Feb. 1956, 13–45.

Elvis Presley: Hero or Heel? (magazine). 1956. (With life-size photograph.)

"Elvis Presley Imitation in Spirit and Flesh." *Rolling Stone*, Mar. 23, 1978.

Elvis Presley in Hollywood (magazine). 1956.

"Elvis Presley Is Dead." *London Daily Mirror*, Aug. 17, 1977, 1.

Elvis Presley Memorial Edition Magazine. Ideal Publishing, 1977, no. 3 Special Edition.

Elvis Presley, Pat Boone, Bill Haley (magazine). Dec. 1956.

"Elvis Presley Returns to the International." *Las Vegas Star*, Aug. 14, 1970.

Elvis Presley Song Hits (magazine). 1965.

Elvis Presley Speaks! (magazine). 1956. (With a hundred Elvis photos for twenty-five cents.)

"Elvis Presley Special Edition." *Country Music*, Dec. 1977.

Elvis Presley, the Amazing (magazine). Great Britain, ca. 1956, 64 pp.

"Elvis Presley, the King Comes Back." *Faces*, Dec. 30, 1975.

Elvis Presley: The Life & Death Of (magazine). Manor, 1977. (Collector's issue.)

"Elvis Presley to Wed Again," *Silver Screen*, Mar. 1974.

"Elvis Presley's Dope Doctor." *High Times*, Nov. 1980.

"Elvis Presley's Songs of Inspiration." Memphis: Elvis Presley Enterprises, Inc., 1989.

Elvis Remembered (magazine). Ideal's Celebrity Series, 1979. (With thirty-five color pinups).

"Elvis Returns Home—Plane Deal Is Off." From the Memphis Public Library and Information Center, Feb. 14, 1975, np, na.

"Elvis Rocks and Rolls Again in the City of High Rollers." Las Vegas: UPI, Jan. 27, 1972.

"Elvis Sang—And the Girls Squealed, Squads of Police Kept Singer's Blue Suede From Being Trampled." *Houston (TX) Press*, Apr. 1956, 1.

"Elvis Sends 6,400 Here Into Frenzy." *Oakland Tribune*, June 4, 1956, 1, 13.

"Elvis Still Dead? The Latest Word . . ." *USA*, Nov. 1–3, 1991.

Elvis: The Hollywood Years (magazine). 1956.

"Elvis the Ingenious." *Harper's*, Apr. 1957, 86.

Elvis, the Intimate Story (magazine). 1957.

Elvis, The King Lives on Poster Magazine (Special Anniversary Edition). 1978. (Opens to become a two-sided seventeen-by-twenty-two-inch color wall poster, with rare Elvis photos.)

Elvis the King: Memorial Collector's Edition. Pasadena, CA: Wellington-Hall Publishers, 1977.

Elvis, the King Returns (magazine). 1960.

Elvis: The King Returns. New York: Edgar Pub. Corp., 1980.

Elvis: The Legend Lives On. New York: Manor Books, 1978. (With color wall poster.)

Elvis-the-Record (magazine). Smith-Lacker-Davis, Inc., 1980. (Editor, Billy Smith, Elvis's cousin.)

"Elvis, the Swingin' Kid" (comic book). Great Britain, (with eight pages of photographs of Elvis in the Army. Other *comics* that Elvis was shown: "Career Girl Romances," 1966; "I Love You," 1966.)

Elvis, the Trials and Triumphs of the Legendary King of Rock & Roll (magazine). Issued by *Tattler*, May 1976. (Plus cover.)

"Elvis Through the Years, January 8, 1935–August 16, 1977" (songbook). Shaltinger-International Music Corp., 1977.

"Elvis Tribute" (recording). Host Jimmy Dean, NBC, Jan. 8, 1978.

"Elvis: True King of Rock 'n' Roll," *Detroit Daily News*, Aug. 17, 1977. (Courtesy William A. Clark.)

"Elvis Used Out-of-Town Sources for Drugs." *Knoxville News Sentinel*, Jan. 18, 1980.

"Elvis vs. Belafonte." *16* (magazine), July 1957.

Elvis vs. the Beatles (magazine). 1956, no. 3.

"Elvis Weds in Quickie Ceremony!" *Movie World*, Nov. 1974.

"Elvis' Wine Tips From Beyond the Grave" (a spoof). *The Wine Spectator*, Mar. 15, 1992, 5.

Elvis Yearbook (magazine). 1960.

Elvis Years (magazine). Sterling, 1979. (No. 1, 1956–77; no. 2, 1977, a tribute to Elvis, 1957–77, with 1001 "facts" about Elvis, with thirty-two color portraits and a color pinup section.)

Elvis Yesterday . . . Today (magazine). 1975.

"Elvis's FBI File." Washington, DC: Elvis File, 1992.

Escott, Colin, and Martin Hawkins. *Catalyst: The Sun Records Story*. London: Aquarius Books, 1975.

———. *Good Rockin' Tonight*. New York: St. Martin's Press, 1991.

———. *Sun Records. The Discography*. Bollersode, West Germany: Bear Family Records, 1987.

"Examiner Is Firm: Heart Disease Fatal to Presley." *American Medical News*, Oct. 12, 1979.

Exclusively Elvis. Fall 1987, no. 3, "Ten Years Later." (With photos from the collection of Jim Curtin.)

Eye (magazine). Hearst Publications, May 1968, no. 3.

Farmer, Paul. "Elvis at Home." *New Statesman*, Mar. 15, 1963.

Farren, Mick, and Pearce Marchbank. *Elvis in His Own Words*. New York: Omnibus Press, 1977. (No sources to quotes given.)

Filiatreau, John. "The Farewell." *Akron (OH) Beacon Journal*, Aug. 1977.

Filler, Martin. "Elvis Presley's Graceland: An American Shrine." *House and Garden*, Mar. 1984, 140–47.

Films and Filming. Aug. 1966. (With Elvis on cover.)

Finkelstein, Sidney. *How Music Expresses Ideas*. New York: International Publishers, 1952, 109.

Firth, Simon, and Andrew Goodwin. *On Record*. New York: Pantheon Books, 1990.

Flake, Richard. "Velvet's Items Up for Bidding." *Elvis World* 19 (May 5, 1991): 9.

Flip (magazine). July 1969; Feb. 1972; Mar. 1974.

Flippo, Chet. *Your Cheatin' Heart: A Biography of Hank Williams*. New York: Simon and Schuster, 1981. (A look at how Williams's country music may have influenced Elvis.)

Folk and Country Songs. (Many issues from 1956 to 1959 have Elvis on the cover and Elvis's songs inside.)

Fortas, Alan. *My Friend Elvis*. Nashville: 1987.

Francis, Thomas J. Letters to the author dated May 30, June 6, June 15, July 31, 1991, Scituate, MA.

Freud, Sigmund. *A General Introduction to Psychoanalysis*. 1916–17.

———. *The Interpretation of Dreams*. 1900.

Frew, Timothy. *Elvis*. New York: Mallard Press, 1992.

Friedman, Favius. *Meet Elvis Presley*. New York: Scholastic Book Services, 1971.

Frith, Simon. *Sound Effects: Youth, Leisure, and the Politics of Rock 'n' Roll*. New York: Pantheon, 1981, 165.

Frith, Simon, and Angela McRobbie. "Rock and Sexuality." *Screen Education* 29 (Winter 1978/1979).

Fusion (magazine). Aug. 22, 1969; no. 39, Aug. 21, 1970; no. 73, "Elvis Presley: The King as a Subject," 1972.

Gardner, Hy. "Glad You Asked That: 'Reprint of 1956 Elvis Presley Telephone Interview.'" *Knoxville News Sentinel*, Nov. 29, 1977, sec. 2, cols. 1–3, p. 23.

Geller, Larry, and Joel Spector with Patricia Romanowski. *If I Can Dream—Elvis' Own Story*. New York: Simon and Schuster, 1989. (An egotistical look from Geller about Elvis's relationship with and dependence on him.

Geller, Larry, and Jess Stearn. *The Truth About Elvis*. New York: Jove Publications, 1980.

Gibson, J. Robert, and Sid Shaw. *Elvis*. New York: McGraw-Hill Book Company, 1985.

———. *Elvis: A King Forever*. New York: McGraw-Hill, 1987.

Gillett, Charlie. *The Sound of the City: The Rise of Rock and Roll*. New York: Outerbridge and Dienstfrey, 1970. (The author believes RCA was Elvis's ruin.)

Girard, Fred. "Thousands Attend Events Marking Elvis's Death." *Knoxville Journal*, Aug. 17, 1983, sec. B, p. 6.

Glade, Emory. *Elvis, a Golden Tribute*. Wauwatosa, WI: Robus Books, 1984.

Globe (newspaper, Boston):

—"Aerosmith, Marky Mark Share Award Spotlight." Apr. 14, 1992.

—Arnold, Donald. "Post Office Takes Its Walk Down Lucrative Lane," pp. 1, 12, and "Elvis Has Been Sighted in St. Vincent," p. 46, Jan. 8, 1993; "Elvis Sightings Climb Nationwide," Jan. 9, 1992, 12.

—"Digesting Di, Bigfoot & Elvis." Diane White, Jan. 18, 1993, 34.

—"DJ Jay Gordon Makes Elvis His Business." Apr. 3, 1992.

—"Falling for the myth that Elvis was a copycat." Apr. 15, 1992, 22.

—"Michael Jackson to re-edit racy video." Nov. 16, 1991, 1, 14.

—Supreme Court. Mar. 3, 1992, 3. (Re: Scientology.)

—"Think Twice, Elvis Bashers." Jan. 19, 1993. 52.

Gold-leaf piano:

—Brodnax, Phillip III. Correspondence between Kathleen Knight of Nantucket and author, many letters, signed affidavits, numerous personal interviews, phone conversations, 1991; letter dated Mar. 12, 1991.

—Coltharp, Russell, Coltharp Piano World, Memphis, TN. Letters dated June 3, 17, 1991, two pages; Sept. 25, 1991, shipping document to Country Music Hall of Fame; numerous phone conversations; two personal visits, June—July, 1991.

—Graceland correspondence. See Morgan, Todd.

—Hames, Thomas A. Letter dated Sept. 20, 1977, one page.

—Keyboard Systems. Letters to author dated July 6, July 23, 1991, each one page.

—McCarthy, Anita, Clark Tower Business Service. Letter to author, Aug. 8, 1991, Memphis, TN.

—Memphis Symphony League. Letter to author, July 1, 1991.

—National Security Trust. Letter dated May 2, 1991.

—"Organo, Complete Service Manual." Printed in fifties.

—Sales slip from Willie E. Shephard, Aug. 25, 1977.

—Smith, Gene. Affidavit, cover of Organo manual.

—VanStory, Marcus. Affidavit dated May 2, 1991, two pages.

—Weisensteiner, Roger H., Kimball Piano. Letter, July 10, 1991, to the author.

Goldman, Albert. *Elvis.* New York: Avon Books, 1981.

———. *Elvis.* McGraw-Hill Book Co., 1981. (Exaggerated.)

———. *Elvis, the Last 24 Hours.* New York: St. Martin's Press, 1990.

———. "Elvis, the Party Years." *Rolling Stone,* Oct. 29, 1981.

Goldmine (magazine, Krause Publications):

—#12, "For Elvis Fans Only," 1976.

—#16, "Elvis Presley, X-rated Rockabilly," 1977.

—#18, "King Elvis Presley Rocks," 1977.

—#19, "Elvis Presley Is Eternal: The King of Rock 'n' Roll, 1977.

—#20, "The Other King of the Twist, Elvis Presley," 1977.

—#24, #28, #30, "Elvis Presley," 1978.

—#39, "Elvis Presley," 1979.

—#44, #47, #54, #55, "Elvis Presley," 1980.

—#56, "Special Elvis Presley Issue," 1980.

—#59, #66, "Elvis Presley," 1981.

—#76, "Special Country & Rockabilly Issue," 1982.

—#80, "Annual Elvis Special," 1983.

—#92, "Elvis Presley"; #105, "A Guide to Elvis' Films," 1984.

—#117, "Elvis Presley"; #133, "Elvis Presley, Southside Johnny Talks About Elvis"; #141, "The Sun Sound," 1985.

—#149, "Elvis Presley Session Background"; #167, "Elvis Presley," 1986.

—#169, "Elvis Presley's Generosity Lives On," 1987.

—#239, "Rarest Elvis Presley Disc," 1989.

Goodman, Charles. "Priscilla explains decision on Graceland." *Memphis Press-Scimitar,* May 4, 1982, 5.

Gordon, Jay. "Elvis: The Sixties Years." *American Pop* 20 (1991): 1–2.

Graceland. West Germany: Elvis Fan Club, 1979.

Graceland Express, 6, no. 1 (Apr. 1991). Elvis Presley Enterprises.

Graceland News, 10th Anniversary Collector's Edition, 1987, includes:

—Cooke, Josh. "The Joker and the King," 1987, 4.

—Morris, Bill. "Remembering the Good Times with Elvis," 10–11.

—Pomus, Doc. "Dreams Do Come True," 14.

—Pritchett, Aunt Nash. "Words of Comfort," 6.

—Smith, Aunt Lorraine, Beth Pease. "Elvis Stood for Love," 35.

Graceland: The Living Legacy of Elvis Presley. San Francisco: Collins Publishers, 1993.

Grant, R. G. *The 1960s.* Mallard Press, Brompton Books, 1990.

Green, Douglas. *Country Roots.* New York: Hawthorn Books, 1976.

Greenwood, Earl. "Elvis Presley's Special Gift. *Movie Screen,* May, 1960.

————. "Elvis Telephones a Message to His Friends." *Movie Mirror,* Aug. 1959.

Greenwood, Earl, and Kathleen Tracy. *The Boy Who Would Be King.* New York: Dutton, 1990.

Gregory, James. *The Elvis Presley Story,* with an Introduction by Dick Clark. New York: Hillman Books, 1960.

Gregory, Neal and Janice. *When Elvis Died.* Washington, DC: Communications Press, 1980; New York: Pocket, 1982.

Griffin, N. *To Bop or Not to Bop.* New York: 1948.

Gripe, Maria. *Elvis and His Friends.* New York: Delacorte, 1976.

Grissim, John. *Country Music: White Man's Blues.* New York: Paperback Library, 1970.

Grove, Martin. *The King Is Dead, Elvis Presley.* New York: Manor Books, 1977.

————. *Elvis—The Legend Lives.* New York: Manor Books, 1978.

Guralnick, Peter. *Elvis, the Great Performances,* Vols. 1 and 2 (videos). In each ten-page introductory essay. Jan. 1990.

————. *Feel Like Going Home.* New York: Harper & Row, 1989.

————. *Good Rockin' Tonight* (foreword). See Escott/Hawkins.

————. Letters to author dated Aug. 1, Aug. 31, Sept. 30, 1991.

————. *Lost Highway.* Boston: Godine, 1979; New York: Harper & Row, 1989. (A purist's view of Elvis-can-do-little-wrong.)

————. "Million Dollar Quartet." *New York Times Magazine,* Mar. 25, 1979, 28–30.

————. *Searching for Robert Johnson.* New York: E. P. Dutton, 1989.

————. *The Sun Years* (foreword). See Escott/Hawkins.

————. *Sweet Soul Music.* New York: Harper & Row, 1986.

Guterman, Jimmy. *The Best Rock 'n' Roll Records of All Time.* New York: Carol Publishing Group, a Citadel Press Book, 1992.

Haining, Peter, ed. *Elvis in Private.* New York: St. Martin's Press, 1987. (With twenty-nine articles from Todd Slaughter's collection.)

Hall, Claude. "Phillips, Presley, Cash, Sun." *Billboard,* Dec. 27, 1969.

Hamblett, Charles. *Elvis the Swingin' Kid*. Mayfair Books, 1962.

Hammontree, Patsy Guy. *Elvis Presley: A Bio-Bibliography*. Westport, CT, and London, England: Greenwood Press, 1985.

———. See Tharpe, Jack L., ed., *Elvis: Images and Fancies*. Essay.

Hand, Albert. "Elvis" specials each year, 1963–82, for the Elvis Presley Fan Club of Great Britain. (Loaded with photographs.)

———. *Elvis Monthly*. 1956–88, yearly.

———. *The Elvis Pocket Handbook*. Summer 1961. (One hundred pages.)

———. "Meet Elvis, Star Special #1." Great Britain, 1962. Fifty-two-page booklet.

Hanna, David. *Elvis: Lonely Star at the Top*. New York: Leisure Books, 1977 paperback.

Hansten, Philip D. *Drug Interactions*. Philadelphia: Lea and Febiger, 1979.

Harbinson, W. A. *The Illustrated Elvis*. New York: Grossett & Dunlap, 1975; revised edition, 1977.

———. *The Legend of Elvis Presley*. London: Treasure Press, 1975.

Harms, Valerie. *Trying to Get to You: The Story of Elvis Presley*. New York: Atheneum, 1979.

Hawkins, Martin, and Colin Escott. *Elvis: The Illustrated Discography*. London: Omnibus, 1981. (Originally published in 1974 as *The Elvis Session File: 20 Years of Elvis*.)

Head, Edith. "Elvis Tribute," host Jimmy Dean (recording). NBC, Jan. 8, 1978.

"Heartbreak, Hound Dogs Put Sales Zip into Presley Products." *Wall Street Journal*, Dec. 31, 1956, 1, 8.

Heilbut, Tony. *The Gospel Sound*. New York: Simon and Schuster, 1976.

———. *The Gospel Sound: Good News and Bad News*. New York: Simon and Schuster, 1971.

Helpern, Milton, with Bernard Knight. *Autopsy*. New York: St. Martin's Press, 1977.

Hemphill, Paul. *The Nashville Sound: Bright Lights and Country Music*. New York: Simon and Schuster, 1970.

Henkel, David K. *Official Price Guide Rock and Roll*. New York: House of Collectibles, 1992.

Hep Cats (magazine) 2, no. 2 (Dec. 1957).

Hep Cats Review, Feb. 1957, (Special issue on Elvis Presley.)

Hill, Ed, as told to Don Hill. *Where Is Elvis?* Atlanta, GA: Cross Road Books, 1979.

Hill, Wanda June. *Elvis Face to Face.* Privately published, 1985.

Hillburn, Robert. "Eternal Revenue: Why Elvis Is Worth More Now Than the Day He Died." *Los Angeles Times Magazine*, June 11, 1989.

"His Best Friend Explodes the Lies About Elvis" (Bobby "Red" West) *Movie Mirror*, Dec. 1958.

Hit Parader (many issues picture Elvis on the cover, 1956–72):
   —"Elvis Presley," Sept. 1960, Apr. 1966, Mar. 1967.
   —"Elvis Presley Meeting the Press," Dec. 1972.
   —"A Tribute to Elvis Presley," Jan. 1978.

Hodenfield, Chris. "Elvis at the Movies ..." *Florence (TX) Morning News*, Oct. 5, 1977, 14.

Hodge, Charlie, with Charles Goodman. *Me 'n' Elvis.* Memphis: Castle Books, 1984.

Hollywood Rebels (magazine). 1957.

Hollywood Studio Magazine:
   —"Elvis Presley." June/July, 1984; Apr. 1986.
   —"Elvis Spectacular King of Rock, His Legacy Lives On." Sept. 1977.

"A Honeymoon for Barbra and Elvis." *Movie Stars*, Sept. 1975.

Hopkins, Jerry. *Elvis: A Biography.* New York: Simon & Schuster, 1971, New York: Warner Books, 1971. (Serialized in *Look* magazine on May 4 and 11, 1971).

———. *Elvis, the Final Years.* New York: Playboy Paperbacks and Playboy Publishers, 1981; New York: St. Martin's Press, 1980.

———. "The Hidden Life of Elvis Presley." *Life*, May 4, 1971, 32–52.

———. *The Rock Story.* New York: New American Library, 1970.

Hopper, Hedda. "Angela Lansbury Quits Stage for Presley Film." *Looking at Hollywood*, Mar. 15, 1960.

Horsley, Edith. *The 1950s.* Mallard Press, Brompton Books, 1990.

"Hospital Drama of Rock King/Elvis Is Dead," *London Daily Express*, Aug. 17, 1977, 1–2.

"How the '50s Dream Turned into the '70s Tragedy." *Midnight Globe*, Sept. 20, 1977.

Hunter, Derek. "Trouble in His Paradise?" *Movie News*, May 1966.

Hurst, Jack. *Nashville's Grand Ole Opry.* New York: Abrams, 1975.

I Love You #60, Here Comes Elvis (magazine). 1966.

Jacksonville (FL) Journal:
—"Elvis' Performance Satisfied (Judge) Gooding" (editorial). Aug. 11, 1956, 1, 3.
—"Elvis Presley Collapses." Feb. 24, 1956, 7.
—"Troubles Mount for Elvis in Jax." Aug. 10, 1956, 1–2.

Jahn, Mike. *Rock from Elvis to the Rolling Stones.* New York: Quadrangle, 1973.

Jazz and Pop (magazine). Interview with Elvis. Oct. 1969.

Jefferies, Al. An article about Elvis's death. *The Globe,* Aug. 10, 1982.

Jennings, C. Robert. "There'll Always Be an Elvis." *Saturday Evening Post,* Sept. 1965.

Jicha, Tom. "Dick Clark Rips Elvis' Manager." *Beacon Journal* (Akron, OH), Jan. 16, 1993.

Jorgenson, Ernst, Erik Rasmussen, John Mikkelson. *Elvis Recording Sessions.* Stenlos, Denmark: JEE-Productions, 1977. Reprinted with a foreword by Lee Cotton as *Reconsider Baby. The Definitive Elvis. Sessionography, 1954–1977.* Ann Arbor, MI: Pierian Press, 1986.

Judge, Frank. "He Helped Elvis to fame." *Detroit Daily News,* Aug. 19, 1977, np.

Kaiser, R. B., "Rediscovery of Elvis." *New York Times Magazine,* Oct. 11, 1970, 28–29.

Kaplan, Michael. "Royalty, Inc." Unknown 1991 magazine article.

Katz, Ephraim. *The Film Encyclopedia,* New York: Putnam Publishing Company, a Perigee Book, 1979.

Kay, Elizabeth. "Forever Elvis." *New Times,* Nov. 13, 1978, 36–50.

Kelly, Joe. *All the King's Men.* New York: Ariel Books, 1979. Distributed by Simon and Schuster.

Kelly, William P. "Running on Empty: Reimagining Rock and Roll." *Journal of American Culture,* Apr. 1981, 152–59.

Kennedy, Caroline Bouvier. "Graceland: A Family Mourns." *Rolling Stone,* 248 (Sept. 22, 1977).

Kent, Nick. "Roy Orbison: The Last Interview." *The Face,* Feb. 1989, 39.

"King Elvis Is Dead." *New York Sun,* Aug. 17, 1977, 1–2.

King, Dr. Martin Luther, Jr.:
  —Obituary. *New York Times*, Apr. 7, 1968.
  —Speech delivered on Aug. 28, 1963, during civil rights march on Washington, DC. ABC-TV newscast.
Kirkland, K. D. *Elvis*. Bison Books, 1988.
Klein, George:
  —"Interview for the Record." *Memphis Record*, June 1979.
  —*Elvis, the Great Performances* (record), Vol. 1, 2 (narrator).
  —Questionnaire from author filled out Aug. 21, 1991.
Klein, Joe. "Tupelo Fair: From Jack to a King." *Florence (TX) Morning News*, Oct. 5, 1977, 19–29.
Kricun, M. E. and V. M. *Elvis, 1956 Reflections*. Wayne, PA: Morgin Press, Inc., 1992.

Lacker, Marty. "Interview for the Record." *The Record*, May 1979.
Lacker, Marty and Patsy et al. *Elvis, Portrait of a Friend*. New York: Bantam, 1979, paperback; Wimmer Brother Books, Memphis, TN, 1979.
Landau, Jon. *It's Too Late to Stop Now*. San Francisco: Straight Arrow, 1972. (An appraisal of Elvis's 1971 Boston concert.)
Langley, Leonora. "Priscilla Presley, How to Live with a Legend." *Woman's Day*, Nov. 27, 1990, 42, 46, 48.
Latham, Caroline. *Priscilla and Elvis*. New York: Signet Books, 1985.
Latham, Caroline, and Jennie Sakol. *"E" Is for Elvis* New York: Nal Books, published by the Penguin Group, NY 1990.
LaVere, Stephen. *The Blues* (photographs). San Francisco: Pomegranate Artbooks, 1989.
Lazar, Jerry. "Elvis Presley and the Mass Media." *Crawdaddy*, Nov. 1977, 17–19.
Ledger-Enquirer (L.A. newspaper):
  —"Elvis Seen as Symbol of Our Times." Nov. 30, 1956, 6.
  —"Hollywood Is Talking About: Presley Rage Spreading to New Lipstick Shades." Nov. 25, 1956, D-5.
  —"Manager Talking New Movie for Elvis After Fans Riot at New York Opening" (at Paramount Theater) and "Pelvis Rocking Merchandising World . . ." Nov. 19, 1956, 16.
Leech, Mike. "He Was Like One of the Guys." *US*, Aug. 24, 1987.
Levitson, Jay B., and Ger J. Rijff. *Elvis Close-up* New York: Simon and Schuster, 1988. (Photographer Levitson's three-day look at Elvis in Las Vegas, August 1956.)

Levy, Alan. *Operation Elvis.* Hardcover, 1960; published in England with another cover; soft cover, 1962.

Lewis, Flanzy. "The Presley Imitators." *Preview*, July 1978.

Liberace:

—"Fabulous Wardrobe." Robert J. Peer, *TV Headliner* 2, no. 3 (Mar. 1956): 12–14, 16, 18.

—"Greatest Stage Show in Our History." *Minneapolis Builders Show Guide*, Mar. 12–20, 1960.

—"Guards His Piano." Jack O'Brien, *Dodge City (KS) Globe*, Oct. 23, 1947.

—Letter from the Colonel (Tom Parker). Apr. 17, 1979. (Courtesy Liberace Museum, Las Vegas).

—*St. Louis Globe Democrat*, Apr. 25 and Apr. 26, 1946.

—Interview with Glenn O'Brien. *Las Vegas Evening News*, Feb. 6, 1987.

—"Liberace." James Agency, Los Angeles, program from 1985.

—"Liberace." *Milwaukee Journal*, Dec. 12, 1947.

—*Liberace.* Bob Thomas. New York: St. Martin's Press, 1977.

—*Liberace: An Autobiography.* New York: G. Putnam & Sons, 1973.

—"Liberace and Elvis." *Curtain Time*, Apr. 28, 1956.

—"Liberace, Elvis Presley Team in Impromptu Act." *Los Angeles Times*, Nov. 16, 1956, part 3, p. 7.

—"Liberace Is Hillbilly—for $50,000 a Week." *Los Angeles Mirror*, Apr. 21, 1955, 1, 15.

—The Liberace Museum. Various pamphlets, postcards, news releases, letters—courtesy of Patricia Jarvis, archivist, Liberace Foundation for the Performing & Creative Arts, Las Vegas.

—"Liberace Now Has $250,000 Palace." Lee Belser, *Los Angeles Mirror*, July 14, 1961.

—"Liberace on Living in the Limelight." *San Antonio Light*, Feb. 8, 1987, M1–M3.

—"Liberace Performs Only on His Own Pianos." Press manual, 1967–68 season.

—"Liberace Wears $2,000 Silver Lamé Formal Suit." "Names in the News," newspaper from Ogden City, UT, Apr. 21, 1955, np.

—"Liberace's costumes are optical fantasies." Rhonda M. Hopp, news article, Cleveland, OH, Aug. 29, 1980, 4.

—"Longhairs Says 'Tut, Tut.'" Beulah Schact, *St. Louis Globe Democrat*, Apr. 26, 1948.

—"The Million Dollar Wardrobe." Liberace program, 1980–81.

—"A Passion for His Piano." Wambly Bald, *New York Post*, Nov. 7, 1947, np.

—"Priceless Personality, Piano Please Patients." Chet Klingensmith, *Message-Signaleer* (Fort Monmouth, NJ), Oct. 29, 1947.

—"Trading Trademarks." *This World*, Nov. 25, 1956, np.

—*The Wonderful Private World of Liberace*. Liberace. New York: Harper & Rowe, 1986.

Lichter, Paul. *The Boy Who Dared to Rock: The Definitive Elvis*. New York: Dolphin Books, 1978.

———. *Elvis in Hollywood*. New York: Fireside Books, 1975; Simon and Schuster, 1976.

———. *Elvis Presley, Behind Closed Doors*. Huntingdon Valley, PA: Jesse Books, 1987.

Life:

—"The Army's Sergeant Elvis Comes Back Home to Girls ..." Mar. 14, 1960.

—Hirshberg, Charles. "The Ballad of A. P. Carter." Vol. 1, no. 16 (Dec. 1991): 114.

—"Elvis, a Different Kind of Idol." Aug. 27, 1956, 101–9.

—"Farewell Squeal for Elvis." Oct. 6, 1958, 17, 77–78, 80.

—"Farewell to Priscilla, Hello USA." Mar. 14, 1960, 97–98.

—"40 Years of Rock & Roll." Special issue, Dec. 1, 1992.

—Goldman, Albert. "Elvis Presley at Las Vegas." Mar. 20, 1970, 17.

—"Howling Hillbilly Success." Apr. 30, 1956, 64.

—"Idols Team Up on TV." May 16, 1960, 103–4.

—"The King's Ransom," Aug. 1984.

—"Love Me Tender" (ad, Time-Life Music). Feb. 25, 1993.

—Owen, Elizabeth. "The King's Ransom: Elvis Presley Lives On as a Billion-Dollar Business." Aug. 1984, 76–84.

—"Private Presley's Debut." Apr. 1958, 117–18.

—"Rock-a-bye role for Presley." Oct. 10, 1960, 121.

Liffey, Anna. "Tom Jones Begs Elvis ..." *Screen Stars*, Sept. 1973, 22–25, 66–67.

"Lisa Marie Presley." *Us*, Feb. 13, 1984, 56–61.

"Long Live the King." *Art and Auction*, Dec. 1991, np.

Look:

—"Elvis and the Fräuleins." Dec. 23, 1958, 113–14.

—"Elvis at 21: The Days of Innocence." Apr. 4, 1979, 18–23.

—"Elvis Presley, He Can't Be but He Is." Aug. 1956, 82–85.

—"Face Is Familiar." Dec. 11, 1956, 130.

—"The Hidden Life of Elvis Presley." May 4, 1971, 33–52, and cover photo; and May 11, 1971, Part II.

—Morrison, Carol. "Great Elvis Presley Industry." Nov. 13, 1956, 99–107.

Love, Robert. *Elvis Presley*. Watts Publishing, 1986.

Loveless, Mary. "The King's Ransom—Elvis for Sale: Who's Taking Care of Business?" *Memphis*, ca. June 1991.

Lowrey, Ray. "Elvisburgers" (cartoon). In *This Space to Let*. London: Abacus/Sphere, 1986; originally in *New Musical Express*, Jan. 8, 1983.

Loyd, Harold, and George Baugh. *The Graceland Gates*. Memphis: Modern Age Enterprises, 1978.

———. *Elvis Presley's Graceland Gates*. Franklin, TN: Jimmy Velvet Publications, 1987.

Loyd, Harold, and Lisa deAngel. *Elvis and His Fans*. Memphis: ca. 1980.

Lydon, Michael. *Rock Folk*. New York: Dial Press, 1971.

MacDonald, Dwight. "A Caste, a Culture, a Market." *The New Yorker*, Nov. 22 and 29, 1958.

Maine Antique Digest. "The Classic American Guitar Show." Aug. 1993, 36-A, 37-A.

Malone, Bill. *Country Music U.S.A.: A Fifty Year History*. Austin, TX: University of Texas Press, 1968.

"The Man Would Be King." *Us*, Mar. 19, 1990.

Mann, May. *Elvis and the Colonel*. New York: Pocket Books, 1975.

———. *Elvis, Why Don't They Leave You Alone?* New York: Signet Books, 1985.

———. *The Private Elvis*. New York: Pocket Books, 1977 edition. (This book's position is that the Colonel is a genius.)

Mansfield, Rex and Elisabeth. *Elvis the Soldier*. West Germany: 1983.

Maraniss, David. "Throngs Still Flock to the Street Where Elvis Lived." *Cleveland Plain Dealer*, Aug. 11, 1991, 5–7

Marcus, Greil. *Dead Elvis*. New York/London: Doubleday, 1991.

———. "Dead Elvis." *Interview*, Nov. 1991, 30.

———. "In Late February . . ." *Interview*, May 1992, 64.

———. *Mystery Train: Images of America in Rock 'n' Roll*. New York: E. P. Dutton, 1975. (An excellent book about the early days of Elvis and Sun Records.)

———. "Spirit and Flesh: Elvis Mattered." *Florence (TX) Morning News*, Oct. 5, 1977, 23–25.

———. "William Eggleston's View of Graceland: The Absence of Elvis." *Artforum*, Mar. 1984, 70–72.

Marsh, Dave. *Elvis*. New York: Rolling Stone Press, 1982.

Martin, Blake. "Exposed: The Strange Cult of Rock-and-Roll." *True Strange*, Dec. 1957.

"Marvel Family, The" (comic). A Fawcett Publication, vol. 6, no. 31 (Jan. 1949).

Matthew, Neal (member of the Jordanaires). *Elvis: A Golden Tribute*. Memphis: 1985.

Matthew-Walker, Robert. *Elvis Presley: A Study in Music*. Kent, England: Midas Books, 1979. (Much trivia. Not recommended.)

Mayr, Dallas. "Elvis Presley." *Penthouse*, Aug. 1978, 37–38.

McKee, Margaret, and F. Chisenhall. *Beale Street Black and Blue*. Baton Rouge, LA: Louisiana State University Press, 1981.

Melly, George. *Revolt Into Style*. Harmondsworth: Penguin, 1970.

Melody Maker:
—"Elvis Presley." July 21, 1956, 3.
—"Let's Be Fair to Mr. Presley." Dec. 1, 1956, 8.

Memphis Press-Scimitar:
—"Army, Navy Recruiters Make Offers to Elvis." Robert Johnson and Thomas N. Pappas, Dec. 1957.
—"Audience Pullers." Aug. 5, 1955.
—"Carter Says Elvis Is Symbol." Aug. 18, 1977.
—"Doctor Group Shuns Elvis Issue." Nov. 2, 1977.
—"Elvis Acting Still Limps After 10 Years, 12 Movies." John Knott, June 10, 1966.
—"Elvis Adds 'Lisa Marie' to His Fleet of Planes." Orville Hancock, nd, 1975.
—"Elvis Admitted to Baptist Hospital." Apr. 1, 1977.
—"Elvis At Home: Hospital on Call." Apr. 6, 1977.
—"Elvis Becomes Owner of Airline Corvair." Orville Hancock, June 11, 1975.
—"Elvis Bigger Than Ever." Dick Kleiner, Dec. 12, 1965.
—"Elvis Buys Manager $1.2 Million Plane." James Kingsley, July 27, 1975.
—"Elvis Captures New Fans." Malcolm Davis, Feb. 26, 1961.
—"Elvis' Death Report Blames Heart, Liver." Beth J. Tamke, Aug. 27, 1977, front page.

—"Elvis Dies Quickly at Graceland After Suffering Heart Failure." Ron Harris and Tim Schick, Aug. 17, 1977, 1.

—"Elvis Escapes Breakup Blame." Alice Fulbright, 1975.

—"Elvis Fans Caught by Wedding Hoax." Charles Goodman, July 12, 1976.

—"Elvis Film Sets Record in Crowds . . ." July 10, 1957.

—"Elvis Is 'Shocked' at Musicians Quitting." Bill E. Burk, Sept. 21, 1957.

—"Elvis Makes Quiet Visit to Tupelo." Dec. 30, 1970.

—"Elvis Plays Santa Claus . . ." James Kingsley, Dec. 1971.

—"Elvis Ponders Tour of World." James Kingsley, Aug. 1, 1969.

—"Elvis' Popularity Puzzling to Hollywood 'Insiders.' " AP, May 1967, np.

—"Elvis Presley Clicks." Oct. 20, 1954.

—"Elvis Presley in Hospital Here." Oct. 15, 1973.

—"Elvis Presley No-Shows RCA Recording Session." Feb. 2, 1977.

—"Elvis Presley Now a Lawman." Oct. 12, 1970, np.

—"Elvis Presley Now Biggest Star." Edwin Howard, Sept. 7, 1965.

—"Elvis Turns Down Contract for Five Million in Las Vegas." James Kingsley, Aug. 10, 1969.

—"Elvis Was to Wed on Christmas Day." Aug. 17, 1977.

—"Elvis' Whim Caters to Car Shopper's Fancy." Robert Kellett, July 29, 1975.

—"Elvis Will Make More Personal Appearances." John Knott, Dec. 1, 1968.

—"Elvis' Will Names 3 Close Relatives."Lawrence Busier, Aug. 23, 1977.

—"Elvis Wins Love of Ann-Margaret." Nov. 8, 1963.

—"Fans Cheer Screen." Mar. 9, 1971, np.

—"Fat and Forty—But Also Sold Out." Sept. 7, 1976.

—"Final Glimpse of Fallen Star Lures Faithful." William Steverson, Aug. 18, 1977.

—"Funeral Sermon Has Encouragement." Deborah White, Aug. 19, 1977.

—"Hayride Show Signs Elvis Presley." Oct. 13, 1954.

—"Hucksters, 49,200 Elvisites Whoop It Up." Jane Sanderson, Mar. 18, 1974.

—"In a Spin." July 28, 1954.

—"Interview with Sam Phillips." Walter Dawson, Aug. 20, 1977.

—"It Looks Like Romance for Presley and Ann-Margret." Bob Thomas, Aug. 8, 1963.

—"It Won't Be Long Now . . ." Paul Vanderwood, Jan. 8, 1957.

—"The King Delights His Subjects." Mar. 17, 1974.

—"A Lonely Life Ends on Elvis Presley Boulevard." Clark Porteous, Aug. 17, 1977, front page.

—"Many Are Cashing In on Memory of Elvis." Amanda McGee, Sept. 5, 1977.

—"Marine Wants Elvis' Apology on Gun Threat." Mar. 25, 1957.

—"Memphis Boy, Elvis Presley, Signs Contract with Gleason." Robert Johnson, Jan. 11, 1956.

—"Memphis' Elvis Outdoes Caruso in Record Sales." Feb. 6, 1957.

—"Memphis Singer Presley Signed by RCA Victor . . ." Robert Johnson, Nov. 11, 1955.

—"Multiple Drugs May Be Ruled as Cause of Elvis' Death." Beth J. Tamke, Oct. 19, 1977.

—"New Fame Failed to Change Elvis' Love for His Mother." Thomas Michael, Aug. 15, 1958.

—"Parker's Wedding Gift for Presley." Dick Kleiner, Hollywood, May 19, 1967.

—"Pity Poor Elvis, So Say Reds." AP, July 22, 1977.

—"Presley Autopsy May Not Be Made Public." Aug. 26, 1977.

—"Presley Carries More Weight at Opening Night in Las Vegas." Mar. 14, 1975.

—"Presley Sales Spin to Tune of 76 Million." July 1957.

—"Presley's big $55,000 Yacht . . ." Feb. 15, 1964.

—"Priscilla Presley Gets a Kiss and a $1.5 Million Settlement." Oct. 10, 1973.

—"Pvt. Elvis Begins Army Life in Sentry-Guarded Barracks." Louis Silver, Mar. 24, 1958.

—"Rumors Fly Along As Girl's Family Goes to See Elvis." Dec. 10, 1976.

—"Secluded Elvis Hailed as Best." Scott Ware, Jan. 9, 1975.

—"She's Too Much . . ." Bill Evans, Feb. 5, 1969, 1.

—"Skitch Henderson Calls Elvis the 'Beethoven of His Field.'" Margaret McKee, Feb. 3, 1967.

—"Sparks Become an Elvis Admirer . . ." Fred Sparks, Jan. 7, 1956.

—"St. Jude Gets Elvis Yacht . . ." Feb. 15, 1964.

—"These Reports True—Elvis and Dewey Had a Falling Out." Robert Johnson, Aug. 1957.

—"3 Charged in Body-Stealing Plot." William Steverson, Aug. 30, 1977.

—"Thru the Patience of Sam Phillips . . ." Robert Johnson, Feb. 5, 1955.

—"Tributes Paid to Elvis Throughout World." Aug. 18, 1977.

—"Tupelo Builds Fund for Elvis Memorial." Michael Arnold, Aug. 20, 1977.

—"TV News and Views." Robert Johnson, Dec. 3, 1956.

—"Wedding Is Typically Elvis—Quick, Quiet and in Style." Thomas F. BeVier, May 2, 1967, front page.

—"Well Again, Elvis Quits Hospital." Nov. 2, 1973.

—"What's the Fuss About?" James F. Page, Dec. 12, 1957.

Meyer, Alan. "A Living Tribute to Elvis." *Teen*, Feb. 1978.

Miller, Douglas T., and Marion Nowak. *The Fifties: The Way We Really Were.* New York: Doubleday, 1975.

Miller, Jim. *The Rolling Stone Illustrated History of Rock & Roll.* New York: Random House, 1976.

"Millions Mourn Presley." *New York Post*, Aug. 17, 1977, 1, 9, 10, 33.

Modern Screen:

—"Elvis Presley! Who Is He? Why Does He Drive Girls Crazy?" Aug. 6, 1956, 41, 90–91.

—"I Flipped When Elvis Held Me . . ." (a fan's comments). Oct. 1956, 37, 90–92.

—"Louella Parsons in Hollywood. Open Letter to Elvis Presley." Sept. 16, 1956, 16.

Monnery, Steve, and Gary Herman. *Rock 'n' Roll Chronicles, 1955–1963.* Stamford, CT: Longmeadow Press, 1991. (With Elvis on the cover.)

Moody, Raymond, Jr. *Elvis After Life.* Atlanta, GA: Peachtree, 1987.

Morgan, Todd, from Graceland, Division of Elvis Presley Enterprises, Inc., Memphis. Letters to the author. June 10, 1991, two pages; July 18, 1991, three pages; Sept. 2, 1991, one page.

Morrison, Jim (1943–71):

—Cohn, Nick. *Awopbopaloobop Alopbamboom.* New York: Weidenfield and Nicolson, 1989.

—Crosby, David, and Carl Gottlieb. *Long Time Gone.* Heinemann, 1989.

—Doe, Andres, and John Tobler. *The Doors in Their Own Words.* New York: Omnibus Press, 1988.

—Dylan, Jones. *Jim Morrison, Dark Star.* New York: Viking Studio Books, 1990.

—Farren, Mick. *The Black Leather Jacket.* Plexus, 1985.

—Jahn, Mike. *Jim Morrison and the Doors.* New York: Grosset and Dunlap, 1969.

Morthland, John. "Elvis Has Left the Building." *Stereo Review,* Jan. 1978, 108–9.

Motion Picture (magazine):

—"Elvis Presley. The Big Noise from Tupelo." Dec. 1956, 40–43, 60–61.

—With Elvis pinup section. 1959.

Movie Life:

—What Liz Will Teach Elvis About Love." Nov.

—"The Whole Shattering Story, Adoption Plans for Elvis' Baby Daughter." 1973, 30–31, 62, 64.

Movie Stars:

—"After Five Years—Elvis Learns Whose Child . . ." 1973, 26–27, 60, 62.

—"Elvis Tells Daughter She'll Have a 'New Mother.'" Feb. 1976.

—"Priscilla Presley's Own Story," Ellen Grant. Nov. 1973, 30–31, 50, 52.

Movie Teen. Special Elvis issue. 1961.

Movie Teen Illustrated (first printed an Elvis article in 1959):

—"The Dramatic Battle Inside Elvis." Apr. 1962, 20–21.

—"The Elvis Party, Just His Name Fires Up a Party." Apr. 1962, 22–23, 47.

—"Is Elvis' Magic for Sale?" Elvis Special #3, Apr. 1962, 30–31.

—"Will We Ever See Elvis Again?" Amy Wakely. Apr. 1962, 24–25.

Movieland:

"Elvis, 'The Doctors Told Me I'd Die!'" 1972.

—"The Inside Story of Elvis' Wedding." Aug. 1967.

—"Why Elvis Can't Marry Linda." May Mann, Sept. 1973, 24–25, 54.

Musician: Player & Listener (magazine). 1982. ($50.)

Nash, Alanna. "The Private Man." *Akron (OH) Beacon Journal,* Aug. 1977.

Nash, David. "How Great Thou Art." *Florence (TX) Morning News,* Special Edition, Oct. 5, 1977, 27.

National Enquirer:
—"Elvis & His Mom Were Lovers." Feb. 18, 1992, front page, 23–25, 31.
—"Elvis' 3-day drug orgy left a teen fan brain-damaged and near death." May 17, 1992, 10.
—"Exclusive . . . ELVIS the Untold Story . . . The Last Picture." Sept. 6, 1977, 1, 20–25.
—"Why Elvis Killed Himself, the Proof at Last." Feb. 25, 1992, front page, 26–27.
—"The woman Elvis really loved—and his brutal rape of Priscilla." Mar. 3, 1992, 7.

National Examiner:
—Elvis half-page postage-stamp ad. Jan. 12, 1993, 9.
—"Elvis has been sighted . . . in St. Vincent." Jan. 12, 1993, 32.
—"Elvis Is Alive." Oct. 4, 1988, front cover.
—"Elvis Is Guiding Lisa Marie from Beyond the Grave." Jan. 12, 1993, 17.
—"Weird Cult to turn Elvis home into a Heartbreak Hotel?" Mar. 17, 1992, 19.

NBC-TV. "Evening News," Aug. 17, 1977 (recording); Jay Leno on "The Tonight Show," Jan. 6, 1993, gave a comedy segment titled "If Elvis Were Amish." (Not funny, Jay.)

Nelson, Pete. *King! When Elvis Rocked the World.* London and New York: Proteus Books, 1985.

"New Elvis Presley Story, The" (radio reel). TM Programming, 1981.

"New Frontier." *Curtain Time* (Las Vegas), Apr. 25, 1956, 22, 38.

New York Times:
—"Elvis Presley. Lack of Responsibility Is Shown by TV in Exploiting Teenagers." Sept. 16, 1956, Section 2, p. 13.
—"Elvis Presley Rises to Fame as Vocalist Who Is Virtuoso of Hootchy-Kootchy." June 6, 1956, 67.
—"Hometown Honors Presley." Sept. 27, 1956, 42.
—"Memphis Coliseum Renamed for Presley." Jan. 4, 1967.
—"Movie Renamed to Fit New Presley Record." Sept. 10, 1956, 55.
—"Presley Involved in Memphis Fight." Oct. 19, 1956, 53.
—"Presley Receives a City Polio Shot." Oct. 29, 1956, 33.
—"Presley Rolls in Clear . . ." Oct. 19, 1956, 16.
—"Presley Signed by Ed Sullivan." July 14, 1956, 33.
—"Presley Termed a Passing Fancy." Dec. 17, 1956, 28. (Stated by a Greenwich Village minister.)

—"Presley Tops Hit Parade on Beatles' Home Grounds." June 10, 1965.

—"Punch Misses Presley." Nov. 24, 1956, 16.

—"The Screen: Culture Takes a Holiday." Nov. 16, 1956, 23. (Blasts Elvis's *Love Me Tender.*)

New Yorker (magazine):

—"Elvis! David!" June 24, 1972, 28.

—"The Current Cinema." Vol. 23, Nov. 1956, 196–97.

Newsweek:

—"GI Jive." Nov. 5, 1956, 67.

—"Hero Worship." June 11, 1956, 66–67.

—"Hillbilly on a Pedestal." May 14, 1956, 82.

—"Inextinguishable." Aug. 27, 1956, 68.

—Lardner, J., "Devitalizing Elvis." July 16, 1956, 59.

—"Mud on the Stars." Oct. 8, 1956, 58.

—"No Takers." Feb. 18, 1956, 58.

—Orth, M. "All Shook Up: Heartbreak Kid." Aug. 27, 1977, 46–49.

—"Presley Sells Profit." Feb. 18, 1957, 84–85.

—"Question and Answer." July 23, 1956, 69.

—"Return of the Pelvis." Aug. 11, 1969, 83.

—"Shows of the Week." June 18, 1956, 14.

—"Spoils of Elvis." Jan. 30, 1978, 58.

—Williams, Dennis, and Kay Veazy. "Did Elvis Die from Drug Abuse?" Jan. 28, 1980, 35.

Nichols, Mrs. Willie Jane. Interview with author by telephone from Nashville, TN, June 1991.

Nixon, Anne E., and Todd Slaughter. *Elvis, Ten Years After.* Great Britain: 1987.

Nolan, Lewis. "Tickets to Elvis Concerts Spawn Scalping." Memphis Library & Information Center, Mar. 8, 1974, np.

Noland, Hal, and Sean Shaver. *The Life of Elvis Presley.* New York: Time Publishing, Inc., 1979. (With over a thousand photos by Shaver; text by Noland, Charlie Dodge, Dick Grob, Billy Smith.)

Nuttall, Jeff. *Bomb Culture.* London: Paladin, 1969.

O'Curran, Charles. "At Last! The Truth About Elvis Presley." *Melody Maker,* July 27, 1957.

Official Elvis Presley Album. Derby, CT: Charlton Pub., 1956.

Oliver, Paul, Max Harrison, and William Bolcom. *The New Grove Gospel, Blues and Jazz.* New York: W. W. Norton & Co., 1986.

Oregonian (newspaper, Portland):

—"And Now, the King: Elvis stamp makes its debut." Jan. 8, 1993.

—"The King Still Reigns—as loyalists hail commemorative stamp." Jan. 10, 1993.

Osborne, Jerry. *Elvis Presley and the Beatles (Official Price Guide to Memorabilia of)*. New York: House of Collectibles, 1992.

Osborne, Jerry, and Bruce Hamilton. *Presleyana*. Chicago: Follett Publishing Co., 1980.

Pageant (magazine):

—"Elvis, the Unhappy Man Behind the Myth." Aug. 1973. (On cover.)

—"Elvis, a New Love/a New Career." Mar. 1974. (On cover.)

Palmer, Robert. "Big Boss Man: Working with the King." *Florence (TX) Morning News*, Oct. 5, 1977, 22, 26.

———. *Deep Blues*. New York: Viking, 1981. (A look at Elvis and the blues tradition.)

———. *Jerry Lee Lewis Rocks*. New York: Delilah Books, 1981.

———. "Sam Phillips: The Sun King." *Memphis*, Dec. 1978.

Pareles, Jon, and Patricia Romanowski, eds. *Rolling Stone Encyclopedia of Rock & Roll*. New York: Rolling Stone Press, Summit Books, 1983.

Parish, James Robert. *The Elvis Presley Scrapbook*. New York: Ballantine Books, 1975.

Parker, Ed. *Inside Elvis*. Rampart House, Ltd., 1978.

Parker, Tom. "Elvis Exclusively." *TV Guide Presents Elvis Presley*, RCA Victor GB-MW-8705 (45 rpm), 1956.

"Paternity Suit Filed Against Elvis Presley." UPI, *Los Angeles Times*, Aug. 15, 1970.

Pattison, Robert. *The Triumph of Vulgarity: Rock Music in the Mirror of Romanticism*. New York: Oxford, 1987.

"Paunchy Elvis Still King." *Knoxville News Sentinel*, Feb. 14, 1977, Knoxville, TN, 2.

Pearlman, Jill. *Elvis for Beginners*. Allen and Unwin, 1986; University of Mississippi, 1981.

Penthouse (magazine):

—"Elvis Presley." June 22, 1987.

—"Elvis Presley at Forty." Jan. 15, 1975.

—"Elvis Presley: How Did He Die?" Jan. 28, 1980.

—"The Elvis Presley Legend . . ." Aug. 21, 1978.

—"Elvis Presley: Ten Years Later . . ." Aug. 17, 1987.

—"The Fight Over Elvis Presley's Estate." Oct. 6, 1980.

—"Priscilla Presley & Her Life with Elvis." Dec. 4, 1978.

—"Remembering Elvis Presley . . ." Oct. 10, 1977.

People (magazine):

—"Colonel Parker Made Elvis Golden; Now a Memphis Court Wonders If He Fleeced Him Too." Aug. 31, 1981, 18–21.

—"Elvis Presley . . ." Nov. 13, 1975. (Elvis on cover.)

—"Elvis' Baby Girl: This month Lisa Marie turned 25 and inherited her dad's $100 million estate." Mar. 1, 1993, 2, 66–70, and front cover of Lisa.

—"The Elvis Legend, One Year Later." Aug. 21, 1978.

—"Elvis Was the Light That Shined on Everybody."Aug. 21, 1978, 20–25.

—"The 50 Most Beautiful People in the World, 1992." Mar. 4, 1992, 119. (Segment on Priscilla Presley.)

—"The Geisslers Corner an Elvis Market." Oct. 10, 1977, 31.

—"The King Is dead, but Long Lives the King in a Showbiz Bonanza." Oct. 10, 1977, 28–31.

—"King's Ransom" (p. 107) and "Elvis and the Colonel, the Untold Story" (about the TV movie, p. 15). Jan. 11, 1993.

—"Mailhouse Rock." Jan. 27, 1992, 44–45.

—Rayl, S. "Did Colonel Parker Take the King for a Ride?" Dec. 1, 1980, 40–41.

—"Remembering Elvis—Imitators, fans and rip-offs launch a billion dollar industry." Oct. 10, 1977.

—"Stitches in Time: The Hollywood Pioneers." Jan. 27, 1992, 64.

Perkins, Carl. *Disciple in Blue Suede Shoes*. Grand Rapids, MI: Zondervan, 1978.

Peters, Richard, with the Official Elvis Presley Fan Club of Great Britain. *Elvis: The Golden Anniversary Tribute*. Salem House, 1985; Great Britain, Pop Universal/Souvenir Press, 1984.

Philadelphia (PA) Inquirer, The (newspaper):

—"Elvis Gets to Allen—So? . . ." July 2, 1956, 22.

—"Rock 'n' Roll Earful Shatters Critic." June 6, 1956, 36.

—"Sullivan's $50,000 Boy Cut Off Amidships." Sept. 10, 1956, 26.

Photoplay:

—"I'm Coming Home!" With a letter from Elvis dated Feb. 1, 1960, from Bad Nauheim, Germany. Mar. 1960, 19, 21, 73.

—"Pinups of Elvis." Vol. 50, Dec. 1956, 40–41.

—"Please don't forget me while I'm gone!" Oct. 1958, 37, 74–75.

—"Presley Takes Hollywood." Vol. 50, Dec. 1956, 42–43, 93–94.

Pike, Charles. "Elvis Presley—'The King' Comes Back." *Faces* (magazine), Dec. 30, 1975.

Platinum (magazine). "King Elvis." Vol. 2, nd, ca. 1977. (All photographs.)

Pleasants, Henry. *The Great American Popular Singers*. New York: Simon and Schuster, 1974.

Pond, Steve. *Elvis in Hollywood*. New York: New American Library, 1990.

Presley, Dee. Interview with author. Nashville, TN, July 15, 1991, by telephone.

Presley, Dee, et. al. *Elvis, We Love You Tender*. New York: Delacorte Press, 1980.

"Presley doctor faces charges." *The Patriot Ledger* (Brockton, MA). Mar. 24, 1992, 2. (Under "Nation.")

"Presley Draws 50,000 Persons in Three Shows." Chicago news article from the Memphis Library, June 18, 1972.

Presley, Elvis. *Elvis Answers Back*. Lawndale, CA: Sound Publishing Corporation, 1956.

Presley, Elvis. "Last Will and Testament of Elvis A. Presley." Mar. 3, 1976. (Thirteen pages.) (*Note:* The year "1976" is crossed out and "1977" is put in its place. Many sources keep the 1976 date. The corrected version is distributed by Graceland. No initials are correctly placed under the crossed-out date.)

———. Letter to Pres. Richard Milhous Nixon. Dec. 1970.

"Presley Fans Gather." *Knoxville News Sentinel*, Jan. 8, 1977.

"Presley Gets Better and Better." *Picturegoer*, Jan. 25, 1958.

"Presley Leaves Hospital Hurriedly to Avoid Fans." *Knoxville News Sentinel*, Apr. 5, 1977, 7.

"The Presley Pressure Can Fracture Anybody" (editorial). *Florida Times-Union, The* (newspaper). Aug. 10, 1956, 6.

Presley, Priscilla Beaulieu, and Sandra Harmon. *Elvis and Me*. New York: Berkley Books, 1986 paperback; G. P. Putnam, hardcover, Sept. 1985. (Excerpted in *People*.)

"Presley 'Sends' Throngs With Bumps, Grinds." *San Francisco Examiner*, June 4, 1956, 1.

Presley, Vester. *A Presley Speaks*. Memphis: Wimmer Brothers Books, 1978.

Presley, Vester, and Nancy Rooks. *The Presley Family Cookbook.* Memphis: Wimmer Brothers Books, 1980.

"Presley's Body Lies in State." *London Evening Standard,* Aug. 17, 1977, front-page story.

Preview. "Elvis Presley—Who Can 'Protect' Him Now?" Feb. 1977. (Also on cover.)

Primus, Claire. *Elvis—"The King" Returns.* New Hampshire: Edgar Publishing Corporation, 1960.

Private Lives (magazine). "Elvis Presley: Music to Sin By—Is Rock 'n' Roll Making Savage Sex Sinners of Simple Teenagers? Is Young Elvis Presley the Answer?" Dec. 1956.

Psychic Reader (Santa Rosa, CA). "Elvis, the Channel." Apr. 1987, 26.

Pugh, John. "Rise and Fall of Sun Records." *Country Music,* Nov. 1973.

Quain, Kevin. *The Elvis Reader.* New York: St. Martin's Press, 1992.

Rabey, Steve. *The Heart of Rock and Roll.* New Jersey: Fleming H. Revell Co., 1986.

Randall, Nancy. "The men who shot Elvis." *Nine-O-One Network,* July/Aug. 1987, 10–13.

RCA Victor. Record catalog to promote records and tapes by Elvis. 1965–73.

"Ready for the Junk Heap." *Super Rock* (National Newsstand Publications), No. 4, Dec. 1978.

Record (published by *Rolling Stone*). "Elvis Presley: Sex and Sin." No. 1, Nov. 1981.

Record Time–TV Movies (magazine). 1960.

Record Whirl (magazine). 1956.

Reggero, John. *Elvis in Concert.* New York: Delta Special Lorelei, 1979. (Introduction by David Stanley.)

Reible, John. Las Vegas News Bureau. Letters to author about Elvis's Vegas performances dated July 16, July 27, July 30, and Nov. 26, 1991, Las Vegas, NV.

Reid, Jan. *The Improbable Rise of Redneck Rock.* Austin, TX: Heidelberg Publishers, 1974.

Reid, Vernon. *Elvis Is Dead.* New York: Famous Music Corp., 1990.

Rejoice! Summer 1988 edition has the following articles:
—"The Blackwood Brothers." Charles Wolfe, 27–29.

—"Elvis and Gospel Music." Cheryl Thurber, 5–9.

—"The Gospel Christian Singers . . ." Tom Hanchett, 38–39.

—"The Iconography of Elvis." Charles Reagan Wilson, 32–33.

—"Singing with the King." Don Cusic, 10–13.

—"60 Years of Black Gospel Quartet . . ." Kip Lornell, 14–17.

Ribakove, Sy and Barbara. *Folk-Rock: The Bob Dylan Story.* New York: Dell Publishing Co., Inc., 1966.

Ridge, Millie. *The Elvis Album.* New York: Gallery Books, 1991.

Rijff, Ger. *Long Lonely Highway: A 1950s Elvis Scrapbook.* Ann Arbor, MI: Pierian Press, 1988, reprint.

Rijff, Ger, and Jan Van Gestel. *Florida Close Up.* (Photography by Jay B. Levitson of concerts in Jacksonville, FL, 1956.)

Rivera, Geraldo. "The Geraldo Rivera Show," Feb. 17, 1992. (With Joe Esposito, Dee Presley, and others.)

———. "Now It Can Be Told" and other "Geraldo Rivera Show" TV dates have covered a possible cover-up regarding the death and life of Elvis, 1991–Apr. 1992.

———. Host of "20/20" special program "The Elvis Cover-Up," aired on ABC-TV, Sept. 13, 1979.

Rock (tabloid): Oct. 11, 1970; Feb. 15, 1971; Mar. 1, 1971; June 21, 1971; Aug. 30, 1971; Dec. 25. 1971; Feb. 28, 1972; Mar. 13, 1971; Sept. 25, 1972; "The Exploitation of . . . Mar. 25, 1974," ; July 5, 1974.

Rock and Roll Roundup (magazine). 1957.

Rock and Roll Stars #1: The Real Elvis Presley Story (magazine). 1956.

Rock and Roll Stars #2: Elvis Answers 10 Important Teenage Questions (magazine). 1957.

Rock and Roll Stars #3: Elvis in the Army? (magazine). 1958.

Rock Legends (magazine). "Elvis Presley: The Original Idol" and "Elvis Presley Discology." No. 1, 1989.

"Rock 'n' Roll Battle. Boone vs. Presley." *Collier's* 138 (Oct. 26, 1956): 109–11.

Rock 'n' Roll Battlers (magazine). 1956.

Rock 'n' Roll Jamboree (magazine). 1956.

Rock 'n' Roll Rivals (magazine). 1957.

Rock 'n' Roll Years. New York: Crescent Books, 1990.

Rock Scene (Four Seasons Publishing). "Elvis Presley Tribute," Feb. 1978.

Rolling Stone (magazine):

"Blue Hawaii," Sept. 22, 1977.

—Colonel Parker article. Jerry Hopkins, Sept. 22, 1977.

—"Duets." May 17, 1979.

—"Elvis Anthology: From Memphis to Myth." Jim Miller, Apr. 11, 1974.

—"Elvis in Hollywood." July 12, 1969. (On cover.)

—"Elvis Presley." #52, #59, #66, #70, 1970; #261, 1978; #312, #325, 1980; #352, 1981; #508, 1987; #576, 1990.

—"Elvis Presley Dead, 1935–1977." #248, 1977.

—"Elvis Presley: His Life & Movies." #344, 1981.

—"Elvis Presley: imitations in spirit and flesh," Mar. 23, 1978.

—"Elvis Presley in Concert." #98, 1971.

—"Elvis Presley in Hollywood." #37, 1969.

—"Elvis Presley, RCA, 1956." Nov. 14, 1991, 124.

—"Elvis Presley: The Party Years." #355, 1981.

—"Elvis Presley's From the Heart . . ." Apr. 2, 1992, 50.

—"Elvis's Stamp of Approval." Michael Goldberg, Mar. 19, 1992, 18.

—"50,000,000 Elvis Fans Can't Be Wrong." Nov. 14, 1991, 137.

—"'Graceland: A Family Mourns." Caroline Bouvier Kennedy, #248, Sept. 22, 1977.

—"King Death." Oct. 23, 1975. ("Applause for the Angel of Death.")

—"The King might be . . ." May 20, 1992, 12.

—"Rare Elvis Presley photos." #506, 1987.

—"The Selling of Elvis Presley." #248, 1977.

—"Son Seals: Born Into the Blues." Robert Palmer, Mar. 23, 1978.

—"Tales from the Crypt." Dec. 14, 1978.

Rook, Jean. "Black Satin Sheets Didn't Help Elvis." *Knoxville News Sentinel*, Nov. 16, 1983, sec. 1.

Rooks, Nancy, and Mae Gutter. *The Maid, the Man, and the Fans.* New York: Vantage Press, 1984.

Rosenthal, Marshall. "Chicago to Get Long-Delayed Chance to Re-access Elvis, Once Called 'Fad.' " *Chicago Daily News*, June 8, 1972.

Rovin. Jeff. *The World According to Elvis.* New Hampshire: Harper Paperbacks, 1992.

"Russian Leader Boris Yeltsin . . ." *Boston Herald*, July 8, 1991.

Ryan, T. C. "Rock 'n' Roll Battle: Boone vs. Presley." *Collier's*, Oct. 26, 1956, 109–11.

Sager, Mike. *Philip Morris Magazine*, "Blue Guitar." Summer 1991, 12, 14. (About B. B. King.)

San Francisco Chronicle (newspaper):
—"Arrest in Memphis Row . . ." Oct. 19, 1956, 1, 6.
—"Elvis Hits and Teenagers Turn Out." June 4, 1956, 20.
—"Elvis Tangles with a Defiant Husband." Nov. 23, 1956, 29.
—"Elvis to Star in Film with Jayne Mansfield." Oct. 9, 1956, 25.
—"Girls Smear Elvis' Cadillac." Oct. 22, 1956, 4.
—"Love Me Tender at the Fox." Nov. 23, 1956, 21.
—"Presley Leaves You in a Blue Suede Funk." June 5, 1956, 19.
San Francisco News (newspaper):
—"Elvis-Pelvis Debate Rocks 'n' Rolls On." June 22, 1956, 9.
—"Elvis Shmelvis: It's Elvis." June 4, 1956, 11.
—"Is Pelvis Elvis Another Frankie?" (compared to Sinatra).
    June 8, 1956, 9.
—"What Makes Elvis Roll On." Oct. 15, 1956, 1.
—"What Makes Elvis Presley Tick—No. 2, 'Can't he'p it . . . Ah
    Just Love That Boy.' " Oct. 16, 1956, 1.
—"What Makes Elvis Presley Tick—No. 3, the Pelvis Explains
    That 'Vulgar' Style." Oct. 17, 1956, 1.
Saturday Review (magazine):
—"Nights of the Living Dead . . ." May 3, 1978.
—"SR Goes to the Movies." Dec. 8, 1956, 30. (Review of *Love
    Me Tender.*)
Sauers, W. *Elvis Presley. A Complete Reference. Biography,
    Chronology, Concert List, Filmography, Discography, Vital
    Documents, Bibliography, Index.* Jefferson, N.C.: McFarland
    and Company, Inc., 1984. (Very incomplete.)
Saunders, Laura. "Sell Me Tender." *Forbes*, Feb. 13, 1984.
Schryers, Fred. "What Price Glory?"*Crawdaddy*, Nov. 1977,
    35–36.
"Scientology Group Starts Media Attack on Time Magazine." *Wall
    Street Journal*, May 29, 1991, 13.
Scott, Vernon. "Elvis Ten Million Dollars Later." *McCall's*, Feb.
    1963, 90–91, 124–29.
———. "Memphian Who Revolutionized Pop Music: Elvis
    Presley Was First; All Others Are Carbon Copies." UPI,
    Sept. 25, 1968.
Seigenthaler. "Elvis a Puzzle in Early Days." *Nashville
    Tennessean*, Aug. 16, 1978, sec. 2, p. 40, col. 5.
Sha-Boom (magazine): #1, Jan. 1990; #2, Feb. 1990; #3, Mar. 1990;
    #5, May 1990; #7, July 1990.
Shaver, Sean, and Hal Noland. *The Life of Elvis Presley.*
    Memphis: Timur Publishers, 1979.

Shaw, Arnold. *The Rockin' 50s*. New York: Hawthorn Books, 1974.

Shaw, Sid. *Elvis in Quotes*. Elvisly Yours, 1986.

Shearer, Lloyd. "I Remember Elvis." *Parade*, Jan. 1978, 4–9.

Shelton, Robert, and Burt Goldblass. *The Country Music Story*. Indianapolis, IN: Bobbs-Merrill, 1966.

Shreveport (LA) Times (newspaper):
   —"Everybody and His Dog Turns Out for Elvis." Pericles Alexander, Dec. 16, 1956, 10A.
   —"Mass Hysteria, Frenzied Elvis Fans Rock Youth Center." Bob Masters, Dec. 16, 1956, 1A.

16 Magazine:
   —"Are There Two Elvis Presleys?" Mar. 1964.
   —"Elvis Presley." Jan. 1961; Feb. 1963; Mar. 1963; Sept. 1964; Mar. 1965; Aug. 1965; Mar. 1969; Apr. 1969; Aug. 1973; and in *16 Magazine*'s 1963 and 1965 "Annual Spectacular."
   —"Elvis Presley: 101 Pix of Elvis." Apr. 1963; Nov. 1963.
   —"Elvis Presley Revealed." Mar. 1962.
   —"Elvis Presley's 101 Untold Secrets." June 1964.
   —"How It Feels to be Kissed by . . ." Jan. 1965.
   —"Inside Elvis Presley by the Girl Who Knows Him Best." May 1959.
   —"A Salute to Elvis Presley." Winter 1966.
   —"Two Years with Elvis Presley." Dec. 1962.
   —"What Is Elvis Presley Hiding?" Oct. 1965.
   —"Why Did Elvis Kiss Ann-Margret Goodbye?" July 1964.

Slaughter, Todd. *Elvis Presley*. Suffolk, England: Richard Clay, Wyndham, 1977.

Smith, Billy. "The Last Days." *The Record*. June 1979, 8–10.

Smith, Joseph. *The Day the Music Died*. New York: Grove, 1981.

Smith, Lorraine. "Some Hard Times." *The Record*, May 1979, 21.

Smith, Wendy. "Staying power of Elvis viewed through humor" (a review of *Dead Elvis*). *Cleveland Plain Dealer*, Nov. 10, 1991.

Snow, Hank. "*Hank Snow Souvenir Photo Album*. 1955. (Tour brochure of the Hank Snow tour caravans in which Elvis participated.)

Sobran, M. J. "Elvis' Demise." *National Review*, Oct. 17, 1977, 185–86.

Song Hits (magazine):
   —"Elvis Presley: Dying at the Box Office." Jan. 1967.
   —"Elvis Presley." Nov. 1972.

Sotheby's. "Collector's Carousel," lot #469, New York: June 22, 1991. (Letter written by Elvis in 1976.)

"Souvenir Folio Concert Edition." (From 1970 to 1977, Las Vegas and the rest of the nation; published by Colonel Parker.)

Souvenir Photo Album: Elvis Presley, "Mr. Dynamite," Nation's Only Atomic Powered Singer (magazine). 1956.

Spin (magazine):
—Elvis interview. Apr. 1987.
—"Elvis Presley." July 1989.

Spokane (WA) Review (newspaper):
—"Presley Whips 12,000 Into Near-Hysteria." Aug. 31, 1957.
—"Well-Guarded Elvis Arrives 'Safe.' " Aug. 30, 1957.

Stambler, Irwin, and Grelun Landon. *Encyclopedia of Folk, Country, and Western*. New York: St. Martin's Press, 1969.

Stanley, Billy, with George Erikson. *Elvis, My Brother*. New York: St. Martin's Press, 1989.

Stanley, David, with David Wimbish. *Life with Elvis*. New Jersey: Fleming H. Revell Co., 1960.

Stanley, Rick, with Paul Harold. *Caught in a Trap*. Dallas: Word Publishing, 1992.

Stanley, William Job, Jr. *Elvis: His Last Tour*. Star Fleet Publishing, 1977.

Star Hits (magazine). "Elvis Presley." Nov. 1987.

Stardom (magazine). 1960.

Staten, Vince. *The Real Elvis: Good Old Boy*. Dayton, OH: Media Ventures, 1978.

Stern, Jan and Michael. *Elvis World*. New York: Alfred A. Knopf, 1987.

Stern, Jess, and Larry Geller. *The Truth About Elvis*. New York: Jove, 1980. (The "religious guru" Geller claims Elvis was near to godlike. Not recommended.)

Stoker, Gordon. "14 Very Good Years." *The Beacon Journal*, May 3, 1991, sec. D, p. D2.

Storm, Tempest. *The Lady Is a Vamp*. 1987. (Storm writes of her affair with Elvis in 1957.)

Straw, Syd. "Listening to Elvis." In *Luxury Condos Coming to Your Neighborhood Soon*. Wyoming: Coyote, 1985.

Stuller, Jay. "Legends That Will Not Die." *Saturday Evening Post*, July/Aug. 1985, 42–49.

Sullivan. "The Ed Sullivan Show." Letter to author, Oct. 14, 1991.

Sumner, J. D., and Bob Terrell. *Gospel Music in My Life*. Nashville, TN: Impact Books, 1971.

Sun News, (Myrtle Beach, SC:
—DuBard, Trip. "All Shook Up? Elvis Returns!" p. C1, and "Elvis Lives" ad, Jan. 6, 1993, 3C.
—"Elvis isn't licked yet, but stamps will go on sale at noon." Jan. 7, 1993, C1, C3.
—"Family Circus" (Elvis cartoon). Dec. 22, 1992, 6C.
—"For 29 cents and a dreamy wait, you could rekindle love for Elvis." Jan. 9, 1993, C1, C2.
—"The King: Elvis Presley Would Have Been 58 Years Old Today" and "The King: Gone but not forgotten . . ." (front-page color shot with Ann-Margret). In Entertainment Guide, Jan. 8, 1993, 1–2.
—"See Elvis for Free at Nixon Library." Jan. 7, 1993, 2A.
—"10,000 Elvises spotted in Memphis." Aug. 12, 1993, 2A.
"Sun's Newest Star." *Cowboy Songs* (magazine), June 1955. (Elvis's first national article.)
Swift, Pamela. "Presley's Druggist." *Parade*, June 8, 1980, 16.

Tathem, Dick. *Elvis: The Rock Greats*. London: Phoebus, 1976.
Taylor, John Alvarez. *Elvis, the King Lives*. New York: Gallery Books, 1990.
Taylor, Roger. *Elvis in Art*. New York: St. Martin's Press, 1987.
Taylor, Ron. "Elvis Bilked Out of Millions, Report Charges." *Atlanta Journal-Constitution*, Aug. 2, 1981, sec. A.
Teen (magazine):
—"Elvis Presley." July 1962; Sept. 1969.
—"Elvis Presley, Ricky Nelson & Dick Clark." June 1958.
—"Elvis Presley vs. Harry Belafonte." No. 1, June 1957.
—"Elvis Presley's Newest Movie . . ." Dec. 1965.
—"The King of Rock 'n' Roll . . ." Jan. 1958.
—"The Private Hours of Elvis . . ." June 1963.
—"Top Pop Poll: Elvis Wins . . ." Apr. 1959.
—"Will the Army Change Elvis?" June 1958. (Feature story and cover.)
Teen Bag Presents the Elvis Presley Story (magazine). No. 1, 1977. (With three hundred photographs and a wall poster.)
Teen Greats (magazine). No. 3, May 1978.
Teen Set "Yellow Submarine" Special (magazine). "Elvis Presley: The King Is Still Very Much Around." 1968.
Teen Talk (magazine):
—"Elvis Presley: A Living Tribute." No. 1, Jan. 1978.
—"Elvis Presley Searches for God." Dec. 1976.

Teen World (magazine):
  —"Elvis Anniversary Special." Aug. 1965.
  —"Elvis Presley." Aug., Sept., Oct., Dec., 1964; Feb., June, July, Sept., Oct., Dec., 1965; Feb. 1966; June 1973; Aug. 1974, Mar. 1975.
Teenage Rock and Roll Review (magazine). Oct., Dec., 1956.
Tharpe, Jac L., ed. *Elvis: Images and Fancies.* Jackson, MS: University Press of Mississippi, 1979/1981. (Academic.)
"The Man Who Would Be King." *Us.* March 19, 1990.
Thompson, Charles C. II, and James P. Cole. *The Death of Elvis: What Really Happened?* New York: Delacorte Press, 1991.
Thompson, Patricia, and Connie Gerber. *Walking in His Footsteps.* Towery Press, 1981.
Thornton, Mary Ann. *Even Elvis.* New Leaf Press, Inc., 1979. (A religious book of sorts.)
Thorpe, Susan Adler. "Presley's Physician Derided." *Atlanta Journal-Constitution.* Oct. 25, 1981, sec. A.
"Thousands give Elvis a sad, tender farewell." *Detroit Daily News*, Aug. 19, 1977, 1A.
Time:
  —"Combat the Menace." Apr. 1957, 58.
  —"Elvis." June 19, 1972, 49–50.
  —"Elvis Aeternus." June 19, 1972, 28.
  —"Forever Elvis." May 7, 1965, 61.
  —"G-Man Blues." July 24, 1978, 23.
  —"Hound Dog Days in Memphis." Aug. 28, 1978, 22–23.
  —"Junkie King." Jan. 28, 1980, 70.
  —"Lonely and Shook Up." May 27, 1957, 101.
  —"A Medical Accident?" Mar. 16, 1992, 56.
  —"People." Oct. 29, 1956, 47. (About parking-lot incident in Memphis.)
  —"Return of the Big Beat." Aug. 15, 1969, 57.
  —"The Rock Is Solid." Nov. 1957, 48–49.
  —"Scientologists and Me." May 6, 1991, 57.
  —"Scientology, the Cult of Greed." Richard Behar, Special Report, May 6, 1991, 50–57.
  —"Sweet Music." Oct. 8, 1956, 96, 98, 100.
  —"Teener's Hero." May 15, 1956, 53–54.
  —"Yeh-Heh-Heh-Hes, Baby." Aug. 18, 1956.
Tio, M. M. "Otis Blackwell: The Power Behind Elvis." *Essence*, May 1978.
"To Elvis with Love." *McCall's*, July 1978.

Tobler, John, *Who's Who in Rock & Roll.* New York: Crescent Books, 1991.

Tomlinson, Roger. *Elvis Presley.* Great Britain: 1973.

Tommy Sands vs. Belafonte and Elvis (magazine). 1957.

Torgenson, Ellen. "Elvis." *TV Guide*, Feb. 10, 1979, 26–29.

Torgoff, Martin, ed. *The Complete Elvis.* New York: Delilah Books, 1982. (Much interesting data.)

Torres, Ben Fong. "Bodyguards Tell 'What Happened.' " *Florence (TX) Morning News*, Oct. 5, 1977, 12, 14.

Tosches, Nick. *Country: The Biggest Music in America.* New York: Stein and Day, 1977.

———. *Hellfire: The Jerry Lee Lewis Story.* New York: Delta, second edition, 1989.

Trevena, Nigel. *Elvis, Man and Myth* London: Atlantic Books, 1977.

Tucker, Stephen R. "Pentecostalism and Popular Culture in the South: A Study of Four Musicians." *Journal of Popular Culture* 16 (1982): 68–80.

Tunzi, Joseph A. *Elvis '69: The Return.* Chicago: J.A.T. Productions, 1990.

———. *The 1st Elvis Video Price and Reference Guide.* Softcover, 1988. (Poorly done and hard to read.)

Tupelo (MS) Daily Journal (newspaper):

—"Cedar Hill Wins $150 Community Awards: Spotlight Today on Presley." Sept. 26, 1956, 1.

—"Elvis, Actress Natalie Wood Are Twosome." Sept. 11, 1956, 11.

—"Elvis Aide Denies Fight Was Stunt." Nov. 23, 1956, 19.

—"Elvis at Milam Junior . . ." Sept. 25, 1956, 11.

—"Elvis Farm Purchase Said Just a Rumor." Nov. 20, 1956, 1.

—"Elvis, Journal Roving . . ." Nov. 17, 1956, 18.

—"Elvis Pondering Major Offer From England." Nov. 11, 1956, 32.

—"Elvis Presley Merchandise Sales Already Topping Davy Crockett . . ." Sept. 27, 1956, 1.

—"Elvis Presley Record Sales Top 10 Million." Oct. 3, 1956, 1.

—"Elvis Presley: The Two-Cadillac Man with a Style Like a Steam Engine." Feb. 15, 1956, 8.

—"Elvis Records Sooth Mental Patients." Nov. 17–18, 1956, 7.

—"Elvis Says He Wants Farm for Father." Oct. 27–28, 1956, 1. (*Note:* father, not mother.)

—"Elvis Sees Draft Call 'Getting Pretty Close.'" Oct. 24, 1956, 1.

—"Elvis Shows Fistic Prowess in Slug Fest." Oct. 19, 1956, 1.

—"Elvis Traffic Brings Ban on Main Parking." Sept. 25, 1956, 1.

—"Favorable Comments on Elvis in New York Times." Nov. 7, 1956, 11.

—"Filling Station Slugger Fired Despite Elvis' plea." Oct. 26, 1956, 1.

—"Girl Doesn't Like Picture, Elvis Settles for $5,500." Sept. 29–30, 1956, 1.

—"GI's in Alaska Ask Bob Hope: When Is Presley Going to Be Drafted Into Army?" Dec. 30, 1956, 5.

—"Gov. Coleman to Visit Here 'Presley Day.'" Aug. 1956, 1.

—"Graham [Billy] Sees Presley as 'Great Evangelist.'" Oct. 30, 1956, 1.

—"Judge Upholds School's Right to Expel Boy for Wearing Elvis Presley Haircut; Mother May Appeal." Nov. 17/18, 1956, 1.

—"Love Me Tender Premiere at Tupelo." Nov. 19, 1956, 19.

—"Movie Renamed to Fit New Presley Record." Sept. 10, 1956, 4.

—"$1,000 a Week for 20 Years for Presley." Nov. 8, 1956, 12. (The story is not true.)

—"Presley Asks $250,000 for 3 Sullivan Shows." Dec. 3,1956, 9. (Not true.)

—"Presley Day Will Emphasize That Tupelo Is Proud of Him." Sept. 21, 1956, 1.

—" 'Presley Homecoming' Theme of Parade on Children's Day." Sept. 8–9, 1956, 1.

—"Presley Rage 'Just Another Phase,' Bing Crosby Says." Nov. 29, 1956, 1.

—"Seven Presley Records Hit Nation with Bang This Week." Sept. 3, 1956, 1.

—"Sullivan Has Presley on Show . . ." Oct. 24, 1956, 6.

—"Teacher Recalls Elvis' Favorite Tune While at Lawhon Was Old Shep." July 1956, 5.

—"20,000 Persons, Mostly Screaming Teenagers, Welcome Presley Home." Sept. 27, 1956, 1.

—"The Welcome Mat Is Out for Presley Homecoming." Sept. 25, 1956, 1.

TV Guide:
- —"Elvis." No. 1925, 1990. (Illustration on the cover with story.)
- —"Elvis: Aloha From Hawaii." Mar. 31–Apr. 6, 1973.
- —"Elvis and Frank Sinatra on cover, May 7–13, 1960.
- —"Elvis and Me." Priscilla Presley, Jan. 30–Feb. 5, 1988.
- —"Elvis, How He Rocked the World." Dave Marsh, Apr. 9–15, 1983.
- —"Elvis Presley." Part 1, Sept. 8–14, 1956, 4–7; part 2, "The Folks He Left Behind," Sept. 22–28, 1956, 17–19; part 3, "He Tells How the Little Wiggle Grew," Sept. 29–Oct 5, 1956, 20–23.
- —"Elvis Presley: Behind the Scenes . . . " No. 1925, 1990.
- —"Elvis Presley: Judging His Music." No. 1567, 1983.
- —"Elvis Presley: The Day Elvis Died." No. 1481, 1981.
- —"How TV Reacted the Day Elvis Died." Aug. 15–21, 1981.
- —"My Life With Elvis." Priscilla Presley. No. 1818, 1988.
- —Seven-page story on the making of the NBC-TV special, Nov. 30, 1968.
- —"Why the Elvis Craze Won't Die." Marshall Frady, Jan. 5–11, 1985.

TV Life. "Elvis Presley's Secret Marriage in Germany." ca. 1961.

TV Movie Fan (magazine). 1956.

TV Movie Men (magazine). 1959.

TV Movie Mirror "Hush-Hush Wedding for Elvis and Cybill Shepherd!" Oct. 1972. (With them on cover.)

TV Movie Screen:
- —"Dear Elvis." Jan. 1963. (Elvis answers readers' questions.)
- —"Elvis Desperate Over Wife's Sexy Binge!" Lara Lawrence, Sept. 1973, 17–20, 55.
- —"Elvis Presley's First Interview as a Civilian!" May 1960.
- —"Elvis Reveals: 'I'm Going to Marry Liz.' " Sept. 1972.
- —"Elvis Weeps for His Little Girl." Jean Lamm, May 1973, 18–20, 66–68.
- —"Secret Wedding for Cher and Elvis." Oct. 1973.

TV Picture Life:
- —"Elvis Learns the Shocking Truth . . ." Amy Rush, July 1973, 17–19, 52–55.
- —"My Daddy's Home Again." July 1976.

TV Radio Mirror:
- —"The Girl Who Got to Presley." Dec. 1956, 28, 84–85.

—"Will Presley Still Be King?" Eunice Field, Dec. 1957, 36–37, 72–73.

TV Star Parade:
—"Cher Found at Graceland! Elvis Reveals New Baby Will Be Born There!" Super issue, Apr. 1977.
—"Priscilla and Elvis Reunited . . ." Sept. 1976.
—"Secret Marriage for Priscilla and Elvis." Jan. 1977.

TV Superstars. "Glen Campbell/Elvis Presley." 1970.

TV World (magazine). Dec. 1956.

U.S. News and World Report:
—"All the King's Men." Dec. 28, 1992–Jan. 4, 1993, 97.
—"Changing the Tune." Dec. 7, 1992, 25.
—"Love Me Tender, Love Me Glued." Science and Society, Mar. 9, 1992.
—"The Debate Over Censorship Goes On." March 16, 1992, 8.

U.S. Postal Service. *Elvis Presley*, a Commemorative Edition. Washington, DC: Jan. 8, 1993, release.

Uslan, Michael, and Bruce Solomon. *Dick Clark's the First 25 Years of Rock & Roll.* New York: Delacorte Press, 1981.

Variety:
—"Around Nashville in Three days." Nov. 14, 1956, 54.
—"As to That Presley Long-Termer . . ." Nov. 7, 1956, 46.
—"Baptist Ministers Sermon vs. Elvis: He'll Hit the Skids." Oct. 17, 1956, 1, 76.
—"Deutsche Pitch for Elvis." Oct. 24, 1956, 78.
—"Elvis a millionaire in 1 Year." Oct. 24, 1956, 1, 78.
—"Elvis Presley—Digitation Churns Up Teen Tantrums, Scribe Raps, So-So B.O." May 30, 1956, 41, 46.
—"Elvis Presley Hits Gold Platter Circle" (with "Heartbreak Hotel"). Apr. 11, 1956, 43.
—"The Elvis Presley Story: He's Making Monkeys Out of Singers." May 9, 1956, 1, 63. (About those who imitate Elvis.)
—"God-Loving Jelly-Kneed Kid: Parker on Presley." Oct. 24, 1956, 78.
—"Halo, Everybody, Halo: Latest Presley Pitch." Sept. 26, 1956, 16.
—"R 'n' R Worth 5 Gold Disc, 450G In 1 Year to Elvis . . ." Oct. 24, 1956, 55.
—"Rock 'n' Roll": Pros 'n' Cons." June 13, 1956, 51, 58.

—"10 Cops for Elvis Park of the 15G Overhead." May 9, 1956, 63.

—"With British Teenage Set." May 9, 1956, 63.

—"You Can't Laugh Off Presley's Phenomenal 10,000,000 Records." Sept. 5, 1956, 1.

Vaughan, Andrew. *The World of Country Music.* England: Longmeadow Press, 1992.

Vellenga, Dick, and Mike Farren. *Elvis and the Colonel* New York: Dell Publishers, 1988. (Authors obviously dislike Parker. Not objective.)

Ventura, Michael. "The Elvis in You." *LA Weekly*, Aug. 14–20, 1987.

Vermorel, Fred and Judy. *Stardust: The Secret Fantasies of Fans.* London: W. H. Allen, 1985.

View. "Elvis 1935–1977," an overview. Tupelo, MS. 1977.

Walker, Alice. *You Can't Keep a Good Woman Down.* New York: Harcourt Brace Jovanovich, 1981, 3–20 ("Nineteen fifty-five").

Walker, Robert Matthew. *Elvis Presley: A Study in Modern Music.* London: Midas Books, 1980.

Walrahf, Rainer, and Heinz Plehn. *Elvis Presley: An Illustrated Biography.* New York: Quick Fox Press, 1978.

Walton, S. B. "Rebel Who Became a Legend." *Saturday Evening Post*, Dec. 1977, 56–57.

"The War of the Generations." *House and Garden*, Oct. 1956, 40–41.

Wark, McKenzie. "Elvis, Listen to the Loss." *Art and Text* (Australia) 31 (Dec. 1988–Feb. 1989): 27–28.

Watkins, Darlene. *Elvis, We Still Love You Tender.* 1988. Distributed by Kisco, Commerce City, CO.

Wecht, Cyril H. "Post Mortem on Elvis Presley Won't Die." *Legal Aspects of Medical Practice.* Dec. 1979.

Welburn, Vivienne. "Elvis: The Way It Was." *Forum 15*, no. 7 (1982): 46–71.

Weller, Sheila. "Priscilla Presley: Surviving Elvis." *McCall's*, May 1979, 20.

Wertheimer, Alfred. *Elvis '56: In the Beginning.* New York: Collier Books, 1979. (Rare photographs. Recommended.)

———. Telephone interview with the author. June 1991; studio visit, NYC, Nov. 1993.

West, Red, Sonny West, and Dave Hebler as told to Steven Dunleavy. *Elvis: What Happened?* New York: Ballantine,

1977. (The inside look at Elvis as seen by his bodyguards. The book that destroyed Elvis's ability to cope.)

Westmoreland, Kathy, and William G. Quinn. *Elvis and Kathy.* Glendale House Pub., 1987.

"Where Elvis Lives." *Reader's Digest,* Aug. 1993, 47–52.

Whisler, J. A. *Elvis Presley. Reference Guide and Discology.* Metuchen, NJ: Scarecrow Press, Inc., 1981.

"Who's Who in the Teen World" (magazine). No. 3, Sept. 1971.

Williams, Roger. *Sing a Sad Song: The Life of Hank Williams.* New York: Doubleday, 1970.

Willis, Ellen. *Beginning to See the Light.* New York: Knopf, 1981.

———. "Rock, etc." *New Yorker,* Aug. 30, 1969, 66, 76–78.

Wilmer, Valerie. *The Face of Black Music.* New York: DaCapo Press, 1976.

Winn, Jan. "A Star Is Born." *New Republic,* Dec. 24, 1956, (Review of *Love Me Tender.*)

Wolcott, James. "Elvis: Shot by His Own Harpoon." *Village Voice,* Mar. 17, 1981, 57.

Wolfe, Charles. *The Grand Ole Opry: The Early Years.* London: Old Time Music, 1975.

Wood, Graham. *An A–Z of Rock and Roll.* London: Studio Vista, 1971.

Wood, William. *Culture and Personality Aspects of the Pentecostal Holiness Religions.* Paris: Mouton Publishers, 1965.

Woolsey, F. W. "Elvis 1935–1977." *Akron (OH) Beacon Journal,* Aug. 1977, 15 pp.

Wooton, Richard. *Elvis.* New York: Random House, 1985.

Woott, Richard, and John Tobler. *Elvis: The Legend of the Music.* Great Britain: Crescent Books hardcover.

"Words and Music." Poppy Press, Sept. 1972.

Worth, Fred L., and Steve D. Tamerius. *All About Elvis.* New York: Bantam Books, 1981. (Facts, trivia.)

———. *Elvis, His Life From A to Z.* Chicago and New York: Contemporary Books, Inc., 1988. (One of the best books for Elvis data.)

Yancey, Becky, and Cliff Linedecker. *My Life with Elvis.* New York: Warner Books, 1977. (Stories about a secretary's life with Elvis. Not well documented.)

York, Max. "The Great Elvis Auction." *The Tennessean Magazine,* Dec. 1977, 44–46.

Young Lovers #18: "The Real Elvis Presley Complete Life Story" (magazine). 1957.

Zmijewsky, Steven and Boris. *Elvis: The Films and Career of Elvis Presley.* Secaucus, NJ: Citadel Press, 1976.

Zoo World (magazine):

—"Elvis Presley." No. 50, Music Award Issue, Jan. 17, 1974.

—"Elvis Presley: How Does He Keep His Sanity?" Sept. 13, 1973.

—"Elvis Presley on Tour." No. 24, Jan. 6, 1973.

INDEX